THE MIDDLE CLASS

THE MIDDLE CLASS

A History

Lawrence James

Little, Brown

LITTLE, BROWN

First published in Great Britain in 2006 by Little, Brown

A CIP catalogue record for this book
is available from the British Library.

ISBN-13 978 0 316 86120 5
ISBN-10 0 316 86120 0

Typeset in Bembo by Palimpsest Book Production Limited,
Grangemouth, Stirlingshire

Printed and bound in Great Britain by
Clays Ltd, St Ives plc

Little, Brown Book Group
Brettenham House
Lancaster Place
London WC2E 7EN

A member of the Hachette Livre Group of Companies

www.littlebrown.co.uk

To Isobel Rose James

Contents

Acknowledgements

First I would like to thank my wife Mary for her encouragement, forbearance and perceptive suggestions at every stage of writing this book. My gratitude to her extends to Siobhan Dundee, Peter James and A. N. Wilson who read the manuscript and offered invaluable advice and exposed deficiencies, errors and infelicities. I am also grateful to my agent Andrew Lownie and Stephen Guise, Iain Hunt, Alan Samson, Linda Silverman and Tim Whiting of Little, Brown for their generous encouragement, help and forbearance.

Perceptive comments, information and advice were also provided by Dr Ian Bradley, Richard Demarco, John Dishman, the Earl and Countess of Dundee, Professor Martin and Eve Edmonds, Professor Clive Elmsley, James Goodsman, Professor John Haldane, Michael and Jenny Halsey, Michael and Veronica Hodges, Edward James, Henry and Ruth James, Dr Charles Kightley, John Laidlaw, Robbie Lyle, Dr Roy Oliver, Dame Kathleen Ollerenshaw, Professor Alan and Dr Anna Paterson, Johnny and Margaret Pattisson, Professor Nicholas and Dr Jane Roe, Professor Jeffrey Richards, Dr Bill Shields, David Vernon-Jones, Andrew Williams and Percy and Isabel Wood. All deserve my thanks.

I would also like to thank the staff at the Bodleian and British Libraries, the Centre of Buckinghamshire Studies, the Guildhall

Library and Record Office, Lambeth Archives, the National Library of Scotland, the National Archives of Scotland and the Wellcome Institute. All have been courteous, helpful and sometimes patient, as have the staff of St Andrews University Library, where I undertook most of my research. In particular I would like to thank Claire Bell, Alice Crawford, Christine Gascoigne, Elizabeth Henderson, Lynda Innocent and Norman Reed.

Tables

My father, a wise and grave man, gave me serious and excellent counsel . . . mine was the middle state, or what might be called the upper station of low life, which he had found by long experience was the best state in the world, the most suited to human happiness, not exposed to the miseries and hardships, the labour and sufferings of the mechanic part of mankind, and not embarrassed with pride, luxury, ambition, and envy of the upper part of mankind.

Daniel Defoe, *Robinson Crusoe* (1719)

Introduction

The middle class created modern Britain, some might say in its own image. Middle-class ingenuity, enterprise and perseverance were the mainsprings behind the eighteenth-century empire of trade and the subsequent Industrial Revolution. The middle class then proceeded to stamp its moral character on the first industrial nation. It decided how and according to what principles it was governed, remade its cities and towns and invited their inhabitants to share the benefits of progress and civilisation. The middle class was on the side of both. It possessed a supreme self-confidence born of the knowledge of past achievements, which in turn rested on the conviction that reason and scientific empiricism offered the best solutions for human problems. And there was the assurance of that Calvinist God who simultaneously rewarded the industrious and insisted that they used their wealth and power to rescue others from ignorance and vice.

Middle-class men and women assumed the right to govern and organise because they were educated, enlightened and forward-looking. Nothing was beneath their attention and nothing beyond their capabilities. This was arrogance on a grand scale, but it was always tempered by a pragmatic spirit of compromise. Even in the heyday of its Victorian supremacy the middle class remained flexible, and it still is. Its members have inherited the impulse to make the world a better place. Passions and energies once concentrated on laying drainage systems and building public libraries are now dedicated to resisting pollution and saving the environment.

Common concerns and visions give a continuity and coherence to the history of the middle class. It is also a narrative full of contradictions and paradoxes. Members of a class which boasted that it represented the 'intelligence' of the nation were inclined to scepticism and contentiousness. There were disagreements over the primacy of individualism, between idealism and pragmatism and between empirical science and religious faith. The impulse to challenge and question meant that the middle class never fell under the spell of any single dogma. Large and influential sections have successively embraced Calvinism, Evangelicalism, Utilitarianism, Liberalism, Conservatism and its recent mutations, Thatcherism and New Labour. Conversion was never permanent; rational minds were always receptive to new ideas and critical of old.

A disposition for debate is one of the reasons why it is hard to pin down the middle class. It has never been a homogeneous body, rather a sprawling, untidy organism in a perpetual state of evolution. The 'middle orders' who emerged between the fourteenth and the eighteenth centuries became the middle class of the nineteenth. The term 'class' was an appropriately modern one, borrowed from the vocabulary of scientists who were endeavouring to classify the natural world according to rational principles. By 1850, the middle class had developed into distinctive layers – an upper, a middle and a lower. This division survives, as does one first identified in the reign of Elizabeth which split society between those who lived by the exercise of their knowledge and intelligence and those who worked with their hands alone. The past and present core of the middle class consists of brainworkers: lawyers, doctors, architects, entrepreneurs, teachers and anyone who has mastered the mysteries of finance.

There are obvious threads which link today's middle class to its predecessors. Chaucer's lawyer, doctor and merchant have the same preoccupations (and peccadilloes) as their modern counterparts. None the less, projecting features of today's world back into the past and reversing the process leads to misunderstanding and distortion. Parallels do exist, but most are on a very basic level. Readers may recognise and sympathise with the private anxieties, vanities and ambitions of previous members of the middle class, but the wider assumptions of their age may often appear alien or bewildering.

Inhabitants of an age which superficially believes in equality and is highly sensitive to the self-esteem of others are bound to be shocked by the hierarchical nature of past society and its attendant snobberies. In this respect, we are out of step with our ancestors, who took these things for granted. Recalling his boyhood in the 1890s, Lawrence Jones, the son of a Norfolk squire, wrote: 'We were not class conscious, because class was something that was there, like the rest of the phenomenal world.' This was accepted by the local parson, the solicitor who handled the elder Jones's affairs, the doctor who tended his family, the retailers who supplied his household, the tenants who provided his revenues and the groom in his stables. Even at this late date, there were a handful of conservatives who still argued that the social order represented God's will.

The nature and machinery of the social hierarchy were understood by novelists and playwrights, for whom the nuances of status and their impact of human relations, particularly courtship and marriage, were a rich source of plots and characterisation. If literature was our only source for understanding our ancestors, we would soon conclude that status dominated their lives. This would be abundantly confirmed by magazines and newspapers, which from the late seventeenth century were crammed with advertisements for objects of desire that were fashionable and, therefore, guaranteed to enhance the status of the purchaser. Middle-class women were and are thought to be particularly susceptible to this form of persuasion.

Status and possessions were inseparable for the middle class. Whatever the sterner moralists like Thomas Carlyle may have said about hard work being its own reward, the middle class wanted tangible ones for their labour. Middle-class men and women were avid materialists, as the purveyors and advertisers of consumer happiness have always known. The middle class has also been engaged in a perpetual search for diversion and succumbed easily to every current fad. At various times, its members were enthralled by the pursuit of the picturesque at home and abroad: photography, cycling, motor cars, stamp collecting, gardening, tennis, golf, bird-watching, jogging and New Age therapies for mind and body. The middle class was always gregarious and enjoyed the company of its own kind. It crowded into genteel assembly rooms, listened to concerts, watched plays and formed clubs and societies which usually blended mental stimulation with conviviality, good food and alcohol. The servants of capitalism were among the most rapacious consumers of its products and I make no apology for examining their spending habits in detail.

An enduring paradox emerges from all this. While the middle class cultivated an image of itself as more useful than and morally superior to the aristocracy, it looked upwards for guidance in matters of entertainment, taste and manners. The richest business and professional men flocked into the countryside, bought properties there and, if they could afford to, lived like rural squires. Lower down the middle-class scale, there was a similar urge to escape the town for that no man's land between the urban and the rustic, the suburb.

Defenders of the suburbs always claimed that they were ideal places in which to bring up children. Family ambition, usually distinguished by the concentration of resources on the education of children, has always marked the middle class. It was both a vindication of a faith in education and an expression of a primal urge to move up in the world. Its intensity depended upon individual temperament, but on the whole and wherever circumstances were favourable the middle-class family was a nursery of ambition. Attending a good school was the first stage in any individual's ascent, which was why the Victorian public schools were so attractive to the middle class. One result was to instil into upper-middle-class boys the ancient chivalric values of selflessness, leadership and duty to others. Oxford and Cambridge played their part and, by 1900, the upper echelons of the middle class were thinking and behaving as a moral as well as an intellectual aristocracy.

The notion of getting ahead made sense only because British society was fluid, and, for all their snobberies, the middle class and the aristocracy accepted newcomers if they had enough money and were prepared to assimilate. How this might be accomplished was explained in those handbooks of taste and etiquette which have proliferated since the fifteenth century. These things still matter, which explains why so many newspapers and magazines with a middle-class readership run columns of advice on social protocol.

I have endeavoured to weave all these themes into a book about the middle class. I shall leave it for my readers to decide whether I have compiled an obituary, or a history which is still unfolding and has a long way to run. The odds are heavily on the latter, for the middle class has never been larger and is multiplying to fill a growing bureaucracy and man the service industries which have replaced the old source of so much of their wealth, manufacturing.

The middle class has never been so secure. Old threats to its security, trade unionism and socialism, were neutered in the 1980s, a decade which ended with the universal triumph of free-market capitalism. The class war between haves and have-nots which has flared up whenever the economy wobbled seems to have ended, although its embers still flickered during the debate on hunting in 2004. The modern middle class has inherited its ancestors' bogeymen. 'Lewd, idle and masterless' youths disturbed the Elizabethan middle orders, hooligans frightened the 'respectable' of Victorian Britain and the inner-city 'underclass' is a source of today's middle-class nightmares. Interestingly, at all periods 'education' was prescribed as one of the remedies of the restlessness of the poorest.

The late-twentieth-century vindication of the economic system that had made the middle class rich was not as much of a source of congratulation as it might have been. There are now elements among the middle class which blame capitalism for the contamination of the environment and economic disparities across the world. The authority of reason and science have been abjured by others who pursue truth and self-understanding through the emotional mysticism of various New Age cults.

None of this surprises me. I have tried to suggest that the middle class has never been static. In unravelling who they were, where they came from, what they wanted and what they accomplished, I have been acutely aware that the middle class has shown an astonishing capacity to seize opportunities and adapt to the new. For these reasons alone, I think it has a bright and fruitful future. Its achievements have been formidable by any standards and, on balance, have added considerably to the sum of human happiness. Today's middle class should feel proud of its collective past.

Part One

Roots and Antecedents: 1350–1720

1

Strings upon a Harp: Order and Change

The richer citizens of Salisbury were a jealous and bad-tempered crew. They quarrelled with the clergy of the cathedral that dominated the city and with each other. In 1447 the backbiting had reached such a pitch that they agreed to discipline themselves and the council decreed a ban on provocative expressions. The forbidden phrases are revealing: 'I defy you'; 'What are you?'; 'I am as rich as you, knave, harlot!'; 'I am as rich as you and greater beloved than you'; and 'I am better of birth than you, and have borne worship and estate of this city and kept it as well as you.' Despite this injunction, wrangling over status continued. 'Turd, fart, for I am worth six of you, you are a fool,' William Boket told the mayor in 1481 and was fined 13s 4d for his insolence.[1]

Insolence of another kind infuriated Robert Broke, a talented lawyer who was five times elected MP for the city of London and chosen speaker for the Commons in 1554. He called himself 'esquire', which was proper for a man who was investing the profits of his practice in land in Shropshire, where he intended to be counted among the gentry. His daughter Mary did not share his pretensions and was courting Richard Mirfield against her father's wishes. Broke investigated the background of his would-be son-in-law and discovered that he was 'a light person . . . of no ability or estimation, nor having any land'. He had 'a bragging manner' and was as 'arrant as any yeoman or other poor serving man'. Broke dismissed with a sneer Mirfield's claim to be a gentleman, remarking that he could discern no difference 'between a beggar and [a] beggarly gentleman'. Mirfield retorted that he was a gentleman and in his native Northamptonshire was 'hitherto reported and known to be of honest conversation and always had a convenient portion of possessions to live according to his degree'. Like his traducer, he augmented his income by using his intelligence: he was a servant to the Bishop of Peterborough and regularly undertook business for him in London. There he had met Mary Broke many times, even though her father had ordered her to walk abroad escorted by his servants, one of whom Broke knocked down.[2]

It mattered greatly who you were in medieval and early-modern England, and it mattered no less that others recognised your status and treated you accordingly. The culture of rank permeated every area of human activity and was often taken for granted. When he made his will in 1528, Sir Richard Knightley wished to be represented on his monument 'according to my degree'. His executors knew he had in mind a stone effigy or brass showing him in armour and surrounded by the shields of arms that advertised his ancestry and connections. This was how his second son, Edmund, appeared on a small brass in Fawsley church, Northampton. For over a hundred years London tombmakers had been mass-producing stereotyped brasses of knights, differentiated only by their size – which of course indicated the length of the patron's purse.

In 1631, John Cudworth, a Lancashire gentleman, instructed his executors to assign revenues for the 'meat, drink and lodging' of his second son, Ralph, 'fitting to his estate and condition'.[3] Again, much was unspoken, but the executors would know how much was needed for a youth who had inherited his father's rank, if not his fortune (which would have largely passed to the eldest son). None the less, he had to maintain appearances so that he could enjoy the companionship of equals and the respect of inferiors, even though as a younger son he would probably have to earn his living.

The law made it an offence for men and women not to dress according to their degree. From 1363 onwards, a series of statutes and proclamations confined specific textiles and furs to certain ranks. The 1465 Sumptuary Act restricted purple silk to noblemen, banned yeomen and those of lesser 'degree' from wearing padded doublets and insisted that labourers and servants wore cloth that had cost less than two shillings a yard. Just a hundred years later, Parliament blamed excessive dress on the 'perverse and forward manners and usage of the people' and feared that, unless checked, overspending on clothes would bankrupt 'light persons' with more money than sense. No one appears to have taken these laws very seriously, least of all the authorities, for there were no prosecutions.

Styles of address emphasised differences of rank. An inferior was spoken to using either his Christian name or 'thou' and answered with 'master' or 'mistress', or the impersonal but formal 'ye'. An Elizabethan labourer addressed a prosperous farmer by his Christian name and surname, or as 'goodman' or 'yeoman', but seldom as 'master', which was usually reserved for gentlemen.[4] Correspondence required an elaborate linguistic punctilio. Although writing to a fellow peer, the Earl of Oxford acknowledged the difference in their ranks when in a letter of 1450 he addressed the Duke of Norfolk as 'Right high and mighty Prince and my right good lord, I recommend me unto your good lordship'. Richard Calle, a bailiff, began a letter to his employer, John Paston, with 'Right worshipful and my most reverent master, I recommend me to your good mastership' and signed himself 'Your poor servant and bedesman'.

Like its language, the imagery of degree was contrived to remind everyone of who stood where in the hierarchy. In 1567 Chief Justice Sir James Dyer told a batch of newly created sergeants-at-law (the counterpart of the modern QC) that 'their habits, port and countenance should be suitable to their degree'. When they travelled to provincial assizes, he urged them to ride at the head of a cavalcade with at least four mounted servants and a sumpter horse for their baggage.[5] The yokels might be overawed and local gentlemen impressed by this display, but if the sergeant was elected to Parliament he and his fellow members stood respectfully bare-headed while the lords sat and discussed a bill.

The theatre of rank was an integral part of everyday life and its performances were constant reminders of the social dispensation. On their visit to Gloucester in the summer of 1535, Henry VIII and Anne Boleyn were greeted by the mayor, sheriffs and aldermen, all on horseback and wearing their scarlet, fur-trimmed gowns, followed by a train of a hundred or so of the richest citizens, all mounted. As the cavalcade entered the city, the gentlemen of the royal household rode behind the mayor and his company. The allusion was clear: the king stood above all in status and authority, but within Gloucester his representatives, the city's rulers, were next in rank.[6] Other arcane rules were applied for other public ceremonies, but the underlying principle was the same: one's place in a procession of civic dignitaries, lawyers or guildsmen and women depended solely upon one's rank. Noblemen, knights, esquires and gentlemen walked or rode in that order after the coffin of a knight and then, some distance behind the cortège, came their servants, whose position was determined by their masters' status. When the Norwich Guild of St George celebrated his feast day, the mayor and alderman rode at the head of the procession to hear mass, wearing their official scarlet robes, and were followed by the councillors, all in the guild's distinctive livery. After the service, they attended the annual dinner, at which guests were seated according to their rank.

Geoffrey Chaucer, the son of a London vintner who had been attached to the household of a royal duchess, was, perhaps for these reasons, acutely conscious of the significance people gave to social rituals and nuances. Among his Canterbury pilgrims was the Wife of Bath, a successful businesswoman who forcefully assumed precedence over her neighbours as they walked down the church nave to receive communion. There were also the Haberdasher, Dyer, Carpenter, Weaver and Carpet-maker, all well-heeled master craftsmen who advertised their wealth with silver fittings on their belts, knives and pouches, contrary to the Sumptuary laws. Each dreamed of becoming an alderman, a prospect relished by their wives:

> To be called 'Madam' is a glorious thought,
> And so is going to church and being seen
> Having your mantle carried like a queen.

As these aspirant ladies took their places in church, they may have glanced upwards and seen the brightly painted wooden angels set on the roof braces. There were nine orders of angels, each with its function and distinctive dress and, whether carved, painted or glazed, they were often rendered playing musical instruments. The symbolism was twofold: onlookers were reminded of the perfect harmony that prevailed in Paradise and that God had divided all creatures into hierarchies. The celestial, angelic orchestra represented God's model for human society in which all Christians strove to achieve order and tranquillity. Whether celestial or earthly, inequality was natural and blessed by God.

The overall form of human society was that of a pyramid with a broad base and narrow apex. A cross-section would have revealed two thin layers at the top and a vast one beneath. This was God's intention, and the wisdom behind it was explained in a sermon delivered by Nicholas Bromyard, a Dominican friar, towards the end of the fourteenth century. He chose an appropriate musical metaphor:

> The order of these various ranks in the community ought to be like strings on a harp. Here it is essential for the purpose of good melody that each string should keep its own place . . . so, in any community each man ought to keep his station – the lower working and obeying, those who are called 'ministers', the lawyers and churchmen, in consulting and praying and speaking, the rulers in ruling and protecting, whose office is like that of a harpist.[7]

Perhaps for this reason a man born to rule, Arthur Prince of Wales, the son of Henry VII, was portrayed in a window in Great Malvern priory surrounded by angelic musicians.

Bromyard's vision of how and why a Christian society should be ordered had its philosophical roots in Scripture, its interpretation by the fathers of the early church, and in Greek and Roman authorities. A synthesis of these sources provided a vindication of the feudal society that emerged during the ninth and tenth centuries. In its earliest, classic form it comprised three, mutually dependent estates or orders. At the top were princes and knights who owned land and guarded the rest of society against external and internal enemies. The second order, ordained churchmen, prayed for everyone and prepared souls for judgment through moral example, teaching and administering the sacraments. At the bottom of the pile was the largest group, the toilers who supported the other two by growing crops, tending livestock and manufacturing tools and utensils. Work of some kind or other was a burden laid by God on all men as one of the punishments for Adam's sin. 'Every man', declared one late-fourteenth-century preacher, had to 'travail in his degree' in expiation of the sin of his common ancestor.[8]

Many, perhaps the majority, of those who laboured with their muscles were serfs. Their lives were circumscribed not only by God's laws, but by man's, which decreed that serfs were confined to the manor on which they were born, were compelled to work unpaid for their lord for fixed periods and paid him fines when they married, when their children came of age and when they died. The serf owned nothing but his belly, observed one thirteenth-century jurist. The serf's legal disabilities did not condemn him to utter poverty. If he was industrious or fortunate, he could accumulate holdings, livestock, farm implements or cash, but, however rich he became, his future and that of his offspring were predetermined by his status.

A serf, the Ploughman, and his brother, the Poor Parson, together with the Knight represent the traditional three orders in *The Canterbury Tales*. Each figure is idealised by Chaucer. Their moral uprightness, dedication to their prescribed social and economic tasks and quietism isolate them from those other pilgrims who are keeping abreast in a competitive world, full of people as cunning, corrupt and ruthless as themselves. There is the sybaritic Monk, that plausible chancer the Merchant, the Sergeant-at-Law and the Doctor who fleece their clients and the two rich peasants, the Miller and the Reeve, who are clambering up the social ladder through theft and fraud. All are creatures of the real world of the 1380s and they had many actual counterparts.

Superficially, fly lawyers and doctors and grasping peasants seemed to be outside the framework of society described by Bromyard, as he and other clergymen were uncomfortably aware. Contemporary preachers were uneasy about the proliferation of businessmen, lawyers and doctors who thrived thanks to their use of applied intelligence, specialised knowledge and a knack of exploiting the opportunities that came their way. Such individuals were sometimes depicted as a threat to the old tripartite order in which there was no obvious place for anyone who lived by the laws of the land or the market place. One cleric declared that knights, priests and labourers had been created by God, while the Devil had created merchants. Moreover, and this was a source of additional distress for conservatives, there was a steady stream of men and women who were using their occupations to move up in rank. Bromyard grumbled about 'merchants and moneyed men' who counted themselves equal to the noblemen to whom they advanced loans.

Complaints about the disintegration of the old social structure and the good fortune and presumption of parvenus were destined to have a long life. In 1536, William Calverley, a Yorkshire gentleman, wrote *A Dialogue between the Plaintiff and the Defendant* in which the former regrets a new world in which, among other enormities, 'rich merchants' were knighted. His protagonist responded by reminding him of a theological and social commonplace. Men rose and fell in the world as a consequence of personal virtue, hard work and the will of God.[9] His ordered universe was not inflexible and, when change occurred, it was with His approval. The hand of God was perpetually at work in human affairs, although the reasons for His intervention were often inexplicable to human intelligence. What was beyond question was that God elevated and cast down men to illustrate two truths: that his power was infinite and that earthly treasure and power were inconstant and ultimately valueless when compared with the bliss of heaven. This message was often conveyed by the image of the wheel of fortune, for ever in motion and indifferent to rank.

Caught by its downward spin, the poet George Ashby resigned himself to his misfortune as he sat in the Fleet prison during 1463. He had known better times as a secretary in the service of Henry

VI and had become a casualty of his deposition by Edward IV two years before. Privation was 'profitable' for Ashby's soul and a salutary reminder of the impermanence of status and wealth:

> fortune left me right sorry
> Showing that this wealth is transitory.

Maybe he had overreached himself in what had been a successful career and had forgotten that 'God's law is man to know his estate.' It was a claim often made by conservatives, but Ashby's experience had prompted him to challenge its validity. He had been an eye-witness to the aristocratic power struggles of the first phase of the Wars of the Roses and they had convinced him that those of the highest rank did not possess a monopoly of wisdom or integrity. Far better, he wrote, for princes to adopt a yardstick of proven moral value rather than rank when selecting advisers and servants. Knights, squires, yeomen and clerks were trustworthy, devoted and honest.[10]

Ashby may have come from a relatively humble background; unusually, his rank and occupation are unmentioned on his brass in Harefield church in Middlesex. Implicit in his verses on public affairs was the belief that virtue and wisdom were not concentrated in the uppermost ranks of society, whose members, according to the three-fold ordering of society, assumed the right to govern. This was a contentious view which gained currency during the late fifteenth and early sixteenth centuries. It was rejected by Henry VIII's coun-cillors Sir Christopher Hales, Sir Anthony St Leger and Richard Rich when they compiled the regulations for King's School, Canterbury, in 1540. They proposed that only the sons of gentlemen should be admitted as pupils. 'Husbandmen's children', they argued, were best suited 'for the plough and to be artificers'. Thomas Cranmer, the Archbishop of Canterbury, disagreed. 'God had given talents to all kinds of people indifferently,' with the result that some of the highest born were 'very dolts'. Neither he nor the objectors had been 'gentlemen born . . . but had our beginning that way from a low and base parentage and, through the benefit of learning and other civil knowledge, for the most part all gentle ascend to their estate'.[11] This was not true – Cranmer was the son of an esquire – but he got his way.

An important issue was at stake. If Hales and his allies were right, then a child's parentage predetermined its future occupation and rank and those who ruled were a closed and self-perpetuating elite. For Cranmer, such restrictions were a denial of God's will because He distributed talent randomly. This being so, pragmatic necessity, in the form of the overall good of the kingdom, demanded that every effort was made to cultivate and harness ability, irrespective of where it was found. New, Renaissance notions of the duty of everyone to develop their innate talents and employ them for universal benefit were blended with the older perception of society as an expression of God's purpose by Christopher St German. Writing in the 1520s, he described human reason as a divine gift and those who made the best use of it, whether jurists like himself or craftsmen, were fulfilling God's will.

Intellectual labour was not only highly desirable, it had become theologically acceptable. This was inevitable on purely practical grounds, for it would have been both impossible and foolish for the church to exclude from the compass of society anyone who lived by his intelligence. As an institution with extensive property, the church had to hire lawyers. Moreover, since the building and refurbishment of cathedrals, churches and monasteries depended almost entirely on lay generosity, the clergy needed the good will and cash of rich men. It welcomed both and was happy to allow patrons to embellish the work they had funded with decorations which proclaimed their piety to the world, often ostentatiously.

On their brass (now somewhat ravaged) at Cowthorpe near York, Judge Brian Roucliffe and his wife hold between them a model of the church he paid for in the 1470s. Sheep, woolsacks, merchants' marks and a shepherd's crook on fifteenth- and sixteenth-century brasses to flock owners and wool dealers in Cirencester and Northleach in Gloucestershire advertise the sources of their wealth, and inscriptions record their contributions to the extension of both churches. Ships, woolman's shears, wine casks and his merchant's mark on the exterior stonework of Tiverton church reveal how John Grenewey, a merchant-adventurer, made his money and, of course, how he spent some of it. Here and elsewhere, the iconography of trade is clear evidence that, whatever misgivings the more reactionary clerics may have had about those who grew rich from business, the church as a whole had no qualms about accepting a share of their profits.

Less obvious than the images of commercial success are those which reveal what we now call social mobility. Lavenham church in Suffolk was in large part a monument to the generous piety of the Spryngs, a dynasty of highly astute clothiers, and its decorations in stone and brass trace their progress up the ladder of rank. Thomas Spryng, who died in 1486, appears on his brass together with the merchant's mark that identified his bales of cloth. It reappears alongside the arms of the de Veres, earls of Oxford, on the stonework of the tower. Merchant and aristocrat not only shared the cost of building the church, they consented to be tied by blood: the second son of the 15th Earl of Oxford married a Spryng. This match confirmed the Spryngs' arrival into the ranks of the gentry. Their new status was duly given permanence on the parapet of the new south chapel where the Spryng coat of arms appears twenty-one times with an inscription that reads (in translation): 'Pray for the souls of Thomas Spryng, esquire, and Alice, his wife, who had this chapel made in the year of Our Lord 1525.' Before God and the world, the Spryngs had announced their new degree and membership of that order which enjoyed social, political and economic dominance.

Not everyone who had made a packet was anxious to clamber up the ladder of degree. In 1633, the antiquary Thomas Gerard noticed that in the Somerset village of Martock there were many 'wealthy and substantial men though not of the best breed' who, although mocked as 'clowns' by their betters, knew they had enough money to be gentlemen if they wished. What did concern these prosperous farmers was that they were treated with respect by their inferiors, and the cynical may have noticed that many of their neighbours who called themselves 'esquire' or 'gentleman' did so entirely on their own estimation.

This fact of life was acknowledged by the 1694 tax on marriages and burials in which payments were fixed according to degree. An 'esquire or reputed esquire owning and writing himself such' was liable for £5, while 'a gentleman or reputed gentleman owning and writing himself such' paid one pound. There must have been plenty of voluntary demotions, as there had been in 1641 when the rate of a poll tax had been set according to rank. An official reported from Cheshire that 'many reputed esquires shrink from their title to be called gentleman and save £5. It were worth any man's laughter to see how these apple esquires that glorified in the title do now assume humility and a lower style'.[12] No doubt once the assessments had been paid, these penny-pinching gentlemen resumed their former degree.

2

Duty and Order: The Hierarchy of Discipline

The tax-evading gentlemen of Cheshire were accustomed to giving orders and having them obeyed. They were a link in a chain of command and correction that stretched from the throne downwards to noblemen, knights, squires, judges, the mayors and corporations of cities and towns, churchwardens, parish constables, overseers of the poor and jurymen. The hierarchy of authority extended into the workplace and household: masters, husbands and fathers gave orders to their employees, wives and children and punished them if they refused, or did so with a bad grace. Just as the local justice ordered a flogging for a thief or beggar, so an employer could beat his servant, or a parent his child.

Defiance and insolence from inferiors was intolerable. A manual on boxing written in 1562 recommended gentlemen to rebuke the 'saucy lout' or 'loitering lubber' with hard blows 'well set on both cheeks'. Adam Eyre, a farmer and officer in Cromwell's army, whipped his servant Joan for 'her slothfulness', but felt ashamed afterwards, 'for my failings in the presence of God Almighty are unquestionably greater than hers are to me'. Thomas Gent, an apprentice printer, was thrashed by his master for his slovenly appearance, and he considered his treatment fair. 'Youth must either be under discipline, or certainly lost,' he wrote forty years later in 1756 when he had his own business and apprentices.[1]

All civil and domestic authority derived from God. Its legitimacy and necessity were explained in one of the homilies that were regularly read in churches as part of the Protestant Church of England rites that had been established by statute in 1559:

> Almighty God has created and appointed all things in heaven, earth and waters, in a most excellent and perfect order . . . In the earth he has assigned kings, princes, with other governors under them in all good and necessary order . . . Every degree of people, in their vocation, calling and office, has appointed them to their duty and order. Some are in high degree, some in low, some kings and princes, some inferiors and subjects, priests and laymen, masters and servants, fathers and children, husbands and wives, rich and poor, the very one have need of the other.

The new Anglican order perpetuated the social doctrines of its Catholic predecessor. And for the same reasons, for the homily continued: 'Take away kings, princes, rulers, magistrates and such states of God's order, [and] no man shall ride or go by the highway unrobbed, no man shall sleep in his own house or bed unkilled, no man shall keep his wife, children, and possessions intact.' This theme was repeated by Ulysses in Shakespeare's *Troilus and Cressida* (1603), when he warns of the anarchy that would follow if 'degree' disappeared.

Those at the bottom of the pile were not instinctively or willingly submissive, far from it. A late-fourteenth-century cleric regretted that they were turbulent and addicted to blasphemy, witchcraft, 'idle plays and japes', wrestling, giving money to jugglers and the 'making of fool's countenances'. Equally deplorable was their 'sturdiness against men of higher estate'.[2] This truculence was also lamented by Thomas Starkey, another clergyman, who observed that his poorer countrymen were 'somewhat rude and sturdy of mind' and, therefore, needed a firm hand.[3] Craftsmen, artisans and labourers and their wives were reluctant to accept their place in the scheme of things, were inclined towards rowdiness and were incapable of self-control. Their characteristics were those of the cussed and stupid cuckoos, ducks and geese in Chaucer's *Parlement of Foulys* (c. 1383) who made such a clamour before the royal eagle, a bird higher than them in 'degree' and by far 'the gentlest' of his kind. This literary comparison sprang to the mind of a Welsh gentleman when he encountered a crowd of anti-tax protesters in Suffolk in 1525: 'With the characteristic of the ignorant' they all spoke at once, 'like a flock of geese'.[4]

Church and state combined to protect such creatures from their own folly, temper their excesses and bind them to some form of social control within the community. Outsiders were always treated with apprehension and brought to the attention of authority. In 1445, the villagers of Honington in Norfolk complained about Robert Growt, who 'lives suspiciously . . . because he does nothing, nor has any land or holding on which he can occupy himself'. He poached rabbits and had somehow obtained some lambs which ate the corn growing in other men's fields.[5] Keeping a close eye on such individuals was one of the purposes of urban religious guilds which fostered piety, harmony and pride among their members. They were charitable bodies that welcomed men and women from every level in society, so long as they could afford the livery. Members also had to uphold the dignity of their guild by seemly behaviour. Brawlers were expelled from the St Thomas's Guild of King's Lynn and gamblers from that of St John the Baptist at Wisbech.[6] Agencies of social control, these fraternities were dissolved in 1547 as part of Henry VIII's reformation of the Church.

Although never its original intention, the final outcome of the Henrician reformation was the creation of Elizabeth I's Church of England, whose doctrines and litany were Protestant. The emphasis of lay devotion shifted from the sacraments to the gospel of the word, preached and privately studied through systematic Bible reading. While the new religion had become widely accepted by the 1580s, its strongest appeal was to literate men and women of superior rank. Their inferiors were largely unworried about salvation and, to the dismay of the godly, preferred to spend Sunday playing football in churchyards, drinking in alehouses or just idling. Those who were coaxed into church found themselves in uncongenial surroundings. They were puzzled or bored by sermons and fidgeted, scuffled, chattered, broke wind and mocked the rites. One Essex man urinated into his neighbour's hat during a service. William Allen, a twenty-year-old from Earl's Colne in the same county, was hauled before the church courts in 1637 for 'pissing in the clock chamber, so that it ran down and annoyed the church . . . [and] easing himself nearby the church door in the churchyard to the great annoyance of the church and the churchyard and the parishioners' noses'.[7] Allen passed from one extreme of profanity to another of piety: in middle age he became a Quaker and, in 1669, wrote a devotional book, *The Glory of Christ's Light*. His betters might have applauded Allen's conversion, had it not been for the fact that he had embraced Quakerism, which was anathema to orthodox Protestants.

Gross irreverence during church services was one of many symptoms of a general spread of restlessness among the lower orders during the sixteenth and seventeenth centuries. There was nothing new in the attitudes of the poor; what caused consternation was the increase in their numbers. Roughly between 1530 and 1650 the population rose from about 2.3 million to over 3.2 million, of whom 40 per cent were under twenty-one.[8] Many could not find permanent work or lacked the means to secure training in a craft and so were impelled towards the margins of society, surviving by begging, petty crime or both. It was the old problem represented by Robert Growt, but on a far greater scale. Thousands drifted towards towns and cities, particularly London, where they were less easy to control than in the countryside. They often walked long distances; a fifth of the beggars arrested in Elizabethan Salisbury had travelled over a hundred miles.

Wherever they wandered, the migrant poor were a permanent source of unease for those in authority. They broke the law, they were difficult to track down and there was no means of knowing whether the country could produce enough food to feed them. A bad harvest, soaring grain prices and famine were the ingredients of large-scale popular unrest. Harvests failed in 1586, 1596–7, 1622 and 1630, causing localised disturbances, and between 1533 and 1630 there were serious riots in Norwich, Gloucester, Basingstoke, Canterbury, Southampton, Leicester and Newbury.

Rage was always directed upwards. In 1598 a Kent labourer declared that the country would be better off under the Spaniards rather than the callous, wealthy men who now ruled it, and in 1630 a Somerset stonemason blamed the present dearth on the 'hard hearts of unfairly rich men', who he hoped would soon be killed. 'It will never be merry till some of the gentry were knocked down,' claimed a miller, and, in 1595, a Kent yeoman foretold a mass uprising, after which 'we should have land cheap and a merry world'.[9] 'Merry' was a word often on the lips of the hungry and discontented; it summoned up a blissful state, either in the past or in the future, in which ale and food were plentiful and everyone was free to enjoy themselves without the constraints of labour or laws. Alcohol helped conjure up visions of a 'merry' world, which was why magistrates and mayors increasingly treated alehouses as sources of sedition as well as rowdiness.

Degree and with it the security of the better off were in peril, or so it seemed. The official reaction was a mixture of coercive and placatory measures: the poor were forced to work or were whipped, and, when food stocks ran low, the government regulated the price and distribution of grain. These aims were combined in a law of 1562 which instructed rural magistrates to compel all unemployed males between twelve and sixty and females between twelve and forty to work in some form of 'husbandry'. If labour was scarce during harvest time, the justices were empowered to draft artisans and labourers to cut hay and corn and place those who refused in the stocks for two days. There were practical as well as moral reasons for such legislation, which were outlined in the preamble to a statute of 1598. Labour in the fields was 'the occasion of the increase and multiplying of people both for service in wars and in time of peace . . . [and the] principal means that the people are set to work, and thereby withdrawn from idleness, drunkenness, unlawful games and all other lewd practices and conditions of life'.[10] Other legal constraints were applied: alehouses were licensed, restrictions imposed on the movement of labourers and servants, fornicators arraigned before the bench and vagrants chivvied and flogged.

Ironically, it was imagined that those who lived outside society had created their own parallel hierarchy. James Awdley's *Fraternity of*

Vagabonds (1575) alleged that there were twenty orders of beggars and criminals, each with its own specialism such as faking madness or infirmity. Another analyst of contemporary crime suggested that this hierarchy existed in a separate, depraved universe. This confirmed what many suspected: the penniless were morally impoverished.

Officially and unofficially the poor were described as 'lewd', 'idle' and 'licentious'. These adjectives were part of a vocabulary of disdain which grew in currency during the sixteenth and seventeenth centuries and included such phrases as 'mean and contemptible persons' and the 'base and unruly people'.[11] Their collective delinquency was the fault of a lack of 'manners', a term which encompassed seemly public behaviour, self-discipline, deference to betters and sexual continence. Viewed from above, the absence or decay of 'manners' became a permanent source of anger and fear. In 1699 William III told Parliament that the poor were a 'burden' and 'their loose and idle life does, in some measure, contribute to the deprivation of manners' which was so noticeable in his kingdom.[12]

Admonishing the manners of the poor and enforcing laws that encouraged industry and punished indolence among them were the responsibilities of unpaid royal officials. In the countryside, these duties were performed by magistrates chosen from the landowning gentry and, in districts where there were none, by the parish vestry. These usually self-perpetuating bodies comprised, in the words of the vestrymen of Layston in Hertfordshire, 'the best sort of inhabitants' of the area, often yeoman farmers. Their overall aims were set down by the vestry of Swallowfield in Berkshire. They promised to do all in their power to assist the sick, disabled and 'honest poor', to make life unbearable for 'common disturbers of the peace and quietness' and expel from the village 'pilferers, backbiters and mischievous persons', who included anyone who questioned their authority.[13]

Such policing was easier in the countryside than in the towns where vagrants were more concentrated and there were more places for them to hide and, sometimes, well-established underworld districts where they would be welcomed. In 1422, a London jury reported that behind the Pye in Queenhithe 'is a privy place which is good shadowing for thieves, and many evil bargains have been made there, and many strumpets and pimps have their covert there'.[14] There were murky corners in Elizabethan Norwich that contained 'safe' houses for juvenile drifters who constantly vexed the authorities everywhere.[15]

Catching, chastising and ejecting the young vagabonds of Norwich were the duties of the mayor and sheriffs, who were the urban counterparts of the rural justice of the peace. In every city and self-governing town, these figures, together with aldermen and councillors, were drawn from prosperous business and professional men. They were self-confident and proud of their civic responsibility. The epitaph of Thomas Hamon who died in 1607 says that he had been six times elected as MP for Rye, had been elected mayor six times and had commanded the local militia. The inscription concludes that his 'prudent courage, justice, gravity deserve a monument of memory'.

Worthies like Hamon regularly advertised their power and pre-eminence through public displays that reminded lesser citizens of their place in the world. The dignitaries of Elizabethan Chester paraded through the streets in gowns of scarlet and violet 'welted with velvet', accompanied by a sword bearer, mace bearer and sergeants-at-arms also carrying maces.[16] The implements of coercion and punishment were a reminder that the chief men in the city were also its magistrates. Urban justice required an impressive setting, so from the mid-sixteenth to the mid-seventeenth centuries town halls and council chambers across the country were rebuilt and refurbished in an august and overawing fashion. At Leicester, the mayor sat on a throne-like seat with pillars on either side looking on to a panelled parlour with coloured glass in the windows.[17]

Many who sat on the bench believed themselves instruments of God's laws as well as the crown's. They were Puritans, members of a busy and clamorous group within the Church of England who hoped to purify it along what they imagined to be scriptural lines by eliminating rituals which smacked of Catholicism, and replacing the authority of bishops with that of congregations. A truly godly church would serve a godly nation that had undergone what the Puritans called a 'reformation of manners'. One of its prerequisites was a systematic removal of those indulgences and pastimes which corrupted the poor. With temptation removed, they would discover religion and learn to be useful.

These two aims were combined by Salisbury Puritans in the 1620s when they proposed that the council offer instruction in crafts to the poor which would be funded by a tobacco tax. In 1632 the Gloucester authorities paid for a lecturer to teach quietism in the city's poorest parishes and three years later appointed an 'overseer of the manners of the poor'. The Puritan Harlakenden family, squires of Earl's Colne, put pressure on churchwardens and constables to evict grazing pigs from the churchyard and ban drinking and playing football on a Sunday. This did not fill the pews, for the refractory walked to alehouses outside the parish.[18]

By attempting to suppress godlessness among the weavers of Essex, the Harlakendens were upholding that fundamental canon of Puritanism: 'By their deeds shall ye know them.' The Puritans believed that an individual's salvation had been predetermined by God and, while no one knew His will, those who considered themselves chosen behaved as if they were already members of a spiritual elite. They endeavoured to live lives of exemplary restraint and piety and, since the Puritan frame of mind acknowledged a perpetual struggle between good and evil, did all in their power to advance the former. Since ignorance, depravity and superstition thrived among the poor, Puritans channelled money into charities that provided the poor with opportunities to become literate, independent and economically useful members of a devout society.

This had been the goal of Mary Collins, a gentleman's wife, who died in 1648 and whose epitaph in Brightling church in Sussex describes her as 'godly, pious and charitable, a true matron unto God's poor children, daily relieving them with food convenient either for their souls or bodies'. The philanthropic impulse was not confined to Puritans; all Christians were under an obligation to fulfil Christ's injunctions to help the unfortunate and simultaneously encourage charity in others. These obligations were set down on the inscription to Robert Grays, a London merchant who died in 1635 and was buried in St Mary Magdalene church in his native Taunton:

This thankful town, that mindful City
Share his piety and his pity,
What he gave, and how he gave it,
Ask the poor, and you shall have it.
Gentle reader, Heaven may strike
Thy tender heart to do the like,
Now thine eyes have read the story,
Give him the praise, and God the glory.

Grays's generosity had plenty of contemporary counterparts. Like Mary Collins, he was practising what would afterwards be called the 'moral economy', that is the tacitly understood obligation of those of higher rank to divert some of their wealth to relieve distress among their inferiors. There was always, then and later, a concern that cash was directed towards the 'deserving' poor who were victims of mischance: when he left £2 to the poor of Wells in 1558, John Heath insisted that none would go to 'strong and sturdy beggars'.[19] Charity of this kind was both an act of Christian mercy and a device that purchased a degree of security, in so far as the poor were never passive and could, conceivably, combine to endanger the safety and possessions of their betters. Almshouses, free schools, annual hand-outs of bread, cloth or fuel, and revenues bequeathed to finance apprenticeships for paupers or dowries to poor girls were an insurance against future unrest.

The private kindnesses of those of superior degree were balanced by their active support of laws that assumed the poor were lazy, feckless, potentially restive and in need of moral direction. This ambivalence was reflected by William Cook, Justice of the Common Pleas, a bright lawyer from a comparatively humble background who was making his way upwards in the world by investing his fees in estates in his native Cambridgeshire in the 1540s. He wanted quick returns and so he evicted smallholders and replaced them with sheep to cash in on the woollen-cloth boom.[20] Cook did not neglect his social duty and earmarked a few acres to provide an annual sum to help the poor, some of whom may have been families whose livelihoods he had destroyed.

They were, he would surely have argued, free to make their way and prosper in a world which rewarded industry and punished indolence. God and the king required men like himself to offer inferiors guidance and reproof, for an education at Cambridge and Gray's Inn had given him greater knowledge, wisdom and awareness of virtue. If he failed to exercise these qualities, then those without them would be cast adrift in a chaotic world. Cook believed this fervently, which was why he had the axiom 'Plebs sine lege ruit' (Without law the common people are overthrown) engraved on his memorial brass in Milton church. He died in 1553, when the Renaissance was beginning to make its influence felt in England, and there is an attempt at portraiture on his memorial. Not surprisingly, his features suggest forcefulness of character, determination and a streak of hardness.

3

Common Consent: Hierarchy and Power

Justice Cook enforced the laws that had been made by men like himself in Parliament. Parliament was the partner in royal government and, in terms of degree, voters and members came from the upper ranks in society. Peers and bishops sat in the House of Lords because of their titles. Members of the Commons occupied their seats for the same reasons as they held authority in town and country: their status, revenues and wisdom. Choosing these men was a haphazard process, for there was no uniform franchise and constituencies varied enormously in population. In 1715 the forty English counties with an overall electorate of 160,000 returned eighty MPs, and 101,000 voters in 205 boroughs returned 409 members. Wales with 28,000 electors sent twenty-four MPs to Westminster, and Scotland with 2,700 a further forty-five. Given a population of just over five million, about a fifth of all men were directly involved in the country's political life.

In theory, voters came from what the 1376 Parliament described as 'les meillour gentz', that is 'the better sort', although the sheriffs who oversaw elections often found them hard to identify. Just over fifty years later there were complaints that electors 'without property of any value' were turning up at county elections, claiming parity with knights and esquires. To rectify this, an act was passed in 1429 which confined the right to vote in county elections to landowners with freeholds valued at £2 a year. This test remained in place for the next four hundred years, despite periods of inflation and an increase in land values. As a result the shire electorate grew: there were 5,000 two-pound freeholders in Kent in 1679 and 6,200 in 1714.[1] Moreover, it was simple for county magnates to create freeholds, known as 'faggot' votes, which they could distribute among their supporters.

The urban franchise was utterly random. In some towns and cities the right to vote was restricted to the mayor and corporation; in 1547 the MP for Much Wenlock was returned by 'common consent of the most and greatest number of . . . burgesses being electors'. Like all urban oligarchies, the burgesses of Much Wenlock were its richest tradesmen. Elsewhere, the franchise could encompass all freemen and householders, many of whom were shopkeepers and craftsmen. This was so in Okehampton in Devon where, in the 1677 general election, one candidate spent £470 in tavern bills to secure the votes of 'the poorer sort of freemen'.[2] Whatever their rank, urban electors expected to be entertained; in the same election Sir William Becker doled out over £436 'to distribute in the inns and alehouses in tobacco' to the voters of Bedford. With tobacco at a shilling (5p) a pound, this represented nearly four tons shared among five hundred electors.

By this date and thanks to the prevalence of bribery, the right to vote had become a marketable asset. In 1681, the fifty electors of Stockbridge in Hampshire invited bids for their votes, expressing a preference for older candidates who 'they think will die sooner that they may choose again'.[3] This made sense, since there were plenty of over-indulgent MPs in Charles II's parliaments. Two who went too far were John Chetwynd, who sneezed to death after taking too much snuff, and Sir Robert Cann, who drank sherry 'morning, noon and night' and died after turning to small beer.[4] Bribes were not always needed: many boroughs were susceptible to arm twisting by the crown or a local landlord.

Corruption pervaded the political culture at every level. In 1690 the mayor of Thetford enfranchised his sons, a seventeen-year-old youth and one 'Hobbs', who seldom went to church and when there spat out the communion wafer, by co-opting them on to the council.[5] Victims of such tricks could have the election overturned by an appeal to the Commons, which had the powers to investigate malpractice by sheriffs. In the autumn of 1640, Bulstrode Whitelocke, a lawyer and one of the defeated candidates at the recent election at Great Marlowe in Buckinghamshire, was approached in his London chambers by 'a country fellow in plain and mean habit'. He claimed that the election had been rigged by the sheriff who had discounted some of Whitelocke's votes in a borough where nearly every adult male was enfranchised, even paupers living in an almshouse. A Parliamentary inquiry upheld the complaint and Whitelocke was duly returned. The evidence presented revealed a considerable degree of popular participation with the four candidates' supporters parading through the streets shouting 'A Whitelocke!', 'A Borlase!', 'A Hippisley!' and 'A Hoby!', and the inevitable dispensing of free tobacco and drinks.[6]

Passions ran high in Great Marlowe because the outcome of a general election would decide the future balance of power between crown and Parliament. Since 1629, when Charles I had decided to break with custom and rule without Parliament, there had been a widening rift between him and many of the men of property and influence who undertook the day-to-day administration of his kingdom. There were several sources of contention: the intrusive influence of the court, fiscal novelties, and fears of a drift towards centralised and autocratic government. Most important in terms of coalescing opposition were widespread suspicions among Puritans and moderate Anglicans that the King was unfit to defend the Protestant faith, that he wished to subvert it and promote Catholicism. Although a large number of Charles's subjects wanted nothing more than to be left alone, they could not ignore developments that threatened the equipoise that had hitherto existed between the monarch and those in the social hierarchy who traditionally supported the figure at its apex. It was their duty to show how the King had gone astray.

There was no written constitution. Parliament had acquired powers in an unplanned way as a consequence of various crises. During the fourteenth century it had gained the right to approve taxation, and censure, remove and punish inept or corrupt royal ministers. In 1399 Parliament had consented to the deposition of Richard II because of his misrule and the accession of Henry IV, who pledged himself to govern fairly. This precedent was pointedly recalled during the 1640–2 crisis when Shakespeare's *Richard II* was revived in some London playhouses. In the fifteenth century Parliament validated the unseating of an incompetent king (Henry VI) and a tyrannical one (Richard III) and authenticated the titles of those who promised to do better (Edward IV and Henry VII). Between 1529 and 1560 Parliament rubber-stamped legislation that severed England's links with Rome, reorganised the administration of the church, confiscated its property and prescribed the nation's faith. Dissatisfied Puritans seized on this precedent to support demands for radical doctrinal changes, including the abolition of bishops.

Although chosen by and filled with men from the upper ranks in society, Parliament did on some occasions reflect the feelings of the masses. A Parliamentary assault on a coterie of venal royal ministers in 1449–50 was backed by popular demonstrations across the Home Counties. A cross-section of society from knights and merchants to weavers and labourers marched on London in 1450, stormed the city and lynched several officials. Jack Cade's rebellion was exceptional in that the rich were invariably apprehensive about any alliance with the masses, who were difficult to control. Having helped purge an unpopular regime, the insurgents turned to looting.

Afterwards, the government blamed the disturbances on disaffected aristocrats and knights who had subverted the common people through a programme of written propaganda, a reminder of high levels of literacy at the time. This explanation fitted the general assumption that, left to their own devices, the masses were intrinsically incapable of organised political action. An official investigation into the large-scale protests against Henry VIII's religious policies in Lincolnshire in 1536 concluded that local gentlemen had been secretly involved, which was why the movement had made such rapid headway.[7] Moreover, bands of rebels had admitted their own deficiencies by pleading with gentlemen to take command of them, which most refused, fearing the King more than the displeasure of the mob. In the 1620s, a spate of riots against field enclosures in Wiltshire were blamed on covert assistance from landowners 'for common people are of slow motion, if not excited by great men'.[8]

There was much excitement among the people as the contest between Charles I and Parliament unfolded during 1641 and the first half of 1642. Londoners favoured the latter, and their violent partisanship unnerved and angered royalists; Lord Clarendon, who witnessed the disorders, later wrote of the 'mutinous and unruly spirit' which expressed itself in 'insolence and sedition'. The 'vile rabble' jeered the King and brawled with courtiers.[9] They were mocked as 'Cavaliers', who responded by calling their assailants 'Roundheads' because apprentices and journeymen cropped their hair. Behind the exchange of insults and the growing popular denunciation of the bishops lurked a fear that the concept of degree itself was being challenged. The assault on the hierarchy of the church was a prelude to one on the civil hierarchy. This was the theme of a satirical Cavalier ballad of 1642 in which the anti-clerical mob boasts:

> We'll teach the nobles how to stoop,
> And keep the gentry down:
> Good manners have an ill report,
> And turn to pride we see,
> We'll therefore put good manners down,
> And hey, then up go we.

Three years into the war between King and Parliament, a Royalist newssheet of 1645 accused the latter of having made an alliance with the 'rout and scum' of the people.[10]

Necessity forced such creatures into both armies, often against their will. Commanders were constantly short of soldiers and had to make do with anyone they could press. Those whose low condition had once barred them from serving in the county militia were drafted and, on the Parliamentary side, sometimes found themselves commanded by men below the rank of gentleman. They served in an army which prided itself on being a godly force, fulfilling God's will and spiritually purifying the kingdom.

Advice as to how this could be accomplished was abundant. The early phase of the struggle between King and Parliament had seen an explosion of religious demagoguery: Puritan preachers of all complexions had flocked to London to encourage the downfall of the bishops and propose ways in which a new, godly order could be established. Sheaves of pamphlets were printed, reproducing sermons, or outlining how the nation might be reborn as a new Israel. A streak of egalitarianism ran through all this literature which argued that the true elect were those who, whatever their social rank, followed the word of God. Those who feverishly studied their Bibles claimed an inviolable right to interpret what they read, setting their own conclusions on a par with or even above those of learned men. During a debate in 1647 on the future of magistrates, two 'mechanics' rejected advice from ministers, 'took snuff' and declared themselves as 'divine as any divines'.[11] After all, anyone who had read that Protestant vade mecum, Foxe's *Book of Martyrs*, knew that it had been poor men and women who had been most fervent and unyielding in their faith during the persecutions of Mary Tudor.

The concept of liberty of conscience and the equality of all godly men and women removed the need for a hierarchy resting on birth, wealth, occupation or education. The old order appeared redundant, especially to those who studied the Book of Revelation and detected in the course of the Civil War signs that cosmic forces were in motion that would transform the world and usher in a new Zion. The collapse of the royal war effort in 1645–6, Charles I's capture and the frustration of his schemes to reopen the conflict with Scottish help revealed the hand of God and were interpreted as portents of further, even more amazing events. What these might be were topics discussed by Parliamentary soldiers who now had plenty of time on their hands. Large numbers were unpaid and, therefore, receptive to suggestions that their efforts in defeating royal tyranny deserved a proper reward. A strong, energetic faction called Levellers emerged with demands for a redistribution of political power in favour of the better-off farmers, retailers and self-employed craftsmen.

The old power structure was defended by senior officers, including Cromwell and his son-in-law, Henry Ireton, in a debate held in Putney church in 1647.[12] Ireton insisted that the lawmakers should remain men 'in whom land is' and in urban corporations 'in whom trading lies' because the 'livelihoods' of all depended upon them. Their judgment was sound and they were not easily swayed. Ireton's adversary, William Rainborow, the son of a naval officer, invoked God's law that all men were 'naturally free', but His will had been overturned by 'old laws'. These prescriptions were part of what the Levellers called the Norman 'yoke' which had deprived Englishmen of the liberties they had enjoyed under the Anglo-Saxon kings. To say the least, this theory took a roseate view of Anglo-Saxon society, but the idea that long ago there had been a golden age when all men were free and equal had a potent appeal, then and later.[13] If such had been the case, concepts of degree and hierarchy blessed by God were alien inventions.

The debate at Putney was never resolved. It was one incident in a short period of intense discussion about how best to order the nation and its faith. Liberty of conscience and notions of universal personal freedom gave a validity to anyone's voice and, seen from above, the commotion threatened stability. Often bizarre sects proliferated – Quakers, Baptists, Fifth Monarchists, Muggletonians, Ranters and Congregationalists – and demanded a complete re-evaluation of the religious and social order. It was rejected wholesale by the Diggers, who adopted a proto-Christian socialism, proclaiming common ownership of land as the only foundation for a truly godly nation. Free thought was running wild and even its advocates paused nervously. When, in 1649, the Diggers began to dig up wasteland on St George's Hill Weybridge, a Leveller pamphlet protested. Levellers 'never had it in our thoughts to level men's estates, it being the upmost of our aim that . . . every man with as much security as may be enjoy his property'.[14]

Security prevailed, or rather those whose security seemed in jeopardy did. The successive administrations of the republic that followed Charles I's execution in 1649 resurrected the somewhat shaken old political dispensation. Dissidents were punished, Parliament passed laws against poaching and to protect the rights of landowners that had a familiar tone, and the influential preacher Puritan Hugh Peter declared that 'a well-monied man that is prudent by God's blessing' and 'gets up above his neighbours' deserved his place in the elect of God and man. After the passage of a new statute against vagrancy in 1656, Quakers protested that under its terms Christ and his apostles would have been arrested.

The governments which upheld old values and remedies were experimental, products of a search for a system that would function without a king at its head. It failed and, after Cromwell's death in 1658, the machinery of the state seemed to be slipping into the hands of professional soldiers, figures from outside the traditional hierarchy, whose power derived from the regiments they commanded. Neither they nor the meddlesome moral legislation foisted on the nation by Puritans were much loved and there was widespread relief when negotiations opened in 1659 for the return from exile of Charles II.

Superficially, the old hierarchy and the principles that justified it were restored in 1660. The Church of England was reinstated and its bishops were zealous in their commitment to the defence and preservation of the authority of their church. Membership of the Anglican church was now, as never before, a statement of loyalty to the crown and acceptance of the prevailing social order. Anyone who repudiated Anglicanism was perceived as a potential source of social and political disruption. The Church of England's old foes, now collectively known as dissenters or nonconformists, were banished to the periphery of society by legislation that excluded from public office anyone who refused to endorse Anglican doctrines publicly. The Test and Corporation Acts bonded the Anglican church to the political hierarchy and kept Congregationalists, Quakers, Baptists and later Moravians outside it. Roman Catholics were subject to the same ban, which extended to Oxford and Cambridge where entry was restricted to undergraduates attesting to the Anglican articles of faith.

Fresh memories of the tumults caused by their preaching in the 1640s and fear of their repetition prompted the persecution of dissenters. There was plenty of passionate defiance: a Surrey man was arraigned before magistrates in 1663 for proclaiming: 'I hope ere long to trample in King's blood and Bishop's blood and I know of six thousand men that will join me in pulling down bishops.'[15] True to their Puritan roots, nonconformists saw themselves as a spiritual elite who placed individual conscience above custom and civil authority. 'Your laws are the devil's laws and you serve the devil . . . and the devil will pay you your wages,' a West Country couple told a local magistrate.[16] Yet while they railed against a state that branded them as wrong-headed and troublesome sectarians, there was nothing dissenters could do to change it.

In 1669 it was calculated that there were about 120,000 dissenters in the country, most of them from the lower orders. Among the nonconformists arrested in Southwark in 1662 were a blacksmith, gardener, yeoman, dyer, cheesemonger, feltmaker and pewterer.[17] Toleration of dissenting worship was allowed in 1689 and the numbers of nonconformists grew; in 1715 it was estimated that there were 180,000 Presbyterians of various sorts, 40,000 Congregationalists and 40,000 Quakers. They gathered in austere surroundings; the Quaker meeting house at Brigg Flats near Sedbergh, built in 1675, has the exterior of a farmhouse and is furnished with plain benches. Elsewhere, lecture halls and chapels have pews and galleries laid out so that the congregation's attention is focused on the preacher. These furnishings convey less of a sense of hierarchy than those in Anglican churches, where the often ornate squire's pew is close to the pulpit, sometimes overlooking the congregation. In many parishes it was common for the poorer members of the congregation to be seated towards the rear of the nave.

High on the chancel arch were the royal coat of arms, a reminder to Anglicans that the monarch was head of their church. A royal church was the partner in royal government; parsons with well-paid livings were often local magistrates and those who were not were still expected to discipline their parishioners. Edward Bennett of South Brewham in Somerset undertook this task zealously according to his epitaph:

> He was no mock priest, but what he did preach,
> By his example also did he teach.
> Error and vice in pulpit and in field
> He fought against and would to neither yield.

Vice and error were hard to uproot and, as in earlier periods, the poor did not take kindly to anyone who tried to hinder their amusements or herd them into church. In 1720 the exasperated parson of Eversholt in Bedfordshire complained to his bishop that his was a 'heathenish and sacrilegious parish where the most laborious ministry and the best example is but washing the blackamoor white'.[18]

Although legally detached from the political hierarchy, dissenting ministers and congregations acted as agents of moral authority. In August 1745 a party of Bedford Moravians 'went to Tilbrook to speak to Presland's wife, for she is a mischievous woman, and will not be obedient to her husband'.[19] Mrs Presland listened to St Paul's strictures on wifely subservience, which, she claimed, were news to her. Learning patience and forbearance were essential for Moravians who, like other dissenters, were profoundly aware of their own sinful leanings. These could be checked only through God's grace, which offered a personal redemption that brought contentment and humility. Among those who sought to teach Mrs Presland the duties of a Christian spouse may have been 'Sister Cherrey', whom her fellow Moravians described as 'very broken and melted at our Saviour's love to be and always thinks herself unworthy of the least mercy, she is a simple heart and is much blessed'.

Prosperity was one of the blessings which many dissenters enjoyed, and for whom it was often seen as a mark of divine favour. One who had done well was described by a colonial official in 1717 as 'a man of very good abilities and estate though a Quaker'.[20] It was obviously puzzling that such a man would allow his creed to disqualify him from enjoying that standing in the world to which his wealth entitled him. Often well to do thanks to trade, dissenters lived in close-knit communities, centred on their chapels and meeting houses and bound together by their sense of righteousness and a rejection of Anglican orthodoxy. None the less, they subscribed wholeheartedly to the commercial ethic that prevailed in the rest of society and the laws which promoted public order and discouraged idleness. Dissenters also applauded the 1701 Act of Succession which upheld Protestant primacy and guaranteed a permanent Protestant monarchy. In time, they developed their own educational system with academies that concentrated on practical and commercial subjects such as arithmetic and science, rather than the study of Classical texts which dominated the curriculum of the universities.

Those who believed themselves blessed were obliged to live abstemiously and honestly. Quakers went so far as to adopt a distinctive, sombre dress and, like other dissenters, had to endure scurrilous accusations of priggishness and humbug. In a ballad of the 1670s with the self-explanatory title 'The Saint turned Sinner; or, the Dissenting Parson's Text under the *Quaker's* Petticoats', a Quaker 'Gospel cushion thumper' is discovered by the local constables lifting the skirts of a draper's wife, also a Quaker.

> The person then confounded
> To see himself surrounded,
> With mob and sturdy watchmen,
> Whose business is to catch men,
> In lewdness with a punk,
> In lewdness with a punk.

Not only is the hypocrite exposed, but he is dragged off to gaol by the officers of the King's justice.

Most Quakers who found themselves arraigned before Charles II's magistrates had fallen foul of laws that restricted their preaching in the interests of public peace. A general desire for tranquillity had been the main reason why the King had been welcomed home in 1660. Old contentions as to how exactly the balance between the power between the crown and Parliament should be weighted were suspended in the interests of stability. They resurfaced in 1685 on the accession of Charles's Catholic brother, James II. His disregard for constitutional and legal precedent and clumsy attempts to reintroduce

Catholics into public life lost him the loyalty of nearly all the aristocracy, gentry, municipal corporations, lawyers, public servants and army and naval officers. Deprived of the support of those on whom the crown depended for running the state, James's regime fell apart within a month of an invasion by William of Orange in November 1688. The Dutch prince had been invited by English dissidents, mostly noblemen, for whom the coup d'état that followed presented an opportunity finally to resolve all outstanding constitutional dilemmas.

The transfer of power and the constitutional arrangements agreed between William III and Mary II and Parliament in 1688–9 were celebrated by future generations as the 'Glorious Revolution'. It was a talismanic compromise that simultaneously ended the strife of the previous sixty years and left Englishmen free to focus their minds and energies on what they did best: making money at home and overseas. In essence the settlement upheld individual legal rights and liberties and established Parliament as a permanent and, as it turned out, dominant partner in government. Henceforward, all political life revolved around Parliament; its business increased dramatically with over 2,500 laws being passed between 1690 and 1714. Equally important was the popular perception of what had been achieved by the Glorious Revolution. The English now considered themselves a privileged people whose unique rights made them superior to other nations, particularly those Continental states ruled by autocratic princes whose authority rested solely on divine sanction. There was much self-congratulation: according to their governor, the inhabitants of New York boasted in 1719 that they were 'free-born Englishmen'.[21] A few years later, Voltaire wrote admiringly and enviously of England as a 'land of liberty'.

Paradoxically, the land of freedom was still one in which power was concentrated in the hands of rich and eminent men. They continued to dispense justice, elect MPs and frame legislation. In 1700 the provincial bench was occupied by rural landowners or urban oligarchs who enforced laws based upon assumptions that had been held for over a century. Those whose rank isolated them from the exercise of power remained free to express their disapproval of their betters and did so frequently and violently. In 1715 Parliament had to pass a Riot Act which gave magistrates the power to order soldiers to fire on rioters who had refused to disperse. Troops were kept busy for the next hundred years dealing with protests against food shortages, the enclosure of common land, regulations for the treatment of the poor and compulsory militia service.

The hierarchy of authority had proved remarkably durable. Its justification had changed and it now rested on pragmatic rather than supernatural grounds, although there were still plenty of squires and parsons who were convinced that their place in society and authority derived from God. What mattered was that those who exercised power did so in ways that benefited a nation which was growing richer and, therefore, needed internal stability. Moreover, it was taken for granted that governance was the concern of those with intelligence and understanding. Like much else that was unquestioningly accepted, this assumption was a basis for everyday jests. One revealing joke circulating in the early 1700s described how a coach containing three MPs crashes and overturns. A nearby rustic refuses to help the passengers with the excuse, 'My father always advised me not to meddle in state affairs.' In similar vein, a pair of countrymen find themselves in a theatre for the first time and hurriedly leave, one remarking, 'Come, Hodge, let's be going . . . the gentlemen are talking about business.'[22]

Not everyone knuckled under. The stubbornness and insolence of the lower orders had been regretted by late-medieval and Tudor commentators. During the reign of James I, one 'Greenhoe', a scrivener, was arraigned before the Earl Marshal's court for declaring that Sir Humphrey Ferrers 'was a base fellow, a base knight and no honest man . . . I am as good a gent born as he, for his ancestors were but king's farriers and by that means got their name as Ferrers.'[23] In 1647 men like Greenhoe offered a more serious assault on the hierarchy of authority. As Levellers they pleaded for a broadening of the hierarchy to include yeomen farmers, independent craftsmen and shopkeepers. Within eighty years these men would be described as 'the middling sort', which was why later historians have regarded the Levellers as the first spokesmen for the political rights of the middle class.

The real voice of the future middle class belonged to Henry Ireton, who insisted that the men who owned land or controlled the nation's trade were to be trusted because their stake in the country qualified them to make judgments in the best interests of all. He made no mention of their superior learning and wisdom which, perhaps, were tacitly understood. Ireton's case was vindicated by experience: the system worked and served the nation well. Furthermore, and this was as persuasive as empirical arguments in favour of the hierarchy of power, English society was fluid and flexible. The hierarchy was never exclusive or self-perpetuating. Irrespective of birth, anyone with talent, initiative and good luck could progress upwards and receive as one of his rewards participation in the exercise of authority over others.

4

Those of Eminent Blood: The Gentry

If one was to devise a game based upon snakes and ladders in which players strove to advance themselves in late-medieval and early-modern England, the winners would be those who made it into the gentry or, and this was a long shot, the aristocracy. Upward movement would depend upon inherited capital, generous kinsfolk and friends, a wife with an ample dowry, a capacity to make the most of opportunities for enrichment, natural intelligence and education. Sickness, accidents, infertility, lawsuits and the caprices of the market would propel the player downwards. The cast of a die would represent the incalculable elements of good luck (which contemporaries would have called 'Providence') and personal temperament. Fundamental to the rules of the game was the universal acceptance of the fact that society was open; it was possible, if not always easy, to climb one or even more rungs in the ladder of degree.

There were hurdles. Myths had been invented which invested the degrees of gentlemen, esquires, knights and noblemen with a peculiar mystique. Their bloodline stretched back to the Creation when Adam's second son, Seth, had been blessed by his father and God. Seth was the progenitor of all who were 'gentle'. His brother, the murderer Cain, cursed by God and his father, was the ancestor of all 'churls' in whose blood ran his inclination towards wickedness. This division of humanity into the 'gentle' and 'ungentle' was explained by Juliana de Berners, a knight's daughter and prioress, in her *Book of St Albans*, which was written at the end of the fourteenth century. It was printed in 1486 and, probably because it contained a mass of useful and recondite information on hunting and angling, went through six editions in the next hundred years.

Dame Juliana's digressions on the scriptural origins of the gentry and the source of their inherited virtue were repeated with elaborations by Gerard Legh in his *The Accedens of Armory* (1562), a popular handbook on heraldry. The author was a herald, an occupation that entitled him to call himself a gentleman, although he had once worked as a draper in London alongside his father, who was an illegitimate son of one of the Leghs, a knightly Cheshire family.[1] None the less, Legh felt obliged to promote the notion that the gentle owed their elevated position and moral qualities to their common ancestor Seth. Jesus, he added, was a gentleman because his genealogy, as given in St Matthew's gospel, traced his ancestry back to King David.

Legh also produced a secular vindication of the moral superiority of the gentle. He conjured up a vision of a remote age when everyone had been considered equal. Then the people had chosen leaders of outstanding 'virtue' which they transmitted to their offspring. They followed their parents' example and 'retained the favour and reverence of the people' and so perpetuated their exalted status.[2] It followed then that, like their forebears, the gentry of Elizabethan England were genetically qualified to rule.

This was a flattering notion and had a long life. Ambrose Barnes, a Newcastle merchant who died in 1710 aged eighty-three, recalled in his memoirs that he came from 'a good' rather than 'a great and high family'. Nevertheless, his birth was advantageous, for those of 'low descent [are] . . . commonly of base, mean spirit, not fit for raised stations; but those of better original . . . naturally aspire to things worthy of themselves'.[3] Not only were the low-born predisposed towards turpitude, they were incapable of exerting authority over others. 'What a disparagement was it to the government and the King's authority' to appoint a former carpenter, William Partridge, as governor of New Hampshire, complained his superior, Lord

Bellomonte, in 1700. 'A mechanic and mean governor' could never be respected by colonists who remembered how he had once earned wages for manual labour.[4]

Respect for such niceties seemed incongruous during a period when more and more men from widely different backgrounds were laying claim to gentry status. William Shakespeare, the glover's son from Stratford, was one, and, like every other new gentleman, he procured a coat of arms as proof of his elevation. It was given to him in return for a fee by a herald, a member of the College of Arms that had been established by the crown in 1483. It issued coats of arms, the official imprimatur of gentleness, and from the 1530s onwards heralds regularly traversed the country to scrutinise the claims of gentlemen and strip impostors of their titles. They had some surprises: after asking a Middlesex backwoodsman to show him his coat, a herald was offered an article of clothing.

As keepers of the gate that separated the gentle from outsiders, the heralds faced an increasingly delicate task as more and more wanted to pass through it. A common way to secure a fee and satisfy a would-be gentleman was to ignore ancestry and emphasise virtue and public esteem. Robert Sotheby, a Yorkshire yeoman, obtained his coat of arms because the herald judged that he was 'descended of a house unde-famed and has long used himself honestly and discreetly'.[5] Like every other new gentleman, Sotheby was reminded that he had entered an estate with an illustrious reputation which he had to live up to. The grant of arms described them as 'tokens of prowess and valour' and told their owner that gentleness had the mystical power to 'stir and kindle hearts of men in imitation of virtue and nobleness'. If he wished to advertise the heroic, martial antecedents of his degree, and most did, the freshly created gentleman had himself portrayed on his tomb in armour. This atavistic conceit persisted well into the seventeenth century when armour was rarely if ever worn on the battlefield.

Did anyone believe this stuff? In his survey of England published in 1577, William Harrison concluded that the whole business was a racket:

Whosoever studies the laws of the realm, who so abides in the University (giving his mind to his book), or professes physic and the liberal sciences, or so beside his service in the room of a captain in the wars, or good counsel given at home, whereby the commonwealth is benefited, can live without manual labour and thereto is able and will bear the part, charge and countenance of a gentleman, he shall for money have a coat of arms bestowed upon him by the heralds who in charter [grant] of the same do of custom pretend antiquity and service and many gay things and thereunto being so good cheap be called master, which is the title that men give to esquires and gentlemen.[6]

The world at large connived at this charade. One of the rogues in the comedy *A Merry Knack to Know a Knave* (1594) announces that, thanks to his 'gay apparel', he has successfully masqueraded as a 'landed knight' and defrauded some London merchants. The deception worked because:

> 'Tis strange to see how men of our knowledge live,
> And how we are hated of the baser sort,
> Because, forsooth, we live upon our wit;
> But let the baser sort think as they will,
> For he may best be termed a gentleman,
> That, when all fail, can live upon his wit.[7]

A confidence trickster active in the 1570s did just this. 'Using as he could courtesy, and being gentlemanlike attired', he persuaded a party of clothiers to set him at the head of the table in the inn where they were staying. His conversation was agreeable, everyone ate and drank well until the gentleman suddenly vanished, leaving his companions to pay his reckoning.[8] Counterfeit gentlemen and women fascinated playwrights and their audiences. In Thomas Middleton's *Michaelmas Term* (1607), Helgill, a pander, persuades a 'Northamptonshire lass' who wants to become a gentlewoman that all that is needed is for her to acquire new clothes. 'Remember a loose-bodied gown, wench, and let it go; wires and tires, bents and bums, felts and falls, thou shalt deceive the world.' Her wardrobe later convinces his reprobate master that she is 'a gentlewoman of great house'.

This must have been a common form of imposture. A contemporary slander case involved a respectable elderly widow being called a 'base slut' and 'baud' whose 'fine clothes were brought at the pawn-brokers'.[9] Outward appearances had to be complemented by confidence and bearing, as Shortyard, a merchant's servant, explains elsewhere in *Michaelmas Term*: 'let a man bear himself portly, the whoresons will creep to him o'their bellies, and their wives o'their backs: there's a bold grace expected throughout all the parts of a gentleman'.

Behind the satire was a disturbing question. As the estate of the gentry became more and more crowded, was gentleness falling into decay? Its ancient values and the gulf in outlook between gentle and non-gentle were invoked by Lady Alworth in Philip Massinger's comedy *A New Way to Pay Old Debts* (1625). 'Common men make sordid wealth the object, and sole end of their industrious aims,' she declares, whereas 'those of eminent blood' prefer to enlarge their honour. Honour was the vital ingredient in the chemistry of gentleness.

Honour had many facets. Valour was essential: in the past members of the first estate had been warriors, trained to use weapons and inspire others by their courage and indifference to death. A gentleman had to be brave which was why, when insulted, he defended his character with sword or pistol in that ultimate test of personal honour, the duel. Even though he might never lead others in war, the gentleman was expected to acquire those skills that were invaluable on the battlefield. He hunted, fenced and, if he was rich enough, learned how to tilt in full armour, although tournaments were passing out of fashion by the end of the sixteenth century. Accustomed to giving orders and with some skill in arms and horsemanship, gentlemen were the natural choice to command the county militia and, by 1700, when England possessed a navy and standing army, to command sailors and soldiers.

Another source of honour was ancestry. The accumulated honour of generations was a source of pride and gave its owner a powerful sense of what was expected from him. This was the theme of the epitaph of Lionel Tollemache, who died in about 1550 and whose tomb was set up by his great-grandson in Helmingham in Suffolk:

Baptized Lyone Tollemache my Name
Since Normans Conquest of unsoyled Fame
Shews my Descent from Ancestors of Worth;
And that my Life might no belye my Birth,
Their Virtues Track with heedfull steps I trod,
Rightful to Men, Religious towards God.

Traducing a gentleman's birth stripped him of honour. In 1631, Thomas Ewbancke, a Northumberland gentleman, complained that he had been slandered by Robert Brandling, another gentleman and sheriff of the county. In language 'not befitting a man of his place and quality', Brandling had called Ewbancke a 'bastardly rogue' whose father had been a 'knave' and mother a 'whore'. He repudiated these slurs by insisting that his parents had been 'well known to the best of the County Palatine of Durham always to have lived in good estimation and credit'.[10] What better recommendation could there be for a gentleman? But if Brandling had been right, it was impossible for a man with such flawed origins to call himself gentleman, irrespective of his merit and conduct. There was a rash of similar contemporary cases which suggests some of the old gentry and aristocracy felt resentment towards interlopers. Their mood was sensed by Sir Francis Bacon, who remarked that 'Men of noble birth are noted to be envious towards new men when they rise.' Tension was unavoidable: 'For the distance is altered; and it is like a deceit of eye, that when others come on, they think themselves go back.'

Those coming on were unstoppable. They were undeterred by fairy stories about Adam's paternal blessing, or fables about an ancient elite of instinctive virtue; indeed, once they became gentlemen some were happy to accept these fictions. Nor were they unduly discountenanced by the 'old' gentry's ancestry fetish that was expressed in various satisfying but harmless ways in the late sixteenth and early seventeenth centuries. Excessive heraldic ornamentation became popular on tombs and Sir Edward Dering of Pluckley in Kent faked monuments to his medieval forebears and had them placed in their local church in the 1630s. Some with 'old' blood obsessively investigated their pedigrees, resorting to invention when all else failed. The Lumleys of Durham traced their ancestors back to Adam, prompting James I to remark: 'I did na ken Adam's name was Lumley.'

Assimilation into the gentry required the adoption of distinctive forms of behaviour and habits of mind. These could be acquired through study of the growing literature devoted to teaching men and women correct forms and manners. More was required than a mastery of etiquette; gentlemen were expected to be cultured and witty. Chaucer's squire composed verses and songs and recited and sang those of others. His contemporary Henry Bolingbroke (the future Henry IV) played the recorder, was fluent in French and Latin, listened to and commented on theological disputations and was a passionate bibliophile.

The library and university were as appropriate places for the gentleman as the stables, tiltyard or tennis court. Indeed, the consensus of Renaissance opinion was that enlightenment drawn from the didactic works of Greece and Rome was of as much importance to a gentleman as the mastery of the rapier or lute, if not more so. A balance existed between physical and mental exercise. In what turned out to be a seminal guide for the conduct of a gentleman's life, *The Boke named The Governour* (1530), the courtier and diplomat Sir Thomas Elyot pressed his readers to acquire 'understanding' through study and contemplation. In a revealing comparison, he likened the enlightened gentleman to one of the higher orders of angels who were 'most fervent in contemplation' and, therefore, 'highest in glory'. The fruits of intellectual enquiry were wisdom, self-knowledge and contentment, qualities essential in a man who ruled others. 'By means of their excellent wit, showed through the glass of authority', 'learned and cultured gentlemen' were able to direct 'others of inferior understanding' towards the 'way of virtue and commodious living'. If he followed Elyot's advice, which was backed by ample citations from Classical authorities, the gentleman would become a counterpart of Plato's philosopher prince whose authority rested on superior percipience.

'Learning, wisdom, authority and wealth' were embodied in the magistrate, according to William Lambard whose handbook for local justices was first published in 1581. These qualities gave the JP the ability to arbitrate in petty disputes as well as to correct lawbreakers.[11]

For Elyot and Lambard, the degree of gentleman carried with it an obligation to maintain civil order and create what Lambard called 'universal unanimity' among the population. This responsibility had a powerful and enduring influence on the upbringing and outlook of gentlemen; they were not just an ornamental noblesse d'épée, but men whose learning, wisdom and judgment gave the nation stability.

The gentleman had not only to aspire to high ideals, he was expected to be restrained and fastidious in his manners. Decorum did not come naturally, if the incivilities listed in the literature of courtesy are anything to go by. Fifteenth- and sixteenth-century textbooks on etiquette strongly suggest that there was an inclination towards coarseness that needed constant admonition. Eating habits in particular needed refinement, for, according to Erasmus' *De Civitate Morum Puerilium* (translated and published as *A Lytell Booke of God Maners for Children* in 1532), a gentleman was identified by how he ate. Workmen thrust their fingers into dishes and tradesmen wiped their noses on the sleeves of their gowns. Elsewhere, gnawing bones was forbidden and one manual noted that the precise carving of meat distinguished a gentleman from labourers who hacked at joints with their knives. This was so intolerable that one nobleman sacked a servant who sliced his meat with a pocket knife, which was the 'cognisance of a clown'.[12] Other giveaway signs of the bumpkin had to be shunned. There were warnings against picking noses and blowing them on table linen, probing ears for wax and rolling it into pellets, scratching testicles, picking teeth with knife points, spitting and farting. 'Belch thou near no man's face with corrupt fumosity,' advised Hugh Rhodes's *Book of Nurture* (1577).

Despite an abundance of guidebooks, standards of propriety were never universal. Gentlemen swaggered, swore, brawled and caroused with abandon. In his diary, William Coe (1662–1729), a Cambridgeshire gentleman, owned to all these transgressions together with gambling and the regular enjoyment of 'filthy songs and discourses'. With some like-minded companions he spent the entire afternoon of 13 May 1694 in 'lewd, wicked and profane discourse'.[13] Coe was a member of that durable race of bucolic gentlemen whose ranks would include Henry Fielding's Squire Western in the eighteenth century and the hunting cronies of R. S. Surtees's Soapy Sponge in the nineteenth.

Such creatures delighted sophisticated London theatregoers from the 1600s onwards. 'You must pardon my father; he's somewhat rude, and my mother grossly brought up,' explains the young Sir Abraham Ninny in Nathan Field's *A Woman is a Weathercock* (1612). This couple had been born and brought up in East Anglia, but their son, who had broken a leg while playing 'football' at Cambridge, fancies himself a polished gentleman. He reveals otherwise when, in response to the question, 'What countrymen were your ancestors?', he answers indignantly, 'Countrymen! They were no countrymen. They were gentlemen all: my father is a Ninny and my mother was a Hammer.'[14]

One suspects that the actor who played Ninny adopted a broad rural accent. By this time, south-eastern English was acquiring associations with gentleness and Ninny's Fenland twang would have made his affectations all the funnier for London audiences. None the less, country accents were acceptable among gentleman. 'Corrupt in speech, be sure I am,' declared Hugh Rhodes, the author of the *Book of Nurture*, but his Devonshire burr did not prevent him from securing a post at the court of Elizabeth I.[15] What mattered was that a gentleman's speech should be comprehensible, according to Edmund Coote's *The English Schoole Master*, which appeared in 1596 and soon became a basic text for teaching correct English usage. Coote vilified the 'barbarous speech of country people' which was riddled with dialect words such as 'yerb' for herb or 'ship' for sheep and therefore unintelligible to strangers. Correctness of pronunciation was essential for a gentleman who had to be understood in whatever company he found himself. His words were to be uttered in a measured and modulated tone and accompanied by graceful gestures. Clumsiness and fidgeting, like dialect words, were hallmarks of the uncouth.

The line between gentle and non-gentle bisected society. 'Art thou an officer?' asks Ancient Pistol when he encounters the disguised Henry V on the night before Agincourt. 'Or art thou base, common and popular?' The King was not only a gentleman, but stood at the pinnacle of a hierarchy that stretched down through the aristocracy to the country squire. The internal barriers of this hierarchy were jealously guarded: a gentleman who forgot his position and challenged the Earl of Northumberland was reprimanded by James I for 'high insolency' and another who called out the Earl of Sussex was imprisoned and compelled to apologise for his temerity. Familiarity was frowned on. Gervase Holles noted approvingly that his kinsman, the 1st Earl of Clare (1564–1651), was 'of the most courteous and affable disposition, yet preserved exactly the grandeur and distance of quality'.[16]

Distinctions in life were preserved after death. At Ewelme in Oxfordshire, the elegant alabaster effigy of Alice Duchess of Suffolk who died in 1475 lies on a high, canopied tomb chest, its sides decorated with painted shields that reveal her illustrious ancestry. Her father, Thomas Chaucer esquire, the son of the poet and several times speaker of the House of Commons, appears armoured on a brass on another raised tomb, also richly embellished with heraldry. This wealthy and well-connected landowner and his daughter lie close to the altar, the holiest part of the church which they helped build. Further away, in the nave, is the smaller brass to Thomas Broke, an esquire and minor royal official who enjoyed the custody of the hunting park at Ewelme. He too wears armour (with a huge tournament helm behind his head) to announce his degree and is surrounded by shields, but his tomb cost a fraction of those of the Duchess and her parents.

Differences in wealth usually coincided with differences in rank within the gentle classes, but not always. Thomas Chaucer, although an esquire, was richer than many knights and, perhaps, than a few impoverished peers. It is hard to discover how much the gentry and aristocracy were worth. Fiscal evidence based upon self-assessed tax returns is bound to be skewed for that reason, but it does provide an indication of the pattern of wealth distribution. In 1436, the year of Chaucer's death, the land tax revealed that the aristocracy possessed between three and four million acres, which provided them with a combined income of £78,000. The total rent roll of knights, esquires and gentlemen with yearly revenues of between five and one hundred pounds was £113,000 from about five million acres, roughly 45 per cent of the land under cultivation. The remainder was in the hands of the crown (5 per cent), the church (between 20 and 25 per cent) and yeoman farmers with annual incomes of under five pounds.

Little changed in the next two hundred years. An estimate made in 1669 gave the gentry 43 per cent of the land.[17] In the 1690s a herald, Gregory King, calculated that there were 2.4 million who paid taxes and rates; between 12,000 and 13,000 were landed gentlemen, between 140,000 and 180,000 farmers with holdings yielding up to £84 per year, and the rest were professional and business men, clergy and shop-keepers. There were three million, about 60 per cent of the population, who were too poor to pay any taxes or rates, including 700,000 wholly or partly supported on poor relief. King's figures ignored higher clergymen (archbishops and bishops received between £450 and £7,000 a year depending on their sees), lawyers and merchants, whose revenues were equal to and sometimes greater than those of some aristocrats and gentlemen. There were also a substantial number of gentlemen who supplemented their incomes through law, commerce and speculation, and younger sons of gentlemen who kept their father's rank but earned their living.[18] These evaluations ignore inflation, the sale to laymen of monastic estates in the mid-sixteenth century and large-scale land reclamation in the seventeenth.

Gentry fortunes were never static. They were subject to the mischances of sudden death, childlessness, infant mortality, the lack of male heirs, bankruptcy, excessive gambling, bad investments and the burden of dependent relatives. There were 557 gentry families in Yorkshire in 1557 and 679 in 1642, totals that reflected the growing numbers of gentlemen throughout the country. And yet, during the same period, 181 families died out in the male line, leaving their estates to be distributed either to daughters, if there were any, or among cousins or nephews. Thirty families vanished, presumably leaving the county or slipping down the social ladder as a consequence of impoverishment or some unforeseen catastrophe.[19] 'I was my father's heir,' lamented William Grismond as he waited for execution. He was a rich young gentleman who, according to a broadsheet of 1650, had been found guilty of murdering a poor local girl whom he had seduced.[20] Between 1618 and 1668, a total of 141 'gentlemen of quality' left Bedfordshire, some no doubt having lost their lands as a consequence of backing Charles I. The loss was more than made good by incomers who had made money from law or trade.[21]

Just as the internal divisions of the aristocracy and gentry were reflected in church monuments, so was their transience. At Ashby St Ledgers in Northamptonshire the floor is inlaid with brasses to various Catesbys, an ambitious dynasty prominent locally and nationally. There is Sir William, a household officer of Henry VI and MP whose fortunes faded after the eclipse of the House of Lancaster. His son William, an unscrupulous lawyer, sought to restore them. He made himself indispensable first to the influential Yorkist magnate William Lord Hastings and then to Richard III. In 1484 Catesby was lampooned with two more of Richard's henchmen, Sir Richard Ratcliff and Lord Lovell:

> The Cat, the Rat and Lovell the dog,
> Rule all England under the hog.

After the death of the 'hog' (Richard III) at Bosworth, Catesby was beheaded, though his epitaph puts his death a week before the battle, no doubt to protect the reputation of his family. Subsequent Catesbys prudently avoided high politics; Richard performed the routine duties of a gentleman, serving as a magistrate, sheriff and MP. He died in 1553 and is commemorated by the largest and most handsome brass which shows him standing on a cat – the doggerel had obviously been forgotten. Richard's great-grandson Robert, a Catholic, joined the Gunpowder Plot of 1603 and was killed resisting arrest, and Ashby St Ledgers was confiscated by the crown as the property of a traitor.

Robert Catesby's foolhardiness was Brian I'Anson's opportunity. The son of an officer in Henry VIII's navy and a prosperous London draper, he purchased Ashby St Ledgers in 1612 as part of a programme of investment in land. His carved monument of 1634 shows him, his wife and children at prayer. I'Anson was a familiar figure, the merchant-turned-gentleman whose pretensions invited satire. Here is Sir Lionel Rash, a rich London entrepreneur, celebrating his elevation in *The City Gallant* (1614):

... I have worship now in the right kind; the sword of knight-hood sticks still upon my shoulder and I feel the blow in my purse, it has cut two leather bags asunder. But all's one, honour must be purchased. I will give over my city coat and betake myself to the court jacket. As for trade, I will deal in't no longer ...

He then sets out to buy some rural property, fitting for his new status.

The I'Ansons did not turn their backs on trade. They married the daughters of merchants as well as of gentlemen, and launched at least three younger sons into commerce; one joined the East India Company in the 1680s. Others were directed towards the law and the church, including Dr Henry I'Anson of All Souls College, Oxford who 'died poor' according the family pedigree.[22] It also lists deaths in childbed and infancy and members of the family who disappeared from view. Close to the I'Anson memorials is a marble tablet in the fashionable Classical style with putti to Joseph Ashley 'Esquire, Citizen and Draper of London who in the Year 1705 purchased the Manor and Estate of Ashby St Ledgers'. Again the property exchanged hands for City money and, in turn, the Ashleys sold the estate to a family that had made its fortune from a new source of wealth creation, manufacturing industry. In 1903 Ashby St Ledgers was bought by Ivor Guest, Viscount Wimborne, the descendant of Josiah Guest (1785–1852), an ironmaster who developed the massive Dowlais plant in South Wales. Lutyens's memorial to Viscount Wimborne is in the churchyard and completes an extraordinary sequence.

Gentry families came and went, a minute number in a spectacular manner like the Catesbys. Most disappeared because of a lack of sons, which was regarded as a tragedy and was why eighteenth- and nineteenth-century sculptors often included a broken column in the design for the tomb to the last in any line. Of course, accumulations of land remained and passed to heiresses and their fortunate husbands or distant male kin. What the memorials at Ashby St Ledgers demon-strate is the ease with which the gentry replenished their ranks; they were never a closed caste, despite fables about inherited virtues extending back to the Creation.

Moreover, and this had enormous significance for the development of society, the custom of primogeniture dictated that younger sons made their own way in the world. Even on the rare occasions when the eldest son was disinherited, his father felt obliged to provide him with some support. In 1653, Thomas Chamberlain's father wrote in his will that he 'has been stubborn and disobedient to me and deserves nothing'. The family's estate in Oxfordshire passed to his younger brother, but Thomas was given £500, which he took to Virginia where planter society welcomed gentlemen.[23] The colonies had already become a repository for scapegrace sons.

Wholesale and overseas trade, the law, the Anglican church and, from the late seventeenth century onwards, the army and navy were considered ideal professions for younger sons. Fathers made the appropriate arrangements for their tuition or apprenticeship, usually and where funds allowed to one of the prestigious London merchant companies. Not all gentlemen had the capital to ease their younger sons into potentially rewarding careers. 'Squire' Coe, who was occasionally beset by cash problems (he once saved money by cutting off the hair of his daughters to make himself a periwig), apprenticed his eldest son to a Wisbech apothecary in 1708.

Young gentlemen were constantly being dispersed among what by the early eighteenth century was beginning to be called 'the middling sort' or 'the middling station in life'. If they found themselves working with their hands, they forfeited any claims to gentle rank. Physical toil had no dignity, something that it would acquire first from romantics and then from socialists. A distinction was drawn between the useful but inferior 'Mechanical Arts', which were disciplines of eye, hand and muscle, and the equally useful but intrinsically superior 'Liberal Arts'. They were Grammar, Dialectic, Rhetoric, Geometry, Arithmetic, Astrology and Music. These purely intellectual activities were entirely proper for gentlemen. They looked askance at abstract knowledge adapted for practical purposes: a mathematics textbook published in 1714 regretted that young gentlemen were 'so brisk and airy as to think that the knowing how to cast account is requisite for such underlings as shopkeepers or tradesmen, but unnecessary and below persons of plentiful estates'.[24] None the less, there were plenty of gentlemen who kept their own daily account books simply to maintain control over their expenditure.

The emergence in the 1700s of the new profession of architecture confirmed how deep-rooted the distinction between abstract and applied knowledge had become. Firmly among the practitioners of the Mechanical Arts was the 'master builder' whom a guide to occupations compiled in 1747 placed among the 'first rank of tradesmen'. He might design buildings, using pattern books, but his time was largely consumed by calculating the costs of material and labour and even cutting stone. By contrast, the architect lived by his creative imagination, which was rooted in a profound understanding of the present Classical style and its ancient roots. One prominent architect, Sir William Chambers (1723–96), denounced master builders as 'mechanics who assume the profession and arrogate the title of architects' and another, Robert Adam (1728–92), reviled them as 'reptile artisans'. Neither was a gentleman by birth, and as doyens of a new profession each was expressing that form of snobbery which always came easily to arrivistes. Nevertheless, they were airing a social truth: anyone whose livelihood depended on abstract reasoning was somehow superior to those who relied on purely practical intelligence, however useful they might be to society.

Younger sons were acutely aware that they had to struggle in a competitive world in which parental status counted for little. A younger son himself, John Wilson grumbled that his kind existed in a 'state' which 'is of all stations for gentlemen most miserable'.[25] He had been born in 1560, had a niggardly inheritance from his father ('that which the cat left on the malt heap'), and, having failed to secure a fellowship at Cambridge, was forced to make a precarious living as an author, translator and spy. Perhaps for this reason he clung to his status and was jealous of those who had the means to achieve it, in particular the sons of rich yeomen. Unwilling to 'be called John and Robert', the discontented yeoman's son 'must skip into his velvet breeches and silken doublet and, getting to be admitted into some Inn of Court . . . must ever after think scorn to be called other than gentleman'. In the end, Wilson's capacity to make himself useful to powerful men regained him his father's rank; he was knighted and achieved some prosperity.

Although dear to him, Wilson's status meant nothing in the eyes of the law. A man indicted in 1505 as a 'yeoman' and later pardoned as a 'gentleman' was deemed by the judges to be the same person.[26] The peculiar honour cherished by gentlemen extended to everyone else, at least in the eyes of the law. In 1519, Nicholas Vernycombe, a Devon man who described himself as 'accustomed with honest persons in buying and selling and lawfully bargaining', was awarded damages of £10 against a man who defamed him as a 'bond churl'.[27] Everyone was entitled to a reputation for honesty and decency. In 1598 a row in a Malton alehouse over a mouldy herring and a high bill prompted Edward Clynt to tell the hostess, Elizabeth Bownas, that she was an 'arrant whore'. She rushed to the local church court, which restored her reputation for chastity.[28] In theory, the law disregarded differences in rank when assessing the merits of a plea. A Tudor litigant from Derbyshire who described himself as 'a poor man' believed that this would not impede his proceedings against a local squire who was 'a man of great power and substance'.[29] Of course this ignored the fact that the latter could hire counsel who might prolong the case until it became prohibitively expensive.

Gentlemen had long purses. They also had many responsibilities: their idealised exemplar, Richard Steele's Sir Roger de Coverley, sat on the local bench, was chairman of his county's Quarter Sessions and sat in the Commons, where he was applauded for 'explaining a passage in the Game Act' – an easy task for an active and dedicated sportsman. He was 'a great lover of mankind', and a conscientious landlord whose tenants flourished. De Coverley's standing derived from his land: it provided financial security and identified him as a member of the gentry, that body which enjoyed political paramountcy and set the tone of society.

5

Golden Hooks: The Professions

In August 1710 Timothy Burrell, a barrister and Sussex squire, was afflicted with piles. He turned to another professional man, Dr Fuller, and purchased a bitter infusion and 'stomach wine' from him. They proved useless, so he approached Dr Cox, whose cure was also ineffective. In October he returned to Fuller who had in the meantime concocted a new remedy.[1] At least Burrell had been spared those universal nostrums, clysters (enemas) and bleeding.

A lawyer, particularly with an embarrassing complaint, seeking the services of a doctor would have amused contemporaries. Each was a member of profession with a reputation for low practice and high charges. In the lampoon *Hell in an Uproar* (1718), lawyers and physicians explain why they are suffering eternal torment. A lawyer declares:

> I think no men on earth live more profane,
> Than students in the Law, in vice they reign;
> They drink and whore all night; i'th morning rise
> To cozen, swear, and tell a thousand lies
> As long as clients can feed us with the gold.

Equally cynical and grasping are the physicians:

> We come not nigh; but for the gentry; who
> Have golden hooks to bait, we gallop to
> Their homes fast enough, both night and day . . .
> To smell their urine, feel how pulses beat,
> These we can cure, if money comes apace.[2]

These were variations on a well-worn satirical theme. Chaucer's sergeant-at-law and physician were more concerned with filling their pockets than with upholding justice or healing the sick. Doctors were likened by a contemporary preacher to robbers 'who by false subtleties take falsely men's goods'. A physician is shown on a fifteenth-century misericord in St Mary's Beverley as a monkey holding a urine glass while a patient proffers a coin. The venality of doctors was matched by that of the apothecaries who prepared and sold prescriptions. 'A man must live,' explained an apothecary in a satire of 1697 in justification for charging 4s 6d for 'a specific bolus' that was a compound of 'a farthing-worth of crabs eyes in a little London treacle'.[3] There was plenty of such rubbish on the market and plenty of desperate men and women willing to put their faith in it.

Lawyers fared no better. In the popular imagination they were mendacious hair-splitters who connived at prolonging cases to jack up their fees. Audiences who watched *The Three Ladies of London* (1581) had all their prejudices vindicated when a lawyer confides:

> Tush, sir, I can make black white, and white black again.
> Tut, he that will be a lawyer must have a thousand ways to feign:
> And many times we lawyers do befriend another,
> And let good matters slip! Tut, we agree like brother and brother.[4]

Jeering at the vices of doctors and lawyers did not hide the uncomfortable fact that they were indispensable. They applied specialist knowledge and solutions to the tiresome, routine problems of everyday life. People fell sick and suffered accidents, and childbirth was perilous. Everyone who owned property or was engaged in commerce needed legal advice to draw up contracts, covenants, bonds, wills and marriage settlements that were unassailable. If they proved otherwise, lawyers were required to recover debts, enforce obligations and secure compensation for trespasses.

Health, peace of mind and redress for injury were essential, and lawyers and doctors set a high price on them. Paying for the intangible and, in the case of the physicians, for what was too often unreliable aroused resentment among laymen. They were also baffled by incomprehensible jargon which like the conjuror's patter seemed contrived either to confuse or to mislead.

Furthermore, dishonest doctors and lawyers were not satirical fabrications. In 1425 a London parson Robert Scarle was denounced by his neighbours as a pimp who also 'presents himself a surgeon and physician to deceive people with his false cunning . . . by which craft [he] has slain many a man'.[5] Thirty years later, the inhabitants of East Anglia complained to Parliament that they were being vexed by lawyers who 'go to every fair, market and other places where congregation of people is, and stir, procure, move and excite people to make untrue suits'.[6] In 1574 some Londoners were taken in by 'one Pyne', a one-eyed rogue who was pilloried for fraud: his indictment described him as 'an old shifter and pettifogger in attorneyship, but no attorney in fact by the roll'.[7] His imposture was exposed by checking the lists of those who had passed through the four Inns of Court.

Gray's Inn, Lincoln's Inn and the Inner and Middle Temple were associations which offered a mixture of informal instruction and regular bouts of conviviality. They were not professional bodies in any modern sense: they kept registers, but set no exams, issued no qualifications and were unconcerned with standards of private and professional probity. Their principal task was to defend their members' monopolies and exclude interlopers. Doctors, surgeons and apothecaries had similar associations. From 1518 all London doctors were controlled by the Royal College of Physicians, which upheld its prestige by restricting the numbers of licences it issued. Recipients had to be graduates of Oxford and Cambridge, where medicine was a Cinderella subject with a purely academic curriculum. The best physicians, like Sir William Hervey, had to get a practical education in the infinitely more distinguished Continental universities, particularly Padua.

Provincial doctors were licensed either by bishops or by the two universities. Surgery was treated as a craft and controlled by urban guilds, which supervised apprenticeships, set charges and enforced standards. In 1500 the York Surgeons Guild had seventy members including one woman, served a population of about 7,000 and had its own library.[8] Apothecaries were organised along similar lines. These professional bodies devoted considerable passion and energy to disputing clinical demarcation lines. The more numerous surgeons and apothecaries finally won a hard-fought struggle; in 1704 a House of Lords judgment permitted the latter to diagnose complaints and administer treatments as well as supply drugs. This ruling merely acknowledged reality, for by then the apothecaries were attending more than nine-tenths of patients in London alone.

Gregarious self-indulgence was common to all professional bodies from the legal Inns to small urban craft guilds. They were part of an immensely popular culture that expressed itself in regular festivities in which members dressed up, ate huge meals, drank heavily and were entertained by musicians and players. Digestive stamina was one assay of the lawyer whose total of meals consumed in his Inn of Court determined the moment when he was called to a bar, a cere-mony which after 1590 guaranteed his right to plead before the central courts at Westminster and the provincial assizes. Communal dining created a sense of professional brotherhood, fostered friend-ships and, on some occasions, offered informal tuition. When the tables were cleared, novices and experienced lawyers disputed often recondite points of law (Shakespeare's 'quiddities') that were tests of knowledge, of fluency in the archaic Norman-French still used in some courts and of a capacity to think quickly. The more dedicated pupils noted down what was said, particularly by judges discussing precedents.

From the early sixteenth century dinners during the twelve-day Christmas festival were followed by revels. These evolved into sophist-icated affairs with interludes, masques and full-length plays performed before illustrious audiences, including Elizabeth I and her ministers. The Inns were casinos as well as temporary playhouses, for gambling was permitted in their halls during Christmas. On New Year's Day

1668, Samuel Pepys watched the play and was appalled to see 'dirty prentices and idle people' among the dicers and was astonished by a 'profane, mad entertainment' in which the lucky won a hundred pounds in an hour. There was no moral incongruity in august institutions playing host to a pastime that was denounced in pulpit and pamphlet. If challenged, senior benchers of the Inns would have defended themselves by asserting that the practice was established by custom. Tradition was revered by the professions, which fostered an aversion to change of all kinds.

A proper gravity prevailed in the Inns during the rituals and banquets that marked the apogee of a lawyer's career, his installation as a sergeant-at-law. Each year, following the advice of the judiciary and senior members of the Inns, the crown nominated new sergeants whose status entitled them to charge the highest fees and from whose ranks judges were appointed. It was a chance to proclaim the dignity, wealth and self-confidence of the legal profession. The new sergeants rode in cavalcade from their Inns to Westminster Hall, where they were invested with the scarlet hoods and white coifs of their order. Afterwards they presented rings to royal ministers and judges, made gifts to their respective Inns, feasted their fellow members and concluded this ostentatious rite of passage with a great dinner, sometimes attended by the monarch. Like all the ceremonies and festivals that marked the calendars of the merchant companies and guilds, these junketings reminded outsiders that those who held them belonged to exclusive and often exalted fellowships.

William Paston was installed as a sergeant-at-law in 1421. He was in his early forties, had a string of valuable clients from his native Norfolk and had come a long way. His father Clement had been born at Paston in the middle of the last century and was remembered locally as 'a good plain husbandman' who had ploughed his hundred or so acres each spring, 'rode to the mill on the bare horseback with his corn under him' and 'drove his cart with divers corn to Winterton to sell'. He was a prosperous peasant, just like his contemporary, Chaucer's Reeve. Both men were among the hundreds of thousands of beneficiaries of the famines of 1315–22 and the plague pandemics between 1348 and 1375 that had reduced the population from just over five million to less than two and a half. Like their equivalents in today's Third World, the survivors tended to be richer and healthier than their neighbours.[9]

A new economic dispensation emerged and was exploited for all its worth by men like Clement Paston, who had enough capital to acquire land and tenancies in a buyer's market. He expanded his holdings and made a profitable marriage to Beatrix, the sister of Geoffrey Somerton, another rich peasant who had a sideline in selling church pardons to local sinners and giving legal advice to his neighbours. Clement persuaded his brother-in-law to channel some of his earnings into the education of William, who was sent to an Inn of Court. It proved a good investment, for William's practice flourished; he was appointed a judge and, when he died in 1444, had acquired substantial properties in north Norfolk. His eldest son John was anxious to hush up his father's lowly origins and in 1466 persuaded Edward IV's council that his ancestors had always been gentlemen 'descended lineally of worshipful blood since the Conquest' and had been lords of the manor of Paston 'since the time that no mind is to the contrary'. They were not so easily hoodwinked in Norfolk, where Clement Paston's toil in the fields was still remembered; there were even whispers that he had been a serf (unfree bondsman).[10]

A 'fustian-to-velvet' story, Paston's career demonstrated how the law provided a way upwards for the sons of small landowners who were just below the gentry, but had enough spare cash to keep a young man at an Inn for several years. This cost at least four pounds a year and the outlay increased with inflation in the sixteenth century. The returns were good, for England was in the grip of a litigation mania, with about 3,000 cases being initiated annually in the 1440s.[11] The supply of lawyers rose to meet the demand: during the second half of the fifteenth century there were about 1,800, of whom a tenth were considered by the Inns as competent to plead in the major courts, Chancery, Common Pleas, King's Bench and Exchequer. New courts – Star Chamber, Requests, Wards, Augmentations and those attached to subsidiary royal councils at York, Ludlow and Exeter – added to the demand. Between 1590 and 1640 over 2,000 lawyers were called to the bar.[12] About half of these were the sons of noblemen, knights and gentlemen, the rest the sons of merchants, yeoman and lawyers. Dynasties of lawyers were appearing like the Yelvertons of Norfolk, whose sons attended Gray's Inn from the mid-fifteenth to the late sixteenth centuries.

Not all students at the Inns were destined to become self-supporting career lawyers. There was a sprinkling of young men for whom an acquaintance with the law would prove valuable when they came to manage their own estates or were made country magistrates. Justice Robert Shallow of Gloucestershire was one of these backwoodsmen for whom his roisterous time at his Inn had been the equivalent of a year or so at a finishing school for gentlemen, with all the facilities of a modern London club. By the early seventeenth century there were plenty of Shallows at the Inns, for a few terms spent there had become an integral part of many gentlemen's upbringing. In his memoirs, Thomas Godfrey, the second son of a Kent squire, recalled what had become a common educational progress for his kind. From eight to sixteen he boarded at a local grammar school, then proceeded to St John's College, Cambridge and, in 1604, aged nineteen, passed on to the Inner Temple, where his lodgings were 'on the left hand in the Brick Court'. He gained enough expertise to undertake legal work for Winchelsea corporation and audit its accounts.[13]

Openings were plentiful for young lawyers who did not want a career in advocacy. Even a smattering of legal knowledge sufficed to secure a position as a land agent, receiver or auditor to a substantial landowner, municipality or cathedral chapter. All property owners had at some time to resort to someone who understood enough legal terminology to frame documents correctly, register deeds at Westminster, procure official papers or writs from the departments of state and sue debtors. Work of this nature, often for several clients, was the occupation of provincial attorneys or, as they were commonly called, 'men of business'.

Such lawyers were invaluable and made a good living. John Smyth, who was born in 1566 and educated at Derby Grammar School, obtained a place in the household of an ancient aristocratic family, the Berkeleys, through the recommendation of his clergyman uncle. Smyth was bright, agreeable and serious-minded, so Lady Catherine Berkeley selected him as the paid companion to her son during his passage through Magdalen College, Oxford and the Inner Temple. Oxford and London brimmed with temptations for a young nobleman, but Smyth managed to steer his charge clear of any detectable misconduct.

He also absorbed some law and, his trustworthiness proved, was appointed steward of the Berkeleys' extensive Gloucestershire estates and given charge of their legal affairs. Smyth attracted other clients and he soon accumulated enough capital to invest in land for himself. A coming man, he made a good marriage to an heiress whose fore-bears had enriched themselves by wholesale dealing in cloth.[14] He was also a scholar, for he compiled a chronicle of the Berkeley family which included snippets of what we now call oral history, for, dili-gent in all things, Smyth interviewed old men and women to record folk memories that stretched back to the Wars of the Roses, over 150 years before. In every way, he was a far cry from the shysters who alternately amused and enraged contemporary London theatregoers.

Men with Smyth's learning and assiduousness were in great demand during the late sixteenth and seventeenth centuries. Land was gener-ating more and more wealth and its owners could afford to dele-gate the responsibility for its day-to-day management. At the same time as their incomes from agriculture rose, the aristocracy and gentry were finding new ways to spend it. Houses were enlarged, or completely rebuilt in line with the latest Classical styles imported from Italy and France. Vanity, the urge to keep abreast of fashions being set at court (which were of course virtually the same thing) and family pride created a demand for portraits. The result was the emergence of a new breed of professional men, part creative artists and part entrepreneurs. They designed buildings, painted likenesses, carved statues and tombs and laid out gardens that proclaimed their patrons cognoscenti, worthy of admiration and emulation.

To begin with, there was a social ambivalence about the creative arts. Sir Thomas Elyot judged drawing to be a gentlemanly pursuit, to be encouraged in children. The Protestant mind was less open on the subject; a religion that set the word above the image condemned the representative arts as the servant of idolatry and certainly not an occupation fit for a gentleman.[15] Anxious to dispel such prejudices, the painter John Gower defended himself and his calling in a self-portrait of 1579 in which he holds a brush and palette. Above is a balance in which the token of his gentleness, a coat of arms, is outweighed by a pair of calipers, the tools of his profession. The symbolism is explained in an inscription in which Gower confesses that 'youthful ways did me entice from arms and virtue', but, 'thanked be God', he had been redeemed by a 'gift' that would restore his and his family's honour. He was correct; during the next twenty years he painted likenesses of heroes and courtiers and the 'Armada' portrait of Elizabeth I.[16]

Gower competed for commissions in an aesthetic world dominated by artists from the Continent and imported pattern books that illustrated forms and motifs current in Italy. English artists proved good copyists, as Wren noted in 1694, but lacked an 'education in that which is the foundation of all Mechanical Arts, a practice in designing and drawing, to which everyone in Italy, France and the Low Countries pretends to more or less'. This essential accomplishment could be achieved only through prolonged foreign study, preferably in Italy, where the artist could examine Graeco-Roman originals and study how they were interpreted and developed by local artists. Two working tours of Italy undertaken in 1605 and 1614–15 taught Inigo Jones Renaissance forms and, most importantly, the principles on which they were based. He applied them first to the scenery and costumes of royal masques (often in irascible partnership with Ben Jonson) and then to the ambitious building projects of James I and Charles I. His intellectual understanding of Palladian architecture and his authority as surveyor of the King's works made him the first architect in the modern sense of the word: he directed the construction of a building that had been designed as an entity.

Sir Roger Pratt (1620–85) also made the intellectual pilgrimage to Italy. After progressing through Oxford and the Inner Temple, he traversed Europe where he studied buildings and collected architectural books. On his return, he applied what he had observed. Asked by a noble patron to recommend an architect for his country house, Pratt recommended commissioning a man like himself – 'An ingenious gentleman' who had travelled abroad and become 'somewhat versed in the best authors of Architecture: viz Palladio, Scarmozzi, Serlio . . .'[17] The alternative was a distinguished polymath like Wren, whose interest in design was an offshoot from other scientific or intellectual investigations. His genius lay in what fellow architect and savant Robert Hooke called the perfect balance of 'a mechanical hand' and a 'philosophical' mind.

Practical competence without abstract understanding was the mark of the master builder. He was essentially a craftsman who had learned draughtsmanship and knew how to cost raw materials and labour. He kept abreast of Continental trends at second hand through printed pattern books, which also contained motifs that could be reproduced on decorations such as doorways, and church monuments. The master builder's clients were gentlemen, successful professional and business men, and institutions whose budgets did not match those of the crown or landowning magnates, but who wanted imposing buildings or tombs produced in approximation of the latest fashions.

The contrast between a rustic craftsman's rendition of an Italianate cherub on a tombstone in a country graveyard and the same reproduced as part of the plasterwork in a great country house was more than just a matter of understanding. The difference reflected the social gap between the master builder and the architect. The latter depended upon a creative genius, cultivated by study abroad, which enabled him to envisage a complete building and all its embellishments from façades to fireplaces as a harmonious entity. An architect was sensitive to the nuances of his patron's tastes which, from the 1700s onwards, were formed by foreign travel and a desire to be in the forefront of fashion. Rome was the magnet for every gentleman who undertook what became known as the 'Grand Tour'. He often returned home full of ideas for some ambitious project and he naturally consulted an architect who, like him, had seen the wonders of Italy. He got a man of aesthetic discrimination, intellect and imagination who knew what was required of him.

Originality coupled with capacity to respond to prevailing taste was the basis of an architect's reputation and fortunes. In the first decades of the eighteenth century his profession was a collection of individuals without any formal training or association, although by mid-century architects were taking on apprentices. Sir William Chambers became an architect in 1755 purely as a consequence of a private interest in modern languages and architecture, which he had developed through reading during long sea voyages to the Far East. Born in 1723, the son of a Scottish merchant in Gothenburg, Chambers was educated at Ripon Grammar School and then placed in an overseas trading company. He had enough capital to turn a dilettante pursuit into a means of earning a living and, in 1749, began a systematic architectural education. He mastered draughtsmanship at the Ecole des Arts in Paris and studied the new neo-Classical style in Italy. In 1755 he felt sufficiently qualified to set up his own business in London and was soon attracting patrons.[18] Chambers flourished and was knighted by George III, an honour which indicated that architecture was a profession of gentlemen and equal in status to law and medicine.

Other artists were on hand to satisfy new tastes. Noblemen and gentlemen who studied the Classics and wandered among the ruins of Italy fancied themselves as Roman grandees. They imagined that their country houses were patrician villas and filled them and the adjacent gardens with statuary. There was a demand too for public sculpture: marble tombs on which gentlemen posed like Roman senators, and statues to monarchs and the commanders of the armies and fleets that were expanding Britain's overseas trade.

Henry Cheere supplied this new market. He was a talented sculptor in the fashionable Rococo style and an astute businessman who invested his profits from art in property and insurance. The son of a prosperous London haberdasher, Cheere was apprenticed to a joiner in 1718. On completion of his term, he became co-owner of a workshop in Old Palace Yard, Westminster. He soon attracted important commissions, including a statue of Sir William Codrington for the library of All Souls College, Oxford for which he received one hundred guineas (£105) in 1732. The former governor of the Leeward Islands appears in the armour of a Roman tribune with a pile of books at his feet, for he was patron of learning. Cheere's atelier offered a wide range of subjects: there were 'gods and goddesses of ancient Rome' for the gardens at Stourhead, and statues of Classical and historical worthies to embellish the interiors of country houses and church monuments. Some of the carving of these pieces was done by apprentices whose fathers were willing to pay Cheere a hundred guineas for instruction in a workshop that was so prized by the bon ton.[19] Its proprietor, although theoretically a master of a 'mechanical art', was recognised as a gentleman: he became a magistrate and was knighted in 1760.

Like Cheere, the sculptor John Bushnell who died in 1701 treated art as a commercial venture. His career began when he was apprenticed to a sculptor (his master seduced a maidservant and bullied Bushnell into marrying her) and afterwards he proceeded to study in Europe. He set up his business in London and soon caught the notice of rich patrons; among his earliest commissions were statues of Charles I and Charles II that were erected at the Royal Exchange. Bushnell channelled his profits into speculation in the coal trade and, in partnership with two vintners, into a novel drinking booth in the form of a full-scale Trojan horse. This ancestor of a modern 'theme pub' was wrecked in a storm and Bushnell's investments in coal came to nothing. Despite these setbacks, he made enough to leave his two sons an income of £160 a year. Wisely, given their father's misadventures, they chose to live off their annuity in modest and idle contentment.[20]

Early recognition, preferably by a respected connoisseur, was an essential springboard for any artistic career. At the same time, an artist needed money to fund his apprenticeship, or years of self-instruction abroad. George Vertue's 'more honest than opulent' parents somehow afforded to pay for his attachment to an engraver who went bankrupt, to support him for three years of private study and then to pay for a second apprenticeship. In 1709, when he was twenty-five, his talents were discovered and applauded by the German portraitist Sir Godfrey Kneller. His future and his family's survival (by now he was the only breadwinner) was guaranteed: patrons flocked to his studio and he was soon selling prints of celebrities based on Kneller's portraits and past worthies. All were destined to decorate the walls of country and town houses whose owners wanted to display their taste and, where the subjects were public figures, their political loyalties.

In 1713 Vertue branched out into what was about to become an equally fashionable art form, engravings of ancient buildings and antiquities. Under the patronage of Robert Harley, the 2nd Earl of Oxford, he catered for the new taste in antiquarianism with prints of ruins, cathedrals and churches. They hung alongside engravings of statesmen, philosophers, men of letters and the admirals and generals who were making Britain great and prosperous.[21] The popularity of historic images and those of modern commanders reflected a growing national self-confidence and patriotism among the well-to-do, and artists responded accordingly. The resulting engravings were joined by prints of victories on land and sea and still decorate the corridors and bedrooms of some smaller country houses.

George Vertue had one thing in common with William Paston the judge, Sir William Chambers the architect and Sir Henry Cheere the sculptor. They were born into families that believed in diverting what spare capital they possessed into the education of their sons and providing them with assistance as they established their careers. A kinsman gave the future lawyer and land agent John Smyth access to a patron who recognised his personal qualities and helped him on. None of the four was a self-made man, in so far as the expression conveys the idea of rising unaided from extremes of poverty. Such creatures were exceptional. Everyone who entered a profession needed a family with savings and the conviction that cash spent on education and training was money well spent. This was also true of every kind of commerce, although there were charities that paid the apprenticeship fees of poor children in the hope that they would acquire a craft and become self-supporting, thus reducing the numbers dependent on the poor rates.

In terms of the evolution of the middle class, the willingness of parents to invest in their offspring's futures is of enormous significance. It took for granted the existence of an open social order in which there were no impediments to anyone with talent, the capacity to persevere and, of course, a modicum of capital. Obtaining it required hard work, thrift and self-discipline. It was routinely assumed that children shared their parents' ambitions and would comply with their plans. Human nature sometimes saw to it that these did not turn out as intended. James Butler, the son of a Newcastle merchant, disappointed his father, who had wanted him to continue his successful business. At some time in the 1640s, the 'debauched' youth 'extravagantly wasted his fortune and married a common woman in his drink'. After he had been abandoned by his family, Butler's friends 'got him put a master of a small vessel' that was bound for the West Indies in the hope that he might recover solvency and respectability dealing in slaves and sugar.[22] Given the time and place, the prospects for the young reprobate were rather good.

Long-term family aspirations were a powerful driving force. Their fulfilment became a source of pride: in 1739 the forty-year-old James Fretwell decided to compile a record of his family's progress during the past hundred years. His great-grandfather had been a carpenter, 'an honest plain man' from Maltby in Yorkshire whose son followed his craft and then branched out into dealing in timber. Buying and selling was always more profitable than making things. The Fretwells may have had an injection of capital, for the young entrepreneur had married a lady of 'ancient family' called Beard. Their son Richard inherited enough to turn to trading in another essential commodity, horses. The timber business continued with successive fathers supervising their sons' education so that they knew enough to run the firm efficiently. James Fretwell went to grammar school until he was fifteen and was then sent to a tutor in Pontefract to learn arithmetic and geometry, which his father considered invaluable for the timber trade. He may not have shown much aptitude, or else his father became more ambitious for him, for when he was nineteen he was sent to London and, through the influence of his attorney uncle, secured a post as a legal clerk. In the meantime his younger brother had been apprenticed to a grocer. In 1720, when James was twenty-one, the question of his future employment became academic, for his father purchased an estate for £1,000.[23]

The descendants of the 'good plain' carpenter were engaged in wholesale business and the law and the head of the family had become a country squire; his son James, who set down their passage through the world, died in 1772 and called himself 'gentleman'. Unremarked in his family narrative and perhaps taken for granted by him was a hidden history of graft, perseverance, opportunism and the husbanding of resources that provided the seedcorn for the next generation.

The frame of mind behind these activities is glimpsed in thousands of late-medieval and early-modern wills, often by men of comparatively humble degree. The testaments of yeomen and smallholders are crammed with minutely detailed descriptions of arable fields, grazing land, livestock, farm implements, crops (growing and in store), furniture, kitchen utensils and clothing. There are equally precise instructions for their dispersal among members of the testator's family. In 1588, John Pickering, a Swaledale farmer, ordered his small herd of cows ('Taggled', 'Cherie', 'Brock', 'Allblack' and 'Flooreld') to be divided among his children.[24] They were valuable assets whose feeding and care must have consumed considerable energy, physical and nervous.

The products of John Trevellion's labour and, in all likelihood, his father's were listed and split among his sons and daughters in 1552. A Somerset yeoman, he left sums of cash, yearlings, horses, plough wheels and fittings to his four younger sons, all presumably independent farmers. Trevellion's sixth and youngest son was still unsettled in any occupation and so he received the largest bequest of £33 13s 4d, which he could use to purchase either a tenancy and stock it or else an apprenticeship to a shopkeeper or craftsman, with enough spare eventually to set up in a business of his own.[25] With prudence and luck, Trevellion's investment might yield a good dividend. A generation later, William Harrison noticed how shrewd and rich yeomen were buying freehold land from 'unthrifty squires' and paying for their sons to attend grammar schools, universities and the Inns of Court.

6

A Heavy Purse: Buying and Selling

The installation of Sir John Swinnerton as lord mayor of London in 1612 was a triumphal affair. The playwright Thomas Dekker had been commissioned to devise a pageant that would celebrate the dignity of the mayor and the honour of the city and its citizens. The result was a spectacle rich in allegories that flattered Swinnerton and the coterie of opulent merchants who had elected him. The centre-piece was a chariot in which stood Virtue, surrounded by figures representing the seven Liberal Arts. This tableau was drawn through the streets by four horses ridden by Time ('the begetter of things'), Mercury the God of Wisdom, Desire which, inflamed by Mercury, sent men in pursuit of Virtue, and Industry, who appeared as 'an old countryman, bearing on his shoulder a spade, as the emblem of honour'. The four horsemen engendered a love of the arts, commerce, science and knowledge 'which are the stairs and ascensions to the Throne of Virtue, and the only glory and upholding of cities'. The symbolism was explained by Virtue in a speech to the mayor:

> The Liberal Arts wait: from whose breasts do run
> The milk of Knowledge: on which, Sciences feed,
> Trades and Professions: and by them, the seed
> Of civil, popular government is sown.[1]

It was satisfying for London's merchant grandees to know that they were part of an intellectual brotherhood who flourished through the application of those liberal arts that were the foundation of civilisation. There was no shame in the counting house, rather honour. There were also vast profits, for England was in the middle of a period of unprecedented economic growth.

This might have been deduced from the confident mood of Dekker's pageant. Although not conceived as an economic tract, it did point to some of the ways in which the nation's prosperity was increasing. The figure of the rustic labourer was a reminder that agriculture was the ultimate source of all wealth: a rapidly growing population had to be fed and the country's staple export was cloth woven from the wool of native sheep. The overseas cloth trade was notoriously fickle, suffering periodic slumps and booms, but it did underpin the economy for all of this period. At the end of the seventeenth century there were an estimated eleven million sheep in England (twice the number of people) and cloth made up 43 per cent of the nation's exports.

A strong agriculture supplying basic needs and overseas markets provided the wherewithal for growth elsewhere. People had more to spend on entertainment, which for most meant drinking: in 1577 there was one alehouse to every 142 people, and in the 1630s one to every hundred. A new industry, printing, expanded to meet what turned out to be an insatiable market for knowledge and diversion. Between three and four million ballad sheets were printed during the second half of the sixteenth century.[2] As Thomas Dekker knew to his advantage, the commercial theatre was booming; as many as 24,000 people visited the city's playhouses each week in 1600.[3] At the same time, the demand for luxury foods rose. Twenty-one thousand oranges and lemons were on sale in Norwich's St Bartholomew's fair in 1581, and in the next decade over a million pounds of currants from the Mediterranean were being imported into London.[4]

London was the powerhouse of the nation's economic life. It had always been a centre for Continental trade and was emerging as the hub of England's new overseas commerce with the Americas, the Mediterranean, India and the Far East. By 1700 it was a leading inter-

national entrepôt, importing sugar, tobacco and other tropical products and re-exporting them to Europe. London dominated a part of
the country's internal trade: it imported mutton from Gloucestershire
and Northamptonshire, fruit and hops from Kent, grain from the
Weald, barley from Norfolk and coal from Tyneside.

A rich and expanding city was a magnet to immigrants from all
over the country, attracted by higher wages and, like that legendary
incomer Dick Whittington, by opportunities for advancement. They
kept on coming, undeterred by wretched housing, and in 1700
London had become home to 500,000, just under a tenth of the
country's population. It was also a focus for conspicuous consumption, thanks to the spending power of the crown, courtiers, civil
servants, businessmen and, when it was in session, members of
Parliament. Growing numbers of rural gentlemen, often egged on by
their wives, resorted to London as a respite from the tedium of
country life and for a chance to discover the latest fashions and see
the latest plays.

Among the most popular productions were those about the making
and spending of money and, often intertwined, about the adventures
and misadventures of courtship and marriage. These works often
contained undercurrents of moral censure directed against the city's
culture of cutthroat competition and its by-products, rapaciousness
and fraud. A character in the *The Three Ladies of London* (1581) regrets
that there is 'no abiding in the city for Conscience and Love'. In the
course of the play this allegorical pair are overwhelmed by a multi-
tude of commercial deceits, most commonly giving short measure.

Pageants might extol the virtue of trade, but there was always a
lingering ambivalence about the methods of those who enriched
themselves from it. One man's gain was always another's loss, but what
perturbed moralists was the extent of the latter and how it came
about. For the Catholic church, the line between making a surplus
and the sins of avarice was almost undetectable. Preachers denounced
the rigging of scales, bogus claims about quality and durability and,
most frequently, the creation of articifial dearths by hoarding food. In
one parable a greedy grain dealer:

buys corn against the year
And keeps it until it is dear.

The starving poor were sent packing ('Go your way: corn is dear'),
but when the shark faces divine judgment, he too is dispatched –
'Go to Hell; for Heaven is dear.' Chicanery of this and other kinds
was common enough, if the number of cases brought before the
courts was anything to go by.

Trade could harm the soul in other ways. A late-fourteenth-century
preacher was shocked by how young ambitious businessmen
exhausted themselves with anxiety: 'These young men expose themselves in the adventure of their life, suffer many mischiefs, many perils
on land and sea. In the daytime they are so tormented . . . that at
nights they have no rest, they have dreams in plenty and many break
sleep.' These medieval counterparts to the modern 'yuppy' talked
about nothing save how much they were making, or the risks they
were taking.[5] Minds so distracted had no time for contemplation of
the rewards of heaven, or how they might be obtained.

Fluctuations in overseas markets and the ups and downs of
exchange rates were the preoccupations of Richard Fermer. Born in
the 1480s, he had inherited several hundred pounds from his parents,
who had made their money buying wool in Oxfordshire. Richard
entered the same business, but at a higher level as a member of the
Calais Staple Company, which enjoyed the monopoly of exporting
wool to the Continent. He had a keen eye for profit and, thanks to
court connections, secured a contract to supply food and equipment
for the army which invaded France in 1513. Wars always offered rich
pickings for entrepreneurs with enough capital to purchase and deliver
commodities in the huge quantities required by armies and navies.
Having shifted from trading in wool to procuring arms and armour,
Fermer branched out again, this time into land. In 1518 he spent
some time at the Inner Temple and picked up enough law to enable
him to supervise the Northamptonshire estates of the Earl of Derby.

Fermer was already investing in land of his own in partnership with
his younger brother William, a lawyer and minor civil servant. They
wanted the highest income from their investments, even if this meant

evicting tenants and turning their arable plots into pasture for sheep. What marks out this pair from hundreds of other contemporary, hard-nosed entrepreneurs was their loyalty to orthodox Catholicism at a time when the state was stripping the church of its power and rewriting its creed. To an extent, Richard Fermer acquiesced in the new order, for the government considered him reliable enough to sit as a juryman in the trial of rebels after the 1536 Pilgrimage of Grace, which had attempted to reverse the changes. His heart may not have been in the matter, for in 1540 Fermer endured imprisonment and the confiscation of his property for harbouring a priest who had criticised Henry VIII's religious policies. Moreover, and perhaps in memory of his devotion, the Fermers remained staunchly Catholic for the next two hundred years.[6]

This adherence to the old religion makes Fermer interesting because he contradicts the contention that men of his kind found Protestant ethics more conducive to money-making activities, and that there was a close correlation between the rise of capitalism and the spread of Protestantism. This is over-simplistic: both Protestant and Catholic clergymen denounced commercial legerdemain with equal vehemence, in particular usury and practices that injured the poorest. There were plenty of Elizabethan and Jacobean stage villains who got rich by these devices and got their come-uppances to the satisfaction of Protestant audiences.

What Protestantism did offer the businessman was the certainty that divine Providence would assist his efforts, so long as he revered God and kept His laws. Puritans in particular were acutely aware of Providence because of their faith in Predestination. They convinced themselves that the elect had to be men and women of exemplary piety, submission, rectitude and continence, virtues that were rewarded in this life as well as the next. 'This week God was good to me and mine in our peace, plenty, health, friends, good estate and raiment,' wrote Ralph Josselin, a Puritan minister in October 1644. Soon after, he heard that the son-in-law of a local butcher had lost an eye after being accidentally struck by a cleaver. The hand of God was unmistakable and Josselin smugly concluded: 'Let this affliction do them good that have need of it.'[7] In contemporary New England, Puritans sang:

We gather together to ask the Lord's blessing.
He chastens and hastens, His will to make known,
The wicked oppressing, now cease to be distressing.
Sing praises to His name, for he forgets not his own.

Similar sentiments were echoed elsewhere by those who had prospered. John Fryer, the son of a Chiltern farmer and of a mother who had sung psalms in her small shop in Great Marlow, inherited their Puritan faith. In 1720 he was elected lord mayor of London and, looking back on his career as a wholesale pewterer, he concluded that his success had been 'an eminent instance of his [God's] care and providence'.[8] William Cotesworth, a contemporary Newcastle entrepreneur and likewise from a humble background, was also grateful to God and the 'providence of his goodness' for helping him to become the equivalent of a millionaire. Less modest than Fryer, he added that 'a head and genius for business' had also played their part.[9] Fryer was a devout man, brought up to believe in Predestination, but it did not automatically follow that he and others like him applied themselves to their work with an added dedication because they regarded personal success as a promise of future salvation. Survival and family ambitions were equally strong motives for working hard and getting on.

The mechanics of Providence were mysterious. There was a pervasive feeling that it might operate like a ledger in which the credits of faith, regular worship and temperate living were offset by the debits of sinfulness. This balance sheet of Providence was a source of hope and anxiety. Like everyone else, William Coe was thankful for mercies, which included recovery from smallpox as a youth, and afflicted by recollections of past misdeeds such as childhood pranks (leading a blind man into a ditch), resorting to shifty 'arts and ways' when horse trading, and dozing during sermons. Occasional reviews of his treatment by Providence provoked spasms of unease, but never deterred Coe from repeating old lapses or discovering new.[10] Others interpreted the favourable intervention of Providence as a sign that God had chosen them to fulfil a specific but often unrevealed purpose: this was how its workings were seen by Oliver Cromwell.

Living in a universe in which human affairs were governed by the forces of an opaque but not unfriendly Providence had profound and far-reaching consequences, especially for anyone who was making his way in the world by taking risks. It helped individuals endure and come to terms with the myriad setbacks of life: sickness, accidents and the everyday hazards of business enterprise such as shipwrecks or wayward markets. Above all, the idea of Providence provided a collective psychological assurance. Whatever their calling, everyone was in some way fulfilling the will of God, so as long as their endeavours were honest and beneficial, not only to themselves but to the rest of society. Work, which Catholic theology had presented as a punishment for Adam's sin, was transformed into a valuable and wholly laudable part of the divine scheme.

Providence favoured godly nations as much as godly individuals. This satisfying and, as it turned out, highly intoxicating concept had a profound impact in England. It explained the spectacular growth of England's international trade, the extension of its flourishing colonies in North America and the Caribbean, and successive victories over its rivals, the Netherlands, France and Spain. These events were clear evidence that the nation and, it went without saying, the creators of its wealth enjoyed a special divine dispensation. This was why throughout the wars of the eighteenth century each victory, and with it the acquisition of fresh sources of profit, was publicly celebrated with the ringing of church bells and services of thanksgiving. Piety and patriotism were blended into a singular creed that would capture the imagination of those engaged in commerce. In time, this amalgam was enthusiastically adopted by the Victorian middle class.

The Victorian middle class would have applauded the commonsense, practical advice offered to potential businessmen by a handbook written in about 1450. First, it stressed the importance of commercial intelligence: it was vital to investigate markets and evaluate them with an eye to future demand. To meet it, the trader required initiative and capital. If his means were slight, the beginner could invest in 'penny' wares such as purses, knives and looking glasses which could be purchased wholesale for 8d (4p) a dozen and sold for 1d each.

This gave a profit margin of 50 per cent. 'Light winning makes a heavy purse,' promised the author, but warned the fledgling entrepreneur always to keep some cash in hand to replenish his stock.[11]

Whether or not he had read this textbook, Thomas Underhill from Hartlebury in Worcestershire understood the principles behind it. In 1479, he heard how a minor epidemic in the nearby village of Hampton Lovett had left a number of properties vacant. He moved to the village with his family, acquired premises from a widow on favourable terms (tenants were scarce) and set up a tavern which also sold food. Underhill's ale was thin and he overcharged for inferior meat and so his profits were healthy. In 1489 he was described as 'dives' (a rich man), and his neighbours recognised his new standing in their community by making him a churchwarden. This must have been gratifying, not least because his success had aroused much envy, but Underhill's goal was the advancement of his children. His sons attended school and he provided the means for one to train as a priest and two to secure apprenticeships, one as a tanner in Tewkesbury, the other as a stonemason in Bristol.[12]

The Underhills had some grasp of market forces. Exploiting them required tenacity and stamina, both of which were shown by Anne Okely, a remarkable woman who was born in Quinton in Northamptonshire in 1691. Her parents saw to it that she was 'taught and learned the solid and useful accomplishments of her sex, according to their middling station in life'. She married in 1718 a Bedford man who 'through extravagance failed in the world', died, and left her destitute with five children under the age of eleven. Her girlhood instruction must have included needlework, since she was able to support her family as a seamstress: 'She maintained them with bread and clothing only by the coats and garments she made with her own weary fingers, working willingly and incessantly for them early and late.'

Undertaking piecework was a precarious and poor living and so Anne decided to set up her own business. She secured capital through renting part of her house, recovering some of her marriage settlement from her husband's creditors and persuading her father to advance her the sum he had allocated her in his will. With £50 in her purse she went to London, purchased a stock of hats and returned to Bedford where she opened a millinery shop. Among her first customers were some of her friends and during the next thirty-three years the business prospered. One of her sons became a naval officer and another went to Cambridge. Anne Okely's willpower was matched by her physical toughness; for over thirty years she suffered from cancer of the breast, which finally killed her in 1766, and she had been crippled in one arm in her mid-fifties after being struck by a wagon. Astonishingly, 'her knowledge of accounts was scanty'. 'She never knew her stock, she never knew her profits; a stream of cash circulated weekly through her hands out of which she took what she hoped she could afford.'[13] Arithmetic was not one of the feminine accomplishments considered appropriate by her parents.

Family money had helped launch Anne Okely on a career forced upon her by necessity. An uncle's generosity gained John Fryer his apprenticeship to a pewterer in 1685. It turned out to be an unpromising start, for his master had an alcoholic wife and made ends meet by compelling his apprentices to undertake journeymen's work. None the less and despite frail health, Fryer served his eight years and was admitted to the Pewterers' Company. His perseverance impressed another uncle who advanced him £300 to buy premises, and marriage to the daughter of a Buckinghamshire tanner brought him a dowry of £500. Fryer's father-in-law doubled this sum after seeing how he was managing his business. What Fryer called his 'great pains in business' persuaded the uncle who had first invested in it to make him his heir and leave him an estate in Hampshire.[14]

It helped enormously for the entrepreneur to be in the right place at the right time and recognise this fact. A Teesside's yeoman's second son, William Cotesworth, was apprenticed to Robert Sutton, a Newcastle tallow chandler, in the early 1680s. His arrival in Tyneside coincided with an upsurge in the local economy. Coal production was rising to meet the demand of London consumers and this in turn stimulated shipbuilding. Two new industries, salt distillation and glass manufacture, were also taking off. Cotesworth was well positioned to exploit this bonanza: his energy and acumen made him invaluable to the Suttons; he virtually took charge of their business and married his master's daughter. With Sutton capital behind him, Cotesworth first engaged in the Baltic trade, exporting salt from pans he had purchased in South Shields. Next, he moved into mining and through sheer nerve and a degree of intimidation secured a near-monopoly over the region's coal shipments. When he died in 1726, Cotesworth's coal investments were worth £60,000 and he had £4,500 a year from the lands he had been buying with his profits.

A forceful, dynamic figure, Cotesworth upset aristocratic mine owners who, while benefiting from his enterprise, were repelled by his bluntness. A member of the Bowes family sneeringly suggested that this was to be expected from a man whose father had once been a menial. Such gibes stung and, shortly before his death, Cotesworth hoped that this son would follow a 'more polite way of living', and to help him towards it sent him away as a boarder to Sedbergh School.

'Esquire' Cotesworth, as he was eventually called, was as canny in politics as in business. He backed the Whigs on George I's accession in 1714 and may have spied for the government in an area strongly inclined towards the Tories and treasonable Jacobitism. He had backed the right side, and grateful friends at court added to his formidable local clout. His overriding aim, the establishment of his family in the forefront of the north-eastern gentry, was never fulfilled; his sons died young without male heirs.[15]

The Underhills, Anne Okely, John Fryer and William Cotesworth were winners in a competitive society during a period of intense economic expansion. Each needed a mixture of resolution, plausibility and quick-wittedness, for they were engaged in a form of trading that has largely fallen into disuse in much of the Western world but remains common elsewhere. A seller stated his price, which was unrealistically high, and the buyer countered with an offer that was unrealistically low. The pair then haggled, debating the quality of their goods and the current state of the market at the same time as making silent calculations as to how far they could go without making a loss. At last, a price was agreed and arrangements made as to the time of payment. Haggling extended to every form of transaction, although it was considered unseemly for gentlemen, whose nice manners could put them out of pocket. In 1663 Samuel Pepys and some friends agreed that his countrymen ought to imitate the French, who did not 'think it below a gentleman or person of honour at a tavern to bargain for his meat before he eats it'.

7

Dexterous Men: Credit and Money Men

Pepys and his companions probably paid their reckoning in cash, although they could easily have asked the tavern keeper to put the bill on account. He would have agreed if he knew that they had credit, information that could be obtained by discreet investigation and picking up hints from hearsay. A guide to marine insurance, then a novelty, published in 1712 advised the shipowner to visit the Royal Exchange and say what vessel he wished to have covered. Then he had to satisfy himself as to the solvency of the insurers, discovering the names of the 'best men' among them and asking questions about their affairs at the Exchange or near where they lived.[1]

Every form of credit required trust and this had to be reinforced by intelligence. Gathering it was worth the effort, for in the 1710s and 1720s up to 15 per cent of London's outwardly most prosperous businessmen were pursued by bankruptcy suits. Small traders were equally vulnerable; a third of alehouse owners in Kent went out of business between 1595 and 1599. Presumably all had been over-generous in allowing customers to use the slate. In King's Lynn, a port with about 7,500 inhabitants, there was an annual average of over 200 actions for debt in the 1680s. Some of those arrested were eminent tradesmen, but most escaped mandatory imprisonment thanks to bail raised by friends. Bailing out a friend was not altruism; bankruptcy had a knock-on effect as other businessmen were forced to write off debts and so reduce the value of their concerns and, with it, their own credit-worthiness. External market forces which temporarily reduced wine consumption in London in 1651 left vintners strapped for cash, driving them to pay importers 'very slowly'. Credit dried up and multiple bankruptcies followed. 'One durst not trust another,' one London wine merchant noted. 'Mr Ellis is broken for near £15,000, they having his person in prison, upon which here is broken two merchants of this city; men that were engaged for him deeply are now utterly undone.'[2]

Credit was the lubricant of commercial life. In so far as it rested on the principle that money was a utility that could be made to work in the same way as say specialised knowledge or a craft skill, capitalism was an integral part of life. Nearly everyone, whatever their background, who possessed a cash surplus loaned some of it and took some form of interest. Medieval monarchs filled their war chests by borrowing from peers, churchmen and merchants and wealthier peasants made small advances to their poorer neighbours.

Routine business transactions commonly involved credit. Once the seller and purchaser had hammered out a price, an arrangement was made for payment at a future date and the appropriate papers were drawn up. Specie changed hands infrequently, for there was never quite enough in circulation to serve the needs of the nation's economy, and much of it was clipped and, therefore, worth less than its face value. The predominance of credit over coin was reflected in thousands of wills and inventories from every social level. In 1560, Leonard Loftus, a Swaledale grazier who dealt in locally mined lead, left £7 in cash and £300 in assignments made by his customers. The assets of John Denie, an Ipswich butcher, totalled £251, of which £191 were debts outstanding to him when he died in 1590. 'Desperate debts' of £20 comprised nearly half the assets of an Ipswich dyer who died in 1602. He may well have been over-accommodating to local clothiers during a recent recession.[3] The same pattern was repeated further up the commercial ladder: when William Turner, a London merchant, retired in 1671 he had £70 in cash and £25,000 in sums due to him, more than half the value of his business.[4]

Merchants and shopkeepers extending credit to their customers were part of a nationwide network of borrowing and lending. Masters loaned money to their servants and vice versa and wives and husbands cadged sums from each other. One of the customary obligations of kinship was a willingness to make advances to members of one's family. Professionals, clergymen and businessmen with spare capital made loans to friends and colleagues and, like everyone else, took interest. Landowners raised capital through covenants (a mortgage in the modern sense was not legally valid until 1925) against the value of their property; in 1641 the total debt of 121 peers was £1.5 million.[5]

Borrowing and lending was always a fraught business. It presented no problems to the numerate and single-minded Robert Cullum, a younger son of a Suffolk family that inhabited the prosperous borderline between the yeomanry and gentry. He was apprenticed to a London draper in 1607 and over the next eight years carefully invested whatever cash that came his way in small loans. He meticulously recorded his transactions in a book and, by 1615, had saved £92 towards setting himself up in business. Cullum accumulated more capital in the next few years from wages earned working for his old master and a legacy from his father, and most of it was advanced in loans. During 1616 he received £19 in interest and in 1622 the figure was £22, which just about covered his living expenses.

Thrift, and a knack of judging the capacity of his debtors to make repayment, paid off and Cullum launched what turned out to be a very successful drapery business that was soon earning up to £1,000 a year. His reputation attracted apprentices, and he charged £80 for indentures which eleven merchants and country squires thought a fair price for their sons to learn from such a diligent master. Cullum became a leading figure in London's government and, while inclining towards Parliament during the Civil War, did so without excessive passion and so was made a baronet by Charles II on his restoration. Cullum was typical in that he appreciated how his capital could be made to work, but he was unusual in that he understood the mysteries of accounting and could keep track of what he was owed and what he was making.[6]

Astonishing as it may seem, many tradesmen were unexpectedly overtaken by bankruptcy simply because they had the flimsiest knowledge of the gap between their assets and their obligations. In 1727, Defoe urged every businessman to stave off insolvency by systematic book-keeping. 'A tradesman's books,' he advised, 'like a Christian's conscience, should always be clean and neat.'[7] Those of Ralph Josselin were sufficiently comprehensible for him to draw up an annual assessment of what he was making from his Essex lands and what he owed and estimate how much he was worth. He wrote the results in his diary, and the entries hint that the revelation of solvency was greeted with a sigh of relief. In 1662 he wrote, 'my stock is better than last year by some pounds' and in 1665, 'my outward estate will this year appear to be better'.[8]

Debts were a source of perpetual stress. Contemporary diaries reveal five universal preoccupations among the moderately rich: the state of their souls, their health, their family relations, their ability to repay loans and the capacity of their debtors to make a settlement. 'Worldly cogitations' about his debts kept Adam Eyre awake during the night of 15 August 1647 and, in despair, he persuaded himself that the only answer to his financial worries was to leave his Yorkshire farm and go to London to 'seek new fortunes'. He had recently borrowed £50 from a friend and promised to repay £53 2s 6d in a year's time, which represented the more or less usual interest rate of 6 per cent. As if this was not enough, he suffered from sciatica and squabbled with his wife over what he considered her indecent and unseemly clothes. Nevertheless, he found money for tobacco, drinking with friends and small wagers on games of bowls.[9]

The burden of anxiety was sometimes overwhelming. In 1693 a young trader under pressure from poor relations and mounting debts reached the point of utter despair. 'I have been endeavouring and labouring with much difficulty . . . to manage my trade and preserve my credit that my creditors may not perceive my declining condition. But I find that Providence does in many things grievously disappoint.' 'God Almighty is angry with me,' he concluded, revealingly, and contemplated suicide.[10]

Samuel Pepys was periodically distracted by precarious liquidity

in the early stages of his career as a civil servant. Between 1661 and
1663 he loaned £700, the greater part of his savings, to his patron,
Lord Sandwich, and guaranteed a further advance of £1,000 made
to the nobleman by his cousin Thomas. The lack of security made
Pepys uneasy, but Sandwich's agent warned him that his master
would take it 'ill' if any was requested. Pepys said nothing. Although
the loan stretched his resources, it was an investment, for the good
will of an influential man was invaluable, even if he was temporarily
out of pocket. By early 1665 and after some spasms of heartache,
all but £250 of the loan and interest had been repaid. The outstanding
sum was now a mere bagatelle for Pepys, who at the end of the
year discovered that he was worth £4,400, three times the value of
his estate twelve months before. A quarter of the amount consisted
of perks and fees due to him as an Admiralty official at a time when
public servants were expected to supplement their often meagre
salaries by gifts and bribes.

Pepys's yearly calculations were a source of pride. His steadily rising
annual surplus indicated that he was a man of 'credit' and general
'esteem', terms that were synonymous in the eyes of the world. On
the last day of 1666 he walked out from his house in Mincing Lane
on a frosty morning with his servant and headed towards the Royal
Exchange and the city to settle his and his wife's outstanding debts.
Leaving his boy to settle up with the candle supplier, Pepys drank
mulled wine with two young women of his acquaintance, returned
home to his account books and the celebration of a private triumph.
'I am master of a better estate' than ever before, he wrote, and 'abound
in good plate, so as at all entertainments to be served wholly with
silver plates'.[11] The same self-congratulatory sentiments would be
expressed by men of similar standing in the nineteenth and the twentieth centuries.

In all likelihood, Pepys would have obtained his silverware on some
kind of credit. Regional assessments based upon personal inventories
suggest that large numbers of comparatively prosperous households
were purchasing goods on long-term credit. The total debts represented an average of up to a quarter of the value of an individual's
possessions and in some cases considerably more. Taken at face value,

these figures suggest that at least a quarter of the moderately prosperous families in the country were spending more than they earned.[12]
Estimates based on a man's liquidity at the moment of death are
misleading in so far as they ignore his previous or future revenues,
factors that must have been known to those who had given him
credit. Indeed, the extent of debt was a measure of an individual's
reputation for creditworthiness and, it went without saying, of his
stature in the community. None the less, these figures show that the
habit of borrowing had become ingrained among those of middling
and higher degree. Indeed, for a considerable number of them, their
ability to secure credit was both a mark of their status and, paradoxically, the means by which they upheld it publicly.

Credit had its perils. The naive could easily be deceived by the
abstruse legal terminology that was part of its mechanisms, as they
are now. In Middleton's *Michaelmas Term* (1607), the gullible young
Essex squire, Easy, is successively tricked into signing a bond of £200
and countersigning another for £700 as a matter of 'fashion' and
finally unwittingly signs away his inheritance. Others fell into debt
through miscalculation or, and this was very common, over-indulgence,
usually alcoholic. Both these causes of downfall were observed by
Richard Gough, a well-heeled yeoman with antiquarian interests who
compiled a history of his parish of Myddle in Shropshire at the end
of the seventeenth century.

There was the spendthrift George Clive (a distant relation of
Clive of India) who was 'a very bad husbandman' and sold off his
acres to meet debts that finally landed him in gaol. Nathaniel Reve
borrowed £20 to purchase a tenancy of a farm, using his new lease
as security and, unable to repay the debt, went to prison, leaving
his creditor to take over the property. William Heath was too clever
by half. He managed a farm inherited from his wife, improved it
and disregarded the debts that had been run up by his father-in-
law and secured on the property. Heath 'sought rather to avoid and
delay payment . . . by subtle tricks and slights in law' and was bank-
rupted by legal fees. Paternal debts compelled Francis Lloyd to sell
his inheritance, 'but by his labour and industry, and by his parsi-
monious living retrieved all and afterwards became very rich in

lands'. The satisfaction of restoring his family fortunes outweighed any pride in status, for 'there was no servant in the town that went more mean in habit, that fared hardier in diet, or that worked harder at any slavish labour than he did'.[13]

Other victims of debt slithered down the social hierarchy. In Dekker's *The Roaring Girl* (1621) two of the characters encounter a woman slicing tobacco leaves. One observes: 'She's a gentlewoman born, I can tell, though it be her fortune now to shred Indian pot-herbs.' His companion remarks: 'Oh sir, 'tis many a good woman's fortune, when her husband turns bankrupt.'[14] Bankruptcy was a source of shame, for credit rested upon trust and the perceived integrity of the borrower. Trustworthiness was a Christian virtue and so debt was a moral and religious as well as financial obligation. The promise of repayment rested on an oath sworn before God. 'Faith and truth, especially in all occasions of attesting it upon the solemn appeal to heaven, is the great bond of society,' wrote the philosopher John Locke in 1692.[15]

Locke was writing on interest rates at a time when the country was in the middle of a financial revolution that depended upon mutual trust. The changes were the inevitable consequences of the increased scale and sophistication of commerce, particularly overseas trade, and the need to fund the global wars against France between 1689 and 1697 and between 1702 and 1714. As a result of the former, the number of joint-stock companies increased to over a hundred by 1695, and there was a corresponding expansion in new fields of economy activity: marine, life and fire insurance, stockjobbing (dealing in shares) and banking. These were concentrated in London and were the forerunners of today's financial service industries. The emergency war-funding measures gave rise to the Bank of England, which handled the new government stock, massive loans raised from the public with interest rates of between 8 and 14 per cent. The sum of wartime borrowing became the National Debt, which increased in leaps and bounds during the eighteenth century as the result of successive conflicts with France and Spain. Fluctuations in share values appeared in the daily and weekly newspapers that were printed in London and circulated throughout the country by the recently introduced official mail service. Everyone, everywhere, could speculate on the stock market.

A novel source of personal wealth had been created. Shares, whether in government stock or trading companies, were an investment which, like land, provided a secure income. Attitudes towards money changed. In the early 1680s, John Morley, a butcher from Halstead in Essex, secured the contract to slaughter the deer in a nearby park owned by Sir Josiah Child, a perspicacious businessman and chairman of the East India Company. Morley met Child, who asked him how much cash he possessed and was told £120. Child then enquired: 'How much will drive your trade?' 'Twenty pounds,' answered Morley. Immediately Child suggested that the surplus hundred pounds should be invested in East India Company shares. The butcher thought to himself, 'I had rather buy fat sheep, taking East India Company stock to be such iron bricks as are set against chimneys,' but he did as the great man instructed him. What now might be considered an 'insider' deal yielded Morley £60 within a year, thanks to the rise in the value of shares.[16]

Neither conventional loans nor land could have realised such a return in so short a time. Not surprisingly, there were many who were enticed by such profits, but they were not made effortlessly. The investor needed the specialist guidance of a new kind of expert who picked up the gossip in the London Exchange and nearby coffee houses, studied markets and, most important of all, could predict how they might behave. In 1710, Jonathan Swift denounced these 'dexterous men' and railed against the 'contrivance and cunning' of stockjobbers who, like all their kind, resorted to 'unintelligible jargon' to trick the unwary.[17] In the summer of 1720, when manic speculation in South Sea Company shares was at its height, a London newspaper reviled all stockjobbers as parasites, a handful of 'worthless men' who were damaging the nation. After the 'bubble' had burst and thousands had been ruined, the same journal declared that all speculators were selfish and indifferent to the 'misery' created by their activities.[18]

No amount of moral censure could dull the urge to gamble on

the stock market. Swift himself succumbed and, after hearing that Bank of England stock was falling, invested £300 in it, believing that it would soon revive. It did and he made five pounds in a week. Swift was flirting with the enemy. As a Tory, he associated the Bank with the 'moneyed interest' which inclined towards the Whigs and their nonconformist allies. The power of this moneyed interest had become so great that he feared it was supplanting that of land.[19] Swift's apprehensions seemed to be justified. In June 1710 a quartet of prominent businessmen, including a director of the East India Company, warned Queen Anne that if she changed her ministry, credit would collapse, share prices plummet and the Bank of England face ruin.[20] The influence of money was eclipsing that of land and an indignant Swift spoke for the rural Tory squires when he declared: 'Must our laws from henceforward pass the Bank and East India Company, or have their royal assent before they are in force?'[21]

The battlelines were not as simple as Swift depicted them. The influence of commerce and finance was already well entrenched in Parliament and, of course, many country landowners had business interests. Between 1660 and 1690, some 9 per cent of MPs were directly engaged in commerce and 53 per cent were landowners, over half of whom had interests in trade and manufacturing. All would have admitted that it was their duty to do all in their power to promote laws and fiscal policies that helped to enrich the nation. Between 1660 and 1714 over six hundred acts were passed which in some way encouraged the creation of wealth, many of them private bills for 'improvements' such as the enlargement of harbours, making rivers more easily navigable and reclaiming wetlands. Aid given to one economic activity assisted others. The law that established the Greenland Company in 1692 stated that it would secure part of the valuable trade in whale oil, provide jobs for English seamen and benefit the chandlers and victuallers that supplied the whaling fleet.

This was as it should be, thought Defoe, who tirelessly advocated the idea that commerce rather than land was the true source of the country's prosperity. 'An estate's a pond,' he argued, but 'trade's a spring'. Its 'inexhausted current . . . not only fills the pond and keeps it full, but is continually running over, and fills all the lower ponds and places about it'.[22] His conclusion was flattering to those of the 'middling sort' whom he was addressing, for Defoe identified their ambition, graft and enterprise as the bedrock of national greatness and prosperity. Long accustomed to using credit, these people also embraced the new sources of wealth and the security they offered. Among the assets of Richard Halsall, a Liverpool mariner who died in 1731, was £800 invested in the Bank of England which he hoped would provide him with an income when he was either too old or too infirm to go to sea and, afterwards, yield a nest egg for his heirs.[23]

8

Diverse Be Their Wits: The Value and Uses of Learning

National economic growth and diversification had been achieved only because of a sufficiency of educated men and women. From the fifteenth to the seventeenth centuries, levels of literacy rose, faster for men than for women. Analyses of signed documents, while not a precise yardstick, give a fair idea of the proportion of the population that could read and write, although they offer no indication of proficiency in either. In early-seventeenth-century Gloucester, a thriving city of about 5,000, around 64 per cent of men and 4 per cent of women were literate. As might be expected given the nature of their occupations, all wholesale dealers and professional men were literate. So too were 91 per cent of gentlemen and between 70 and 75 per cent of yeomen, craftsmen and retailers. The same pattern was found in County Durham between 1663 and 1689, where every professional could read and write, nearly all gentlemen and master mariners, and between 70 and 85 per cent of yeomen, craftsmen, shopkeepers and, surprisingly, artisans and labourers. Signed wills from New England between 1650 and 1670 suggest that 60 per cent of men and 31 per cent of women were literate.[1]

These statistics indicate that at least two-thirds of men and just under a third of women could read and write in seventeenth-century

England, twice the numbers in the fifteenth century. Not all could read fluently or write legibly. An ability to read and a clear hand were essential for a wide range of occupations, which was why apprenticeship indentures insisted that masters were responsible for the education of their charges. In purely economic terms, an employee who knew his letters was infinitely more valuable than one who did not. The law demanded that a written record was kept of all sales involving goods worth more than ten pounds, internal and overseas trade required extensive documentation, and shopkeepers and craftsmen would expect to correspond with their customers.

This was appreciated by those businessmen responsible for London's poor, who were a reservoir of potential apprentices and artisans. Regulations for pauper children in the Bishopsgate ward in 1699 required them to work between seven in the morning and six in the afternoon with an hour off, for playing and instruction in reading and writing.[2] The intention was twofold: the poor would learn their letters and habits of industry. Furthermore, and this appealed strongly to godly citizens, these children would be able to read the Scriptures.

Teaching the poor could make them more tractable. During the celebrations of Childermas in Gloucester cathedral in 1558, the boy bishop, a pupil at the cathedral school, declared in his mock sermon that 'a good education' helped 'to discourage youth utterly touching vile and vicious manners' and directed it towards 'virtue and virtuous manners'.[3] Gloucester's children were well provided with routes to virtue: the city possessed two grammar schools, where boys studied Latin and perhaps Greek, and a dozen smaller establishments which taught four- to eight-year-olds reading. At every stage, pupils absorbed Christian doctrines, particularly quietism, which fostered submissiveness and civility to one's betters.

Literacy made Christian doctrine more comprehensible, but it could also foment subversion. In 1538, when Henry VIII's ministers placed an English Bible in every parish church, a conservative Sussex parson feared a theological free-for-all once literate laymen began reading. 'Butchers, bunglers and cobblers which have the Testament in their keeping' were best advised to 'deliver it to us gentlemen which have studied therefore'.[4] For Protestants, this was priestcraft at its worst, for it withheld the word of God from ordinary men and women. Two hundred years later an Anglican repeated what had become a fundamental tenet of Protestantism: that print and the vernacular Bible had liberated men's consciences. Before the reformation, 'the common people . . . were on a level with Hottentots and Indian savages; and their priests were little better'.[5] A faith based on scripture rather than sacraments needed an educated laity. Ignorance was the progenitor of superstition, conversion was incomplete without understanding and faith grew through constant reading of the Scriptures.

In the classroom the Protestant ethic promoted a mixture of utilitarian instruction and simple theology, at least for the very young. This was the curriculum of the charity school at Meppershall in Bedfordshire which was funded by two local ladies. In 1698 it had six poor girls and six poor boys taught by 'Dame Gurney' and 'Dame Soale' who were paid by results; one received 3s 4d for ten weeks spent teaching a boy to read. Every Sunday, the pupils learned the Anglican catechism, and the Bible was the text for weekday reading lessons. Using spinning wheels supplied by the trustees and flax and yarn provided by their parents, girls were taught to spin and knit.[6] These accomplishments would make them good housewives, able to supplement the family income as outworkers for textile manufacturers.

Meppershall's dame school was typical of thousands that were scattered unevenly across the country. Many attracted pupils from all social backgrounds. John Fretwell, a timber dealer's son, began his education at the local dame school before proceeding to Doncaster Grammar School, where he spent five or six years poring over Classical texts. In 1713, when he was fourteen, his father sent him to a Pontefract firm to pick up some mathematics. Reading, writing, a familiarity with Classical texts and ideas and basic numeracy were 'as much learning' as his father considered 'necessary for me, and indeed as could be expected for one of my degree'.[7]

Attitudes towards learning were a touchstone of degree. A few years after, when he had purchased an estate, Fretwell senior might have reconsidered his attitude to his sons' education. For the gentry, education had an ornamental as well as practical value, since social convention required a gentleman to display wisdom, wit and taste.

For those who had to make their way in the world, learning was essentially a practical business even though the syllabuses at grammar schools and universities were devoted to the pursuit of abstract knowledge and linguistic precision.

Achievement was the result of effort and willpower, neither of which came easily to the young. Several hours of memorising Latin vocabulary and translating texts required stamina as well as intelligence and it was no wonder that Shakespeare's schoolboy dragged himself to his lessons. There were rewards: the young scholar learned how to think and write with elegance and exactitude and, through his study of Roman authors, was put in touch with other minds and imaginations. Above all, perhaps, he was exposed to the philosophy and values of the ancient world, particularly its sense of public duty and patriotism.

These ideas were understood by the father of the poet Robert Greene (*c.* 1560–93). He was a Norwich man 'who bore office in his parish and sat as formally in his fox-furred gown, as if he had been an upright burgess' and hoped that through learning his son would become 'a profitable member of the commonwealth and a comfort to his age'. It all went wrong, for when Greene reached Cambridge he squandered his time with 'wags as lewd as myself with whom I consumed the flower of my youth'. This was a normal peril of college life which was overlooked by many parents.[8] Like others of his standing, the elder Greene regarded education as an investment that would help his son to prosper.

In young Greene's case, his presence at Cambridge also made him a gentleman, for custom allowed anyone who matriculated from there or Oxford to assume gentle status. The point was made by another Cambridge man, Christopher Marlowe, in *Edward II*, when the clerk Baldock announces himself:

> My name is Baldock, and my gentry
> I fetch from Oxford, not from heraldry.

Greene made a precarious living in the Elizabethan literary world. If his temperament had been different, he might have entered a profession or trade and become 'a profitable member of the common-wealth' and gladdened his father's heart.

Contemporary wills reflected similar preoccupations on the part of fathers who wanted their sons to preserve or advance their standing in the world. In 1523, Marmaduke Constable, a Yorkshire lawyer and landowner, instructed his wife to keep their eldest son James at school and then dispatch him to an Inn of Court, where his uncle would supervise his studies. A hundred pounds was set aside for the 'promotion' of his younger brother, some of which was to be spent on schooling. A hundred or so years later, Nicholas Spencer, a gentleman, instructed his executors to have his second son 'educated in a fitting way to be a tradesman and bound apprentice'.[9]

The poor rarely set any store by education. Their children were a source of immediate income rather than an investment for the future. The sons and daughters of labourers were resources to be exploited as soon as they were physically capable of paid work. The trustees of the dame school at Meppershall were obliged to allow all the pupils a holiday from Midsummer's day to Michaelmas so that they could help their parents during the harvest. Describing his childhood in the 1640s, Thomas Tryon, a weaver's son from Bibury, recalled: 'The first work my father put me to, was spinning and carding, wherein I was industrious and grew so expert that at eight years of age I could spin four pound [of wool] a day which came to two shillings a week.' A few years later, Tryon became a shep-herd's boy, but at thirteen he came to consider 'the vast usefulness of reading' and purchased a primer. He made headway and, having obtained two sheep as part of his wages, he gave one to a 'lame young man who taught some poor people's children to read and write'.[10]

Those with learning ridiculed those without it. The gaffes and gaucheries of the uneducated were a stock theme of seventeenth-and eighteenth-century jokes. Soon after the defeat of the Armada, the mayor of Queenborough in Kent told Elizabeth I: 'When the Spaniards meddled with your majesty, they took the wrong sow by the ear.' A subsequent generation laughed at the rustic who asked whether St Paul's cathedral 'was made in England, or brought from beyond the sea'. A husband rebuked by a rural magistrate for having 'defiled his bed' by getting a girl pregnant interjected: 'You mistake, sir . . . there was no defiling the bed in this case, for it was done in a field.'

The tables were occasionally turned. 'A clodhopper of the real Sussex breed' outwitted a 'clever' lawyer who had asked him to identify his 'sleeping partner' and was told 'Mary, my wife.'[11] The naivety and stupidity of 'clowns' (a contemporary word widely and significantly used to describe labourers and artisans) amused the educated and sophisticated. They still do; who one laughs at and why has always been an indicator of status.

The classroom was a preparation for future life, in so far as the pupil had to submit to the discipline of time and the authority of superiors. Neither was welcomed. A dialogue between pupil and schoolmaster set for translation in Latin by Magdalen College School, Oxford in the early sixteenth century reflects the inevitable tension between the two:

> My father sent me here to learn grammar, thinking that two years at the uttermost three years would suffice . . . Cease you wanton boy, complain no more of this cause that you are in here . . . Though you have been brought up here afore with your mother wantonly, yet I counsel you to put out of your mind that wantonness here, for if you do not, you shall see hereafter that you have great cause to complain.[12]

Recalcitrant and insubordinate pupils were regularly beaten. Instruction was inseparable from chastisement, which was why the popular image of the schoolmaster was a figure brandishing a bundle of birch twigs. Dominies whacking the bare rumps of their pupils appear on fifteenth-century misericords at Boston, Sherborne, Westminster abbey and Norwich cathedral.

Physical correction was integral to a syllabus that required concentration. Hours were consumed memorising Latin vocabulary and mastering syntax and applying what was learned to translation. There was a moral element in many of the sentences that late-medieval schoolchildren had to render into Latin: 'Between two stools falls the arse down' and 'Children that come of good kind should forbear each other and not chide each other like harlots.' 'I have no spending money' and 'Children stand in a row, some well arrayed, some evil arrayed; diverse be their wits' were reminders that free schools took pupils regardless of their parents' background.[13]

Syllabuses changed during the second half of the sixteenth century as the country was infiltrated by Renaissance humanist ideas. Although there was never a universal curriculum, grammar schools always emphasised the study of Classical Latin texts, with Greek and Hebrew for promising scholars whose sights were set on Oxford and Cambridge and possible ordination. The regime followed by George Hoole, the headmaster of Rotherham Grammar School and outlined in his guidebook for schoolmasters, *The Usher's Duty* (1659), was typical, as were his scholastic values. At seven or eight the new boy began memorising vocabulary and the rules of grammar so that within a year or two, when his 'wits are new ripened', he could concentrate on translating prose and verse. 'Pithy orations' from Sallust, Livy and Tacitus were translated aloud in class to encourage confidence. Hoole noticed that such exercises encouraged 'the most bashful and least promising' who discovered that they could 'outstrip their fellows in pronouncing with a courage and comely gesture'.[14]

It was not all grind. Pupils at Sedbergh Grammar School recalled Gilbert Nelson, a 'very pleasant, facetious man' whose 'merry comments' made Terence and Plautus intelligible to the 'weaker capacity of boys'.[15] There were some dragons: in 1710 two brothers at King Edward's School, Birmingham complained of the 'very odd peevish humour' of the headmaster, James Parkinson. Another pair grumbled about his 'harsh humour'. All four were transferred to other schools by their fathers. A fifth pupil, who had absorbed the stoicism necessary to survive in this or any other school, observed that Parkinson was 'no otherwise peevish than other masters are'.[16]

Although both Sedbergh and King Edward's School had been founded as free grammar schools for their immediate locality, they soon attracted boarders whose parents paid for lodging and sometimes instruction. Boys at Sedbergh paid customary gifts of between five shillings and one pound to their usher each Shrovetide, supplementing his annual salary by up to £30. In early-eighteenth-century Bedfordshire schoolmasters at 'free' schools for the poor were charging four pence a week for the children of the better off and also received tips.[17] Paying fees was not a token of a school's social exclusiveness. Rather it reflected academic reputation, as at Sedbergh, or, as in Bedfordshire, the wish of parents to secure an education for their children where it was most conveniently available. As a consequence, the children of local labourers, artisans, shopkeepers, professional and business men, yeomen and gentlemen rubbed shoulders in grammar schools.

Schools of all kinds were randomly distributed, which was why children had to be sent away to board, or else walked several miles to and from school. A pious local squire, Roger Wake, who died in 1503, endowed a school at Blisworth in Northamptonshire that, by 1547, had a roll of thirty pupils, which must have represented all the children in a parish where there were 200 communicants each Sunday.[18] School places were plentiful in early-eighteenth-century Andover, a town with about 6,000 inhabitants and one free school of thirty scholars and two charity schools of sixty-four pupils. By contrast, Fordingbridge with a population of 1,700 had no school, nor was there one in Gilbert White's Selbourne, where there were 500 parishioners.[19]

These discrepancies were the result of chance; one town or village might have one or maybe more worthies who were prepared to finance schools and others had none. In 1717, five poor children from Melchbourne in Bedfordshire were coached in their ABC by a poor widow who was paid by a local landowner, Lord St John. The children of Barton in the same county learned their letters from a Quaker from a nearby parish and at Billington from a 'poor woman'.[20] Lord St John may have made the allowance to the schoolmistress as an act of piety in the hope that her pupils might read the gospels. Or he may have imagined that by providing the poor with education he was somehow furthering the interests of the nation as a whole. The idea that the encouragement of learning produced universal benefits had a long history. In 1406, Parliament had decreed that 'every man . . . of any estate or condition' had the right to procure an education for his sons or daughters at any school he chose.[21]

Masters who accepted illiterate apprentices were legally bound to have them taught their letters. They were also compelled to impose moral restraints on their trainees. These included prohibitions on fornication and gambling, a vice indulged in by Hogarth's 'Idle 'Prentice' in a churchyard while his 'Industrious' companion is in inside, attending a service. The parallel lives of these two young men were a reminder that the system of apprenticeship served a dual purpose: it imposed discipline on the young, who were naturally inclined to waywardness, and benefited the national economy by the provision of a competent workforce, whose members were able to support themselves.

For these reasons the state closely regulated apprenticeships and, wherever possible, encouraged parents to procure them for their sons. As might be expected in a hierarchical society, there were attempts to restrict apprenticeships in the most profitable occupations to the sons of prosperous men. According to the 1563 Statute of Apprentices, overseas traders and merchants in cities and boroughs could only accept the sons of two-pound freeholders as apprentices and in other towns the sons of men with an 'estate' worth at least three pounds. Wholesalers in market towns were permitted to take the sons of artisans, while craftsmen, such as coopers and bricklayers, could take apprentices whose fathers had no property. Young men who disobeyed their fathers and rejected apprenticeships were to be imprisoned until they complied.

Legal constraints were reinforced by economic ones. Only the better off could afford the fees charged for apprenticeships by the proprietors of flourishing businesses. In early-eighteenth-century Oxford the average rate was £12, with two gentlemen paying £35 and £60 for their sons to be bound to a chandler and a milliner respectively. These sums reflected the truth that there was more profit to be made from selling than from manufacturing goods, and so the cost of his indenture was a measure of an apprentice's future earning power. The fathers of apprentice weavers, wheelwrights and tobacco-pipe makers were charged £5, occasionally less.[22] Reductions were allowed for kinsmen who, in some cases, were trained for nothing. Private charities attempted to lower the barrier by funding indentures for poor children, and the state did its bit by encouraging magistrates and overseers of the poor to pay for apprenticeships for orphans and bastards on parish relief.

What appears to be a discarded book or pamphlet lies on the floor near the loom of Hogarth's idle apprentice. What had he been reading? Given his character, it was certainly something entertaining, possibly scurrilous, even pornographic. Such material was plentiful: in 1719 a London bookseller was offering books on 'Onanism', 'Eunuchism' and impotency and, intriguingly, *A Treatise on the Use of FLOGGING for Syphilis*.[23] Less debauched tastes were satisfied by a more conventional London bookseller, William Thackeray, who also supplied stock to travelling chapmen for sale in small towns and villages. The titles were a fair indication of popular taste; there were twenty-one Robin Hood ballads, 'Small Merry Books' (compendiums of jokes), Arthurian and Classical tales, a sheaf of love stories, melodramas, the confessions of criminals and pious texts.[24]

The market for such stuff was already vast and grew as literacy rates rose. To judge from the titles aimed at those in the middle and lower ranks, most read for pleasure, although there was a steady demand for solid, devotional works. Authors, publishers and booksellers quickly exploited this new market. After rejecting a career in the Anglican church foisted on him by his family, John Dunton (1659–1733) launched himself as a popular publisher. A natural entrepreneur, he identified his market of craftsmen, artisans and servants and provided it with what it wanted, cheap books on sex and lugubrious religious texts.

During the 1690s Dunton shifted into another new area, popular journalism. He founded and edited a monthly journal, the *Athenian Gazette*, which was soon relaunched as the *Athenian Mercury*. Its chief feature was 'Nice and curious questions proposed by the ingenious of either sex', which Dunton and his hacks answered with a mixture of commonsense and commonplace religious dogma. There were a few philosophical and scientific queries, but they were outnumbered by enquiries from readers seeking answers to moral and sexual dilemmas. Dunton had invented the 'Agony Uncle', and what proved to be a successful formula was quickly copied. A rival, the *Post Angel*, puffed itself in 1701 as a 'universal entertainment' crammed with news, obituaries, descriptions of 'several late elopements', answers to such questions as why heathens were created and an agony column concerned with 'relations between the sexes'.[25]

Readership of the *Athenian Mercury* and *Post Angel* included a large proportion of men and women from the middle ranks in society. In the former those seeking solutions to their personal problems in 1693 included an orphan girl of 'good family' who had been compelled to work for a living, a bachelor with 'an estate' seeking a wife and a young tradesman tormented by fears of bankruptcy. The *Gentleman's Journal* set its sights on 'gentlemen in the country' and no doubt those who wished to be thought so. Its issues for January and February 1694 offered an eclectic collection of articles on current news, history, philosophy, science (experiments on vipers undertaken in the Paris Academy of Sciences), mathematics and poetry. Backwoodsmen and women read about topics that were being discussed in metropolitan salons and could impress their friends with performances of the songs that were currently in vogue in London, for the journal reproduced the music and lyrics of the latest pieces by Purcell and John Blow.

These weekly and monthly journals were products of what turned out be a revolutionary and far-reaching development: the emergence of a national press. Growing literacy and the need for reliable and frequent commercial intelligence had been the key elements in its evolution. Newspapers proliferated in the late seventeenth and eighteenth centuries and, although most were published in London, they had a national readership thanks to the new postal services. The new press reflected the interests and preoccupations of the gentry and the mercantile community. There were regular reports of diplomatic and military events on the Continent that were useful to overseas traders and commercial intelligence covering current stock and commodity prices, shipwrecks, the departures and arrivals of merchantmen and advertisements for the sale of their cargoes.

Readers also got what became the staples of British journalism: social gossip, scandal, satire, crime (particularly robberies carried out by highwaymen) and sensational murders. In April 1701 the *London Post* described how a newly wed Hampshire blacksmith had murdered his wife and dismembered and burned her corpse; the British obsession with Grand Guignol crime stretches back three centuries. In wartime there were accounts of battles on land and sea, often drawn from official dispatches, that stirred up a patriotic fervour which substantially reinforced that sense of national superiority which grew inexorably throughout the eighteenth century. Political coverage was far less than today, although by the 1720s candidates for Parliament were publishing their manifestos in the newssheets. And then there were those indices of human desire, anxiety and gullibility: advertisements. Two may stand for many others. The first, a puff from 1693, promised users of 'Venetian Wash' that their wrinkles and freckles would vanish at the same time as their mental vigour revived. The second, from 1701, offered 'an immediate cure for the French disease and clap' for a few shillings.[26] If this nostrum failed, there were plenty of others being advertised by apothecaries and physicians.

From 1695 the press was theoretically free from state interference. There were always journalists who danced to the government's tune, either through conviction or for reward. During the eighteenth century there were clashes between editors and ministers who wanted to muzzle newspapers to shield themselves from criticism or ridicule. In 1738, when it was feared that newspapers might succumb to official supervision, at least one declared that the independence of the press was a cornerstone of national liberty.[27] This was already a widely held view and it eventually prevailed.

Seen from the perspective of the evolution of the middle class, the rapid propagation of newssheets and journals had profound repercussions. By 1714, a total of 2.5 million newspapers were sold annually; they provided the foundation of informed political debate to the entire country, accelerated the spread of innovations of all kinds, promoted the free and speedy circulation of ideas and contributed towards the formation of national opinion. This power to inform and stimulate was recognised by Richard Addison in March 1711 when he heard that the circulation of his essays, published every two days, had reached three thousand in London alone. He fancied himself a second Socrates who had taken Philosophy from the Gods 'to inhabit among men'. Addison proudly claimed that he was transferring the subject from 'Closets, Libraries and Schools and Colleges' and setting it down 'in Clubs and Assemblies, at Tea-tables and in Coffee-houses'.

9

Godly Matrons: Wives and Daughters

Alison, Chaucer's Wife of Bath, ended her tale with a prayer:

> and may Christ Jesus send
> Us husbands meek and young and fresh in bed,
> And grace to overbid them when we wed.

These lines concluded a story in which her fellow pilgrims had learned that the thing most desired by women was mastery over men. That was to be expected, since Alison had preceded her narrative with a lengthy vindication of her life and a digression on marriage in general. It was a tour de force in which she recalled her five marriages in terms that make them sound like campaigns, which in a way they were, for in each she had endeavoured to do whatever she pleased, in defiance of her husbands. Throughout, she upheld her own 'experience' against that bedrock of medieval thinking, ancestral wisdom, and at the same time cheekily invoked the 'authority' of the past whenever it coincided with her opinions. This impertinence upset the Friar, who remarked that philosophy and theology were best left to churchmen:

> Let's leave the authorities, in Heaven's name,
> To preachers and to schools for ordinands.

Alison's last husband, a clerk from Oxford, would have said amen to this. He had absorbed that corpus of exemplary anecdote and scholastic abstraction that comprised the church's view of women. Perhaps tactlessly, he shared this knowledge with her by reciting from a long catalogue of wayward and inconstant women extracted from the fables of the Old Testament and Classical literature. In exasperation, she tore three pages from the book and in the subsequent scuffle was clouted with it, leaving her partly deaf.

Alison's hour had not yet come, which may make her an odd representative of those women who occupied the middle ranks of society during this period. Her views were exceptional, although there is plenty of evidence, mostly literary, to suggest there were women like her who spurned the rules and the philosophy behind them. There was no question of Alison's status: two of her husbands had been rich and left her comfortably off. She dressed well, was jealous of her position in her local community and had enough money to undertake long and costly pilgrimages to Rome and Jerusalem. She was a widow of substance and for this reason alone could afford to challenge orthodoxy.

A woman's place in the social hierarchy was fixed by father's or husband's degree and she would expect to share the respect and deference due to him from equals and inferiors. Women took this as seriously as men: a rancorous early-seventeenth-century lawsuit began in Basingstoke parish church after a scuffle in which the wife of an arriviste gentleman pushed herself in front of the sister of another of ancient pedigree.[1] The litigation was undertaken by the husband and brother. According to the law, a woman was under the control and protection of her father until the moment she married, when her husband assumed these paternal responsibilities. The marriage contract permitting, a wife was free to manage the property assigned to her as a dowry, but otherwise everything she owned was at the disposal of her husband. Subject to her husband, a wife enjoyed authority over his household and superintended its day-to-day finances and the discipline of children and servants. After his death, she might continue her business and familial duties as the executrix of his will.

In her husband's absence, his wife was expected to manage his affairs. When her husband John was in London, Margaret Paston took charge of his estates in Norfolk. She consulted with lawyers, negotiated with tenants, and twice, in 1450 and 1470, supervised the defence of two of his properties, Gresham manor and Caistor castle. Before the siege of Gresham, she was busy ordering cross-bows and instructing servants to reinforce doorways. After her private chamber had been undermined and the manor house stormed, Margaret was evicted under protest. Reading through her letters, this clear-headed, resolute and devoted wife emerges as the domin-ant partner in the marriage and the mainstay of a dynasty making its way in a hostile world.

The Wife of Bath was engaged in commerce, for Chaucer remarks that her cloth matched in quality that of Flanders. Whether she was manufacturing it independently or running a business inherited from one of her husband's is not known. Such arrangements commonly occurred at all levels. In his will of 1534 John Weston of Carlton in Lincolnshire referred to a 'great team' of plough oxen that was passed to her eldest son once his mother had 'given up her husbandry'. Clearly the farm had been run by husband and wife as a joint enter prise. In Dunwich in Suffolk, the wives of boat-owners and deep-sea fishermen brewed beer to supplement their husband's income, a practice common everywhere.[2]

Irrespective of how profitable a part she may have played in her husband's affairs, a wife was legally his subject. Her inferior posi-tion, like the overall structure of society, was a fulfilment of God's will as revealed in the Old Testament and St Paul's letters. The former portrayed women as a source of infinite mischief: they were morally frail and fickle and enticed men away from God and His laws. Eve's weakness ('The serpent beguiled me, and I did eat') precipitated Adam's sin and the Fall of Man. Twisting the truth to their purpose, medieval commentators blamed Bathsheba for arousing David's lust, making her the cause of his sin and an accomplice in her husband's murder. Lot's wife follows Eve and rebels against God by disobeying her husband, for which she was punished. To her example was added the fictional one of Noah's wife, who in some fifteenth-century mystery plays was portrayed as a shrew.[3] Her contempt for her husband's God-given authority provided audiences with plenty of knockabout fun, but also reminded them of the Pauline injunction that the Christian wife obeyed her husband. In edifying contrast to the Bible's sirens and harpies was the Virgin Mary, an exemplary figure of purity and passive virtue, a model for all women.

Despite their capacity for moral disruption, women were an integral part of the Christian order. There were orders of nuns who followed a celibate life of prayer, contemplation and charity, often as schoolmistresses. Pious widows could become vowesses, submitting themselves to the discipline of the nunnery and pursuing good works. Female godliness required overcoming that inclination towards sensuality which was imagined to have derived from Eve in the same way as gentleness was inherited from her son Seth. 'Chastity perishes in delicacies,' warned St Bernard of Clairvaux in his advice to women who sought the cloister.

The church found plenty to do for women who remained in the world. Many parish churches were cleaned by members of local women's gilds, who also raised money for repairs and ornaments. Between 1469 and 1472, a Bodmin gild of virgins raised £2 for rebuilding the church, and in 1497 the matrons of Walberswick in Suffolk collected over ten shillings for a new stained-glass window and a painted panel depicting Henry VI, then a candidate for sainthood.[4] Fundraising was a chance for communal beanos and dances and members of women's gilds had the social satisfaction of walking in church processions. No doubt they would have worn their 'best' gowns, girdles and headdresses, treasured items that were specified in women's wills and often bequeathed to elder daughters.

Women enjoying themselves publicly in the interests of the church was permissible. Women doing so for mere personal pleasure was not – although, as the Wife of Bath vehemently declared:

> We cannot love a husband who takes charge
> Of where we go. We like to be at large.

This urge to wander like 'a goose' was to be suppressed, argued the author of *How the Good Wife Taught her Daughter*, a late-fifteenth-century marriage handbook. The gadabout wife who squandered her clothes allowance in taverns and ogled at such street entertainments as wrestling was likened to 'a strumpet and gigglelot'.[5] The impulsive and shameless wife was certain to go astray and, if she was a woman of superior social standing, could easily lose it and sink to the level of a prostitute. No harm in this, thought the Wife of Bath, who, when one of her husbands was in London on business, went strolling, chatting and gossiping:

> All the more fun for me – I only mean
> The fun of seeing people and being seen
> By cocky lads . . .

This assertion of independence was the subject of a French farce translated into English as *Johan, Johan the Husband* and first published in 1533. It is vulgar, rumbustious stuff about a wife who, if she had read them, has rejected the guidebooks to a perfect marriage. She asserts:

> It is mete for women to go play
> Abroad in the town for an hour or two.

Her husband, possibly a retailer or craftsman, objects to her 'gadding' about like an 'Anthony Pig' – animal metaphors were commonly applied to errant wives – and tries to restrain her with blows. She fights back, arming herself with her distaff, and he fears that their brawls will lower his standing in the neighbourhood. Rowdiness was associated with the lower orders. So was lechery, and Johan is further troubled about his wife's confessor, who 'gives absolution upon a bed' and is rumoured to be 'a whore monger' and 'haunter of stews'.

The ribaldry must have aroused belly laughs, but it had a darker side. The cuckold and the husband who could not master his wife (they were often one and the same) were figures of ridicule and creatures from a world in which the divine order had been reversed.

Fights between husbands and wives were a popular theme for the carvers of misericords, and many examples show the woman gaining the upper hand: at Great Malvern in Worcestershire she is whacking her husband with a broken distaff. The kitchen provided a useful armoury: at Nantwich in Cheshire the wife wields a ladle and at Fairford in Gloucestershire a wooden scoop.

Like the Wife of Bath, the wife in *Johan, Johan* secretly confides her grievances and adventures to her 'gossip Margery', a sympathetic neighbour. Given the natural fluidity of tittle-tattle, Johan is likely to suffer further mockery on account of his wife and his standing will droop lower.

The intimate and, for male theatregoers, intriguing exchanges between three gossips was the subject of Samuel Rowlands's comedy *'Tis Merrie when Gossips Meete* (1602). The trio comprise a fifteen-year-old 'maid', a married woman with children who sometimes tends her husband's shop and a widow who has 'try'd all the pleasures every kind of way'. All claim to be 'London gentlewomen born'.

Free spirits, they assemble in an upstairs private room of a tavern to 'drink like men', taking the 'sprightly wine' (claret) by the pint. As the evening draws on they order sausages and are infuriated when their sanctuary is violated by the world of men in the form of tobacco smoke wafting up from below. The wife asserts that she has banned tobacco from her house and does not care whether her husband smells wine on her breath, leaving the audience in no doubt as to who rules her household. Conversation drifts towards men, love and sex. Marriage is praised and there is a reference to the old fable that spinsters are foredoomed to lead apes into hell, a cruel fancy represented on a misericord of about 1520 in Bristol cathedral. The talk drifts towards sexual fantasy. The wife admits:

> I know that beauteous wenches are inclined
> To harbour handsome men within the mind.

Such an Adonis is imagined by the maid:

> I'll have a comely man from head to foot,

> In whose neat limbs no blemish can be spied
> Whose leg shall grace his stocking or his boot,
> And wear his rapier manly by his side:
> With such a one my humour does agree,
> He shall be welcome to my bed by me.[6]

This confession must have aroused the young bloods in the audience. Or were these the hidden thoughts they hoped that all young gentlewomen entertained?

'Tis Merrie when Gossips Meete is part of that vast literature which illustrates, often comically, the inner conflicts of marriage in a period when convention tilted the odds against women. It is significant as social history because the three protagonists, like the Wife of Bath, occupy that section of society that was looked up to. They were the forerunners of those respectable but more inhibited matrons who would gather in Victorian parlours and modern tea shops for refreshment and tittle-tattle. Part of the humour of *'Tis Merrie when Gossips Meete* is the fact that the audience knows that they are women with standards to uphold who were required to complement, even enhance, their husbands' status. To achieve this they needed self-discipline, decorum and modesty, qualities identified by the handbooks on conduct as the prime features of anyone with social aspirations.

The lower orders preferred to follow their instincts rather than any treatise on manners. Not surprisingly there was a rough correlation between social position and sexual activity. Just as the lower orders gobbled their food, spat, scratched themselves and created an uproar in the streets, they were promiscuous and coarsely spoken. By the seventeenth century, the old word 'lewd', which meant lascivious, had become synonymous with 'common' and 'vulgar' and was widely applied to the lower orders.[7] Excusing the 'harlotry' of the Miller's and Reeve's stories, Chaucer observed that they knew no better, for both were churls. The further down the social ladder one went, the greater the sexual excess; illegitimacy rates were highest among the poorest peasants in Halesowen in the fourteenth century.[8] At the very bottom of the pile there were no constraints at all. An analyst of the

Elizabethan criminal class observed that its members grew up 'wallowing in lewd lechery', which they never considered sinful.[9]

The impulse to impose 'manners' on the poor inevitably extended to correcting their sexual morals. In 1529 the authorities in London launched a drive against 'common bauds, strumpets and harlots', who were rounded up, conveyed to Newgate gaol 'in red hoods and carrying white wands'. This charivari was followed by a crowd with 'basins and pans ringing'.[10] Impromptu instruments taken from the kitchen suggest the presence of respectable housewives. Urban purification campaigns gathered momentum after the Reformation with the Puritans taking the initiative. In York in 1572, the Church Commissioners were appalled by the passage through the city of 'King Yule' and his 'Queen', who were part of the traditional Christmas celebrations. They progressed through the streets 'very indecently and uncomely' and committed various 'enormities' on the way, to the amusement of onlookers.[11]

Banning such parades was part of a wider Puritan programme of prying and punishing that began in the 1580s and was at its most intense (and unpopular) during the Interregnum between 1649 and 1660. Greater efforts were made to summon fornicators before the church and civil courts and discover the fathers of illegitimate children. By law, their upkeep was the responsibility of the parish. If their fathers could be identified, the magistrates could compel them to support their child and so save the ratepayers money. A few Puritans went so far as to wonder whether the poor should be discouraged from marrying at all, given that they were so often unable to feed and clothe their children, who would have to become a charge on the poor rates.[12] Unmarried women with 'no man to control them' attracted the scrutiny of the civic powers in Manchester in 1589. Some followed such trades as brewing and baking and were imagined to be drawing away custom from men with families to support, and there were suspicions that these women might also be prostitutes.[13] As with the clampdown on sexual irresponsibility, moral and economic motives were intermingled.

These endeavours to spread the gospel of godly continence had severely limited success. To judge from the numbers of bastardy and fornication cases brought before the courts, the poor continued to pursue their old pleasures with the same carelessness as their ancestors. Many of their betters did the same: cases involving masters seducing their female servants were common enough. The culture of filthy stories and male sexual boasting extended to every level of society. In 1660 Samuel Pepys gladly listened to the 'bawdy' stories told him by a Thames waterman, including one of a female passenger who had asked him for sex and was given 'content'.[14] Together with farting, sex was a staple of contemporary jokes. One, which may have amused women as much as it discomfited men, described two young ladies discovering a gentleman peeing against a wall – a common enough sight. The pair giggle, the man asks them why and is told: 'O! Lord Sir . . . a very little thing will make us laugh.'[15]

As a young man, Isaac Archer would have laughed at such a jest. He was a 'rude, saucy, lascivious' youth who scrumped apples from orchards and succumbed easily to 'lascivious and vain thoughts'. He must have been the despair of his parents, who were 'good' folk of the Puritan persuasion. In time, Archer was ordained as an Anglican minister (to the indignation of his father) and in 1667 he married. He was twenty-six and declared that 'by marriage all my former youthful desires were cured; and my extravagant thoughts ceased'.[16] Sex had clearly been on his mind frequently and his Puritan upbringing made him feel that his thoughts were as sinful as they were persistent.

At the same time as demonising sexual transgression, the Puritan ethic reinforced the notion that those of superior station were defined by their capacity to discipline themselves. Thomas Bulwer, a prominent London apothecary, enjoyed what he described as a 'good report' as the head of family with a reputation for 'honesty, chastity and religiosity'. In 1622 Bulwer's impeccable standing was challenged by Jane Knipe, his former maidservant. She alleged that he and his son were libertines, who consorted with prostitutes, and claimed that his three daughters were whores who 'daubed paint on their faces'. Knipe persuaded a friend, a genuine whore, to declare that young Bulwer had fathered her bastard and the pair collected a mob which made nocturnal attacks on the family's house, pelting it with dung and dirt from the streets. The Bulwers' social standing was in jeopardy and so he resorted to the Court of Star Chamber to vindicate his 'loving and peaceable' marriage and the 'blameless, unspotted and undefiled' reputation of his daughters. All were of marriageable age and their chances of a good match would be reduced if they were suspected of wantonness, or, of coming from a debauched family.[17]

In a contemporary case the servant and mistress of a Westminster vintner disclosed his indiscretions to his intended bride's mother, who called off the wedding. Deprived of a £500 dowry, he married his mistress.[18] A wine seller might marry his servant without fear of social disparagement, but a Puritan preacher warned that the propertied widow who married her groom or the gentleman his cook risked censure and ridicule.[19] Well-born London apprentices felt their present and, more importantly, their future standing might be impaired by a ballad of 1672 in which the city's prostitutes thanked them for their attentions. The offended young men responded in verse:

> Your damned impudence have made you shameless,
> You at your doors stand poxed and painted
> Perfum'd with powder yet with all vice tainted.
>
> 'Tis known that most of us are well bred
> And scorn a giddy multitude to head
> We know we shall masters become in time . . .[20]

Social and moral boundaries did march together and those of a superior station were more vulnerable to moral censure since their position owed much to the appraisal of equals. In 1693 the editor of the *Athenian Mercury* warned a correspondent that his 'fame' would be eroded if he chose to live with a woman to whom he was not married. It mattered little that the couple were faithful, for 'if it may not be fornication, 'tis yet, first, a great folly' that would injure any children the pair might have. Such a union was also illegal and 'heathenish'.[21]

Church and state upheld marriage. Its supernatural resonances, binding sacramental power and pragmatic value were publicly affirmed at every wedding service in every church. Following the canon of the Church of England set down in the words of the Book of Common Prayer of 1660, God had ordained marriage as symbolic of the 'mystical union between Christ and the Church'. It was a sacrament to be approached 'reverently, discreetly, advisedly, soberly, and in fear of God'. 'It was ordained for the procreation of children' and 'a remedy against sin and to avoid fornication; that such persons as have not the gift of continency might marry, and keep themselves undefiled members of Christ's body'.

The service then turned from the spiritual to the worldly benefits of marriage. It provided men and women with 'mutual society, help and comfort . . . both in prosperity and adversity'. With this in mind, the bride and groom exchanged vows: she swore to 'love, honour and obey' and he 'to love her, comfort her, honour and keep her'. The celebrant then prayed for the couple, asking that the wife 'may be loving and amiable, faithful and obedient to her husband; and in all quietness, sobriety and peace, be a follower of holy and godly matrons'. Words seldom heard now had a universal and far-reaching significance then and for over four hundred years. They touched the private lives of millions of men and women by offering an ideal of harmony with each other and God. These vows were of paramount significance, for Christian marriage was both the foundation and cement of a harmonious, godly nation.

The litany may have been that of Cranmer and the Elizabethan Protestant reformers, but the sentiments were older. The first precept of *How the Good Wife taught her Daughter* was wifely obedience:

> Love thou him and honour most of earthly thing;
> Meekly you answer him, not as a shrew,
> And so you may slake his temper, and be his dear darling.

Customary submission did not obviate the fact that marriage was an emotional partnership whose ultimate success depended on mutual tolerance and flexibility. For this reason, guides to marriage offered commonsense suggestions for the fostering of friendship, understanding and compromise.

Unilateral and unconditional wifely submission was dismissed by Edmund Tilney, a sophisticated gentleman who supervised the court revels of Elizabeth I and James I. His *Briefe and Pleasaunt Discourse of Duties in Marriage* (1568) proposed that perfect concord required a balance of interests and wills. 'Equalness causes friendship', he suggested and advised men always to be 'merry and pleasant' to their wives. Husbands had to accept constraints: 'abstain from brawling, glowering and grudging . . . for if the wife first conceive hate, she will never love again'.

It cannot be known how many readers took this and similar counsel to heart. Certainly couples were anxious to learn the arts of marriage, for the marital-guidebook market expanded during the second half of the sixteenth and seventeenth centuries. If digressions on house-hold management and the importance of public seemliness are anything to go by, these treatises were specifically directed towards the gentry, business and professional men and their wives.

From the early 1500s the brasses of such men often portray them and their wives kneeling with books of devotion open on a prie-dieu with sons behind their father and daughters behind their mother, all at prayer. By the second half of the century this fashion spread from brasses to stone monuments. This was a revealing conceit; even before the reformation, private – that is, personal – devotion had been growing in popularity. Households had daily prayers and some had rooms set aside as private chapels. The reformation confirmed this shift towards family worship and the Puritans in particular stressed the family and household as a miniature congregation.

Puritan ministers encouraged this trend with their own handbooks on marriage. The title of the Reverend Daniel Rogers's *Matrimonial Honour: or, The Mutuall Crowne and Comfort of Godly, Loyall and Chaste Marriage* (1642) left readers in no doubt about what was in store for them. It opens with a few shots against the Catholics for their 'deifying of virginity above marriage' and the denunciation of adulterers and 'whoremongers'. Rogers's ideal wife stays at home, where she is perpetually active: 'A chaste wife has her eyes open, ears watching, heart attending upon the welfare of the family, husband, children and servants: she thinks that all concern her; estate, content, posterity: this

rivets her into the house.' Although busy, this paragon has to overcome secret sensual desires and vanity. In particular she has to resist
the temptations of buying alluring clothes: 'abhor all those cursed
colours . . . abhor the Devil's fig leaves'.

For all his scoffing at Catholic dogma, Rogers accepts that all
women retained the characteristics of Eve. It was a view strongly
held by most Protestants. A devotional guide written for women in
1582 recommended prayers to be offered before and after childbirth. They included pleas for fortitude to endure the agonies that
resulted from the sin they had inherited from Eve, and one lamented
'our guilty and polluted nature, like the foul menstruous cloth of a
woman, [that] is washed by the blood of thy son'.[22] Spiritual decon-
tamination was provided by the service of 'churching' in which a
woman was formally 'cleansed' of the taint of childbirth, a practice
that lasted until early in the last century.

Since his audience consisted of men and women who enjoyed
some status in society, Rogers gave some attention to the problem
of marriages across social boundaries. They were a bad thing, he
concluded, for 'cattle of uneven size and stature, strength and proportion draw very ill together in one yoke'. Rogers had borrowed his
farmyard analogy from Sir John Ferne, who in his *The Blazon Gentry*
(1586) had declared that such marriages were the 'unequal coupling
in yoke of the clean ox, and the unclean ass'.[23] For Rogers, temperament as much as background could cause mismatches, for 'When a
poor party meets with a rich; a well-bred with an illiberal, a courteous with a froward; a bountiful with a miserly; a noble with a
base, one from Court with another from the shop or cart . . . what
a disproportion does it cause, and a kind of loathsomeness.'

Where did physical attraction and love come in this scheme of
things? Rogers gave little space to either subject, although he considered that 'sympathy of heart, or amiable qualities' were vital, or else
a marriage would become 'sad bondage'. It was beyond question
that sex was for the procreation of children and to suggest otherwise was tantamount to heresy. Asked in 1695 whether a man and
woman could lawfully avoid having children, the editor of the

Athenian Mercury sharply replied that St Paul had insisted that neither a man nor a woman had power over their bodies. The notion of contraception 'is a shocking of Almighty God'.[24] Man obeyed the laws of the natural world. His submission did not, however, prevent him from boosting his virility. In 1719 a newspaper advertised 'vivifying drops' costing five shillings that simultaneously cured infertility in women and 'potently strengthen and corroborate the parts of generation in men'. The same nostrum was still on sale nineteen years later, so perhaps it worked. If it did not, customers kept quiet, presumably not wishing to publicise their disabilities.[25]

Sterility and impotence were sources of distress. In 1693 a bachelor with 'an estate' that he hoped to pass to 'one of my own blood' wished to know whether, if he married and his wife proved childless, the union would be legally void. With characteristic good sense the editor of the *Athenian Mercury* suggested that the lack of children might be his fault and he would 'lose a good bed-fellow'.[26] This was no comfort for a man of property, for whom marriage was just about getting heirs and, if he could find a rich and well-born wife, the enlargement of income and social advancement.

Marriage and money were inseparable. For those with property and capital, arranging a marriage was a complicated commercial operation that involved the gathering of intelligence about opportunities and, once a union had been tentatively proposed, hard bargaining. The experiences of the Celys, a well-to-do family of wool exporters, may represent those of many other families throughout this period. In the spring of 1482 Richard Cely was looking for a wife. Discussing the matter with his younger brother George in their shared bed, he contemplated the sister of a fellow merchant, who he feared might impose stringent financial conditions. George made a reconnaissance and reported that 'she is as goodly a young woman, as fair, as well bodied and as sad as I have seen . . . this seven year'. Her father asked after Richard's prospects.

Richard Cely was also undertaking his own investigations. At Northleach, he heard from Richard Midwinter, a local wool wholesaler, of a 'young gentlewoman' who had been left £40 a year by her mother and whose father, Thomas Limrick, was 'the greatest ruler

and the richest man in that county'. Richard was immediately interested: he saw Elizabeth Limrick with her stepmother during mass
and ordered some wine to be delivered to her party. Afterwards, he
greeted the two ladies with customary kisses (a familiarity which
amazed foreign visitors) and arranged to dine with them later, offering
a gallon of wine to complement their roast heron. He later wrote
that he had 'right good communication, and the person pleased me
well . . . she is young . . . very well favoured and witty and the country
speaks much good by her'.

In the meantime, Midwinter spoke to her father, no doubt praising
the acumen and wealth of the Celys and probing to discover how
much he would settle on his daughter.[27] Dowries took many forms
– cash, land and assignments of revenue – and were agreed by
contract. Many brides' portions included furniture and household
utensils which their parents had set aside: in 1601 the daughter of
a Staffordshire yeoman presented her husband with a bedstead, feather
bed, napery, pewter ware and £10 in cash. A further charge on the
bride's family was the wedding, which was an occasion for a display
of hospitality that reflected status. In the seventeenth century a
gentleman could expect to spend between twenty-five and two
hundred pounds, a yeoman between five and fifty and a middling
farmer between five shillings and five pounds.[28]

The preliminary exchange of vows between bride and groom
were taken by many to have the same moral weight as the promises they would make on their wedding day. At the end of the
sixteenth century, between 10 and 20 per cent of brides were pregnant when they married, a proportion that dropped slightly in the
seventeenth and rose to a third during the early eighteenth.[29] Proof
of fertility obviously mattered. According to John Aubrey, the professional soldier George Monck (later Lord Albemarle) seduced his
seamstress, Nan Clarges ('she was not at all handsome nor cleanly'),
while he was imprisoned in the Tower in 1644. Her brother later
informed Monck that she had given birth. "'Of what? said he." "Of
a son". "Why then said he, she is my wife".' They married.[30]

Frances Medewell, a thirty-one-year-old widow, was three
months pregnant when she married her second husband, a London

fishmonger, in 1607. Her first had died eighteen months before and her remarriage followed a common pattern: on average widows remarried within nineteenth months of their husband's death and widowers just over twelve months after their wife's death.[31] Two-thirds of widows chose younger single men, a fondness regretted in a ballad of 1625:

> Young maidens are bashful, but widows are bold
> They tempt poor young men with their silver and gold.[32]

One of these young men was William Lilly, a penniless lad who had come to London from Leicestershire in 1602, when he was eighteen. After eight years as a servant to a rich businessman, he married his widow. 'My mistress', he wrote afterwards, 'had been married to old men' and 'was now resolved to be cozened no more.' 'She was of a brown ruddy complexion, corpulent, of but mean stature, plain' and 'with no education'. She proposed, 'saying one day after dinner she respected not wealth but desired an honest man'. She got one for the next six years during which Lilly said they 'lived very lovingly' and he remained faithful. When Mrs Lilly died she left her husband £1,000 which he invested in property. Within eight months he married again and secured a £500 dowry from his second wife.[33]

The well-heeled widow could call the odds, as no doubt the Wife of Bath had. She could bypass the polite rituals, enquiry and negotiation that occurred whenever marriages were contemplated by families. Furthermore, as Mrs Lilly appreciated, she could no longer be 'cozened'. In other words, she was released from that universal maxim that parents knew what was best and profitable for their offspring, who would bow to their wisdom and to convention. Of course, the theories behind it took no account of the contrariness of sons and daughters who chose to follow their passions rather than the commands of parents or guardians. The stratagems and convolutions, comic and tragic, which resulted from headstrong individuals setting love before filial compliance and future security were the stock-in-trade of playwrights and novelists.

In many plots, true love swept aside social and financial barriers.

It also did so in real life, but as a result not of youthful infatuation but of parental calculation. Fathers and mothers with younger sons and daughters were often unable to select partners of equal degree. An analysis of the marriages of offspring of the Lincolnshire gentry between 1612 and 1617 reveals a considerable range of social mobility. One-third of men and two-thirds of women wedded outside their degree, with the latter more often marrying downwards into yeoman and artisan families.[34]

Such unions were not always congenial. In 1693 a lady complained to the *Athenian Mercury* that she had had to spurn a 'very well accomplished' suitor in favour of one who was 'rough and unpolished' because 'a speedy marriage was necessary'. Was it wicked, she wondered, to yearn after 'the genteel sparks'? Was it right for an unmarried lady of 'good family' to hanker after 'a gentleman' who would 'give me as much money, as I would have, to buy me what I want'?. 'A good husband' and a greater devotion to God would cure such fancies. Both ladies might have heeded the advice of another correspondent, 'Arabella', who believed that happiness was the result of 'conscientiously' fulfilling her duties to God and her neighbours.[35] She was doubtless a virtuous consort as well, a true 'Godly matron' and a model for all wives of husbands who enjoyed some standing in society.

Part Two

The Middle Class Emerges: 1720–1832

1

The Gigantic Power of Man: A New Age

On 14 September 1830 the Duke of Wellington visited Manchester. It was an encounter between the past and the present and was riddled with paradoxes. The most modern and progressive industrial town in Britain was playing host to a prime minister who was convinced that only the landed aristocracy could be trusted to govern wisely and fairly in the interests of all. A traditionalist – his enemies would have said an arch-reactionary – was lending his prestige to a celebration of the achievements of the Industrial Revolution that was eroding the political system and values he cherished. But Wellington was always a pragmatist. He knew that his defeat of Napoleonic France in the Peninsular War and, finally in 1815, at Waterloo had depended upon resources created by manufacturing, mining and domestic and international trade. Without industry, there would have been no British Empire. A fellow Tory, the poet laureate Robert Southey, while deploring the moral and physical wilderness created by industry, grudgingly admitted that the 'spirit of trade' had transformed Britain into a global power without equal.[1]

Mancunians were honouring Wellington for his victories, which had decisively ended a hundred-year power struggle between Britain and France. During its final phase, between 1793 and 1815, it had been an ideological as well a commercial war. For conservatives like

Wellington, Waterloo had signalled the rout not only of Napoleon, but of the French Revolution which he had so cynically manipulated. Britain's land and sea victories were also a vindication of the nation's constitution and represented a reverse for those radicals who had hoped to remould it to accommodate French notions of democracy and equality. Neither was much in evidence in Manchester, at least among the bigwigs who attended the banquet given in Wellington's honour by the town's borough reeves. They stood at the apex of a self-perpetuating oligarchy whose authority rested on feudal precedents. Equipped with the powers of a manorial court, they ran a manufacturing town and its satellites with a population of over 100,000 and did so autocratically. The Duke revered ancient systems and refused to tamper with them so long as they worked.

He said as much when he proposed a toast to the borough reeves. Manchester was 'the centre of a great system of commerce' and its rulers 'foster its prosperity and . . . are the persons who protect and excite the industry of the community'.[2] The 2nd Lord Wilton, an etiolated young man who was something of a dandy and happiest on horseback, then delivered an encomium on industry and commerce. It was heartfelt, for the aristocracy was doing well from the Industrial Revolution. Agricultural rents (the workers had to be fed) and revenues from mineral rights were rising and the sale of urban land for commercial and housing developments provided valuable windfalls. Businessmen were flourishing as never before and fortunes were being made. Wilton's reference to the inventor Sir Richard Arkwright who had died nearly forty years before would have been warmly applauded, particularly by Sir Robert Peel, the Home Secretary. His father had used Arkwright's machines in his textile mills and had died three months before, leaving a million pounds, just under half of which went to his son. Set alongside Arkwright (whose own son died a millionaire) was James Watt, which was appropriate given the events of the next day.[3]

At 10.40 the following morning the Duke and Sir Robert Peel, accompanied by local landowners, civic worthies and the directors of the Liverpool and Manchester railway, took their places in elegant carriages, drawn by the locomotive *Northumbrian*. The opening of the first link in Britain's railway network was a splendid gala: there were brass bands, a small orchestra conveyed in an open carriage, flags and thousands of onlookers, some packed twenty deep along the line. Order was maintained by a regiment of infantry, for like most parts of the country south Lancashire had no police force. This exhibition of British ingenuity was also watched by a handful of Continental aristocrats like the Austrian Prince Esterhazy who would tell their countrymen about this wonder of the new technology and the dynamic energy of the nation that was exploiting it.

The locomotive designer, the engineer George Stephenson, kept an eye on his creation on the footplate of the *Northumbrian* at the head of what, for lack of a better word, the *Times* correspondent called a 'cavalcade'. Stephenson was a man ascending in the world thanks to an understanding of machines and what they could do. The son of a Northumberland collier, he once replied when asked his name by a lady: 'Why, Madam, they used to call me George Stephenson; I am now called George Stephenson, *Esquire*, of Tapton Hall, near Chesterfield. And further let me say, that I have dined with princes, peers, and commoners, with persons of all classes, from the humblest to the highest. I have dined off a red herring when seated in a hedge-bottom and I have gone through the meanest drudgery.' He ended this classic soliloquy of the self-made man by observing that there 'was not much difference' between his legion of acquaintants.[4]

During a stop to replenish the engine's boilers, William Huskisson, a former Tory minister, ignored the warning that had been given by the railway company directors, and stepped down from his carriage. He was rather shaky on his legs and was struck and fatally injured by the locomotive. Wellington was shocked and suggested cancelling the journey, but changed his mind after the Manchester borough reeves warned that there would be disturbances if the train did not arrive. The engine chugged on at a steady fifteen miles an hour.

Huskisson's death blighted what would otherwise have been the most spectacular triumph of the Industrial Revolution. It was the climax of a century of unprecedented progress and a perfect example of how men had learned to penetrate the secrets of nature, analyse them and then harness them. Spellbound by the locomotive, the bridges, viaducts, embankments, cuttings and tunnels, the Whig politician Lord Brougham imagined that he had witnessed a victory of man over time and space. 'The gigantic power of man' seemed poised to overcome nature by 'skill and industry'.[5] Another passenger shared his exhilaration. 'What mighty efforts the human mind is capable of,' he concluded, imploring his countrymen to make a journey that so amply illustrated the 'glory and splendour' of Britain and the 'enterprise and perseverance' of its people. They were almost gods, for the locomotive was 'a creature . . . moulded by mortal hands and fully capable of all the physical functions of animal existence'.[6]

Frankenstein's monster is called to mind, and conservative contemporaries indeed feared that machines might supplant and finally dominate their creators. For Southey, the children who worked in the mills 'as part of the machinery' were trapped without hope of betterment within a greater machine of production and consumption. Operative and machine became one, 'employed in continually increasing what it is impossible for him to enjoy'.[7]

The servants of machines, spinners and weavers, who watched the procession of trains may have marvelled at what they saw, but had no cause for jubilation. During the previous few months, they had been busy endeavouring to form trade unions which offered them the only hope of escape from what many called slavery. Propaganda for the new organisations depicted the entire working class as engaged in a struggle for survival against 'wealth and monopoly' and 'avarice and selfishness'. To date, it had been an unequal contest with the workers enduring a steady fall in their standard of living.[8]

One way in which this could be reversed was a complete overhaul of the constitution. It was a cause that was generating more and more passion. Working men pelted one carriage in the mistaken belief that it contained Wellington. Passengers saw onlookers waving tricolours and placards with the slogan 'Vote by Ballot'. Wellington had been hissed at Manchester, as he had been the day before at Stockport. Many of the manufacturers who listened to the Duke or travelled with his party suppressed their hisses. They felt the need for Parliamentary reform as strongly as their employees, but for different reasons. It was an imperative that a modern, progressive nation was governed by a House of Commons elected in a rational way so that the voices of the creators of wealth could be heard and policies shaped according to their interests, which, it went without saying, were those of the country as a whole.

Over the previous forty or so years, the businessmen of Manchester and other industrial centres had been described as part of the 'middle class', a term that became common currency in the next two years during the debates on Parliamentary reform. The phrase had its origins in the labours of eighteenth-century naturalists to classify animals, fishes and plants according to their observable, intrinsic qualities rather than imagined human ones, or their usefulness to man. The natural world was partitioned into broad classes such as birds or fishes, and these were subdivided into genera, species and subspecies.

Comparisons were made with the human order. In 1782 an English commentary on the Linnaean system suggested that grasses were nature's 'plebeians' because 'the more they are taxed and trod upon, the more they multiply'.[9] William Marshall, an agronomist surveying agriculture in the West Country in 1794, treated its inhabitants as if they were plants or birds. The farmers of North Devon were split into 'a lower class' whose members were more 'civilised and intelligent' than the Cornish miners; 'middle and lower classes' who were 'mostly plain, decent looking working husbandmen'; and a tiny 'superior order of farmers'. Marshall also identified various 'species' of rustics in Dorset.[10] Social and biological terms were interchangeable. 'No naturalist can be said to know a plant, unless he knows its rank in the vegetable kingdom,' observed a naturalist in 1828. Revealingly, he employed a mixture of new and old phrases in an appeal to the 'labouring classes' to pursue natural history, which, he argued, would provide them with a 'chance of raising themselves to a higher station in society'.[11]

The all-encompassing labels adopted by science offered a convenient shorthand for describing the biggest social groups and, of course, allowed scope for the presence of species and subspecies. William Wilberforce, the anti-slavery campaigner and MP for York, in 1797 admonished the 'Higher and Middle Classes' for their indifference towards Christianity. This assumed the existence of a tripartite society of broad layers of which the third and lowest was the 'labouring' or 'working class', expressions which were often synonymous with the 'poor'. An elderly Tory, the 1st Earl of Sheffield, took this social dispensation for granted at the end of 1818 when he warned Lord Sidmouth, the Home Secretary, of the present 'violence of [the] middling and lower classes'.[12]

As both aristocrats were uncomfortably aware, this violence was directed towards men like themselves. This animus was increasing in 1830, as the popular demonstrations against Wellington showed. A large proportion of the middle class saw themselves denied the political influence their intelligence, ingenuity and wealth deserved. These qualities were absent from the working class; their lack of education meant their judgment was flawed and they were incapable of ever seeing beyond their immediate, sectional and physical needs. The term middle class and its political ambitions were novelties, but its members had inherited older misgivings about the collective naivety and untrustworthiness of their inferiors.

Their demands for democracy disturbed the middle class. One man, one vote would produce a government that would harm the present economic system, perhaps fatally, by regulations designed to satisfy the short-term interests of the working class. Moreover, and this was very frightening to the middle classes, the rights of property itself might be jeopardised. This anxiety was perfectly understandable when agitators described factories as 'Bastilles', and there were recurrent and not always empty rumours of extremists buying weapons, forging pike heads and boasting that revolution was weeks away. In these circumstances, those with something to lose gravitated towards authority, irrespective of their views on Parliamentary reform. This recognition of interests was implicit in the suggestion made by an army officer after popular disturbances in Leicester at the end of 1830. He recommended that the government should enlist every 'respectable householder', his servants and workmen as special constables in the event of further riots.[13]

These issues must have been the subjects of the thoughts and conversations of the travellers between Liverpool and Manchester in the autumn of 1830. As they approached the powerhouse of industrial Britain, they could not have missed what a later passenger called 'the decayed insignificant borough of Newton'. It sent two members to Parliament, unlike its 'opulent' and 'prosperous' neighbour, Manchester, which sent none. Wellington detected no incongruity and would spend the next eighteen months doing all within his power to resist the reform of Parliament: Manchester's hero became its villain. What turned out to be Wellington's rearguard action amused the Whig wit Sidney Smith, who likened him to Dame Partington. This simple old woman from Sussex had tried to sweep back the tidal floodwaters from her cottage with a broom during the great storm of 1824.

2

Benefits to the Country: Revolutions

While Dame Partington and Wellington were both swamped, the Duke faced the more formidable flood, produced as it was by the confluence of four revolutions. The first two, the Agricultural and Industrial, were strictly speaking an extended period of accelerated transition that began in about 1760 and was over by 1850 when the basic national railway network had been completed. The second two, the American of 1776 and the French of 1789, were dramatic upheavals that transformed the ways in which people regarded themselves and their place in the scheme of things. Both offered new visions of the ordering of society and government along democratic and egalitarian lines and, for this reason, made a powerful impact on many Britons.

Their world was already undergoing far-reaching changes. Technical innovation, efficient deployment of manpower and their upshot, mass production, transformed British society and created a modern industrial nation whose survival depended on manufacturing and commerce. National self-esteem soared; the achievements of new, industrial Britain boosted its people's belief in their unique natural genius and superiority. Material progress and patriotism were blended in a philosophy that justified change and the endeavours of its architects.

Statistics best convey the scale and direction of the changes. Britain's population rose from 10.9 million in 1801, the year of the first census, to 16.5 million in 1831. More and more people resided in cities and towns; their share of the total population rose from 17 per cent in 1700 to 30 per cent in 1800 and 48 per cent in 1840. London absorbed the most, its inhabitants passing the million mark at the turn of the eighteenth century. The demographic shift reflected new patterns of employment. In 1700 some 61 per cent of the adult males worked on the land, by 1760 the proportion had fallen to 53 per cent, by 1800 it was 41 per cent and in 1840 it had dropped to 29 per cent. This rural exodus provided labour for industry whose workforce grew from 23 per cent of males in 1800 to 47 per cent in 1840.

Geology and geography dictated the migrants' eventual destination. Machines needed power, first water and then coal, and so manufacturing was concentrated in areas where both were available. People moved towards the mining and industrial complexes of the Midlands, the North and Clydeside, and high rates of infant mortality and low levels of life expectancy kept up the demand for labour. Between 1789 and 1831 the population of Oldham and its surrounding villages rose from 13,000 to 50,000, about two-thirds of whom were employed in cotton mills, mines and engineering works.

Many of the incomers had been dispossessed by the drive for high yields in agriculture – an expanding population needed cheap and plentiful food. 'Reduced farmers' were among those who beat a path towards the new, water-driven cotton mill established at Deanston in Perthshire in 1785.[1] They must have included Highland crofters, evicted by landlords who were applying new agronomic principles; the sale of fleeces from vast flocks of sheep produced more than rents from subsistence farms. Everywhere, small, uneconomic farms were merged into larger ones whose operating costs were less and yields greater.

Change imposed from above was unwelcome and sometimes resisted. When, on Christmas Day 1821, a Thame solicitor and land agent accompanied by his clerk arrived at nearby Towersey with an enclosure notice to be pinned to the church door, their path was blocked by thirty villagers. Boys waved their hats to panic the agent's horse and his clerk lashed out with his umbrella at several women who were hustling him. In the end the villagers accepted the inevitable and local magistrates imprisoned the leading rioters to remind the peasantry that quietism was in their best interests.[2]

Modern sympathy for the victims of Britain's economic miracle (whose plight takes up an inordinate amount of space in school curriculums) would have puzzled most contemporaries, who regarded the forces of change as an expression of man's capacity to better himself through the application of his natural intelligence and talents. Short-term disruptions were incidental; what mattered were the long-term benefits. This would have been understood by the Thame solicitor, a quintessential middle-class figure serving the interests of progress, and, like other land agents, doing very well from it.

The mood of the times was caught during the annual agricultural show held at Woburn park in June 1800.[3] Landlords and farmers inspected the exhibits to discover what was new and exchange ideas. They admiringly prodded the firm flesh and deep fleeces of selectively bred sheep, congratulated their owners and made arrangements to introduce the new strains into their own flocks. The eighteenth-century counterpart of genetic modification prompted none of today's foreboding; rather it was seen as a shining example of man's capacity to uncover and utilise the forces of nature.

Optimism and self-confidence pervaded the toasts proposed after the vast dinners which ended each day's business. Glasses and tankards were raised to 'Success to Experiments' (science held the key to farming's future) and to the adventurous innovators who were sponsoring them. Among them was William Coke of Holkham Hall on the Norfolk coast. When he died, aged ninety, in 1842, another landowner applauded him for 'applying the whole energy of his mind to the collection and dissemination of all knowledge which he could derive from practical and scientific farmers'. 'Great improvements' were the result which delighted Coke and delivered 'the most incalculable benefits to the country'.[4]

Similar sentiments animated everyone who welcomed canals, railways and any device which increased the pace of production or cut overheads. Heaping praise on the inventions that had revolutionised cotton manufacture over the previous fifty years, the *Scotsman* declared in 1817 that 'Every new application of machinery, every division of the extension of labour has the tendency to reduce the costs of commodities, or to render their acquisition a less difficult task to consumers.'[5] Modern farming put food on the plates of the poor and applied technology and ergomonics put cheap cotton clothes on their backs.

Experiments in agriculture had coincided with two experiments in government, the American and French republics. They and the revolutions that introduced them were inspired by ideas deeply rooted in the British intellectual and political tradition. American rebels quoted John Locke, and the egalitarianism of New England merchants, farmers, shopkeepers and craftsmen had a pedigree that stretched back to the radical Puritanism of their ancestors. When the Scottish radical Thomas Muir was on trial in 1793 for advocating French democracy, the High Tory judge Lord Braxfield cited Montesquieu's praise of the British constitution as evidence of its perfection. Others of Muir's mind accused the government that prosecuted them as betraying the historic liberties of the British people.

This made sense in so far as the public had welcomed the news of the events of 1789. 'Despotism is destroyed,' declared a Bristol newspaper after the fall of the Bastille, and a Bath journal described the behaviour of the French as 'sagacious, consistent and honourable'.[6] The chattering classes in their inns and coffee houses agreed, and many concluded, somewhat smugly, that France was having its long overdue Glorious Revolution. Reason had triumphed: royal absolutism and the powers of a privileged aristocracy and parasitic church had been abolished.

This consensus of benevolent approval was soon torn apart by events in France. The revolutionaries declared a republic, guillotined their king, confiscated swathes of ecclesiastical and aristocratic property, briefly abolished God, fell out among themselves, presided over chronic inflation, and in 1792 began to export the revolution to the rest of Europe at the point of a bayonet. These were the birth pangs of a new age which had a new creed: the Declaration of Human Rights. Henceforward, sovereignty rested solely with the popular will, which was law, and from birth everyone was endowed with natural and inalienable rights.

British reactions veered from sympathetic understanding and admiration to downright horror. The latter prevailed after Britain entered the war against the republic early in 1793. 'The name of Frenchman is already become synonymous with that of Atheist, Murderer, Regicide, and Plunderer in the ears of every friend of Liberty and Virtue,' announced one patriotic newssheet.[7] An increasingly small and continually harassed minority disagreed. France, like America before it, had created not only an alternative political system, but an alternative society. When they ridded themselves of monarchy, Americans and Frenchmen had also shed concepts of hierarchy. Truly fluid and just societies had been created in which, theoretically at least, all were free and equal.

Thomas Paine, an eyewitness to the American revolution, was convinced that America and France had found a formula for universal happiness. He explained why in his *Rights of Man* (1791), which sold over 50,000 copies within two months. Paine is worth reading because he said incisively and passionately what many of his readers felt but could not always articulate. They were drawn from that section of the middle class that included independent craftsmen and shopkeepers. Many were nonconformists legally excluded from any part in the political process. Typical was Samuel Bamford's father, a Methodist of independent mind who successively worked as a schoolmaster, cotton spinner and workhouse manager in Middleton in Lancashire. He studied *The Rights of Man* like a gospel text and discussed his conclusions with like-minded friends, including an apothecary, a shoemaker and a 'weaver and herb doctor'.[8] Similar groups formed part of the network of Corresponding Societies whose members called each other 'citizen' in the French manner. Among the citizen delegates to an Edinburgh 'convention' in 1793 were weavers, shoemakers, a tailor, a school teacher, a bookseller's clerk and a 'teacher of fencing and pugilism'.[9] Although some of these men imagined that they might engineer a violent revolution, most preferred mental to physical combat.

Paine gave them ammunition. He diagnosed the ailments of the old order and suggested a remedy that was both cure and stimulant. The crown and the nobility with all their clients and toadies were drones who impoverished the nation and had to go. Out too would go the principles of hierarchy that they symbolised and the people would become free, happy and more prosperous, as they were in America and France. Paine's image of an indolent, parasitic aristocracy was a theme that was exploited by later radicals and reformers. In 1816 William Cobbett contrasted the small salaries of American officials with the bloated sums paid to sinecurists and courtiers in Britain.[10] A pro-reform handbill of 1831 listed the recipients of taxpayers' cash with droll explanations of their entitlement; Lord Delamare who got £10,000 a year was described as 'a pot companion to George IV'.[11] Such squandering of revenues incensed the industrious middle class as much as the poor.

Those of middling rank were, however, in a quandary when it came to Paine's support for democracy and dismantling the barriers of the old, hierarchical order. His assertion that revolutions released the talents of individuals who had been traditionally overlooked or disregarded appealed to clever men of humble rank and, of course, potential Robespierres. It was wormwood to anyone who believed that the political hierarchy should always remain a replica of the social. 'I prefer a legislature comprising the wealth, the talent and the education of the realm to a Radical Directory of shopless cobblers and shopless apothecaries,' declared one Tory squire in 1820. Invoking memories of events in France twenty to thirty years before, he added that any alteration of the constitution would be bound to elevate 'lawless, creedless, murderous, blasphemous banditti'.[12]

War and the well-reported antics of the 'banditti' who had taken charge in France swayed most of the population away from Paine and, for that matter, from further consideration of political reform. The twin phantoms of invasion (France had pledged to export its revolution to Britain) and subversion by the dwindling number of Paine's sympathisers haunted the country from 1793 onwards. There were two moments of intense anxiety: in 1797 there were two naval mutinies (the one at the Nore ominously set up a 'floating republic'), and in 1798 there was a rebellion in Ireland, backed by French troops.

These episodes and a rash of localised popular disturbances (nearly all in response to food shortages) sent jitters through the upper and middle ranks of society. Menaced by the floating republic at the mouth of the Thames, London merchants, shipowners and insurers hurriedly set up a fund to reward loyal sailors and informers with intelligence of seditious conspiracies. Other Londoners crowded into the ranks of the volunteers, one unit announcing that its members would die to defend the 'tranquillity' of the city and preserve the property of its inhabitants.[13]

Revolution was on the doorstep and Londoners knew what to expect, for the press had been full of lurid accounts of the Jacobin and Thermidorean terrors. Print shops brimmed with cartoons, some reproducing vivid scenes of French anarchy in the familiar streets of London as a warning of what would follow invasion or insurrection, or a combination of both. Billy Pitt's government was delighted. It was winning an ideological war, convincing Britons that their lives and possessions were secure only in a stable, rich and God-fearing nation united to defend its ancient freedoms. Dissenters were ridiculed, intimidated and prosecuted under emergency legislation. State coercion was supplemented by private; formed at the end of 1791, the Association for Preserving Liberty and Property against Republicans and Levellers offered an outlet for patriots who had something to lose.

They found plenty to do and did it with relish. News that Mancunian Jacobins were planning to hold a dinner on the second anniversary of the fall of the Bastille prompted a handbill that invited 'true' Englishmen to demolish the house about their heads, for 'the brains of every man who dined there would be much improved by being mingled with bricks and mortar'. Local innkeepers were understandably reluctant to host such functions. After pro-revolutionaries had provocatively proposed to raise money for the French army in Flanders, two hundred Manchester publicans proclaimed their 'detestation of such wicked and abominable practices' and banned all 'infernal associations' from their premises.[14] This was a wise precaution since all relied upon licences granted by the local magistrates, who were staunch patriots.

In Bath, Dr Harrington, who was mayor between 1793 and 1794, feverishly sniffed out sedition and celebrated his activities with the toast:

> May knaves who plot the State to vex
> Find law provides for all their necks.

Occasionally his zeal overcame his reason. On discovering a notice that a local shop was offering London newspapers with the latest reports of a British defeat at Toulon, he threatened to prosecute the proprietor for 'seditious' libel.[15] The efforts of this busybody physician were widely applauded in the city of fashion. 'Men of rank and distinction' in the public galleries 'huzzaed, cheered and threw their hats in the air' when magistrates delivered a guilty verdict against Thomas Wilde, a tailor and member of a local Corresponding Society.

Throughout the country men of Wilde's persuasion who escaped prosecution for sedition were regularly pelted and buffeted and had their windows broken by 'Church and King' mobs, often under the eyes of magistrates like Harrington. Anglican clergymen in particular were free with their cash when it came to buying drinks for loyal rioters, or funding one of the hundreds of street parties held whenever effigies of Tom Paine were ritually and noisily burned. One victim, a nonconformist Nottingham factory owner, sued the local authorities for their benevolent inertia after his premises had been burned down by a 'Church and King' mob.[16] Ironically, more property was damaged and mayhem caused by defenders of crown, church and constitution than by the small number of British proto-revolutionaries.

The passion and violence of the loyalists were a barometer of the fears of the middle and upper ranks in society. Anarchy beckoned from France, as the civic authorities of Gravesend warned in 1792. If a revolution occurred, the 'lower orders' might gain through 'rapine and plunder' some 'temporary and small advantage', but this would be more than outweighed by the lawless chaos that would inevitably follow, leaving them and their families poorer than ever.

This was not scaremongering: there were over a thousand riots between 1790 and 1810, just under half against high food prices.[17]

Political grievances accounted for a tenth of the tumults and the rest were demonstrations against economic change. Rural mobs tried to impede enclosures and workers displaced by machines broke them to smithereens in attacks on factories. The violence was localised, sporadic and easily contained by the military, but seen from above it sometimes suggested that the country was a hair's breadth away from revolution. After an anti-enclosure riot in Bedfordshire in 1796, a local parson imagined that he had glimpsed something of the chaos that was enveloping France. 'If poor people are suffered to make laws for themselves, we shall shortly have no government in this country.'[18]

Thousands of those who were now being referred to as the middle class would have concurred. They had read enough in their papers to associate the French revolution with bloodshed, anarchy and an utter contempt for the rights of property, and for these reasons alone were prepared to close ranks with the government. They subscribed to patriotic funds for the relief of soldiers' and sailors' widows and orphans, drilled with the volunteers and yeomanry, and stifled their grumbles about the extraordinarily high levels of taxation. Anyone who still felt sympathy with the ideals of the revolutionaries had them dispersed by Napoleon's coup, although there was a coterie of Romantics, most notably Byron, who saw the Emperor as a superman who had extended the boundaries of imagination. The majority view was more down to earth: drunk on the abstractions of the Rights of Man, the Frenchman had woken up to find himself under a military dictatorship. Britain's constitution and ancient freedoms were proving more solid and durable than intoxicating French notions of equality and fraternity. It was a point that was repeatedly made after the war to rebut calls for political reform.

Not only did popular revolution endanger property, it dissolved the deference which those of middle and upper rank still expected. During the 1797 anti-militia riots in Perthshire, parishioners at Dull had insolently turned their backs on their minister as he walked to the kirk. A local laird who identified one of the rioters called to him with a phrase ringing with undertones of future retribution: 'I observe you, James.' 'I observe you too and be damned,' the man answered.[19] Urban disrespect was more threatening. During disturbances in

Huddersfield in 1820, the 'lower orders' were overcome by a 'daring spirit'. 'All subordination and obedience' vanished as working men and women shouted, hooted and hissed the yeomanry who were patrolling the streets. The mob was 'determined to intimidate and frighten' the cavalrymen and 'every well dressed decent man who does not countenance their proceedings'.[20]

This was class war, with those of middle rank aligned alongside the aristocracy against the working class. A year earlier, the extreme left-wing journal *Black Dwarf* had identified the volunteer yeomanry who were officered by landowners as the 'fawning dependants or the supple slaves of the great'.[21] Manufacturers were among the Manchester Yeomanry detachment that became entangled with reform demonstrators during the meeting at St Peter's Fields in 1819 which ended with the Peterloo massacre.[22] It was a dramatic incident that highlighted the vast rift that seemed to be opening between the upper and middle classes and the working.

Among the working class, memories of it lingered for generations. 'Were you at Peterloo?' a heckler shouted at John Duncuft, the successful Tory candidate in the 1847 Oldham election. He was said to have been among the yeomanry troopers and might well have been, for he was a self-made cotton manufacturer who had started his career by buying a second-hand pair of spinning mules. Duncuft denied he had wielded a sabre at Peterloo, but working-class listeners found it easy to believe that he had been there in spirit.[23]

Duncuft's alleged participation in the suppression of a popular rally for reform illustrates the ambiguity of the political position of the middle class and the complexities of its loyalties. He was a man who been made by the Industrial Revolution and who later poured some of his profits into railway speculation. Duncuft also had political ambitions that he was only able to fulfil thanks to the reform of Parliament in 1832, the same cause that had brought crowds of working-class men and women to St Peter's Field in 1819. They had come to hear another man from the middle classes, Henry ('Orator') Hunt, a sometime Wiltshire farmer and political agitator who eventually became an MP and made his living from manufacturing boot polish.

Hunt was a classic 'village Hampden', fiercely dedicated to the protection and advancement of ancient native freedoms and the defiance of anyone or anything that smacked of tyranny. Like so many contemporary radicals, he saw himself as the heir general and defender of Magna Carta, the Glorious Revolution and the Bill of Rights. In the mid-seventeenth century, he would have been a Leveller. Wherever liberty was under threat, Hunt was there. In the autumn of 1830 he was sharing a platform with another middle-class reformer, the editor of the *Lancet* Dr Thomas Wakley, who was standing for election as coroner for Middlesex. For Hunt it was no parochial matter; addressing 'Englishmen loving liberty', he claimed that Wakley's candidature was part of a universal struggle for freedom and pointed them in the direction of France, where the people had just dethroned the *ultra* Bourbon king, Charles X.[24] A vote for the radical and outspoken surgeon would be a further blow against the forces of reaction.

Wakley won and within a few months was throwing himself into the battle for political reform, organising the provocatively named National Union of the Useful Classes. During the winter and spring of 1830–1, similar bodies were being formed across the country, holding meetings and drawing up petitions. A veteran reformer told an assembly at Chelmsford that forty years before men like himself had been denounced as 'mad dogs which were disposed to bite all who came their way'. Now, it was the Tory enemies of reform who were considered 'crazy'. When Tories spoke up for the status quo, their voices were drowned by laughter and catcalls. At Winchester, deference was ditched and Lord Carnarvon's anti-reform speech was barracked. 'It don't matter what he says,' bawled one heckler.[25] Newspaper reports of these meetings noted that the middle class was heavily represented; at Keighley the speakers included a clergyman, surgeon, organist and land surveyor.

All were impatient. They regarded the constitution as an evolving organism that had to adapt itself to a changing economic and social environment in order to function. Its basic machinery was breaking down: in the 1818 general election there had been no contests in over a hundred of the 138 small boroughs and more and more county elections were being stitched up by the equivalent of non-aggression

By heaven's command: the three orders of medieval society

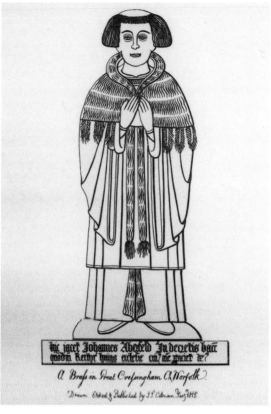

Knights: Armour, sword and the lion symbolising courage convey the conventional image of the warrior on the brass of Sir Robert Bardolph, ?. 1395, Mapledurham, Oxfordshire.

Priests: John Aberfield, *d.* 1518, is distinguished by his tonsure and vestments, Great Cressingham, Norfolk. *(University of St Andrews Library)*

Labourers: three peasants ready for harvesting with their scythes on a late-fourteenth-century misericord at Worcester cathedral. *(The Chapter of Worcester Cathedral)*

A merchant with a forked beard:
Robert Attelath. This brass was engraved
in Flanders in the fourteenth century and
stolen from St Margaret's, King's Lynn,
in the eighteenth. *(University of St Andrews Library)*

A man of law: William Curteys, *d.* 1499,
a notary with his pen case and ink pot
attached to his belt, Necton, Norfolk.
(University of St Andrews Library)

Alternative therapies, *c.* 1490, one physician bleeds his patient, the other
examines his urine in a flask. *(British Library)*

Good wives

Labour and love in the fourteenth century: the good wife spins and is importuned by her husband whose mind is on another of her duties.
(British Library)

Childbirth: the wife cradles a swaddled baby while her maid prepares nourishment; her husband waits outside; late-fifteenth century.
(British Library)

Status mania: with so many from the middling orders moving upwards into gentry, those of ancient blood and long pedigrees responded by displays of heraldry: brass of Sir Thomas Blennerhasset, *d.* 1531, at Frenze in Norfolk.
(University of St Andrews Library)

A middle-class parable, Hogarth's Industry and Idleness, 1747

The industrious apprentice works his loom, while his idle companion daydreams with a tankard labelled 'Spitalfield' (gin?) nearby and a book lying on the floor. His master, rod in hand, appears and will soon deliver correction. *(Bridgeman Art Library)*

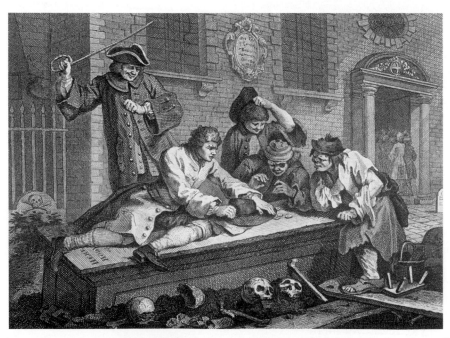

The godly (including the industrious apprentice) enter church while the idler rolls dice on a gravestone with a trio of wastrels. Again punishment looms, this time delivered by the beadle. *(Bridgeman Art Library)*

Virtue rewarded: the industrious apprentice now a rich merchant is installed as sheriff of London. *(Bridgeman Art Library)*

Vice rewarded: after a dissolute life on the margins of crime, the idle apprentice pleads before his distraught, former companion. Private emotion will not deflect him from fulfilling his public responsibilities and the idle apprentice will soon be hanged at Tyburn. *(Bridgeman Art Library)*

A rout at the Vauxhall Pleasure Gardens: respectable patriots celebrate Wellington's victory at Vittoria in 1813 by drinking themselves silly, cavorting and flirting. Fireworks will conclude the evening. *(British Museum)*

The last gasp of an easy-going morality: ladies at an assembly puff cheroots then advertised as preventative to cholera. It is 1832 and such raffishness will soon be frowned upon with the advent of sterner moral codes. *(British Museum)*

The triumph of reform: the new dawn of the middle class is celebrated by an allegorical print. William IV gives his assent to the Reform Act seated on a throne supported by figures symbolising manufacturing, agriculture and the arts. Wellington and the Tories lurk in the darkness of their obscurantism. *(British Museum)*

Chasing the middle-class vote. Fears of the naïveté of the new voters were exaggerated; fears that they would succumb to bribery and free drinks were not. *(British Museum)*

Work by Ford Madox Brown: Thomas Carlyle and the Reverend John Maurice contemplate their countrymen and women in Hampstead. *(Bridgeman Art Library)*

Servants: Dr Adamson's groom waiting with the trap for his master to do his rounds. Nanny is about to take the children for a walk, a housemaid (far right) prepares to go shopping, while the housekeeper and another maid stand in the doorway, St Andrews, 1862. *(University of St Andrews Library)*

pacts between local grandees. General elections were less and less about choosing representatives and more and more about private agreements between 'borough mongers' and anyone who could pay their price. Whatever else it might achieve, reform would restore faith in the system. When the first reform bill was introduced in March 1831, Lord John Russell warned of the 'growing want of confidence' in 'public men'. There was, he feared, a widening breach between government and 'the great mass of the weight and intelligence of the country'.

This gap could be closed by giving seats to 'opulent towns, full of enterprise, industry and intelligence'. Other Whig politicians repeated these points during successive debates, always appealing to the middle classes. They were ideal partners in government, according to the Prime Minister, Earl Grey, who told the highly sceptical House of Lords that they consisted of 'able, and active, and industrious men, who had acquired large property by their habits of enterprise and assiduity, and who had, therefore, the deepest interest in its [the country's] security and preservation'.[26]

Grey was flattering a section of society which was rallying to reform and to his party. There was 'the most extraordinary spirit' abroad, complained the agent for the Tory 4th Duke of Newcastle in May 1831. His middle-class tenants in Newark were refusing to vote for his nominee. The Duke tried arm-twisting: he moved to his seat at nearby Clumber, hoping to overawe the voters, and, when this failed, threatened to evict the obdurate. One defiant elector, 'Thorpe the Confectioner', refused to shift, claiming that he had voted for the Radical candidate only after he had made him blind drunk.[27] A sober independence of mind was shown by Joseph Townsend, a surveyor and land agent with aristocratic clients, who disengaged himself from the irksome business of moving house and rode twelve miles with his father and brother to Aylesbury on the last day of the four-day poll in the shire election. All three voted for the reform candidates and against the wishes of the local Tory magnate.[28]

By chance or historical accident 'Thorpe the Confectioner' and the Townsends had the vote and used it to support Whigs and Radicals. They and like-minded members of the middle class put extra-Parliamentary pressure on the government through political unions. Some like the largest, the Birmingham Political Union, embraced the working class and demanded democracy. A spasm of riots during 1831 and reports of revolutionary conspiracies had the same effect as their counterparts in the 1790s; the middle class remembered its property. While pledging themselves to fight the 'vile oligarchy' blocking reform, middle-class members of the Yeovil Political Union promised to uphold 'peace and good order' and support the authorities in the suppression of popular tumults.[29]

Bath reformers were possibly more radical and certainly more theatrical. Like the French revolutionaries in the summer of 1789, they held their first meeting in a tennis court and dedicated themselves to 'Liberty' and 'Just Rights'.[30] Working-class reformers, already fearing that they would be excluded from the franchise, talked about revolution. In South Lancashire in 1832 some political unions began buying stocks of firearms and swords from local ironmongers.[31] An extremist journal, the *Republican*, self-consciously adopted the French revolutionary calendar: 1831 was 'Year of the People 1'.[32]

The *Republican*'s readership was disappointed. The Reform Act passed in 'Year of the People 2' (1832) set the qualification for the urban vote as ownership of property with a rateable value of ten pounds. It was a hurdle that deliberately excluded most of the working class, and there was unease in some quarters that it had been set too low. Lord Brougham had no qualms, for he was convinced, rightly as it turned out, that old habits of deference were deeply entrenched. 'Respectable shopkeepers and tradesmen', factory managers and even 'foremen' who had the vote would naturally seek the political guidance of 'richer men'. The judicious and prudent influence of 'character and education' would ultimately prevail.[33] So much for Wellington's gibes about an electorate of 'petty tradesmen' and 'shopkeepers'.

From the perspective of the far right, an ex-Guards officer, Lord Falmouth, claimed that the abolition of many proprietorial boroughs was 'legislative robbery' and detected a 'revolution' in the making.[34] He was as wrong as he was silly: what had been established was a new equilibrium between the old landowning order and the middle class. The latter gained immeasurably in self-confidence and self-esteem, having been repeatedly described in a series of superlatives that gave the impression that it represented the collective intelligence, wisdom and energy of the nation. In alliance with a section of the Whig aristocracy – and this coincidence of interests should not be forgotten – the middle class had penetrated the political establishment. This made pragmatic political sense, for in various ways its members now controlled the creation of the country's wealth. This was acknowledged in 1832 and was of enormous significance for the future of the middle class.

In terms of practical politics, there was no revolution – quite the contrary. In all, a third of a million largely middle-class voters were added to the electoral roll, roughly 14 per cent of the adult male population. Since the middle class was increasing in size (between 1824 and 1833 the number of general practitioners, for instance, rose from 5,200 to 8,100), the electorate grew. By 1859 it totalled 1.2 million, just over a quarter of the adult male population. Electioneering followed old patterns. Corruption persisted (the *Scotsman* had naively suggested that the 'middle classes' would never be bribed or intimidated), proprietorial boroughs survived well into the 1880s and there were large numbers of uncontested seats until the first decade of the twentieth century. Surprisingly, given the intensity of the reform debate, a substantial section of the newly enfranchised were insouciant about using their vote. In 1859 only 27 per cent of the electorate voted.[35]

3

Usefulness: Identities and Aspirations

The Reform Act altered the balance of political power, but left the structure of society undisturbed. When Brougham had referred to the capacity of men of 'character and education' to sway their inferiors, he had acknowledged that the old hierarchical order was intact and fulfilling its traditional function of providing moral leadership. Giving a man a vote may have raised his self-esteem, but it did not change his status.

Consider Allen James, an Aylesbury chimneysweep whose address was the 'Common Dunghill' and whose neighbours included a cordwainer and a labourer. Luck had it that they all lived in a borough where every adult male could vote and in the 1818 general election James voted for William Rickman, a local banker and a Whig. James's property was worth more than ten pounds a year and so he kept his vote, and in 1835 he again backed Rickman.[1] He was on the lower fringe of the middle class and would have been deferential to its more substantial members, the town's professional men, wholesalers and brewers, while he would have treated fellow tradesmen and shopkeepers with familiarity. All electors would have acknowledged Rickman their superior, for he was rich, owned nearby estates, called himself 'esquire' and was listed among the nobility, gentry and clergy in the local directory.

The vocabulary of rank with its implications of dignity, moral authority and usefulness had survived. The Industrial and Agricultural Revolutions may have enlarged the middle orders, but they continued to think of themselves and their place in the world in terms familiar to their ancestors. Philip Whitehead, a London merchant who died in 1774, was described in his obituary as the 'son of a respectable tradesman [a tailor] in Westminster' who provided him with 'an education suitable to his birth and circumstances' and then apprenticed him to a woollen draper.[2] Affirming his loyalty in 1794, William Baker, a shopkeeper and grain dealer, declared that he performed the duties of 'my station', which were honouring the King, fearing God and 'quietly [leaving] the care of the State matters to those whom Providence had entrusted with them'.[3]

Recalling his boyhood in north Buckinghamshire in the 1820s, the future Gothic Revival architect George Gilbert Scott described a social order that had been virtually static for two hundred years. He remembered 'an unpicturesque country denuded of its natural aristocracy', a deficiency in part remedied by his parents. His father, a clergyman, and his mother, whose family owned a sugar plantation in Antigua, were both 'well bred' and by nature and upbringing 'gentlefolk'. Their son admired his father's 'gentleman-like address when he encountered those of higher station'.[4] Such a bearing was expected from a cleric of the established church, but now it was also found among those who had no hereditary or occupational claim to it. Thomas Payne, a Pall Mall bookseller who died in 1831, was described as a 'gentleman of his profession' whose 'kindness of temper' and 'gentleman-like suavity of manners' impressed his scholarly customers.[5]

The line between gentle and non-gentle still transected society. But, as the praise heaped upon Payne indicates, notions of what constituted a gentleman had followed lines laid down in the Renaissance. These were echoed by Thomas Allen, a Cambridge graduate and provincial physician, who reviewed his life in 1700 and concluded that 'propagating goodness, brightening thought, correcting errors and false courses in the world' were the obligations of gentlemen like himself.[6] A national survey published in 1731 defined gentlemen as distinguished from 'the common sort' by 'a good garb, genteel air, or good education, wealth and learning'.[7] Above all, the gentleman dedicated himself and his talents to the public good. Virtue disseminated for the general good was a constant theme of epitaphs; one of 1780 from Boston in Lincolnshire may stand for many, in both sentiments and fulsomeness:

> Sacred to the memory of Richard Fydell, esquire, who with great natural abilities improved by a liberal education and with unbiassed integrity sustained and adorned the various and important characters of a British senator, magistrate, a gentleman and a merchant; and in whom (distinguished as he was, by the purity and elegance of his manners, a man of sound piety and enlarged benevolence, happy in himself, and delighting to make others happy) the world saw and admired the fairest example of social and domestic virtue.

Heraldic decorations remind us that Fydell was a gentleman by birth. Ancestry still counted, but education and generosity of spirit counted as much, perhaps more, and they were not necessarily hereditary. The shift of emphasis was recorded in Dr Johnson's dictionary of 1755 in which he stated that the definition of 'gentleman' as meaning 'man of birth' was 'now out of use'. More commonly the word indicated: 'A man raised above the vulgar by his character and post'. Wealth alone did not make a gentleman; Johnson tartly remarked that retired businessmen in rural Twickenham had 'lost the civility of tradesmen without acquiring the manners of gentlemen'.[8]

The path from urban business premises to a rural mansion and its surrounding acres was already well worn by the eighteenth century. Successful professionals and businessmen continued to follow it, imagining like the Twickenham tradesmen that their exodus would transform them into gentlemen. Rich Londoners intent on becoming country gentlemen headed westwards along the north bank of the Thames, the route taken by Thrifty, a merchant, and his ambitious wife in a satirical poem of 1756. She was the prime mover behind this reconnaissance, arguing that her husband's health would benefit from 'exercise and country air'. Jealousy proved more persuasive, for she reminded him that another merchant, Sir Traffic, had bought a house a mile or so from Chelsea.

> Sir Traffic's name so well apply'd
> Awak'd his brother merchant's pride;
> And Thrifty, who had all his life
> Paid utmost deference to his wife,
> Confess'd her arguments had reason,
> And by th'approaching summer season,
> Draws a few hundreds from the stocks,
> And purchases his Country Box.[9]

The eighteenth-century version of today's second home in the countryside was also a reward for a lifetime of hard work. Thomas Webb, a Birmingham businessman who retired in 1819 to Kitwell Park, a red-brick Georgian house, celebrated his achievement of sylvan tranquillity with a poem:

> When business, oft by profit led,
> Employed my labouring hands and head
> A cot, I hoped, on rising ground
> Would at some distant day be found,
> Where I might view in humble pride,
> The vast expanse of Nature wide;
> There know what sweets away from strife
> Attend upon a well spent life.[10]

Webb was satisfied by the view. Other middle-class migrants were not. Owning a gentleman's residence meant that one had to think and behave like a gentleman, which in the eighteenth and early nineteenth centuries involved following the current aesthetic theory that urged the enlightened to remake the landscape and create an artificial natural harmony. In a satire of 1753 'Mushroom', a lawyer's son, renovates the farmhouse where he had been born and which he has just purchased to prove himself not only a gentleman, but a discriminating one. He fails and the result is a hotchpotch of contemporary styles with a Gothic extension next to an Italianate. His gardens contain the obligatory folly, a hermitage ('St Austin's cave') and a bridge 'partly in the Chinese manner'. 'Squire' Mushroom is proud of his contrived Arcadia and 'desires you to repose yourself and expects encomiums on his taste'. The sophisticated reader laughs, the more so since Mushroom remains at heart a bumpkin; his mock-Classical temple 'consecrated to Venus' is where he 'riots . . . in vulgar love with a couple of orange wenches'.[11]

Poor Mushroom knew but did not understand the rules. The bon ton could be merciless when it came to their infraction. Dr Johnson, the son of a provincial bookseller who called himself a gentleman, was particularly sensitive to the nuances of conduct and the injury they could inflict on those who failed to conform to them. In an essay of 1751, he described the fortunes of the second son of a country gentleman who had been apprenticed to a respectable London haberdasher. After four years of diligent application, he returns home and meets old friends. He expects to find local gentlemen keen to pay heed to his advice on money matters and ladies anxious to hear about the latest metropolitan fashions. His talk bores the company at his 'first public table' where a young lawyer and a Guards officer command attention with historical anecdotes and accounts of the court, assemblies of the beau monde and London's pleasure gardens.

Despite his mother's reminder that lawyers and army officers would one day be glad to borrow from him, the young man returns to the city disheartened. Soon after, his elder brother dies 'of a drunken joy, for having run down a fox that had baffled all the packs in the province'. The apprentice becomes the squire and is unhappy in a social limbo. He loathes hunting ('I was afraid of thorns in the thicket and the dirt of the marsh') and, when in London, travels in a curtained sedan chair to avoid being spotted by former friends who want to carouse and discuss local girls. The parable ends with the hero rejecting convention, choosing instead to live according to his own lights, which of course required self-confidence and determination.[12]

A marginally more successful fictional fox-hunter was Mr Puffington.

He was the only son of a Stepney starch manufacturer and his social ascent in the 1820s was described by R. S. Surtees. Like every satirist, Surtees knew that wives were the engine that moved families upwards; Mrs Puffington successively urges her husband to move from the East End to a house in Mecklenburg Square and send their son to Eton and then Christ Church, where he jostled with sporting aristocrats and embraced their habits. 'How proud the old people were of him! How they would sit listening to him, flashing, and telling how Deuceace and he floored a Charley [policeman] and he pitched a snob out of the boxes into the pit.'[13]

Businessmen acquiring country seats, a lawyer's son landscaping the grounds of his, and a manufacturer's son cavorting with blue-blooded swells were nothing new. The middle orders remained in thrall to the aristocracy and gentry, who continued to set the tone of society and to dictate taste and fashion. Even as they were moving towards a collective identity, based upon their usefulness and sense of responsibility, the middle class continued to defer to their betters.

This powerful urge to emulate and imitate was commercialised, ironically, by that quintessential middle-class businessman Josiah Wedgwood, the pottery manufacturer. In 1777 he attributed the popularity of his black basalt 'Etruscan' vases to the fact that 'The great people had these vases in their palaces long enough for them to be seen and admired by the Middling Class of people, which class we know are vastly, I had almost said, infinitely superior to the number of the great.' Mass production satisfied a mass market; for as little as 7s 6d, the tradesman's wife could have on her mantelshelf a vase similar to one in a countess's drawing room. Moreover, since Wedgwood understood the range of middle-class spending power, the barrister's wife could have a larger one for three guineas.[14] In newspaper advertisements, retailers were always inviting the 'nobility' and 'gentry' to examine their wares, or indicating that they regularly patronised their shops. True or not, such claims assured humble shoppers that they were buying goods desired by their betters in premises they frequented.

Like Wedgwood, these shopkeepers were tapping a rich vein of snobbish vanity. It was mocked by Dr Johnson in a piece in the

Idler that described the antics of Sam Softly, a sugar baker who had come into a fortune. To spend it, he had to acquire taste and so with his wife and a few 'select friends' he sets off on a tour of 'the most eminent seats' of the nobility and gentry. When their owners were absent, many country parks and houses were open to the public and so Softly's party had picnics (with tea of course) in the grounds and gardens and then inspected the furnishings, paintings and ornaments. Having seen what was fashionable, Softly and other middle-class tourists could return home knowing exactly what to buy.

Horses and equipage headed most shopping lists. Softly purchased two geldings and a chaise before his excursion, for the nobility and gentry always travelled by carriage or on horseback. The middle class aspired to do likewise, so carriage ownership became a barometer of a city's or town's prosperity. During the last quarter of the eighteenth century, the number of carriages in Edinburgh doubled to just under 1,900. Most of the new owners were merchants, physicians, surgeons, ministers and university professors. In all likelihood, these men subscribed to the city's riding school, established in 1764 under a riding master who was paid £200 a year. This was a large salary, but his pupils wanted the best, for a gentleman was identified by his seat and the ease with which he controlled a horse.[15]

Instruction was also available for those middle classes who wished to discover the correct modes of behaviour and fashions. Handbooks of etiquette continued to enjoy a wide readership and now newspapers and journals offered advice on this subject together with articles on the latest fashions in taste. Everywhere, the emphasis was on an individual's realisation of happiness and promoting it in others. The quest for happiness is 'the first and ultimate object of everyone of us . . . it was for this we were born,' insisted the *Lady's Magazine* of February 1778. The title suggested exclusiveness and therefore attracted many middle-class readers.

Active happiness was expressed through conversation. Its perfect expression was described in a handbook of 1707:

Whilst conversation, ever on the wing,
Delights to rove through all the honied spring,
Like music's voice, harmonious, deep and clear,
Pours all its information through the ear,
Draws out the force of education's plan,
Combines the whole and finishes the man.[16]

The raw material for conversation was provided by collections of epigrams and philosophical sayings and by the press. The fluent young fellows who discountenanced the apprentice haberdasher may well have acquired some of their social sparkle from newspaper reports in the press or from reviews and anecdotes in weekly magazines.

Formal occasions such as assemblies, balls, routs (evening receptions) and supper parties provided the opportunities for conversation. To judge from the literature on the subject, perfect conversation required a pleasant, nimble wit, a store of amusing anecdotes, a knowledge of what was new in the world and an elegance of phrase. By the second half of the century, the social aspirant was being advised to acquire some intellectual ballast. Returning, as it so often did, to a subject dear to its readers' hearts, the *Lady's Magazine* of March 1798 cautioned them against 'vanity, affectation and frivolousness' and reminded them that conversation was 'an index of the mind'. It had to be filled so that a lady's conversation carried some weight, but not too much, for 'pedantry' was to be avoided.

It was not to the taste of Jesse Harden, the daughter of an Edinburgh banker and newspaper proprietor and wife of an artist. In 1810 she complained about a rout in which there was 'nothing to do but chat' in which she became trapped by the 'learned set'. 'Cards and music are quite necessary to make an evening go off,' she concluded.[17] Jesse was right: a balance between erudition and amusement was essential in any entertainment. A guide of 1825 on the management of a household advised the middle-class housewife who wished to hold a 'conversazione' to include card games as an antidote to pedantry. None the less, intelligent conversation had to be stimulated, so she was instructed to scatter the 'newest publications', prints, drawings, fossils and shells on her tables 'to excite attention and promote remark'.[18] The hostess could well have added some of Josiah Wedgwood's basalt or jasper medallions of philosophers, men of letters, Roman emperors and modern worthies.

The wife of say an attorney who held a conversazione along the lines suggested in her domestic vade mecum would have hoped that her guests left describing the ambience as 'genteel'. It was a word that had been in circulation for well over a century and had been defined by Dr Johnson as an adjective suggesting politeness and refinement. Obviously the word had close connotations with the older 'gentility' and 'gentleness', but was not synonymous with gentleman or any of its derivatives. Early in 1776 a London newspaper offered three different properties each aimed at a specific market. There was a 'capital mansion . . . suitable for a gentleman's family' close to Lincoln cathedral, a 'genteel messuage' in Herefordshire and a 'small genteel house' with two rooms in Soho.[19] The last two houses were clearly for those below the rank of gentleman but with claims to respectability – in other words, the middle and lower levels of the middle class.

They were people who set great store by appearance, which was essential to uphold their place in society. In 1767 a junior Admiralty clerk complained that his yearly salary of thirty pounds was insufficient for a 'genteel' bachelor to survive. Unlike a 'labouring man', his occupation demanded 'a tolerable appearance' and his self-esteem 'tolerable' lodgings, either a 'decent' house with an annual rent of twenty pounds, or 'tolerable' rooms let for at least four shillings a week.[20] The genteel were instantly recognisable. In January 1776 a young lady 'genteely dressed in black silk' was attacked by a dog in a London street, and at the end of 1789 'genteel' people gathered in Bath abbey for a service to celebrate the new local Sunday Schools to which some may have subscribed.

The genteel strove to be temperate in their habits, particularly in public and in contrast to their inferiors, who were, as ever, characterised by reckless over-indulgence. Polite abstemiousness did not come easily; in 1786 an evening assembly in Edinburgh was disrupted by men who 'reeled from taverns, flustered with wine', to the distress of the elegant ladies who had gathered there. Standards had risen a few years later, when a local magistrate noted approvingly that 'immoderate drinking' was passing 'out of fashion' among Edinburgh's 'genteel'. They were not killjoys, however, for 'every tradesman in decent circumstances' was serving wine with dinner, something unheard of thirty years before.[21]

Preoccupation with appearance made the genteel susceptible to advertisements that appealed to their insecurity. In 1817 a puff for shoe-blacking reminded potential customers that 'shining' footwear was essential for 'a genteel appearance', for 'this is the law of fashion and must be obeyed'.[22] Genteel followers of fashion were not always what they seemed. During 1838 London policemen were on the look-out for a 'genteelly dressed' young Welsh woman who was wanted for theft and for John Bodle, a former valet and burglar who was 'slender made, of genteel figure', 'very smart in his linen' and of 'affected and effeminate manners'.[23]

Maintaining genteel externals was a source of anxiety, because of what William Cobbett called the 'shame of being thought poor', an unease that could be alleviated only by conspicuous spending. He deplored the middle class's hankering after the paraphernalia of the gentry: money spent on servants, horses, carriages, wine and 'ardent' spirits (that is, brandy) was money squandered. As a result the middle-class family lost its 'independence', which Cobbett saw as the root of 'happiness'. 'Can I do without it? was a question he urged his middle-class readers to ask whenever temptation appeared.[24] 'No' was the common answer, not for any practical reason, but because consumption was inextricably tied up with status. As the Admiralty clerk knew, his wardrobe and address set him apart from artisans (who may have earned as much as him) and the young lady in silk who had the misfortune to be bitten by a dog was a cut above the maid or seamstress in her printed cotton frock.

Cobbett regarded credit as the guilty accessory of self-indulgence, which of course it was. The genteel and those who aped the gentry always ran the risk of over-stretching their resources and succumbing to bankruptcy. It was an incubus that haunted the middle classes, and for some suicide was preferable to the humiliation of the debtors' gaol. In May 1737, Eustace Bugell, a writer and journalist, threw himself from the Greenwich ferry and drowned. His was a genteel but insecure occupation and his credit had dried up, although his pockets contained a gold watch and some change. Friends told the coroner that 'he expected an execution to enter his house . . . which gave him great uneasiness'. The same fears tormented William Alchorne, a city businessman who shot himself and died soon after in January 1819. He admitted that 'he and his family were ruined and he expected to be in prison for life', and he had told his partner that his 'private affairs were much embarrassed'.[25] He was spared gaol, but his family was left with the disgrace of a coroner's verdict which assumed that most suicides were the consequence of insanity.

Living genteelly with a thin purse was misery. In 1777 it broke the spirit of an unknown young lady who had been 'genteelly starving on a small annuity [fifteen pounds]' with a maiden aunt, proud of the family's tenuous aristocratic connections. She looked for employment in 'some genteel business', or as a last resort as a lady's maid. The old lady 'flew into a passion, and told me that there had not been *trade* in her family for these two-hundred years'. After narrowly escaping a dubious career as a mistress (a gentleman lodging near by attempted to lure her into his bed), the young lady finally secured a place as a maid with a 'good' family. She was persuaded to take the plunge by a greengrocer who had mistaken her for a servant; in appearance the shabby genteel were hard to distinguish from housemaids.

Her new job was a liberation. 'Instead of being condemned to a life of pride, poverty, idleness, nastiness and misery, supported only by the consideration of being nobly born . . . I was now honestly and usefully employed . . . there was nothing to rob me of my happiness but the idea of being a *servant*'.[26] This confession appeared in the *Lady's Magazine* and one wonders how readers would have reacted to it. Did it imply that being genteel was a state of mind rather than a reflection of income? Was the young lady right to jettison her genteel status, and was its loss offset by prospects of future usefulness and greater comfort? Certainly she had convinced herself that usefulness opened a door to happiness.

★

Whatever their feeling about taking a position as a servant may have been, the wives and daughters of middle-class men would have applauded the young lady's views on usefulness. It was a quality of which the middle classes were immensely proud; they were of service not only to themselves but to the rest of the world. This was why Dr Wakley had classified them as the 'Useful Classes', and his fellow reformers contrasted the fruitful industriousness of the middle classes with the flânerie of the aristocracy. Yet, paradoxically, the better-off members of the middle class were spending money and energy affecting the tastes and buying the trappings of an apparently idle nobility. Of course imitation of externals did not mean an endorsement of attitudes. In Disraeli's *Coningsby* (1844), the Manchester cotton manufacturer Mr Millbank does not shed his reformist opinions on purchasing an estate, far from it. As events prove, he is playing the nobility at its own game, for his property gave him influence in a nearby rotten borough.

Furthermore, and this is sometimes lost sight of, the aristocracy and gentry were in the forefront of the industrial and agricultural change, providing capital and using their social prestige to promote beneficial inventions. Five dukes presided over the Society Instituted at London for the Encouragement of Arts, Manufacture and Commerce, and its subscribers included country squires as well as businessmen. All funded prizes for innovations in agriculture and industry and their society symbolised an ideal of co-operation between the middle class and the aristocracy in pursuit of the national good. Aristocratic participation in such bodies was essential for their success. Hesitant support for a Mechanics Institute in London in 1823 was blamed on the public's reluctance to back any project unless 'led on and directed by the aristocracy of wealth and rank'.[27]

Usefulness was not confined to the middle classes, however much they liked to think otherwise, nor was it manifested only in supporting public enterprises or generating wealth. Perhaps the best definition, embracing private and public life, was given by Robert Southey in 1829 when he outlined the goals of the 'good and wise man'. He had:

To do his duty first to his family, then to his neighbours, lastly to his country and kind; to promote the welfare and happiness of those who are in any degree dependent upon him, or whom he has the means of assisting, and never wantonly to injure the meanest thing that lives; to encourage, as far as he may have the power, whatever is useful and ornamental in society, whatever tends to refine and elevate humanity . . .[28]

This commonplace recipe for a perfect life could have been written at any time during the previous three hundred years. Its repetition indicates how deep-rooted ideals of service had become.

No area of life was exempt from the principle of service. Daily drudgery could be useful, if the worker had a proper attitude. Among a series of model letters compiled by an Anglican cleric in 1784 to help those who fumbled with words was one from a hypothetical young gentleman apprenticed to a grocer. He vows 'to follow some useful business in this world' and its value was explained in another letter, composed for a merchant paying suit to a lawyer's daughter. Commerce is to be admired, for it 'supports the interest, and promotes the glory of the nation', and through it 'the industrious poor are honestly employed and . . . acquire comfortable subsistence'.[29]

It was a point worth making. There were still pockets of that old snobbery that looked askance at trade. Richard ('Beau') Nash (1674–1762) once told Oliver Goldsmith of how a monthly assembly was held in the town hall of a market town 'to encourage that harmony which ought to subsist in society'. It was 'conducted with such decency, decorum and politeness' that the local nobility and gentry attended. In time some ladies began to object to the presence of tradesmen's daughters and gentlemen announced their aversion to dancing with them. The tradesmen were indignant. They were self-sufficient 'men of worth' who retaliated by cutting off the gentry's credit and demanding a quick settlement of debt; for the middle class money was always power. A rapprochement was achieved through the mediation of a nobleman, who explained that it was absurd for the two parties to be at loggerheads since each depended on the other. The moral of the tale was obvious and timeless: without mutual co-operation between its different segments, society would dissolve into chaos.[30]

There were tremors and tensions within the middle class because of disagreements about the relative usefulness of its members. In 1750 Dr Johnson observed a 'tendency of those engaged in all occupations to denigrate others and exalt their own profession'. For example, the 'studious and speculative' considered themselves superior and happier than those engaged 'in the tumult of public business'.[31] Dr Johnson was among the former, but any jealousy he may have felt was tempered by the knowledge that the rewards of commerce were offset by its risks. Like every other newspaper reader, he would have seen the weekly lists of bankrupts.

Followers of the liberal professions were ambivalent towards the profit motive. In 1816, Richard Reece, a distinguished physician, regretted that medicine was being 'disgraced' by 'a spirit of trade which has put the profession on a level with the avocation of the lowest mechanic'.[32] His rage was directed against urban physicians and apothecaries who connived to enrich each other at the expense of the sick and doctors who published medical treatises in the press that were in fact 'genteel advertisements for fees'. These base stratagems were considered unseemly for a profession whose impulse was the 'welfare of mankind'. Reece was over-idealistic, for even the best doctors did all they could to procure patients and fees, not always honestly. None the less, he had raised an important issue that would continue to exercise medical minds: were members of what was one of the largest professions just like everyone else employing their talents to make a living? Or did the nature of their calling elevate them and secure rewards that could not be registered in an account book?

Prejudice of another kind was directed towards a new profession, engineers. A memoir of James Watt (1736–1819) suggested that his life and character were proof that 'mechanical pursuits' were not incompatible with fine feelings and gentlemanly courtesy. The contrary assumption was commonly accepted on historical grounds. In the past those engaged in 'the really useful arts' had been 'slaves and degraded classes of men'.[33] Correcting this bias was one of the aims of the *Mechanic's Magazine* founded in 1823 and it was soon boosting the confidence and pride of its readers. It is not, ran one early article, a rich scabbard that makes the sword 'but the edge and temper of the blade'. 'In like manner, it is not money or possessions that makes a man considerable, but his virtue.'

Whether or not the engineer possessed virtue, or whether he deserved the same respect as say a banker, were irrelevancies for William Wade. He was a journalist who had made a name for himself exposing political corruption and in 1833 he published an analysis of the middle class which offered it a new, corporate identity that dispensed with old notions of hierarchy and rank. They had become redundant in a modern, industrial world where the bond of 'capitalism' united the former middling orders into a single unit. Wade defined capitalism as wealth employed practically and productively. Its value was self-evident and it had always been the lubricant of civilisation: without it, he asked, could man 'have built the Pyramids, St Paul's, Westminster Abbey, New London Bridge, or constructed the Manchester railway'?

All members of the middle class were capitalists, not because they had surplus cash for investment (many did not), but because they were engaged in the generation of wealth. The vast network of capitalism extended beyond those engaged in the funding, production, distribution and sale of goods to all professions. By curing the sick, the doctor made it possible for men and women to work. The web also encompassed all who encouraged consumption. 'A jeweller employed in chasing a ring for a finger, or a silver show buckle may be the cause of increased industry in the manufacturer and agriculturalist' because 'men can only be induced to labour by something they prize'.[34]

Wade's theory was also a call for unity. A year before, the Reform Act had given a measure of political power to the middle class. They were the masters now, but to exercise authority the middle class needed a common will. Assuming, as Wade did, that getting and spending were the overriding preoccupations of the middle class, then economic interest was the cement that would bind its members together. There was some truth in this: the middle class had multiplied and enriched itself thanks to recent agricultural and industrial growth. Its members tended to favour innovation and justified it as progress.

They were impatient with whatever impeded progress. Conservative appeals to 'the wisdom of our ancestors' failed to convince the middle class, particularly during the debates over political reform. In a collection of essays published in 1825, the radical philosopher Jeremy Bentham (1748–1832) likened the nation's history to an evolutionary progress, with each generation increasing the general store of knowledge and experience. Change was natural and desirable since it was a process of betterment. Antiquity did not justify the continuation of institutions and habits of mind. During the 1820s and 1830s the politically conscious middle class of Whig and Radical inclinations saw themselves as modernisers, clearing away anachronisms of every kind from rotten boroughs to the exclusion of non-Anglicans from universities.

Modernisation involved restricting the ancient powers of the aristocracy and the established church at the same time as preserving the social and economic status quo. This involved a delicate balancing act, as conservatives pointed out. Tampering with one part of the system could jeopardise the whole and open the way to what the middle class did not want, revolution from below. Wade was essentially correct when he identified common economic aims as the bonds that united the middle class, although, as events proved, its members regularly fell out when it came to which economic policies were best for the country.

Other issues divided the early-nineteenth-century middle class. Some middle-class men expected to be treated as gentlemen, others did not or took refuge in the belief that a gentleman was defined by his conduct rather than by birth, education or wealth. Practitioners of the 'liberal' arts still considered themselves superior to those who followed the 'mechanical'. When Wade's book appeared, the medical profession was at loggerheads over the exact status of its various branches. There was no religious or political consensus among the middle class; it was split between Tories, Whigs and Radicals and between Anglicans and dissenters. Middle-class men and women argued over slavery, how best to alleviate poverty and sundry lesser issues of taste, morality and behaviour.

4

Genteel Chimney Pieces:
Patterns of Consumption

The eighteenth- and early-nineteenth-century middle class expended as much time, energy and ingenuity on spending money as they did earning it. Never before in Britain had one's place in the world depended on how one dispersed one's income. Money purchased the myriad stimulants to that individual pleasure whose fulfilment became a philosophy of life.

A child's guide to this new world of consumption written in 1791 urged the young to cultivate taste and refinement, which were the essence of 'civilisation'. Illustrating the chapter 'Man in a Civilised State' is an engraving of a man and a woman walking their dog along an urban street against the background of a cathedral, a modern bridge being crossed by a stage-coach and the masts and spars of ships at a distant quayside. Religion, efficient transport and commerce are the foundations of modern civilisation and the couple its representatives.[1]

Their clothes indicate that they belong to the upper tier of the middle orders, but where are they going? The dog suggests a stroll for the health of body and mind. The nascent Romantic movement was strongly recommending rural walks during which the rambler's imagination could be aroused by the contemplation of picturesque landscapes or ruins. Views of majestic mountains or tranquil rusticity were reproduced in the engravings that hung on the walls of this couple's house. It will also contain chinaware, glassware and ornaments chosen by the wife, whose friends will congratulate her on her discernment when they call for morning tea and chatter. One complemented the other, and both were pleasurable, inspiring an amateur poetess to write:

> Oh thou! The fountain of that stream, whose power
> Bestows delight at morn's awakening hour
> And after when the beams of daylight fail
> Renew'st thy flow of fragrant beverage,
> With thee through life securely can I pass . . .[2]

Most people went through life seldom tasting tea, for it was an expensive and therefore exclusive drink. National consumption was two pounds a head in 1800, twice as much as that for that other middle-class stimulant, coffee.[3] This would have been regularly drunk by the lady's husband when he visited a coffee house to meet friends, discuss business and glance at the daily newspapers. He will be a member of one or more all-male clubs and associations, formed to foster friendship through the convivial exchange of knowledge and opinions. Not all are high-minded or sedate. In November 1783 Parson Woodforde spent a restless night at the King's Head in Norwich thanks to a meeting of the Thumb Club, which dispersed the following morning. 'They hallowed and hooped all night, broke above 12 shillings worth of glasses and bowls.'[4]

There were decorous entertainments that the pair could enjoy together. If they lived in or visited London, they could go to one of the many pleasure gardens and in nearly every provincial city and town there were theatres and assembly rooms for conversation, concerts, cardplay and dancing. Possessions and recreation cost money, but the price was worth paying, for the embellishments of the civilised life will bring this pair private contentment and public respect. Seeking pleasure was integral to human nature, argued a defender of music in 1817, and 'with proper regulation' was a source of infinite happiness, satisfying the 'bodily senses, or imagination, or both'.[5]

Gratifying the senses became big business in the eighteenth century. Literature, the theatre and to a lesser extent painting and sculpture increasingly depended on middle-class patronage. The number of theatres rose rapidly; in the provinces a playhouse became a totem of civic distinction and simultaneously announced the presence of a thriving and prosperous community with sophisticated tastes. These new theatres were profitable investments: a hundred-pound share in the theatre and assembly room built in Sheffield in 1761 yielded an annual 6 per cent dividend and almost doubled in value within sixty years.[6] Auditoriums were enlarged to meet rising demand, with the big London playhouses seating over two thousand by the end of the century.

Economics dictated what was staged. Playwrights and impresarios like David Garrick discovered what the public wanted and supplied it. On the whole, theatregoers were happiest with what was familiar and easily digested, so this was not an age of adventurous or provocative drama. Audiences liked variety, in particular Shakespeare in abridged and sometimes sanitised versions, romances, farces and topical satire. Fops, faddists and foreigners, who on the English stage included Scots and Irish, were regularly ridiculed. Samuel Foote's *The Register Office* (1751) amply catered for prevailing tastes and prejudices. Its scenario was a famous London labour exchange where servants were hired and the characters included a caricatured Frenchman, a prickly Scot full of his ancient pedigree and an illiterate Irishman who tells the audience that he was born in 'an inland seaport town'. During the second half of the century medleys of plays, dances, tableaux and musical interludes grew in popularity.

Theatrical programmes convey the flavour of middle-class preferences. In the first week of 1787 Bristol's Theatre Royal presented *Henry IV, or the Humours of Sir John Falstaff* (no doubt an edited and adulterated version), a dance called 'La Jardiniere Italien' performed by Master and Miss Mitchell and 'several elegant pieces on pianoforte' played by an 'amazing phenomenon' who was a four-year-old boy who had previously appeared before Louis XIV and Marie Antoinette as well as the 'chief musical cognoscenti of England'. After sharing the pleasures of the illustrious, Bristolians came down to earth with a vulgar bump with *Peeping Tom of Coventry*, a comic opera. The next week's programme consisted of a new comedy, *He Who Would Be a Soldier*, the 'Duchess of Devonshire's minuet' and, since this was the Christmas season, a pantomime, *Robinson Crusoe*.[7]

Middle-class taste was uniform and universal. In January 1817 Aberdeen's Theatre Royal presented *Macbeth* (surely a truncated version) which was followed by several songs and a farce, *A Lovers' Quarrels*. The following evening's programme was a comedy, *The Honeymoon*, a new farce, *Past Ten O'Clock on a Rainy Night*, an opera, *The Foundling of the Forest*, and another farce.[8] Similar repertories in which the sentimental, comical and domestic predominated were clearly just what audiences would pay for.

Patriotism was also exploited by managements. In what were the forerunners of the cinema newsreels, London theatres staged realistic reconstructions of British victories overseas. In September 1793 Astley's Amphitheatre in the Strand, which specialised in this sort of thing, produced tableaux of the recent siege and occupation of Valenciennes by British troops. These were followed by 'Harlequin's medley', comic dances and *The Tipsy Woodcutter*, a 'musical piece'. Not far away, Sadler's Wells was also offering vignettes from the war, a tightrope walker and a 'New Comic Extravaganza'.[9]

Rival playhouses with competing repertories provided the middle class with what it now took for granted in every area of individual consumption, choice. It was not a novelty, but what had changed significantly was the sheer variety of goods and services on the market. They were the result of the growth of overseas trade, domestic manufacturing and the ability of distributors to send goods cheaply and efficiently to every corner of the country. These developments had made the middle orders richer than ever: they had more spare money and were determined to spend it on the comforts, entertainments and commodities that took their fancy.

International trade was filling shelves and transforming diets. In 1793 an Aberdeen grocer was advertising Malaga grapes, pistachio nuts, sago, tapioca, French and Spanish olives, coconuts, Barbados rum and Indian arrack. The Aberdonian housewife could choose from five varieties of China tea and, if she was thrifty, some cheaper 'green tea' at four shillings a pound.[10] She and her daughters would have worn dresses made from North American cotton, probably woven in Lancashire or the Lowlands, and, for formal occasions, Indian muslin. The less well off were also indulging the new consumerism. In the early 1790s a Fife minister noticed that during the previous thirty years his parishioners had discarded the traditional plaid and bonnet for coats of English cloth and cut and tricorne hats, and servants were carrying that former token of exalted status, a pocket watch. In a nearby parish, the minister regretted that the poorer members of his congregation were vying with each other to buy fashionable clothes that were 'often above their station'.[11] Consumerism was a leveller, but not to the extent that it would become during the second part of the twentieth century.

Consumerism increased the numbers of the urban middle class; more shops meant more shopkeepers. In 1801 Southampton with a population of 8,000 supported over three hundred retailers, drapers and milliners. Thirty years later, the 26,000 inhabitants of York were served by 274 tailors and breechmakers, ninety-six grocers and fifty-four chemists. New-style retail warehouses appeared, the counterpart of today's supermarkets, which, like them, relied on a fast turnover to keep prices down. Ordinary retailers branched out into every kind of commodity. In 1773 William Robertson, an Elgin merchant, advertised guns, pistols, ironmongery, japanned tea trays, 'Things in the Birmingham and Sheffield Way' (that is, metalwares and cutlery), tortoiseshell ware, paper, cheeses, pickles, anchovies, wax and 'a neat assortment of Staffordshire and glass wares'. A mail order service was available for customers in outlying districts.[12]

With such selections of goods available, shopping became an engrossing and popular pastime for the middle classes. In late-eighteenth-century Edinburgh 'the daughters of many tradesmen consumed the mornings at toilet, or in strolling from shop to shop'.[13]

Window shopping had arrived, with its delights of imagining what one could buy if one had the money. Shopping expeditions and the problems of choice were increasingly described in diaries and letters. In August 1804 Jesse Harden lingered over pelisses in an Edinburgh dressmakers, selecting one in brown and purple silk at six guineas after rejecting another at eight guineas as too expensive and spurning cheaper ones as 'common'.[14]

Men were also obsessive shoppers, none more than the Reverend John Woodforde. Details of his purchases on expeditions to Norwich have equal prominence in his diary with his other favourite indulgences, food and wine. In January 1778 he was tempted to purchase a pruning knife and two razors at the 'New Birmingham shop' for half a crown. Excursions in 1781 yielded among other things a 'very genteel cork screw' and tobacco, paper, nutcrackers, a humming top, scent, needles, a candlestick and 'an ivory thing to wind silk or thread' which were among the eclectic wares stocked by a Mr Baker. Some of these items were presents for friends, servants or his sister, for whom he once bought stays and 'a neat ostrich feather' to adorn her riding hat. At £1 13s 6d this was a luxury, although a rural clergyman with a rich living had to uphold appearances. Interestingly for a servant of the state church, Woodforde surreptitiously patronised smugglers. In 1777 they supplied him with tea, Indian silk handkerchiefs and an anker (eight-and-a-half gallons) of rum, although in the following year he redeemed his disloyalty by subscribing five pounds to the fund for the army in North America.[15]

Woodforde represented another new phenomenon: the impulse buyer. As retailers' stock became more extensive and alluring, it was easy for the shopper suddenly to discover a need of which he or she had hitherto been unaware. The middle classes were particularly vulnerable, for they had credit, which made it harder to resist temptation. Past luxuries became present necessities, much to the horror of that enemy of credit and consumerism, Cobbett. Travelling across southern England in the 1820s he was dismayed by the ways in which farmers' wives were embracing urban middle-class habits and tastes. The farmhouse now had a 'parlour' and was filled with 'showy chairs and a sofa . . . prints in gilt frames' and 'some swinging bookshelves with novels and tracts'.[16] The mistress of the household would have seen things very differently; her husband was doing well from the new agriculture and her furnishings and ornaments were both a sensible way in which to spend extra cash and a proper reflection of her family's standing in the world. What was more, the retailer in the neighbouring market town had assured her that such articles were purchased by the gentry.

Cobbett's disapproving eye also detected further evidence of the new consumerism. Prosperous farmers were rebuilding their houses in the modern style, which he found unwelcoming. Their owners would have disagreed and the tide of opinion was on their side. A revolution was under way in which the middle orders were migrating to new developments that provided airy, spacious and comfortable houses with imposing and elegant façades. In 1763 Edinburgh's 'people of quality and fashion' had been content with houses that thirty years later were regarded as fit only for 'humble and ordinary' people.[17] In the meantime their betters had moved to the modern residences being built in the 'New Town'.

This was one of many late-eighteenth- and early-nineteenth-century speculative building ventures aimed at a middle-class market. New accommodation of all kinds was being constructed everywhere on an unprecedented scale: between 1791 and 1800 a total of 188,000 new houses were built, between 1821 and 1830 it was 480,000 and between 1831 and 1840 around 586,000.[18] This massive enterprise profited investors and absorbed as much labour as manufacturing, employing legions of bricklayers, masons and carpenters. At the height of the boom the construction industry was employing 15 per cent of the male workforce.

Land speculators, architects and builders both flattered the middle class and paid careful heed to its preferences. There was an inclination towards pseudo-aristocratic grandeur: new developments were clustered around 'squares' or set in 'parades', 'rows', 'terraces' and 'places'. Their names had royal and patriotic resonances. Edinburgh's New Town had its Hanover Street, and Clifton, overlooking Bristol, had Rodney Place and Cornwallis Crescent in celebration of a victorious admiral and general. There was something distinctly aristocratic in the overall appearance of the houses. A Bristol merchant who returned to his home in Windsor Terrace saw a stately line of houses, punctuated by tall Corinthian pilasters and surmounted by colonnaded parapets, which together suggested the façade of a nobleman's country seat. The countryside permeated the new suburbs with trees and gardens in squares; like the squire, the merchant or lawyer could see greenery from his windows. It was what the middle class wanted and the developers obliged. John Lockier, a mahogany importer who financed Clifton's Royal Park, took care that his properties had agreeable views towards the hills of Somerset.[19]

The middle classes also wanted their new environment to be quarantined from the hurly-burly of crowds and the stench of industry. Many developments had covenants that forbade buyers or tenants from selling alcohol, converting their property to playhouses, schools or chapels, manufacturing glue, or setting up forges. In industrial centres like Leeds, houses were deliberately sited to the leeward of prevailing winds so that their owners were not plagued by smoke, odours and the clamour of industry. The domestic world was gradually separated from that of work.

Communities were changed by these arrangements. A guidebook to Leeds published in 1806 described a social geography created by recent building. 'In St Peter's Square, the houses are equally remote from splendour and meanness' and 'occupied by persons of the middle ranks of society'. The High Street was home to 'the sons of Labour'. Some of the houses built for the 'middle ranks' came complete with fittings; an advertisement of 1778 described a property containing cooking ranges, coppers, stoves, shelves, sinks and rooms for a butler and housekeeper with tables and cupboards for glass and chinaware. The living rooms contained 'genteel chimney pieces' finely carved in marble. External offices included stables, a saddle room, granaries and a brewhouse and, of course, accommodation for servants. The gentleman merchant could expect to pay between six and nine hundred pounds for such houses, but most preferred to rent them.

★

The middle-class inhabitants of the parades, rows and squares that were springing up in the most prosperous cities and towns enjoyed each other's company. They found it in assembly rooms, designed to accommodate refined people and entertain them politely. The combination of ambience and activity was summed up by an inscription on the foundation stone of Newcastle's assembly room, which was opened in 1773:

> In an age
> When the polite arts
> By genteel encouragement and emulation
> Have advanced to a state of perfection
> Unknown in any former period;
> The first stone of this edifice
> Dedicated to the most elegant recreation.[20]

Inside was a large room for balls and concerts and a smaller one for reading books and newspapers, drinking coffee and playing cards. Admission charges kept out the hoi polloi and ensured that investors in the project got a return on their £20,000.

Such places of amusement naturally drew the socially ambitious who would afterwards impress their equals and inferiors with tales of who they saw or met. The fictional Mr Smith was one of this kind. He lodged with the Branghtons, a shopkeeper's family, and one of their daughters told Evelina, the eponymous heroine of Fanny Burney's novel, that he 'is like one of the quality, and dresses fine, and goes to balls and dances, and everything quite in taste; – and besides, Miss, he keeps a footboy of his own'. Evelina, a knight's daughter, is not so easily fooled and she immediately identifies Mr Smith as 'low bred'. A ticket to a ball in an assembly room was not a passport to the beau monde and it certainly did not entitle its owner to think himself part of it.

Mr Smith reveals his faults when he makes up a party, including the Branghtons, for a summer evening's indulgence in the Vauxhall pleasure gardens. After listening to music and watching the cascade, the group take supper. Much to Evelina's annoyance, her companions grumble about the price of their meal and speculate on how much profit the caterer is making. Trade talk is vulgar, but worse follows. The shopkeeper suggests revisiting the gardens on the last night of the season. 'Why, Lord, it's the best night of any; there's always a riot, – and there the folks run about, – and such squealing and squawling! – and all the lamps are broke.' This chatter further detracts from Evelina's pleasure. For her, the joys of the gardens lay in their appeal to her senses and imagination ('The hautboy in the open air is heavenly') and this has been spoiled by banal conversation.

Assembly rooms and, to a lesser degree, pleasure gardens were settings contrived to encourage that elegantly turned and amiable conversation which was integral to public pleasures. They were commercial entertainments open to anyone who could afford a ticket, allowing men and women of different rank to mix freely, if not always comfortably. The Vauxhall gardens were egalitarian, for entry cost a shilling, which was a day's wage for an artisan; the Ranelagh was more sedate, charging half a crown. The surroundings and company were as important as the content of the entertainment. Phillippa Knight, a young lady who was one of a party that attended a subscription concert in Cambridge in 1809, was delighted by the pink stucco of the chamber and its crimson sofas, chandelier and mirror. The music was 'very good', she added, but the greatest pleasure was flirtatious chatter during the interludes with the alluring 'chevalier', a foreign gentleman.[21] Assembly rooms, pleasure gardens, theatres and concerts were always convenient places for assignations and dalliance, which of course added to their attractiveness, particularly for the young.

Behaviour was regulated, at least for the middle and upper ranks of society. The niceties of public conduct had been outlined at the beginning of the century by Beau Nash, whose father, he admitted to Goldsmith, had been a member of the 'middle ranks' of society. Nash's protocols had first been tested at Bath which, after Queen Anne's visit in 1703, became a magnet for gouty and bilious invalids with full purses. As the city's master of ceremonies, Nash curbed what he called the 'Gothic haughtiness' of the blue-blooded by imposing restrictions on flamboyant clothes and insisting that the

Squire Westerns moderated their language and appetites. Rank and precedent were respected (balls always opened with a minuet danced by 'a pair of the highest distinction'), but each visitor was expected to adhere to prescribed daily routines such as afternoon public promenades.

Alcohol dissolved conventions. A New Year's masquerade in Edinburgh in 1827 was poorly attended with the usual Harlequins and Columbines and some Vestal Virgins 'who dealt in glances, and ogles, and sighs, and wishes and words ill-suited to the purity of their positions'. Guests in the guise of 'Irish thieves' created uproar. A reporter was amazed that there were no fights, which were to be expected given the 'violent effects which are sometimes produced by the exhilarating juices of Charles Wright's champagne'.[22] The middle classes were not universally inhibited by codes of public decorum.

Ideally, public diversions agreeably filled otherwise idle hours, provided the means of cultivating and extending friendship and were a chance for the vain to flaunt themselves. When these entertainments involved the creative arts, there was an element of individual improvement. Paintings exhibited at say the Vauxhall gardens did more than please the eye or provide a topic for conversation; purists hoped that their examination would inspire contemplation and its child, moral uplift. In his *Two Discourses* (1719), the portrait painter Jonathan Richardson placed artists on a level with poets, historians, philosophers and divines because they instructed as well as pleased. The enlarged vision and sensibilities of the gentleman connoisseur increased his capacity to influence the 'common people' for the better.

Music too had its moral usefulness. In 1821 an anonymous commentator deplored the social exclusiveness of the best of London's subscription concerts and demanded their extension to the middle classes. The 'solid opulence of trade' needed the same stimuli for 'intellectual cultivation' as the nobility. It was essential for 'the respectability as well as the strength of the country' that its 'mercantile classes' became 'an order distinguished by mental attainments as by the acquisition of wealth'.[23] This was grossly unfair to the large numbers of middle-class men and women who sang, played instruments and held private concerts for family and friends and, equally, to those who sketched, visited exhibitions and purchased prints.

5

Improvement in Friendship and Knowledge: Association and Reading

Three years' exile in England in the 1720s convinced Voltaire that it was a 'nation of philosophers'. He moved in circles where men of learning investigated, speculated, debated, corresponded and wrote books and pamphlets. Laurence Sterne gently ribbed the intellectual spirit of his times in *Tristram Shandy* (1759–67), when he observed that 'our knowledge physical, metaphysical, physiological, polemical, nautical, mathematical, enigmatical, technical, biographical, romantical, chemical and obstetrical, with fifty other branches of it (most of 'em ending as these do in *ical*)' was ascending towards an acme of 'perfection'.

Optimistic men of the upper and middle orders would have agreed with Sterne, even if his tone was flippant. Omniscience had not yet been achieved, but it seemed within man's grasp. The rapid accumulation of knowledge was leading to an unprecedented understanding of his nature, of the mechanisms of his world and of the God who had created both. In 1828 an anonymous zoologist exalted his subject because it directed the student towards 'the contemplation of man, the image of the Creator of all'. In time, the novice would understand that 'man presents, in the varied and extensive combination of his powers, that balance of perfection, which independent of mental endowment, stamps him the head of his own, as of every other class'.[1]

The inquisitive also uncovered ways in which to enrich themselves and the nation. The Society Instituted at London for the Encouragement of Arts, Manufactures and Commerce rewarded the curious and patient for discoveries that raised yields or industrial production. No field of enterprise was beneath its concern; in 1797 it gave a prize for a new foot lathe and offered another of fifty guineas to anyone who found a means to distil a proof spirit 'from articles not the food of man or cattle'.[2]

The example of the London patrons of applied science was copied elsewhere. In 1817 the Highland Society of Scotland awarded fifty guineas to James Smith, an engineer, who over the previous ten years had devised and tested a reaping machine that cut an acre in an hour. Throughout its development, Smith had been helped by Monteith farmers. 'The liberality and zeal in the cause, which they evinced on every occasion, would have done honour to the most favoured sons of liberal science.'[3]

Associations of like-minded men, like that which rewarded Smith, were the advance guard of progress. They attracted men from the higher and middle orders of society who sincerely believed that through sharing and discussing ideas they could simultaneously cultivate their own enlightenment and benefit society as a whole. This was the dream of Maurice Johnston, a barrister, who founded the Spalding Gentlemen's Society in 1710. He wanted it to be a 'useful' association of 'men of professions' who would meet regularly 'for the sake of improvement in friendship and knowledge'. Members gathered at Mr Younger's coffee house (London fashions had penetrated the Fens), read newspapers and journals and conversed. In the next twenty years, the society acquired a library, a museum and a second-hand Grimaldi harpsichord for occasional concerts.[4]

Archaeology, history and natural history eventually dominated the proceedings, but there were also presentations on the murder of an English traveller by a highwayman in France, a local watchmaker's device for draining the fens and a display of books printed by Caxton.

Each subject must have sparked off lively discussions. The story of the highwayman might have prompted comments on the prevalence of domestic crime, how best it could be controlled and comparisons between Britain and France. Patriots would have boasted that throughout the country men like themselves could associate freely and speak their thoughts fearlessly. This was denied by the French because the state and Catholic church combined to restrict the expression and circulation of ideas and opinions, which was why Monsieur Voltaire had been forced to come to England.

Britons never missed a chance to congratulate themselves on their liberty and its fruits. It permitted genius to flower with results like the watchmaker's pump. Speculation along similar lines might have followed the examination of the old books. Print had been indispensable for human progress and how blessed the nation was to have a free press. The Gothic woodcuts would have been considered curious, but barbaric in form and execution. Their naivety would have provoked comparisons with the accomplished engravings of the celebrated George Vertue, one of the Spalding Society's metropolitan members. The Gothic may have had a champion in the Reverend George Stukeley, an antiquary and architect. His house in Stamford, built in the 1740s, included the novelty of mock-Gothic features, eccentricities that in forty years would become the height of fashion.

The debates and fancies of the learned, largely upper-middle-class members of the Spalding Gentlemen's Society were echoed across the country. In Norwich the new botanical society heard lectures on optics, hydrostatics and pneumatics during 1738.[5] The latest discoveries and theories were aired. In January 1824 the Bristol Philosophical Society ventured into that hazardous no man's land between science and dogmatic religion when they heard a paper on the unearthing of the skeleton of an ichthyosaurus. At Hull during the same month, a geologist described the origins of secondary rocks, reassuring his audience that theories about their formation did not contradict the Creation as related in Genesis. The London Astronomical Society held its monthly meeting in Lincoln's Inn and presented medals to such luminaries as its retiring secretary, Charles

Babbage, the future inventor of a prototype computer. Afterwards, the chairman gave a 'most eloquent, learned and interesting address of considerable length' on calculating the movements of comets. When it was over, members adjourned for a 'social and elegant' and very welcome dinner at the nearby Freemasons Tavern.[6]

Conviviality was inseparable from scholarship. A perfect balance of the two is portrayed in Reynolds's *Members of the Society of Dilettanti* (1779), where there is fruit and wine on the table. The scholars are alert, and, appropriately for a body formed to study Classical art, two are examining antique rings. In stark contrast, Hogarth's *A Midnight Modern Conversation* (1730–1) depicts a meeting of minds that has ended in a drunken pandemonium: one man lies sprawled across a bottle-strewn floor, another has collapsed in a chair, a third lurches from a table and everyone's wig is askew. Hogarth returned to the theme of unrestrained sociability in *Night* (1738), in which a pair of befuddled Freemasons are edging their way homewards. The brother being struck by piss and turds dropped from a chamberpot was an unpopular Bow Street magistrate.[7] It has been estimated that as many as twenty thousand male Londoners made similar journeys home from their clubs and societies each night.[8]

A handful may have attended august meetings of erudite men, but most were returning from small, semi-formal gatherings in inns and taverns. Innkeepers had recognised the urge for exclusive, masculine sociability among the middle classes and welcomed clubs and societies, so long as each member agreed to buy at least a quart of beer.[9] Many innkeepers set aside special rooms for these gatherings. Goldsmith's fictional but typical Harmonical Club for the promotion of friendship and affability had been founded by a landlord with an eye to a free-spending, captive market.

The Harmonical Club's meeting opened with a discussion of 'the topic of the day' which, given it was 1759, might well have been the campaign against the French in Canada. Whatever it was, this subject was soon exhausted and conversation drifted towards the trivial as members smoked and drank. 'Mr Bellows-mender' hoped that 'Mr Curry-comb-maker' had not caught cold going home and the latter replied asking whether his son had recovered from a cough. Dr Twist related an anecdote about an MP he knew well, and 'Bag-man' (commercial traveller) trumped it with a 'better story' of a lord of his acquaintance. A breeches-maker told a ghost story that he had read in the papers earlier in the day, while a pedlar and a Jew were arguing over religion. As conversation became rambling and slurred, a song was called for.[10]

This was how the lower reaches of the middle class relaxed. Interestingly, the taste for gossip, preferably scandalous, about the famous extended upwards. At a meeting of the Royal Academy Society in January 1793 the portraitist John Hoppner recounted his visit to the Duke of Clarence (the future William IV), whom he found 'uncommonly illiterate' and whose mistress, the actress Mrs Jordan, was dull, unable to talk of anything but the stage. Tittle-tattle was followed by mimicry, performed by another member, a comic actor.[11]

At the beginning of the century, a new form of association had appeared that quickly attracted the middle class, gentry and nobility, Freemasonry. It caught the spirit of the age: its aim was universal harmony, although women, menial servants and illiterates were disbarred. Freemasons gathered for the common pursuit of virtue, wisdom and happiness, which the Grand Architect of the Universe wanted all men to possess. While masonic bonds and rituals had tenuous historical links with the medieval craft guilds, Freemasonry was non-sectarian and its intellectual basis was rational. Rank was temporarily shed within the lodge and members passed upwards in the masonic hierarchy only through an understanding of arcane mysteries of the craft.

Ceremonies were held in temples designed to remind masons that their Grand Architect endorsed the layered society that existed outside. Aristocratic masons were the squares (that is, foundation) and brothers who earned their livelihoods 'by application of peculiar arts, manufactures and commerce' were the angles of the edifice. A masonic handbook of 1759 instructed members to be 'submissive to superiors, courteous and affable to equals, [and] kind and condescending to inferiors'.[12] Unlike its Continental counterpart, British Freemasonry was never identified with egalitarianism or radicalism.

Ritual was followed by beanfeasts like the one that the pair in Hogarth's engraving had just left. The masonic blend of the serious and the self-indulgent was captured in 1799 by a mason who relished both and celebrated them in a song that began:

> Merry masons drink and sing
> Come, then brothers, lead along
> Social rites and mystic song . . .[13]

One hopes that this merriment did not end in Hogarthian disorder. Hogarth's images of sociability were deliberately paradoxical: what was intended to elevate men frequently left them prostrate, squabbling and incoherent. This was at odds with the overriding aim of associations of all kinds: the achievement of a small scale of that harmony that ought to prevail in society as a whole. The spirit of association was proof that Britain had abandoned its recent, violent past of religious fanaticism. It was as barbaric as Gothic woodcuts, for men were now directed by reason, regarded by many as God's greatest gift, and reached truth through rational debate rather than private revelation. Intelligent men were now free to discover themselves and explore the world without reference to theological dogma. Moreover, voluntary associations of free men added to the new national self-image of an open, progressive nation.

Like Tristram Shandy's Uncle Toby, the middle class believed that every man had a right to his 'Hobby-Horse'. Men with hobbyhorses filled associations, particularly the philosophical, antiquarian and scientific. How hard and persistently their hobby-horses were ridden depended upon the intensity of individual passion and resources. This was the age of the middle-class amateur scholar who believed that, as well as exercising his hobby-horse, he was contributing to the growth of knowledge and, therefore, the overall betterment of the world. He was a 'useful' creature.

Usefulness took many forms, not all of them obvious. The wonderfully named Reverend Clayton Mordaunt Cracherode (1730–99) was a scholar hermit, a bachelor of 'sound' judgment and 'excellent' taste which he could well afford to indulge. He had an allowance of £600 a year from his family estates and a further £100,000 invested in government stock. A substantial part of this income was spent on modern paintings and sculpture, ancient coins, medals and fine books, including a vellum New Testament once owned by Anne Boleyn. Cracherode seldom moved outside a circle of cognoscenti, or for that matter beyond his home in Queen Square, London. None the less, he had a sense of public duty, serving as a trustee of the British Museum to which he bequeathed his books and prints.[14]

Cracherode was one of that remarkable breed of Anglican clerics who were the backbone of scholarship. A few had rich livings that allowed them ample time and money to pursue their interests while curates undertook the parochial chores. The Reverend Norton Phillips preferred chasing butterflies with a net and keeping caged finches to mundane parish affairs and his parishioners who, unlike his singing birds, were 'often big, ugly, and incapable of being taught anything'.[15]

Amateur archaeological and scientific research attracted the self-taught as well as clerics, lawyers and surgeons whose minds had been trained in other disciplines. The antiquary Thomas Fisher was the son of a Rochester bookseller and spent nearly fifty years of his life as a clerk and then as a searcher of records for the East India Company. One of its directors had secured him the post in 1786 when he was fifteen, soon after his father's death. His mother joined him in London, fearing that he might slip into debauched company. She rented lodgings in Hoxton, and Fisher lived there for the rest of his life, cared for first by his mother and then by his unmarried sister.

Fisher showed a talent for draughtsmanship and developed a passion for the past. He found plenty of time to tour the country, visiting churches and making notes and sketches. From the age of eighteen, he contributed his observations to learned journals and later published a survey of monuments in Bedfordshire churches, illustrated by his drawings. Superficially, Fisher's was a quiet, genteel middle-class life of a man lucky enough to ride his hobby horse at a gentle canter. He also fulfilled the public responsibilities of a middle-class man in moderate circumstances: he was a fervent and active campaigner against slavery, supported missionary societies and, just before his death in 1836, was elected one of the guardians for the Shoreditch workhouse.

Amateurs like Fisher were expected to be gentleman purists and Anglicans. His Congregationalism and commercial work as an artist excluded him from the rather stuffy pantheon of the Society of Antiquaries until the last year of his life, when he was elected a fellow.[16] This honour would certainly been denied to two other scholars of even humbler background than Fisher, Henry Hinton, an ironmonger, and his friend James Hunt, an apothecary's apprentice. Between 1795 and 1820, they traversed Oxfordshire and Berkshire collecting material for a projected history of the two counties. The pair were among the first practitioners of that popular middle-class Victorian pastime, brass-rubbing. Both had been caught up in the current passion for the Gothic that was then being generated by Sir Walter Scott's romantic medieval novels.

Amateurs' discoveries were announced either before learned societies or in the correspondence columns of the well-established *Gentleman's Magazine*. Its readers' forum proved immensely popular and was widely copied. The *Gardener's Magazine* of 1827 contained readers' advice on the eternal problem of the eradication of pests, and the November 1828 edition of the *Magazine of Natural History* included amateur ornithologists' letters on the 'manners' of the nuthatch and the 'manners and economy' of the pied wagtail. Both writers were following in the footsteps of that brilliant naturalist the Reverend Gilbert White and, like him, were increasing man's knowledge of the world.

Useful knowledge was the staple of the press. By the mid-eighteenth century it had established its central and enduring position in national life. More and more newspapers were being published in London and the provinces (there were more than fifty local papers in 1750) and titles were multiplying. In 1776 it was estimated that twelve million newspapers were printed each year and, since copies were kept in coffee houses, reading rooms, inns and taverns, overall readership was far higher.

The middle class were avid newspaper readers. They craved knowledge about domestic affairs, politics, commercial intelligence, diplomacy, wars and the fortunes of Britain's expanding empire. Some newspapers ran special 'American affairs' columns. Newspapers were also market places in which wares and services were advertised. Opinion was less prominent than in today's press; readers were left to evaluate events, either on their own or in discussion with family and friends. Thanks to the press, inns, societies and clubs became arenas of political and social debate. The complementary freedoms of association and the press now made it possible to talk about public opinion in a modern sense.

The expansion of the press and its readership was a revolution, comparable in impact to the appearance of the wireless, television and internet during the twentieth century. Newspapers created a national consciousness: Britons now knew more than ever before about what was happening everywhere in a world where their country was of more and more account. This information was transmitted swiftly so that remoteness no longer excused ignorance or indifference to matters of national concern. Within five days of Waterloo, Aberdonians had news of the battle and its outcome. Truly national politics could now flourish: during 1831 and 1832 supporters of reform in say Chelmsford could follow the activities of like-minded men in every other part of the country.

Trends in taste and fashion fanned out from London and were at the fingertips of anyone who wanted to embrace them, wherever they lived. In 1773 middle-class men and women across the country were invited to subscribe to the new *Westminster Magazine or The Pantheon of Taste*. Its publishers promised 'propriety', anthologies of verse, 'belles lettres' and a 'faithful picture' of a period that 'has made quicker progress towards the extremes of refinement and gallantry' than any of its predecessors. This was an enticing menu for anyone who wished to keep abreast of fashion and make sense of his times.

Similar journals proliferated, packed with essays on philosophy, politics, literature, the arts, religion, geographical and scientific discoveries and the latest modes. New novels were serialised: during 1777 subscribers to the *Lady's Magazine* read Rousseau's *Emile* in monthly episodes and simultaneously traced the movements of George III's army in North America. This eclectic mixture worked, as it still does in the magazine supplements to modern papers.The monthly *Gentleman's Magazine* founded in 1731 had a print run of 15,000 within ten years.

Like theatre managers, newspaper proprietors stayed in business by identifying and supplying what was a largely middle-class taste. Commercially useful facts such as Virginia tobacco prices and lists of bankrupts needed some seasoning and editors appreciated the flavours that appealed to readers' palates. Prurience and a capacity for moral outrage were satisfied by reports of murder trials, divorce proceedings involving adultery, duels and high-life scandal. One story of 1796 may speak for many others. It described the suicide of 'a young gentleman' and 'heir to a fortune' who, shortly before his death, had 'been in company with two girls of the town in Covent Garden'.[17]

By this date, a section of middle-class newspaper readers may have taken secret comfort from an example of the wages of sin being remitted in full. Whereas earlier in the century reading was for pleasure and information, there was a strong and growing belief that moral content was the ultimate yardstick for all kinds of literature. It went without saying that the moral criteria were Christian.

However much they might have curtailed creativity, authors and publishers had to take account of such demands, for the middle class represented their largest market. Commercial publishing was thriving: by the 1790s there were nearly a thousand booksellers scattered among three hundred cities and towns with the biggest concentration in London. Save for pamphlets, sermons, plays and slim collections of verse that sold at sixpence or a shilling each, books were still comparatively expensive and beyond the budgets of most middle-class families. Among the books published in the first fortnight of April 1767 were the sixteenth and final volume of a history of the modern world for two guineas, a study of electricity by Dr Joseph Priestley at one guinea, a collection of designs for builders at twelve shillings, and a collection of Italian madrigals at half a guinea. Novels were far cheaper: bound in plain boards they cost between three and five shillings each. In 1825 a twelve-volume set of Scott's bestselling Waverley novels cost four shillings each in boards and the six volumes of his medieval 'romances' with engravings two guineas.[18]

The price of books was not an insurmountable hurdle to the middle-class reader. Circulating libraries provided his needs. Some booksellers had their own libraries: Bell's in London had a stock of 8,000 and Sibbald's in Edinburgh 6,000. In 1820 the middle class of the rich commercial port of Liverpool supported two libraries and two newsrooms. The grandest, the Athenaeum, was an imposing Classical building that contained a newspaper room and a library with 10,000 books which could be read in a 'respectable and pleasing room'. The five hundred 'proprietors' paid two-and-a-half guineas a year for this comfort and seclusion. A guinea each was paid by the eight hundred subscribers to the Lyceum, which contained a 21,000-volume library, a newsroom with British and foreign newspapers and magazines and a coffee room.[19] The patrons of these libraries represented less than 1 per cent of the city's population.

An analysis of books borrowed from a Bristol circulating library between 1773 and 1784 reveals the middle class's thirst for factual knowledge. Six thousand history books were loaned, 3,000 'belles lettres' and between a hundred and a thousand works of philosophy, natural history, theology, law, mathematics and medicine.[20] The preoccupation with history was in part curiosity, part patriotism and part the belief that the lives and deeds of great men of the past were an inspiration. Addison had gone so far as to suggest that merely contemplating the images of distinguished figures was spiritually rewarding. Many concurred, which was why Wedgwood mass-produced 'exact and durable' facsimiles of 'antique medallions' showing the features of 'illustrious men'. Great Romans were understandably popular in an imperial nation. In 1775 a set of Roman profiles on playing cards was advertised as invaluable 'for inclucating the most necessary virtues into the minds of youth'.[21] Perhaps so in theory, but it is hard to imagine the young gamester pausing to examine the image of Pompey.

'Belles lettres', which were so much in vogue in Bristol, were compilations of prose and verse selected by editors who, readers were always assured, were men of discrimination. Their efforts were summed up by Jane Austen in *Northanger Abbey* (1818): 'some dozen lines of Milton, Pope, and Prior, with a paper from the Spectator, and a chapter from Sterne'. The reader was spared the chore of trawling through longer works and was assured that these snippets had been chosen for elegance of style and capacity for moral uplift. There was nothing vulgar to bruise the sensibilities.

The popularity of such anthologies was a measure of the middle class's increasing concern with the moral tone of fiction. Revealingly, a review of *As You Like It* in 1796 praised the play's 'fine vein of moral and pathetic reflection' and its author's 'elegant and sterling wit', but added that 'as in all the plays of Shakespeare' it was 'debased by low quibble and coarse pleasantry'.[22] Novels were now expected to teach lessons in morality and conduct. A reviewer of three new novels by Maria Edgeworth published in 1812 looked back on earlier fiction and complained that Fielding's *Tom Jones* and Smollett's *Peregrine Pickle* were marred by 'gay immoralities' that 'debauch youthful imaginations'.[23] Cobbett warned middle-class readers of the snares of *Tom Jones* which encouraged every lad to think of himself as the hero and every girl to imagine herself Sophie Western. Such fancies would justify headstrong behaviour and a contempt for virtue.[24] None the less, there were sections of the middle class who were prepared to jeopardise their children's morals at the expense of a good story. In the 1790s a London bookseller noticed that poorer farmers who had once entertained themselves at their firesides by reading ghost stories from chapbooks were now listening to their sons and daughters reading *Tom Jones* or *Roderick Random*.[25]

Thomas Bowdler (1754–1825) recalled his father reading Shakespeare aloud to his family during winter evenings. An occasional invalid, Bowdler spasmodically practised medicine and convinced himself that he had a 'hereditary desire to be doing good'. It expressed itself in membership of associations for prison reform and the redemption of London prostitutes and, notoriously, in his sincere endeavours to purify literature. Bowdler is now remembered for his ten-volume edition of Shakespeare's works, expunged of all passages 'unfit to be read aloud by a gentleman in the company of ladies'.

Out went 'words and expressions, which are of such a nature as to raise a blush on the cheek of modesty' or make the reader falter through embarrassment.[26] Just before his death, Bowdler vetted Gibbon's *Decline and Fall of the Roman Empire*, excising whatever he judged 'irreligious' and 'indecent'. It was work well done, for he argued that Gibbon's 'improper language and erroneous principles' would place a 'useful' book beyond the consideration of any 'friend of decency' whose fine principles would, therefore, isolate him from a work that 'improves the understanding by the communication of useful ideas'.[27]

By no stretch of the imagination was Bowdler a creature of the Enlightenment into which he had been born. His belief that an improper moral outlook or scurrilous material devalued any work of literature, however well written or percipient, would have astonished members of the Spalding Gentleman's Society. They would have detected hints of a vulgar Puritan zeal in Bowdler's desire to interfere with writings that were admired by the learned and discerning. Yet this Puritan zeal was resurfacing in a less pugnacious but equally dogmatic form during the second half of the eighteenth century. It was called Evangelicalism and attracted those middle-class men and women who would have been thankful to Bowdler for allowing them to read Shakespeare without discomposure. A cultivated, prominent and highly active Evangelical, Hannah More (1745–1833), accepted that while it was part of the nature of poetry to arouse the passions, its overriding purpose was to lead its readers towards Christian 'virtue'.[28]

Miss More and those of her frame of mind were sowing the seeds of anti-intellectualism and a philistine distrust of all the creative arts. Their enjoyment was inferior to the satisfaction of a simple, heartfelt faith and the fulfilment of the duties it imposed. Many Evangelicals suspected that the arts were corrupt distractions and would have applauded Thomas Carlyle's father's assertion that 'Poetry, Fiction in general [are] . . . not only idle, but false and criminal.'[29] Sydney Smith wondered whether Hannah More's Evangelicalism was stifling the pleasures of the eye and mind that had so long engaged the middle and upper classes. He was right – she and her kind were leading the middle class away from the assembly room, the picture gallery, the library and the pleasure garden towards the church and chapel.

6

Worthy Labours: Christianity, Coercion and Charity

One Sunday in the spring of 1800, the curate of Weston Zoyland in the Somerset levels decided to preach a sermon, something he was not obliged to do. A yokel warned him off: 'You can't preach today, for there's our goose sitting on twelve eggs up in the pulpit and she won't hatch till Thursday.'[1] Hannah More (who lived twenty or so miles away) would have been scandalised; for her and other Evangelicals the broody goose was further proof of a widespread insouciance towards Christianity that often verged on contempt.

James Bowdler (1746–1823), Thomas's elder brother, would have shared her dismay. His life and preoccupations represented a novel, vigorous spirit that was permeating wide sections of the middle class. Evangelicalism lay at its heart, a personal spirituality that combined the confidence of salvation with an urge to remould the world. Throughout his life, Bowdler wanted 'to be useful to the society he laboured to improve'.[2] He was kept very busy, for the country seemed to be teetering on a precipice; the lower orders were growing in numbers, dissipation and rowdiness. They needed to be rebuked and instructed in Christian doctrines that would induce self-control and submissiveness. This was the task of pious, high-minded men like Bowdler.

He was a well-to-do, generous lawyer who joined associations whose aims were the spiritual and social priorities of Evangelicalism: the Society for the Suppression of Vice and organisations dedicated to the revitalising of the Scottish Episcopalian church, the education of the poor and the spreading of Christianity to everyone, every-where. Towards the end of his life, Bowdler concentrated his energies on procuring funds for additional churches and free pews for the poor so that they could find 'the means of grace'. Within four years he had enlisted the support of the Prime Minister, Lord Liverpool, and over a hundred peers, bishops and MPs. Bowdler also procured the prestigious patronage of George III's second son, the Duke of York. It says much for the residual awe in which royalty was held that the Duke's prestige held good even though he had recently been involved in a scandal in which his mistress had been accused of trafficking in army commissions. York's name, if not his morals, helped the cause and in 1818 the government agreed to finance a programme of church building in urban areas.

Bowdler believed that the new churches would provide the poor with 'the means of grace', that private revelation of salvation through the redemptive powers of Christ which he had himself experienced. It was a conversion shared by other Evangelicals; the sheer joy of the moment of deliverance was captured in Charles Wesley's hymn:

> Long my imprisoned spirit lay
> Fast bound in sin and nature's night;
> Thine eye diffused a quickening ray –
> I woke, the dungeon framed with light;
> My chains fell off, my heart was free,
> I rose, went forth and followed thee.

This sense of personal liberation complemented and reinforced that older Protestant faith in Providence. It was still as strong at the beginning of the nineteenth century as it had been in the seven-teenth. On 10 June 1819, Charles Churchill, a prosperous London woodbroker, noted in his diary that it was the second anniversary of 'my providential rescue from a watery grave'. It was also the eleventh birthday of his daughter 'little Ellen' and, therefore, 'another day of Providential Mercy'. On New Year's Day 1830 he entered his forty-sixth year and, surveying his past life, acknowledged 'with the deepest thankfulness the goodness of God, in the lot that has fallen to me – while I have been fostered and increased – so that misfortune has not come to me'.[3] If it had been otherwise, Churchill would been comforted by a verse from Cowper's moving Evangelical hymn 'God Moves in a Mysterious Way':

> Judge not the Lord by feeble sense,
> But trust him for his grace;
> Behind a frowning providence,
> He hides a smiling face.

Not every Christian could discern this benign countenance. In 1819 John Beveridge, a Southwark shopkeeper, shot himself after several months in a 'melancholy state' induced by a burglary on his premises. He scanned the Bible for guidance and among the papers found near his body were two notes. One read: 'Beveridge God has determined your fate from the beginning,' and the other: 'There must be a God, look at the creation of all mankind.'[4]

Conservative Anglicans would have blamed Beveridge's misfortunes on 'enthusiasm', a term applied throughout the eighteenth century to any Christian who let his heart override his reason. All nonconformists were enthusiasts, which explained their moral shortcomings and why they were confined to the margins of civil society. Anglicans were open-handed, free and 'genteel' in their spending and were altogether more agreeable.[5] They also had political power and the prestige that went with it; only in 1828 were Charles II's Test and Corporation Acts repealed and dissenters admitted to public life. Sectarian animosities ran deep and Anglicans protested vehemently. In 1834 the Reverend John Gray, a fellow of Magdalen, declared to an Oxford congregation that if dissenters were allowed into the universities they would become 'seminaries of profane learning'. Protestantism would be undermined by 'Jews and Papists' and nonconformists would work to overthrow the established church.[6]

The Church of England was an arm of the state. Its clergy were figures of local authority, sometimes even magistrates, and by definition were gentlemen, even though the majority had incomes that could hardly support a gentlemanly way of life. The richest owed their positions to strings pulled by kinsmen or influential friends. Preferment came through acquaintance with political powerbrokers rather than through piety or a mastery of Scripture. The social gospel of the Anglican church was what it had always been: quietism. There were still clergymen who imagined that the earthly hierarchy extended to heaven, a fancy repeated by John Webb, a parson antiquary, in 1805 in his epitaph of a 'deaf mechanic':

> Sweet rest be thine upon the bed of clay
> Till the last trump proclaims a rising day;
> Then may'st thou mount (thro' mercy), and obtain
> A lowly station with the ransom'd train,
> And gain in realms of light a humble seat
> Where bliss inferior is still bliss complete.[7]

The goose in the pulpit was a reminder that there were plenty of Anglican clergymen who took a leisurely approach to their pastoral duties. When they preached, it was invariably what Goldsmith called 'dry, methodical and unaffecting' stuff. 'An address to reason and not to passion' was not, he thought, the best way of overcoming vice, whose roots lay in uncontrolled passion. Evangelicals concurred. For their enemies within the Church of England, enthusiasm was a rejection of reason, even a return to the disruptive zeal of the Puritans. In 1821, a Lincolnshire curate complained to his bishop of the tumults caused by 'organised banditti of strolling Methodists' and 'impious Ranters' who were spreading the born-again gospel among local labourers.[8]

Public commotions were not commonly associated with Methodism. Historical wisdom has long held that the field and marketplace evangelism of John Wesley and his adherents averted popular revolution by converting the poorest to what was essentially a quietist faith. This can never be proved, but Wesley's preaching captivated the middle classes as well as the poor. Patterns of conversion reflected the local social dispensation. In the textile districts around Keighley, two-thirds of the Methodists were weavers. Less than a tenth were labourers. Direction of the fledgling Methodist congregations was largely in the hands of those who already enjoyed local status: in 1763 the Keighley chapel's trustees included an innkeeper, a clockmaker, three yeomen and a farmer.[9] Wesley never advocated egalitarianism, and born-again Christians acknowledged custom by looking to the leadership of their betters.

Both Methodism and Anglican Evangelicalism insisted that submission and salvation were inseparable. The late-eighteenth-century Sunday School movement not only brought poor children to Christ, but taught them their place in the world and the need to show gratitude to their benefactors. Addressing a congregation of subscribers to Manchester Sunday Schools in 1789, a pupil declared that all who attended them:

> Should thank the hands from who our favours flow:
> For by their goodness we may here improve,
> And bless the worthy labours of their love.[10]

Most of the listeners were middle-class men and women, and within the next few years the frightening news of the upheavals in France would have been proof that their donations to the Sunday Schools had been money well invested.

Contemporaries believed that the various Christian revivals had an overall calming effect on the poor. But the quietist message needed constant repetition. In Birmingham in the 1820s a parson regularly reminded his Sunday School classes that, when they grew up, they had to be content with that station which God had assigned them.[11] Another cleric, preaching at a service to celebrate Oxford's Sunday Schools in 1835, praised them for perpetuating the social and economic order. The offspring of the 'humbler classes' were being prepared 'for their future services and situations in life', so that they could support themselves and their country. These youngsters were spiritually equipped to spurn the 'mischievous' propaganda of radicals bent on fracturing 'those dependencies of one man upon another's assistance' that held society together.[12]

At the height of the working-class agitation in 1817, a radical had told the Home Secretary, Lord Sidmouth, that he had 'hitherto worked hard for his family, attended church, and lived peacefully with his neighbours'. He now repented his flirtation with politics (transportation was beckoning) and 'assured his lordship that he would return to his church and never leave it again'.[13] How John Bowdler and other Evangelicals would have rejoiced at this pledge; it was proof that their demands for more Sunday Schools and churches would save the nation by saving the souls of the poor.

Doses of Methodism and Evangelical Anglicanism were an antidote to sedition, but they were never prescribed systematically or universally. There were large pockets of irreligion across the country, particularly in industrial districts, which were a source of heartache to Victorian evangelists of all denominations. Furthermore, in periods of acute economic and social tension, the government's intelligence services and military capacity proved more than adequate in suppressing and deterring unrest.

Guiding the godless and intemperate towards the pew was not enough. Their propensity for wickedness had to be engaged head on and forcefully, a task voluntarily taken on by the Society for the Suppression of Vice founded in 1802. Within two years it had twelve hundred members, most of whom, like John Bowdler, came from London's Anglican upper-middle class. At their first meeting they declared war on non-observance of the Sabbath, blasphemy, swearing, pornography and those vipers' nests of temptation: public houses, brothels and gambling dens. Members snooped, reported transgressions to the authorities, facilitated prosecutions and clamoured for stricter laws and punishments. In the early 1820s pressure from the Society persuaded the government to include severe clauses in the vagrancy laws against nude bathing, indecent exposure and passionate canoodling in public by courting couples.[14]

That urbane Whig, Sydney Smith, scented a whiff of humbug. He suggested that, while sincere, the Society's members were doing more harm than good. Their activities gave the impression of the 'haves' ganging up against the 'have-nots', given that gamblers in taverns were harried and rich men playing cards in private houses were unmolested. The whole business was ultimately self-defeating. 'You may drag men into church by main force, and prosecute them for buying a pot of beer, – and cut them off from the enjoyment of a leg of mutton; – and you may do all this, till you make the common people hate Sunday, and the clergy, and religion, and every thing that relates to such subjects.'[15]

Wiser Evangelicals agreed, as did anyone who believed in liberty and tolerance. There was something distasteful about a body that policed public morals by informers. The poor were surely more responsive to persuasion and good example than to threats. By 1830 the Society had become a shadow of its old self with less than a quarter of its original membership, although it would battle on for a further fifty years. Its determination, vigilance and Parliamentary successes encouraged other, more philanthropic and largely middle-class organisations such as the (Royal) Society for the Prevention of Cruelty to Animals, which was founded in 1824.

There was agreement between all engaged in redeeming the poor that the lower classes were innately delinquent and unable to discern between right and wrong. This was common knowledge according to an Edinburgh attorney defending a carpenter accused of wife-beating in 1815:

> People in that rank of life are less accustomed than those in the higher ranks to lay a restraint on their passions, and they never think of dissembling the feelings which arise in their minds. Hence they indulge in coarseness of language and of behaviour, which would be quite intolerable in the higher ranks. A blow given by a person in a low rank of life neither indicates, nor is understood to imply, such a degree of hatred and dislike, as, in the higher ranks, might be indicated by an angry word.

The wife's lawyer riposted that differences of rank did not eradicate common sensibilities to pain, and all men, whatever their station, shared a revulsion to 'base and unmanly' violence against women.[16] He won his case.

Those who sympathised with the aims of the Society for the Suppression of Vice believed that 'coarseness' was endemic among the lower orders, and its manifestations were a source of daily and unavoidable distress to the more sensitive and godly members of the middle class. This was why the Society tried to rid the streets of noisy revellers, whores, brawlers and braggarts. Just as Thomas Bowdler was making literature wholesome for middle-class readers, James Bowdler and his colleagues were making the nation's streets and open spaces safe for middle-class shoppers and promenaders. Success was minimal and, in time, other organisations took up a struggle that has turned out to be unending. Equally durable has been the debate among the middle classes as to what extent the criminal law was an agency for enforcing morality rather than protecting persons and property.

Both were in greater jeopardy than ever in the eighteenth century. Crime was increasing at an alarming rate, partly as a consequence of the overall rise in the population and partly as a by-product of economic upheaval. Evidence for the crime wave was often anecdotal, but nevertheless compelling. In 1800 it was estimated that in London alone the total value of petty thefts was £710,000, pilfering from docks and river boats £800,000, burglaries and highway robberies £220,000 and the proceeds from counterfeiting and forgery £220,000.

The scale of the crime wave unnerved the middle and upper classes and Parliament reflected their fearfulness by legislation that extended the range of felonies punishable by hanging. Using the simple psychological formula that pure fear overcame greed, it was imagined that the public death throes of say a housebreaker or a counterfeiter would frighten potential criminals. Maybe it did, but the would-be miscreant could take heart from the fact that the machinery of law enforcement was ramshackle and so the odds on escaping justice were in his favour.

The property-owning classes faced a dilemma. Hanging the odd burglar or pickpocket manifestly failed to safeguard a man's silver-ware or pocket watch, but the alternative of a regular police force was abhorrent. Omnipresent policemen and their official prying were features of Continental despotisms and, therefore, unwelcome in a nation proud of its liberties. The answer was a compromise that satis-fied traditions of freedom and at the same time offered protection for property: voluntary associations.

Their activities filled the advertisement columns of newspapers. One in the *True Briton* in January 1797 may speak for many others: the Chiswick Association for the Prosecution of Thieves and Felons announced a reward of three pounds for the arrest of a runaway apprentice, Thomas Gardener, formerly of 'Slut's Hole' in Chiswick. He was twenty, 'a very audacious fellow', and had burgled the prem-ises of a butcher, who was a society member.[17]

The butcher was a subscriber to one of many hundred similar local associations. Their members were men with most to lose from crime: of the 108 subscribers to the South Shields association for apprehending felons, nearly three-quarters were shopkeepers, or owners of commercial or industrial premises. Yearly subscriptions ranged between five shillings and a guinea and associations mustered between twenty and a hundred members. They hired solicitors to circulate handbills, insert advertisements in the press and distribute details of the losses, suspects (if any) and rewards to magistrates and parish constables.[18]

It is impossible to calculate the success of these hit-or-miss meas-ures, although associations somehow managed to recover property and secure the arrest of thieves. The proliferation of these associ-ations was a measure of the deep fear of crime among the well-to-do. The most frightening bogeyman was always the burglar, forcing his way through windows, skylights or cellars, taking what he could find and disappearing into the night. During the first three weeks of July 1826, two housebreakers, an artisan and a carver and gilder, nipped in and out of houses in Edinburgh's fashionable New Town. They stole silverware from a dentist, a gilt-buttoned coat from a lawyer, plate and linen from a perfumier, a tartan cloak from a merchant and a brown silk umbrella from a gentleman.[19]

To deter such intruders, the middle classes kept fierce dogs and had loaded pistols to hand, sometimes by their bedsides. An Aldgate merchant's son used one to shoot dead an intruder one night in July 1789, claiming he was about to rape his sister. The dead man was nowhere near her room, but the jury of local shopkeepers and businessmen believed him and returned a verdict of justifiable homicide.[20] A few years after, a judge vindicated the right of every man to defend his property with firearms.[21] Countrymen protected their premises and grounds with man-traps and spring-guns that, when triggered, peppered thieves and poachers with grapeshot.

Rural crime was as hard to contain as urban. During the winter of 1819–20 the countryside around Shere was terrorised by a gang of poachers and thieves who robbed 'poor cottagers' and set fire to the barns of the rich. Local gentlemen and farmers offered rewards for informers, but faced a wall of silence and had to ask the Home Office for a promise of pardon for a stool pigeon who peached on his cronies. It was always tempting bait when conviction meant either the gallows or transportation.[22] A regular, rural constabulary was an obvious remedy, but the victims of these outrages would have rejected it because it smacked of say Prussian or Neapolitan tyranny.

It would be tempting to imagine that the Shere gang were poor men risking their lives and freedom to sustain their families at a time of agricultural recession. If this was so, they would have fitted the modern picture of the contemporary criminal as a man or woman driven to robbery or prostitution in order to survive in a brutally competitive society that extended no pity to losers. Contemporaries would have been astonished by this explanation; they blamed crime on moral rather than economic determinism. Greed, laziness and a lack of self-discipline created criminals and not the defects in a system that offered work to anyone who genuinely wanted it. Furthermore, court records of the period strongly suggest that the poor preyed on the poor.

There were some who stole to stay alive. In 1819 two brothers, Joseph and John Windmill, pleaded poverty to excuse their impersonation of a gentleman's servants to obtain lamb, suet and flour on credit. John claimed he was 'very much in distress' with just four shillings a week to live on. The magistrates ordered the pair to be publicly whipped in Aylesbury.[23] Such mitigating pleas were uncommon in Buckingshire even at a time of high unemployment.

Justifying their strictness, the justices might have quoted from the observations of Sir Frederick Eden, the chairman of the Globe Insurance Company, who had undertaken a methodical survey of the country's poor during 1794 and 1795, years of severe food shortages. Eden would have explained the theft of lamb as an instance of the unrealistic dietary expectations of the poor. They liked roast meat, although it was beyond their budget, and shunned 'cheap and agreeable substitutes' that they could afford. 'Improvidence' and 'unthriftiness' rather than low wages were the cause of destitution.[24]

Plenty of soup was Eden's answer to hunger, as it was of the middle class then and later. He offered his own recipe for a gruel made from ten pounds of grain, four 'red herrings' and some herbs which, he claimed, could feed sixty-four paupers. Nourishing broth could save souls as well as bodies. A 1795 recipe for potato soup promised that its consumption would stop the poor from drinking large amounts of beer which was the consequence of eating too much roast meat, bacon and bread.[25] 'Windywash' was what the poor called these unappetising potages. By a bizarre paradox, thin soups were routinely portrayed in contemporary patriotic cartoons as the Frenchman's staple, while Britons dined on roast beef.

There was little meat for the paupers of Nantwich in 1815. The overseers of the poor took the line that indulging their preferences encouraged waste and 'habits of idleness and dissipation'. There were ninety persons depending on poor relief in the parish, more than twice as many as there had been thirty years before. Charges for maintaining these paupers had increased proportionally and were now nearly nineteen pounds a week, which had to come from the poor rates.[26] The experience of Nantwich was being repeated across the country and vexing the middle classes, whose rate bills were soaring.

Mass poverty, like rising crime, hit the pockets and upset the equanimity of the middle class. Both raised questions that were aired and debated in journals and pamphlets from the late eighteenth century onwards. How was it possible that an advanced commercial civilisation found itself burdened with an ever-growing population of paupers? Were they a permanent by-product of agricultural and industrial change or would they disappear when these changes had run their course? If not, how could the numbers of the poor be reduced and their conditions improved? Considerable faith was placed in the national capacity for ingenuity. In February 1828 the *Mechanic's Magazine* extolled the virtues of a new potato-grinding machine that would 'improve the resources' of the country by providing potato flour to improve the diet of 'the labouring and most useful classes'. More windywash.

It was imperative to devise answers, for the scale of the problem was increasing and, whenever there were lay-offs and shortages, the poor refused to be passive. Angry letters written by labourers to squires, parsons and farmers during the rural disturbances of 1830 threatened arson, even murder. Here and during other protests there was a strong undercurrent of resentment: the poor were victims of an unfair and heartless system that rewarded their superiors, and offered them the alternatives of drudgery or starvation. Methodist preachers and Sunday Schools had failed to dispel this sense of injustice that surfaced whenever times were bad.

Solutions to the problems of crime and poverty provoked new contentions that divided the middle classes. There were appeals to the heart. Conservatives and Christians of all persuasions invoked the old moral economy and argued that the poor would always remain dependent on the compassion and generosity of the rich. During food riots in the Midlands in 1766, one mob was told: 'You cannot but conceive that the better sort of people in this place have some feeling for your distress. We have always our hearts as well as our purses open for your relief.'[27] Here as everywhere the 'better sort' were local landowners, clergymen, farmers, professional and business men and shopkeepers. Their names and how much they paid could be read in lists of subscribers to impromptu relief funds that were published in the press.

Those who opened their purses were performing a Christian duty, revealed by Jesus' example and St Paul's injunction to the Galatians: 'Bear ye one another's burdens, and so fulfil the law of

Christ.' Christian benevolence had practical benefits for the nation as a whole. As a royal chaplain explained to a congregation of city magnates in 1835, they had a responsibility 'to meet the necessities of those by whose industry they exist'. Private philanthropy advanced the general good of society, and this far outweighed the fact that its recipients might include the odd 'dishonest idler'.[28]

Reason scoffed at such sentimental appeals. Private charity and the state's poor law apparatus crippled the economy by absorbing capital that could be more fruitfully dispensed elsewhere, or so the political economists claimed. Their arguments had to be taken seriously for they were the outcome of the scientific research of men like Eden who methodically investigated subjects and analysed their data dispassionately. In the process, the political economists led by Adam Smith believed that they had uncovered infallible laws which held the key to future growth and prosperity in a capitalist society. Both required a universal, competitive free market in commodities and goods and a state attached to the principles of laissez-faire, that is non-intervention in the mechanisms of trade, especially the laws of supply and demand. Individuals and not governments knew what was best for them and how best to spend their money.

Ameliorating poverty paralysed the labour market. So long as the wages of able-bodied workers were augmented by the state or charity, workers had no incentive to shift to areas where they were needed. Idleness was rewarded, industry devalued and the productive capacity of the nation diminished. There were doubts as to whether it could keep pace with a growing population, but these were removed by the inexorable calculus of Thomas Malthus. His *Essay on Population* (1798) suggested that nature would intervene when the population outstripped food resources. Mass famine would restore a natural balance. Cobbett mischievously suggested that, if Malthus' natural laws really did exist, then the poor would not wait for starvation but would seize whatever they needed.

Drones were not to be tolerated in any form in a nation where mass production depended on the full utilisation of every source of labour. An unknown disciple of Adam Smith, praising the Highland clearances, was dismissive of the evicted crofters as:

> A hardy, but not industrious race of people scattered over the various glens and sides of mountains, raising without much labour a small quantity of inferior oats of which they made their cakes and of barley, from which they distilled their whisky, added little to the industry or to the wealth of the empire.

Economic forces, unfettered by sentiment, would transform the 'lazy', the 'idle' and the 'sheep stealer' of Scotland and, for that matter, the fit paupers of the rest of England into useful workers.[29]

Charity did not wither in the face of the arithmetic of the political economists. It was deeply rooted in the middle classes and had been reinvigorated by Evangelical ideals. In August 1805, the *Lady's Magazine* advised a lady 'of elevated rank' who had just inherited an estate to show every kindness to the poor. Cottagers were to be treated with 'lenity' and their rents kept to levels that 'their industry can realise in these hard times'. Such compassion towards individual human suffering owed something to the Romantic movement and ran counter to all the assumptions of the political economists.

They were best ignored, according to Mrs Parkes's guidebook of 1825 for newly married, upper-middle-class housewives. She told them to disregard the carping of 'political economists' who criticised 'the charity of English women'. It was source of national pride and a source of happiness that aroused 'the best feelings with which their hearts can be animated'. She recommended visits to the poor in their homes 'to get full knowledge of their circumstances', but warned that such expeditions should be confined to the countryside. The haunts of the urban poor were clearly hazardous.[30]

Significantly, Mrs Parkes considered that active charity was a source of happiness equal to any that might be gained within the conventional social arena. Her views reflected the extent to which the Evangelical frame of mind had gained ground among the middle class over the previous thirty years. There had been a retreat from attitudes and diversions that could have been described as hedonistic. Wilberforce, perhaps the most influential Evangelical of his generation, while regretting the degree to which the upper and middle classes pursued sensual pleasures, did not think that their 'temperate' enjoyment detracted from Christian virtue.[31] Hannah More was not so sure. She had misgivings about what society deemed 'pleasant', but which she had found to be brittle and inimical to 'genius, feeling, truth and principle'. In her experience (she had mixed in the same circles as Dr Johnson and Garrick) the 'taste of general society is not favourable to improvement', and 'habitual levity' inhibited the development of sincere faith.[32]

It was that faith which was being mobilised against irreligion, ignorance, moral delinquency and, since these vices were most prevalent among the indigent, poverty. In their widely different ways, members of societies to suppress vice, promote education, catch thieves and establish Sunday Schools were striving after two common goals, pulling society back from the brink of chaos and the redemption of individuals unable to help themselves. These ambitious projects relied on old notions of Christian social responsibility and well-tried methods of payment and, most important of all, persuasion. Early-nineteenth-century philanthropists hoped that they could remake the working classes through encouraging them to adopt middle-class attitudes towards work, thrift, temperance, Bible reading and Sunday observance. This was not condescension, although it has been called so and worse; a great number of men, women and children of the labouring classes recognised that they were being offered the means to a better life and often welcomed efforts to lead them to it.

There was an alternative to a revived and often gentler campaign to extend manners. It required intellectual rather than emotional commitment and a degree of cold disinterest. Middle-class men or women could accept as proven the theories that had evolved alongside the demographic and economic changes they explained. If they did so, they acknowledged the supremacy of laws that provided the basis for the rational supervision of society and preserved order and prosperity.

The poor family crying out for sustenance, spiritual revelation, moral discipline and education for its children was a unit of production upon which the nation's fortunes rested. This family's fate depended on the unfettered progress of economic forces and not the intervention of well-intentioned humanitarians with religious tracts and recipes for broth. The useful class faced a dilemma and was bombarded with contrary arguments that were equally compelling. But there was agreement on one point: a new society was emerging and its future could be determined by that faith, willpower and human ingenuity which the middle class believed it possessed in abundance.

Domestic Happiness: Marriage, Children and Morality

Domestic Happiness, thou only bliss
Of Paradise that has survived the Fall!

Hannah More approvingly quoted Cowper's lines at the beginning of her *Strictures on the Modern System of Female Education* (1799), another addition to the growing library on marriage and women's place in the scheme of things. Neither she nor the poet ever married, but they recognised wedlock's importance as a sacrament that provided mutual fulfilment, a sound basis for the raising of children and a cornerstone of society in an orderly Christian nation.

For the last reason, marriage continued to be closely regulated by church and state. The 1754 Marriage Act defined marriage as valid only when formalised by Anglican rites; Quakers and Jews were exempt, but all other nonconformists had to be wed in church. This monopoly put fees in the parson's pocket, irritated the poor who had hitherto often been content with informal partnerships, and angered dissenters for whom it was another reminder of their creeds' assumed inferiority. One of the act's unlooked for by-products was a steady stream of elopements across the border into Scotland, where this legislation did not apply.

The law continued to make separation difficult and expensive (less so in Scotland) and, save where specific contracts had been made beforehand, gave a husband considerable control over his wife's property and person. He could do whatever he liked with her chattels and any property or money that came her way after marriage, even if she had earned it herself.

A husband could, although this was rare, openly sell his wife without the intervention of the law. In August 1836 a man in his early forties with a 'shabby genteel exterior' appeared at the Islington cattle market with his wife, who had a halter around her waist. He offered her for auction, opening the bidding at five shillings, and she was bought by a young man of 'decent appearance' for twenty-six. The vendor went on his way saying he had got rid of a 'troublesome, noisy woman'. To judge from the eyewitness description, he and the buyer may have been from the lower-middle class.[1] The so-called 'ancient' right of a husband to chastise his wife was passing into abeyance, a Scottish jurist noted in 1846, not because of a change in the law, but because of a shift in public attitudes.[2]

Other old conventions reinforced the law, in so far as the wife was expected to be subordinate to her husband's desires in all things. She remained confined to her own sphere, the home, where she supervised the household and the early education of her husband's children. For these tasks she had been prepared from girlhood and was conditioned to believe that marriage was the proper consummation of her life. It could not be otherwise, for women's minds were considered intrinsically different from those of men and best suited to practical affairs. 'Greater things are generally the subject of men's study,' argued a child's introduction to the contemporary world written in 1791. 'Lesser things were the study of women,' for God had given men 'a more extensive understanding, and stronger powers of mind'.[3] It was a theory that prevailed, virtually unchallenged, well into the next century, when John Stuart Mill declared that the ideal female education was 'of sentiments and not of understanding'.

The middle-class wife of this period lived under constraints similar to those imposed on her predecessors. She was part ornament and part co-operative and passive helpmate. 'Mira', the authoress of a guide to marriage published in 1756, advised the newly wed bride to 'let the inward satisfaction of the change of her condition glow on her cheeks and sparkle in her eyes; but let her tongue keep a modest reserve'. By nature more patient ('a damnable mistake' has been written in the margin of the copy of this book I consulted), a woman always allowed her husband free rein in those areas that traditionally were his prerogatives. She had a right to her opinions, but, if they clashed with her husband's, she kept them to herself.[4]

As well as avoiding contention, the wife had to budget carefully and not show an over-fondness for pets. As proof of this, Mira cited a wife whose 'Miss Chloe', a 'harlequin bitch', had 'all the best bits at table' and slept on the bed. The husband departed 'for the favours of a chambermaid'. The fault plainly lay with the wife, and contemporaries would have regarded her behaviour as further proof of the ease with which women in general surrendered to their fancies. Husbandly forbearance was also stretched by costly excursions to spas, which required new wardrobes, and excessive outings to masquerades, balls and assemblies, where honour and virtue were compromised.

An alternative, if more constrictive diversion was paying and receiving visits. According to Mira, this 'is now become the chief occupation of degrees of women', the wives of the 'middling gentry' travelling by carriages, the 'lower sort' on foot. Taking tea and conversing with friends at home superseded that 'gadding about' and trips to taverns that had peeved husbands in earlier generations. Wives were now kept within the orbit of the home, where of course they and, more importantly, their furnishings and possessions were under critical scrutiny. All reflected a capacity to stay abreast of fashion and, of course, status. 'Old plate marks ancestral dignity,' observed Mrs Parkes in her vade mecum for brides of 1825, and therefore was worth displaying prominently.[5]

Furnishings, ornaments, drapes and wallpaper were the backcloth for female conversation. It was not always domestic. In 1773, a young lady forced to stay at home because of illness yearned to see her friends again for a gossip:

To talk of the beaux and to laugh at their ways
Is a topic which pleases our visiting days.[6]

Not all visitors were welcome, and their patter could be tiresome. In the same year a lady in a provincial town complained about 'prim, antiquated widows' and 'stale superannuated virgins' who called on her in search of dinner. 'They enter your house without hesitation; they address you immediately with the most accomplished gossiping eloquence and spin out their insignificant stories till your meat is just ready to make its appearance on your table.'[7]

Successful entertainment of all kinds depended upon the middle-class wife's ability to discipline her servants. Mira advised 'sweetness and affability' and an avoidance of favouritism as the keys to compliance. The more realistic Mrs Parkes advised vigilance and strictness, citing the instance of a wife who had spent a morning paying visits and returned home to find that preparations for dinner had been desultory; there were insufficient chairs for guests and the fish and soup were cold. Laundries needed close surveillance for they were where the under-employed loitered to gossip and sometimes worse – in one Northumberland country house the laundry was also a brothel.[8]

The mistress of the household also needed to prevent female servants from aping the fashions of their betters. It was easy to discourage muslins and silks and equally easy to encourage familiarity, particularly with personal maids who could slip into the role of confidante. During the divorce proceedings against Cassandra Ricketts, a barrister's wife, in 1798, her maid testified that, while undressing, her mistress had confessed her adulteries 'in such language as the deponent could not repeat'.[9]

Choosing servants was a wife's responsibility and a chancy business, despite the existence of agencies and a system of references. An exemplary guide to family budgeting written in the 1820s suggested that a middle-class household with three children and an annual income of £250 could afford one maidservant who was paid sixteen pounds a year. Other fixed items were £134 for food, fuel and cleaning materials, £36 for clothes (the wife may well have made some of her own and her children's), £25 for rent, rates and taxes and £10 10s for school fees.[10] A family in the highest layer of the middle class with £1,000 a year could afford a coach, two horses, a groom, footman, cook, and a nursery and housemaid whose wages bill was £220. The lowest paid, the nurserymaid, received £10 10s a year.

There were plenty of servants who were paid far less: Mrs Ashford, who came from a 'middling' family that had fallen on bad times, was paid £6 10s a year as housemaid to a bank clerk's family in the early 1800s.[11] She was good at her job and changed households several times before marrying an older servant, a widower who had some savings invested in government stock. In time she re-re-entered the middle class, helping her second husband to run his small business.[12]

It was possible to prosper below stairs if a servant had the right attitude. This was summed up in an imaginary exchange between an ideal maidservant and her father written in 1784. The prim girl declares, 'I hate idleness, and am determined to be usefully employed' and learn from the example of her mistress, who gives leftover food to the poor and subscribes to schools for their children.[13] On hearing of her promotion, her father warns her that her new 'station' within the household might provoke envy and so she was to be 'meek and agreeable' to her underlings.

As in the past, the pious and disciplined household was a microcosm of society as a whole, but human nature saw to it that exceptions were plentiful. Husbands were henpecked and there were plenty of idle, saucy, drunken and pilfering servants. And there were employers whose priorities were summed up in the diary of Charles Churchill, a London wood-broker. On 11 July 1830 his dog Bruin attacked the cook 'most savagely' and his wife was 'knocked up with fright'. He added: 'the dog otherwise quite well'.[14]

Churchill was not a harsh man. His diaries reveal a godly and affectionate husband and father who enjoyed 'a calm and happy life'. He owed much of his contentment to his wife Sarah, who presided over a smoothly run household (Bruin apart) and presented her husband with a reposeful sanctuary when he came home from work. His happiness was hers and she could increase it and her own by the stimulation of what Mrs Parkes called the 'agreeable' strains in his character. More than ever, the wife enforced seemliness within the home. Mrs Jorrocks demanded that her husband, a retired London grocer, abandon his 'low-life stable conversation' when at home. It was becoming a place with standards and codes of conduct that were laid down by the wife. Domesticity had arrived.

Evangelicals considered the home to be the seedbed of godliness, and in this context the wife was paramount. It was in the nursery that spiritual awareness first took root and it was the highest duty of motherhood to cultivate it. Women were perfectly fitted for this task, thought Hannah More, because of their unique religious passion. If they exercised it, the home became a miniature church or chapel, the Victorian 'sacred' hearth sanctified by Christian devotion.

There were volumes of advice on the conduct of a Christian household and on how parents, in particular mothers, should instruct their offspring. Perhaps the most revealing vision of the Evangelical home is in Mrs Sherwood's novel *The History of the Fairchild Family; or The Child's Manual* which first appeared in 1818. Melodramatic and, for modern readers, grotesque, it provides a fascinating insight into the Evangelical view of how the young should be brought up, as well as a picture of everyday life within what the authoress considers an ideal household.

Mr and Mrs Fairchild are a middle-class couple living in the countryside. If he has any employment, it is not mentioned, although he has enough money to keep a pair of servants and provide funds to pay the wages of teachers in a local school for poor boys. Maybe Mr Fairchild is a rentier with an income from government or commercial stock. He teaches Latin to his only son, Henry, who, although just out of the nursery, wants to be a clergyman. Translation errors are punished by whippings (performed by a servant), a diet of bread and water and the repetition of prayers for humility.

Lucy Fairchild, aged nine-and-a-half, also needs a regimen of prayer, for she is sulky, refuses to clean her room and envies the 'fine things' enjoyed by Augusta Noble, the daughter of Lord and Lady

Noble who live near by. Once a year, the Fairchilds visit the Nobles, whose 'smooth white stone' house is set in a park. The Noble children are pampered and have plenty of toys, unlike their young visitors. The elder Noble boy tells his younger brother: 'When our parson dies, you shall be parson, Henry, but I'll never go to church when you preach.' Such impiety is unsurprising since their mother, Lady Noble, 'would even mock religion and religious people' in the presence of her children.

Grisly nemesis overtakes the Nobles. Augusta, defying her mother's warning and unchecked by her impious governess, is burned to death after playing with candles while Lady Noble is at the card table. A vindictive, Evangelical God visits the sins of the parents on the children. Divine vengeance also fell directly on sinners, as Methodist journals gleefully reported. Quoting from them in 1808, Sydney Smith cited instances of a clergyman struck dead at a card table and a man dying after swearing at a cock fight.

Mrs Fairchild used the misfortunes of the Nobles to admonish her offspring about the evils of ambition. It is 'the desire to be greater than we are' that makes people 'unhappy, and discontented with what they are and what they have'. This was not a message that would appeal to the middle class – not even Evangelicals, who, like the Puritans, still saw the fulfilment of ambition as a mark of providential favour.

What does one make of such stuff? Clearly the piety of the Fairchilds is to be admired and imitated and, usually in less extreme forms, set the tone of many middle-class families from the 1820s to 1914. At the turn of the century, the mother of T. E. Lawrence followed a similar regime of family prayers, Bible reading and moral exhortations that would have pleased Mrs Sherwood. She had presented Evangelicals with an image of a model family, united by faith and with parents keen that their children should grow up with a powerful urge to follow Christ in every aspect of their lives and spread His word to those who knew nothing of it. In the frontispiece of Mrs Sherwood's *The History of Milner, A little Boy who was not Brought up according to the Fashions of the World* (1825), the six-year-old hero is shown reading the Scriptures to a group of haymakers.

★

Mrs Sherwood's own upbringing had been nothing like this. Born in 1775, the daughter of a moderately successful Anglican clergyman, she was sent to a boarding school that catered for middle-class girls. Her teachers included a 'simpering Englishwoman, very like a second-rate milliner in those days', a 'slovenly, rather handsome' French girl and a Swiss lady scarred by smallpox.[15] She did not say whether these mentors fostered her religious life. This was not the function of conventional schooling, much to the regret of Maria Edgeworth. In her novel *Vivian* (1812), the hero, aged thirteen, is sent to Harrow 'to make a man of me'. Hitherto guided by his mother, he later confesses that he was 'made ashamed of everything good I had learned at home; and there I learned everything bad, and nothing good . . .' Thomas Arnold's moral reformation was twenty years off, and public schools were, in Sydney Smith's words, institutions in which 'every boy is alternately tyrant and slave' and where he could discover 'premature debauchery'. 'In great schools', Dr Samuel Solomon warned parents in an envoi to his popular handbook to health, older boys guided younger towards masturbation.[16]

Parents were prepared to take this risk, for private boarding schools of all kinds were proliferating. Where the great public schools were concerned, snobbery had long provided the impulse for many middle-class parents to enrol their sons. In a satire of 1738, Mrs Stitch the tailor's wife was delighted to be able to answer a 'tea-table gossip's' enquiry about her son's health: 'He is at boarding school with Master such-a-one (son to her husband's best customer) . . .'[17]

Middle-class parents were also concerned with securing an education which not only satisfied the universal wish for a smattering of Greek and Latin but offered some vocational instruction. For this reason advertisements for schools stressed practical and vocational courses. In 1789 Mr Grist's school for 'young gentlemen' at Long Ashton near Bristol promised the sons of the city's professionals and businessmen the standard English, Latin and Greek, penmanship, accounting, geography, astronomy and land surveying. The registration charge was a guinea and boarding and annual tuition fees were fourteen guineas, the annual cost of a housemaid and a tenth of the family's food budget. Navigation and book-keeping were on the curriculums of other schools, and one at Scorton in North Yorkshire provided German and French, which were 'absolutely necessary, not only to a commercial but a polite education'.[18] Leavers' career prospects were advanced, which was a good return on parental investment.

With plenty of choice, children were frequently moved from school to school. Samuel Elliot, born in 1807, the son of a London clock-maker, attended a local school until he was seven, when he went to an establishment in Suffolk where he suffered under a clerical usher. This 'great brute' inflicted beatings that left 'large bruises on my body'. 'My father called for an explanation,' and Mrs Elliot had to restrain him from thrashing the cleric. Young Elliot was transferred to Eton, where he remained for four years before going to a London boarding school for a further four.[19]

Samuel Elliot was being prepared for work; he eventually became a maker of scientific instruments. Joshua Parsons's father, a Somerset maltster, wanted to place his son in a profession and laid out consid-erable capital to this end. First, Joshua was sent to board at the Baptist school at Radley in Oxfordshire in the 1820s. The school prospectus promised a 'more comprehensive' system of education than its rivals and 'moral vigilance'. Fees were between twenty-five and sixty guineas, with further charges for Greek, Latin and math-ematics. After Joshua left Radley, his father funded him for nine years during which he was apprenticed to an apothecary and under-took training at a London hospital and medical school.[20] In 1837 Joshua qualified, aged twenty-three, and began practice in a village close to his home.

Girls were prepared for the world of marriage and home. In an advertisement of 1827, typical for the time, the Misses Harrison's school for ladies in Durham promised tuition in reading, writing, grammar, history and plain and ornamental needlework. 'Parlour boarders' (who lodged with the proprietors) were charged fifty guineas a year and there were extra charges for optional geography (a guinea), singing and piano playing (two-and-a-half guineas) and japanning and painting velvet (£1 12s). Parents were assured that 'religion and morality' were central in the school's life.[21]

★

Pupils at the Misses Harrison's school dreamed of husbands rich enough to allow them to remain at home as mistress of the household. This was how the wives of aristocrats and gentlemen lived and men from the better-off middle classes wanted their wives to confine themselves wholly to domestic matters. A totally dependent wife concerned solely with household and family was a sign that a man could support all by his own efforts; a wife who worked was a public admission that her husband was not earning enough to make ends meet. This ideal of a wife as purely a homemaker gained considerable ground as the nineteenth century progressed and became a status symbol among the middle classes.

Economic realities, not least those periodic slumps in trade which often lowered middle-class incomes, compelled some middle-class women to work and gain a degree of independence. Some had their own independent businesses, like George Holyoake's mother who in the 1820s simultaneously tended to eleven children and ran her own button-making workshop in Birmingham. George's father, who considered himself middle-class, was employed as a foundryman and attempted to establish his own business manufacturing buttons using a punch powered by a steam engine.[22] The wife of James Williams, a stonemason, kept a shop in Wickham Market in Suffolk while her husband was developing his flair for sculpture. By 1845, he had enough capital to establish his own business in Ipswich which employed nineteen hands. It flourished, for Williams was adept in reproducing those medieval styles which church builders and restorers were now demanding.[23] Mrs Williams was her husband's business partner and no doubt, once his enterprise was profitable, she withdrew to managing the household.

Other wives were compelled by their husbands' fecklessness to become the full-time family breadwinner. Euphemia Vallance supported an idle husband and three children, whom she brought up in a 'respectable manner' by running a butcher's shop in Ayr. Ten years of hard graft were endangered in 1828 when her drunken husband began insulting her customers, but this was Scotland and so she was able to sue for divorce.[24] Here and in similar cases, the wife paid a daily allowance to her husband, which was invariably spent on drink.

Wives in this position attracted pity; self-reliant, unmarried women were considered eccentric. Eyebrows were raised in Sussex when two 'genteelly educated ladies', Mrs Sarah Spenser and her sister Mary, decided to take up farming. Family mischance had left them with £300 a year, and convention dictated either marriage or permanent quarters in the household of a relation. Instead, they ran a profitable farm and were derided by their neighbours, who called them 'Man Mary' and 'Captain Sally', nicknames that hinted at another sort of scandal. None the less, this pair maintained social contacts with the local gentry until they died in the early 1780s.[25]

Man Mary and Captain Sally may have amused the Sussex yokels, but they were not exceptional. The 1841 census revealed 22,900 female farmers in Britain, roughly 7 per cent of the total.[26] Most were either widows or unmarried daughters who had inherited their father's property, like Thomas Hardy's Bathsheba Everdene in *Far from the Madding Crowd* (1874), whose refusal to take a husband struck her neighbours as perverse. This census, the first to enquire into occupation, also revealed 2,000 women horse and cattle dealers (5 per cent of the total) and 14,500 women engaged in what was officially described as 'medicine' who were midwives and nurses.

The only profession open to middle-class women was teaching. In 1841 there were 21,100 women employed in education, more than twice the number of men. They included teachers in dame and private schools like two spinster sisters, Eliza and Emma Hook, who ran a day school in Devizes in the early 1840s that gave them a joint income of about £200 a year. An enterprising pair, they also turned their hands to selling confectionery, glassware and 'Berlin' wool for tapestries.[27]

There were also governesses, a species that inhabited a social limbo. In most households, the governess was a 'genteel upper servant' who was expected to possess the 'dress and demeanour of a lady' coupled with the 'meek and pliant spirit' of a sycophant, according to a survey of the teaching profession written in 1839.[28] This was true, but the post of governess was the only alternative for an impoverished, well-bred young lady.

★

One area which the governess did not touch upon in her lessons was sex. 'False delicacy in parents and teachers' thwarted the perfectly understandable enquiries of children on this subject, with the result that they picked up snippets of information from servants or older boys and girls. The consequence was 'unspeakable evils to mind and body'. Far better, one teacher argued, that they learned about reproduction from his kind, who would answer questions 'without any prurient excitement of imagination'.[29]

In fact, there was an abundance of information on this subject available during this period for curious children, those intending marriage and those already wed. *Aristotle's Master-piece*, a general technical guide to procreation, had appeared at the close of the seventeenth century and remained in print for the next. Equally well read was Dr Samuel Solomon's *A Guide to Health, or Advice to Both Sexes*, which was first published in 1782, cost three shillings and went through sixty-six editions by 1817. Pamphlets on birth control, written by freethinkers and radicals, circulated widely from the 1820s onwards and, although aimed at the working class, must have been read by the middle classes.[30] Contraception was a vital matter for everyone who aspired to a 'genteel life', argued a radical journalist in 1826. Husbands and wives whose 'most virtuous and praiseworthy efforts are perpetually made to keep up the respectability of the family' could so easily slip into insolvency and loss of status if they had more children than they could afford to support.[31]

Children were the natural and highly desirable outcome of marriage – on this everyone was agreed. A further but now less well-known consensus was that women as well as men enjoyed sex. Female sexuality was freely admitted in both *Aristotle's Master-piece* and Dr Solomon's medical vade mecum. Both publications had a wide circulation and give the lie to the mistaken assumption that the early Victorian married woman was expected to regard sex as a duty to be endured and a distraction from her prime responsibilities as guardian goddess of home and family.[32]

Dr Solomon repeatedly emphasised the physical delights of lovemaking. 'Amorous pleasure' provided 'blissful moments' thanks to an 'ardent desire to give and receive something essentially pleasing'.

Orgasm was a 'short epilepsy', he believed, but he added that too many produced debility, which of course could be remedied by doses of Balm of Gilead at half a guinea a bottle. It was relentlessly advertised throughout the book as a cure for all distempers, save the imbecility, pimples and the shrinking penis that were the result of masturbation, which Solomon in common with other contemporary physicians considered corrosive to physical and mental health.[33]

Doctors also frowned on birth control since it impeded the forces of nature, although, unlike today, clergymen of all denominations had nothing to say on the subject. Two forms of artificial contraception existed at this time: the condom made of sheep gut, that 'armour' against the pox used by Boswell, and the sponge on a ribbon that was inserted before intercourse and removed afterwards, which was recommended by one writer to middle-class couples.[34] There was also coitus interruptus, known as the 'Coffee House' ('to go in and out and spend nothing'), and abortion, which became a crime only in 1803. Before, abortionists had advertised their services or concoctions openly in the press: in 1796 Mrs Ringenberg, a 'herbalist' of Pimlico Gardens, offered treatment for female disorders including 'obstructions' and 'irregularities' and promised that 'secrecy may be depended on in every case'.[35] Similar advertisements, couched in more circumspect language, appeared throughout the next century.

There is plenty of evidence that the means of contraception were available at the time if you knew where to look, but none to suggest how many middle-class couples resorted to them. The proportion may have been very small and remained so until the 1870s when rubber condoms came on the market and the birth rate began a slow and what turned out to be irreversible decline. A statistician analysing trends in the birth rate in the 1880s noticed that it was the middle classes who were having fewer children.[36]

Birth control and the enjoyment of sex do not accord with the conventional historical picture of marriage in the decades immediately before Queen Victoria's accession. In social and moral terms, many features were already in place for that peculiar Victorian exaltation of family life which Tennyson would epitomise as 'Household happiness, gracious children, debtless competence, golden mean'. This was the Christian ideal of married life that middle-class couples would strive after and enjoy and the working classes emulate. It also provided the environment in which children spent their earliest years.

The elevation of marriage was part of a wider remaking of the moral landscape. It had been under way since the end of the eighteenth century and, powered by Evangelicalism, it gathered momentum in the first quarter of the next. Writing in the 1840s and looking back to his youth sixty years before, Francis Place noticed a general tightening of sexual disciplines. He remembered a 'want of chastity' among girls, many the daughters of respectable London tradesmen who were destined to marry respectable men. They drank rum and milk in pubs, smoked pipes, sang ribald ballads and watched 'lewd plays and interludes' on the stage.[37] All this would now be abhorrent, thought Place, although his impressions alone are not evidence for a total moral reformation. Scatological and sexual jokes may have been removed from the 1832 edition of Joe Miller's *Complete Jest Book*, but there were still at least fifty-seven London shops selling pornography in 1834.[38] Seven years later, it was still possible for the French can-can to make its debut in the city despite a chorus of fury from the 'respectable' community.[39]

Middle-class voices were part of this clamour, but it would be wrong to imagine that they were upholding a specifically middle-class morality. Evangelical aristocrats were the among the most prominent and strident early- and mid-Victorian advocates of decency and purity. The 8th Duke of Argyll (1823–1900) was president of the Society for the Encouragement of Purity in Literature, and Lord Campbell of St Andrews (1779–1861), a successful lawyer and son of a Fife minister, spent his seventy-ninth year steering an obscene publications bill through Parliament. Lord Robert Grosvenor MP (1801–93), the son of the 2nd Marquess of Westminster, was a strict and therefore highly unpopular champion of extreme Sunday observance. In 1860, Lord Lovaine MP, the future 6th Duke of Northumberland, expressed the revulsion towards bare-knuckle prize fights felt in some sections of the middle class. No one layer of society could claim the new moral sensibilities as its own.

8

A Post Hoffice Directory . . . Man: Snobberies

John Bell KC of Gray's Inn died aged seventy-one in 1836 after a
remarkable career at the Bar. He had buck teeth, was short and round-
shouldered and his club foot made him walk with an ungainly limp.
When he pleaded it was painful to listen, for he spoke his 'native
Cumberland' dialect with a severe stammer. Yet he told a 'plain tale
in a plain manner', had a sharp intellect and his discretion and judgment more than compensated for his linguistic infirmities. He left
an estate worth £80,000 and was warmly remembered for his cheery
affability.[1]

Another professional man who died the same year was less fondly
recalled. Dr Pelham Warren, sometime member of Trinity College,
Cambridge, Fellow of the Royal Society and of the Royal College
of Physicians, made 'no contributions to medical science except a
paper on headache'. 'His manners were peculiar and not always
pleasing, being generally cold, and sometimes abrupt. He took a
prodigious quantity of snuff, and was plain and untidy in dress . . .'
Dr Warren was fifty-eight when he died, but looked older, perhaps
because for many years he had taken 'no more exercise than walking
from carriage to sick chamber'.[2] In other words, he was stout.

Bell and Warren occupied the upper stratum of the middle class
and their education and professions made them gentlemen. Yet their

idiosyncrasies place them beyond the pale of the conventional. Their obituaries give no clue to the intensity of their religious convictions or the regularity of their church attendance. Did they prefer the race meeting, the cricket match, a prize fight or even a public hanging to a gathering summoned to promote some humanitarian cause or petition to Parliament? Many middle-class men did, then and later. It is hard to imagine that either made a favourable impression at any polite assembly, or were agreeable figures beyond their professional circles; indeed Dr Warren's acerbity must have sometimes embarrassed his friends.

None the less, this pair are important for two reasons. They remind us that, while there were common patterns of conduct and outlook within the middle class, there was never uniformity. Individual quirkiness is therefore valuable because it reveals much about forms that were considered normal and therefore seldom referred to; those who neglected or ignored the rules drew attention to them. The fact that Bell and Warren infringed conventions of speech, appearance and manners was worth mentioning and many readers may have considered that Warren's lapses diminished his social standing. In Mrs Gaskell's *Cranford* (1850), the local doctor was an excellent clinician 'but as a man – or rather, I should say, as a gentleman – we could only shake our heads over his name . . . and wish he had read Lord Chesterfield's letters in the days when his manners were susceptible to improvement'.

Today, no one reads Chesterfield's admonitions to his bastard son. Our age is uncomfortable with formality and unwilling to judge people by how they dress and speak. To do so is considered one of the worst forms of prejudice – snobbery. Yet, in so far as it was an open recognition that society was stratified and that differences of behaviour and education mattered, snobbery was endemic among the middle and upper classes of eighteenth- and early-nineteenth-century Britain. Nuances of dress, diction and manners were the touchstones by which social position and often moral worth were assayed. There was nothing new in this; what Jane Austen took for granted had been tacitly understood by Chaucer and Shakespeare. While optimistic commentators and philosophers proclaimed the advent of a truly modern age, stripped of the shackles of the past, those prime beneficiaries of the change, the midde class, were content to live according to social codes with their roots in the Middle Ages.

What is more, these conventions derived from those traditionally followed by the aristocracy. Yet, paradoxically, the tribunes of the middle class were denouncing the concept of an aristocracy as outmoded and inimical to progress. The term encompassed not only diehard Tory lords blocking political reform but other elites that laid claim to privileges which were justified solely by custom and antiquity. In 1828 a young apothecary's apprentice denounced the Royal College of Surgeons as a 'refuge of aristocratic pride and assumed sanctuary of purity of morals and good breeding'. This bastion of ancestral wisdom was about to crumble because an impatient nation was poised 'to confound in one universal ruin all corporate privileges and monopolies'.[3] Dr Warren shared these sentiments, for he did not tolerate 'aristocratic impertinence', which he reproved with 'caustic bitterness'. Like so many middle-class professional men he would not countenance that superiority assumed by those who owed their eminence to string pulling or membership of self-perpetuating, exclusive institutions such as the Royal College of Surgeons or a corruptly elected House of Commons.

The tone of Dr Warren's put-downs may be easily imagined, but how did he deliver them? We cannot know for certain: the first recordings of the human voice date from the 1880s and anecdotal evidence of the accents of individuals is scattered. Enough exists to suggest that in the 1830s speech had yet to define class in the way that it did later, although John Bell's Cumberland vowels were clearly unusual in a courtroom.

There was no universal, instantly recognisable middle-class or aristocratic accent. Dr Johnson noted that Lord Chesterfield rhymed 'great' with 'state', while the Speaker of the Commons, a northerner, rhymed it with 'seat'.[4] Disraeli observed that his colleague the 14th Earl of Derby (1799–1869) spoke a neutral English and that his son, the 15th Earl (1826–93), had a Lancashire twang.[5] The father had attended Eton and Christ Church, his son Rugby and Trinity

College, Cambridge. In *Middlemarch* (1871–2) George Eliot remarks that the speech of Fred Vincy revealed that he 'has kept college company', but she may well be projecting back thirty years the Oxford and Cambridge drawl of her own time. King William IV used 'ain't' and 'you was' for you were. Both were eighteenth-century constructions and passing out of usage along with 'yaller' for yellow, 'cowcumber' for cucumber, 'ra-ally' for really and 'ooman' for woman.

None the less, incorrect pronunciation and awkward syntax were impediments for anyone making his way up in the world. Slow, stumbling, ungrammatical speech, dialect words or phrases, aitches dropped or added and the replacement of 'g' with 'k' as in 'nothink' declared humble birth or limited education, or both. Certain words had vulgar connotations and were best shunned, so that inebriated was preferable to 'drunk'. Euphemism was occasionally taken to extremes, as it was by a genteel spinster who called a cock a 'hen's companion'.[6] If this was not enough, there were further, revealing snares for the socially ambitious, the pronunciation of the names of carriages. A phaeton was articulated as 'fe-a-ton', a brougham as 'broom'.

Mastering such niceties was essential for members of the middle class who wished to impress equals and superiors or to obscure lowly birth. 'Meritorious people who have risen by their own exertions' were tormented by 'the fear of being thought vulgar', according to an etiquette guide of 1834.[7] Such books still enjoyed large sales among those who wanted to avoid the socially revealing solecism. Its utterance or a regional accent were not insurmountable hurdles; John Bell won his cases in a Cumberland brogue. And there were some who did not give a damn, like R. S. Surtees's aitch-abusing London-grocer-turned-master-of-foxhounds. 'I'm only a tradesman – a post hoffice directory, not a peerage man,' he announces in *Handley Cross* (1843). He spurns iced champagne with 'I havn't got so advanced in gentility to like my wine froze.'

If speech was not an infallible yardstick of social standing, appearance was. Dr Warren's dishevelled and presumably snuff-stained clothing did not befit a physician, or so his obituarist thought. He was right, since dress and grooming were commonly accepted as an indication of background, occupation and even trustworthiness. In 1817 working-class radical plotters were taken in by the fashionable outfit, 'genteel appearance' and 'good address' of Oliver the Spy, a Home Office agent posing as a middle-class sympathiser.[8] A few years later, George Holyoake was intrigued by a young grinder who turned up each morning for work in a Birmingham foundry wearing a well-cut black suit. He changed into working clothes and, in the evening, would 'wash, dress and leave . . . like a gentleman'.[9]

An appeal by a weaver for parish assistance for his aged mother and epileptic sister was rejected by Bolton magistrates in 1838 on the ground that he looked 'too clean and decent' to need charity.[10] While rarely mentioning provincial accents, contemporary police wanted notices always distinguished 'genteel' suspects by their apparel. A commercial traveller who had absconded with two hundred pounds of his employer's money was identifiable by his new black coat and waistcoat and striped trousers.[11]

This rig was becoming the normal wear for professionals and businessmen and their clerks. It was worn by the slim and suave Dr Mello, a physician in Surtees's spa town of Handley Cross who believed that a proper appearance inspired patients' confidence. His black suit was well tailored, his boots shone and his linen was immaculate – 'turned-back cambric wristbands displayed the snowy whiteness of his hand, and set off an antique ring or two'. There were four frills to his shirt front and, when visiting patients, he sported a gold-topped cane. His portly and shambling rival, Dr Swizzle, adopted another style of dress, then still fashionable among middle-class men, of contrasting coat and trousers. 'A country-made snuff-coloured coat, black waistcoat, and short greenish drab trousers . . . were the adjuncts of his short ungainly figure.' The condition as well as the cut and quality of a man's wardrobe were also giveaways of status and solvency. Dickens's 'shabby genteel' characters wore shiny, sometimes darned and often crumpled suits, and their linen was yellowed and frayed. Even in poor repair, their sombre suits declared that they were clerks who were expected to have a businesslike appearance.

There were dandies among the middle class and vain men who dressed so as to raise their status a notch or two. In *Dr Thorne* (1858), Anthony Trollope describes Mr Gazebee, a London lawyer, as a 'very elegant young man'. When he rode in Rotten Row, 'you would hardly have taken him for an attorney'. We may be certain that Gazebee was a manly figure; for the previous sixty years male fashion had emphasised a well-turned calf, a narrow waist and broad shoulders. As masculinity in dress advanced, ostentatious dandyism retreated. This was to be expected, since the flamboyance of the macaronis of the 1770s and their successors had provoked allegations of effeminacy and even a tendency towards the abominable 'Italian vice', as sodomy was often called.

If male fashions were expressions of the temper of the times, and there are good reasons to believe that they were, then a revolution was under way. The gradual extinction of extravagant colours, embroidered coats, laced cuffs and wigs was a rejection of artificiality and self-indulgence. According to the *Lady's Magazine* of November 1798 the new and, therefore, desirable man had stepped on to the stage with:

> An air that's gay and yet severe;
> An awful, but an easy mien.

And, the amateur poetess was happy to say, there was no hint of 'foppery' in his dress. A new earnestness and sobriety was already gaining ground. It permeated every level of the upper and middle orders in different ways and with widely varying degrees of intensity.

Part Three

The Triumph of the Middle Classes: 1832–1914

1

Work: Middle-Class Values

The Victorian age will not go away, nor will the legacy of its middle class. It dominated society and produced a social and moral environment that has not entirely disappeared. Whenever Britain undergoes one of its periodic fits of moral introspection, the codes and certainties of the Victorian middle class are invoked, either in admiration or in horror. Mrs Thatcher was an admirer and said so with characteristic vigour during the 1983 election campaign when she repeated what she had learned from her grandmother, a child of Queen Victoria's reign.

> We were taught to work jolly hard. We were taught to prove yourself; we were taught self-reliance; we were taught to live within our income. You were taught that cleanliness is next to godliness. You were taught self-respect. You were taught always to give a hand to your neighbour. You were taught tremendous pride in your country. All these things are Victorian values. They are also perennial values.[1]

Afterwards she corrected herself, replacing 'values' with 'virtues'. They were not peculiarly Victorian, having their roots in Classical and Judaeo-Christian recipes for the perfect life, and had offered models for human conduct since the Middle Ages. Neil Kinnock, the Labour leader, perversely mistook virtues for the sources of vice, defining 'Victorian values' as 'cruelty, misery, drudgery, squalor and ignorance', conditions that the Victorian middle class did all in its power to eliminate. Ironically, Kinnock had attended the University of Wales, one of the many Victorian institutions founded to spread knowledge among all classes.

While it is hard to be dispassionate about Victorian creeds, it is impossible to deny Victorian energy, in particular that of the middle class. The evidence is everywhere. Victorian factories, railway stations, commercial offices and private houses still crowd our townscapes, although far less so than fifty years ago. We are the inheritors of Victorian civic and private benevolence. It has provided us with parks, libraries, museums, town halls, hospitals, universities, schools, churches, swimming baths, public lavatories, horse troughs and those now derelict drinking fountains with brass scoops. These conveniences perfectly reflected that Victorian blend of compassion and practicality. With clean water to hand, the thirsty working man would not squander his earnings on beer; refreshed and sober he would return home to his family and perhaps place the money he had saved in the Post Office savings bank, another Victorian innovation. Like him, we drink water that has been purified in plants designed and built by Victorian engineers.

The middle class had a controlling hand in all this. Demography had made it possible for the middle class to exert an extraordinary social, cultural and political influence. Its members ruled cities and towns, where, by 1901, four-fifths of the population lived. Urban expansion had been rapid: in 1861 there were 141 towns and cities with between twenty and one hundred thousand inhabitants, in 1881 there were 245. These figures reflected an equally sharp increase in the overall population, which rose from 26.7 million in 1841 to 41.7 million in 1901.

As entrepreneurs and manufacturers, the middle class created modern, urban Britain, and on the whole central government was happy to let them mould its environment. In what was some of the most influential and far-reaching legislation ever passed, Westminster

delegated extensive powers to elected councils. These were dominated by a middle class with a compelling faith in its own capacity
to make the world a cleaner, healthier, more secure and better-
educated place. It started with the urban infrastructure, laying drains,
purifying water and paving and lighting streets. Then it turned its
attentions to civic amenities such as baths, libraries, parks, museums
and the supply of gas and electricity. These often massive programmes
of regeneration and modernisation enhanced the middle class's image
of Britain as a progressive and civilised nation.

It was fitting that such a country strove for the overall improvement of everyone. This was why in 1861 a Tory barrister and Liberal
coal merchant joined forces in Leeds to persuade the council to
fund a free public library.[2] A thriving manufacturing city could not
tolerate ignorance, nor reject the demands of working men to acquire
knowledge, which was of course the springboard for physical and
moral improvement. The issue was thrashed out within a recently
completed town hall, one of the grandest in Britain. As they entered,
Leeds councillors looked up to see allegorical statues of Progress,
Art and Commerce set above the entrance. Like the great houses
of aristocracy and gentry which overlooked the countryside, public
buildings commissioned by the middle class advertised its confidence
and power.

Civic patrons invited architects to contrive designs that reflected
the glories of the great cities of the past. On laying the foundation
stone of Birmingham's municipal offices in 1874, the radical mayor
Joseph Chamberlain likened his fellow citizens to the 'free and independent burghers' of medieval cities on the Continent and modern
civic buildings to the 'magnificent palaces' of those times. The new
structure symbolised both Birmingham's pride and the 'welfare and
happiness' of its people.[3]

Ironically, the architecture of progress and optimism looked back-
wards. Even when they employed modern materials, iron and plate
glass, Victorian architects plundered the past for styles. It was not that
they lacked imagination; the buildings and sculpture of the past had
resonances that were in tune with the present. A Doric arch with

columns forty feet high confronted the passenger at Euston station. Inside were mosaic pavements and Romano-Ionic columns adorned with bas-reliefs, each representing a city served by the London and North Western Railway. The architecture and ornaments of Classical triumphalism had been recreated in homage to the achievements of the present. What was more, and this was often unsaid, for all their genius the Greeks and Romans could never have harnessed steam and built railways. (Erected in 1836, the Euston arch did not survive the decay of the railways and was demolished by philistines in 1961.)

A few minutes' walk away is St Pancras station, designed by Sir George Gilbert Scott and constructed between 1868 and 1874. Again the traveller is overawed by what one admirer called the 'palatial beauty, comfort, and convenience' of a building that blended English and Continental Gothic styles. Nothing could be too sumptuous or ornate for passengers, and such stations proclaimed the reliability and financial soundness of the railway companies. These qualities were also expressed in the architecture of business houses, whose offices resembled the palaces of Italian Renaissance princes complete with marble floors. Some firms chose the pseudo-Gothic style which conveyed the stability and grandeur of a cathedral. Step into an old-fashioned city bank and one enters a banking hall that blends solidity and dignity with restrained opulence; the St Andrews Square Edinburgh branch of the Bank of Scotland is a marvellous example. Like others of its genre, this building has that sense of permanence vital for any enterprise whose fortunes rested on public trust.

These cathedrals and palaces of commerce were adorned with statues that revealed the hopes and ideals of the middle-class businessmen who commissioned them. Symbolic figures of Peace, Plenty, Industry and Science decorated the terminus at Paddington, completed in the early 1850s. During the second half of the century, imperial images appeared on more and more buildings. Farmers carrying sheaves of wheat, gold miners, foresters, ploughmen and shepherds were the icons of Australia, New Zealand, Canada and Cape Colony. Britain was an imperial as well as a global trading power and its dominions and colonies were a source of customers, raw materials and pride.

Visionaries who had led and enriched the nation were also depicted on the powerhouses of commerce. Their features appear on stone medallions set in the walls of Bradford's Exchange (1864–7) so that cloth brokers would daily remember the dreams and labours of those Titans who had made them and their country pre-eminent and prosperous. There are the explorers who had opened the world to British trade: Raleigh, Drake, Cook and Anson. Then there was Lord Palmerston, the Whig Foreign Secretary and Prime Minister, whose warships made the world safe for British businessmen and who courted their votes by defiance of Continental despots and support for such liberal heroes as Garibaldi. National genius was celebrated by a galaxy of inventors – Stephenson, Watt and Arkwright – and the champion of free trade and tribune of the middle classes, Richard Cobden.

'All good architecture is the expression of national life and character,' John Ruskin (1819–1900) told the Bradford worthies after they had consulted him about the design for their new Exchange. The country's leading art guru was right: the sum of Victorian building reflected the nation's congratulatory self-image.

Victorian architecture is assertive in scale, profusely decorated, sometimes vainglorious and supremely durable. Whatever else they may have had doubts about, the Victorians believed in the future; their structures were made to last. Yet, while Victorians copied the past, they imagined that they could improve on it with results that can be seen in thousands of restored medieval cathedrals and churches.

The Victorians believed they could surpass their ancestors because they were more inventive, had novel materials and had mastered the techniques of industrial production. A survey of the railways published in 1852 boasted that Euston's mosaic pavement had been made from a modern conglomerate: 'patent metallic lava'.[4] Much of St Pancras and so many other mock-Gothic buildings were constructed with mass-produced bricks and paved with mass-produced Minton tiles.

This presumption of the superiority of the modern was strong among the middle classes. They had been emboldened by political reforms

in the 1830s and fancied they were entering a new age. Its architecture might be borrowed from antiquity, but its spirit was modern,
universal and symbolised by steam. 'Feudality has gone for ever,'
concluded Thomas Arnold, the headmaster of Rugby, after he had
seen his first train, and Thomas Carlyle agreed. Steam power was
'overturning the whole old system of society' and opening the way
for 'Industrialism and the Government of the Wisest'.[5]

The middle-class rank and file echoed the opinions of their intellectual mentors. Listen to the address of T. J. Green, chairman of the
Bedford, London and North Western Railway, at the opening of
the local branch line in 1846:

> As members of a vast commercial empire we know the great
> advantages arising from the cheap and rapid interchange of
> agricultural produce, the minerals and the manufactures of this
> country, and the prosperity and happiness that result from it.
> And as members of this enlightened community, we must feel
> how the cause of morality is advanced, how science is promoted
> and how society is improved by the quick and easy commun-
> ication this afforded between all its members.[6]

Mr Green was a Bedford fuel merchant who was investing in land.
His was the authentic, self-confident voice of a vast proportion of
the middle class engaged in commerce.

Others recoiled from a world of machines and money-making
and escaped into a medieval one, largely of their own invention.
Disraeli wrote novels in which young noblemen dreamed of reviving
medieval society and reclaiming the aristocracy's traditional responsibilities for the weak and poor. Like his creator, Coningsby believed
that 'Man was born to adore and obey.' John Keble and his Tractarian
disciples agreed in principle and urged the Church of England to
rediscover its medieval Catholic inheritance. Forgotten liturgies and
rituals would regenerate both the church and people. In 1848 the
Pre-Raphaelite Brotherhood believed that they had uncovered a lost
purity and idealism in art and endeavoured to reproduce it. Arthurian
legend was chosen by Tennyson as the source for what he hoped

would be the great epic poem of his age, the *Idylls of the King*.

We know exactly what Disraeli, Keble, Tennyson and the Pre-Raphaelites looked like because they were not so detached from the present as to shun the camera. Photography appeared in 1839 and immediately caught the middle-class imagination in the way that railways had in the previous decade. Thomas Rogers, a young hosiery wholesaler, spent the large sum of twenty-eight shillings and sixpence (over twice a labourer's weekly pay) on a daguerreotype of his sweetheart in 1844. Four years later he spent a similar sum on one of his mother.[7] The desire to possess a truthful, scientific likeness of a loved one was irresistible. If anything symbolised Victorians' intense emotional attachment to the family, it was the proliferation of photographs of fathers, mothers and children, aunts, uncles and so on. By the mid-1840s photographic studios were opening in provincial towns to satisfy a market that turned out to be insatiable. What started as a middle-class luxury was soon available to the working class. In 1855 the pioneer war photographer Roger Fenton was badgered by navvies in the Crimea, all demanding likenesses to send home. Photographs now cost as little as five shillings and were within the budget of all but the poorest. This pattern of invention and eventual mass consumption was repeated with bicycling. It became the middle class fad in the 1870s when the 'ordinary' (that is, penny-farthing bicycle) cost £12 10s and was a highly desirable status symbol. In the next decade the familiar, two-wheeled 'safety' bicycle with pneumatic tyres was developed and prices fell. By 1905 the cheapest bicycle was five guineas and could be afforded by shop assistants, elementary school teachers and skilled artisans and mechanics.

Such men and women joined one of the hundreds of cycling clubs which sprang up across the country and whose membership had reached over 20,000 in the early 1880s. Parties of cyclists pedalling along country roads were as important in their way as steam engines had been fifty years before. Many cyclists carried cameras which now cost as little as twelve shillings and sixpence. Cheap bicycles and cameras were a vindication of liberal capitalist theory which had long claimed that the benefits of industrialisation would filter downwards to all classes. They did, but slowly and unevenly, leaving many among the working class frustrated and impatient.

Revealingly, this process of manufacturers developing inexpensive products for a mass market failed to repeat itself after motor cars made their first appearance in the early 1890s. There was a collective commercial myopia, with early car manufacturers concentrating solely on a luxury market. In 1901 Wolseley advertised its latest model as 'suitable for a gentleman's use' (this would have caught the eye of Mr Toad) and rival 'electric carriages' were puffed as 'the only motor vehicles for fashionable use', which was why Queen Alexandra and a string of peers and peeresses had purchased them.[8] The upper reaches of the middle class were tempted: doctors, clergymen, bankers and country squires were buying cars in Norfolk in the early 1900s.[9]

The car makers' lack of foresight and adventurousness was criticised by *The Times* in 1912. Why, it asked, was there no 'sufficiently enterprising' manufacturer producing motors for between one and two hundred pounds? In America there were 600,000 cheap cars on the roads, many owned by 'superior working men and small tradesmen'.[10] Such a market existed in Britain, but so far there was no 'democratic' motoring. An American manufacturer, Henry Ford, had been quick off the mark with his famous Model T or 'Tin Lizzie', which was deliberately aimed at the middle classes. In 1911 his Dagenham factory was mass-producing cars that sold for as little as £125 and, of the 12,000 cars that sold for under £200 in 1913, nearly two-thirds were Fords.

The missed chances of the embryonic British car industry were significant. They were further symptoms of a malaise that had infected the economy during the last quarter of the century and from which it seemed unable to recover. Patterns of international trade were changing and to Britain's disadvantage: its share of an admittedly expanding global market shrank; exports stagnated and imports rose; and during the 1900s America and Germany overtook it in terms of industrial capacity. The first industrial nation of 1815 had become the third by 1914.

It was hard to fathom why this was so, since domestic levels of consumption were rising. Perhaps the most convincing explanation

was that many British boardrooms had succumbed to a mental sclerosis that closed minds and fostered caution. British industrialists stuck
to what they knew and what had made them rich, leaving American
and German companies free to make the running in the development of new technologies, materials and sources of power. In 1877
two rival American corporations, Bell and Edison, contended for the
establishment of a telephone network in Britain. When, in the mid-
1890s, British municipalities decided to electrify their tramways, they
had no choice but to turn to American companies for the machinery
and expertise.[11]

The second Industrial Revolution needed a skilled and versatile
labour force. Britain had neither, for unlike its new rivals it neglected
scientific and technical education. Universal elementary schooling
had been introduced in 1870, but the curriculum was confined to
basic literacy and numeracy. A disregard for science was also evident
in municipal grammar and public schools, where the emphasis was
on the Classics. Furthermore, the growth in aggressive trade unionism
among skilled workers was creating an intractable workforce that
resisted flexibility on the production line, a problem that seldom troubled American employers served by plentiful and docile immigrant
labour.

Britain was cushioned from the consequences of its economic
shortcomings by the phenomenal profits of the financial service
industries and shipping and by dividends from overseas investments.
In 1913 the total of British capital invested abroad was £3,780
million. British engineers might not have been able to invent a telephone, but British investors were able to fund new telephone companies from Chile to Egypt. Much of this capital was middle-class
savings and surpluses made during the first stages of the Industrial
Revolution. Earlier, this capital had largely flowed into domestic
enterprises. The portfolio of the Jowetts, a Leeds mercantile dynasty,
was typical. In the 1840s they owned shares in the local gas company,
the Leeds and Yorkshire Assurance Company, the Leeds New Baths
Company and local railways. The next generation, guided by a London
stockbroker, shifted funds into American railroad stock.[12]

★

Like the rest of the middle class, investor and adviser were deferring to the sovereignty of the market. Capital moved to wherever it could earn the best returns. The principle of free trade applied to every commodity and its adoption in the second quarter of the century was hailed by the commercial middle class as the key to Britain's dominance of world markets. And so it was, given that before 1880 British manufacturers and exporters had no serious competitors.

Free-market economics blended with the gospel of work was as close as the Victorian middle class came to an ideology of its own. They were complementary ideas: the competitive market provided opportunities, and hard work was the only way to exploit them. 'Produce! Produce!' trumpeted Thomas Carlyle (1795–1881) in *Sartor Resartus* (1834). He repeated the message in his steam-hammer prose many times, sanctifying it with invocations of the old Puritan work ethic he had learned from his father, an Ecclefechan stonemason. 'Blessed is the man who has found work, let him ask no other blessedness.'[13] This was just what the middle class wanted to hear and explains why it revered Carlyle as its sage and prophet. Work delivered what its members cherished: riches, status and self-respect.

Carlyle appears with the Christian Socialist the Reverend Denison Maurice in Ford Madox Brown's *Work*, painted between 1852 and 1865. The pair, both workers of the intellect, are contemplating a Hampstead street late on a summer's afternoon. Immediately before them is physical labour: a gang of workmen excavating a drain or a gas main. They are elevated by their toil, which benefits their countrymen. In 1866 the Evangelical hero Lord Shaftesbury declared that 'manual labour' was compatible with 'moral dignity'. Praising the new industrial schools in which young workers studied during the evenings, he observed that 'the discipline of pots and pans, humble as it may appear, is found to be nobly instrumental to the acquisition of learning'. Work, Shaftesbury concluded, delivered the poor from degradation and immorality.[14]

In the middle distance of Madox Brown's picture are a gentleman and lady on horseback. They may be members of the aristocracy, whom Carlyle despised as drones, or, just as likely, a successful professional man and his wife; Hampstead was already attracting commuters.

The aristocracy fitted awkwardly into the middle-class universe of work and production, and some thought it was superfluous. 'I have no mind to force myself into a set of indolent, corrupt aristocrats whom as a class (forgive me) I hate and despise with my whole being,' the lawyer John Coleridge (1828–94) told his father in 1855.[15] The venom of a clever man who in time would become lord chief justice and a peer was understandable. The Crimean War was in full swing and the country was stunned by press reports of chronic mismanagement by a largely aristocratic officer corps, whose members purchased their commissions, and a civil service whose officials got their jobs through influence. Privilege was impeding efficiency; no businessman would have tolerated such bungling.

Several other figures in Madox Brown's picture are ambivalent. In the far distance are a soldier and two volunteers and a string of sandwich-board men carrying election posters. Their contribution to work is hard to pinpoint, save that the former defended the state and the latter were lowly servants of its political system. Two figures in the middle ground are voluntary exiles from Carlyle's world of work. A pot-bellied and perhaps hard-drinking idler smoking a pipe lounges against a tree and a bare-footed flower girl in a torn dress hurries past. They may be unemployed or unemployable and the girl is barely surviving on the margins of society, perhaps occasionally slipping into casual prostitution.

What were Carlyle and Maurice saying? The latter might have pointed to this pair as evidence of the inequalities of capitalist society and the inequities produced by unbridled competition. Carlyle would have depicted them as victims not of the system, but of an inborn and indelible tendency to laziness. As proof of the existence of genetic inclinations to vice, he might have cited the opinions of his friend James Stephen (1829–94), a young and brilliant jurist. He had witnessed the trial of the Rugeley general practitioner Dr William Palmer in May 1856 and concluded that the career of this middle-class mass murderer was 'one of the proofs of a fact which many kind-hearted people seem to doubt, namely, the fact that such a thing as atrocious wickedness is consistent with good education, perfect sanity, and everything, in a word, that deprives men of all excuse for crime'.[16]

Palmer had spurned productive work, as Carlyle and a substantial body of the middle class would have understood it, by forsaking medicine for a life of chance and transitory rewards in horse racing. His trial had attracted enormous attention: there were plenty of lurid details to excite the prurient and it focused attention on a moral dilemma. Did creatures like Palmer have an inherited disposition for vice, as Stephen suggested? Or were they capable of repentance and regeneration, as Evangelicals would have insisted? It was a question that was invariably raised whenever the middle class debated ways in which their inferiors could be reformed or improved.

The middle-class work ethic had become part of the law in 1834. The Poor Law Act had been contrived to make life so wretched for the able-bodied poor that they had no other choice but to join the labour market, often on the most unfavourable terms. The management of the new workhouses (the poor damned them as 'Bastilles') was in the hands of the middle class, and the attitude of many Poor Law administrators was summed up by George Warry, a barrister and owner of a small estate in Somerset. He supervised the Bridgwater workhouse and was an apostle of work, as he explained in 1837:

> We war against the idle, the dissolute and improvident and we hesitate not in the application of a pungent, yet wholesome remedy to their complaint. The unpleasant nature of the remedy has a multiplied efficacy. It removes the disease, it prevents its recurrence, it stimulates to industry, it improves the morals, it adds comfort to the cottage.[17]

Warry worked hard, examining files and writing reports, often by candlelight. A creature marinated in Benthamite theory, he never visited the workhouses he ran and saw no need to. His regime of Spartan rations, the separation of families and the reformative therapy of the treadmill shocked his colleague James Bowen, a self-taught engineer who had once built an iron bridge at Lucknow for the East India Company. He organised a campaign against Warry, using all the customary instruments of middle-class protest: letters to the press, pamphlets and petitions to Parliament.

The clash between the two is a reminder that the Victorian middle class was never united when it came to social policy. Warry followed his intellect: he was a Whig who sincerely believed in the discipline of work, the supremacy of the market and the Benthamite nostrum that the 'greatest happiness of the great number' was the touchstone of public good. The Tory Bowen was ruled by his heart, which told him that modern, scientific theories should not entirely displace the old moral economy that required the rich to treat the poor with humanity.

There was much Bowen and Warry would have agreed on. They prized individual liberty and considered individuals better qualified than the state to judge what was for the general good. Freedom embraced the right of any man to go as far as his talents allowed, which was why the middle class was so hostile towards anything that smacked of aristocratic privilege. There was an equally strong antipathy towards centralised government. When, in 1856, Parliament made it compulsory for every area of the country to maintain a police force, the reaction in some quarters was hysterical. 'If the police of the country were to be managed by the Home Secretary's department and if all the teachers of education in the country . . . were in the hands of the government, a more despicable despotism would not exist,' warned George Hadford, the Liberal MP for Sheffield.[18] He would have been laughed at ten years later when the practical value of the police force was beyond doubt. None the less, misgivings lingered. In 1860 the conservative *Saturday Review* accused detectives investigating the Road murder of intruding into the life of a respectable family, seeking vulgar press publicity and too easily assuming the guilt of a suspect.[19]

Even the most extreme libertarians were forced to concede that the state was essential. A competitive nation needed courts to arbitrate, uphold contracts, collect debts and prosecute criminals. Commerce depended on the postal system and a stable currency. Individual security required a police force and national security the armed services, in particular the Royal Navy, which protected Britons abroad and waged war on slavers to the applause of the Evangelicals.

All this had to be paid for, mainly by middle-class taxpayers, and their representatives were forever demanding that ministries cut costs and avoid waste with the same vigour as any manufacturer.

Liberal-minded men agreed that the balance between individual rights and the power of the state, combined with a Parliament elected by informed men of property, had made Britain the most civilised nation in the world. This was why Palmerston periodically lectured Continental autocrats on the virtues of constitutional government and why the middle classes lionised liberal nationalists like Kossuth and Garibaldi. Yet many liberal thinkers like Carlyle distrusted democracy because they feared it would replace the rule of the enlightened with what John Stuart Mill called the 'tyranny of the majority'. The pass was sold between 1867 and 1885 with the extension of the franchise to most working men, the equalisation of constituencies, the secret ballot and the outlawing of electoral bribery and intimidation.

The middle classes and their parties, the Liberals and Conservatives, successfully accommodated themselves to democracy. Urban working-class voters tended to elect middle-class MPs, who made up an increasing proportion of the Commons; in 1865 half the members came from landed backgrounds, in 1885 a quarter. Cabinets remained predominantly aristocratic, more so for the Tories than the Liberals. Of the eleven members of the Marquess of Salisbury's inner cabinet of 1900, six were peers.

Fears of class politics voiced in the 1870s proved premature, although both parties had to woo the new voters. In the process laissez-faire dogma was whittled down and the free market constrained in ways that would have been unthinkable thirty years before. In 1870 and 1883 Parliament compelled tram and railway companies to offer low fares for commuting workmen. Specifically anti-capitalist parties emerged only in the 1890s and made sluggish advances. In the 1900 general election the new Labour Party gained two seats with less than 2 per cent of the popular vote.

The middle class was never entirely happy with ideologies and blanket solutions. Rather, its members preferred causes with moral or, better still, religious overtones. Men and women combined to preach temperance to the poor, send missionaries to Africa and Asia, rescue prostitutes and save children from depravity and ignorance. Collective action was complemented by individual: ideally the philanthropist not only attended mass meetings to reform the licensing laws but entered the home of the habitual drunkard to coax him into signing the pledge.

This passion to engage in the world and improve it overwhelms Lancelot, the hero of Charles Kingsley's *Yeast* (1851). 'Still he felt in himself a capacity, nay, an infinite longing to speak; though, what he should utter, or how – whether as a poet, social theorist, preacher, he could not decide.' On a practical level, Samuel Beesley, a middle-aged Banbury confectioner and Evangelical, made up his mind in 1841 to give 'moral and religious instruction' to the prisoners in Banbury gaol. Each Sunday he spoke to each of them, heard their bleak life stories and awakened their consciences.[20] Similar 'work' was undertaken by thousands of others who trusted to their own faith, their strength of character and the sheer rightness of their message. Beesley would have understood the lines from Elizabeth Barrett Browning's *Aurora Leigh* (1856):

> A red-haired child
> Sick in fever, if you touch him once,
> Though but so little, as with a finger-tip
> Will set you weeping; but a million sick . . .
> You could as soon weep for the rule of three
> Or compound fractions.

Warry, the Poor Law bureaucrat, would have been genuinely puzzled. Like others schooled in the theories of political economy he treated the problems of society en masse and thought of them solely in terms of statistics. Facts were all that mattered to that man 'of realities', the manufacturer Thomas Gradgrind MP, in Dickens's *Hard Times* (1854), who, like all creatures of satire, had plenty of living counterparts. Yet he and Warry shared with Beesley an urge to curb the worst excesses of industrialisation, rescue its victims and draw them into civilised, productive society. The achievement of these goals exercised the intelligence and energy of the politically active middle class, who put themselves forward for elections to local councils, health boards and school boards.

Middle-class participation in public life weakened some old certainties. Free competition and laissez-faire were not universal cure-alls. Self-interest was not always enlightened, and its extremes merged into selfishness. Take Henry Sibley, a Luton farmer, who like many with spare cash had taken advantage of the housing boom between 1830 and 1850. He owned fifty cottages which yielded a total annual rent of £165 and were among the worst slums in the town.[21] There were thousands of other high-density, jerry-built developments in every city and town, constructed with an eye to a quick profit and no thought for any sort of infrastructure. Not only the poor suffered from open sewers and contaminated water. Microbes did not distinguish rank, and cholera and enteric fevers killed the middle as well as the working class.

Eliminating water-carried distempers was one of the responsibilities of the public health boards created under the terms of the 1848 Public Health Act. Mr Sibley objected to the creation of such a board in Luton, rightly fearing that it might exercise its statutory powers and demolish his hovels. He lost and the town gained its health board and a medical officer of health who, like Dr Lydgate in *Middlemarch*, may have been one of those young, idealistic, articulate and impatient doctors whose job it was to advise health boards and implement the law.

Plenty of them were active in Victorian public life, and the career of one may represent many others. In his early years as a general practitioner in north Somerset, Dr Joshua Parsons showed a taste for liberal politics, campaigning for the penny post and against the Corn Laws, which showed independence of mind, for they were strongly supported in farming areas in the 1830s. New causes presented themselves thirty years later when he took over a practice in the small town of Frome, where he became medical officer of health and a champion of better water supplies and a cottage hospital. He died aged seventy-eight in 1892 while collecting samples of polluted water from a well at a local farm. His devotion to public medicine was inherited by his son Henry, who became medical officer of health for Goole and senior medical officer to the Local Government Board.[22]

Energetic men of strong character like Parsons made the laws passed in Westminster work. Local pride also played its part: backers of the free library in Leeds pointed out that similar institutions existed in Manchester and Sheffield to the shame of their city, which would be branded as reactionary and penny-pinching. Foul water and stinking drains were an affront to a civilised people, the more so since they were easily eradicated. Revealingly, Victorian middle-class tourists were always fussing over the plumbing arrangements in Continental hotels and inns.[23] A flushing lavatory had become a yardstick of civilisation.

Civic regeneration in the last quarter of the century witnessed local authorities trespassing in areas hitherto the preserve of private enterprise. By 1909 there were 327 county and urban local author-ities in England and Wales, of which 232 ran companies supplying water, 106 gas, 83 electricity and 24 tramways.[24] This proliferation of monopolies would have shocked free marketeers of sixty years before. Gasworks and pumping stations (many now lovingly preserved by the heritage industry as monuments to technology rather than civic philanthropy) were the outward signs of sixty years of progress.

These structures were misleading, in so far as much remained to be done. In 1900 there were still vast areas of dilapidated working-class housing whose occupants were underfed, sickly and with strik-ingly low life expectancies. At a time when imperialists boasted of the manly vigour of the 'imperial race', there were well-founded fears that it might be in a state of terminal degeneration. A socialist Robert Blatchford sourly observed that the sun which never set on the British Empire had never risen over the slums of Britain.

Had municipal philanthropy and private charity failed? Or, as many wondered, had the task of civilising industrial Britain been too great? It could be completed only by the agencies of the state drawing on the resources of a taxation system contrived to redis-tribute wealth. The twentieth century opened with the middle class in a quandary. It backed away from Joseph Chamberlain's 1903 proposal to fund social reform by imposing tariffs on imports and was uneasy five years later when David Lloyd George raised taxes on incomes and property to underwrite a new state welfare programme. The middle class's allegiance to free trade (and of course cheap food) and the rights of property proved stronger than its sense of social responsibility. In the general election of January 1910, the swing against the Liberal government was highest in predominantly middle-class constituencies.[25]

For the previous seventy years the middle class had enjoyed unparalleled power over the lives of others, mostly those beneath it. Whether as employers, shapers of public opinion, voters, elected officials or public servants, its members had been able to compel the rest of society to accept its assumptions and ambitions. Pragmatists tended to outnumber idealists. More time was spent at meetings of school boards in the 1870s and 1880s on discussing finance, teachers' salaries and reducing waste than on any other subject. When architects and builders submitted tenders for public utilities, the law acknowledged ratepayers' interests and insisted that the contract always went to the lowest bidder. The public purse was not bottomless; the middle class demanded value for money and extended commercial economic commercial principles to every communal project, regardless of its social value.

There was a strong element of old-style paternalism in all this activity. The successful businessman who devoted his spare time and spare money to the moral and physical generation of his city was in spirit the heir of the paternalist squire. Both men listened to their consciences and hoped to make the world a better place. In private, the civic grandee may have considered the aristocracy redundant, but he unconsciously followed its code of noblesse oblige. On a humbler level, the mining engineer, colliery agent, butcher and clergyman elected to the Willington (Co. Durham) school board in 1877 tacitly acknowledged that their status imposed an obligation on them to serve their small community. The compass of this sense of social responsibility was widening: women and working men voted in school board elections and stood as candidates.

The prevailing religious and moral codes of the Victorian middle class made social indifference impossible; the weak and poor were never isolated or left to their own devices. The middle classes refused to abandon the rest of society to the physical and moral consequences of industrialisation. Middle-class men and women put pressure on the state and local government and offered their time and money to create what they regarded as a humane, contented and civilised society. This was not pure altruism. The middle class benefited from pure drinking water, gas-lit, paved streets and libraries. Social reform from above pre-empted unrest (and there was plenty of this), and there was always the inner unease felt by so many of those whom industry and capitalism were enriching.

2

Exclusiveness: Social Arithmetic

In 1911 the Norwood Conservative Association gloomily noted that 'a considerable element of the working class' was settling close to Loughborough Junction station. These potential Liberal or Labour votes were offset by an influx of nearly 1,900 lodgers who had registered as Tories. They were young city clerks accommodated by lower-middle-class families with similar loyalties.[1] Everywhere constituency associations were undertaking what were in essence social surveys to assess local support. Such exercises were a comparative novelty, the result of profound changes in patterns of occupation and social geography.

A social map of early-Victorian Britain would have been uncomplicated. Swathes of solid colour across London and the industrial conurbations of the Midlands, South Wales, the North and Clydeside would have distinguished the largest class, the working. Many workers lived in single-occupation communities devoted to shipbuilding, textiles and mining that survived well into the second half of the the twentieth century. Less dense blocks of the same colour would have marked the rural working class, whose numbers continued to decline. In country and town the predominant pigment would be speckled with dots of another colour representing an unevenly distributed middle class. Nearly everywhere the classes mingled. In

1845 the planners who laid out the Grand Junction Railway's new town at Crewe took it for granted that skilled and unskilled workers would live alongside supervisory and clerical staff, with the latter paying higher rents for roomier houses.[2]

Within sixty years Britain's social geography had been transformed. A map of 1900 would have revealed areas like Norwood where the middle class were in the majority. Fashion, convenience, a transport revolution and the expansion of white-collar jobs had created clusters of urban middle-class housing. The process of relocation started in the 1840s when 'villa mania' captured the imagination of the better off and swept them towards semi-rural suburbs. A gulf opened between the worlds of work and of family. The comfortable suburban villa presided over by a wife wholly dedicated to her husband's welfare was a haven where he relaxed and enjoyed the private pleasures of family life. His new life had other attractions: wholesome air and comparative safety, for proximity to the slums was proximity to hooliganism and street crime.

The new world of the suburbs was revealed to R. S. Surtees's Soapy Sponge when he made an excursion into Middlesex in the early 1850s. From Oxford Circus his horse omnibus trundled along to the Edgware Road, where the city's 'brick and mortar' and terraces gave way to detached houses with gardens and iron railings. Open country soon appeared, punctuated by what Sponge called an 'exclusiveness of villas', each in its own grounds and surrounded by fields. The richer you were, the more you craved privacy in a house that was not overlooked. The word 'villa' suggested the peaceful, rural sanctuary of a well-to-do Roman citizen who had escaped the hurly-burly of the city. Pockets of tranquillity still existed among the villages of Middlesex for the cost of a shilling return fare, but not for long. Brick-and-mortar, terraced London was surging outwards and would soon encompass the isolated villas. Their owners trekked deeper into the countryside and commuted by rail.

Sponge had had a glimpse of the future. The urban exodus gained momentum after 1860, particularly around London. A combination of speculative building ventures, cheap fares and railway expansion created acres of fresh suburbs. They abutted the new tracks that were encircling the city and snaking southwards into Kent and Surrey. 'We have a nice little back garden which runs down to the railway,' proudly declared Mr Pooter, that comical anti-hero of late-Victorian suburbia. His 'nice six-roomed residence' was called 'The Laurels' in Brickfield Terrace, Holloway. It was a terrace house with grand pretensions (steps up to a door that had a small portico and tinted glass panels) and was one of thousands built to house London's swelling army of office workers.

At the turn of the century there were already 22,000 clerks and their families living in Camberwell.[3] They lived well away from the smoke and vapours of industry which the prevailing winds blew eastwards; the East End was always the unhealthiest as well the poorest quarter of London. In 1895, Thomas Ling, a grocer from Streatham, described it as 'typical' suburb of over fifty thousand, most of whom paid yearly rents of between forty and four hundred pounds. It also contained a 'small colony' (an instructive phrase) of working-class men and women who served as gardeners, coachmen and laundresses.[4] Camberwell and Streatham were part of a block of eighteen predominantly middle-class London constituencies formed by the 1885 Redistribution Act. They appear on the maps published in the press after each general election as solidly Conservative: a close and long-lasting correlation between social and political geography had appeared.

Older patterns in which middle and working classes lived in the same vicinity persisted. Just as in the Third World today where high-rise luxury apartments look down on squatter camps, there were localities where slums lay close to the homes and businesses of the rich. Kensington was split between an elegant middle-class south ('Stuccovia') and a seedy working-class north. Slums were universal, even in picturesque cities and towns. Remembering his travels through southern England in the middle years of the century, the showman 'Lord' George Sanger observed that the starkest social contrasts he had seen had been in cathedral cities. There was little sweetness and light in Barchester, rather 'piety and learning' at the top and 'at the bottom . . . dirt, degradation, misery and evil of the most appalling kinds'.[5]

The market ultimately decided how the classes were dispersed. Speculative builders costed their developments carefully, calculating how much potential tenants could afford in rents and fares. For this reason alone, the new suburbs were bound to be exclusive. In 1865 a London factory worker rejected the idea of commuting 'like the clerks in the city' on the ground that his uncles had tried it and found the several miles' walk too exhausting. Trains and buses were too expensive and he found it hard to fathom their timetables.[6]

Twenty years later, when cheap statutory fares had been introduced, he might have thought differently. Even so, the housing market did not favour working-class budgets. A private slum demolition and redevelopment programme of 1865 went awry because weekly rents of four to five shillings a room (with free gas) were beyond a workman's pocket. Reductions to half a crown a week tempted a few tenants, but not enough for investors to secure the 3.5 to 4 per cent return expected from such projects.[7] Inevitably, commerical builders plumped for the profitable middle-class market, and it served them well.

Co-ordinating a social geography of Victorian Britain would have been a tricky business, for the boundaries between and within classes were blurred. Each contained its own hierarchy based upon income, pretensions, self-esteem and the esteem of others. For instance, where did a sometime grocer-turned-stationmaster belong in the triple-tiered society? Was he a 'have' or a 'have-not'? He lived in what his daughter remembered as an 'artisan' estate in London in the early 1900s, but wore a frock coat and silk hat when he went to church on Sundays. His wife joined other church-going matrons to sew clothes for poor children and her husband thought of himself as 'upper working class'.[8] His neighbours may well have thought differently.

Stepping back fifty years, what was the precise position of Joseph Barber, a Luton labourer who lived with wife, ten-year-old daughter and a young female lodger? The women made straw bonnets and the household's weekly earnings were forty shillings.[9] Of course this ménage was vulnerable to trade fluctuations, but in good times its combined income equalled that of some schoolmasters, many innkeepers and a handful of poorer curates. Yet Barber would have raised his hat to a curate, however impoverished, and have treated a threadbare schoolmaster with respect.

The compilers of the ten-yearly census attempted to rationalise class divisions, sometimes eccentrically. In 1851 seventeen categories of employment were specified, but the administrative category brackcted senior civil servants with naval dockyard labourers. A decade later, organ-grinders and buskers were treated as professional men, presumably because they earned their living through the exercise of a specialist, non-manual skill. Lawyers and doctors must have been furious.

Even without the unwelcome intrusion of hurdy-gurdy men, the ranks of the professional middle class were filling up at an unprecedented rate. More people needed more doctors, the railway and construction industries needed legal advice and architects and engineers, and a global trading nation required financial specialists. The expanding agencies of local government also absorbed professional men. The new demands of the private and public sectors were reflected in the statistics (see Table 1).

Table 1: Number of members in the professions, 1861 and 1901

	1861	1901
Clergy	19,200	25,200
Physicians and surgeons	14,500	23,000
Barristers and solicitors	14,400	21,000
Teachers	110,300	230,000
Mining and civil engineers	4,400	11,000
Dentists	1,600	5,300
Accountants	6,300	12,500
Actors	2,200	12,500[10]

Some professional men would have been uncomfortable about the inclusion of teachers. They were certainly the poorest 'profession'; most elementary school teachers earned less than a hundred pounds a year, making them scarcely better off than say gas fitters or scaffolders. More significantly, teachers were not subject to a professional association with statutory power to assess qualifications and dictate standards. Rather, the National Union of Elementary Teachers founded in 1870 and renamed the National Union of Teachers in 1889 was a trade union, solely concerned with terms of employment.

Actors also seemed beyond the orbit of the professions. In 1885 a commentator remarked that anyone could call themselves an actor or an artist. The standing of a professional man rested on the judgment of his equals, not on self-evaluation, and submission to social as well as vocational disciplines. Each profession 'possesses an etiquette – an unwritten code of conventions . . . designed to maintain a high standard of professional conduct, and to preserve them as employment for honourable men'.[11]

Vocational competence and private integrity were the distinguishing qualities striven after by the voluntary professional associations founded during the previous seventy years. The institutes of civil engineers (1818), architects (1834), mechanical engineers (1847), surveyors (1868), chartered accountants (1880) and auditors (1885) defined their professions in terms of tested ability and personal scrupulousness. A non-interventionist state welcomed these bodies and invested them with powers to set public examinations, mark them and issue qualifications. The Law Society, established in 1843, was given control over solicitors' exams in 1877 and the legal authority to discipline and punish the dishonest and negligent. The 1858 Medicine Act delegated the policing of all doctors to the British Medical Association, whose General Medical Council could suspend or expel members for clinical mistakes and moral turpitude. In 1878 a similar law was passed regulating dentists.

New laws embodied old concepts, for they assumed that physicians and lawyers were gentlemen. Insobriety, peculation and sexual misbehaviour were as much grounds for investigation as vocational shortcomings. This dual emphasis on impartially assessed competence and private rectitude added enormously to the prestige of the professions, the self-regard of their members and the respect of the public. This was particularly true for doctors, since the introduction of stringent self-regulation had coincided with the appearance of new methods of diagnosis and treatment that extended their capacity to cure patients.

In numerical terms, the professions were a tiny elite of the middle class and just over 3 per cent of the country's workforce. But, by their own and the rest of society's estimation, they were at the apex of the middle class and within touching distance of the aristocracy: prominent physicians, jurists and architects were regularly ennobled and their children married into the nobility. There was some huffing and puffing by those at the top (a favourite theme of Trollope), but in the end they acquiesced. When the future Prime Minister Lord Salisbury chose to marry the daughter of a judge, his father had to swallow his objections.

By far the largest proportion of the middle class was employed in manufacturing, handling other people's money, transport and the distribution and selling of goods. A contemporary statistician estimated that between 1851 and 1881 the total of people engaged in 'dealing' of one sort or another had risen from 547,000 to 924,000, bankers, accountants and commercial clerks from 44,000 to 225,000 and managers of building operations from 15,200 to 55,500.[12] This trend continued: in 1911 the middle class represented 11 per cent of the working population, over twice what it had been sixty years before.[13]

As it grew, the middle class was reshaped. Its structure was still pyramidal, but the base was being broadened by a legion of clerical workers, teachers, commercial travellers, shop supervisors and small-scale retailers. There were over 600,000 shops in Britain in 1911, one to every fifty-nine of the population. Most were small family newsagents, tobacconists, barbers and licensed grocers serving working-class communities. Their owners were sometimes hardly better off than their customers, but they were already being described as part of the 'lower-middle class'. Like the suburbs to which its members gravitated, this sector of the class was a relatively new social phenomenon, but its importance was quickly appreciated. Lower-middle-class opinion, aspirations and spending power became a matter of serious concern for politicians, newspaper proprietors, journalists and retailers.

As it grew larger, the middle class grew richer. Its share of the nation's wealth is indicated by two comparative analyses made in 1886 and based upon income tax returns (see Tables 2 and 3).[14]

Table 2: Distribution of wealth, 1843

	Approximate nos (million)	Income (£ million)		
		Agriculture	Industry	Total
[A] Taxpayers with over £150 p.a.	1.0	63	165	228
[B] Upper and middle class with under £150 p.a.	1.0	20	62	82
[C] Manual labourers	5.5	42	80	122

Table 3: Distribution of wealth, 1883

	Approximate nos (million)	Income (£ million)		
		Agricultural	Non-agricultural	Total
[A] Upper and middle class with over £150 p.a.	1.4	90	486	576
[B] Upper and middle class with under £150 p.a.	1.5	23	84	107
[C] Manual labourers	11.5	76	445	515

A more detailed anatomy of purely middle-class earnings at the turn of the century shows new trends, in particular the drop in revenues from land and the rise in those receiving fixed salaries in the public and private sectors (see Table 4).[15]

Table 4: Taxable income, 1891–2 and 1904–5 (£ million)*

	Land and property	Revenues from stocks	Business and professional	Salaries
1891–2	170.4	37.0	296.0	35.0
1904–5	162.2	41.0	365.0	51.0

*These figures were based on incomes of over £150 p.a., the tax threshold.

These figures need cautious treatment. Victorian taxpayers assessed themselves and naturally underestimated their incomes, and some employers obligingly reduced salaries to £149 a year, one pound below the threshold. Misleading the Treasury was relatively low on the middle-class scale of venality. A distinguished London solicitor once advised a client to tear up a cheque for two thousand pounds owed to the Inland Revenue on the grounds that it was ignorant of the debt and its discovery would only stir up trouble.[16] Consciences were sometimes pricked, and the personal columns of the press regularly printed acknowledgments of anonymous sums sent to the Revenue by guilty taxpayers.

Individual honesty aside, the sets of figures on page 261 indicate a disparity between earnings and social status. Its nature is revealed by income-tax returns from the Devizes district (a rare survival) covering the middle years of the century. Among the exempt were Thomas Moore (1779–1852), 'gentleman' and biographer of Byron who also called himself 'poet' and whose annual civil list grant was one hundred pounds, the same as the income of a solicitor's clerk. There was also a surgeon who said he never received more than £125 a year, and various teachers and a curate who were getting between fifty and a hundred pounds. By contrast there were beerhouse owners with incomes of forty to ninety pounds, blacksmiths with between forty and eighty, and a pig killer with between £120 and £160. Firmly within the middle class were a bank manager, a solicitor, a civil engineer, a newspaper owner, a brewer, several builders and various retailers with between £150 and £600.

In terms of financial survival, the great division was between those whose fortunes depended upon external commercial circumstances and those who lived off fixed salaries, although these too could be terminated by recession. None the less, clerical civil servants and white-collar employees of the Post Office, railway companies, banks, some financial houses and local authorities had the security of fixed pay and promotion structures that guaranteed progressive rises for the diligent. Businessmen had opportunities to earn more, but even the most enterprising were always hostages to economic forces: a Devizes silk manufacturer's income swung from £169 to £400 within a decade.

Achieving permanent solvency was always a difficult matter, as Mr Micawber knew to his cost. Flexibility and a capacity somehow to absorb fluctuations in income were keys to survival. Both were shown by Nathaniel Knee, who earned eighty-seven pounds a year as a schoolmaster between 1852 and 1855, seventy-three pounds as a clerk between 1855 and 1857 and £140 as a commercial traveller and distributor of baby linen between 1857 and 1860.[17] Changes of occupation and fortune were everyday and not always happy events for a large section of the middle class. At all levels, individuals were undone by such uncontrollable and unforeseen circumstances as recessions, sickness, injury or dismissal. When wages were cut or factory hands laid off, local shopkeepers soon felt the pinch. The middle class was not immune from redundancies. Over-recruitment by Scottish banks forced many clerks to emigrate to Canada, and an overestimate by training colleges of the jobs available led to a surplus of element-ary school teachers in 1910 and 1911.[18]

Moreover, as readers of Trollope would have known, there were men destined to succumb to some destructive flaw in their char-acter. Overspending did for Edwin James, a solicitor's son, starry QC (he was crown counsel in the Palmer case) and MP for Marylebone. Fittingly for a pillar of London's professional middle class, he had rooms in Pall Mall, close to his club, Brooks's. His pretensions outran his income and in 1861 he was forced to flee with debts of a hundred thousand pounds. He qualified for the American bar in New York, but on returning to England in 1872 discovered that his past delinquencies had permanently excluded him from his profession.

Knee and James inhabited opposite poles of the middle class, but they shared a common dependence on market forces. If the former could not sell enough of his stock, or if James's fees failed to keep pace with his outlays, they were in trouble. Thrift offered some hope in lean times, but the money markets were capricious and sometimes merciless. The railway stock bubbles of 1835 and 1845–6 (precursors of the similar dot-com collapse of 1998) were signal reminders to middle-class investors of what could go wrong. The year 1866 provided further warnings with the successive collapses of the financial house of Overend and Gurney with liabilities of £10 million, of the railway contractors Peto and Betts with £4 million and of the English Joint Stock Bank with £800,000. The last had been an amalgamation of smaller banks in south-eastern England and among its Bournemouth depositors were a number of speculative builders.[19] At a stroke their operations were in jeopardy and they and their sub-contractors faced losses, possibly bankruptcy.

Set a generation before, Mrs Gaskell's novel *Cranford* (1863) depicts what must have been one of thousands of individual tragedies that followed the collapse of banks. Miss Matilda ('Matty') Jenkyns, a generous-hearted lady with shares in the 'Town and County Bank', becomes penniless overnight, and, as she remarks, so did possessors of the bank's now worthless notes. Genteel poverty has been replaced by the threat of utter indigence, but, supported by friends, she can make a living by selling tea. It could have been worse: 'The small dining parlour was to be converted into a shop, without any of its degrading characteristics . . .' In sharp contrast to today, the state stood aloof from such calamities. The Bank of England firmly refused to shore up Overend and Gurney, arguing that if it did, it would be driven to bail out other mismanaged or unlucky banks. Depositors and investors like Matty Jenkyns had to take care of their own affairs; saving money was risky even in an age that prized thrift.

The middle-class taxpayers of Devizes spent more on food than their neighbours and consequently were bigger and healthier. In 1864, when the president of the British Medical Association spoke of the 'well-fed middle and higher classes and the moderately-fed or ill-fed labouring classes', he was repeating a well-known fact of life. It was not absolute, for, as he pointed out, there were regional variations. The badly paid West Country labourer on average ate a pound of meat a week, the better off Yorkshire textile worker seven pounds, but their wives and children had far less on the universal principle of necessity, which insisted that the breadwinner needed the most nourishment.[20]

What people ate and how regularly dictated their state of health and life expectancy. In the mid-1880s the overall death rate among the professional class was twenty-two per thousand, seventy-one among artisans. Infant mortality figures emphasised this link between diet and survival: 59 in a thousand children died before their fifth birthday in middle-class families, 110 in the working class. The middle class lived longer; 158 in a thousand of the professional class passed sixty, and 63 in the working class. Social geography played its part in the calculus of survival; at the turn of the century infant deaths in Glasgow were eight per thousand in middle-class Kelvinside, thirty three per thousand in the working-class tenements of Cowcaddens.[21]

Such statistics confirmed the everyday experience of life. Among the middle class and the medical profession in particular such statistics were a source of apprehension and a spur for action. There was some consolation in the fact that conditions were getting better, although there was disagreement over the scope and pace of improvement. Professor Leone Levi, a commercial lawyer and statistician, spoke for the optimists in 1886 when he reviewed fifty years of progress. 'The labouring classes were much more elevated in character, intellectually, socially and politically,' he declared, and were healthier and stronger than ever.[22] Capitalism was at last working for the benefit of all, contrary to what had been expected in the bleak days of the 'Hungry' 1840s.

Yet physical inequalities persisted, and some believed they were widening. During 1899 army doctors sent away between a quarter and a third of recruits because of various infirmities. Nearly all the unfit were between seventeen and twenty-five, and an occupational analysis of those turned down revealed that 36 per cent of artisans and servants were unfit, 34 per cent of 'shopmen and clerks', 33 per cent of labourers, 28 per cent of students and 'professionals' and 21 per cent of men engaged in heavy manual work. Forty clinical reasons for rejection were specified: the commonest were falling below the required height, chest measurement and weight (11 per cent), defective vision (4 per cent) and tooth loss or decay (2.5 per cent).[23] A combination of an inadequate diet and lack of medical attention was weakening the poor.

Dietary deficiencies and lingering ailments were rooted in child-hood. A survey undertaken in Edinburgh in the early 1900s contrasted children from Bruntsfield, where nine-tenths of families lived in houses with three or more rooms, with Canongate, where the proportion was under a quarter. The better-nourished middle- and upper-working-class boys and girls from Bruntsfield were ruddier-cheeked, taller and stouter than their contemporaries from Canongate, where the school doctors described the population as 'thriftless and inefficient'. At fifteen a lad from Bruntsfield was up to five pounds heavier than one from Canongate, and a girl twelve.[24]

What made such disparities disturbing was that they were being uncovered after sixty years of cheap food and minimal inflation. Free trade appeared to have fulfilled the dreams of its champions. Industrial Britain was able to feed itself and incidentally the hundreds of thousands of horses that were the basis of its transport systems. Not only did its exports earn the wherewithal to pay for its food, agricultural and technical developments were adding to its variety and making it more plentiful. During the last quarter of the century steamships brought cargoes of grain from the North American prairies and frozen and canned meat from Australia, New Zealand and Argentina. Tinned and processed food appeared on grocers' shelves and was affordable even for the poorest; in the 1890s a can of sardines cost tuppence ha'penny.

Food purchases made up the largest single item in the budgets of each class. Comparative and hypothetical analyses made in 1901 show that a married civil servant with two servants and a salary of

£180 a year paid about £160 a year for feeding his household and a further £20 for drinks, including fifty-four bottles of whisky (£8 2s) and 108 of claret (£6 15s). A lower-middle-class cashier to a firm of London solicitors with £160 a year, a wife and two children spent £47 9s on food a year and a skilled workman, married with three children earning about £90, spent £32 12s 6d.[25] Neither bought much drink; had they done so, they would have quickly slipped into debt.

The cashier and the workmen were lucky in that they had thrifty wives who hunted for bargains. The wife of the former saved money by buying groceries from larger stores for cash, and her husband purchased New Zealand mutton cheaply at the Leadenhall market before he caught his train home. His wife could make an eight-pound leg (four shillings) last three days: on the first it was roast with vegetables, on the second cold with salad and on the third its remnants were served up as a hash. The workman's wife also shopped prudently and her 'docile' husband was happy to carry the parcels of food home if the search for savings involved a long walk. By using the cash-only, open-air London street markets where prices were a half to a third less than in shops, she secured mutton and beef for between threepence and sixpence a pound depending on cut, fish for the same price and imported tomatoes for tuppence a pound. Like her lower-middle-class counterpart, she made a joint last for three days.

The arithmetic of shopping was unfavourable to the feckless and poorest who made day-to-day purchases on 'tick', often in the tiniest possible quantities. Those who bought foodstuffs by the halfpenny's or farthing's worth ended up paying far more than those who bought in bulk. Moreover, if complaints by doctors were to be believed, the cheapest comestibles were often the least nutritious. At the turn of the century, medical journals were full of complaints about the working-class preference for fine white bread and rejection of grainier, wholemeal loaves. There were also well-founded alarms about the microbes lurking in badly processed or potted foods.

Even the most prudent family always had to be careful. The annual budget for the lower-middle-class household allowed for a margin of just over six pounds to meet such emergencies as medical treatment, and that for the working-class, three pounds. Friendly societies and mutually supportive benevolent clubs such as the Freemasons and, for the lower-middle class, the Buffaloes, Ancient Druids, Odd Fellows and Foresters offered some immediate relief in the event of the sickness or the sudden death of a breadwinner. None the less, many middle and even more working-class families lived on tight budgets with a disturbingly narrow margin between survival and insolvency. This was why moralists constantly preached the virtues of thrift and temperance; they were as good for the body as for the soul. Yet even in the most abstemious and carefully managed households, fluctuations in the cost of living could mean disaster, which explains why food prices were a source of such bitter political contention.

3

A Good Time Coming: Class Politics, 1832–1885

Polling day in Barchester was rumbustious fun. Bands played and crowds of people paraded, sporting ribbons in the candidates' colours: red for Sir Roger Scatcherd the Liberal and yellow for Mr Moffat the Tory. Both were middle-class, the former a stonemason-turned-railway-contractor and the latter the son of a rich London tailor. Each had promised electoral 'purity', but their agents knew what the locals expected and had surreptitiously instructed publicans to have plenty of free beer in hand for the hoi polloi and brandy and rum for their betters, whose votes would decide the contest. Speech-making was confined to personal polemic, although Scatcherd's supporters flourished banners with the free-trade slogan 'Peace abroad and a big loaf at home'. Not far away in his castle, Lord Courcy discreetly pulled strings for his candidate, just as his ancestors had done for centuries. And why not? Moffat was a reliable fellow and about to marry Courcy's niece. As for his background, he was rich and the aristocracy had to make personal accommodations with the middle class, just as it had made a political one in 1832.[1]

Reading Trollope's account of a provincial election in the early 1850s it is easy to forget that the Reform Act had ever been passed. Fiction mirrored reality. A contemporary commentator lamented the prevalence of corruption and a mass of middle-class electors who treated the vote as a disposable asset that could be sold to the highest bidder, irrespective of his principles. Shopkeepers and ten-pound householders of the 'lower class' were the easiest to bribe.[2] They were also vulnerable to working-class intimidation. In that hotbed of volatile radicalism Oldham, workers picketed the premises of shop-keepers with Whig or Tory sympathies and warned them that they would lose custom if the poll books revealed they had voted for either party. Prudent retailers displayed placards advertising their backing for the working man's candidates.[3] The secret ballot of 1870 put an end to such arm twisting, although as late as 1886 there were tales of Tory landlords evicting farm labourers suspected of having voted Liberal.[4]

The disenfranchised expressed their feelings with fists, cudgels and brickbats. Violence was deeply embedded in early-Victorian polit-ical culture and would remain there for sixty years. In 1835 elec-tion disturbances at Wolverhampton left one cavalry charger dead and five rioters wounded by carbine fire. Meanwhile at Selkirk and Jedburgh mobs bombarded candidates with icy snowballs and stones and smashed windows before hurriedly summoned dragoons arrived.[5] Election riots occurred in Nottingham in 1865, 1870, 1874 and 1885, when at least 150 demonstrators were injured in battles with the police, and there was one in Cardiff in 1886.[6] Lesser forms of violence persisted: in 1892 London Unionists complained that the Liberals were hiring 'roughs' from the 'disenfranchised classes' to disrupt meetings and frighten away the 'decent classes'.[7]

Dismissive and provocative, the language of class antipathy and loathing was also part of political culture. Undercurrents of social resentment and envy were a part of life, much to the regret of politicians who saw one of their prime responsibilities as fostering a spirit of mutual co-operation and national unity. These were difficult to sustain during economic crises, when there were blatant inequalities of sacrifice and discomfort; hard times were always harder for employees than for employers. Redundancies and wage cuts were often the beginning of a journey that ended with the calculated humiliations and privations of the Poor Law system. Passions were not calmed by appeals from above to show forbearance in the hope of better times ahead.

Working-class patience was frequently stretched to breaking point in the 1830s and 1840s, a period of alternate booms and slumps. Not only the working man faced a precarious future. Industrialists feared that the country's economic potential was being stifled by the landowning aristocracy which was using what was left of its power to protect agriculture. Expensive food forced up wages and production costs. Each group reacted aggressively to safeguard its livelihoods and the upshot was intermittent, bare-knuckle social conflict.

Three political figures personified an extremism rooted in panic: the Tory MP for Lincoln, Colonel Charles de Waldo Laet Sibthorp, the Liberal member for Birmingham, John Bright, and Feargus O'Connor, who sat for Nottingham. Sibthorp was at odds with his age, devoting much of his vast reserves of spleen to denunciations of the railways and the commercial middle class. One had eradicated the rural arcadia he loved and the other was chipping away at the authority and rights of men like himself, a country squire and Anglican. Bright wanted to topple Sibthorp and all his kind. God had instructed him to chastise the aristocracy, overthrow the Church of England and deliver the nation into the capable hands of middle-class businessmen. In the spring of 1848 he was challenging the game laws and Sibthorp arose to defend the rights of the aristocracy on their own land. No doubt waving his famous quizzing glass, he asked what did a Quaker textile manufacturer know about a gentleman's sport? Nothing, for he could not distinguish between 'a pointer and a pig'.[8] Members were delighted, as they usually were whenever Sibthorp spoke, although few took him seriously. The new satirical magazine *Punch* adored him as an unwitting source of copy.

A month after his clash with Bright, the colonel shifted his sights to a tribune of the working classes, Feargus O'Connor, the Chartist firebrand who advocated revolution. The Chartists had just presented a petition to Parliament demanding one man one vote with five million mostly bogus signatures, including Sibthorp's. It had been backed by a mass rally at Kennington, and mayhem was anticipated.

Londoners prepared for street fighting, and Sibthorp, a Peninsular veteran, smelt blood. He was disappointed when the demonstration fizzled out. In the Commons lobby he overheard O'Connor express his relief that the Chartists had not crossed the Thames. Sibthorp accosted him and growled that he was sorry there had not been a fight, for 'you would have got the damnedest hiding mortal men ever received'.[9]

Sibthorp, Bright and O'Connor were intemperate spokesmen for their classes, taking their cues from the transient circumstances of their times. They distorted and exaggerated social, political and economic tensions to the point where it seemed that the nation was split into three hostile and irreconcilable classes. This message was repeated in Disraeli's *Sybil* (1845) and Mrs Gaskell's *Mary Barton* (1848), novels set in a polarised industrial north. It represented what Disraeli famously described as the 'two nations', the rich and the poor, 'between whom there is no intercourse and no sympathy; who are as ignorant of each other's habits, thoughts, and feelings as if they were dwellers in different zones, or inhabitants of different planets'. Collision seems unavoidable and occurs in the melodramatic climax of *Sybil* when some of the poor ('a grimy crew') storm a castle, loot its wine cellars, set it alight and are driven off in the nick of time by the local yeomanry.

Here was a middle-class nightmare: a plundering mob of incendiarists inflamed by socialism and stolen alcohol. For some of Disraeli's readers the destruction of Mowbray castle was credible, particularly in the light of newspaper reports of the Chartist insurrection at Newport in Monmouthshire in 1839 and the violent, extended strikes in the North-West during the autumn of 1842. It must have been unnerving for respectable travellers to watch battalions of infantry and batteries of cannon arriving at Euston to entrain for Manchester, the more so since working-class onlookers booed and jeered the defenders of order and property.

Both seemed imperilled. In 1840 the textile workers of Oldham paid a penny each to hear a lecture on 'The Impending Ruin of the Middle Class' delivered by a socialist fresh from Paris.[10] Two years later, a Chartist newspaper gleefully reported that the 'middle classes and shopkeepers' of Wolverhampton were in a 'feverish excite-ment' as policemen, dragoons and cannon poured into their town to protect them from striking miners. Their fears soon evaporated: some colliers were overawed by this show of strength and willpower, broke ranks and 'truckled' to the 'respectables', much to the disgust of militants.[11] It was the same whenever Chartists went on the rampage; the government always had sufficient forces to cope with what were always localised outbreaks of violence.

Such incidents dismayed many Chartists as much as they scared the prosperous. The overall aim of Chartism was to remake the consti-tution in a way that would give the working class a deciding voice in government. Once the Commons' benches were filled with working men it would be possible to overturn the Poor Law and provide employment and economic security for all. The trouble was that the Chartists never agreed how this might be accomplished. Those of O'Connor's mind imagined that they could bludgeon their adver-saries into submission, while others believed that dignified demon-strations and appeals to reason and fair play would persuade their rulers that working men had a right to the vote and were fit to use it wisely.

There was little chance of this so long as Chartism was associ-ated with tumults and revolutionary rhetoric. What, for instance, would a well-to-do sympathiser have made of the impending apoca-lypse predicted by one Chartist leader soon after the Kennington fiasco in 1848? 'The aristocracy of money and land are now engaged in their last struggle against the middle and working classes; the capitalist and land-owner against the shop-keeper, farmer and working man.' The time had come for the lower-middle class to recognise where their true interests lay and defect to the working class as the Parisian bourgeois had recently done.[12] This was whistling in the wind: six weeks before, London shopkeepers had joined the rest of the middle class and flocked to police stations to enlist as special constables and defend the city against the Chartist mob. As for the Parisian middle class, it would soon be cheering as troops smashed their way through the barricades. Within a few years Chartism had withered; its newspapers had nothing to offer the working class but advice on emigration. Those who stayed behind redirected their passion and energies into the Co-operative movement and trade unionism.

Chartism was in large part a desperate reaction to what contemporaries called 'hard times' when 'trade' was 'slack', in other words when productive capacity exceeded demand. The trade cycle of alternate boom and recession could be broken, argued supporters of free trade, if there was an abundance of imported, cheap food. Labour costs would stabilise and British products would become more competitive, earning more than enough abroad to pay for imported food. This formula for national growth was presented by the Anti-Corn Law League, founded in 1839. It was directed by Bright and Richard Cobden, a calico printer who was happiest tending his farm in Sussex.

Getting rid of the Corn Laws was more than economic commonsense. For Cobden, Bright and many of their adherents this legislation symbolised the continued power of the aristocracy and its repeal would truly mark the ascendancy of the middle class. The League's stance and language were therefore combative. Tory protectionists and the nobility in general were caricatured as pantomime villains, cunning, mercenary and bent on blocking the path to national prosperity. 'Lords and great proprietors of the soil' were locked in a life-or-death struggle with the 'commercial and industrial classes', the League declared in 1845.[13] It was funded by industrialists and made converts among professional men, retailers, wholesalers who imagined, rightly as it turned out, that their fortunes would be improved by free trade. The League lobbied MPs and the press, issued pamphlets and sent propagandists across the country. They were not welcomed in the countryside, but attempts were made to enlist farmers by promises to end the game laws.

Working men were lured by promises of a golden age just around the corner. Its blessings were outlined in one of the League's many songs:

> There's a good time coming, boys,
> A good time coming;
> Throughout the world Free Trade shall be

> The Universal policy.
> In the good time coming!
> Every land shall be at peace
> And commerce flourish stronger . . .[14]

These were weasel words, claimed O'Connor. He warned working men not to be deceived by the League's propaganda. 'High Wages, Cheap Bread and Plenty to Do' were catchphrases spun by the bosses 'to subjugate labour to the caprice of capital'. Bad times were ahead when the workman would have no choice but to 'starve or make a stipulated amount of profit for his master'.[15]

In 1846 Sir Robert Peel's government repealed the Corn Laws, dividing the Tory Party in the process. 'Rats!' Sibthorp shouted at the apostates, including Gladstone, who was on the first stage of his political odyssey towards radical Liberalism. The League had won, or so it imagined. In fact what had happened was a re-enactment of 1832, with the landowners bowing to middle-class opinion rather than hazarding a prolonged trial of strength that might end with the loss of what remained of their influence. It survived undamaged, as both Bright and Cobden subsequently recognised. The aristocracy remained a force to be reckoned with in every area of national life, and for the next thirty years Bright continued to denounce it. Surveying the political landscape in 1863, Frederick Harrison, a young, radical barrister, wrote about 'our aristocratic rulers'.[16] To the despair of men of his convictions, the middle-class electorate was on the whole satisfied with this dispensation of power.

A year after the Corn Laws had been revoked, the Ten Hours Act was passed. Cobden and Bright were furious at an act of sacrilege against the creed of laissez-faire. Cobden sniffily remarked that workers who found shopfloor conditions uncongenial should emigrate. Karl Marx wryly observed that restrictions on working hours were the aristocracy's revenge on the manufacturers for the repeal of the Corn Laws. It was an instance of tit-for-tat that seemed to support his embryonic theories of predestined class antagonism and its outcome. The landowning aristocracy would surrender ground to the middle class which, as it grew richer, would edge into power.

In turn, it would confront the working class or proletariat in a conflict that would end with the disintegration of capitalism, sundered by its own irremovable contradictions. The working class would take power and establish a just system that would provide perpetual prosperity and contentment. This prognosis assumed that events in Britain during the 1840s would be repeated in other developing industrial societies. The decade had been an aberration in British history, but what Marx deduced from it cast a long shadow across the modern world which only faded in the closing years of the twentieth century with the implosion of Europe's Communist states.

Like Disraeli and Mrs Gaskell, Marx had misinterpreted the issues and events of the 1840s. Each had imagined a crudely divided society engaged in a three-cornered fight for survival and supremacy. It was a simplified view from which stereotypes inevitably emerged that took on a historical life of their own. The heartless manufacturer who thought only in terms of profit and loss and ruthlessly exploited his underpaid and underfed hands in a 'satanic' mill has become embedded in folk consciousness. He did exist, but there were also plenty of paternalist employers who provided such amenities as baths and schools for their operatives.

At this period most industrial enterprises were small-scale, with an average of between ten and twenty employees. Bosses were not distant Olympian figures. George Holyoake recalled the three co-owners of the Birmingham foundry where he worked in the 1830s. There was Samuel Smith, a Unitarian and 'a placid gentleman' who spoke kindly to his men and slipped them advances whenever trade was slack and their wages fell. Timothy Hawkes, a Methodist, was also generous-hearted and paid daily visits to the sickbed of one of the hands who had been fatally injured in a workshop accident, often bringing gifts. By contrast, William Hawkes was overbearing, miserly and addressed staff harshly.[17] As makers of parts for steam engines (for which there was a growing export market) they would have been in favour of free trade and, as humane Christians, the former two would have abhorred the cruelties practised in some workhouses and supported popular demands for their investigation and elimination. This pair might also have been sympathetic to schemes for the moral and physical improvement of the working class, perhaps even giving them the vote.

Just as middle-class stereotypes dissolve under close inspection, so do working-class. The skilled mechanics who worked alongside Holyoake were paid considerably more than unskilled labourers. Foremen, engineers and craftsmen employed in coal mines received between twenty and thirty shillings a week, twice the wages of labourers and three times those of women and children. In Lancashire in 1860 skilled foundrymen and pattern makers were earning up to thirty-four shillings a week, colliers between eighteen and twenty-five, and unskilled men between fourteen and eighteen. Those at the lower end of the scale had to depend on income from wives and children to reach the thirty shillings a week that was judged sufficient to maintain a couple with three children.[18] Discrepancies in income split the working as they did the middle class. In proportional terms the gulf between the engine driver and the crossing sweeper was as great as that between a QC and a provincial solicitor's clerk.

The working class was not the homogeneous 'poor' of Disraeli's two nations nor one tightly packed layer of a triple tiered society. It had its own hierarchy with ranks as closely defined as those within the middle class. There were differences of outlook, ambition, temperament, patterns of consumption and moral codes. Consider Catherine Baxter, a widow of Haddington in Lothian who was prosecuted in 1858 for banging on the door of a public house, throwing stones at it, swearing in the street and causing a fracas in a tobacconist's. The court heard that she had five previous convictions for similar offences committed during the previous nine years.[19] She was one of Disraeli's 'poor' and Marx's working class. So too was George Rix, a trade union leader who in 1880 urged his members to 'Unite for mutual intercourse, instruction and information, knowledge is power. Leave off smoking and tippling and get to reading, thinking and asking.'[20]

Perhaps the most accurate portrayal of Victorian society was the cartoonist George Cruikshank's representation of Britain as a massive conical beehive.[21] Drawn in 1840, it was an image of mutual co-operation and support: on every level men and women were working with brains and hands in pursuit of a common prosperity. It is revealing, not only of the validity of this icon but of the mentality of its members, that in the 1850s London trade unionists chose the *Beehive* as the title for their journal.

The intermittent commotions and rant of class politics of the 1840s ended with the decade. Charles Kingsley sighed with relief and, as an Anglican parson who sympathised with the working class, was pleased to discover a refreshing new spirit abroad. In the 1858 preface to *Alton Locke* he noticed a return to the old ideal of moral responsibility among young men of the middle and upper classes. They showed 'humanity' towards their inferiors, were liberal and courteous and above all mixed freely among working men with whom they shared 'the common ground of manhood'. If this mood prevailed, 'the last remnants of class prejudices and class grudges' would vanish within a generation.

That manly Whig grandee Lord Palmerston concurred. There was now harmony throughout the country, he told the Commons in 1850. 'Every class in society accepts with cheerfulness a lot which Providence has assigned to it and simultaneously each individual strives to improve himself . . . by preserving good conduct and by steady and energetic execution of the moral and intellectual faculties with which his creator had endowed him.' Here was Cruikshank's beehive throbbing with fruitful activity.

Prosperity fostered this purposefulness. From 1850 until the mid-1870s Britain enjoyed a boom. It opened with a fanfare of self-congratulation, the Great Exhibition of 1851. The world was invited to admire the genius of Britain's industry, witness the benefits of free trade and learn what could be accomplished by a free people guided by an elected government. The crowds in the Crystal Palace were evidence of the new social accord. 'Whoever thought of meeting you here?' ran the caption of a *Punch* cartoon which showed a group of craftsmen and labourers with their families encountering an elderly gentleman in court dress with his elegant daughters and granddaughters. One tiny lad in a smock is offering a posy to one of the girls, while a smartly dressed and distinctively bourgeois Mr Punch beams down from a gallery.

The workmen had taken advantage of one of the cheap day-return fares offered by the railway companies to visitors to the Exhibition on those days when the admission charge was cut from a pound to a shilling. These days were chosen by Queen Victoria for her visits to the Crystal Palace so that she could mingle with her subjects when the 'extremes in the order of society . . . meet in the intellectual ground that has been opened to all'.[22] On a smaller but equally significant scale, the Banbury flower show of 1856 was described by the local paper as 'One of those happy occasions when rich and poor mingle freely together and when young and drink deep the draughts of delight from a common spring.'[23]

In 1860 another public entertainment aroused different emotions. Thousands of the 'worst ruffians' in London joined their betters on a railway excursion into Hampshire to watch the Sayers–Heenan prize fight. The high-minded protested and the Prime Minister Lord Palmerston answered them with a spirited defence of 'an exhibition of manly courage, characteristic of this country'. His countrymen ought to have felt pride, for the French press had described the match as a signal display of the 'national character for . . . indomitable perseverance'.[24] It was typical Palmerstonian stuff, and it pleased the voters. There was already a vigorous streak of belligerent patriotism in the middle class and it had expressed itself vehemently during the Crimean War and the suppression of the Indian Mutiny. Within a generation it would crystallise into the jingoism that infected all classes whenever British armies were in action, or when imperial interests appeared threatened.

The pacifist Bright had been saddened to hear that his fellow Mancunians had cheered when news of the death of Czar Nicholas I was announced in the theatres in 1855. For Bright this applause was shameful in a Christian country, even though the majority of his fellow believers were convinced that Britain's arms in Russia and India had God's blessing. In a nation that believed it was fulfilling divine will, it was inevitable that God was at the heart of political life.

Scripture was invoked to justify policy, parties made alliances with various denominations and clergymen regularly intervened in political debates. Some may have gone further: the 1882 Corrupt Practices Act treated spiritual inducements to electors as a form of bribery.

Individual politicians prayed for divine guidance and were not embarrassed to say so. Only a 'signal favour . . . of the great Supreme' had delivered Bright from a three-year enervating sickness, he informed a Birmingham audience in 1858. A Congregationalist minister who heard him believed that he was briefly in 'the presence of the Eternal'. Bright then revealed what God had spared him for and plunged into a denunciation of aristocratic 'privileges', singling out Anglican bishops for special vituperation.[25] Privilege based upon inherited status, custom or both was the common enemy of nonconformists and the Liberal Party. History made them natural partners, for in the past each had fought against a self-perpetuating political and religious establishment. 'Is it not a singular thing', Joseph Chamberlain reminded the National Liberal Club in 1886, 'that of all the great movements that had abated the claims of privilege or destroyed the power of tyrants, which have freed the nation or classes from servitude or oppression or raised the condition of the great mass of people there is scarcely one that has owed anything . . . to the great ecclesiastical organisation which lays claim to national authority and support?.'[26]

Denominational antipathy spawned sectarian bigotry. Like religious affiliations it crossed social boundaries and permeated politics at every level. When he campaigned as a Liberal in Beverley in 1868, Trollope was told that he would be unwelcome in either of the town's two Anglican churches. In 1877 the nonconformist majority on the Stoke-on-Trent school board refused to appoint a bright girl as a pupil-teacher because she was a Catholic. Methodists on a Sheffield school board rejected another girl for a similar post in 1881 on the ground that she was the daughter of a publican. Justifying the decision, Alderman Clegg alleged that all public houses were 'undesirable' places.[27]

The Liberal Party needed middle-class nonconformists like Clegg. For twenty years the party had offered a haven for all dissenters and the causes they cherished, notably temperance, the disestablishment of the Anglican churches in England, Wales and Ireland and the confiscation of some of their assets. This was the objective of the Liberation Society, which embraced Wesleyans, Baptists and Congregationalists, was underwritten by a handful of rich industrialists and helped the Liberals at elections. In 1872 Chamberlain told his Birmingham constituents that 'For years we have served the Liberal party; we have been hewers of wood and drawers of water.'[28] These exertions were rewarded: the Irish Church was disestablished; the Anglican grip on Oxford and Cambridge was finally removed; and temperance legislation introduced. The Liberals also satisfied middle-class meritocrats (and opened paths upwards for their sons) by replacing backstairs influence with examinations for most civil service posts and abolishing the purchase of army commissions.

Self-preservation kept the Church of England firmly within the Conservative orbit. Strongest in the countryside, the Anglican church still enjoyed immense social prestige which attracted socially ambitious members of the middle class who found the egalitarianism of the chapel uncongenial. The Evangelical wing of the church continued to be the spiritual heirs of Wilberforce. Church of England Evangelicals were as vigorous as ever, claimed the Reverend A. W. Thorold, a future bishop of Winchester, in 1868 and they were heavily engaged in campaigns 'against brutish ignorance, against selfish luxury, against vice and evil of all kinds [and] against rationalistic and Romish aggression'.

At the same time Anglicanism was fending off nonconformist sallies. After the Tory victory in the June 1886 election, the Church Defence Institution announced with relief that it had been a reverse for nonconformists who had intended to demolish 'a structure of venerable antiquity' that was vital for 'cementing the framework of English society' and 'promoting the existence of kindly feelings between all classes'.[29] The Anglican–Conservative entente complemented the latter's new image as the party that respected the wisdom of the past and promoted national unity. These ideals would make the Tories the party of 'one nation' which appealed to voters of all backgrounds who wanted stability and the preservation of the social fabric.

Toryism had had a rough passage. Later characterised by Disraeli as a 'heartless oligarchy', it had wandered forlornly in the political wilderness; the Conservative general election victory in 1874 was its first for thirty-two years. The party survived because it had kept a core of middle-class voters. They voted Tory because doing so ran in the family or because of attachment to the church, other loyalties (grammar schoolboys in Rochdale traditionally backed the party) or deference. Conservatism was always a magnet for those ambitious middle-class men who set great store by social contacts with the rural magnates who dominated the party. It attracted the railway contractors Robert Stephenson and Thomas Brassey, and Sir William Armstrong (1810–1900), a Newcastle grammar schoolboy, engineer and founder of the Elswick Ordnance Company which manufactured artillery. Moreover, as Disraeli recognised, there was a vein of pacificism running through Liberalism which went against the grain of large sections of the middle classes who were proud of Britain and keen for it to count for something in the world.

Self-interest drove nearly everyone connected with the drink trade into the arms of the Tories, their only defence against the Liberal–nonconformist temperance lobby. The chapel became a Liberal citadel, the pub a Tory. It was an invaluable alliance, for in many urban constituencies publicans, wine merchants, brewers, coopers, maltsters and hop dealers made up between 10 and 15 per cent of voters, enough to tip the balance in a close contest.

In 1867 and 1885 the political significance of the public house increased immeasurably with the extension of the franchise to nearly all the urban and rural working class. The electorate had been increasing steadily since 1832 as rising prosperity propelled more and more householders over the ten-pound threshold, many of them skilled artisans. The question was whether to lower the property hurdle and admit the entire upper and eventually the middle and some of the lower echelons of the working classes.

On the whole, and guided by Lord John Russell, a patrician Whig, and Gladstone, who considered himself middle-class in spite of his landed estate, the Liberals favoured an enlarged franchise. There were misgivings across the political landscape in which old fears were revived of confiscatory legislation being introduced by a Parliament largely chosen by working men. 'An indiscriminate enfranchisement' would sweep aside the collective influence (and wisdom) of 'all the manufacturers, merchants, tradesmen, farmers and landowners', argued the *Saturday Review* in 1873. Workingmen would be seduced by 'demagogues and jobbers' and property and capitalism be imperilled.[30] Others contended that the working classes had amply proved their capacity for sound judgment. A Leeds councillor suggested in 1866 that the middle class had nothing whatsoever to fear from 'the men who formed their cooperative societies and mechanics institutions, [and] the two-hundred-and-fifty to three-hundred-thousand men who are training youths in our Sunday Schools'.[31] However sober and devout such creatures were, giving them the vote made many Liberals nervous. One described it as 'a leap in the dark' – which it was, but not in the way that he had imagined, for Gladstone had considerably underestimated the numbers who would be enfranchised.

The new voters behaved responsibly. During the 1884 debate on the franchise, a Liberal MP praised the 'rare discretion' of the working-class electors. Rather than 'deluging this House with mechanics and working men' they had elected representatives from a class 'many points above them'. So long as that class, the middle, could keep the confidence of the working, matters would go well for the country, argued another speaker.[32] Forty years before, only the most sanguine optimist would have imagined that progress towards democracy would have been such a trouble-free journey. Few would have dared to prophesy that, superficially at least, the middle class would be one of its beneficiaries. The other was the reinvented Tory Party, a prediction that would have provoked ridicule in the 1840s.

4

Private Property Is Public Robbery: New Politics and Old Tensions, 1886–1914

Modern politics were a phenomenon of the late-Victorian age. They had evolved rapidly, were the offspring of democracy and technology and their development coincided with the quickening tempo of change in every area of human activity. Daily life was becoming more complex, hectic and fraught, at least for those who could remember gentler rhythms. In 1910 the seventy-nine-year-old Frederick Harrison confessed to being overwhelmed by modernity:

> Railways, motors, photographs, telegraph, telephone. Electric trams, taxi-cabs, bicycles, perambulators, lucifers [matches], typing machines, cheap postage, – all bring in their worries and confusions. We are whirled about, and hooted around and rung up as if we were all parcels, booking clerks, or office boys.[1]

Oddly for a political journalist, Harrison ignored the new, clamorous mass-circulation press. It was perhaps the most important novelty in the now familiar paraphernalia of modern political life. Steam printing presses, the telegraph and railways had injected a new pace and immediacy into politics. Newspapers gave politicians the means to appeal directly to the entire country, transforming the provincial public meeting into a national platform. In 1880 speeches delivered by Gladstone to audiences in Midlothian were reported and relayed to the rest of the country the next morning. Party leaders treated the nation as their constituency, toured the provinces and made speeches, often to audiences of thousands. Disraeli, Gladstone, Chamberlain, Lord Salisbury and later Lloyd George and Churchill were more familiar figures than say the two Pitts or Sir Robert Peel.

The communications revolution coincided with rising levels of literacy. In 1899 some 97 per cent of the predominantly working- and lower-middle-class recruits to the army could read and write, 1 per cent could only read and 2 per cent were illiterate. Mass literacy meant an ever-expanding market for newspapers and magazines: the number of titles increased from 1,583 to nearly 5,000 between 1861 and 1900.[2] Circulation figures soared: in 1870 the daily print run for *The Times* was 63,000, a third of that of its cheaper rival in the middle-class market, the *Daily Telegraph.* A portent of the future was the half-million daily sales of *Reynolds Weekly*, which cost a penny.[3]

Growth was most dramatic at the turn of the century, with the appearance of mass-circulation dailies aimed at the lower-middle and working classes. They proved an insatiable market. In the first decade of the twentieth century, the *Daily Mail* had 900,000 readers, the *Daily Express* 425,000, the *Daily Chronicle* 400,000 and the *Daily News* 320,000. By contrast, the combined readership of *The Times, Telegraph* and *Morning Post* was 290,000, most of whom came from the upper echelons of the middle class.[4] These readers disdained the new press for its sensationalism, vulgarity and tendency to hysteria. Yet while Lord Salisbury dismissed the *Daily Mail* as a paper written by and for 'office boys', he had, however reluctantly, to heed its opinions if his 'villa Conservatism' was to keep its hold on the suburban, lower-middle class.

Villa Conservatives were among the readers of a sheaf of new weekly magazines that provided a pot-pourri of politics, reviews and illustrated serials and short stories blended to appeal to middle-brow tastes. The contents of *Black and White*, first published in 1891 and costing sixpence, included fiction by Robert Louis Stevenson and

J. M. Barrie, domestic and international news stories, interviews, sports reports (the Henley Regatta and the annual Eton and Harrow match), poetry and reviews of the arts. For female readers there was a survey of the spring fashions presented by the large London department stores and, in serious vein, an account of a Salvation Army hostel for prostitutes. Nearly every piece was accompanied by photographs or line drawings. *Black and White*'s politics were Conservative. In 1900 it claimed that 'The average recruit to Socialism . . . remains raw, wild and unkempt with his hand against his neighbour . . . Socialism and crime go hand in hand.'[5]

Democratic Britain had inherited a fiercely partisan press. Proprietors and editors were free to ride their own hobby-horses and did so, constrained only by the pressures of reader loyalty and advertising revenue. Mass opinion was malleable, volatile and susceptible to press campaigns which isolated injustices and demanded remedy. At the turn of the century, the *Daily Mail* successfully struggled to have a telephone installed in every police station. The press flaunted its political bias openly and often fervently. In 1910, *The Times, Telegraph, Morning Post, Daily Express, Daily Graphic* and *Daily Mail*, with a combined readership of 1.76 million, supported the Conservatives and Unionists. The Liberals were less well served with the *Daily Chronicle, Daily News, Morning Leader* and *Star*, with a total circulation of 1.32 million.[6]

These papers depicted a political world that is recognisable today. There were two parties, the Conservative–Unionist coalition and Liberals, each with its own apparatus of national and local associations. The latter undertook the huge task of listing sympathetic electors, ensuring that they registered and getting them to the polling stations. All this could be accomplished only with the help of women: they were the footsoldiers of the party machines, collating lists and addressing envelopes. A guide for party agents published in 1894 admitted that constituency parties could not function without them.[7] The author also recommended employing publicans, schoolmasters and blacksmiths to collect details of voters in the countryside, rather than squires and farmers. The management of a mass electorate gave women and the lower-middle class the chance to engage actively in political life, admittedly on a humble level.

The new politics required MPs to keep in closer touch with their constituents. They regularly addressed meetings at which resolutions were passed and duly reported in the local press to remind the public what the parties stood for. In 1886 South London Tories heard their MP allege that Liberal proposals for reducing pub opening hours were 'subversive of local liberty'. During 1911 successive meetings of the Norwood Conservatives denounced the Irish Home Rule and National Insurance bills and predicted that reform of the House of Lords would send shudders of horror across the Empire.[8] Members also enforced party discipline, withdrawing support from a councillor whose attendance record was dismal.

Local party associations tended to reflect the local hierarchy; in the 1880s South London Conservative Association' office-holders were mostly professional men, including a QC (who gave five guineas to party funds), two architects and a civil engineer. But there was room for a publican, a reminder of the confluence of interests between the licensed trade and Conservatism, and the fact that parties could never afford to appear socially exclusive. To swell the numbers of lower-middle- and working-class recruits, the South London Tories cut the cost of annual subscriptions from five shillings to one.

Party associations cemented political allegiance through entertainment. At the end of the century the 350 members of the Gloucester Liberal Association held fortnightly smoking concerts, a winter ball and a summer dinner. Women members organised bazaars, held teas and a yearly garden party.[9] The Conservatives were most adept at mixing politics with conviviality. The party's social prestige and aristocratic ambience continued to draw the upwardly mobile, providing the means for them to mix on familiar terms with county magnates and business and professional men who comprised the upper strata of provincial towns and the suburbs. As Mr Pooter would have told you, these things mattered to senior clerks and junior ones too, and of course their wives. When he (as a representative of London's 'Trades and Industry') and his wife were invited by the Lord Mayor to a ball at the Mansion House, the pair were overjoyed, and were indignant when their names were omitted from the lists of guests published in the local paper afterwards. Scottish Pooters were luckier, for their and their wives' names appeared in a press report of a meeting of the Edinburgh Western District Conservative Association which listened to a lecture on the ascent of Mont Blanc in February 1880. A fortnight later they were entertained by a talk on 'The Chemistry of Rubbish'.[10]

In smaller, provincial towns deference was still strong and still helpful to the Conservatives. The 'well-to-do' in Wiltshire (mostly farmers) gravitated towards the party of the squire and parson, as did the 'genteel'. As elsewhere 'every tap room' generated 'Tory propaganda'.[11] The drinking man's party provided a jolly evening for 150 members of the South London Conservative associations who had bought tickets for a smoking concert held at the Lord Stanley public house in 1887.[12] The Tories were skilfully blending politics with the flourishing tradition of male camaraderie through the licensed Conservative and Unionist clubs which helped to bind the urban lower-middle- and working-class voter to the party. Both were attracted to the party's muscular and manly image, which was embedded in the culture of the public house and closely associated with racing and football.[13] Despite Lord Rosebery's turf successes, the Liberals were widely believed to have a Puritanical aversion to sport.[14] The Tory voter was frequently reminded that his party was defending his pleasures from the restrictions that the Liberals and their teetotal one-sip-and-you're-damned allies were forever proposing. A fictional working man's pub reverie written in 1905 said it all: '. . . I'll sit and drink my beer and smoke my pipe, and talk and laugh and chaff and feel as happy as a little king. What right has anyone to stop me . . .'[15] The shopkeeper and clerk would have concurred; Mr Pooter and his companions enjoyed a beer after their weekend strolls.

In 1905 a working man was more likely to have been contemplating the security of his job rather than his pint, for the country was emerging from a recession. For the previous thirty years economic growth had been fitful and recessions had alternated with booms. Agriculture had succumbed completely under the pressure of imported foodstuffs; revenues from land dropped from £69 million in 1881 to £53 million in 1899. In rural Cardiganshire the population fell as families emigrated to industrial South Wales or America and would not recover until the mid-1950s.[16]

Erratic demand and keen foreign competition drove manufacturers to pare down production costs by shedding staff and reducing wages. Old tensions resurfaced, dramatically after a 5 per cent wage cut for Lancashire textile workers in 1878. An eight-week strike exploded into violence: rioters armed with poles, files, pokers, hatchets, packets of cayenne pepper and firearms assaulted employers and fought policemen. A mob stormed and burned down the house of one intransigent mill owner and sexually assaulted his female servants as they attempted to escape. Calm was restored only after a squadron of lancers dispersed crowds. The underclass (casual workers and rowdies) were blamed for the violence and hands accepted a further clipping of their wages in the following year. In the 1880 general election they dutifully voted for candidates who were also employers.[17]

Was this an isolated incident, or were these the first shots in a reopened class war? If the latter, the working classes were better prepared then ever to defend their interests. For the previous thirty years they had been experimenting with collectivism through the Co-operative movement and trade unionism. The former had been encouraged by the middle classes, since it rested on principles they endorsed: self-help and thrift. Trade unionism was a different matter. On the one hand, the fledgling unions of skilled working men won respect on account of their high moral tone – members were encouraged to abstain and seek intellectual improvement. On the other, the unions' belief in solidarity and its corollary, the closed shop, challenged the customary right of employers to run their businesses as they saw fit.

Trade unionism flourished in an uncertain economic climate. In 1880 membership stood at about 750,000 and by 1914 had spiralled to 4.1 million, of whom the majority were unskilled workers of both sexes. Strikes multiplied and were often accompanied by threats of violence, which drove some anxious magistrates to reinforce the police with troops. A hundred soldiers were rushed from Plymouth to Bridgwater in 1896 after a small-scale strike by bricklayers had led to a riot.[18] Far larger contingents were needed between 1910 and 1913 to cope with national strikes by miners and railwaymen. Jittery middle-class householders in industrial areas prudently purchased revolvers.[19]

The sheer numerical strength of the unions, their capacity to discipline their members, the proliferation of strikes and sporadic disturbances associated with them intimidated all sections of the middle class. It was not just the confrontation between capital and labour, although this was worrying enough. More disturbing was the wider conflict between that individualism prized by the middle class and the new concept of collective solidarity that was at the heart of trade unionism. If a trade union was to function, every member had to set aside the rulings of his own conscience in the interests of the majority. Worse still, from a middle-class perspective, was the tentative alliance between the unions and the newly fledged socialist parties that were making headway in the 1890s. Their promises to reconstruct the social order prompted hysteria in some quarters. Socialist radicals were 'debauching the Have-Nots with intoxicating doctrine, backed by bribes taken out of the pockets of Haves', shrilled one Conservative journal in 1895.[20] A novel but still distant danger to property had appeared.

Middle-class faith in individualism was, however, not so unyielding as to prevent employers from forming their own protective organisations. They portrayed the unions as unrepresentative and overbearing bodies that spread discord and injured their members and the nation through unrealistic wage demands. At its second annual conference in 1894, an employers' group, the National Free Labour Association, denounced the 'meddlesomeness and tyranny' of the unions and the 'class hatred' they were generating. The 'best men could always command the highest wage' and presumably could secure it through old-style, man-to-man bargaining with their bosses, rather than relying on a union negotiator. Delegates listened to a sympathetic letter from the Conservative leader Lord Salisbury deploring secondary picketing. A message from Herbert Asquith, the Liberal Home Secretary, was evasive.[21]

A Liberal minister could not afford to side openly with masters against men. Fin-de-siècle Liberalism was in a quandary: how did it satisfy its old, predominantly middle-class nonconformist constituency at the same time as engrossing as much as possible of the new, working-class vote? Finding a balance was made immeasurably more difficult by Gladstone's championship of Irish Home Rule. British voters were either indifferent or hostile; his first attempt to pass a Home Rule bill in 1886 had split the Parliamentary party and driven the Unionist defectors, led by Chamberlain, into the arms of the Conservatives. The outcome was a landslide victory for the Conservatives and Unionists with a 7 to 13 per cent swing against the Liberals in the largely middle-class seats in London and the Home Counties.[22]

Home Rule strained the Liberal–nonconformist alliance. In Scotland the kirk was disturbed by the prospect of Ulster Presbyterians coming under Catholic government, an anxiety shared by Methodists. Old nonconformist rallying cries had few resonances with the mass electorate. Although a matter of concern to the congregation of an Ebenezer chapel in North Wales, the disestablishment of the Welsh church was an anachronistic irrelevancy to the English urban voter. Another cause close to the nonconformist heart, temperance, earned the Liberals the reputation of busybody killjoys among the working classes.

Conservatives and Unionists never missed a chance to label their opponents as interfering 'faddists' desperately trying to satisfy single-issue fanatics. 'The temperance folk may take heart,' said one Tory polemicist during the 1892 election. 'All things shall be given to them if they support Home Rule. Welsh, Scots disestablishers likewise.'[23] There was Tory contempt too for the Liberals' increasing reliance on rural seats on the Celtic periphery. 'Blaengwrach, Llangdinangelyng-Ngwynfa . . . Benbecula, Pabbay' were the places that the Liberals depended on for a majority, sneered one Tory journalist during the January 1910 election. What right had the inhabitants of these back-waters 'to override the great, prosperous, enlightened and familiar constituencies' whose sophisticated voters understood 'the running of a great empire'? He had in mind the middle-class, Conservative electors of London and the South-East.[24]

Celtic votes helped win the 1892 election for the Liberals, but a second Home Rule bill was vetoed by the House of Lords. This assertion of aristocratic power propelled the Liberals towards radical reform, and in the process they reinvented themselves as a populist social democratic party with a platform designed to win working-class votes. It was a gamble, for the new radicalism was bound to alienate middle-class voters who detected the thin edge of a socialist, collectivist wedge. The former Liberal Prime Minister Lord Rosebery saw the new course as a 'negation of faith, of family, of property, of monarchy, of Empire'.[25] His party's long and mutually satisfying love affair with capitalism seemed on the rocks; in 1914 over thirty Liberal businessmen protested that the party had replaced the principles of Cobden with 'ill-considered and socialistic policies'.[26]

Gladstone had begun the lurch leftwards in 1886 when he set about mobilising the masses. He foresaw the arrival of a new polit-ical arena in which the 'masses' engaged the 'classes'. For him and his moral heir, David Lloyd George, the Liberals were the cham-pions of the masses and were fighting to overthrow a formidable, callous and cunning plutocracy of the peers and super-rich busi-nessmen, financiers and entrepreneurs. Their prototype was Melmotte in Trollope's *The Way We Live Now* (1874–5) and their real-life succes-sors included millionaires like Cecil Rhodes who had made their fortunes overseas. These moneybags were greedy and pampered, used the House of Lords to flout the wishes of the people and, some Liberal radicals imagined, secretly pulled the strings of government to make themselves richer. *Punch* cartoonists portrayed them as over-weight figures wearing silk hats, smoking cigars and sometimes with semitic features.

Squeezed between the super-rich and the increasingly assertive working classes, the middle classes needed a refuge. It was offered by the Conservatives, ironically since Lord Salisbury was an old-fashioned patrician devoted to perpetuating a structured, hierarchical society governed by men of his breed and temper. His knowledge of the middle-class mind was limited and it was rumoured that he depended upon the 'judgment and sentiments' of Queen Victoria as a guide to what the middle classes were thinking. This was curious, given that her social contacts were either with the nobility or with servants, but Salisbury may have imagined that the Queen's devotion to duty, her religious faith, her belief in hard work, the 'intensity' of her family affections and her ability to combine an august exterior with an 'element of homeliness' were middle-class qualities.[27]

Whatever its source, Salisbury's insight into the middle-class mind was acute. He and his party offered just what was needed for a country facing unquiet times: unity, stability, order and an invigorating dose of imperialism, although this lost its tang during the anti-guerrilla operations at the close of the Boer War. This recipe appealed to all levels of a middle class that wanted to preserve the status quo and were apprehensive about the restlessness of the workers and the strength of their unions. Pledges of caution and security gave Conservatives and Unionists victories in the 1895 and 1900 elections, when they collected up to two-thirds of the middle-class vote.[28]

These voting patterns were symptoms of a severe bout of nervousness. It was worst among the lower-middle class. 'In feverish hordes, the suburbs swarm to the polling booth to vote against a truculent Proletariat,' wrote C. F. G. Masterman in his analysis of Edwardian society published in 1909. There was a widespread exhaustion with the importunity of the unemployed and the poor, who were constantly demanding relief that had to be funded by middle-class ratepayers and taxpayers. They had constructed a bogeyman: 'a loud-voiced, independent, arrogant figure with a thirst for drink, and imperfect standards of decency, and a determination to be supported at someone else's expense'. If it was not provided, he would snatch it, providing the suburban householder with his most terrifying nightmare. 'He would never be surprised to find the crowd behind the red flag, surging up his pleasant pathways, tearing down the railings, trampling the little garden; the "letting in of the jungle" upon the patch of fertile ground which has been redeemed from the wilderness.'[29]

Perhaps this was far fetched. Yet in 1911 the catechism of the twenty or so Socialist Sunday Schools on Clydeside included 'Private Property Is Public Theft' and defined 'classes' as 'rich and idle people who claim all things as by right'.[30] A genuine, anti–capitalist party, Labour, had entered into an electoral alliance with the Liberals in 1906 and secured thirty seats, an increase of twenty-eight on their 1900 total. Between 1906 and 1910 there were nearly 5,000 strikes, which accounted for the loss of 26.5 million working days. The clerk in Streatham needed protection and the Conservatives offered it, as well as a sense of superiority. 'He is proud when he is identifying his interests with those of Kensington, and indignant when his interests are identified with those of Poplar,' observed Masterman. The 1908 election for the London County Council gave the lower-middle class a chance to express its exasperation. After twenty years in power the radical Progressive Party was trounced and the authority passed into Conservative hands.

Three times during the decade the middle classes voted in general elections that were in effect referendums, the first two in 1906 and January 1910 on economic issues, the third in December 1910 on a constitutional one. Towards the end of the 1902–3 recession Chamberlain proposed a revolutionary formula designed to re-invigorate manufacturing industry, tighten imperial bonds and finance a basic welfare programme. Foreign imports, including foodstuffs, would be taxed and Britain become the hub of an imperial free-trade area. It was a bold initiative, but it fragmented the Conservative Party, which was racked by internal wrangling (much as it was over Europe in the 1990s). Businessmen were largely unconvinced, and the middle and working classes feared that higher food prices would stretch family budgets to breaking point. Anxieties combined and the Liberals secured a landslide victory in 1906 which confirmed the nation's faith in free trade.

Cheap food in the shopping bag was one matter, backing the new radicalism of the Liberals was another, especially when it raised middle-class tax bills. When he presented his 1909 budget Lloyd George stressed that he intended to squeeze the richest, which he did: higher rates of income tax were imposed on incomes of over £5,000, a levy was placed on land values, petrol duties were increased and the cost of a car licence rose from two guineas to forty pounds. The middle and lower ranks of the middle class also had to pay more. They were the majority of the one million income tax payers who faced an increase from one shilling to one shilling and tuppence in the pound and additional duties on tobacco and alcohol. This raised the tax bill for a white-collar worker on £160 a year from eight pounds to nine pounds and four shillings, irrespective of how much he smoked or drank. This was bad news for families whose annual budget margin was between five and ten pounds.

Naval expenditure soaked up some of the new revenues, but Lloyd George emphasised that most would be poured into a 'war budget' for the campaign against 'poverty and squalidness'. It was rejected by the House of Lords. In January 1910 the Liberals asked the country to consent to the principle of wealth redistribution implicit in the budget. Taking the London and Home Counties seats as a barometer of middle-class opinion, its response was distinctly hostile, with Liberals and Labour losing 103 seats.[31] Nevertheless, the Liberals stayed in power, but only thanks to the support of Irish Home Rule MPs.

In December 1910 the Liberals asked for a mandate to abolish the House of Lords veto. The 'Peers against the People' election was a bad-tempered contest, riddled with the language of class animosity. Lloyd George and Churchill set the tone and were accused of inflaming class hatred by demonising the aristocracy.[32] Rallying Fife Tories in Anstruther, the Marquess of Tullibardine announced himself as 'a Tory, a laird, the son of a duke [and] therefore a blackguard' and was greeted with cheers and laughter.[33] Others were unamused by the recrudescence of vitriolic class politics. Sir Henry Newbolt, the bard of muscular imperialism, denounced what he called the 'persecution of particular classes' and the 'destruction of sympathy between the rich and the poor'.[34] The right-wing *Blackwood's Magazine* reminded the middle classes that the peerage was their ally. The Lords veto was all that stood between the country and socialism – 'a widespread deluge in which not only our political institutions but our personal liberties would perish'.[35]

Again the swing went against the Liberals, though less so than earlier in the year, and again it was most pronounced in largely middle-class constituencies in the South-East. Residual, middle-class antipathy towards the aristocracy helped the Liberals keep some northern, urban seats and everywhere the Conservatives were handicapped by their ambivalence towards free trade.[36] Yet the party had recovered from the signal reverse of 1906 and managed to regain the loyalty of a huge swathe of the middle classes.

In what must have been one of the wryest political paradoxes of all time, old men and women in rural North Oxfordshire heaped blessings on 'Lord George' for their new weekly pension of five shillings. Only a lord, they claimed, could have been so generous. The gratitude of these pensioners was recorded by Flora Thompson, a village sub-postmistress and daughter of an artisan. She was intellectually curious and had a streak of independence; when asked by the squire's wife to join the Conservative Primrose League, she refused, saying her father was Liberal. One form of deference bowed to another, for the lady told Flora that she would have to seek her 'parents'' permission if she wished to join. In later life Flora became involved in Labour politics.

Flora Thompson was one of many men and women from the lower levels of the middle class and the upper of the working who were being drawn into political life. At a national level it was now dominated by professionals and businessmen; in 1910 just over two-thirds of Liberal MPs were from manufacturing, commercial, professional and service backgrounds. In the following year, the Conservatives replaced Arthur Balfour, a leader with close aristocratic ties, with Arthur Bonar Law, a Scots Canadian businessman. In 1912 and as a favour to Labour, MPs were given an annual salary of £400, roughly the income of a rural solicitor and twice that of a senior clerk in the city.

Salaries were welcome to a new group of MPs, Labour and left-leaning Liberals who had been entering the house during the previous twenty years. Their roots were in the working and lower-middle classes (often clerks in local or national government service) and their learning had been acquired at the board school and from evenings spent studying, or attending lectures in institutes dedicated to opening the minds of the poor. William Bowyer, the son of a

Battersea ironmonger's clerk and a Post Office clerk, consumed books by H. G. Wells and George Bernard Shaw, companions to what he later called his 'liberation'.[37] Serious-minded young autodidacts discussed the new ideas they were discovering. Eric Makeham, an ex-Battersea grammar schoolboy and London County Council (LCC) clerk, addressed his staff debating society on 'How Shall We Save the Family' and concluded that socialism alone could create a fairer society; he joined the Fabians in 1908. Another LCC clerk, William Kent, participated in earnest discussions at the YMCA, attended lectures ('Should Christians Smoke') and read socialist journals. After 1914 he drifted towards pacifism and spiritualism.[38] Like many others of his kind, he strayed far from the conventional religious faith of his parents.

A nonconformist upbringing, a decent education (many of these young men had stayed at school until fifteen or sixteen), a faith in their own and their countrymen's capacity for self-improvement, an interest in current social and political preoccupations and an urge to become part of the forces for change nudged such young men and women leftwards. Teachers were part of this ferment; in 1911 their union protested against plans to make them civil servants and so debar them from political activities.[39] It was an overreaction; a considerable tolerance was shown by the civil service and local government towards politically active employees.

It was certainly extended to Philip Snowden (1864–1937), a junior civil service clerk. His father was an artisan and lay preacher who could not afford to have his bright son articled to a local solicitor. It is unlikely that he would have flourished in a provincial lawyer's office, for Philip was steeped in the passionate radical and dissenting traditions of Lancashire. As a young man he threw himself into temperance crusades and would later recall hearing an old orator who had been an eyewitness to Peterloo and remembered his words. 'As I saw the cavalry striking down unarmed and peaceful people, I swore eternal enmity to Toryism in all its ways.'[40] Snowden's political heritage steered him towards the new Labour Party and he was elected MP for Blackburn in 1906. He would serve three times as chancellor of the exchequer in Labour governments and was created a viscount, which might have astonished the veteran of Peterloo.

Popular Conservatism was producing a new breed of Tory, self-made men of lower-middle-class origins who had made their way in local government. The son of an Easingwold farmer, Henry Wilson (1859–1930) began his career as a railway clerk in Leeds. In the evenings he studied to qualify as an accountant and became president of the local branch of the Accountants Society. A teetotaller and devout Anglican, Wilson was an energetic figure who devoted his spare time to unpaid public service, which earned him the trust and respect of his community. He taught in Sunday Schools and the Young Men's Bible Classes, joined the Volunteers and was active in the Foresters and Oddfellows, the last three providing him with fruitful business connections. Unpaid public service opened the path into local politics and Wilson was elected a Tory councillor in 1890 and five years later was chosen party leader on the council. The old Liberal–Radical alliance was losing public confidence, and in 1907 the Tories secured a majority on Leeds council.

Wilson was the no-nonsense tribune of a new populist Conservatism. Middle-class ratepayers wanted value for money and Wilson gave it to them by imposing tight control over wages. His astringencies led to clashes with striking gas and tramway workers in 1913, and he had to be given armed police protection after strikers had attempted to murder another councillor and thrown a bomb at a power station. Wilson beat the unions and in 1922 was elected MP for Leeds. His was the authentic voice of a new Toryism which set a high value on individual self-reliance and property ownership. In 1928, when advocating private home ownership, he declared to Leeds council: 'It is a good thing for people to buy houses. They turn Tory directly. We shall go on making Tories and you [Labour] will be wiped out.'[41]

Of course there were house-owning, middle-class Labour voters and council tenants who supported the Conservatives, but these exceptions did not invalidate Wilson's thesis. Class politics were back and were becoming deeply embedded. Until the final decade of the century, an individual's social background was invariably the touchstone for his political allegiance. The middle classes tended to be Conservative, partly because of the sea change within the Liberal Party and partly because they believed that they would suffer materially if the Labour Party and its trade unionist allies gained power.

5

Dangerous Classes: Correction and Compassion

One afternoon in March 1846 a public footpath off the main street of Tranent was blocked by a swarm of drunken, swearing colliers. They had gathered to watch and wager on a fight between a pair of gamecocks provided by two labourers.[1] Respectable passers-by steered clear of this crowd and, even though cockfighting had recently been made illegal, protests would have been foolhardy. Eight years before, an RSPCA constable had been killed in a fracas at a cockfight in Hanworth in Middlesex.[2] And serve him right, the Lothian pitmen would have thought, for the law against cockfighting was a further example of the rich outlawing the pleasures of the poor.

Obscenities were shouted at 'a gent' by a couple in Spitalfields after he had drawn a policeman's attention to their furtive loitering late one September night in 1845.[3] Their reaction was to be expected in a notoriously unruly and dissolute district where the middle classes endured every kind of vexation. Boys hurled stones and brickbats at shopkeepers' doors, windows were regularly broken, the respectable were taunted by gangs of youths and every night drunken men and women brawled and cursed. Distressing encounters with members of the rowdy working class were a fact of life for the middle class; they occurred everywhere at any time. One hot Saturday evening in July 1872 a barrister caught the London-to-Harrow train and found the first-class carriage full, so he moved into the second-class section. Scattered through both classes was a party of 'respectable but undoubtedly noisy mechanics' singing and breaking windows. His request for them to remove their feet from the seats got an insolent response and the guard ignored the incident.[4]

It was just as bad in the countryside and provincial towns. In 1838 the new curate at Southery in the Norfolk fens discovered a godless community of drunks, gamblers and poachers. When he informed the magistrates about illicit beer houses, the villagers came to his house at night, stripped his garden, stole poultry and untethered his horse, which ran off. After two years he left this 'stronghold of Satan' where resistance to Anglican moral discipline remained strong. In 1876 one of his successors noted that there were only three surnames in the parish, which he considered evidence of isolation, intermarriage and 'many serious evils'.[5] 'Lord' George Sanger was sickened by the casual violence at fairgrounds in the 1840s. At Stalybridge he witnessed Lancashire miners kick to death a gingerbread seller and at Lansdown Hill the fairground was stormed and vandalised by a mob led by 'Carroty Kate', who was the 'terror of every respectable person in Bath and its neighbourhood'.[6] Her band may have swelled the crowds who flocked to Devizes to see a man hanged in 1838. Bedlam overwhelmed the small town, according to the governor of the gaol, who reported 'the most disgraceful and indecent behaviour' and scenes of 'beastly drunkenness and debauchery'.[7]

The public peace of Victorian Britain was brittle. The common perception of the period as a golden age of exemplary tranquillity when the edicts of God and the state were universally observed and authority revered is a distortion. The crime reports in any newspaper and the records of prosecutions in the minor courts reveal a fractious and often brutal society. It is equally wrong to blame crime and public disorders solely on poverty and helplessness. The majority of those convicted for assault, housebreaking and theft at the Dumfries sheriff's court between February 1837 and March 1838 had occupations. There were gardeners, servants, weavers, apprentices, a clockmaker and a bookseller.[8] They were not well paid, but neither were they destitute. Sixty years later, London youths found guilty of assaults and what we now call 'street crime' were all employed, admittedly in low-paid jobs.[9] Whatever else they may have been, their commotions were not the protests of starvelings. Like so many others of their kind who appeared before the courts, these young men were conservatives rather than rebels. Getting belligerently drunk and creating a rumpus in the streets had been the recreations of their forebears and they saw no reason to break with tradition.

Another bugbear for the middle class was the professional thief who believed that crime's rewards outweighed its risks. A gang of burglars, most in their twenties, who terrorised Kent and Sussex in 1850 and 1851 accumulated hauls of cash, silverware, watches, guns, jewellery and clothing stolen from public houses, shops and farms. Armed with pistols, swords and crowbars, they threatened and sometimes wounded their victims. At Frimley vicarage one member of the gang shot dead the parson after he had fired on them. The murderer was hanged and his accomplices transported.[10] Readers of *Oliver Twist* (1837–9) would have recognised their type and the underworld they emerged from. Many of its real inhabitants were there because it offered them a better living than they could have achieved by working.

Another alternative to work (or the workhouse) was begging. Often taking ingenious forms, it was universal, although mendicants tended to concentrate in cities and towns where their prosperous and sometimes conscience-stricken middle-class targets lived. One described a stroll through London in the 1860s during wh°ich he was badgered by 'urchin' crossing-sweepers, assailed by the 'whining interruptions' of a 'sturdy Irishman who is always starving' and, as he ate lunch in a restaurant, his every mouthful was observed by 'a whole family of ragged vagabonds' gathered outside.[11] Equally tiresome and intrusive were the prostitutes touting for business in the larger towns and cities. The potential for annoyance and danger was everywhere.

The middle classes had the will and the means to cope with both. Through such voluntary bodies as the RSPCA and various temperance associations, they lobbied for legislation to regulate public behaviour and, as magistrates and judges, rigorously enforced such laws, old and new. The property hurdles for jury service guaranteed that middle-class concepts of morality prevailed in the higher courts. Jurymen empanelled in Glasgow during 1890 represented a cross-section of the middle class from stockbrokers and manufacturers through to electrical engineers, commercial travellers, teachers and retailers.[12] All could be relied upon to uphold the rights of property and the rights of individuals like themselves to walk the streets unmolested.

Licensed anarchy in the shape of semi-ritualised and usually violent folk festivals was stamped out by magistrates in partnership with the new police. The lower orders did not forgo their customs willingly; dragoons were needed to suppress the last bull running through the streets of Stamford in 1838. A more widespread source of tumults, traditional inter-village or inter-town football matches, persisted into the 1860s. Mass and sometimes bloody free-for-alls, these events were suppressed by a combination of resolute magistrates, police truncheons and, at Derby, soldiers.[13] Outlawing excessive displays of working-class boisterousness was part of a wider, middle-class campaign to create a polite, decorous and, therefore, civilised nation.

Coercion worked, but a better cure was to channel the energies and passions of the working class towards closely regulated spectator sports. The framework of modern mass sport was erected in the 1860s and 1870s in an endeavour to provide excitement and diversion for urban working men without the risks of partisanship spilling into violence. The Football Association and Rugby Football Union supervised leagues and organised matches between teams who played according to strictly enforced national rules. Overall control was in the hands of the middle classes: between 1888 and 1915 some 85 per cent of football club directors were middle-class.[14] This was unsurprising, since football was good for business. It generated beer sales (some unconvincingly argued that spectators preferred to watch the game sober), sold newspapers and, by the early 1880s, was making money for railway companies which laid on 'football specials' with cheap fares.

Old passions were redirected, but never exorcised. Late-Victorian football crowds pelted players, harangued and sometimes fought with each other before, during and after matches and cursed referees. 'A gang of the great unwashed' hurled snowballs at visiting fans during the FA cup semi-final between Small Heath and West Bromwich Albion in 1886 in what turned out to be a prelude to a pitch invasion and full-scale battle.[15] Such unruliness was typical and commonplace; as an exercise in social discipline, the creation of mass spectator sport turned out to be a disappointment.

The middle classes took such setbacks in their stride. With an often superhuman self-confidence, they maintained the struggle to create a tractable, well-scrubbed, sober and godly working class and integrate it into the nation. Physical regeneration complemented moral. In 1892 an enthusiast praised public baths as 'an instrument of the most powerful order for elevating the masses and stimulating the desire for improvement. To make a habitually dirty man clean is to create in his inmost soul . . . a desire to rise out of the squalor and filth with which he may ordinarily be encompassed.'[16] Sobriety, literacy and thrift would work similar miracles. Gymnastics, playgrounds, parks and open spaces would reduce hooliganism, argued *The Times* in 1898, although it placed more faith in astringents. 'Drilled and subject to officers who are merciless to loutish turbulence', the young ruffian would soon cease to be 'a pest to society'.[17]

Preventive rescue was always considered the best option. This was why in 1879 a party from the Northampton School Board inspected the Oxford Industrial School where the children of the 'dregs of the population' (thieves and prostitutes) were being trained to become productive and honest citizens. The visitors were impressed with what they saw: children 'who would otherwise grow into criminal and dangerous classes' (an illuminating phrase) were being led away from vice. 'Better to save them from falling, than to punish them for falling.'[18] It was a mantra exploited by charities that cared for destitute children. Both Lord Shaftesbury and Dr Barnardo reminded middle-class donors that their money would curtail the proliferation of the 'dangerous classes'.[19] In 1900 the treasurer of the Edinburgh branch of the NSPCA told its annual general meeting that the society was stemming the flow of poor children into 'the criminal class'. Glaswegian members were told that prompt action by two volunteers had saved a thirteen-year-old girl who had been found in the company of prostitutes and packed her off to an industrial school.[20]

Uncorrected children and the hungry poor could easily metamorphose into that demon of the middle-class imagination: the callous and desperate robber. His menacing form appears in *Punch* cartoons in 1862 when London was briefly terrorised by a spate of muggings by 'garotters' who preyed on the respectable, even in the West End. The image was of a burly, muscular footpad armed with cosh, knife or pistol and with brutish, simian features and the shaven head of a convict. Cartoonists also depicted middle-class men and women nervously venturing abroad in protective groups laden with firearms, swordsticks and cudgels.

Multiplied many thousand times, the lurking mugger or burglar became the mob. Its potential for malevolence and destruction was frighteningly brought to life in the spring of 1871 with press reports of the Paris Commune. The *Illustrated London News* published engravings which showed 'quiet and respectable' Parisians desperately trying to escape from the city, and there were images of unkempt, ragged and ruffianly communards. 'Order, law, trade and even religion have been trampled on by the canaille,' declared the journal, which singled out the savagery of 'abominable and unsexed women'. Could it happen in Britain? The pessimistic *Saturday Review* detected parallels between the French mob and the British, although the latter was just a 'tumultuous gathering of useless, obnoxious people' with no purpose save to fight the police. By contrast, the French mob was driven by socialism, which must have been of little comfort to the magazine's middle-class readers.[21]

The British middle class never had any qualms about defending themselves and their property. As in earlier periods, a large number of householders kept loaded firearms in readiness for resisting housebreakers. In September 1854, their patience exhausted by the depredations committed by three hundred Irish navvies, a party of Lauder men armed with guns attacked their camp. Shots were fired, but no one was hurt and the authorities took no action.[22] Had they done so, these vigilantes might have invoked the scarcity of policemen as an excuse for their actions, but even when police numbers and efficiency had increased, the middle class insisted on the right to possess guns.

'Why should not Englishmen arm themselves?' demanded an MP in 1893 after the government had introduced a bill to tighten the lax licensing system for revolvers. The house was sympathetic and the bill was abandoned.[23] During the previous year, thirty-one burglars had been arrested carrying pistols and in 1897 the streets of Clerkenwell were disturbed by 'pistol gangs' of youths armed with cheap revolvers. One of their chance shots killed an eleven-year-old girl.[24] In 1902 a Glasgow policeman was wounded by a burglar armed with a revolver he had stolen from a middle-class house. Its owner, a widow, had kept the weapon by her bedside.[25] Revolvers were freely available for the anxious property owner: a department-store advertisement of 1896 offered a Webley for three pounds. Given the abundance of firearms, it is astonishing that there was so little gun crime in Victorian and Edwardian Britain.

A degree of security could also be purchased indirectly through subscriptions to charities dedicated to the relief of poverty and helping men, women and children who had the will but not the wherewithal to escape from crime and vice. Charities provided a conduit for money to flow from the rich to the poor. Between 1851 and 1898 the well-to-do middle-class congregation of St Mark's Audley Square raised £500,000 for local Sunday Schools, youth clubs, a library and a gymnasium for the poor who lived in the slums behind Grosvenor Square. The effort owed everything to the parson Joseph Ayre, whose industry, earnestness, 'fine presence and polished manners' won the hearts of the 'very elite of society'.[26] On a national level the amount dispensed by charities increased from £6.5 million in 1900 to £8.6 million in 1913.

The impulses behind middle-class philanthropy were the same as ever. On a purely personal level there were what a member of the Bristol Samaritan Society described as those 'delicious emotions excited in our hearts by the consciousness of doing good'. Baser instincts were also gratified. In 1858 a clergyman denounced donors whose immediate response to an appeal was 'Show me the subscription list, will it be published?'[27] Charities offered snobs a chance to identify themselves with the illustrious whose names always headed these lists and who dominated committees. Annual meetings and fundraising events were opportunities to mingle with aristocrats, even royals, which was gratifying to anyone making his way up in the world. Joining the board of a charity marked the 'arrival' of many a businessman.

Some donors wanted anonymity. 'Benevolence assumes its purest form when its author is not only unrequited but unknown,' claimed a speaker at an RSPCA meeting in 1845.[28] Givers were sometimes persuaded to regard their benevolence as an investment. In the 1870s temperance organisations promised manufacturers that their gifts would reduce wage bills on the ingenious grounds that if the workers did not drink they would have more to spend on necessities and, therefore, have no need of higher wages.[29] Shock tactics also opened cheque books and purses. In 1903 members of the Holborn Deanery Association were horrified by Dr Scharlieb's vivid eyewitness account of the lives of prostitutes who were wandering the nearby streets. Her revelations of 'white slavery' prompted one man to offer a hundred pounds immediately and, by the end of the meeting, a further twenty had been pledged to save these girls.[30]

Solicitude for those who had strayed and ameliorating the miseries of the poor were Christian duties. Unlike ourselves, the Victorians and the middle class in particular believed they inhabited a world created by God in which good and evil coexisted. The latter was always formidable in its depth and scope, but was never unconquerable. When evil seemed at its worst, public response was surprisingly measured. Crimes that today would generate mass hysteria and anguished national self-examination were treated with a remarkable dispassion. In 1861 two eight-year-old boys were convicted of abducting a two-year-old, stripping him, beating him and finally drowning him in a brook near Stockport in Lancashire. It was uncannily like the 1993 Bulger murder, but the public and the press stayed calm. Before sentencing the pair to five years in a juvenile reformatory, the judge observed that they were 'utterly neglected and uneducated', with consciences calloused by brutal sports and habits.[31] This was simultaneously proof of the depravity still embedded in a civilised, Christian nation and a spur to those who sought to emancipate such creatures from a physical and cultural environment that had made it possible for them to commit homicide without understanding what they were doing.

An awareness of God was essential to this release. In 1841 a fifteen-year-old girl incarcerated in Banbury prison for robbing her father admitted that she had attended Sunday School, but she was ignorant of God, Christ, Adam and Eve. She did, however, know that the wicked would go to hell, which says much about the nature of her instruction. An Evangelical prison visitor was heartened and set to guiding her towards atonement and forgiveness.[32] Reports published by charities contained many heart-warming stories of the salvation of souls restored to God; even the Stockport child murderers could find God and learn His commandments.

Redemption and regeneration were matters of personal choice. Anyone who did not reject vice lived with consequences that were tantamount to exile from society. This was the conviction of Josephine Butler (1835–1906), the wife of an Anglican schoolmaster/cleric who devoted the middle years of her life to the repeal of the Contagious Diseases Act, which compelled prostitutes in garrison towns and naval ports to undergo regular medical inspections. Like so many middle-class Christians engaged in the purification and regeneration of the wayward poor, she believed that 'Depriving God's creatures of free-will, of choice and of responsibility' was 'the greatest crime of which earth can witness'. To remove choice from even the most wicked and degenerate was to deny both their humanity and the doctrine of free will.[33]

If the wrong choice led to further miseries, so be it. At a meeting held in Gloucester in 1872 in support of Mrs Butler's campaign, the middle-class audience was shocked when a doctor declared: 'It is the duty of the medical man to alleviate human suffering irrespective of moral considerations.'[34] He had challenged his listeners' collective assumption that the suffering referred to, venereal infection, was the direct result of the victim's preference for promiscuity rather than chastity. Like alcoholism, the pox was both self-inflicted wound and punishment for sin.

It followed that, to be effective, the goal of charity was to bring recipients into the fold of society, something that could be achieved only if they adopted that quintessential middle-class virtue, self-help. Evidence that they had and were moving towards independence provided charities with the publicity they needed to attract patrons and donors. No one wanted their money squandered on lazy recidivists. Save in the instances of the young, the old and the permanently infirm, private charities therefore endeavoured to apply the principles of the Poor Law by giving relief to those whose misfortunes were temporary and reversible. Dependency was to be avoided at all costs.

Weeding out work-shy spongers was one of the prime objectives of the Charity Organisation Society (COS), which was founded in 1869 to co-ordinate and concentrate the distribution of funds in London. Subscribers paid a guinea a year, confident that it would be wisely spent, for the society intended to 'cut off charity from the worthless and direct it to the deserving'. In practice this involved making loans to men and women who showed a determination to help themselves. While other charities represented a middle-class insurance against the proliferation of the 'dangerous classes', the COS offered an investment in thrift, honesty and sobriety.

Evaluating the worthiness of claimants was the work of volunteers in the society's branch offices. Through interrogation and investigation they sifted the 'deserving' from the 'undeserving' poor. In 1877 the former included a fifty-year-old Wandsworth billsticker and carrier who had requested a ten-pound loan to buy a horse. He had twelve children, earned one pound fifteen shillings a week and was found to a 'very steady, hardworking honest man'. His three oldest sons, all employed, lent him two pounds and the society eight, which he eventually repaid. Here was a glowing example of that blend of mutual support, economy and the urge for betterment that distinguished the middle classes. In stark contrast was a heavy-drinking Newington sawdust dealer who asked the COS for two pounds to buy a donkey, although he had already borrowed the sum. No cash was forthcoming for an impudent cadger.[35]

Lifelines were lowered only to individuals committed to helping themselves. An article of 1891 on a Salvation Army hostel for some of London's 'fallen women' emphasised how they they were over-coming degradation by the cultivation of self-esteem, an essential ingre-dient of that integrity which eventually would impel them towards honest work and a place in the community. Exterior cleanliness was vital to this process and here the bath house proved invaluable. 'Dirt and vice in low places, dirt and slipshod morality in places not quite so low, go together as invariably as berry and flower.' An illustration showed a well-dressed, respectable lady inspecting the premises.[36]

She was one of the many middle-class women who dedicated passion, energy and time to that area of philanthropy for which they believed themselves best suited: the rescue of prostitutes. It was a task hallowed by Christ when he forgave Mary Magdalen and was best undertaken by women. In 1855 the undergraduates who founded the Cambridge Female Mission hired a woman to undertake the actual approaches to prostitutes because they rightly feared the 'impropriety and danger of attempting to touch the evil directly'.[37] Contrary to what is often imagined, the nature and extent of the evil was familiar to the middle classes. Victorian squeamishness about sexual matters did not extend to prostitution, which was a subject widely aired in the press and in the literature issued by charities.

This knowledge, compounded no doubt by what they had seen on the city's streets, persuaded a body of middle-class women in Birmingham to visit brothels, prisons and magistrates' courts in a campaign aimed at saving as many prostitutes as they could. During the 1880s the elegantly dressed (she believed that charity work was no excuse for dowdiness) Mrs Hallowes regularly visited brothels during the mid-afternoon slack period and took tea with the girls. They chatted about current affairs, for she believed that religious exhorta-tions might alienate her listeners.

Those of her tea-time companions who had retained some of their innocence were invited to Mrs Hallowes's house and, if they wished to repudiate their past, were taken to the local Reform House for rehabilitation.[38] Here, former prostitutes were trained for domestic work so that they could become household servants. Every charity bent on reclamation measured its successes in terms of how many beneficiaries found useful work. In 1900 boys at the NSPCC home at Murrayfield in Edinburgh 'were taught what a manly thing it was to be a soldier' and their martial ambitions were encouraged by a pipe band.[39]

The former Birmingham prostitutes attended Bible classes, learned how to sew and were introduced to the sedate world of middle-class leisure. They heard lantern-slide lectures on foreign missions, played parlour games, listened to the gramophone and went on outings to museums and the countryside. A party of ex-prostitutes enjoying tea with a solicitor's wife before being taken to a local art gallery was a perfect instance of private charity and municipal bene-volence working in tandem. Respectable and, it was hoped, invig-orating recreation was offered by an Anglican ladies' group who provided country and seaside holidays for London 'factory girls'. Founded in 1888, this charity expected the girls to pay a propor-tion of their rail fare, although in some instances it had to provide them with boots, clothing and 'what to them was an almost unheard-of, quite unnecessary luxury, a night dress'. It was noted with satis-faction that the town girls chose not to wear their 'showy' clothes when strolling down a lane or along the seashore.[40]

Discovering girls who slept in their underwear or nothing at all may have come as a shock for rural parsons' wives. Whatever else it may have achieved, charity work taught the middle classes about the realities of everyday life among the poorest of the working class. Personal visits were actively encouraged by charities, encounters that in part narrowed the demographic gap that was widening between the better off and the poor. Crossing the social divide was an unpleasant duty for the fastidious, for poverty was noisome. 'I dreaded and loathed the smells of their cottages,' Edmund Gosse wrote, recalling visits to the poor with his father. In later life, a young middle-class girl from Notting Hill recollected that her clothes were permeated for days with the odours of the play centre for poor children which she visited in the 1880s. Likewise, Lawrence Jones had a memory of the 'strong smell of corduroys and sweat' that emanated from the 'workhouse boys' whom his father entertained yearly in his manor house in the 1890s.[41] No wonder the middle classes set such store by bath houses.

By the beginning of the twentieth century more and more respectable outsiders were braving the miasmas of want. A growing number of officials and voluntary social workers entered the homes of the poor to offer gifts, encouragement and admonitions. Public officials such as school attendance officers and health visitors joined voluntary social workers, and the efforts of all were co-ordinated. Whenever the NSPCC came across neglected children they alerted the police and pressed for the prosecution of parents.

The burden of paying for welfare was moving away from charities towards national and local government. Council rates in England and Wales rose from £35 million in 1901 to £56 million in 1913, of which a third went towards elementary education. In the financial year from 1913 to 1914 the government's welfare budget was £20 million, much of which went in old-age pensions and unemployment pay. A large proportion of this money came from the middle classes, who suspected that it was being dispersed among many who would have been considered undeserving if judged by the criteria of charities. Some on the right queried whether the principle of concentrating more and more resources on the poor was doing more harm than good. In 1911 Sir Robert Baden-Powell, the hero of Mafeking and self-appointed saviour of Britain's youth, declared that:

> Over civilisation threatens England with deterioration. Free feeding and old-age pensions, strike pay, cheap beer and indiscriminate charity do not make for the hardening of the nation or the building up of a self-reliant, energetic manhood. They tend, on the contrary, to produce an army of dependents and wasters.

Baden-Powell was contributing to a debate that had been raging for over a decade. At its heart was the question whether past, present and future measures for the alleviation of hardship were bound to fail simply because of the sheer scale of the problem. Recent investigations and collations of statistics by such social analysts as Sidney and Beatrice Webb and Seebohm Rowntree indicated that the problem of poverty was far greater than had ever been imagined. Their conclusions also upheld the contention that the gulf between the rich and poor was opening, although there was no agreement about where precisely the boundary between wealth and poverty was drawn. Furthermore, as the temperance lobby had always maintained, privation was often the consequence of perfectly adequate wages frittered away on beer and gambling.

Addiction to both remained strong. In the first decade of the twentieth century an annual average of about 35.5 million barrels of beer was consumed, the equivalent of roughly thirty-six gallons for each man, woman and child in the country. The total spent on betting increased slightly from £4.9 to £5.5 million, totals that ignored illegal gambling. Crime figures were creeping up: the total number of convictions in all courts rose from 665,000 in 1908 to 857,000 in 1913. In 1902 about 90 per cent of the 172,000 men and women in gaol were from the poorest classes.

Familiar bogeymen continued to torment the respectable. During the hot, dry August and September of 1898 the inner suburbs of London suffered an explosion of hooliganism that was sensationally reported in the popular press. 'Tuxy' Girdle's gang, all in their early twenties, terrorised the New Kent Road; the 'Dick Turpin' gang of school and errand boys plundered in Highgate; and a Lambeth magistrate deplored the 'extraordinary amount of ruffianism' that was engulfing the borough. Like the Mods and the Rockers and the Skinheads of the 1960s and 1970s, the hooligans of 1898 were distinguished by their clothes and hair, which was close-cropped with a small patch on the crown pulled down in a donkey fringe over the forehead. The Spartan rigours of prisons and reformatories made little impression on these creatures. After twenty-six convictions for drunkenness and assault, William Mallinson, a lathe worker, remained, in the words of a police witness, 'the absolute terror of respectable people in Kensal New Town'.[42]

The press worked itself into a fury and the middle class took fright. A substantial section of society – male, in its teens and early twenties and with low-paid, unskilled jobs – was slipping out of control.

If this was not enough, there was the larger and ultimately more significant issue of the long-term survival of Britain in a new century. There was the stark clinical evidence that a high proportion of children of the poorest sections of the working class were physically debilitated and that infant weaknesses would follow them into adulthood. That 'Anglo-Saxon manhood' which imperialists of all complexions thought to be the backbone of Britain was in danger of being eroded unless far-reaching remedies were applied quickly. Charities turned their attention to child welfare, in particular the training of mothers, and the state responded with infant-health programmes.

Behind these activities was a new source of disquiet. War was beckoning and there was a mass of young men incapable of facing up to its rigours. What reformers called the 'condition of England' question was a matter not just of producing stronger, healthier children, but of the country's survival in a hostile world. Given the nature of the problems, it was perhaps inevitable that pseudo-Darwinian theories crept into social thinking. Eugenics offered one solution as Dr William Inge, Professor of Divinity at Cambridge, explained to a meeting of the Eugenics Society in 1909. There was now a physical divide between rich and poor. 'The well-to-do classes in this country are, on average, the finest specimens of humanity which have appeared since the ancient Greeks.' But their birth rate was declining, while that of the 'lowest classes' was soaring and producing offspring whose 'average physique is exceedingly poor.' 'Eugenic practice, and, ultimately . . . eugenic legislation' were the only solutions. The medical writer and proto-sexologist Havelock Ellis went further and proposed the sterilisation of the 'unfit'.[43]

Twenty years before it would have been impossible to conceive of an intelligent, well-educated audience nodding with approval as a clergyman of the established church proposed state-imposed selective breeding among humans. Yet, for all their appeals to modern science and reason, the Eugenicists were unconsciously expressing that sense of insecurity that had always troubled the middle classes. If anything, their fearfulness was increasing; not only was poverty (and with it social envy and resentment) still deeply entrenched, there were new anxieties about whether their countrymen were up to winning a war. Seen from the perspective of the early twentieth century, the middle classes' efforts to improve the lives and environment of the poor had been a quantitative failure.

Measured on a qualitative scale, the result was very different. There is no reason to disbelieve the reports published annually by charities with their stories of rehabilitated drunkards, wife beaters, prostitutes, thieves and vagabonds, or of men, women and children who had been assisted in their passage upwards in the world. However Panglossian it may sound and however much we may be repelled by the assumptions of those who administered Victorian charities, they did help make the world a better place. Although they provided only a brief respite from hunger, the eggs, scones, sugar, tea, cocoa and Bovril collected by the ladies of the Buittle kirk guild and distributed to poor families in Leith in the winter of 1903 were welcome.[44] Given the scale of so many charities, mishaps and scandals were inevitable. During the 1870s patients at the Bristol free fever hospital faced long waits for treatment at the hands of physicians with abrupt manners and a faith in such discredited nostrums as bleeding. Even more disturbing was the sight of one surgeon 'clad in a germ-ridden gown, smoking a cigar above the operating table'.[45]

No doubt there were protests and remedial action. Of course complacency and apathy existed among the middle classes, but, on balance, they were outweighed by the determination of those who believed that individual action could make a significant difference. The poor were not cast adrift in a sea of their own follies. The knowledge that there was still so much unaccomplished did not dishearten middle-class philanthropists, nor did it weaken their faith in themselves as the godparents of a new Utopia. Here is Mrs Allan Bright, the wife of a director of a Liverpool metalware company and president of the National Union of Women Workers of Great Britain, addressing its annual conference in 1913. United in will, members would 'sweep away the dark clouds of ignorance', overcome disease, hunger, overcrowding and all that hindered 'the building up of character' among the poor. Collective resolve was matched by personal action. Mrs Hylton Dale told the assembly that she had purchased 'baby comforters' (that is, alcohol- and opium-based sedatives) and sent them to cabinet ministers with the challenge: 'These are illegal in France: why not in England?'[46]

6

Put Your Playthings Away:
Faith and Morals

While it is easy for us to understand and even sympathise with the charitable instincts of the Victorian middle classes, their spiritual world is dusty, remote and incomprehensible. Its physical features are familiar enough: churches restored or rebuilt with dark interiors partially lit by stained-glass windows full of whiskery patriarchs, androgynous angels and bland representations of Christ. The tunes and words of Victorian hymns retain their former power to stir our feelings, but the serious literature of faith is opaque and forbidding. We cannot engage with collections of sermons, prolix theological texts and contributions to those inter-denominational disputes that consumed so much clerical passion and time. Religious novels, compulsory reading on Sunday afternoons and bestsellers in their time, are literary curiosities more likely to raise a smile than a tear. Yet the trappings and creations of Victorian spirituality convey one important message: belief in God and His word was normal.

Victorian Britain regarded itself as a Christian nation. Its collective faith was a source of strength and justified the belief that the country was a chosen agent of Providence. In the autumn of 1857, when things were going badly in the Indian Mutiny, a day of atonement and prayer was decreed. Congregations fell to their knees, acknowledged the nation's sinfulness and pleaded for the restoration of God's favour. Yet, paradoxically, Britain was an open society in which all opinions could be expressed freely, although freethinkers and atheists had occasionally been prosecuted in the 1840s. This would have been unimaginable forty years later when unbelief had become respectable and the proponents of new, scientific and empirical philosophies regularly engaged in public debates with the defenders of revealed, dogmatic Christianity.

Comic magazines may have scoffed at Darwin's theory of man's descent from monkeys, but if he was right the Scriptures were riddled with fancies and man was not a unique creation in God's image. Natural selection rather than divine sanction dictated the ordering of the universe, a conjecture that pleased some of the commercial middle classes who had always believed in competition as natural. Science and sceptical enquiry demolished the miraculous and superstitious elements in Christianity, which was a relief to many clergymen and intelligent laymen who no longer had to uphold what they had privately imagined to be unproven and unprovable. Pruning the dead wood of myth and untenable supposition led to new, flexible creeds in which believers stressed the existence of God and the value of His moral laws. The theists kept their God, the agnostics wavered and the atheists rejected Him.

The publication of Darwin's *Origin of Species* (1859) and the extended debate it provoked was part of a sea change in the intellectual atmosphere of the country. Doubt came out of the closet, although asking questions could be awkward, even dangerous. An Anglican parson told an upper-middle-class schoolboy that God existed simply because 'The world was so wonderful that somebody even more wonderful must have made it. Hence God.' 'But then, who made God?' the boy countered. His mentor was outraged; only the Devil could have put such a thought into the mind of a boy from a respectable, Christian family. As the boy realised afterwards, he had 'pried below the surface of belief . . . I had not known where to stop short of a logical consequence'.[1] Faith ought to have halted such probing. And it did for many, although, as Ruskin once observed, the middle classes were reluctant to examine or discuss exactly what they believed in.

John Taylor had no such inhibitions. His autobiography was a commentary on the state of his soul after 1840 when, aged twenty-nine, he had found divine grace. Ten years later, he asked: 'Who am I? Where am I – How am I – in the sight of God?' His own self-analysis revealed a sober man who worked hard for his family, shunned 'worldly' company, applied the principles of his faith to his duties as an attorney and coroner for Oldham and, by example, raised the 'tone' of his neighbourhood. His belief in God gave him strength in adversity. After his daughter Gertrude had died aged a few days, he consoled himself with the thought: 'If there are saints in Heaven, Gertrude must be among them.'[2] A comforting speculation that was visually rendered in those marble child-like angels which appear on so many gravestones of infants in Victorian cemeteries.

Taylor discovered salvation through Anglicanism; William Smith was converted at a revivalist Methodist meeting in the 1840s and spent the rest of his life preaching the gospel of redemption through grace. Religion made him respectable. It admitted him to the company of 'the best men and women' in his home town of Wellington in Shropshire. He recalled with pride the praise of a local attorney who had told him: 'William, I have watched you for years and never saw you in company that I would be ashamed of myself.' Piety was a passport to prosperity. Successively employed as a turnpike supervisor, shopkeeper, Post Office clerk and land agent, Smith wrote: 'one door closed after another opened, as all things work together for good to them that fear the Lord'.[3]

Taylor wrote his memoirs in the 1880s, and Smith completed his in the opening years of the twentieth century. They were conventional, middle-class believers whose faith and views of the universe and of their place in it were unshaken by contemporary theological or philosophical controversies. God had created them and their world and laid down the rules that guaranteed earthly happiness and eternal life. Their beliefs permeated the complementary worlds of worship and labour, whose oneness was celebrated in a hymn:

> Work shall be prayer, if all be wrought
> As Thou wouldst have it done:

> And prayer, by thee inspired and taught,
> Itself with work be one.[4]

All work was of equal value to a God who continued to bless the social order. Religion remained a social cement, as another hymn proclaimed:

> God has given each his station:
> Some have riches and high place,
> Some have lowly homes and labour;
> All may have his precious grace.
>
> And God loveth all his children,
> Rich and poor, and high and low;
> And they shall meet in heaven
> Who have served Him here below.

More middle- than working-class worshippers sang these verses. The presumption that Britain was a Christian nation rested on the fervour of a middle-class minority rather than the professed faith of the masses. This disturbing fact was revealed one rainy Sunday in March 1851 when England's Christians went to church and chapel to be counted. The tally caused consternation: 7.26 million adults were at prayer that day, 10.67 million were not. A further million children were estimated to have attended Sunday School. The pews were most crowded in rural areas and provincial cities and towns and emptiest in the industrial conurbations. In Manchester and Tower Hamlets scarcely a third of the mainly working-class population attended a service. Understandably, given the result, no further religious censuses were held, which was just as well given that anecdotal evidence suggested a gradual decline in churchgoing during the second half of the century. This was confirmed in 1910 when a survey of Protestant churches, chapels and Sunday Schools in Wales revealed that only 40 per cent of the population owned up to any religious belief.[5]

In 1851 roughly half the worshippers were Anglicans, the rest nonconformists and Catholics. That maestro of episcopal silliness, William Wilberforce ('Soapy Sam'), the Bishop of Oxford, smelt a rat and told the Lords that the smaller dissenting sects had treated the survey as 'a trial of strength' and exaggerated the size of their congregations. 'Many of their ministers were not of the same rank of life as the clergy of the Established Church,' which explained their ungentlemanly conduct.[6] In his own diocese, the parson of Chipping Norton blamed packed chapels on local manufacturers who gave preference to fellow nonconformists when it came to jobs.[7] In rural parishes, fear of the disapprobation of squire and parson propelled tenant farmers and labourers (who were often still restricted to the pews at the back of the nave) into church.

Allegations of rigging were a further token of the animosities that split the Victorian churches. Each denomination claimed a monopoly of truth, and sectarian partisanship was endemic, vinegary and occasionally violent. Passions could run so high that the middle class even suspended its abhorrence of public violence. Unbelievably, Lord Francis Osborne, the high-church rector of Great Elm in Somerset, became involved in a fracas with parishioners on the village green after he had refused burial rites to a Methodist in 1874. Another respectable local figure, his bailiff Mr Titt, stripped to his shirt and weighed in, to the delight of his master who shouted, 'That's it, Titt, give him a licking!'[8] In 1894 middle-class nonconformists pelted the police in Weston-super-Mare when several of their number were prosecuted for refusing to obey the vaccination law on grounds of conscience.[9] Closed minds were usually mean-spirited. 'His death will be no loss to anybody, for he was a rank but amiable infidel, and most dangerous person,' ran the *Church Herald*'s obituary of John Stuart Mill in 1873. At the same time, Welsh nonconformists boasted that 'The chapel has stood between Wales and Heathenism.' Welsh Anglicans riposted: 'The Chapel stands between Wales and Religion.'[10]

All denominations agreed that it was imperative to cultivate the faith of the young, a duty that conscientious middle-class parents took very seriously. A Christian education was founded on the discipline of Sabbath observance, which began the previous afternoon when Mama swept toys from the nursery:

> Haste, put your playthings all away,
> To-morrow is the Sabbath day,
> Come bring me your Noah's ark,
> Your pretty, tinkling music-cart.
> Because my love, my love you must not play,
> But keep holy the Sabbath day.[11]

Sundays provided one otherwise pious man with the 'gloomiest recollections of childhood'. Games, walks and books were banned with the exception of such uplifting works as *Pilgrim's Progress* and tracts full of the 'dreary wastes of sermonising and controversy'.[12] During the second half of the century these were augmented by Christian weeklies with poems, short stories and serials, all with a high moral content.

Boredom could be as corrosive as intellectual uncertainties. In later life, the children of early- and mid-Victorian Britain looked back on long and hectoring sermons with horror. Sir Herbert Maxwell spoke for a generation when he wrote of his boyhood in the 1850s:

> . . . I was more conscientious than devout. At no time in my life have I enjoyed public worship or found it refreshing, as many people do. I was always glad, not when they said unto me, 'Let us go into the house of the Lord,' but when, service being over, I was at liberty to depart. I attribute this as a natural reaction from the excessive amount of church going I had been put through as a child.[13]

Old dogmas reiterated at length and often bombastically alienated the educated middle class at a time when doubt was being aired openly and gaining credence. Invocations of hell and damnation in an icy chapel one November Sunday in 1884 incensed an Aberdeen student who found the preacher's delivery as repellent as his 'old, harsh bitter unsatisfying Calvinist theology'.[14] Such diatribes were fit only for unsophisticated congregations 'in some obscure part of the Highlands'. Dragooned by his mother into the London meeting house of one of the glummer dissenting sects in the early 1890s, William Bowyer recalled polemics against other denominations whose followers would be bound for hell. A twisted theology had affected the physiognomy of his fellow worshippers, all of whom seemed to be 'deformed or undersized, flat-chested or round shouldered, red-nosed and skinny'.[15]

The decay of old orthodoxies and the haemorrhage of worshippers paralysed the churches. The malaise and its causes had been evident for some time: in 1854 two Oxford parsons regretted that the middle classes in their parishes were either too 'worldly' or distracted by other things to attend church.[16] In 1870 J. B. Sturrock, the minister of Paisley, blamed 'materialism' and 'Pantheism' for the disappearance of conventional beliefs among 'all classes of the reading public'.[17] New weekend recreations proved more attractive than sermons; in 1911 a Glaswegian minister regretted that his middle-class parishioners were being lured away from the kirk by motoring and golf.[18] One answer was for the churches to offer counter-distractions. In 1904 the Church of Scotland's Young Men's Guilds organised group tours to Whitby and Amsterdam and in the following year trips were planned to the Highlands and, rather daringly, Paris.[19]

Excursions and high jinks were not an antidote to doubt, although they fostered a community spirit among worshippers. C. F. G. Masterman suspected that the middle class were losing their confidence in the 'arcane and unreal forms' of worship and were no longer willing to swallow traditional dogmas. Moreover, the growing number of alternative faiths (some secular) provided the middle class with a choice denied their ancestors. In 1914, Dorothy Sayers, a clergyman's daughter and future crime novelist, then at Somerville, was questioned by an aunt on her 'soul's welfare'. It was the sort of subject dear to 'earnest people of narrow experience', and Dorothy answered as tactfully as she could. What she had learned counted for nothing and what mattered was what she discovered for herself by evaluating what was being offered, including Christianity.[20] Significantly, it was now permissible to poke fun at religion. In 1895 a *Punch* cartoon showed a schoolboy leaving church with his smartly dressed middle-class parents. The son addresses his mother: 'Mamma, didn't the vicar say that the natives of Gongalooloo wore no clothes.' 'Yes, darling.' 'Then why did papa put a button in the bag.'

Despite falling congregations and challenges to Scriptural verities, Christian ethics remained supreme. They were enforced by national and local associations, often closely connected with churches, which served as a moral gendarmerie. Their largely middle-class membership was primarily concerned with the suppression of licentiousness, in particular invitations to sexual promiscuity in the form of pornography. The ideology behind this activity was a blend of Old Testament injunctions, current medical alarms about the mental and physical consequences of masturbation and a general apprehension that, if unchecked, sexual licence could somehow debilitate the nation. Marie Lloyd was wrong: a little bit of what you fancy did not do you good. Preserving national continence depended on the co-operation of the Home Office, police, magistrates' courts and of course laws that defined public morals.

Framing this sort of legislation was difficult since it intruded on individual liberty and taste. During the debate on the 1857 Obscene Publications bill, two illustrious jurists, Lords Brougham and Lyndhurst, wondered whether certain Renaissance paintings and the poetry of Rochester, Congreve and Wycherley might become liable for prosecution.[21] And not a moment too soon, declared the bill's sponsor, Lord Chief Justice Campbell. 'Cackling like an old hen', he read erotic passages from a recently published translation of Dumas' *The Lady of the Camellias*, an example of a kind of literature that he believed 'more deadly than prussic acid, strychnine, or arsenic'. Overblown language had always been part of the vocabulary of censorship, and on this occasion it carried the day; the bill was passed. It had been supported by the *Daily Telegraph* with a report of young men and women from the 'respectable classes' staring at allegedly indecent prints and pictures displayed in the windows of London shops.

When did curiosity become an urge for gratification? This was not clear in the act, which had to be fine-tuned by Lord Chief

Justice Cockburn in 1868 when he defined 'obscene' as 'tending . . . to deprave and corrupt those whose minds were open to such immoral influences'. He had in mind the young and the working classes.[22] This was presumably why vigilance associations secured the prosecution of cheap translations of Boccaccio and Rabelais rather than more expensive versions. This notion that the working classes were peculiarly susceptible to sexual images and erotic literature had a long life. During a 1931 prosecution of a seller of saucy French postcards ('Jeunes Filles Modernes'), one lawyer commented that 'A costermonger, for instance, might be more easily corrupted in that way than a highly educated man.'[23] This had been the hope of the accused, who had waved the pictures at young working men with the promise, 'These are really hot.' A police inspector who approached his stall to examine the photos was mortified: 'I could see hair showing around her private parts.'

Despite the watchfulness of purity campaigners, this kind of material remained freely available. Between 1858 and 1880 moral vigilance associations secured the confiscation of a quarter of a million pornographic images.[24] Some may have passed through the hands of 'a tall ugly' boy at Eton who in the late 1850s was distributing 'evil books and prints' and offering 'pornic experience' to anyone who would listen. One who shunned his wares did so because of the influence of his parents who, he thought, 'trusted their son to keep himself clean'.[25] In the early 1900s, 'smut' was a popular topic among teenage Post Office clerks who furtively pored over photographs of nudes, probably from various 'Etudes d'après nature' collections imported from France, where the law treated them as 'art'. In Britain they were pornography, a judgment that extended to literature and led to the banning of a translation of Zola's *La Terre* in 1888.

Another French import, the can-can, was among the displays that incensed Liverpool's Society for the Suppression of Vicious Practices in 1857. It was one of the entertainments staged at the Lime Street Hop, which was a cross between a cabaret and night club, and its patrons included men 'with highly respected positions' in the city. Its owner defended the propriety of his establishment by every night playing the National Anthem before closing time. His enemies suspected, quite rightly, that the Lime Street Hop was a place of assignation and was frequented by prostitutes. Men and women were among the audience of a similar dive in Great Charlotte Street where, among other diversions, they enjoyed watching 'poses plastique' including a naked couple posing as Adam and Eve.[26]

Both places of amusement had been open for several years. Along with other 'notorious houses', they had attracted the attention of vigilantes not on account of the pleasures they offered, but because of the rumpus created by their departing clients in the early hours. Some were so drunk that they could not distinguish between who was and who was not a prostitute. Respectable women returning home from parties and concerts were regularly 'insulted'. It was not so much a matter of purifying the city as of saving the neighbourhood. This was also the case around Piccadilly in 1856 where a respectable area was in peril of becoming a red-light district. The root of the trouble was that landlords got higher rents from brothels and gaming dens. Some held out, like the widow of 'a respectable tradesman', but she found that potential lodgers were deterred by the presence of whorehouses in the street. Pressure was put on the police by the rector and churchwardens of St James, Jermyn Street, with help from the Society for the Suppression of Vice.[27]

Alerting the authorities to blatant immorality was the result of often painstaking sleuthing in areas and on premises where wantonness was suspected. During the summer of 1896 purity campaigners ventured into London's music halls and were shocked beyond their greatest expectations. They subsequently presented their findings to the local magistrates in an effort to have the licences of these premises revoked. Marie Lloyd, clad in knickerbockers and singing 'Give it a wink', upset the wife of a Baptist minister, but this vigilante recovered her equilibrium sufficiently to count the number of girls drinking with 'swells' and 'fast men'. Other vigilantes were shocked by Miss Lloyd's appearance as a schoolgirl singing 'I asked Johnny and I know now' and another chanteuse singing a ballad about a girl crossing a stile with the chorus 'And what I saw I will not tell'. Most mortifying of all, two female vigilantes were mistaken for loose women.

One, frowning at the debauchery around her, was approached by an elderly man who asked her to look 'a little more cheerful' and offered to buy her a drink. The other, Miss Read of the Social Purity Branch of the Women's Temperance Association, was evicted by the manager of the music hall on the ground that she appeared to be 'looking for men'.[28]

Delivered in a po-faced manner, this evidence caused amusement in court and no doubt to readers of press reports of the case. The music halls got their licences from magistrates who appreciated the difference between vulgarity and depravity. Undeterred, the purity campaigners battled on. In 1911 the London Council for Public Morality, formidably backed by three bishops and a trio of public school headmasters, protested to the Home Secretary about the contents of London shows. There were also protests against 'indecent' advertisements and a new source of temptation, the 'sex novel'. There were misgivings too about a new backdrop for carnality, the darkened cinema.[29] In 1915 and 1916 the National Union of Women Workers had ten agents, seven of them spinsters, patrolling London's picture houses. One visited the Palladium in Brixton, where she was appalled to see 'young couples who do not come to see the pictures' smooching in the gallery and noted that the boxes 'facilitate indecency'.[30]

Only through such watchfulness was Babylon kept at bay. The nation was always vulnerable to moral subversion, and to suggest otherwise, however mildly, invited charges of tolerating degeneracy. There could be no moral neutrality in a country whose imperial destiny was unfolding. From time to time there were lurid warnings that the British Empire could easily follow the Roman and enter a spiral of decline if sexual profligacy was not checked.

It is impossible to gauge the depth of middle-class sympathy for the moral policing of society. Censorship appealed to the pious and patriotic, and there was a strong feeling that Britain had to project a wholesome image to the world because it was a beacon of civilisation and progress. In this context it was revealing that 'filth' and its derivatives were the words universally used by purity campaigners whenever they encountered sexual images or literature. Hygiene and chastity were complementary and equally desirable, although it was easier to provide clean water than to uphold standards of propriety and modesty.

There were middle-class males who patronised music halls and establishments like the Lime Street Hop, purchased pornography and frequented prostitutes. Counting them was impossible, although they occasionally emerged from the shadows when the providers of their pleasures were prosecuted. During the trial in 1894 of a quack who had made a small fortune selling bogus cures for syphilis, it was stated that his customers included university students, businessmen, commercial travellers and a clergyman, the last revelation causing a 'sensation' in the court. The *Lancet* report of the case concluded that there were always men 'unashamed' of their vices but 'ashamed' of their consequences, which was why they resorted to charlatans rather than doctors.[31] In his previous criminal existence this snake-oil salesman had been a pornography dealer, advertising his wares in public lavatories.

This sordid figure was a creature of the 'naughty' Nineties. As purity campaigners were uncomfortably aware, they were not just naughty in a music-hall sense of a slight loosening of corsets. The decade saw the appearance of the 'new' (that is, emancipated) woman, the loucheness of the Aesthetic movement and the downfall of its lodestar Oscar Wilde in 1895. His trial was a signal reminder that 'art' could easily slip into forbidden territory. *Punch* caught the tenor of middle-class revulsion at his crime:

> If such be 'Artists' then may Philistines
> Arise, plain sturdy Britons as of yore,
> And sweep them off and purge away the signs
> That England e'er such noxious offspring bore.

Similar indignation was provoked by the growing literary candour. Mary Oliphant, the authoress of the children's *Tell Jesus* (1864) which sold 300,000 copies in fifty years, denounced Hardy's *Jude the Obscure* (1896) as 'an assault on the stronghold of marriage' and full of 'grossness, indecency and horror'.[32]

Although unaware of it, Mrs Oliphant was fighting a skirmish in what turned out to be a rearguard action that would end with the case against the publication of *Lady Chatterley's Lover* in 1960. Then, the prosecution counsel famously asked the jury whether they would let their domestic servants read the novel, unconsciously echoing the Victorian purity lobby's belief in the innate corruptibility of the working classes. This was pure silliness. So too, in a different way, was the heavy-handed imposition of Old Testament codes on a country that was slowly drifting away from dogmatic religion. The enforcement of the great Thou-Shalt-Nots did not win over the sceptical or indifferent and left the lasting impression that 'middle-class' morality was essentially repressive and vindictive.

7

To Live Decently before His Fellows: The Triumph of the Public Schools

The ideals and architecture of the Victorian public schools were Gothic. It was a style exactly appropriate for institutions that imagined themselves the inheritors of ancient traditions of faith and learning. Rural isolation, grandiose chapels and cloisters suggested monastic brotherhoods striving after purity and knowledge. Pinnacles and parapets overlooked playing fields where young men took rigorous exercise, grew strong and absorbed codes of selflessness and fair play. This too was distinctly Gothic, in so far as strength and stamina tempered by a sense of personal honour and concern for others were regarded by the Victorians as the ideals of Christian chivalry. This Gothic moral revival was as appealing to the middle class as its aesthetic counterpart, and it had a long life. In 1929 Dr Cyril Norwood, headmaster of Harrow, compared the ancient ideal of chivalry with 'the ideal of service to the community' that was cultivated in public schools. 'It is based upon religion: it relies largely upon games and open-air prowess, where these involve corporate effort . . .'[1] From this union of monastery and Camelot emerged the paragon whose virtues were recited by Canon Joseph McCormick in a sermon preached to Cambridge undergraduates in 1892. 'The true Christian is the true gentleman – the honest, upright, God-fearing man, who will take no advantage of the innocent, and who will be just as straight in religious opinions and practices as in the concerns of daily life.'[2]

The new idealism of the public schools struck a chord with middle-class parents. More and more of their sons and, from the 1870s onwards, daughters were being sent to such schools. Older schools expanded to meet the demand and new ones were founded. By 1912 there were 127 fee-paying schools with a total of 36,000 pupils, mostly boarders, and numbers were steadily rising. Fees varied according to a pupil's age and the school's academic status. In the 1890s two middle-ranking boys' schools, Ardingly and Felsted, charged between twelve and twenty-one guineas a year. Denstone charged thirty-four guineas, forty-eight if a boy lodged with the headmaster. Parents of girls at North London Collegiate, a day school, paid between fifteen and twenty-one pounds a year, depending on their daughter's age.

A public school education was comparatively inexpensive by today's standards: the average termly fee was the same as the cost of a case of vintage brandy or a pair of superior binoculars. A yearly bill of twenty to forty pounds was well within the budget of say a successful doctor or dentist with an income of six to seven hundred pounds. The schools themselves were economically viable. In 1891 a small North Devon boys' school was put on the market with annual receipts of £558, of which £250 was profit. It had a roll of thirty-four, eleven of whom boarded for thirty guineas a year.[3]

What did the middle classes expect for their investment? They believed that their children would flourish at schools where the moral tone was lofty and where they would be safe from the contagious corruption that had tainted public schools a hundred years before. In a closely regulated environment boys and girls would learn how to integrate with what one champion of public schools called their 'corporate life' and so prepare them to take their 'place in the world'. Lessons in 'discipline, responsibility and devotion to a common cause' were an introduction to the outside world, for the public school was a microcosm of a nation that cherished these virtues. Within what was in effect a moral fortress, individuals discovered a sense of proportion, seriousness of purpose, emotional autonomy and an 'economy of sentiment' that made them proof against 'ill founded and hysterical enthusiasms'.[4] It went without saying that these qualities were fostered in a strongly Christian atmosphere, usually Anglican.

Advertisements for public schools offered the middle class tangible benefits. The socially ambitious could feel confident that their children would acquire social graces and make friends within a pure environment. Exclusiveness counted and was exploited by some schools. In 1898 a 'high-class, well known ladies school' moving to new premises on the south coast advertised places for 'well-connected girls'.[5]

Parents anxious about the future economic status of their offspring were promised intensive coaching for public examinations. Over forty years before, the middle class had been clamouring for competitive examinations as the fairest and most efficient method of recruiting public servants. Once the system had been installed, there was a demand for schools that concentrated on intensive coaching for these tests. Private schools responded and crammed pupils for the papers set by Woolwich, Sandhurst and sections of the domestic, colonial and Indian civil services. In 1906 a secure, well-paid future was offered to 'the sons of gentlemen' with a scientific bent by Seafield Park School near Fareham where they would be brought up to scratch for the entry exams set by the Indian Public Works Department.[6] By this date, the examination craze had extended to the professions and universities, which began to require dispassionate evidence of achievement and potential in the form of matriculation certificates issued by the various examination boards.

Less bright pupils joined classes for the army exams, while academic pupils were fine-tuned for Oxford and Cambridge. The cleverest chased scholarships, nearly all in Classics, and winning them was commonly seen as a measure of a public school's excellence.[7] The dominance of Classics at the two universities dictated curriculums, not only for star pupils. One army officer recalled tedious hours spent swotting for the Sandhurst exams in the 1890s. Two-thirds of his time was consumed by composing 'mediocre Latin elegiacs and Greek iambics', construing and rote-learning passages from set texts. The rest of his study was dedicated to a smattering of history, geography and maths and to translating written French (not a word of the language was ever spoken in the classroom).[8]

Hours spent studying dead languages was just what middle-class parents wanted. Giving evidence before a Parliamentary commission on education in 1866, a businessman with a son at Rugby dismissed the notion that men of his background had no time for the Classics. He was uninterested in 'commercial education' and insisted that what his son was learning would immeasurably help him 'keep his position in society'. Like the majority of fathers who were sending their sons to schools such as Rugby, he hoped that his son would emerge as a gentleman. 'Liberal education makes . . . the gentleman,' claimed Cardinal Newman, exactly echoing the dogma of late-medieval and Renaissance educationalists. 'It is well to have a cultivated intellect, a delicate taste, a candid, equitable, dispassionate mind, a noble and courteous bearing in the conduct of life; — these are the connatural qualities of a large knowledge; they are the objects of a University.'[9] If he had not already absorbed most of these qualities, the product of the post-Arnoldian public school was susceptible to them. Middle-class parents whose livelihoods depended upon industry and commerce were glad to have their sons taught the virtues of the Renaissance gentleman.

A Lambeth builder told the commission that men of his rank could easily afford twenty pounds a year for a boy's schooling and that he was keen for French to be taught on practical grounds.[10] Latin was 'serviceable', for it made children 'more sharp and intelligent' and he was spending twenty pounds a year to have his son's mind honed at one of the schools recently founded by Canon Nathaniel Woodard (1811–91), a Sussex cleric.

Woodard was the St John the Baptist of the public schools, tirelessly persuading the middle and lower sections of the middle class that it was their duty to send their sons to one of the schools he was founding. He fervently hoped that he could entice the middle classes away from nonconformity towards Anglicanism through a network of independent boarding schools. The son of an impoverished squire, Woodard was determined that, though his schools would widen the clientele for boarding education, they should not threaten the social order. The schools were therefore stratified according to parents' status and earnings. The top layer accepted only the sons of clergymen and gentlemen who paid between thirty and fifty guineas a year until they were eighteen and could proceed to university. The second stratum was for sons of 'trades classes' who paid eighteen guineas and left at sixteen for careers in commerce. The lowest stratum of schools took the sons of mechanics, small shopkeepers and clerks who earned less that a hundred and fifty pounds but could somehow afford twelve guineas a year. Schooling ended for these boys when they were fourteen. Woodard privately confessed that the monastic ethos of his schools would rescue boys from the 'noxious' influences that he imagined pervaded the homes of anyone in trade.[11]

Woodard was able to make headway in establishing his schools and in persuading the middle classes to patronise them because of a revolution that was transforming both the image and the reality of the public schools. It had begun in 1828, when the Reverend Dr Thomas Arnold was appointed headmaster of Rugby, and gained momentum during the next thirty years. Old schools were remodelled and new ones established on Arnoldian principles. The process was like a religious revival: Arnold was its high priest and its acolytes were his ushers, who departed, became headmasters and imposed his orthodoxies on their schools. Like their mentor, Arnold's apostles dreamed of regenerating not only their pupils but the nation by teaching the middle classes a philosophy that blended Anglicanism with a romantic notion of chivalry that embraced self-denial, purity of soul, fitness of body and the compassion of the strong for the weak. In time, this amalgam became known as 'muscular Christianity'.

Arnold's renovation of Rugby was a reaction to the moral decay of the public schools. There was a distinctly ancien-régime flavour to their ambience: masters were detached, distant figures who allowed boys considerable licence to run their own affairs, often anarchically. Intervention was risky since pupils defended their liberties pugnaciously. There were fourteen public school rebellions between 1793 and 1832, including four at Eton and two at Rugby, and at each school headmasters had to summon troops to restore their authority. Defenders of this turbulent, dog-eat-dog ethos argued that it was a perfect preparation for the mutable adult world of perpetual struggle. Boys suffered plenty of hard knocks, but enduring blows to body and self-esteem was preferable to being cocooned in an over-supervised 'mock Utopia', suggested one of Arnold's critics.[12]

Arnold intuitively understood that the middle classes wanted Utopia for their sons. He provided them with a structured, orderly society in which their innocence could be defended against sexual corruption. He and his followers sincerely believed that regular attendance at chapel and guidance from the pulpit could stiffen resistance to sinfulness. Testosterone-fuelled violence was directed towards and burned out on the playing field. Competitive team games also reinforced loyalties to house and school, and their strict rules and emphasis on fair play taught self-control. Revealingly, Arnold banned aristocratic field sports from Rugby, so that boys no longer appeared with their horses, hounds, sporting guns and gun dogs. Their owners may have been beyond redemption, unlike Arnold's favourite pupils, who were the sons of country gentlemen of moderate means and sober habits. Appropriately enough, Tom Brown – whose fictional rites of passage at Arnold's Rugby were set down by Thomas Hughes (an alumnus of the school) – came from just this background.

Tom's Brown's Schooldays (1859) described a self-contained, tightly disciplined, stratified community. Arnold had made senior boys partners in running the school and created a hierarchy of service and virtue. On the lowest level the new boy learned submission as a fag undertaking chores for his seniors. If he showed the qualities that won the approval of his superiors (both masters and prefects), he moved upwards to learn the responsibilities of authority as a prefect. Special insignia denoted an individual's place in the pecking order: at Rugby accomplished rugby players received a velvet cap with gold tassels which gave exemption from fagging. Physical prowess was a measure of virtue, for the boy who had been 'capped' was expected 'to live decently before his fellows' and publicly uphold the rules of 'good form'.[13] Other schools copied Rugby, creating a ruling elite of prefects, monitors, praepostors and, of course, crack games players.

Every public school invented its often idiosyncratic honours systems, with 'colours' awarded for players in school or house teams. Recipients wore a regalia of caps, distinctive ties and blazers and sometimes enjoyed arcane privileges. The middle-class boy learned from experience how to exist and flourish within a hierarchical society in which, theoretically, perseverance and decency were rewarded. The regalia of comparative rank also fostered the corporate identity of school and house and evolved into that peculiar advertisement of a man's place in the world, the old school tie, with its variations for outstanding games players. It mattered not only to belong, but to be seen to have belonged. Belonging was also expressed by a school's peculiar slang, mastering which was one of the first duties of a new boy. Institutional loyalty and bonds of brotherhood were also fostered through the rituals of founders' days, special anniversaries and ceremonies where prizes were given and the scholars delivered orations in Greek and Latin.

These shared rituals reinforced the overriding objective of the post-Arnoldian public schools, the creation of a moral aristocracy whose members were gentlemen, irrespective of their background or antecedents. In the words of Dr Edmond Warre the headmaster who raised the moral tone of Eton between 1884 and 1905, the public school alumnus was 'on the side of good'. He did good in the world and set it an example, for his conversation was 'clean' and his energies were directed towards whatever was 'innocent . . . wholesome and unselfish'.[14]

This paragon would have been a keen games player. Team games were central to the life of the new public schools; some said that they dominated it. They were right in so far as the values of the playing field were integral to the concept of the Christian gentleman. He placed team before self, humbly submitted to the judgments of referee or umpire and played fairly according to the rules. In the process he accumulated honour, irrespective of his batting average, wickets taken or tries scored. He also overcame physical and mental pain and was the better for it. 'What man who rows does not exult in the mighty swing of the trained arms and the speed, though the skill and strength involved pain?' Edmond Thring, headmaster of Uppingham, asked a congregation of Cambridge undergraduates. This was because 'lesser pain may underlie great joy, and indeed produce it'.[15] How Thring would have applauded the ex-public schoolboys who founded the I Zingari cricket club and insisted that members who had been struck by a ball never paused to rub the bruise.

Playing the game well was good for the soul as much as for the body. Hitherto, the middle-class male had not been noted for his physical exertion. Necessity compelled him to ride and walk, and if he lived in the countryside he might shoot, fish and hunt. Now, thanks to the public schools, middle-class boys were being invited to take regular, often violent exercise playing soccer, rugby and cricket. They found all to their taste and continued to play as adults. In the 1870s university rugger appeared and fifteens were formed from trainee and practising doctors at the London teaching hospitals (for example, Guy's and Bart's) and from among civil servants and lawyers. The Rochdale Hornets, founded in 1871, included a local magistrate, watchmaker, shopkeepers, a merchant and solicitors and managing directors. Ex-pupils of Sheffield Collegiate School banded together in 1857 to play football. The club had a high prestige thanks to what a local newspaper called 'the character' of its players, who were 'almost exclusively of the middle class'.[16]

These manly fellows, like their counterparts in public schools, were playing the game for its own sake and their rewards were personal fitness and a feeling of having done their best. Winning was secondary, or was it? There was a contradiction within the mid-Victorian world of middle-class games. While the dedicated player gained respect for his generous spirit, there were inter-house and inter-school competitions with trophies to be won. Patterns of competitiveness were reproduced in the outside world where, by the 1870s, local and national rugby and football leagues ran their own contests. Boys and men were overcome with tremulous excitement before matches, and then as now speculation about a team's or a player's performance was a major source of everyday masculine conversation.

The third quarter of the nineteenth century saw cricket, football and rugby pass from the public schools into the mainstream of British culture. The number of clubs affiliated to the Football Association rose from fifty in 1871 to over ten thousand in 1905. There was pressure for competitive games to be introduced into the new elementary schools where drill (that is, physical jerks) was the only form of exercise for working-class children. School boards were sympathetic and middle-class enthusiasts gave money for playing fields because they would encourage an instinct for fair play among the poor, as well as toughen them up.[17] By the first decade of the twentieth century, games were part of the syllabus in nearly every elementary school.

Expansion brought with it conflict. The middle-class vision of the playing field was a testing ground for moral virtues and was reserved for amateurs with spare time to play and train. The adept working-class rugger or soccer player wanted to be paid, if only in the sense of compensation for time off work and for the costs of travel. The middle class saw this as the first stage of a downhill slide towards professional players, who would threaten the moral ethos of sport. In 1894 a Rugby Union official and old Haileyburian expressed the fear that professionals would 'play very keenly without quite the spirit of the game'.[18] Four years later, the world of rugby divided along social and geographical lines. The Rugby Football Union remained. Middle-class, amateur and public-school orientated, it dominated the south, with strong outposts in South Wales, the Midlands and the Borders, while the Rugby League was working class, professional and dominated the north. The same split occurred within soccer, with the proliferation of clubs from industrial areas employing professionals.

The erosion of the amateur spirit was widely lamented. In 1912 a former headmaster deplored 'professional athleticism, [the] craze for record breaking, and the deification of champion performers', which were symptoms of the 'decay of strenuous national vigour'.[19] There was plenty of such hand-wringing, and the MCC (Marylebone Cricket Club) insisted that 'players' (that is, professionals) had separate changing rooms from 'gentlemen' (that is, amateurs), an arrangement that lasted until the middle of the twentieth century.[20] A gentleman was designated on the score card by his name and his initials, a player by his surname alone. The middle class's objections to professionalism and razor-edged competitiveness seemed uncharacteristic since it had always believed that competition was natural and essential for the creation of wealth and the advancement of mankind. But, thanks to the ideology of the public schools, sport was an exception to this rule. If not quite sacred, it had acquired a nobility that would be tarnished by money and the urge to win at all costs. Like the medieval knight, the true sportsman sought nothing more than honour and reputation.

Superficially, this antipathy to professional sport appeared to reflect a wider hostility to money-making that was embedded in the culture of the late-Victorian public schools. It has been argued that they turned generations of middle-class boys away from the commercial world in which their fathers had flourished towards careers that allowed the Christian gentleman to follow his conscience and do good. High-mindedness was not compatible with chasing profits, and the public schools had resurrected an old and now largely dormant social prejudice against trade. This apparent shift in attitudes has been described by Correlli Barnett, who imagined that it led to a decay of the inventiveness and entrepreneurial spirit that had underpinned the Industrial Revolution. Economic sclerosis and the decline of British global power followed close behind.[21]

This places a heavy responsibility on the public schools and flatters the capacity of schoolmasters to influence the upper echelons of the middle class. Yet the registers of public school alumni suggest the opposite. Judged by their subsequent careers, public schoolboys had a strong spirit of enterprise and were willing to engage in business, particularly in the growing number of foreign and colonial ventures. Of the thirteen boys who enrolled at Repton during the academic year 1854–5, the subsequent careers of ten are recorded. There were three lawyers (one became a judge in Madras), two graduated from university (one taking a post as an interpreter in

China), two went into business, one became a dentist, one was commissioned in the army and another emigrated to New South Wales. A similar pattern emerges from the thirty-seven boys who entered Repton in 1880–1.

Army commission	2
Business	10
Engineering/Science	1
Law/Medicine	5
University	15

Among the rest were a schoolmaster, an artist and an Indian administrator.[22]

Similar preferences were found among the old boys of Sedbergh and Haileybury, both schools with a predominantly middle-class intake. The subsequent occupations of Sedbergh's class of 1884–5 were:

Army commission	2
Business	16
Engineering/Science	3
Law/Medicine	7

The rest included two at university, two architects, a civil servant and educational administrator. Among those engaged in business were a coffee planter in India, a real-estate dealer in the USA and a farmer in Tasmania.[23]

Haileybury's class of 1888–9 reveals the same pattern:

Army commission	4
(one in the Anglo-Egyptian army)	
Business	15
Law/Medicine	4
Engineering/Science	2
Home/Imperial government	4

The remaining dozen included two clergymen, a schoolmaster and an architect. As with Sedbergh, overseas ventures proved alluring; old

Haileyburians turned to tea planting in Ceylon, banking in Brazil and Bombay, fruit farming in California and ranching in Oregon.[24] At a time when more and more British capital was flowing abroad, young public schoolmen were following it to run the enterprises it was funding.

There had been no appreciable drift away from business nor a rush into occupations such as administration and teaching where the opportunities for doing good were more obvious. It was a slightly different matter with the universities, traditionally a stepping stone to holy orders. Of the twenty-one freshmen who entered Gonville and Caius College, Cambridge in 1849–50, ten were ordained and nine were evenly split between teaching, the civil service and the law. Of the remaining two, one (a clothier's son) proceeded to work with Brunel and the other became manager of the Brazil Telegraph Company.[25] Within forty years during which the college, in common with others, had expanded, the pattern had changed. The breakdown of the fifty-eight members of the class of 1886 to 1887 was:

Army commission	3
Business	6
Engineering/Science	4
Law/Medicine	20
Church	15
Teaching	4

Of the rest, one graduate followed his father as editor of the *Leeds Mercury* and another became a plantation overseer in British Guiana, where he died in a shooting accident.[26]

By this date the public schools had achieved a near monopoly of Oxford and Cambridge. Of the twenty-one Gonville and Caius freshmen in 1849–50, one-third had attended public schools and one-third had been educated privately by tutors. In 1886–7 thirty-four out of sixty-one came from public schools, seven from urban grammar schools and none had had private tuition. The middle class had clearly been converted to boarding, although there were several instances of fathers transferring their sons from one public school to another, presumably in the hope of better results. Investment in education often fulfilled dynastic ambitions: the careers of the

Gonville and Caius men include several examples of sons following their fathers into law and medicine. There were also some shifts in status within the middle class: the son of a chief engineer for the Midland Railway became a barrister and the son of a corn merchant a solicitor. And there were movements from professions to commerce: a clergyman's son took a post as a grain broker in Canada. Wherever they ended up, the products of the public schools and universities almost universally remained within the middle class.

Like their equivalents at public schools, a large body of university graduates passed into the world of middle-class work, for which their education had not been a direct preparation. This was not a handicap, for they possessed something that was more highly valued than vocational training. They had acquired what Newman had called 'liberal or gentlemen's knowledge', which he defined as knowledge purely for 'its own end'. Its fruits were prudent and dispassionate judgment, a degree of caution in all things and a sense of moral responsibility. Between them, Arnold and Newman had taught the heirs of industrial Britain to regard themselves as a moral elite with special responsibilities to themselves and the outside world. Themes of continuity, moral uprightness and future public service and eminence mingle in the speech of welcome given by the warden of St Mary's College to freshmen in Compton Mackenzie's *Sinister Street* (1913):

> You have come to Oxford . . . some of you to hunt foxes, some of you to wear very large and unusual overcoats, some of you to row for your college and a few of you to work. But all of you have come to Oxford to remain English gentlemen. In after life when you are ambassadors and proconsuls and members of Parliament you will never remember this little address which I have the honour of delivering to you. That will not matter, so long as you always remember that you are St Mary's men and the heirs of an honourable and ancient foundation.

The aside on fox hunting was a reminder that the aristocracy had not been completely ousted from Oxford and Cambridge or the

A monument to the industrial age: the Cannon Street terminus of the South Eastern Railway in 1866. The style is Renaissance derivative, but the materials (glass and iron) are modern. *(Illustrated London News)*

Steam, ingenuity and progress: laying the track for a new inner-London railway line in the early 1860s. Such operations involved extensive demolition of houses, but aroused no middle-class protests, unlike road construction in the 1990s. *(London Transport Museum)*

The pleasures of progress: William Powell Frith's *The Railway Station* of 1863 shows middle-class passengers and their luggage. *(Bridgeman Art Library)*

First Class – The Meeting by Abraham Solomon: a wealthy father listens attentively to a young naval officer while his daughter listens admiringly. Perhaps he has returned from the Crimea and certainly he is a gentleman and therefore a suitable match.

(Bridgeman Art Library)

Commuting, 1906: City clerks read their newspapers untroubled by a workman.
hundred years later their successors will endure the same discomforts. *(Illustrated London News)*

Rush hour: office workers and buses cross London Bridge in about 1890.
(Guildhall Library, City of London)

Holiday time for the middle class

A trip round the bay, St Andrews. *(University of St Andrews Library)*

A sedate promenade at Minehead: in some resorts the local authorities segregated the 'respectable' from noisy, working-class day trippers. *(University of St Andrews Library)*

Highland adventure: passengers embark at Iona *(University of St Andrews Library)*

High jinks. four clerks enjoy a day out at Worthing. *(University of St Andrews Library)*

The suburbs

An escape from the city: the new suburb of Bedford Park at Turnham Green in 1879. Exteriors and interiors were inspired by the nascent aesthetic movement and the setting is rural. *(Illustrated London News)*

A half acre of heaven for the lower-middle classes: a suburban garden in 1905. *(Getty Images)*

The poor man at his gate: a posed photograph of the 1860s which shows
a respectable lady in a crinoline visiting a labourer's family bringing gifts and advice.

(Time Life Pictures/Getty Images)

Manly relaxation: a mid-century cricket match between Sussex and Kent.
(Bridgeman Art Library)

New pleasures: a quartet of golfers arrive by car at the Old Golf Course at St Andrews in 1904. At least one Presbyterian minister blamed golf and motoring for falling congregation

(University of St Andrews Library)

public schools, far from it. They shared both with the upper-middle class and sections of its better-off middling ranks. In terms of power and wealth, the middle class had gradually supplanted the old aristocracy of pedigrees and acres, but they desperately wanted to absorb its finer qualities and, by doing so, justify their ascendancy.

Although their pupils represented less than 1 per cent of those receiving schooling in 1912, the Victorian and Edwardian public schools were the nurseries of the men who would exercise authority and whose opinions counted during the next half-century. Former public schoolboys filled cabinets, governed the Empire, commanded its armies and navies, dominated boardrooms, crowded the judicial bench and were the mandarins of the civil service. In 1939 between 68 and 80 per cent of the higher civil service, judiciary, bishops and directors of banks were the alumni of late-Victorian and Edwardian public schools. It seemed only right and proper that a former public schoolboy, Rupert Brooke (1887 1915), who combined athleticism and aestheticism with fresh virginal good looks, became a national icon for youthful courage and self-sacrifice in the early stages of the First World War.

Of course there were rebels who found the pressure to conform cloying, refused to knuckle under and despised the system. Alec Waugh, whose *Loom of Youth* (1917) was published when he was nineteen and serving in the trenches, used his experiences at Sherborne to expose the often corrosive tensions between athleticism and aestheticism. Another young officer, Robert Graves, wrote scathingly about his time at Charterhouse in his autobiography *Goodbye to All That* (1929). Yet Waugh later confessed to having been happy at Sherborne. Thousands like him acquiesced and made the best of things (learning this was perhaps the most valuable feature of a public school education) and suppressed their miseries and discontents. They believed that they had benefited, and sent their own sons to public schools.

Critics of the public schools detected an inbuilt conservatism and philistinism. The encouragement of quietism, corporate conformity and a reverence for peculiar traditions (often invented and comparatively modern) were the seeds of stagnation. Furthermore, the manic pursuit of athleticism generated undercurrents of antipathy towards whatever was creative, imaginative or intellectual. Headmasters and boys were suspicious of 'cleverness', which they considered far less worthy than 'character' moulded on the playing field. The gospel of robust Christian manliness was sometimes overwhelming, which may be why in 1891 a Devon boarding school promised that 'Young and delicate boys receive special care.'[27] Elsewhere, others of this disposition did not receive such consideration, as John Bejetman (Marlborough in the early 1920s) remembered:

> The dread of beatings! Dread of being late!
> And, greatest dread of all, the dread of games![28]

The consequences of that moral care which involved the preservation of what headmasters imagined to be boyhood purity had results that are difficult to evaluate given the general reticence on this subject in so many autobiographies.[29] A doctor's son, John Addington Symonds believed from experience that 'many forms of passion between males are a matter of fact' and encountered plenty at Harrow in the 1850s, where he also discovered that the headmaster Dr Vaughan had a clandestine passion for one boy.[30] Seventy years later, Robin Maugham, found transient adolescent homosexuality common both at his preparatory school and at Eton.[31] E. W. Benson, an Arnoldian missionary, was pleased that he had only a few cases at Wellington when he was headmaster in the 1870s, thanks to stiff doses of sermons and dormitory patrols by matrons. He did expel three boys for having sex with a fourteen-year-old maidservant, but was shocked to find that his predominantly aristocratic governors treated the scandal with indifference or benevolent amusement.[32] No wonder Arnold feared that noblemen's sons were a source of moral pollution.

Private schools of all kinds reinforced existing social barriers. The concept that education could be used to promote social equality was alien to the Victorian middle classes, although most of them passionately believed that schooling was a vehicle by which poor but able individuals could rise within society. The orthodox view and the thinking behind it were expressed by a judge in 1860 when he decided a case involving an old provincial free grammar school that wanted to take fee-paying boarders. Mixing the sons of poor and rich men was unwise, for the former would be resentful and, ultimately, isolated, for there was a 'tendency for the higher classes to exclude the lower'. Segregation was preferable.[33]

Middle-class parents concurred, sometimes for different reasons. Wealthy men did not want their sons to go to local schools and pick up the local brogue. Even parents who could not afford fees and had to send their children to board schools were sensitive on this point. In 1881 the Horsham school board proposed to make St Mark's 'a better class school' by raising the small weekly charge to attract 'middle-class' parents.[34] Anxieties about social contamination may have persuaded the school boards of York and Warrington to ban some of the poorest children because of their 'undesirable manners and conversation'. Where sufficient endowments were available, some grammar schools upheld the tradition of an open door. In 1911 thanks to local authority assistance, Bradford Grammar School could offer between 160 and 170 free places and the recipients secured a disproportionate share of the academic honours.[35]

Like many other grammar schools, Bradford modelled itself on the post-Arnoldian public schools. Paradoxically its rituals and hierarchies would have been familiar to the lower-middle-class and working-class scholarship boys. Late-Victorian Britain saw a proliferation of cheap weekly magazines for boys in which stirring yarns of pluck and audacity on imperial frontiers rubbed shoulders with tales of public school life. Public schools were the scenario for full-length novels such as Kipling's *Stalky and Co* (1899), and in the next decade the adventures of their pupils became a staple of penny comics such as *Gem* and *Magnet*, home to Greyfriars and Billy Bunter. The elementary school and errand boy shared at a distance a world of eccentric beaks in mortar boards, swishing canes, dorms, tuck-boxes, fagging and nail-biting moments in closely run house matches. It was exciting and often funny and not unrealistic stuff, and made public school a part of the culture of all classes.[36] This literature may even have helped spread the lofty ideals which the public schools had come to represent. As Bunter knew too well, the greedy, caddish and deceitful always got their come-uppance. Dr Arnold would have approved.

8

The New Woman: Marriage and Its Alternatives

The accession of Queen Victoria made no difference to the status and treatment of women. The Queen's private life followed the pattern of marriage and motherhood that was preordained for middle-class women. In the middle years of her reign this model of the perfect female existence began to change, but slowly. Even though women were engaging in spheres of activity hitherto reserved for men, marriage and rearing children remained the feminine ideal. Frances Buss, the pioneer of women's education and founder of the North London Collegiate School, insisted that its middle-class girls attended only in the mornings, leaving the afternoons free for them to learn their future domestic responsibilities from their mothers. A guidebook for holidays for that new breed, single working women, published in 1887 had the inscription 'Victoria, Wife, Mother and Queen' on its cover, an instructive order of occupational precedence.[1]

One of the contributors to this pamphlet was proud to call herself a 'brainworker', a category of woman that would have been extremely rare and frowned upon fifty years before. Physical labour was another matter. It was forced upon working-class wives by economic necessity and, as philanthropists and reformers were forever warning, was detrimental to the welfare of their families. The middle-class wife was exempt from the burden of paid work: she was supported and protected by her husband. In return, she was revered as the goddess of the hearth who provides a comfortable and tranquil refuge from the hurly-burly of work. She supervised servants and the purchase of victuals, bore children, guided her sons through infancy and trained her daughters for their eventual duties as wives and mothers, and played the hostess. Above all, as Ruskin observed in *Sesame and Lilies* (1865), her life was wholly devoted to her husband's happiness and in this she gladly embraced 'self-renunciation' and what he called 'the modesty of service'.

Ruskin's paragon was judged by how well she carried out her domestic obligations. David Copperfield's first wife Dora failed to carry them out properly and her death removed an obstacle to his contentment, although he had been enchanted by her ornamental qualities. Glamour could never compensate for deficiencies in domestic competence, not least that touchstone of the good wife, her capacity to discipline children and servants. Cleaning the middle-class house, keeping it warm, feeding its inhabitants and washing their clothes were labour-intensive activities. Servants were essential. Their grind diminished somewhat towards the close of the century with improvements in gaslights and the appearance of the Ewbank cleaner, the gas stove and, in wealthier households, electric lighting. Changes in fashion also reduced the workload, particularly the pruning of those dust-collecting knick-knacks and framed family photographs so cherished by the middle classes. What one architectural critic called the 'simplicity and taste' of the Edwardian home meant, among other things, that it was easier to clean.[2]

Most middle-class families employed servants. In 1891 around 10 per cent of London households (roughly equivalent to the city's middle class) had resident servants. Of these, 6 per cent had one, and 4 per cent had two or more, and there were many wives who had part-time charwomen and laundresses.[3] Permanent servants were expensive; they expected annual pay rises, and wage levels were increasing (see Table 5).

Table 5: Annual wages of permanent servants, 1871 and 1907[4]

	1871	1907
Cook	£15 0s 0d	£19 5s 0d
General servant	£12 14s 6d	£18 0s 0d
Housemaid	£10 0s 0d	£15 0s 0d
Nursemaid	£13 0s 0d	£15 16s 0d

These figures excluded the cost of uniforms, food and laundering.

Hiring, firing and overseeing servants was a fraught and time-consuming business. The best came with a 'character' from a previous employer which testified to their industry, diligence, sobriety and tractability. Country girls of twelve to fourteen were preferred as novices because it was believed they had been brought up to be deferential. These virtues were uncommon and commanded a higher price that most middle-class budgets could not afford. Instead, there were the equivalents of 'that stupid girl Sarah', Carrie Pooter's general maid, who could be negligent and intrusive, threw tantrums and once was slapped by Mrs Birrell the charwoman whom she had accused of being drunk. Idle and temperamental servants were commonplace, a topic of everyday conversation between their mistresses and the source of that peculiarly middle-class source of amusement, the servant joke. A favourite theme was the exasperation of the employer and the careless servant's capacity to blend innocence with pertness. It appeared in a *Punch* carton of 1895 in which a young middle-class wife is reprimanding a maid: 'Susan, just look here! I can write my name in the dust on the top of this table.' 'Lor, mum, so you can! Now I never had no edjercation myself.'

Dealing firmly with Susan and her kind was something for which the young wife ought to have been prepared. The numberless vexations of everyday domestic life were tiresome, but the housewife had the compensation of knowing that she was fulfilling what her husband and society expected from her. Contemporary Darwinian theories and the findings of proto-psychologists suggested that she had inherited the innate qualities needed for her position in the world: tenderness, selflessness, generosity of spirit.

New science seemed to reinforce old conventions. Yet both were open to question. Individual women of intelligence and determination, of whom Florence Nightingale was the most famous, were making an impact on national life. Unmarried, Florence Nightingale concurred with the general view that for women marriage was 'a promotion which creates new duties', but she also believed and proved that she had what she once described as 'high purposes for mankind and God'. Many other upper-middle-class women sympathised with her aspirations and frustrations and found plenty of male allies. Once they turned their attentions towards entering the professions, these women encountered conservative men determined to defend their traditional preserves to the last ditch.

There was a further challenge to the orthodoxies concerning a woman's proper place in the world, paradoxically based upon scientific efforts to analyse the female character. It was argued that on the whole women were more patient, painstaking and willing to please than men. This conclusion was good news for the nation's economy since these were just the qualities needed for the routine, menial office work which men shunned. The rapid growth of commercial and public bureaucracies and the appearance in the mid-1870s of the mass-produced Remington typewriter coincided to provide a genteel employment for lower-middle-class teenage girls. In 1861 there had been fewer than five hundred female clerical workers, by 1911 there were just under 140,000. Most were shorthand typists, confined to the lower reaches of the office hierarchy and paid less then men performing similar tasks.[5] As a further reminder of their helotry, women were excluded from some occupations; they could undertake routine book-keeping, but not audit the result, for accountancy was a male profession.

The admission of young women into the masculine world of business and public administration was a concession to necessity. The home and not the office remained the focus of a woman's aspirations. This message was reiterated in the growing number of cheap weekly magazines that first appeared in the 1890s and catered for lower-middle-class girls and housewives. In 1898 an article provocatively titled 'Do Men Like Clever Girls?' in *Home Sweet Home* offered its readers a summary of feminine perfection:

> About medium height, with a smiling, cheerful face, rather pretty. Neatly and tastefully dressed. Lovable, good-tempered, and sympathetic. Fond of home, and chiefly interested in making it the brightest of all homes. Thinks her husband the dearest old boy in the world.

By contrast the 'clever' girl was bored by domesticity and thought 'household drudgery' beneath her.[6] The inference was that she was unlikely to find a husband and that, if she did, he would soon be disgruntled.

Even the clever girls who had secured a measure of independence as teachers, typists or telephonists could not deny their instincts. They liked nothing better than getting home to busy themselves with cooking, tidying and rearranging the furniture.[7] This form of self-fulfilment was exactly what young men dreamed about when they looked for a wife. In 1916 wives in waiting were reassured by verses in *Girls Weekly*:

> The girls that get married are home girls
> Girls that are mother's right hand
> Their fathers and brothers can trust in
> And little ones understand.
>
> The girls that get married are wise girls
> Who know what to do and to say
> Who drive with a smile or a soft word
> The wrath of the household away.[8]

Popular journalism was joining forces with another, equally powerful agent for social conformity, parental pressure. The upbringing of a middle-class girl was an apprenticeship for marriage; it was her destiny and the means by which she justified her existence and took her place in the world. The state concurred, and in the early 1890s educational planners stressed the importance of 'domestic' subjects within the curriculum of elementary schools, including the preparation of household budgets.

Marriage still meant dependency and submission, though less so than in the past. There were gradual piecemeal adjustments to the law which gave women a measure of freedom from the worst excesses of domestic oppression. The Married Women's Property Acts of 1870 and 1882 reduced a husband's power over his wife's assets, and the 1857 Divorce Act made separation easier, but only marginally so. A double standard still prevailed, allowing a husband to divorce his wife on the ground of her adultery alone, while she had to prove adultery together with either cruelty, desertion or incest. This legal disparity remained until 1937. There was some relief for wives who were regularly maltreated by their husbands: the 1878 Matrimonial Causes Act gave magistrates the power to issue separation orders and secure maintenance payments from convicted wife beaters.

Contrary to general opinion, wife beating was not a wholly working-class vice. Divorce proceedings revealed many instances of middle-class wives suffering at their husbands' hands and sometimes fighting back. In 1861 Mrs Butler, the wife of a Midlands businessman, sued her husband on the grounds of his adultery with a prostitute and assaults going back two years. She resisted, once pulling his whiskers, and there were exchanges of hurled crockery and cutlery. The judge dismissed the case because he thought her 'hysterical', an adjective commonly attached to women whenever their passions or frustrations got the better of them, or if they were highly strung. He also expressed the hope that the pair 'would live together happily'.[9] Revealingly, husbands' complaints about the neglect of household duties were a common source of friction.[10]

It would be perverse to base any anatomy of Victorian middle-class marriage on the evidence presented in the divorce courts, but the sheer diversity of human temperament meant that marital tensions were inevitable and commonplace. Many had to remain unresolved, for divorce proceedings were expensive and, since they were widely reported, a public humiliation. Other escape routes existed. In the 1850s an anonymous doctor perplexingly observed that every practitioner he knew in London had at some time been forced to suppress suspicions that his patients included husbands who had poisoned their wives and wives their husbands.[11]

This was a murky and intriguing area, although forensic suspicions were understandable. Poisons were easily obtainable and it was often difficult to distinguish between the symptoms of fatal intestinal distempers and those of poisoning, as Dr Palmer knew to his profit. There were desperate middle-class wives prepared to risk the gallows to be rid of husbands. Florence Campbell's first husband, a Guards officer, who was regularly drunk and no less regularly beat her, died aged twenty-eight from a stomach complaint that was conveniently blamed on his alcoholism. Her second husband Charles Bravo, a barrister, died in April 1876 from antimony poisoning and Florence was suspected of murdering him. She had had an affair with her physician, Dr James Gully, and there was evidence that Bravo knew and was furious. Gully had treated her for one of her miscarriages; pregnancy and childbirth were always dangerous and often fatal for many women, which may be why Florence may have terminated her marriage.[12] If she did, there was insufficient evidence to prosecute her, although the public thought otherwise. Florence Maybrick's husband, a Liverpool businessman, was a valetudinarian who suffered from acute dyspepsia and beat her. She was found guilty in 1889 of his murder by arsenic poisoning, having allegedly distilled it by boiling fly papers. Like Florence Bravo, she was having an affair which may have been an inducement to remove an unwanted and unlikeable husband.[13] Each case gave some weight to the unknown doctor's surmise and provided harrowing evidence of the lives of middle-class husbands and wives trapped within loveless and turbulent marriages.

Newspapers chronicled the miseries and penalties of mismatches. There were overbearing husbands and intelligent and independent-minded wives who were unwilling to obliterate their personalities in the ways suggested by Ruskin (whose own marriage failed) and other gurus. When reduced to first principles, their strictures rested on a genetic willingness of women to serve their husbands and of course on Biblical convention. The former was shaky science and the latter's authority diminishing.

Changes in attitudes towards women, notably in relation to what part they should play in society, were under way by the early 1870s. Orthodoxies were challenged, revised and sometimes overturned. The movement gathered momentum and, in retrospect, its benefi- ciaries could claim that it was the first stage in a revolution that would end a hundred years later in total female emancipation. By the 1890s the 'new woman' had emerged and her sisters proclaimed themselves unshackled from an oppressive past. One, writing in 1903, declared that 'The most old-fashioned girl of our time would certainly have ranked as a "revolted daughter" or a "new woman" a hundred years before.' Nowadays, Jane Austen's Elizabeth Bennett would have fled her claustrophobic home and 'foolish idle mother' and embarked upon a career. Her sister Mary would have proceeded to university.[14] When at Girton, the Edwardian Mary Bennett would have ridden a bicycle, argued the merits of female suffrage, smoked cigarettes, sympathised with the anti-corset movement and seriously contemplated the theories of those on the far left who pilloried marriage as a hybrid between domestic servitude and prostitution.

Conservatives were shocked by the outlook and behaviour of the new woman. Yet she was the product of evolution rather than revo- lution. Her antecedents lay in the contradictions at the heart of earlier visions of womanhood. In the abstract, women were revered as sublime beings who possessed wisdom, creativity, energy and, some argued, an innate high-mindedness that made them the natural balance to the pervasive, mid-century materialism.[15] None the less, they needed constant male supervision and their intelligence and talents kept within the bounds of custom. Even when its rules were partially suspended, prejudice remained. Florence Nightingale had been allowed to nurse convalescents at Scutari, but the army author- ities insisted that she and her middle-class companions tended the rank and file and not officers. It was feared that, for all their sense of vocation, these young ladies were covertly seeking husbands.

The moral dilemma over what might or might not be appropriate work for women was compounded by figures like Miss Nightingale. She was a middle-class spinster, a creature who lived on the margin of society. Her social isolation was described by the novelist George Gissing (1857–1903): 'A feeble, purposeless, hopeless woman' who was ordained to suffer from 'the conviction that in missing love she had missed everything'.[16] The number of spinsters was increasing, thanks to the demographic imbalance between the sexes: in 1901 women outnumbered men by a million. This, coupled with the fact that the average age for marriage was between twenty-five and thirty-five, had created a reservoir of labour.

Universal application of the laws of supply and demand to middle-class women was impossible. Protective fences were erected by the professional men and university dons, and there was always the delicate question of whether the nature of a woman's work demeaned her status. Was it right, for instance, for a girl from the middle class to enter nursing, a 'vocation' that in pre-Nightingale days had been filled with an uneducated 'inferior class of women'? The answer was a hesitant yes, in so far as by the mid-1860s new training programmes being introduced into the London hospitals and copied elsewhere gave nursing the status of a profession.

Tending the sick was one thing, diagnosing and curing them another. Early reactions to the prospect of women doctors ranged from acceptance through condescending amusement to obstructive indignation. It required audacity, determination and sheer persistence for Mrs Elizabeth Garrett Anderson (1836–1917) to qualify as a physician in the face of the intransigence of much of the medical establishment. Sophia Jex-Blake (1840–1912), the sister of a headmaster of Rugby, was grudgingly allowed to study medicine, but was refused a degree by Edinburgh University. There was something distinctly unjust and spiteful about such posturing, and it failed to deter middle-class girls from enrolling for medical courses. It took twenty years for the medical schools to come to terms with reality; in 1895 the universities of London, Durham, St Andrews, Edinburgh and Glasgow granted degrees to women doctors. At Glasgow they represented 10 per cent of the medical graduates that year.

This progress had been possible only because of a change of mindset among the better-educated middle classes. The intellectual catalyst was the traditional liberal concept of benevolent progress. In his *The Subjection of Women* (1869) John Stuart Mill argued that, like so much else the modern age was discarding, the inferior status of women was a relic of the unenlightened past. It was a survival from the period when male 'superior strength' alone was the source of authority, an arrangement that its possessors thought natural and desirable. Female subjection had become less brutal and now men treated a woman 'not [as] a slave but [as] a favourite', but she remained an inferior being. Her liberation and elevation to equality were imperative and the logical consequence of that wider economic, political and mental emancipation that had been under way for most of the century and which had been embraced by the middle class. It was already in progress, for there were plenty of 'clever and experienced women of the world' who commonly advised their husbands on private and public matters. No one could question the capacities of the female mind, and its continued enslavement on the ground of archaic convention was as unjust as it was wasteful.

Women themselves sensed this and exploited the traditional middle-class vehicles of persuasion – associations, public meetings, pamphleteering and fundraising – to press their case. Free access to education was immediately identified as the key to emancipation: privately financed women's colleges were established at Oxford and Cambridge in the 1870s. Male reactions were largely hostile or asinine. In 1871 the Oxford Union voted by nineteen to thirteen to keep women out of the university, and in 1897 Cambridge undergraduates celebrated the senate's refusal to allow women to take degrees by suspending an effigy of a female on a bicycle from a college window. To judge from her knickerbockers she was unmistakably a new woman.[17] The crustier dons (the majority) were obstructive and often rude. In 1870 Ruskin endeavoured to exclude women from his Oxford art lectures. 'I cannot let the bonnets in,' he announced, adding that what he was about to say would prove of 'no use to the female mind'.[18] This tradition of incivility was upheld by the Cambridge medievalist G. G. Coulton, who in the late 1920s pointedly began his lectures to a mixed audience with 'Good morning, gentlemen.'[19]

Oxford and Cambridge were embattled outposts. The new, provincial universities founded from the 1870s onwards with private and later state finance accepted the principle of equality. In Birmingham in 1893 the proportion of male to female students was 365 to 335, and at Aberystwyth in 1913 it was 441 to 173. Here, just under a quarter of all students were supported by college and county scholarships.[20] There was, however, a striking imbalance in universities with a technical and scientific bent: at Sheffield in 1911 there were forty-eight women students and over a thousand men. Even though they upheld the ideal of gender parity, a condescending spirit existed in such colleges. At Birmingham in 1901, when a female graduate was presented to the chancellor Joseph Chamberlain the men shouted, 'Go on, Sir, kiss her.' This opponent of women's suffrage refused.[21]

This pattern of first acknowledging the potential of the female intelligence and then accepting its deployment in areas hitherto the preserve of men was repeated elsewhere. The Pharmaceutical Society admitted women with little fuss in 1879, after accepting the common-sense line that if they had passed the exams they deserved to practise. Practical considerations dictated the appointment of women sanitary inspectors by local authorities in London and the provinces in 1894. Their sphere of action was however limited to premises such as laundries where most employees were female and to visiting the bedridden wives of the poor where 'propriety' was essential.[22]

Victorian feminism was entirely a middle-class phenomenon. Yet there were many middle-class men and women unconvinced by feminist arguments. Older notions of women's place within society remained strong and were nowhere more forcefully expressed than in the divided medical profession. An appeal for recognition made by the female doctors of Elizabeth Garrett Anderson's London Hospital in 1895 convulsed the Royal College of Physicians. One fellow sneeringly remarked that women had been allowed to study medicine only so that they could survive 'independent of marriage' without the fear of poverty. Teaching and nursing were their natural métiers. Another male doctor alleged that they lacked the the imagination to create or

advance knowledge. There were cheers from the sidelines. A correspondent in the *Lancet* blamed the 'new woman' for the rumpus and
jeeringly added that she was a 'morbid' character who should be
directed towards 'morbid anatomy'. A throat and ear surgeon insisted
that the female doctor 'unsexes herself' and defied that 'divine wisdom'
that decreed her confinement to the home.[23] The *Practitioner* found
this fogeyism ridiculous and likened it to the 'last desperate flourish
of the mop by the Mrs Partingtons of medicine.[24] The comparison
with the figure who was a metaphor for the enemies of political
reform sixty years before was apt; in time the diehard physicians, like
the diehard Tories, were engulfed by the tide.

Even the most obscurantist medic could not deny the usefulness
of women in public life so long as they restricted themselves to
certain forms of philanthropy. It was agreed that the middle–class
woman had a capacity to transcend class and could speak frankly and
sympathetically with her working-class sister on domestic and family
matters. Her natural sympathies and compassion encouraged her to
do battle against the exploitation of women, either as workers or as
prostitutes. Experience in this field alone justified women's entry into
the political arena. If, as J. S. Mill argued, women's emancipation was
part of the natural flow of progress, then they deserved the vote.

This principle was tacitly admitted in 1870 when women
ratepayers were allowed to vote in and stand for elections for local
school boards. Three were elected at the end of the year.[25] The 1888
local government legislation gave the vote to women householders.
There were 600,000 of them in London in 1907, when roughly a
fifth voted in the council elections.[26] Yet these precedents and the
widening participation of women in the local party organisations
counted for nothing when it came to the next step, the extension
of the Parliamentary franchise to women. Its eventual achievement
has been thoroughly described and analysed.[27]

Votes for women was an issue that initially cut across party lines
(Disraeli was for and Gladstone against), but both parties regarded
it as a peripheral matter that would not attract votes from a male
electorate. This apathy was not shaken by the traditional middle-
class political apparatus of journalistic persuasion, lobbying, demon-

strations and public meetings. The systematic violence employed by the Women's Social and Political Union was a resort of desperation. Between 1912 and 1914 the pent-up frustrations of Mrs Pankhurst's 'militant' suffragettes erupted into arson, smashing windows and acts of vandalism. The campaign ran against the grain of traditional middle-class political protest and failed to remove the impasse. Any concession was a gamble for the Liberals, whose share of the vote had slumped in the two elections of 1910 and might continue to drop, for Asquith feared that by enfranchising women he would swell Tory majorities.[28] Did he, like so many opponents of the suffragettes, imagine that women would either be swayed by their emotions or follow their husbands' wishes on polling day?

It was the wartime exertions of women that secured those under thirty the vote early in 1918. One of the first and probably the most significant consequences of the female franchise and women MPs was the Sex Disqualification (Removal) Act of 1919. Henceforward, gender was not a bar to public offices, to 'any civil profession or vocation' or to the granting of degrees.[29] Oxford revised its statutes accordingly the following year, leaving Cambridge to hold the fort single-handedly until 1947. In the meantime all the male professions were gradually and not always graciously opened to women.

Dismantling the hurdles of law and custom was accompanied by an equally far-reaching revolution in women's aspirations and self-esteem. Pioneers like Mrs Garrett Anderson opened the middle-class girl's horizons, persuaded her to challenge antique shibboleths about her sex and demonstrated that the intelligent and persevering woman could sustain herself within the male world. The models and dreams of the younger generation of new women were presented in the *The Girl's Realm* annual which first appeared in the 1890s and was aimed at teenage middle-class girls. The pages of the 1904 edition reveal a woman's world that would have been unimaginable forty years before. There were pieces entitled 'What Girls are Doing' with portraits and biographies of women graduates, musicians, the first Australian woman barrister and two girls who had rescued people

from drowning. Alongside were articles on Helen Keller, women graduates from Trinity College Dublin, reports from prominent girls' schools,
and tips on that robust pastime for ladies, poker-work. If girls had any
misgivings about their mental and physical stamina, they could take
heart from G. A. Henty's *A Soldier's Daughter* (*c.* 1895) and discover a
spirited lass who was learning how to box and knew how to put some
backbone into a wobbly subaltern and save the North-West Frontier
from a Pathan uprising. The new girl could beat the boys at their own
game, empire-building.

The readers of *The Girl's Realm* were healthier, more ambitious
and more adventurous than their grandmothers. Nothing was more
symbolic of the freedom, vitality and independence of the new
woman than her bicycle. Cycling mania overtook the country in
the mid-1890s. It was a predominantly middle-class phenomenon,
thanks to the price of bicycles, although manufacturers puffed their
models with claims that they were ridden by titled ladies. The middle
class was reassured that its current object of desire was also eagerly
sought by the aristocracy. Society ladies, leading actresses and luminaries of the Primrose League expressed their enthusiasm for their
bicycles in *Wheelwoman*. Another cycling magazine had an instructive short story in which the seventeen-year-old Clara pleads with
her stick-in-the-mud father to buy her a machine. She reminds him
that the squire's wife and a neighbouring noblewoman are pedalling
along the local lanes. Unimpressed, he gives way only when she
suggests that cycling would be a cheap alternative to the balls and
parties that he is obliged to hold to help his daughter find a
husband.[30]

There were further calls on the pockets of middle-class husbands
and fathers. The fashion industry promoted cycling outfits; red was
a modish colour in 1896. It did not seem to fit with the modesty
expected of the female cyclist, who was warned against brazenness.
Wheelwoman's censure of the 'loud-voiced, loudly dressed demois-
elle, who rides with arms akimbo and challenging stare' suggests
that such hussies frequented the highways in notable numbers.[31]
Complete decorum was impossible. Recommending exercises for
calves, *Beauty and Health* admitted that 'Since the advent of the

bicycle and the rainy day skirt, it has been permitted to women to acknowledge they now have legs.'[32]

The bicycle engendered a new social freedom. 'The girl of today is not only more industrious, but through cycling derives health and pleasure, to say nothing of the social intercourse among the sterner sex, that her mother, unfortunately for the poor thing, never experienced.'[33] What was applauded by a cycling weekly was considered contagious decadence elsewhere. Mrs Challoner Chute, a purity campaigner, warned churchwomen in 1895 that the single female cyclist was the outrider of moral disintegration. Her play-thing was a form of conspicuous consumption by the rich that would lead to the neglect of the poor and the advance of socialism.[34] The rest of the middle class was more indulgent to the cycling fad. Two months after Mrs Chute's jeremiad, the appearance of a French woman cyclist in knickerbockers pedalling along Rotten Row caused little more than a 'flutter of mild protest' from bystanders.[35]

This bold spirit may well have wished to drive a car. Motoring was recommended to readers of the *Wheelwoman* in 1896. 'Women of today lead broader and freer lives,' it claimed, and urged them to supplement cycling with skating, tennis, golf and hunting.[36] A gen-eration before, middle-class men had taken up bracing physical exer-cise; now their daughters and granddaughters were toughening up. Female athletic zeal matched male. In 1903 *Beauty and Health* told 'physical culture girls' that it was their duty only to marry men as pure and healthy as themselves. They were the daughters of a new era. 'Just think of it girls! You are in the "heyday" of youth . . . fair, beautiful and whole.'[37] It was very uplifting and a trifle naughty: exercises were illustrated by photographs of women in bloomers, combinations and bathing suits. No doubt some of these exercises were performed by women who attended the meetings of the network of societies organised by the journal. *Beauty and Health* also backed the anti-corset campaign that had been started in 1894. The demands of fashion proved more compelling than those of health or comfort and women remained laced in. It was estimated that five million corsets were sold annually.

★

Beauty and Health offered its readers circumspect advice on sexual problems. Children were still the prime purpose and focus of marriage. Exact knowledge of how they were conceived was haphazardly acquired by middle-class girls, some of whom approached their weddings only dimly aware of the mechanics of reproduction. This was a taboo subject among a class which admired female nudity (minus pubic hair) in art, read detailed reports of rape and sexual murders in the newspapers and discussed the problems of prostitution. It was the same with defecation. Matters concerning sewage disposal were freely aired, but young girls visiting friends felt constrained not to ask where the lavatory was.[38] If they found the courage and were in an upper-middle-class house, they would have been told that the lavatory for ladies was on the second storey, while that for men was conveniently sited on the first. Men still came first in the matter of plumbing arrangements.

Ignorance and reticence were in marginal decline by the 1890s.[39] Systematic sexual education for the young was still unthinkable because the admission that children might have sexual instincts was a violation of their innocence. Those who were curious were overcome by inhibitions. In 1921 a middle-class girl who was about to be married confessed that she was reluctant to approach even her 'most intimate relations' with enquiries about sex.[40] As in earlier periods, other children and servants were the conduits of information. M—, who was born in 1885, learned from a servant, and discovered 'queer unhealthy ideas and curiosities' when she was about fourteen from another middle-class girl of the same age.[41]

M— married in 1910 and her barrister husband understood about contraception. The couple used condoms, but these failed and she was soon pregnant. By this time it was estimated that 15 per cent of middle-class couples were practising some kind of contraception, and the proportion was increasing rapidly.[42] Birth control was now easier and more reliable than at any previous time, thanks to the mass-produced rubber sheaths that appeared on the market in the 1870s and were sold in barbers' shops. In 1883 a French visitor was amused to see condoms on sale in Petticoat Lane decorated with the heads of Queen Victoria and Mr Gladstone.[43] Was this a joke, or were these figures symbols of the product's reliability? Pamphlets on contraception were available and, surprisingly, did not attract much attention from purity vigilantes. If her husband co-operated, the new woman now could limit the size of their family.

The spread of birth control was reflected in a falling middle-class birth rate. The average size of a family fell from 6.1 in the 1860s to 2.4 by 1915 and analysts agreed the decline was most pronounced among the middle classes. This was the conclusion of the 1904 royal commission on the 'physical deterioration' of the nation, which was alarmed by the low birth rate among the 'superior' (that is, middle and upper) classes.[44] A closer examination of the statistics revealed the sharpest fall among the families of professional men, followed by those of civil servants and the lower-middle classes.[45] If contraception was being resorted to, and there is every reason to believe that it was, then it was a habit that was spreading from the top downwards. The attitude of the medical profession was confused. There were doctors who rejected birth control on eugenic grounds and general practitioners who advised middle-class wives to have fewer children to safeguard their health, but forbore to explain how this could be achieved. These doctors did not preach what they practised, for it was noticeable that like other professional men they were having smaller families.[46]

The state was disturbed by the decrease in the middle-class birth rate, which seemed to threaten what contemporary eugenicists believed to be the fittest breeding stock in the country. An attempt to reverse the trend was made in the 1911 budget, which offered an annual ten pounds' allowance to the fathers of families with children under sixteen. Given the tax threshold of £150, this was a clear inducement to the middle classes to enlarge their families. It failed, as did the warnings of doctors and churchmen opposed to contraception on doctrinal grounds. By 1919 it was calculated that 40 per cent of all married women practised birth control.[47]

Clerical opponents of birth control cited the Old Testament ordinance that procreation was the sole purpose of sexual intercourse. Two-thirds of a sample of forty-five American middle-class married couples surveyed in the 1890s agreed, but over a half added that sex was pleasurable for both parties.[48] No equivalent British enquiry was made, but there is no reason to imagine that, if it had been, the results would have been radically different. The Victorian middle-class bedroom remains a secret place, but there is nothing to suggest that it was always a joyless one. Lucy Baldwin, the future Prime Minister's wife, may well have lain back and 'thought of England', but others of her class were more responsive.

Writing in 1930, the novelist Ford Madox Ford pinpointed 1895 as the beginning of 'our own familiar, if inchoate modernity'. It was the year when the new woman was coming into her stride and, in an oblique acknowledgment of her potential, Ford observed that he would rather be ruled by his great-granddaughter than by his great-grandfather.[49] His preference was not shown by all the middle classes, yet by 1914 they had acquiesced with varying degrees of grace to the partial emancipation of women. Its tempo would be quickened by the demands of an unlooked-for national emergency, the First World War. Yet the mobilisation of women between 1914 and 1918 was the culmination of a process that had been gathering momentum for at least forty years. In essence, the emancipation of women was the inevitable outcome of middle-class liberalism, which insisted that natural talent should not be impeded and that progress required the jettisoning of notions whose only validity was their antiquity. There was also the free market; the intellectual arguments in favour of female emancipation coincided with economic changes that offered respectable jobs to mainly lower-middle-class women.

In 1861 the total employed in genteel occupations, including nursing, shopkeeping, millinery and dress-making, was 381,000. By 1911 this figure had risen to 959,000, just over a tenth of whom were clerks, typists and telegraphists.[50] The number of women doctors rose slowly; there were twenty-five in 1881 and 477 in 1911, less than a tenth of the total of female photographers. Work opportunities may have expanded and women may have acquired greater confidence and independence, but marriage remained the middle-class ideal.

9

Be Imaginative: Diversions, Mostly Outdoors

Mobility was freedom. It was prized by the middle classes, for whom it offered one of the greatest sources of private happiness: holidays were anticipated, enjoyed and then remembered. The pleasure of abandoning, however briefly, the daily world of routine became more acute as the pace and pressure of work increased. Everyone seemed afflicted with what Matthew Arnold's Scholar-Gipsy identified as a consuming malady:

> this strange disease of modern life,
> With its sick hurry, its divided aims,
> Its heads o'ertaxed, its palsied hearts.

Not surprisingly middle-class men and women treated holidays as therapy. Fresh air, sea bathing and vigorous exercise revitalised the muscles and organs of the sedentary urban man, and his wife enjoyed a respite from the fatigue of running a household. Jaded senses were stimulated by seeing great buildings and works of art of the past and the contemplation of sublime land- and seascapes. 'Mountain and moorland!' declared an enthusiast for lonely grandeur. 'The words breathe a fair freedom, a liberty of sight, sound and form . . . who would not be better and wiser for one blue day in the hills.'[1]

Until the last decade of the century, when railways had penetrated every quarter of the Continent and package holidays were being arranged by tour operators, foreign travel was adventure. The early-Victorian wanderer in Greece was also an explorer on the frontiers of civilisation. If he followed the advice of Murray's handbook, he slept cocooned in calico with a muslin net draped over his head to repel mosquitoes and fleas and carried firearms for protection against bandits as well as for sport.[2] The extremities of Europe were still dangerous, as was the Orient, where only the intrepid ventured in search of mystery and sensuality. Wherever he went, the middle-class traveller approached his journey with a blend of excitement, trepidation and, often enough, an overbearing sense of national superiority.

Like their earlier and later counterparts, Victorian and Edwardian tourists carried mental portmanteaus full of preconceptions, expectations and anxieties. Guidebooks prepared visitors for inconveniences and local quirks. Austrian customs officers would do their duty with 'civility and despatch' only if they were bribed, and landlords and waiters in the Pera district of Constantinople were shockingly ignorant of the whereabouts of the British legation.[3] Most tiresome of all was the pettiness of Continental bureaucrats who seemed bent on restricting the right of free-born Britons to go wherever they wished. Early editions of Murray's handbook to France repeatedly pleaded with visitors to show restraint rather than 'pugnacity' whenever they were delayed by Napoleon III's gendarmes or officials. Furthermore, the middle-class Briton believed he had the right to air his prejudices, regardless of local sensitivities. In France and Italy parties of tourists strolled around cathedrals and churches during services, interrupting the ceremonies with chatter and leaving congregations in no doubt of their contempt for Catholicism.[4]

As well as discourtesy, the British abroad were noted for their aloofness, which was largely the consequence of a wilful ignorance of their hosts' language. This made intimacy with foreigners rare and, in any case, most tourists were more interested in the distant rather than the present culture of the places they visited. In 1869, the snobbish travel writer Augustus Hare encountered a 'kind, vulgar' London couple in a Pisan hotel and discovered that the husband survived in France and Italy with one phrase: 'Lait, pain, thé, boungjour, toodyswee'.[5] One suspects that this pair, in common with so many other tourists, wanted the excitement of staying in a foreign country while still surrounded by some of the familiar features of home. In 1890 Swiss, German and Italian hotels were advertising for middle-class patrons with promises of 'sanitary arrangements' that were 'perfect', English-speaking staff, 'English comforts' and a resident English chaplain. The Grand Hôtel Royal in Naples reassured the fastidious that it had been 'specially selected' by the International Sanitary Commission when they had stayed in the city.[6] There was solace too in such names as the Hôtel Victoria in Baden Baden, or the Hôtel Grande Bretagne in Genoa, where the guest was guaranteed isolation from 'the odours and noise' of the port for just six shillings a day.

Hotel and inn were bases from which tourists emerged to satisfy their curiosity and indulge their fancies. The interests of the middle-class holidaymaker at home and abroad were reflected in guidebooks and the illustrated articles on travel that were a mainstay of weekly journals such as the *Graphic* or *Illustrated London News*. If he was not undergoing a cure, the traveller hoped to have his imagination aroused and knowledge enlarged. Greece satisfied these needs in abundance. Britons could speculate on the roots of their own civil-isation as they admired the ruins and surveyed a country that had once been inhabited by the warrior heroes, philosophers and writers whose deeds and words they had studied at school. Even without their historical associations, such sights enriched the soul, as Edward Lear explained: 'You have majestic cliff-girt shores, castle-crowned heights, and gloomy fortresses; Turkish palaces glittering with gilding and paint, mountain-passes such as you encounter in the snowy regions of Switzerland; deep bays and blue seas, with calm bright isles . . .'

Humanity too was picturesque, for the Greeks exhibited a 'variety of costume and pictorial incident'.[7] Even more exotic were the Anatolian Turks: 'At home in the wilds, should the Mussulman be seen, picturesque in his attire, sculpturesque in his attitude, with

dignity on his forehead, welcome on his lips, and poetry all around.'
After a day among such splendid fellows, the traveller could return
to his lodgings and indulge his mind with a 'calm communing with
nature, and the silent observation of men and things'.[8]

Complementary excursions of body and mind were the ideal to
which middle-class travellers aspired. It impelled Thomas Rogers, a
London businessman with a taste for antiquities, to take the early-
morning train for Gloucester in August 1855. After a brief visit to
the cathedral, he caught a connection to Chepstow and next morning
walked to Tintern, where he sketched the ruined abbey made famous
by Wordsworth's poem and Turner's painting. He returned to London
late that night, having spent over fourteen hours in railway carriages.[9]
It was worth the discomfort and Rogers subsequently abandoned his
office for brief antiquarian expeditions into Rutland and
Northamptonshire. For this latter trip he may well have equipped
himself with the Reverend C. H. Hartshorne's *Funeral Monuments in
Northamptonshire* (1840), which invited readers to take leaps of historical imagination. Looking at the effigies of medieval ladies, it was easy
to picture them in their times, Eleanors and Phillippas 'whose regal
eminence was enhanced by their lofty deeds'.

This was the romantic Gothic world of Scott, and it was dear to
the heart of the middle-class tourist who wanted to see the buildings and countryside where the high drama of history had been
staged. Where better to undertake such a pilgrimage of the imagination than Scotland, where the wild and remote landscapes of the
Midlothian novels were now accessible thanks to the railways. The
revealingly titled *Black's Picturesque Tourist of Scotland* (1882) asked
visitors to let their fancies run free when they approached Aberfoyle,
the haunt of Rob Roy. 'If the tourist be imaginative, he may picture
to himself Helen MacGregor standing on one of the eminences and
demanding of him what he seeks in the country of the MacGregors.'

Awesome Highland scenery, castles and ruined monasteries were
the backdrop to the sort of history that captivated the Victorian
middle class. It was pure theatre, a sequence of dramatic tableaus,
which was why historic genre paintings of the most moving and
arresting episodes were so popular. Forty thousand prints of MacLise's

Death of Nelson and *The Meeting of Wellington and Blücher after Waterloo* were distributed among the predominantly middle-class subscribers to the Art Union of London in 1875 and 1876.[10] Each picture represented a milestone in the nation's progress towards its present eminence, which added to the prints' attractiveness.

The ferocity of the past, particularly its politics, was now distant. History's most violent and irrational moments could be seen in the art gallery or imagined in Highland passes, and afterwards the spectator could go on his way thankful that he lived in enlightened and tranquil times. The middle class's perception of history was also nostalgic: the apparently gentle tempo and simplicity of the pre-industrial past compared favourably with the noisy and insistent rhythms of their own times. This contrast was most striking in the country-side, where the visitor glimpsed the measured world of the pre-industrial past.

It was 'quaint' which, together with 'picturesque', was a word that peppered travel literature. Old mills and half-timbered cottages were quaint, so were their inhabitants, particularly when they wore traditional peasant costumes, as they still did in rural Europe. Depictions of countrymen and women in their local costumes were widely reproduced in guidebooks, in travel articles and on postcards. At home there were kilted Highlanders, Welsh women in cloaks and tall hats and fishermen and fishwives in their working clothes, all favourites of artists and photographers.

There was also the contrived arcadia of Kate Greenaway (1846–1901), who illustrated children's books with figures of girls in eighteenth-century mop caps and bonnets taking tea on rural lawns or in bright, plainly furnished rustic parlours. Together, these scenes symbolised joyful, ingenuous childhood and, of course, the simplicity of a vanished world. Generations of middle-class children were brought up with Greenaway's pictures and country holidays. Both generated a taste for the rustic: in 1912 Heals the furnishers were tempting middle-class customers with a recreation of a country parlour. 'Nice, old fashioned Windsor chairs standing on a red-tile floor, a sensible oak table – everything very clean, business-like, domestic'.[11]

Ironically, given that this was a period in which rural Britain appeared to be in terminal economic decay, the middle classes were idealising it and its inhabitants. Artists like Sir George Clausen (1852–1944) painted men and women labouring in the fields in what turned out to be a highly popular genre. There were no equivalent studies of industrial workers. The middle classes also took steps to see that arcadia was preserved to their liking: they combined to form the Commons Preservation Society in 1865, the (later Royal) Society for the Protection of Birds in 1889 and the National Trust in 1895.

These bodies and romantically inclined tourists were unconscious contributors to the notion that the countryside represented the essence of Englishness. Its ingredients were outlined by that tireless rambler and champion of the bucolic G. K. Chesterton (1874–1936), when he was asked to explain what was 'precious' about a village. It was so because the 'naturalness and the integrity of roofs and walls seemed to mingle naturally with fields and the trees; the feeling of preciousness of the inn, of the cross-roads, or of the market cross . . . the normal, the English, the unreplaceable things'.[12] It was this Eden that young middle-class poets evoked in the trenches during the First World War. This had been where they had once enjoyed their summer holidays and represented all that was good and enduring in their homeland. It was the England of the magical cadences of George Butterworth's *The Banks of Green Willow* and Vaughan Williams's *Pastoral Symphony*.

Nostalgia needed prompting, which was why middle-class tourists returned home with pictures and souvenirs that were displayed in their homes. Memory alone could not be trusted: Thomas Traill, an Edinburgh physician visiting London in 1844, wrote down a list of all the pictures he saw in the National Gallery with remarks on each. Elsewhere his diaries contain exact drawings of antiquities.[13] By the 1880s photographs had become the preferred form of record and were mounted in albums whose inspection was a form of family entertainment. They contain images of family groups posed in some picturesque location and commercially produced plates of dramatic landscapes (waterfalls were popular) and ruins. Within a few years and to satisfy an expanding market, penny postcards appeared. There was hardly a village post office that did not sell them, and they were sent in millions to friends and kinsfolk to show where the holidaymaker was and what he or she was doing. Messages about the weather predominate alongside expressions of satisfaction.

Compact box cameras and roll film, cheaply available by 1900, added to the store of permanent memories of travel and moments of happiness. The urge to acquire them was expressed by a keen cyclist/photographer in 1897:

> But when you mount your steed
> And across the country speed,
> Pray do not leave your camera at home;
> The pictures you obtain,
> As mementoes will remain
> Of the scenery through which you love to roam.[14]

There were trophies too. Keepsakes and trinkets inscribed with their place of origin were sold at popular resorts, particularly by the seaside, to be taken home and placed on tables and mantelshelves. Middle-class holidaymakers on the Norfolk broads in the 1890s were promised opportunities for painting, brass rubbing, bird watching, flower pressing and butterfly collecting. Lepidopterists would have the pleasure of winter evenings spent poring over the specimens they had netted in the reedbeds.[15] It was an indulgence shared with collectors of fossils, shells, semi-precious stones, birds' eggs and plants which were carried home to be classified, labelled and tidily placed in cabinets and cases. Nature was an infinite resource for the middle-class tourist.

Technology had given men and women the capacity to plunder nature as well as gain access to remote beauty and ancient monuments, at home and abroad. Railways, steamships and latterly bicycles, automobiles and motor buses created mass tourism. Above all, it was the train which enabled the middle classes to travel cheaply, quickly and in varying degrees of comfort to wherever they chose. The railway companies recognised an insatiable demand and exploited it for all it was worth. A typhoid epidemic in Worthing in 1893 was estimated to have cost the London, Brighton and South Coast Railway £15,000 in lost fares.[16] Many would have been day returns, sometimes incorporating the entrance charge to some local amenity, and concessionary tickets that allowed the holidaymaker to explore the countryside using local branch lines.

Rail journeys were slow and frustrating. In 1874 it took fifty-eight hours from London to Milan (seven guineas first class, five second) and a London family taking a holiday in Cornwall in 1895 departed from Waterloo just before six in the morning and reached Penzance nearly fourteen hours later. The Paris boat train from Victoria took nine hours, including the Channel crossing, but was good value with the third-class return costing thirty-three shillings and threepence, less than half the weekly salary of a commercial clerk.

The efficiency of rail services varied enormously. In the wake of the collapse of one railway company in 1866, there were fears that others had overreached themselves financially and were being compelled to reduce overheads.[17] Then as now, the consequences were exhausted staff, overcrowded carriages, delays and accidents. Excessive commuter and excursion traffic contributed to a crash at Sydenham one July afternoon in 1870. Shortly before, an eyewitness had noticed the 'furious impatience' of the 'genteel crowd' returning from day trips to Epsom and the Crystal Palace.[18] Nothing incensed the middle classes more than kicking their heels on platforms waiting for overdue trains, or being squeezed into carriages, which must have been a misery for women in crinolines and bustles.

All were grumbled about in a sheaf of letters to *The Times* in 1872, most from travellers on the busy London-to-Portsmouth line. They groused about signal mishaps, mechanical failures and casual drivers whose banter with station staff delayed departures.[19] At least one commuter accepted his misfortunes with resignation, drolly observing that 'You get rid entirely on this line of the restless spirit of the age.' Distress and exasperation continued. In 1892 London commuters formed the Railway Travellers Association to wage war against overcrowding, restrictions on season tickets and acts of 'injustice and tyranny' committed by the rail companies and their employees.[20] Victory is still far away.

Behind the moaning was the disturbing knowledge that mismanagement and technical faults caused accidents. During 1872 over eleven hundred people were killed in railway accidents and three thousand injured.[21] So common were these events that the *Annual Register* only bothered to list major crashes and derailments: there were ten in 1876 which killed twenty-six and injured a further fifty. All travellers were vulnerable: among the casualties of a collision near Bath were day-trippers returning from an excursion. Such disasters, and for that matter the sinking of pleasure craft, were a fact of Victorian life. Sixty hundred and forty passengers and crew were drowned off Woolwich in 1878 when the paddle steamer *Princess Alice* sank after it had been rammed by a coalship.

Most of the dead were trippers returning from an excursion to Gravesend. The seaside was the most popular destination for excursions and holidays for all classes throughout this period and well into the next century. Railway companies joined private investors and local authorities in promoting resorts and expanding their facilities. Within forty years of the railway reaching the decorous Regency sea-bathing resort of Worthing in 1845, it had acquired additional hotels, esplanades, bandstands and a pier. The railway's arrival at Aberystwyth in 1867 was the impetus for similar improvements including mineral baths, new hotels and boarding houses and horse-drawn and later motor buses that carried visitors to nearby beauty spots. By 1900 films were regularly shown at the New Market Hall. The most prestigious and, therefore, expensive accommodation was always closest to the beach. Morris's Temple Hotel in Aberystwyth provided lady guests with 'Garibaldian' and 'Turkish' costumes so that they could take the short walk to their bathing machines with modesty.[22]

Perhaps the most celebrated image of the Victorian middle classes by the seaside was Frith's *Ramsgate Sands* (1854), in which well-dressed families crowd the beach and mamas coax nervous toddlers to paddle in the sea. It was a scene that touched a chord with the middle classes: the London Art Union bought the print rights in 1859 and had fifteen thousand copies made.[23] The original was purchased by Queen Victoria. According to a contemporary guide, Ramsgate was 'more aristocratic' than neighbouring, boisterous Margate, which attracted lower-middle- and working-class day-trippers from London.[24]

The reassuring presence of their own kind mattered immensely to the middle class. In 1891 potential visitors to Scarborough were told that their peace would not be disturbed by 'vulgar' day-trippers from the industrial towns of Yorkshire, and at Great Yarmouth only the 'better class of visitors' were permitted to stroll along the promenade.[25] They were of course distinguished by their dress: ladies carried parasols, men wore boaters and light summer clothing (including sporting striped blazers), and their sons sailor suits. Even dogs proclaimed social standing. 'Nobody who is anybody can afford to be followed about by a mongrel dog,' declared a breeder of pedigree dogs in 1896. Ornamental breeds such as bulldogs and collies were the most fashionable, and some cost two thousand pounds or more.[26] The late-Victorian canine hierarchy was one of the many visible reminders that how one spent one's money was, as ever, a determinant of social status.

This was also true of holiday accommodation. Hotel owners exploited this and their advertisements emphasised luxuries of a kind that few of their middle-class patrons would normally have enjoyed at home, such as electric light. A holiday was a chance to move up a notch in society, if only briefly. The Metropole Hotel at Brighton was pure make-believe: guests could imagine themselves in the château of an arriviste millionaire for whom ostentation and taste were synonymous. The five-storey hotel opened in 1890 and its range of styles from Louis XIV to Moorish conveyed opulence. Marble and plasterwork were everywhere, and visitors could stroll in an Italian garden. Chandeliers lit the lofty, centrally heated public rooms, electric lifts carried guests to their bedrooms which were lit by electric light. All overlooked the sea and had running hot, cold and sea water.[27] The Brighton Metropole created a middle-class dream world which was repeated at other resorts, where massive, ornate hotels looked seawards across esplanades and promenades.

Wherever one stayed, the annual holiday had become an essential part of middle-class life. In 1887 young professional women were urged to spend a fortnight either at the seaside or hiking in the countryside, where they would enjoy fresh air and wholesome food. Living expenses were as little as eighteen shillings a week.[28] A hypothetical budget for a lower-middle-class family of four in 1901 included five pounds to cover two weeks at the seaside in the boarding house.[29] In 1900 the British spent £38.9 million in hotels, loding houses and restaurants and by 1914 the total had risen to £64.7 million.[30]

Recreation sometimes created social friction. The middle classes could be surprisingly militant in defending what they took to be their right to enjoy themselves. When, in 1884, the 1st Lord Sackville installed barriers to prevent riders and perambulators from entering his park at Knole, middle-class protesters from nearby Sevenoaks demolished them and for several nights made a rumpus outside his house, once defiantly singing 'Rule Britannia'. One demonstration was led by a solicitor's clerk on horseback. He claimed to be defending ancient rights of way, while Sackville said he was protecting his privacy from London day-trippers.[31] In 1890 Edinburgh trade unionists objected to the local authority converting some of the city's open spaces into golf links. 'Golf was for the [middle] classes,' claimed one, although the golfers riposted that the game was open to all classes, which was hard to believe given that annual club fees were half a guinea, there were additional fees for competitions and the cheapest clubs cost between five shillings and seven and six.[32]

Motoring generated the bitterest social tension. When, in 1905, Richmond magistrates fined a lady driver five pounds for driving at just over the twenty-mile-an-hour limit, what her husband called the 'great unpaid' in the court room laughed and jeered.[33] Middle-class rural magistrates encouraged working-class policemen to conceal themselves behind bushes and trap speeding motorists in the knowledge that their evidence would be accepted unquestioningly. The guerrilla war against speed was a reaction to accidents: in 1911 there were 184 deaths from accidents involving cars and motor buses and over five thousand injuries.[34] In the same year, three thousand motorists were charged with speeding in London alone.

These statistics reinforced the animus against the motor: it was the plaything of the rich which enabled them to display the careless arrogance made famous by Mr Toad. His obsession with speed was the common vice of all motorists, whom one countrydweller considered philistines, utterly indifferent to the beauty of the landscapes they rushed past.[35] What hurt most was the plutocratic image. The hostility towards what he called 'automobilism' would evaporate only when it became a middle-class pastime, argued a speaker at the 1902 annual dinner of the Automobile Association.[36] He was correct, but he would have to wait twenty years for the middle classes to become addicted to cars.

Motor enthusiasts were already gathering for events such as endurance trials. Edwardian motor rallies were a novel feature of the older and deeply rooted culture of shared enthusiasm and conviviality. It existed at all levels and served all kinds of interests. These ranged from the intellectual and artistic (provincial antiquarian, amateur theatrical and musical societies) to the predominantly lower-middle-class Ancient Druids, Oddfellows, Foresters and Buffaloes who blended mutual assistance with regular beanos. Rail travel added to the pleasures of association, providing opportunities for excursions, usually annual and held during the summer. Sunday School parties visited the seaside and enjoyed picnics, antiquaries undertook expeditions to country houses and were given tea by the owners and Buffalo lodges exchanged visits and played cricket matches.

Rail excursions in cheerful and like-minded company became integral to the holiday season and were eagerly anticipated. So too were the static social occasions: annual carnivals, fêtes, galas, flower shows, tea parties organised by communities and voluntary associations. These beanfeasts were the Victorian age's counterpart to the older holidays held on saints' days but, unlike them, they were closely regulated and therefore more seemly occasions. The middle classes saw to that. They had a guiding hand in all these festivities, partly because they took pleasure in them and partly because their encouragement was a social responsibility. An event like a carnival attracted people from all backgrounds and generated an atmosphere of harmony, a fact often mentioned by the local bigwigs whose speeches opened the proceedings. Chances to moralise were never missed. At the fête held by the local Buffalo lodge at Andover in 1881 the mayor thanked the hosts and added that such bodies were of universal benefit, for they helped create 'better husbands, better parents and better members of society'.[37]

Village fêtes (often held in the grounds of the manor house or parsonage) and the harvest festivals represented attempts by squires, clergymen and the richer farmers to neuter the traditional excesses which had ended in drunkenness and fornication.[38] Now, the harvest home, like so many other annual jamborees, concluded with fireworks and the National Anthem. In time, these occasions like their urban counterparts came to be revered as authentic survivals from 'Merrie England'.

Just as there were calendars of local annual events, there was a national one. It operated on two social levels. For those at the apex of society there was the exclusive London 'season', a sequence of sporting contests such as the Henley Regatta, the opening viewing of the Royal Academy exhibition, balls and receptions. The overall tone was distinctly aristocratic, particularly the ritual quest for suitable husbands by mamas and their daughters, but the socially ambitious upper-middle classes could elbow their way in if they were rich enough. Connections were a marketable, if expensive, commodity. In an advertisement of 1892 two anonymous titled ladies promised to take girls into their houses and groom them for society in return for a fee of between one and two thousand pounds.[39]

The annual Canterbury Cricket Week was open to all. In August 1881 a reporter noted that 'different' classes mingled easily, and accompanying drawings showed a pair of clergymen in a gig, a middle-class family and soldiers ogling a passing girl. There was plenty of fun, with military bands playing in the afternoons and productions by local amateur dramatic societies in the evenings.[40] On Derby Day in 1893 what another journalist called a 'great democracy' assembled, encompassing costermongers, creatures from the margins of criminality and figures displaying 'the dullness of respectability'.[41]

The classes also mixed on those occasions when ordinary people had the chance to witness the public drama of history. Thomas Rogers endured a four-hour queue in an 'awful crowd' to see the Duke of Wellington's lying in state in November 1852. It was 'a grand sight but not worth the trouble', he wrote afterwards, but he had recovered his spirits sufficiently to watch the Duke's funeral procession two days later.[42] As part of a wider policy to encourage the nation to identify more closely with the monarchy, royal occasions became increasingly theatrical and elaborate. Samuel Elliott, a London clockmaker, was impressed by the 'magnificent display' of fireworks on the evening of the Prince of Wales's marriage in 1863.[43]

Gorgeous pageantry marked the Jubilees of 1887 and 1897 and the coronations of 1902 and 1911, all of which were celebrated in cities, towns and villages. Crowds watched processions of civic dignitaries (a reminder of social hierarchy) and heard patriotic speeches. Afterwards, they listened to bands, ate, drank, lit bonfires and watched fireworks. The middle classes affirmed their loyalty and civic duty by subscribing to these festivities and sometimes funding gifts for poor children so that they too could feel pride in their country and its Empire. Blending patriotism with a chance of a grand day out, thousands flocked to Portsmouth to watch reviews of the Home Fleet, perhaps the greatest spectacle of the age.

Like the extended holiday, a day out to see battleships was a treat for the middle classes. It was not, many would have argued, an indulgence, for the weight and repetitiveness of work more than justified intervals of relaxation, even idleness, in unfamiliar surroundings. To abstain from such breaks was unhealthy, and, to judge by the sheer number of advertisements for tonics and universal panaceas, there was a strong streak of valetudinarianism running through the middle class. Certainly, if the use of the adjective 'bracing' in puffs for resorts is anything to go by, a holiday was an investment in good health as well as a reward for industriousness. Nothing better symbolised the middle-class ideal than the pier along which the visitor could stroll inhaling ozone while simultaneously being entertained.

As Jerome K. Jerome's three men rowing up the Thames discovered, holidays and excursions were adventures in which the unexpected could occur. A boating trip, like an excursion to a London exhibition or a Primrose League tea party, was a relief from monotony. The industrial age did not invent drudgery and routine, but it did make them more intense for everyone who had to earn a living. Holidays were vital, which was why so much disposable middle-class income was spent on them. Ironically, those who upheld the work ethic and strove to earn more found themselves spending more and more to alleviate fatigue and boredom. This circle of ever-increasing effort and compensating diversion became a pattern of life for the middle classes and was one of the nineteenth century's legacies to the twentieth.

10

Philistines: Middle-Class Cultures

In his essay *Culture and Anarchy* (1869) Matthew Arnold famously labelled the middle classes as philistines. Philistine stigmata were narrow-mindedness, self-satisfaction, greed and toleration of ugliness in art and architecture. Above the philistines were the aristocracy, whom Arnold labelled 'barbarians', a caste distinguished by their panache, free indulgence of passion and detachment from the rest of the world. Beneath the philistines were the 'populace', who together with the barbarians were beyond redemption. Arnold held out some hope for the philistines, whose aesthetic salvation could be achieved if they discarded their materialism and embraced the virtues of the ancient Greeks. 'Human life in the hands of Hellenism', he believed, 'is invested with a kind of aërial ease, clearness, and radiance; they are full of sweetness and light.'

Arnold was one of a succession of pundits who told the middle classes what was beautiful and what was not. Pugin, Ruskin, Arnold and later William Morris guided their readers towards what was pure and pleasing to the eye and reminded them that great art had a moral dimension which cleansed and uplifted the spirit. The middle classes listened avidly, particularly the socially ambitious who wished to be accepted as discerning patrons. They absorbed the principle that the aesthetic qualities of a work of art were secondary, though closely allied to its power to instruct or narrate; art of the right kind made people better. Millais' *Boyhood of Raleigh* (popular with middle-class buyers of prints) told the story of how the imagination of a future empire builder was first aroused and was a reminder that late-Victorian boyhood needed similar stimulation to great deeds. It was an inspiring scene that still decorated schoolrooms until the middle of the twentieth century. Sometimes the message was immediate. William Frith's *The Road to Ruin* of 1887 was an updated *Rake's Progress*, with scenes of gambling undergraduates, a race course, the arrival of bailiffs, a young bankrupt and his family exiled to France and, finally, a pistol lying on the table in a garret.

Art was also about spending money. All levels of the middle class patronised the decorative arts. The richest commissioned architects to build their houses and bought paintings and sculpture to fill them, and those with less to spend purchased reproductions and mass-produced furniture and ceramics. Whatever their budget, the middle classes were conscious of fashion and, since art provided those domestic embellishments which advertised status, followed it. The aesthetic ideals extolled by Arnold and other gurus were translated into commodities. *Culture and Anarchy* helped usher in the revived Queen Anne style of the 1870s (Osbert Lancaster's 'Pont Street Dutch'), whose airiness and simplicity was a reaction against the oppressive and fussy Gothic. Arnoldian sweetness and light permeated the Queen Anne houses in the Bedford Park estate at Turnham Green, a speculative venture contrived to attract sophisticated upper-middle-class customers. A satirist summed up the joys they would encounter in:

> a village builded
> for all who are aesthete
> Whose precious souls it did fill
> with utter joy complete.
>
> For floors were stained and polished
> and very hearth was tiled
> And Philistines abolished by Culture's gracious child.[1]

The eighteenth-century tradition of cultural correctness was flourishing. Consumers preferred not to trust to untutored instinct and followed the dogmas of experts. An aesthetic misjudgment was as much a social solecism as serving fish before soup. As in all matters of fashion, the transient ascendancy of the latest style usually involved the denunciation of its predecessor. The clean, crisp lines of the detached Edwardian house were a welcome 'change from the reign of hybrid villadom' and the 'degraded productions of the Victorian era', proclaimed the *Studio* in 1905.

Different aesthetic philosophies informed these judgments, but the purpose was always the same: the cultivation of a taste that would excite respect and admiration. Rembrandt etchings, cheap prints, William Morris wallpapers or mass-produced dinner services were displayed in houses where they simultaneously announced the owner's spending power and discrimination. The set for Somerset Maugham's play *Smith* (1909) was specified as 'the kind of drawing room which every woman of the upper middle class has in London', one which reflected 'excellent taste of a commonplace sort'. There was 'good china' in the cabinets and prints of Italian masters on the walls.[2]

It was easy for the designer to have created an authentic drawing room. Illustrations of its furnishings could be found in magazines catering for readers preoccupied with the trappings of status. Designers and manufacturers treated the words 'good' and 'fashionable' as synonymous and rightly believed that many of their customers were anxious to keep abreast of the latest modes. Furniture in the 'new designs of 1886' advertised in the autumn of that year probably differed little from that of 1885, but whatever novelty it possessed counted with consumers.[3] By 1900 reproduction seventeenth-century furniture was all the rage. Gillows of Oxford Street offered individual items and complete interiors for customers who wanted instant décor created by experts. This service had been patronised by royalty and the peerage, which was still a touchstone of excellence for the middle-class buyer with social pretensions.[4] If late-Victorian and Edwardian advertising copy is to be believed, there was a breed of hostesses who were forever telling visitors that their drawing rooms were replicas of those of minor royalty. Likewise, their husbands may have boasted that they owned the same car that had been chosen by the Prime Minister and a handful of noblemen. Aristocratic choice remained a criterion of desirability for the middle classes.

They were also influenced by foreign travel, which opened their eyes to new objects of desire. In Robert Tressell's *The Ragged Trousered Philanthropists* (1907), Mr Sweater, a provincial businessman, had seen a room in Paris that had taken his 'fancy'. It was 'a sort of *Japanese* fashion' with stencilled decorations on the wall which he wanted reproduced in his new, prestigious house. In fact the motifs were Moorish, but what mattered for Sweater was that they were fashionable. The craftsman employed to produce the templates turned to one of the many handbooks available to builders and decorators for models.

A grasping and hard man, Sweater exactly fitted Arnold's definition of a philistine, save that he was not entirely immune to 'sweetness and light' in so far as he had some notions of art, if only of the I-know-what-I-like nature. Guidance was available for men of his kind. The Art Union was dedicated to 'propagating a taste for art among the middle classes' and did so through making available cheap prints by leading artists.[5] In 1867 it was offering reproductions of Maclise's *Death of Nelson*, Parian-ware busts of Queen Victoria and the Princess of Wales and bronze statuettes of a wood nymph. A few years earlier the Art Union had joined forces with the National Society for the Education of the Poor in the Principles of the Established Church to distribute prints of William Hilton's *Crucifixion*, which it described as 'a scene on earth leading heaven-ward'.[6]

The influence of the Art Union declined in the last quarter of the century as more commercial enterprises entered the art market. The subjects chosen for mass-produced reproductions reveal a range of middle-class taste that tended towards the conformist and cautious. There was a fondness for pictorial narrative, historical and romantic scenes and portraits, conventionally pretty or awesome landscapes, nostalgia and sentimental religious images that verged on the mawkish. Among the prints released in 1894 were *A Highland Glen* and *A Surrey Pinewood*, and conversational pieces included *The Bethrothed* and *The Child Handel*.[7] Next year, twenty-four coloured photogravure prints of 'female celebrities' were being sold at twelve shillings each. Among them was Lord Leighton's *Desdemona*.[8] In 1901 dealers were offering engravings of the reliefs of Kimberley and Ladysmith for patriots, the evergreen *Boyhood of Raleigh*, representations of Regency coaching scenes and images of sporting dogs and grouse moors. Prices ranged from half a guinea to ten. For those with larger purses and loftier notions of connoisseurship, there were reproductions of old masters from public and private collections, including Rembrandt's *Anatomy Lesson*.[9]

Such prints, often in heavy frames, together with contemporary furniture and pottery, are found today in antique shops and markets which have become museums of late-Victorian and Edwardian middle-class taste. The assumptions behind mass-market aesthetics were simple and were expressed in an advertisement of 1878 for Christmas cards promising images of flowers and pictures which told stories to please 'all classes, for all can understand and *feel* them [my italics]'.[10] Favourable reactions could be guaranteed by almost photographic exactitude and technical adroitness that rendered a subject 'lifelike'. A review of *A Drizzly Day*, exhibited at the Royal Academy in 1885, praised 'its living horses and its admirable effect of weather'.[11] Flair was not enough: artists needed integrity and moral vision. The 1886 obituary of the painter J. W. Waterhouse praised his honesty, his directness and the 'moral qualities' of his works.[12]

By the time of Waterhouse's death the Aesthetic movement was gaining ground with its gospel of 'art for art's sake' and often for the sake of provoking others. It was a concept which mystified and perturbed the mass of the middle classes, who considered it conceited indulgence. In its exaggerated form Aestheticism was mocked in Gilbert and Sullivan's *Patience*, and the Wilde scandal confirmed that its cultivated decadence merged naturally with depravity. Middle-class hostility towards anyone and anything connected with 'art for art's sake' was channelled through *Punch*, which never missed a chance to poke fun at Aesthetes, their appearance (flamboyant bohemian with beards and large floppy hats) and their pretentiousness. In a cartoon of July 1914 the Aesthete husband instructs his wife to hang out the washing according to a 'harmonious colour scheme'. The frivolity of the Aesthetes was dangerous in that it denied art's capacity for moral improvement. Furthermore, what they produced was sometimes difficult to comprehend.

The middle classes wanted the security of the familiar. The result encouraged the mediocrity that was apparent in the works displayed in the Royal Academy's summer exhibition of 1914. There were no surprises, one critic noted, just an accumulation of the 'solid and respectable' that was guaranteed to appeal to the 'widest possible public'.[13] A similar caution permeated middle-class tastes in architecture. The early twentieth century had seen the architect replacing the speculative builder as the middle classes demanded 'more artistic' houses, but they felt nervous about designs whose originality might be considered eccentric.[14]

Middle-class faith in the moral power of art was the impulse behind the establishment of civic art galleries and museums during the last quarter of the century. Dispensing moral enlightenment through free access to art was part of the middle class's civilising mission: municipal corporations and rich individuals funded the new galleries and exhibits that filled them. As always with such enterprises, prestige was a priority. After praising an exhibition of works by local watercolourists in 1878, the *Glasgow Herald* hoped that it would 'improve public taste' and act as forerunner for further shows. It added that the city could not afford to lag behind Edinburgh or London in its patronage of art.[15]

Civic art galleries were successful beyond the dreams of their sponsors. Leeds Art Gallery, which opened in 1888, had an average of 20,000 visitors a year, and West Bromwich Art Gallery, opened in 1898, had had 150,000 within fourteen years. In 1899 Edinburgh Museum and Art Gallery had just over a third of a million visitors.[16] Modern restorations and notions of curatorship have often radically altered repositories that reflected the tastes of Victorian donors and city fathers. Older readers may remember the results, magpie-like accumulations that ranged from stuffed birds to ancient artefacts unearthed locally by middle-class amateur archaeologists. Alongside eoliths and shards were 'curiosities' brought back from distant lands by travellers and imperial soldiers. Mughal swords and armour from India and weaponry from Central Africa were displayed in the Albert Gallery and Institute at Dundee (now the Macmanus Gallery), which was founded in 1867 to promote 'science, literature and [the] arts'.

Like many other contemporary temples to improvement, the Albert Gallery was a solid building with an arched and tiled entrance hall that calls to mind a chapel. Art was to be revered in sumptuous surroundings. Inside, middle-class tastes prevailed. From the past there were seventeenth- and eighteenth-century European canvases (landscapes, still lifes, Classical and Biblical incidents) donated by a civic-minded local collector. The present was represented by celebrated artists and familiar subjects (Dante Gabriel Rossetti's *Dante's Dream on the Day of the Death of Beatrice*) and a sequence of stained-glass windows designed by Sir Edward Burne-Jones and executed by William Morris's studio. They were commissioned in 1889 for Dundee's Town House and declared that the city's jute barons were not philistines.

Later generations dismissed their aesthetic values, often with a snigger of contempt. In 1934 works by masters lionised by the Victorian middle class were auctioned for less than a tenth of their original prices. Friths that had been sold for up to five hundred pounds went down to forty.[17] A few years later, a new curator of a Midlands municipal gallery seeking space for works by contemporary artists was willing to give older works away, including watercolours by Cotman.[18]

Like art, literature was a commodity which was marketed for middle-class consumption. 'Literature nowadays is a trade,' Jasper Milvain tells his mother and sisters at the beginning of Gissing's *New Grub Street* (1882). Only the 'tradesman' who gave consumers what they wanted achieved fame. For instance, religious stories 'sold like hot cakes' for Sunday School prizes, and Milvain suggested that one of his sisters might try her hand at writing them, 'out-trashing the trashiest'. His own infallible formula was 'the upper-middle class intellect', which conveyed the feeling that a novel 'has a special cleverness' with a careful balance between the 'solid' and the 'flashy'.

Confirmation of Gissing's cynical view of literature appeared the next year with the publication of Trollope's posthumous autobiography. It contained a recital of the ergonomics of composition (daily targets of words written) and a balance sheet which revealed that Trollope had made £70,000 in a thirty-year career. During its final ten years he had written sixteen novels, some of which he candidly admitted had been of indifferent quality. Even so, the middle classes purchased them, as they did the works of Sir George Meason (1818–1901), who, like Trollope, knew the market and exploited it. Meason began life as a engraver, but during the 1850s he turned to writing and illustrating the cheap official guides for travellers issued by railway companies. He produced ten in all and had made a fortune that allowed him to retire in comfort in 1870. The rest of his life was dedicated to animal charities, including the London Home for Lost and Starving Dogs.[19]

There was money to be made from books. Middle-class readers were hungry for knowledge and entertainment. For the young there were bloodthirsty penny-dreadfuls, which were frowned upon, and wholesome tales of adventure and Christian sacrifice, which were recommended by responsible parents. There were simplified manuals covering every area of human knowledge and a range of serious, escapist and romantic novels to appeal to every level of concentration and intelligence. The classics remained highly popular; in 1914 eleven publishers were offering editions of *Pride and Prejudice*. The greater part of contemporary fiction was ephemeral; a glance through publishers' advertisements in the press reveals authors and titles that have now been completely forgotten. Among the novels released in the summer of 1914 were G. F. Turner's *The Real Virgin*, which was described as a 'Ruritanian' romance, and *Megan of the Dark Isle*, which was 'a pleasant dull story of North Wales, of its peoples and its legends'.[20] Bestsellers flourished and then vanished, like the *Ingoldsby Legends*, which was first published in 1840 and sold 425,000 copies within fifty-five years, a quarter of them the sixpenny 'people's' edition which first appeared in 1881.

Literary fashions were inconstant. It would be impossible to generalise about the middle-class taste in fiction, although there was a consensus that its moral content should reinforce prevailing codes. Bad men and women were unmasked and suffered the consequences of their misdeeds or shortcomings. The homily element was strong in fiction aimed at those one commentator called the inhabitants of 'genteel villadom' who were addicted to the antics of 'high society'.[21] Curiosity, escapism and prurience merged in the serials published in *Home Sweet Home* during 1898. *A Man's Vengeance, Marguerite's Proposal, A Woman Scorned* and *Crimson Band* ('a story of mystery, love and feeling') conveyed lower-middle-class housewives into a romantic world of country houses and glittering balls where raffish officers and rakes prowled. Ultimately the moral order prevailed: chastity and marital fidelity were upheld and bounders got their deserts.

The law and the circulating libraries were the guardians of literary morality. In 1909 the powerful leading circulating libraries imposed a voluntary censorship over new books. Middle-class sensibilities were the only criterion for deciding what was 'doubtful' or 'objectionable' and therefore banned.[22] Among the casualties was George Cannan's novel *Round the Corner*, which appeared in 1913 and was praised for its frankness by one critic.[23]

It was a caustic survey of middle-class hypocrisy as reflected in the history of the worldly, easygoing Anglican clergyman who embraces high-church ritualism and whose children are distinguished for their waywardness. Most of the plot covers the last quarter of the nineteenth century and is a retrospective rant against Victorian society and its values, an Edwardian prototype of John Osborne's *Look Back in Anger*. What was best left unsaid is exposed, particularly police corruption and the sheer nastiness of the anti-Catholic bigotry that was so easily whipped up by nonconformists. The parson's scapegrace son Fred gets the daughter of a lodging-house keeper pregnant, but she is bundled out of the way so that he can marry a girl with material prospects. When his son is born, he gives the mother fifty pounds for his education and the advice: 'Don't make him a gentleman. Put him in trade. If he's any good he'll get out of it. If he's only middling good, he'll stay there and marry and die respectable.' An artist who believes in art for its own sake, Fred rages against the commerical pressures that crush 'the sheer delight of exercising talent'. It is easy to see why *Round the Corner* was excluded from the shelves of the lending libraries. Subscribers from Kensington or Camberwell for that matter would have been incensed by this anatomy of the 'respectable' and the frustrations caused by slavish adherence to social and moral convention.

The middle classes did enjoy reading about themselves and their betters, but without having to swallow bitter affronts to their collective character. Money, marriage and the nuances of status and manners were the dominant themes in domestic fiction. Readers were invited to identify themselves with characters and their predicaments. The alternative was adventure in the real and invented worlds of Dumas (*The Three Musketeers* was the childhood favourite of Dorothy Sayers and Malcolm Muggeridge), Rider Haggard, Kipling and Anthony Hope. Ruritania and suburbia met in the unlikely yet plausible context of Sherlock Holmes's lodgings. Conan Doyle's sleuth was as much at home safeguarding the honour of European princes as investigating crimes in Norwood or Harrow. He was a complete, modern professional man with a faith in intellect, science and reason (God was nowhere in his scheme of things) and an agent of retribution who protected society from the predators on its margins and sometimes in its midst.

Holmes's cases were adapted for the theatre, fitting easily into popular genre of melodrama. After 1850 the theatres had endeavoured to shed their reputation for vulgarity and noisiness and regain a middle-class audience, which they did, leaving the working classes to beat a path to the music halls. Luring the middle classes into playhouses involved contriving programmes that adhered to the canons of propriety, pleased the eye and never overtaxed the brain. Like art and literature, the theatre was a mirror of morality. Actors were the 'great teachers of humanity', one critic observed, and it was their duty to promote 'one standard of morality . . . the morality which every properly disposed man and woman strives to assert within their homes'.[24]

Shakespeare was always safe, if scrupulously edited, and provided opportunities for gorgeous costumes and pageantry which were the theatrical equivalent of popular historical paintings. Such spectacles were necessary to compete with Astley's Amphitheatre and its imitators which offered re-enactments of imperial battles, complete with redcoats, machine-guns and, of course, hordes of natives.

While it might be morally desirable, turning the stage into a pulpit was bad business. Impresarios and theatre managers knew that profits depended upon diverting or enchanting audiences, rather than engaging their intellects, exciting their indignation or exposing them to unpleasant realities. 'No rude breath of the outer world' was permitted inside the playhouse, lamented one critic in 1893.[25] In 1909, Sir Herbert Tree, the actor–manager, told a Parliamentary commission on censorship that playwrights were nervous about discussing serious subjects. 'The tragedy of great passions has been tabooed, while French farces have been favoured,' he added. It was not just fear of the Lord Chamberlain's blue pencil. Theatregoers preferred 'cheerful harmless plays', observed a financier who invested in productions.[26] The result was pabulum for the middle classes to consume before a late-evening supper: melodramas, romances, domestic comedies, pantomimes and, of course, Gilbert and Sullivan's gentle and genteel musical satires. These spawned many more musicals with carefree, romantic themes and effervescent libretti, such as the Edwardian 'girl' series which included *The Girl Behind the Counter* and *The Girl in the Taxi*.

These had the merit of holding the attention of audiences. According to the playwright Sir Arthur Pinero (1855–1934), the middle classes had a low boredom threshold and, therefore, listnessness had to be averted by crisp dialogue, well laced with repartee and bons mots. Only an upper-middle-class or aristocratic scenario could provide a suitable vehicle for such material. Pinero was convinced that the 'inarticulateness, the inexpressiveness, of the English lower-middle and lower classes – their reluctance to analyse, to generalise, to give vivid utterance to their thoughts or their emotions' exiled them from the stage.[27]

Stark reality was unwelcome. Ibsen's dissections of social and marital tensions got a hostile reception (*Ghosts* was banned in 1891 because it reflected on the consequences of hereditary syphilis), although a loophole in the laws allowed his plays to be performed before audiences who had joined the Independent Theatre Society. The society's members were liberal intellectuals, receptive to new ideas, particularly when they questioned social orthodoxies. The long struggle between the avant garde and upholders of the status quo had begun, and at a time when the middle classes were suspicious of all forms of creative novelty. Ford Madox Ford suspected that the spiteful treatment of Whistler's *Chelsea Old Bridge*, *Hedda Gabler* and Hardy's *Under the Greenwood Tree* reflected a wider middle-class inclination to equate creative innovation with revolution and socialism. That section of society which had once displayed an openness towards new ideas now distrusted them as 'subversive of morality and the security of society'.[28]

The new century saw a hesitant shift towards plays which engaged contemporary problems. John Galsworthy's *Justice*, which appeared in the West End at the beginning of 1910, was a sombre exposure of the penal system. One critic wondered whether the drama marked a watershed. In the future an excursion to the theatre would be undertaken out of a 'sense of duty' rather than in pursuit of amusement.[29] *Punch* defended the pleasure seekers and responded to *Justice* with a sneer in the form of 'Gloom: A Drama of Modern Life' in which one character declaims that the workhouse is 'the symbol of the system, the embodiment of all the maddening hypocrisy of existence'. The following week *Punch* redressed the balance with a parody of the sort of play its readers enjoyed, 'Major Manifold's Marriage'. Its vacuous persiflage included the line: 'A man isn't a man until he's married.'[30]

By now theatres were competing with cinemas. These had first appeared in 1896 and enjoyed what was surely the most spectacular growth of any industry in Britain. In 1914 well over a thousand cinemas entertained an audience of between seven and eight million each week. Picture houses were concentrated in cities and towns (Manchester had over a hundred and Glasgow and Birmingham over forty) and their clientele were largely members of the lower-middle and working classes who paid as little as three pence for a seat. The

'Bijous' and 'Olympias' which were springing up offered their customers an ambience of what one proprietor called 'cosy refinement' with red plush, marble, electric lights and mirrors in the foyer.

The higher reaches of the middle class were frosty towards a form of mass entertainment that from its infancy had deliberately sought to captivate the working class. Cinemagoers watched two-hour programmes of newsreels (among the earliest was footage of the 1897 Jubilee procession and the battle of Spion Kop in 1900) and fifteen-minute 'shorts'. Their story lines were naive and written to satisfy a narrow range of basic emotions: Edwardian cinemagoers wept, laughed, trembled with fear and gasped in wonderment. Producers and cinema proprietors believed that this was what the working class wanted, although the owner of Hammersmith's Electric Theatre was proud that his customers included 'the elite of Kensington' who arrived in motors and carriages.[31] Between 1911 and 1913 British directors turned toward full-length films, selecting scenarios that had proved their popularity on stage: *David Copperfield*, the melodrama *East Lynne* and *Richard III*. These may have attracted a superior audience, but by now the cinemas were showing a growing number of American films which appealed strongly to working-class tastes.

Domestic life was a money spinner for novelists, playwrights and film directors. So long as the subject was treated sympathetically (gently mocked rather than ridiculed), the middle classes were happy. The intimacies of the home deserved to be treated reverentially, for it was the focus of the middle-class world. It was simultaneously a moral bulwark, a sanctuary from the restless universe of labour, an academy where children learned their first and most lasting lessons and a source of pride to its owner. In 1900 the novelist Arnold Bennett, a solicitor's son from Stoke-on-Trent, described it as 'one of the most perfectly organised microcosms on this planet'.

It is a fountain of refinement and consolation, the nursery of affection. It has the peculiar faculty of nourishing itself, for it implicitly denies the existence of anything beyond its doorstep, save the Constitution, a bishop, a rector, the seaside, Switzerland,

and the respectable poor. And its exclusiveness is equalled by its dogmatism . . . This is right: that is wrong – always has been, always will be. This is nice: that is not nice – always has been, always will be.[32]

The economics of the building trade meant that mass-produced middle-class houses looked alike, an arrangement that satisfied builders, purchases and tenants. In the 1880s an eight-roomed house costing between £350 and £450 came with coloured glass in the doorway, mahogany stair-rails, a tessellated hallway, a gas stove and a bathroom. 'City men' were invited in 1906 to buy identical detached six-room houses ten minutes from the station in a 'nice country town' twenty-five miles from London. Each cost £285 or a balance of 10 per cent and the rest paid over twenty-one years. Buyers got six rooms, a bath, a mock-Tudor gable, an ample porch and a garden.

The interior of the terraced house of the clerk or the larger 'residence' of his boss was the domain of the housewife. In larger, upper-middle-class houses she had her own territory (drawing and dressing rooms and boudoir) and her husband had his, the study, and smoking and billiard rooms. Wives chose furnishings and their custom was feverishly sought by manufacturers and department stores which, from the 1890s onwards, offered interest-free credit. In 1895 rival London firms were offering twenty pounds' worth of purchases for between eleven and fifteen shillings a month. An oak or mahogany sideboard cost twenty-six pounds ten shillings, a couch nine pounds, a dining table six pounds fifteen shillings, an easy chair five pounds and a kitchen chair just under two.

These objects of desire provided the backdrop for the formal visit at which hostess and guests wore 'tea gowns' and gossiped. It was not all empty chit-chat; in 1898 the 'wife of a professional or businessman' was advised to widen her conversation beyond fashion to include 'various topics of the day'. These may have added sparkle to enliven what Mr Pooter called 'pleasant' parties at which friends gathered, ate, drank and played parlour or card games. In households which possessed that prized symbol of refinement, a piano (in 1894 prices ranged from ten to a hundred pounds with a twenty-pound Erard having the recommendation of the maestro Paderewski), there were musical entertainments. Nothing is more evocative of middle-class domestic culture than the vividly coloured covers of song sheets and the comical and sentimental lyrics they contained.

The jovial male culture of cheery companionship flourished. The lower-middle classes in particular were attracted by the Volunteers (nearly a million men passed through their ranks in the second half of the century) and those bodies which copied Freemasonic objectives and formulae. Oddfellows, Ancient Druids and Foresters, and Buffaloes all adopted hierarchies, titles and regalia in pursuit of a jolly time and mutual assistance. Meetings were a happy blend of solemn rituals and indulgent cheerfulness. 'The punchbowls were kept in working order, also a plentiful supply of champagne' at a session of the Shrewsbury Buffaloes in 1882. Buffaloes also enjoyed excursions and inter-lodge cricket matches. The names chosen for their lodges – 'General Scarlet' ('a great Christian soldier and a hero of the Crimean war') and 'Empress of India' – echoed popular late-Victorian patriotism.[33]

Commercial travellers, a growing and distinctive group within the lower-middle class, also borrowed from the Freemasons, forming protective associations. These negotiated with hoteliers and railway companies to secure favourable terms for their members, who carried identity cards with photographs.[34] The bonds of common employment extended to entertainments. During 1907 and 1908 the four-hundred-strong Edinburgh and Leith Commercial Travellers Association held concerts, including one for 'indigent' members, whist drives, ladies' nights, lectures ('Scottish Song and Story') and recitals. Instrumental pieces and songs by Mozart, Chopin, Gounod and Dvořák featured at a ladies' night in 1913.[35]

Amateur pianists performing Chopin to an audience of commercial travellers and their wives was a fragment of a vast, heterogeneous middle-class culture. Its sheer diversity reflected the spending power of the middle class, the need to fill spare time and the conviction that the arts contributed to the betterment of the individual and society. Market forces and individual choice dictated nearly everything that was written, produced and performed, a fact of life that angered contrarian Aesthetes, who insisted that authors and artists should express their personal passions, rather than temporise with public morality and commerical pressures. Many artists were happy to accept conditions as they were and made small fortunes doing so. The portraitist Sir Hubert von Herkomer (1849–1914) accepted commissions from aristocrats and middle-class businessmen, illustrated books and towards the end of his life was involved in theatrical productions and film-making.[36]

Social boundaries sometimes ran parallel with cultural, but not always. Virginia Woolf's upper-middle-class family visited picture galleries and attended public lectures on learned subjects, but also indulged in parlour theatricals and went to Christmas pantomimes, that most enduring Victorian middle-class ritual. Yet, and this became more and more pronounced in the new century, the middle and lower ranks of the middle class tended to reject and deride novel forms of art and literature. According to E. M. Forster, *Punch* led the chorus of the new philistinism, always on hand with the 'snigger of the suburban householder who can understand nothing that does not resemble himself'.[37]

The avant garde Omega workshop founded in 1913 was disappointed by the middle-class response to its offer to decorate London flats in the post-impressionist manner. Revealingly, its first patron was Lady Hamilton, the aristocratic wife of a general. Equally revealing was the *Daily Mirror*'s gibe that the result was a 'futurist nightmare'.[38] Better to seek the 'Æsthetic Conversion' advertised by Heals in 1912 together with a sketch of the result, a drawing room in the mock-eighteenth-century 'Colonial Adam' style.

Middle-class aversion to modernism allied with prudery in 1908 when Epstein was commissioned to produce sculptures for the façade of the new headquarters of the British Medical Association in Agar Street. Male and female nudes symbolising aspects of medicine prompted outbursts from the National Vigilance Association, a Catholic priest and the Metropolitan police. The doctors were taken unawares, having not seen Epstein's preliminary sketches, and hurriedly convened to decide what to do with the result. In the meantime the prurient collected in the Strand to stare up at the sculptures, some with binoculars the better to see breasts and penises. *The Times* was disdainful and warned the medics to ignore the 'philistinism and hypocrisy of a portion of our middle class'. After a droll debate, the BMA voted in favour of the statues. Educated, professional men distanced themselves from a mixture of vulgarism and coyness which was now identified with the lower ranks of the middle class.[39]

A new aesthetic and intellectual hierarchy had emerged, and within a few years its divisions received the labels high-brow, middle-brow and low-brow. These three orders have endured, unlike Epstein's statues. The statues were vandalised and were removed in 1937 after the BMA's premises had been purchased by the government of Southern Rhodesia.

11

Am I Making Progress?: Happiness, Identity and Prospects in 1914

Happiness seemed abundant during the last weekend of June 1914. The weather was warm, and professional and business men grumbled about the convention of wearing frock coats and stiff collars. Women were luckier; at the end of the month the summer sales began, with enticing offers of cool seaside or riverside outfits. Holidays were imminent: a fortnight's golf on the Belgian coast for five pounds, ten days in the Alps for just under seven and the Royal Hotel at Whitby, which promised an 'atmosphere of great refinement' for the sedentary. At the Oval, thirteen thousand spectators watched Surrey score 502 for six against the county champions Middlesex. Sporting, social and academic rituals were duly performed. Public schools held their end-of-term speech days. At Haileybury, a proconsul of Empire told boys and parents that there was 'no nobler service' than governing the 'warm-hearted and acutely observant' races of India, who admired the character of the public schoolboy. In Edinburgh, the chairman of governors of Fettes regretted that supertax and death duties prevented rich businessmen from founding schools. The parents applauded.[1]

Such vexations were pinpricks. The middle classes seemed happy, perhaps happier then they had ever been. Unlike dissatisfaction, which is always clamorous and sometimes visible, contentment is often unnoticed and therefore taken for granted. We know from experience that there are large numbers of people who enjoy their lives or convince themselves that they ought to. Such commonplace reactions to circumstances as 'mustn't grumble' or 'can't complain' indicate a degree of satisfaction and the feeling that it is somehow wrong to air one's discontents. Individual misery can be detected and even quantified, but collective happiness remains a black hole of history. Its presence can be sensed, but it defies measurement.

Photographs can help. By 1914, the snapshot taken by the cheap camera had become a medium for recording and preserving middle-class happiness. Virginia Woolf's family took photographs of themselves whenever they were on holiday and enjoying themselves. The results have become icons of a lost world of carefree pleasure. Laughing cyclists pose by their machines outside a country pub, motorists in caps and goggles sit proudly in their cars, families enjoy picnics in meadows and children paddle in the sea. Momentary happiness caught by the camera is not evidence of unending bliss, although the sheer number of snapshots taken suggests a middle-class addiction to amassing memories of pleasure.

These images can be deceptive. We know from elsewhere that the families strolling along seaside promenades had briefly separated themselves from occupational and domestic routines that were exhausting and tedious. Happiness was compensation, as a clerk living in the London suburbs understood, when he balanced the joys of owning a house in the suburbs against the inconveniences of commuting and work:

> He leaned upon the narrow wall
> That set the limit to his ground
> And marvelled thinking of it all,
> That he such happiness had found.
>
> He had no word for it, but bliss
> He smoked his pipe; he thanked his stars;
> And, what more wonderful than this?
> He blessed the groaning, stinking cars

> That made it doubly sweet to win
> The respite of the hours apart
> From all the broil and sin and din
> Of London's damned money mart.[2]

Not all villa owners who caught the 7.30 from Penge each morning felt this way, but it is important to remember that many did. Money was central to middle-class contentment; it enabled the happy clerk to buy or rent his home, sustain his family, fund the ambitions of his children and take them on annual holidays. He may also have had enough to indulge in the new craze of stamp collecting which was popular with middle-class males, particularly commuters. Until the 1960s stamp shops were scattered across the city and some were sited close to suburban stations. The issues of the British Empire were always the most popular.

The ability to maintain a family and have enough spare cash to buy the latest Rhodesian stamps or other objects of desire was known in the 1990s as the 'feel good' factor. It is a new name for an old phenomenon, a form of collective euphoria created by individuals with money to spend (or access to credit) and a wide range of goods to spend it on. Judged by these economic criteria the middle classes had every reason to feel happy in 1914. Inflation was minimal, their disposable incomes were rising, there was a reservoir of domestic labour available (though it was less cheap and tractable than in the past) and the choice of goods and services was widening. Nothing better illustrated the trend in middle-class consumption than children's toys, whose range and sophistication had grown over the previous thirty years. There were delicately painted and prettily dressed dolls for girls, and painted model soldiers and brightly coloured tinplate ships, cars and aeroplanes for boys. These were still expensive luxuries, but the experience of the last century had demonstrated that one generation's luxury became affordable to the next.

Hoardings and advertisements in the press urged the middle classes to spend more. Copywriters played on wants and anxieties. The process of ageing could be halted or reversed by unguents and potions that restored lost or greying hair, or banished wrinkles. Patent medicines replaced lost energy and vitalised inert bowels and overworked livers, and nutritious Bovril and cocoa provided instant stamina. 'Life is only worth living when the liver is right' insisted the manufacturer of a nostrum that guaranteed its constant welfare. Prepared foods for infants and children promised strong and healthy offspring. They grew up in a household from which patent cleaners had banished dirt (and disease) and, if Sunlight soap was used in the laundry, all the family had 'the joy of sweet, clean clothes'.

Women made themselves attractive through cosmetics, perfumes and corsetry engineered to produce what was considered an alluring figure. Men were constantly reminded that well-tailored suits and clean shirts were the outward signs of commercial ability and success. Speculative builders advertised new houses in suburban communities surrounded by fields and woods. A Carron fireplace gave an aura of 'cheerfulness' to the new home, and its owner's cultural aspirations could be fulfilled only by a 'Metrostyle Pianola'. Alongside this claim was a drawing of a lady in an evening gown playing the automatic piano while her husband in evening dress listened attentively. They were followers of what, in 1912, a clergyman called 'the practical gospel of well-being', a modern doctrine that exposed its devotees to 'the ceaseless pressure of material interests'.[3] This could be endured, even welcome, since the accessories of 'well-being' were the tokens of status, which itself was a source of happiness. It was satisfying to have what everyone else had, better still to have more.

There was a correspondence between what advertisers promised to provide and the basic components of middle-class happiness. They were good health, robust children, cleanliness of person and surroundings, smart clothes and a comfortable, well-furnished home in agreeable surroundings. With perhaps the exception of freedom from dirt, all were timeless and would endure for the rest of the century. The bellows-driven 'dust extractor' of 1913 was puffed in much the same way as an electric-powered vacuum cleaner ninety years later: both assured a spotless home in which children were protected from germs. Like every other constituent of happiness, these gadgets could be purchased, which was why economists have alleged that consumption lay at the heart of happiness. Behavioural scientists demur. Between 1961 and 1987 incomes in Japan rose steadily, but, in so far as this could be quantified, there was no commensurate upsurge in happiness.[4]

Was this so among the middle classes of late-Victorian and Edwardian Britain? One ought to pause before transferring data obtained through the apparatus of late-twentieth-century social surveys to previous generations, although some things are constant. Early-twentieth-century women's journals claimed that preparing meals that were appreciated by her family was one of the greatest sources of satisfaction to a woman, a fact which has unsurprisingly been confirmed by modern consumer research.[5] A triumphant cook reminds us that there are other yard-sticks by which human happiness can be measured than what was provided by the market. If it was severely restricted, as occurred during the two world wars, happiness did not disappear. People made do with just enough to eat, found they could endure the cold and were still able to enjoy friendship, conversation, reading and the contemplation of the sublime.

Myriad variations of individual ambition, expectation and temperament always set thresholds of contentment and render it impossible to calculate precisely the overall happiness of a class which by 1914 numbered two million. Moreover, there have always been disagreements over what constitutes happiness. In the nineteenth century, Continentals blamed the high suicide rates in Britain on excessive freedom, a spirit of enquiry and exaggerated expectations of life. These were the qualities which the British middle class believed offered the best chances of happiness for everyone.[6] Protestantism also contributed to this urge for self-destruction since it fostered melancholic spiritual introspection among the educated. This would have astonished clergymen, who believed that they provided that true and permanent happiness enjoyed by those who served God and expected salvation.

Victorian Protestant attitudes to happiness were ambivalent. Finding God, following His commandments and believing in His powers of redemption were essential for personal happiness. Self-denial was virtuous, envy and avarice were sinful, but individual prosperity was blessed if it had been earned. This stricture had no appeal to those who had suffered deprivation in early life and compensated for it by purchasing whatever they wanted. The self-made man wanted to proclaim his success, and this was most satisfyingly achieved through conspicuous consumption or, for that matter, generous gifts to charities.

That old Puritan correlation between money in the bank and spiritual worth worked in contrary ways. It instilled in the successful man a sense that his wealth was deserved and it drove those who had failed to the extremes of despair. This was dramatically illustrated at the beginning of the great agricultural slump when farm bankruptcies soared. In 1879 and 1880 some 2,300 farms went bust and just over two hundred farmers took their own lives.[7] A similar rise in the suicides of farmers occurred during and after the outbreaks of foot-and-mouth disease in 2000 and 2001. The earlier calamity was the product of natural and economic forces beyond the victims' control. They believed otherwise, and judged themselves by prevailing, middle-class codes. Unpayable debts carried a burden of guilt which was a compound of having failed oneself and one's dependants and, perhaps, of having wasted one's life.

Such considerations spring to mind when considering an analysis of suicides which occurred between 1878 and 1883. The highest rates were among men active in the victualling trade, chemists, shop-keepers and commercial travellers. All were engaged in highly competitive and economically precarious activities. Just below innkeepers and dealers in spirits were doctors and barristers, whose suicide rate reflected the pressures of 'prolonged mental work and concentrated attention'. Interestingly, suicide was commonest among males aged between fifteen and twenty whose careers were beginning and among those between forty-five and fifty when they were coming to an end.[8] Despondency was most intense among those facing the future and those contemplating what they had accomplished. Debility and incurable illnesses added to the anxieties of the old.

Understanding of the causes of what we now recognise as clinical depression and nervous exhaustion was limited and dogmatic.

Whatever its reason, suicide was commonly seen as the consequence of madness. The moods and eccentricities caused by fear and anxiety were routinely diagnosed as the symptoms of insanity, as were the spasms associated with fevers, and under the Lunacy Laws rendered the victim liable to confinement in an asylum. This tended to be permanent, since no differentiation was made between acute, temporary and recoverable cases. For middle-class families madness was a source of shame, as lunacy was thought to be hereditary. The deranged were either kept hidden, like Mrs Rochester, or certified and exiled.

Callousness was the product of ignorance. Until the general publication of Freud's researches and theories in the 1900s, knowledge of the mechanisms of the brain was scanty and psychoanalysis unheard of. Freud's observations aroused enormous interest among the educated middle class, for whom they offered a key to understanding emotions and behaviour. Moral absolutes lost some of their old force. The mischievousness of children could now be explained as a natural consequence of their peculiar mental life and not the result of a wilfulness rooted in original sin that needed to be contained and reprimanded.[9]

The welfare of their children was a responsibility which was an alternating source of happiness and anguish to the middle class. It was incumbent upon parents to secure the best education and opportunities for their children, and, if funds were short or a breadwinner died or absconded, this obligation was passed to grandparents, aunts, uncles and cousins. William Bowyer's father managed to find enough spare cash from his income as an ironmonger's clerk to fund an extra two years of schooling which made the difference between a dead-end job as a messenger boy and a clerkship with the potential for promotion. In H. G. Wells's *Anne Veronica* (1909), Mr Stanley, the heroine's solicitor father, planned and financed what he considered 'brilliant careers' for her brothers, one in the Indian Civil Service, the other in the motor business. They were shrewd choices: the latter was expanding and, by the time he was thirty, the administrator would have a salary of a thousand a year. Of course, not all sons were so compliant. A friend tells Mr Stanley: 'My son wanted to marry a woman of thirty in a tobacconist's shop . . . We fixed that.' 'Fixing' the careers and marriages of the young was a fraught and exasperating business, as Mr Pooter discovered when he tried to settle the future of his son, Lupin.

Lupin Pooter does eventually secure a well-paid 'situation' (a wonderful period word) in a City firm. He tells his astonished father: 'I want to go *on*.' Movement onwards and upwards was lubricated by the principles of self-help, a philosophy which the middle class believed had been the mainspring of their fortunes and happiness. Self-help offered a lifeline to anyone, however poor, who had the will and wit to advance himself. As in modern America, the message of the rich to the poor was: pull yourselves together and follow our example. How to do so was explained by Samuel Smiles in his *Self Help* of 1859 and repeated by a host of imitators. One, the anonymous compiler of *Small Beginnings or the Way to Get On*, published in the 1880s, identified the middle class's 'persevering industry and well directed skill' as the foundations of their success. These qualities flourished in a nation which had hallowed 'honourable ambition'. 'The application of industry, intelligence, and skill to the ordinary pursuits of life under God's blessing' was the foundation of future 'honour and influence'. How happy Britain was to be a nation where 'talent and genius', combined with 'integrity', were always destined to be rewarded.[10]

Optimism and an absolute faith in human character permeated these books, as they did the collective mind of the middle class. 'Go on and prosper' was the valediction given to a young commerical traveller by his first boss in 1858, and it must have been repeated many times and in many forms over the next fifty or so years.[11] It went without saying that endeavour and perseverance would be rewarded with prosperity and happiness. 'Am I making progress?' asked an advertisement for the Pelman School of the Mind in 1913. The uncertain, and there must have been many, were invited to subscribe to *Brain Power*, which was guaranteed to set 'ambition stirring'. Followers of Pelmanism would soon discover new powers of initiative, concentration and 'salesmanship' which would eliminate luck as a factor in their advancement. Banishing luck involved a course of simple memory tests and exercises, including skipping with a rope. Thousands of hopeful men and women were taken in.

Philosophies of self-help took for granted a hierarchical, multi-layered but open society in which talent and hard graft were rewarded. Dress proclaimed one's place in the world. After he had secured an office job in London, D. H. Lawrence's brother William returned home to stroll through the streets in a silk hat, frock coat and yellow kid gloves and, in his words, 'astonish the natives' of the Nottingham mining village.[12] *Punch* cartoons provided a crude guide to who stood where in the social order. Aristocrats were identified by coronets, robes and a backdrop of grouse moors and the middle classes by suits, collars and ties, homburgs (silk hats for professional and business men) and boaters in summer. Working men wore cloth caps, collarless shirts and hands thrust into the pockets of dishevelled trousers. The middle classes stood out in other ways; they were were taller and sturdier than their inferiors. In 1904 the average height of a thirteen-year-old boy at Rugby was five feet one inch and he weighed ninety-eight pounds. His contemporary at a Salford board school was four feet five inches tall and weighed seventy-nine pounds.[13]

Clothes and physique marked an individual's position in a complex pyramid. A vertical cross-section was made in 1910 by an academic who uncovered six basic layers determined by income, education, occupation and perceived intelligence. At the apex were the 'rich' with incomes of over £2,000. Below them was a middle class with three distinct tiers. The highest included senior civil servants and professional men who had attended public school and university and had salaries of between £600 and £2,000. Next came business and professional men with incomes of between £300 and £600 a year who had been educated at grammar schools and took an informed interest in public affairs. Underneath them was the lower-middle class which comprised shopkeepers, clerks, printers and commercial travellers who had been to elementary schools. They earned between three and five pounds a week and had 'superficial opinions on all subjects' abstracted from the popular press.

Just below them was a border zone between the middle and working class inhabited by skilled artisans, clerks and foremen who lived in five-roomed houses with 'homely but comfortable furniture' and earned between two and three pounds a week. They had 'simple' minds. At the bottom of the pile was a working class of unskilled and casual workers, office boys and shop assistants of 'low' intelligence and wages – between eighteen and twenty-five shillings a week.[14]

Other, subjective criteria separated the classes, particularly manners and fastidiousness. Middle-class inmates in an Edinburgh lunatic asylum protested at having to share accommodation with the poor. They were 'riff raff', a 'stinking low set' and 'a shade removed from the beasts of the fields', whose eating habits were revolting.[15] Recollecting his boyhood in a terrace of 'spec' houses in Battersea in the 1890s, William Bowyer noted that the lower part of the street was on the verge of becoming a slum. Front doors opened on interiors of 'indescribable filthiness' with 'half-naked, dirty children crawling about the thresholds'. At 'our end' were 'respectable' families of clerks and artisans who were concerned with cleanliness and 'the future'.[16] It was a familiar picture: the middle classes possessed self-respect because they were clean, seemly in their behaviour and had foresight. The working class was dirty and did not care about tomorrow.

The middle classes were keen to keep a distance between themselves and such creatures. The daughter of a merchant navy officer brought up in a Liverpool suburb remembered that her mother warned her to restrict her contacts to 'nice' people, who included a schoolmistress, a music teacher and a dressmaker.[17] In the countryside, codes of medieval precedence still obtained. A farm worker's daughter recalled the seating arrangements in an Essex church at the beginning of the twentieth century. In the front pews 'were the local farmers, the local bigwigs, you see, posh people'. Behind sat shopkeepers 'and people who were considered to be a bit superior to others', and in the rear were the poor, including her mother.[18] If she joined the Mothers Union, she would have been urged to instil obedience into her children, for it was well known that the working classes were slack in disciplining their offspring.[19]

Everyone agreed that the aristocracy occupied the summit of

society. For Virginia Woolf, it was a truly Olympian position. After a visit to the Cecils in 1903, she likened them to Zeus, Bacchus and Pan, enjoying 'a happy luxurious life with all the best of everything at their command'.[20] It was an abundance and omnipotence to which many upper-middle-class families aspired. Others shied away because the aristocracy seemed frivolous and obsessed with field sports. By contrast, families like Virginia Woolf's cultivated the serious and often intense world of the intellect. In time, she would gravitate towards a circle of men and women from similar backgrounds who deliberately exiled themselves from the coarsening world of earning and spending and devoted their lives to art and literature. The Bloomsbury Group could afford this indulgence because its members enjoyed incomes derived from the investments and ultimately labour of their middle-class parents and grandparents. They did not have to work to survive and, therefore, their lives were akin to those of the philistine aristocrats and plutocrats whom they despised.

Cultural predilections or their absence split the upper-middle class. In E. M. Forster's *Howards End* (1910), the high-brow Schlegels are chaffed by the Willcoxes, whose money was made in the City. Theirs was the dismissive voice of reactionary philistinism: 'Equality was nonsense, Votes for Women nonsense, Socialism nonsense, Art and Literature, except when conducive to strengthening character, nonsense.' The aesthetes had their own snobbery. One, travelling south from London by train in 1914, deplored the 'red houses in rows' and the semis with their monkey-puzzle trees and 'vulgar' rhododendrons. Once 'a beautiful county', Surrey was in the hands of 'lovers of golf and whisky'.[21]

Professional men continued to defend their territories jealously. In 1900 a doctor complained about hospital administrators who intruded on clinical matters. 'Skilful dissectors of balance sheets' should automatically defer to clinicians.[22] There were similar objections to doctors being placed under the control of non-medical administrators when the National Insurance Act became law in 1910.[23] The row has smouldered ever since.

Behind the medics' prickliness was the sense of self-esteem shared by other professional men: they were the elite, not just of the middle classes but of the entire country. Their intelligence, wisdom and responsibility had been the foundations of national and imperial success. Their influence was everywhere and beneficial; writing in 1920, E. M. Forster acknowledged that the middle class had become the 'dominant force in our country' and its characteristic 'solidity, caution, integrity [and] efficiency' were now accepted as the main-springs of Britain's greatness.[24] The cost, Forster believed, had been the smothering of imagination and creativity.

Middle-class self-assurance and its frequent companion self-righteousness were strongest at the top. At all levels it coexisted with a strain of nervousness that expressed itself in a desire to keep the company of one's own kind. Straying beyond familiar circles caused embarrassment. The insurance clerk Leonard Bast in *Howards End* is ignorant of what is expected of him when he takes tea with the Schlegels, and his gaucheries convince him that he ought to have stayed away. He imagines that he is somehow the equal of his host-esses, but is unequal to their ambience. Mr Willcox the businessman would not have invited him: 'Your servants ought to have orders not to let such people in.' They should be allowed a contented exis-tence within the boundaries of their own world. 'I look at the faces of the clerks in my office, and observe them to be dull, but I don't know what's going on beneath.'

Very little, believed Malcolm Muggeridge. He had been born in 1903, grew up in a semi-detached house just beyond Croydon and convinced himself that he was under the 'general anathema of being *petit bourgeois*'. He detested his surroundings: 'Hateful, despicable, ridiculous little houses with preposterous names like The Elms, Chez Nous, the Nook; with tradesmen's entrances when there was scarcely room for a tolerable front door and mock-Tudor beams and gables'. It was a world of tensions in which 'we were snobs in relation to our neighbours, and anti-snobs in relation to those above and below us in the social scale'.[25] The nuances of status were acutely felt; Muggeridge's mother confided to him that her dream was to go to church on Sunday mornings alongside her husband in a top hat with her five sons behind, each in an Eton collar and jacket.

In Muggeridge's case, lower-middle-class self-hatred was fostered by paternal socialism. Having discarded the suburban stereotype he invented another: 'a real worker sitting in braces in front of a roaring fire and drinking cups of strong tea which his missus had just prepared for him. A . . . figure straight from *Sons and Lovers*.' It was appropriate that this early contribution to the twentieth-century romanticisation of the working class came from D. H. Lawrence. Lawrence's father was a colliery foreman, and for a time his mother kept a small shop which placed his family somewhere in that no man's land between the working and the lower-middle classes. A scholarship led him to Nottingham High School, where he wore the regulation Eton collar but felt isolated among companions who sneered about him eventually ending up 'down pit'. Not surprisingly, he loathed class divisions and the harm they inflicted on those who hoped to transcend them. In *Women in Love* Birkin declares, 'We are all different and unequal in spirit – it is only the social differences that are based on accidental material conditions.'

Yet the differences were important for the lower-middle class. Like Leonard Bast, many of them existed frighteningly close to what Lawrence called 'the abyss' (that is, the working class) from which they had emerged and into which they could easily descend. Personal shortcomings (often related to alcohol), debts and outside economic pressures provided the impetus. During the recession of 1903 the *Decorators' and Painters' Magazine* warned the owners of small businesses to avoid buying cheap materials on credit from persuasive commercial travellers, a sure path to bankruptcy. Young men entering the building trade were directed towards clerkships in the Post Office and local government, where they enjoyed security of employment.[26] The proprietors of corner shops were compelled to extend credit to working-class customers and simultaneously faced fierce competition from larger concerns, including, in industrial areas, the Co-op. If the lower-middle class possessed capital, it was frequently tied up in small houses which were rented to working-class tenants. Living on narrow margins themselves, the landlords were ferocious in demanding rents and lacked the means to maintain their properties.[27]

Clerks and petty capitalists had a tribune in Horatio Bottomley

MP, whose *John Bull* (founded in 1906) gave a voice to what he called the 'small man'. Forthright and irreverent, the weekly enticed readers with competitions, hired Frank Harris to review books and campaigned against profiteers. It championed the victims of credit and exposed mail–order companies which sold shoddy suits to clerks desperate to keep up appearances. Its readers were also anxious about improving themselves and their families, for *John Bull* regularly advert-ised cut-price editions of Dickens and children's encyclopaedias.

The encyclopaedias in the clerk's home were a tribute to a faith in the nostrums of self-help which, in turn, rested on the dicey notion that talent could sweep aside the barriers created by birth. In theory, the Education Acts of 1870 and 1902 had given fresh impetus to upward social mobility. In 1909, the Archbishop of York announced that he would welcome working–class men as ordination candidates, with a preference for those who had had a 'good' education at secondary school.[28] The door was open, but very narrowly. What the Archbishop termed a good education was available only to the chil-dren of families which possessed sufficient reserves to finance one or two years' additional schooling beyond the statutory leaving age of fourteen.

Higher learning also required capital. In 1912 fees for the University of Bristol's engineering course were twenty-six pounds five shillings a year, with a reduction to fifteen guineas for students whose parents' income was less than £350. Glasgow Technical College charged an average of twelve guineas a term and teacher training colleges between sixty-five and seventy pounds for two-year courses. Maintenance added to bills. At St Andrews students in university halls of residence paid between forty-five and seventy-five pounds a year rent, and annual tuition fees were twelve pounds. Taking into account a personal allowance of thirty pounds a year, the parents of a son or daughter undertaking a four-year honours course would expect to pay a total of at least £250, the price of an automobile.

Limited private and public awards were available. In 1898 London County Council offered twenty-five pounds a year to young women wishing to study the teaching of 'domestic economy' at Battersea

Polytechnic for two years. Recipients would need extra to feed and clothe themselves. State assistance was minimal: in 1911 an annual government grant of £114,000 was distributed among fifteen universities.

Getting on required capital, whether it was invested in education, professional training or the establishment of a small business. Those who did not possess or could not borrow this vital ingredient for mobility tended to stay where they were, whatever their talents or ambitions. Among the working class, there were cultural and familial pressures to stay put, particularly the tradition of sons following fathers into skilled manual work. Getting on the first rung of the ladder was perhaps the hardest step of all, requiring considerable drive and ability: D. H. Lawrence was one of the three miners' sons who passed the examinations for Nottingham High School between 1882 and 1899. His schoolmates included the sons of colliery clerks and managers, farmers and shopkeepers. All no doubt wanted their boys to get on or at least retain the social standing of their parents, and all had the wherewithal to make the necessary investment.

These factors, particularly the lack of capital reserves, hindered upward social mobility. Marriages offer a clue to its prevalence. An analysis of occupations in registers of marriages between 1899 and 1914 suggests that 20 per cent of couples were moving upwards and 25 per cent downwards. In rural areas the figures were lower.[29] Of course, these documents provide no evidence relating to the future fortunes of the newlyweds, but superficially they indicate a relatively static society. The Lawrence brothers were an exception; if your father came home from work with dirty hands, it was likely that you would too.

Yet the middle class continued to grow. That suggests a degree of recruitment from outside which would increase as the century progressed. This enlargement coincided with a dilution and, ultimately, diminishment of its influence in society. This, like that catalyst for so much future change – Britain's entry into the war on 4 August 1914 – could not have been foreseen by the middle-class men and women who enjoyed themselves during the high summer.

Part Four

Stress and Survival: 1914–2005

1

People Seem to Lose their Way: Continuity and Change, 1914–1951

Few among the exultant crowds which massed in Trafalgar Square on 4 August 1914 and over the next four weeks waved Union Jacks at departing soldiers had the slightest inkling of the nature of the war that was beginning. Nor could they have imagined the sacrifice and discipline that would be needed to win it. One onlooker in London that August evening observed that the people around him were 'delighted at the prospect' of the war, and the subsequent stampede to the army recruiting offices showed that there was no lack of volunteers glad to fight it.[1] Patriotism dissolved class differences. 'The clerk in straw hat and blue serge, who yesterday would greatly have resented being pushed in the chest by a social inferior who notes his proportions in a clumsy hand, now smiles cheerfully.'[2]

Khaki did not prove a leveller. The civilian social order was reproduced in the trenches. It was assumed that young upper-middle-class men like Rupert Brooke with their 'education and refinement', physical stamina and 'élan' were natural officers, just as the squire's sons had been in the past.[3] The public schools had seen to that, and their idealism was vindicated at the front. 'Every public schoolboy is serving,' wrote one, and one in six gives up his life. 'They cannot be such bad places after all.'[4] Another insisted that when the working-class soldier is commanded by 'a typical Public School boy or University man as an officer, his happiness is complete'.[5] The upper-middle classes had at last gained equality with the old aristocracy and gentry; thanks to Dr Arnold and his successors, they had proved themselves 'natural' leaders.

British tactics and German firepower soon drained the reservoir of public school subalterns, and battalion commanders were compelled to fill their places with lower-middle- and working-class rankers who had brains and initiative. 'Temporary gentlemen' took over platoons and companies. Their rough table manners and colloquialisms shocked public schoolmen, one of whom was horrified to see brother officers flirting with 'shopgirls' while on leave. Some of the inter-lopers in the mess played the chameleon. One recalled: 'I came to appreciate many things that count, and despite a board school educa-tion, I found myself unconsciously acquiring a knack, or habit of that other accent which differs so utterly from the one that the average Londoner uses.'[6]

Wartime status disappeared with demobilisation, and temporary gentlemen soon discovered that the subaltern's pip was not a pass-port to social advancement or a better job. Some were compelled to become railway porters, cabmen and, in one case, even an organ grinder. George Bowling, the hero of Orwell's *Coming Up for Air* (1939), summed up their plight: 'We'd suddenly changed from gentlemen holding his Majesty's Commission into miserable out-of-works whom nobody wanted.' Pleas for work from temporary gentlemen were a common feature of newspaper personal columns. Many were married men and glad to take whatever was available; in April 1920 an ex-officer and former salesman was content to take a job as a storeman.[7] Permanent' gentlemen were equally desperate. In October 1919 a public school officer and 'all-round athlete' begged for someone to 'risk' employing him.[8] The middle-class experience of starting life again in the 'Land fit for Heroes' could be as bleak as that of the working class.

The war had had an impact on everyone's lives and its social effects have been well analysed.[9] Given that modern, total war is a test of national unity and collective will, Edwardian Britain had performed remarkably well. Mass patriotism fuelled determination, although morale was showing signs of fatigue during the final year of the war. The mobilisation of man and woman power and the state's assumption of control over industry, agriculture and transport had required the submissive co-operation of all classes. They recognised the gravity of the emergency and did what the government ordered, paid more taxes and surrendered cherished individual freedoms. Above all, the people had faith in their rulers, although afterwards doubts surfaced. These were reflected by Orwell's overview of the war, written in 1940: 'The thick-necked cavalry generals remained at the top, but the lower-middle classes and the colonies came to the rescue.'[10] He had in mind the clerks who had swarmed out of their offices in 1914 to join the 'Pals' battalions of Kitchener's volunteer army and troops from the white dominions. These men had saved the aristocracy and upper-middle classes from the consequences of their ineptitude. It was a common view between the wars and not without truth.

Total war had played havoc with the economic orthodoxies of the Victorian middle classes. Minimalist government and free-market capitalism were suspended. A command economy took their place: the government dictated what was manufactured and grown, rationed food and fuel and fixed prices. Taxation soared, so did wages and inflation. The middle classes had to acquiesce, but by 1918 many were stunned and full of foreboding. Once the masters of an economic system that worked to their advantage, they were now the victims of one in which the dice seemed loaded against them. Hysteria infected some and it focused on the trade unions, which by sheer numbers and ruthlessness were securing for their members an increasing share of the nation's wealth. 'A triumphant proletariat' was now poised to 'live luxuriously on the plunder of the helpless classes'.[11] 'Hobnailed trade unions' had brought the middle classes to their knees. 'War has extinguished civilisation.'[12] Worse still, a Communist revolution was just around the corner, if the headlines of the Conservative press were to be believed, which they were by many during 1919 and 1920.

These were false alarms. The Edwardian social hierarchy was intact and healthy. The future looked bright for public schools, according to the headmaster of Charterhouse, who predicted in 1919 that more and more parents would seek places for their sons.[13] At the dedication of Cheltenham's war memorial the following year, Field-Marshal Sir William Robertson told a new generation that they were destined to be 'leaders of men', keeping faith with the 670 Cheltonians who had been killed in battle.[14] Power would pass naturally and easily into the hands of their survivors. They may have been among the senior civil servants observed making their way along Whitehall one morning in the early 1930s. They were mature men between forty and sixty-five, 'well dressed in a quiet style' as was to be expected from 'able, cultivated men of the upper middle class'. Half an hour earlier, junior civil servants had turned up for work: 'a picked sample of the great class loosely known as the "lower middle class", solid, decent, kindly, trustworthy'.[15]

Deference was still expected and practised. A 1931 manual for trainee nurses instructed them to address doctors as 'sir' and treat them with 'proper respect'. 'Familiarity' towards patients and the use of 'terms of endearment' were outlawed.[16] 'Refinement, politeness and dignity' were essential to salesmen, advised a guide of 1931. 'Convey the fact that you are a gentleman, and usually customers will treat you as one.'[17] At the bottom of the pile, unquestioning quietism was still a way of life, as one working-class boy later recalled. 'If you were born into the class I was born into you accepted it, you were automatically submissive in your attitude. And yet we didn't seem to be envious. If a coalowner lived on the outskirts of a village . . . we accepted it.' Authority was also accepted. Caps were raised to the schoolteacher and 'a sort of reverence' was shown to the local policeman. 'Submissiveness was born into you because of your status.'[18] Such attitudes were by no means universal in a period when class war was preached by the extreme left and strikers and the unemployed clashed with the police, but it is worth remembering that they existed.

The complementary hierarchy of authority and its legal apparatus were still in place. At its apex was the monarchy, which had gained in public affection thanks to the upsurge in patriotism during the war. Between 1914 and 1918, King George V had symbolised national and imperial unity, and during the unquiet years that followed he represented steadiness and calm. A conservative, down-to-earth and dignified patriarch with a high sense of duty, the King personified old middle-class virtues and, like so many of his middle-class subjects, was an avid stamp collector. Thanks to intense, often sycophantic and trivial press coverage of its activities, the royal family was projected as a model for all families. It was, but not in the intended way. The froideur between the King and a Prince of Wales who preferred the louche pleasures available to the young and rich mirrored a wider post-war conflict between the generations. It concluded, appropriately, in 1936 when Edward VIII set emotion above duty and forfeited his throne and the respect of millions conditioned to expect better of royalty.

The moral order which the royal family now represented had taken a hard knock during the war. A century of human progress had been brutally terminated and optimism had perished on the battlefield, along with other reassuring Victorian orthodoxies. Intellectuals in arms sensed the change. 'God as an all wise Providence was dead; blind Chance succeeded to the throne,' Robert Graves wrote afterwards. A mental chasm had opened up, with those at home worshipping God and adhering to virtues that 'the fighting forces mocked, such as High Endeavour, Humility, Thrift, Prudence, Sobriety'.[19] Middle-class self-assurance had been dented and its members felt cast adrift and carried along by unfamiliar currents towards an unseen and possibly frightening destination. Noël Coward caught their mood in his 'Twentieth Century Blues' of 1932:

> In this strange illusion
> Chaos and confusion,
> People seem to lose their way.

Judged by the anxieties of the self-styled 'nouveaux pauvres' and the nihilism of the survivors of the mass slaughter of the war, the world had been or was about to be turned upside down. Those born before 1890 were out of touch with a new, alien world. In 1931 a senior schools inspector appealed to older teachers not to grimace whenever their pupils mentioned 'jazz' or wince when they talked about the 'movies' and 'modern dancing'.[20] American films and ragtime had made their debut before the war, but this was irrelevant to an older generation which blamed the conflict for everything that seemed wrong with the present.

Young middle-class couples who danced to Alexander's Rag Time Band in 1914 were the heirs of an age of unparalleled progress which had showed every sign of continuing. After 1918 the middle classes were less cocksure and during the next twenty years their anxieties were confirmed by a wayward economy, mass unemployment and chronic instability in Europe. Progress seemed to have been arrested and the prospect of tomorrow was unnerving. 'Look for the silver lining' ran the opening line of a popular song of the 1930s; for many it was hard to discern. The war had weakened confidence, as Bertrand Russell observed on the fortieth anniversary of its outbreak: 'A great war would mark the end of an epoch and drastically lower the general level of civilisation.'[21] 'Never such innocence again', wrote Philip Larkin in his evocation of Edwardian Britain, 'MCMXIV'. He could easily have added: 'Nor ever such confidence'.

No one knew what to put in its place. Over the next ninety years middle-class men and women who believed themselves duty bound to engage with the world and bring it to its senses faced a stream of collective and individual dilemmas. Did they make a bold break with the past and embrace the exciting ideologies now offered by the extremes of right and left and construct totally new moral, political and social orders, like those in Lenin's Russia and Mussolini's Italy? The democratic socialism of the Labour Party tempted sections of the middle class who, after the 1931 economic crisis, convinced themselves that capitalism's faults were irredeemable and its decline irreversible. Many who strode leftwards were propelled by anger and pity at the cold-hearted treatment of the unemployed and by an admiration for the forthrightness and vitality of the working classes.

Labour converts like Hugh Gaitskell and Richard Crossman (both

Wykehamists) were the mental descendants of those upper-middle-class men and women who had followed their consciences and placed their time and talents at the disposal of the unfortunate. Middle-class socialists were often infected with the twin vices of intellectuals, impatience and an urge to dominate, which was galling for their working-class colleagues. A former Oxford don, Crossman noticed in 1953 that intellectuals of his generation were regarded as 'thrusting outsiders' by working-class members of Labour's National Executive.[22] This antipathy persisted when the party was in power. During a cabinet discussion on royal revenues in 1969, Jim Callaghan defended the royal family. 'I think [Prince] Philip is a fine fellow,' he argued in a speech that denounced the 'sentiments of middle-class intellectuals'. Crossman was appalled. Yet he never shook off the snobbery of his upper-middle-class upbringing: he thought Keir Hardie had been an instinctive 'patrician', considered Gaitskell '*bourgeois*' and sneered at the 'deeply *petit bourgeois*' domestic arrangements of Harold Wilson at Number Ten.[23]

In the 1930s many of the middle classes who shifted leftwards were animated by a fear of the radical right which was making so much headway on the Continent. The need to resist Fascism and Nazism sent middle-class volunteers to fight Franco in Spain between 1936 and 1939. Four anti-Fascists, Kim Philby, Guy Burgess, Donald Maclean and Anthony Blunt, went further and placed themselves at the disposal of Soviet intelligence. Their impeccable public school and Cambridge credentials gained them places in the Foreign Office and intelligence services. It was as unthinkable as it was inexplicable that this quartet should embrace an ideology so inimical to their class, which was why their treason has fascinated later generations. Home-grown Fascism had hardly any appeal to the middle classes, not least because Sir Oswald Mosley's British Union of Fascists was soon associated with riots and vicious Jew-baiting in the East End.

The vast majority of the middle classes stayed put and trusted in old creeds and parties. They hoped that something would be salvaged from the past and adapted to fit modern circumstances. If left to its own devices, perhaps with some help from the state, capitalism could cure itself. Political and economic experiments were dangerous, not least to property. 'Safety first', a slogan coined by an advertising agency for the Conservatives in 1929, caught the mood of the middle classes. They voted overwhelmingly for Ramsay MacDonald's coalition (largely Liberal and Conservative) in 1931 and for Stanley Baldwin's Tories in 1935. According to that novelty of the time, the public opinion poll, the Conservatives had a majority of over 50 per cent in February 1940. Caution was the watchword for the nine to ten million who were in work during the 1930s and were buying cheap cars and houses in the expanding suburbs. As George Orwell observed of the suburban car owners, they were 'Tories, yes-men and bum suckers' prepared to 'die on the battlefield' to save Britain from Communism.[24] Their votes kept centre-right governments in power between the wars and in 1939 they went to war to save Britain and Europe from Nazism and Fascism.

Among the older generation there was a hankering to preserve the old moral order and pretend that the war had never happened. Sir William Joynson-Hicks (1865–1932), a former solicitor and temperance fanatic, had a try at putting the clock back when he was home secretary between 1924 and 1929 and made an ass of himself. He was applauded by moral absolutists who spent the inter-war years and, for that matter, the rest of the century endeavouring to halt what they feared was a slide towards national decadence and promiscuity.

They were kept busy, pestering the Home Office and the police and writing furious letters to the press. 'Bestiality' was how a surgeon described sunbathing and swimming by suspected nudists at the Welsh Harp reservoir in North London in 1930. 'Anon' of Hendon called the spectacle 'filthy and disgusting', and prejudices mingled in the outcry of onlookers who were horrified to see 'white girls' swimming close by two 'very dark skinned men'. Everyone was sufficiently covered to satisfy the police. Behind this affront to the suburbs was Harold Vincent, a cashiered army officer who gave his occupation as 'Reformer' and whose campaign for nudism had led to many earlier skirmishes with the law. Once, he was charged with indecent exposure after standing naked at a window with a large card inscribed 'Throw away your clothes'. Mrs Virago (*sic*) of Gloucester

Place was not persuaded and alerted the police, complaining that he could be seen by her servants![25]

Newspapers and their readers took a prurient interest in the sunbathers and in anything else that was risqué. In 1931 the romantic writer Mrs Alexander McCorquodale (Barbara Cartland) promised forbidden thrills when she told the gossip column of the *Daily Sketch* that her forthcoming novel *Sweet Punishment* contained characters who 'do not adhere to a strict moral code'.[26] This revelation no doubt had the paper's lower-middle-class readers flocking to their subscription libraries. The saucy contents of the magazine *Razzle*, which first appeared in 1934, flouted even the loosest moral code and the Home Office was bombarded by demands that it be banned. Among the indignant was the headmaster of Harrow, who may have been outraged by a cartoon which showed a naked couple in bed with the woman remarking: 'Oh darling, you look a terrific cad without your school tie.' Save for a prosecution by the Dartford police, no official action was taken.[27]

Tolerance levels were rising. Apart from sexual jokes, there was nothing in *Razzle* that could not be found in more respectable journals aimed at middle-class audiences. Advertisements for lingerie became more daring and photographs of girls in the new, revealing swimming costumes appeared everywhere. Glamour shots of girls in their underwear were regular features of the middle-brow *Picture Post* launched in 1938, and one reader congratulated the editor for being 'frank and sensible enough to print pictures of attractive girls, who also feel no shame'. Photographs of American female wrestlers were too much for another reader, who judged them 'not fit for boys and girls to look at'.[28] Twenty-five years before, pictures of girls posing in camiknickers would have been unthinkable in a magazine designed for family reading. These images and an increasing candour in public discussion of sexual matters were signs of a wider moral relaxation.

Pragmatists sensed the temper of the times and cautiously began to redraw the moral map and establish new bearings. Church leaders continued to act as the nation's moral tribunal, and among the bishops there was a tentative shift towards more liberal attitudes. In

1930 the Church of England withdrew its objections to contraception and the government gave permission for local authorities to provide contraceptive advice in their welfare clinics. Modern, middle-class parents were advised to be clinically frank when asked about sex by their children and to avoid confusing them with 'ethical' considerations. 'Knowledge itself cannot imply sin.'[29] Adjustments which favoured women were made to the divorce laws in 1937. Not all the guardians of the country's morals were happy with the rewriting of old codes; in 1952 the Headmasters' Conference informed the Royal Commission of Divorce that it was 'pointless to give instruction to children about marriage years before they are likely to marry'.[30]

Old proscriptions remained and were sternly upheld. In 1928 Radclyffe Hall's lesbian apologia *The Well of Loneliness* was banned. James Douglas (1867–1940), the editor of the *Daily Express*, proclaimed that he would sooner give 'a phial of prussic acid' to a 'healthy boy or girl' than hand them a book that was 'moral poison'.[31] Hardly any of his lower-middle-class readers would have had any idea what lesbianism was. Police surveillance and prosecution of homosexuals intensified during the 1930s. In 1933 the Recorder of London was infuriated by the insolence of twenty-seven men (mostly hotel workers and waiters) who had just been convicted of homosexual offences in a house in Holland Park. They were convinced that they were doing no wrong, considered their arrest 'an infringement of their liberty' and 'glory in their shame'.[32]

Those among the middle classes who were alarmed by the encroachments of decadence were reassured by the emergence of a new and potentially very powerful force for good, the British Broadcasting Corporation. Its charter of 1922 gave the BBC a monopoly of domestic broadcasting and financial independence in the form of the annual ten-shilling licence fee paid by everyone who owned a radio. At first, sets were expensive (and unreliable), but by 1939 a receiver cost five pounds and could be obtained through hire purchase. Radios were designed as items of furniture to be placed in sitting rooms, where, as contemporary advertisements show, they were listened to by families. The wireless quickly became a new focus for family life and remained so until the mid-1950s, when it was supplanted by the television.

Few forms of entertainment have proved so popular or spread so rapidly. Four million licences were issued in 1931 and well over ten million in 1947. The weekly circulation of the *Radio Times*, which provided schedules of BBC programmes, passed the million mark in 1930 and continued to rise. The BBC's first audiences were mainly middle class: a survey of licence-holders made in 1931 revealed a concentration in London, the South-East and the Midlands where between 10 and 15 per cent of families had sets.[33]

They listened to programmes whose content and tone reflected the ideals of the first director-general, John Reith (1889–1970). He was a natural autocrat cast in the late-Victorian mould, the son of a Presbyterian minister with a strong streak of Puritanism and a passion to enlighten and improve mankind. Under his rule, the BBC upheld traditional decencies and continued on a grand scale the civilising mission of public art galleries, museums, concert halls and mechanics' institutes. Reith and his immediate successors recognised the enormous power of the wireless as a force for good in public life, far exceeding that of the press. It could shape the moral and cultural tone of the nation just as the 'received pronunciation' of its announcers established what would become a uniform accent for anyone with social and intellectual pretensions. Above all, the mind of the masses could be opened and useful knowledge disseminated in ways that would have amazed and delighted the Victorians. Never before had there been such an opportunity for the high-minded upper-middle classes to convert so many to their tastes and values.

Their vision and priorities permeated the programme schedules. One week's listings may stand for many others. Between 6 and 13 November 1938 there were talks on gardening, 'economy in the kitchen', missionary work in South Africa, Alexander the Great, how people caught diseases and a report from American by Alistair Cooke. There was a production of *A Winter's Tale*, a dramatic serialisation of *The Cloister and the Hearth* and daily readings from *Mr Sponge's Sporting Tour*. Classical music was strongly represented with concerts and recitals and, given that the BBC had to satisfy less demanding tastes, there were performances by dance bands (Mantovani) and cinema organists. Each day there were prayers and religious services. The only outside broadcast that week was the relaying of Neville Chamberlain's speech at the Lord Mayor's banquet.[34]

The cultural balance changed after 1939. National morale depended on servicemen and civilians getting more of what they preferred rather than what was deemed good for their souls. There was more light music, particularly from American-style swing bands, comedy shows (*ITMA*) and *Housewives' Choice* and *Workers' Playtime* injected a daily bounce into the lives of those labouring on the home front. Propriety was always upheld. The band leader Geraldo was ordered to alter a line in a song from 'Why don't we do this more often, just as we do tonight?' to 'Why don't we do this more often, just as we're doing today?'[35] News bulletins were truthful and impartial and there-fore respected. Reith had successfully defended the BBC's political neutrality, often in the face of stiff opposition. As early as 1933 Tories were grumbling about left-wing bias and have been doing so ever since.[36]

Despite concessions to mass taste, the Reithian BBC remained an essentially middle-class institution. It did all in its power to fulfil its charter obligations to educate and improve the nation, objectives which the educated middle class had traditionally believed to be as vital as they were worthy. Listeners were given a menu of what was nutritious and devised to cultivate the palate with a limited amount of pabulum. Those who preferred the latter tuned in to Radio Luxemburg, a commercial station with an American diet of adver-tisements and popular music. It was popular with a working class that was by now addicted to Hollywood films.

This was an age uncorrupted by cultural relativism; the BBC unashamedly dispensed middle-class culture and did so with flair and imagination, particularly in programmes aimed at children. In June 1947 'schools' programmes included an orchestral concert and *The People of Windmill Hill*, a dramatic piece by the distinguished archaeologist Jacquetta Hawkes which described the lives of the earliest Britons. During 1946 and 1947 *Children's Hour* (between five and six in the afternoon) included dramatic serialisations of *Pilgrim's Progress* and C. S. Forrester's *The Commodore* and the gentle humour and whimsy of Wurzel Gummidge and *Toytown*. For thrills there were the adventures of Norman and Henry Bones ('boy detectives'), and considerable airtime was given to natural history with *Nature Parliament* and *New from London Zoo*. There must be a correlation between these programmes and the growing interest in and concern for the environment among all levels of the middle classes during the second half of the century.[37]

Children's Hour was broadcast on the Home Service, that station which cultivated an educated, middle-class audience in the same way as its successor Radio Four does. As its name suggested, the Light Programme was easier listening, while the Third Programme (founded in 1946) was lofty in subject matter and tone. Its audience were expected to display considerable intellectual stamina (three- to four-hour productions of plays without intervals) and possess a store of recondite knowledge. Dennis Potter (1935–94), a miner's son and grammar schoolboy, found the Third Programme's outlook 'paternalistic' and 'stuffily pompous', but admitted that, despite this, it encouraged his own intellectual awakening.[38] I can still remember the excitement of hearing Donald Wolfit in Marlowe's *Tamburlaine* in the 1950s. I also enjoyed comedy shows and the nightly cliffhanger *Dick Barton, Special Agent*.

At its inception the BBC was seen as having the ability to bind the nation together. At times between the wars national cohesion had been brittle. At the end of his journey through England in 1933, the novelist and broadcaster J. B. Priestley concluded that he had traversed two nations, one thrusting and vibrant, the other moribund. The former was the land 'of arterial and by-pass roads, of filling stations and factories that looked like exhibition buildings, of giant cinemas and dance halls and cafés, bungalows with tiny garages, cocktail bars, Woolworths, motor coaches, wireless, hiking, factory girls looking like actresses . . .'[39] Large fragments of this townscape complete with Art Deco and neo-Egyptian cinemas can still be seen along the A4 between Hammersmith and Uxbridge. North and east of a line drawn between the Severn and the Humber was the other Britain, a country isolated by the poverty and hopelessness created by the decay of staple industries and long-term unemployment.

The chasm remained even after a partial economic resurgence. By 1935 between 8 and 11 per cent of the workforce in London, the South and the Midlands were without jobs, compared with between 20 and 31 per cent in Wales, the North and Scotland.[40] Two different nations were inhabited by two distinct races. During 1940 and 1941 the army medical services noted that recruits from the South, the South-West and the Midlands were taller and sturdier than those from the former industrial heartlands.[41]

In 1940 there was desperate need for these two nations to unite. Invasion was a possibility and Churchill reminded everyone that the country was fighting for its life. Class divisions weakened the nation. 'Forget your old school tie,' ran a line in Billy Cotton's 'We Must All Pull Together'. It was a theme that would resonate throughout the war. Official propaganda identified class divisions as a stumbling block to victory: notions of hierarchy created discord and jealousy. For the more radical working-class soldier, the officers' mess became a symbol of exclusiveness that perpetuated discredited notions of hierarchy and status. Class was a brake on national efficiency, particularly because it frustrated natural talent. Among the working class and sections of the lower-middle class, there was a visceral feeling that the old ruling class had betrayed the nation between the wars: it had failed to manage the economy or preserve the peace of the world. This resentment surfaced in 1941 after pressure had been put on the BBC to curtail broadcasts by J. B. Priestley in which he had dealt sharply with the old guard and with middle-class prejudices. There was an outcry in the popular press. One protester claimed that the 'La-De-Dahs' had silenced Priestley to protect themselves, while another praised Priestley's vision of a new Britain simply because it was 'not what the Carlton Club would want'.[42]

Priestley's dreams were Labour's. The party promised the lowering of social barriers as part of its blueprint for peacetime regeneration. By the winter of 1942–3, when it was clear that Germany would be beaten, more and more men and women were looking to their own and their country's future. They wanted rewards for their sacrifice and would not tolerate a rerun of the inter-war years. Peace would mark the birth of a new, fairer and more closely knit society in which ability would count for more than birth, in which a good education would be regarded as a right and in which wealth would be more equitably distributed. In July 1945 just under half the electorate endorsed the New Jerusalem and gave Labour a landslide victory.

A form of classlessness was already in place thanks to wartime food and fuel rationing, clothes coupons and universal 'Utility' standards of clothing and furniture. Queues emphasised the new equality. The middle-class housewife could no longer phone the butcher or grocer with her daily order and have it delivered. Instead, she waited in line with everyone else, sometimes for hours and with the nagging anxiety that stocks would run out.

These wartime inconveniences continued after the war, when the regime of prohibitions and controls was kept as part of Labour's plan for economic recovery. Resentment was universal and strongest among middle-class housewives, who were denied choice and forced to contrive menus from dull and often scarce ingredients. Wartime surveillance of the public was maintained, with the police recording the reactions of shoppers to rationing and to the many new restrictions imposed after 1945. Their reports were a catalogue of irritation and occasional outbursts of fury; the comradeship of the queue was one of shared grousing. During the summer of 1945 the 'forbearance' of Edinburgh housewives nearly snapped when fresh limitations on fats made baking all but impossible. The housewives' mood was 'almost revolutionary' after the introduction of bread rationing in 1946, and many wondered whether conditions were worse than they had been during the war.[43] Patience ran thin everywhere as the prices of unrationed food rose and there were shortages; particularly vexing were the limited supplies of soap, which made it hard to keep homes and clothes clean.

The thriving black market offered an escape from the oppression of Labour's command economy. 'All classes' in Edinburgh were resorting to it during 1946. 'It was common knowledge . . . that without a "little extra" of all commodities, life would be become impossible,' the city's chief constable concluded. Early the next year, his counterpart in Dundee admitted that it was no longer possible to control the illicit market in petrol coupons.[44] Spivs in Dundee and the rest of the country had plenty of middle-class customers with flexible consciences and the resources to pay for goods that had been smuggled or fallen from the backs of lorries. Perhaps for the first time in their history, the middle classes became accomplices in mass law-breaking. Some did very well from the black economy: in 1949 Conservative Party canvassers encountered smallholders who were worried about the government taxing their profits from clandestine sales of food.[45] They deserved some sympathy, not least because of their ingenuity in evading the army of official snoopers who enforced the rationing regulations.

There were consolations for the middle classes. The years of compulsory abstinence coincided with a revolution that began with the 1944 Education Act and ended in 1948 with the introduction of the National Health Service. For Labour, its welfare legislation was a settlement of outstanding scores from the pre-war years. Henceforward, the working-class fears of poverty, sickness and unemployment were banished. Benefits were universal and shared by the middle classes, who, of course, help fund them through taxation. In August 1946 a cartoon in the *Daily Express* showed a middle-class husband and wife and four children arriving home from their holidays to find an overgrown sunflower in their garden with the label: 'Family allowance 5/- per child'. It was paid to families with more than one child under sixteen, so the wife could expect an extra fifteen shillings a week.

If these children proved their academic suitability by passing the Eleven Plus exam, they got a free place in a local grammar school and, if they secured a university place, their fees would be paid by the local education authority, which would also pay a maintenance grant assessed on their parents' income. The theoretical objective was a truly meritocratic society in which talent could soar, unpinioned by parental background or income. Paradoxically, the middle classes were the first beneficiaries of a system designed to assist the working classes. Between 1936 and 1945, around 36 per cent of children born to salaried fathers undertook higher education, a proportion which increased to 47 per cent in the next ten years. During the same period the numbers of students from working-class families rose slowly from 7 to just over 10 per cent.[46] Conservative soundings of middle-class opinion during 1949 found general approval for the health service, which many saw as Labour's greatest achievement.[47]

Universal free education and the welfare state represented the convergence of many ideals which had their roots in the past. Although superficially a denial of the middle-class belief in self-help, the welfare systems of the 1940s were inspired by those Victorian middle-class theories of social responsibility which, in turn, traced their ancestry back to Evangelical philanthropy and the concept of the moral economy. The passage of the clever but poor boy through grammar school to university was a success story that would have pleased middle-class philanthropists from the fifteenth century onwards.

There was, however, an enormous difference: good was now achieved through the state rather than through the individual with a kind heart and a sense of duty to mankind. Moreover, individual philanthropists of the past had always been acutely conscious that gifts to the hapless could easily create a supine dependency on the part of the recipient. This disturbed Sir William Beveridge, whose 1942 proposals for the alleviation of poverty were the foundations of the welfare state. Born in 1879, the son of an Indian administrator, Beveridge was the embodiment of the patrician upper-middle class of his generation (Charterhouse and an Oxford First), with a string of influential academic and civil service posts. True to his late-Victorian liberal mindset, he intended that his plans for the welfare state should provide a safety net and never become a substitute for industry and self-reliance.

Labour also addressed two other legacies from the inter-war years, infirm industries and the chaos that was imagined to be the outcome of a lack of central economic and environmental planning. The need for the latter was undeniable: in 1933 an estate agent had offered for sale 'Unspoilt hill top: suitable for bungalow'.[48] Saving the countryside proved far easier than reviving decrepit industries. Mining, transport, power supplies and other basic industries were nationalised and regulations imposed on the private sector to improve its efficiency and productivity. Until the privatisations of the 1980s and 1990s the British economy was a hybrid of free-market capitalism and publicly owned and funded enterprises. Labour pledged itself to holding down unemployment (3 per cent was regarded as the maximum level), a promise that would compel later governments to subsidise ailing industries to preserve jobs.

The economic world formed a hundred years before by the middle classes had been transformed beyond recognition. Laissez-faire had been buried, the free market had been bridled and the state financed a welfare system that eliminated the multiple sufferings that had been the by-product of the Industrial Revolution. The middle classes now existed in a society which its architects hoped would be fair, contented, meritocratic and homogeneous. Yet notions of status and all that went with it had not disappeared. As in 1919, there were former officers who expected that their wartime standing entitled them to better jobs.[49]

2

Make the Good Life Better: Prosperity and Permissiveness, 1951–1979

Nineteen-fifty-one was an unnoticed watershed for the middle classes. It was the year in which the balance of political power tilted back in their favour. Experiments in egalitarianism and compulsory austerity were entering their final days against a background of meat shortages and rising prices. The middle classes had had enough. In March, the Edinburgh branch of the Housewives League declared that socialism had failed and that it was time for a return to free enterprise.[1] It reappeared in October when its champions, the Conservatives, won the general election. They stayed in power for the next thirteen years, during which they terminated rationing, dismantled much of the apparatus of state control over trade and presided over an unprecedented boom which enriched not only the middle classes, but a large swathe of their working brethren.

Middle-class cultural values enjoyed a momentary success that year: the Festival of Britain of 1951. Its chronicler Michael Frayn percipiently characterised it as an overwhelmingly middle-class affair, reflecting the preoccupations of one of its busiest sub-species.

. . . Festival Britain was the Britain of the radical middle-classes – the do-gooders; the readers of the *News Chronicle*, the

[*Manchester*] *Guardian*, and the *Observer*; the signers of petitions; the backbone of the BBC. In short, the Herbivores, or gentle ruminants, who look out from the lush pastures which are their natural station in life with eyes full of sorrow for less fortunate creatures, guiltily conscious of their advantages, though not usually ceasing to eat the grass.[2]

Given the well-meaning paternalism of its godparents, the Festival was a blend of earnest improvement and those self-conscious madrigals-and-maypole-style diversions which had been cherished by the herbivorous middle classes since the time of William Morris. The modern world was represented by the Dome of Discovery on the south bank of the Thames. It was filled with informative exhibits celebrating British explorers, modern scientific research and the advance of beneficial knowledge. There was also an exhibition of paintings and sculpture which balanced representational works that the layman could comprehend with others that would certainly puzzle him, such as Eduardo Paolozzi's abstract structures.[3] The five-year-old Arts Council encouraged a scattering of miniature provincial festivals across the country, often loosely attached to routine annual events such as gymkhanas, fairs and cricket matches. At Woodstock there was a pageant with folk dancing, in Scotland there were traditional gatherings and in Wales choral singing festivals.

It was all very British in a cosy sort of way, but with little to attract the working classes, who looked to America for their daily entertainment, and with nothing to attract that other subspecies of the middle class whom Frayn called the 'Carnivores'. According to him, they embraced Evelyn Waugh, who deplored the Festival, readers of the *Daily Express*, those listed in the Directory of Directors and all within the upper echelons of the middle class who imagined 'that if God had not wished them to prey upon all smaller and weaker creatures without scruple he would not have made them as they are'. The future belonged to the carnivores, for whom the Festival was a costly indulgence undertaken by those who were forever foisting their ideas and tastes on other people without ever asking them what they actually wanted and, more importantly, were willing to pay for. Rows between the Festival's adherents and deni-grators opened what turned out to be an enduring cultural rift that would divide the middle classes for the rest of the century.

Television widened this split. It had first appeared in 1936 and was welcomed as a medium with a greater potential than wireless for moulding the nation's cultural and moral identity. For this reason, the BBC had a monopoly of transmissions. In 1953 the Conservative government proposed to end this arrangement and introduce commercial stations funded by advertising revenues on the American model. Sixty per cent of the country favoured this innovation, but the educated middle classes were aghast: Britain's cultural traditions were in peril. Luminaries such as Beveridge and E. M. Forster combined with the National Union of Teachers and the Workers Educational Association to defend the BBC and save the country from a deluge of low-brow, made-for-television entertainment produced in Hollywood. Many old-school patrician Tories joined the protests because they resented America's global dominance and suspected that the national identity was about to be extinguished.[4] We must be ourselves, one declared in the Lords, adding: 'we do not wear ties [with] nude blondes'.[5]

In the same debate, friends of the BBC argued that it provided programmes like *Children's Hour* and religious services which no moneybags would sponsor, that it was impartial and governed by trustworthy men. Beveridge appealed for television to be employed 'to make men more intelligent, to be better in their judgement of entertainment, music and everything else'. Reith in volcanic mood warned of the 'moral hurt' about to be inflicted on the nation and likened commercial television to the intrusion of 'a maggot . . . into the body of England'.[6] Throughout the exchanges in Parliament and outside there were assertions that the profit motive tainted whatever it touched. To entice mass audiences, commercial televi-sion would have to appeal to the lowest common denominator, which was a guarantee of programmes that were banal or crudely sensational. Hollywood films were vivid proof of this. *Punch* produced a cartoon which showed a Rodinesque figure gawping at a screen with the caption 'The Non-Thinker'.[7] Conservatives placed their faith in what one called the 'good sense and maturity' of viewers.[8] Others were more trenchant, accusing their opponents of overbearing elitism, of depriving their countrymen of choice, and by implication of suggesting that the majority were incapable of choosing wisely.

Commercial television was approved by Parliament and in September 1955 Independent Television made its first broadcast. After pompous speeches, music by Elgar and the National Anthem, a tube of SR toothpaste encased in ice appeared on the screen and an upper-middle-class voice proclaimed that it was 'tingling fresh'. The BBC's riposte to this bathos was the dramatic death of Grace Archer while rescuing horses from a burning stable in *The Archers*. Within three years, ITV had secured 72 per cent of the national audience with, as the Jeremiahs had predicted, a diet of American imports and such home-made imitations of American programmes as *Opportunity Knocks*. As one former BBC employee observed: 'The public likes girls, wrestling, bright musicals, quiz shows and real-life drama. We gave them the Hallé orchestra . . . and visits to the local fire station.'[9] Revealingly, the BBC was soon engaged in a ratings war in which it attempted to lure audiences away from ITV with programmes with a mass appeal, many imported from America. To help fund hospital soap operas, money was diverted from the Third Programme.

The battle for commercial television had been a clash of two middle-class dogmas. On the one hand there was the free market and, on the other, the assumption of a section of the middle classes that they were ideally qualified to oversee the cultural and educational life of the nation and guide it towards enlightenment. Both notions were products of the nineteenth century, and the latter was embodied in the BBC's charter. It took for granted the existence of a 'superior' culture, which was desirable because it elevated the mind and soul, and of an 'inferior' one, which merely titillated the naive. The free marketeers countered with a form of relativism: all types of diversion had an equal value in so far as they provided enjoyment. To insist that one was better and then impose it on the country was a denial of personal freedom. It smacked of the kind of authoritarianism symbolised by the 'Ministries of Culture' then active in countries of the Communist bloc. This was how ITV's audiences saw it. In 1962 after the predominantly upper-middle-class Pilkington committee tentatively suggested that commercial companies raised their intellectual standards, a *Daily Mirror* headline declared: 'Pilkington tells the public to go hell'.[10]

Moreover, and this counted for something in a country fresh from a decade of enforced denial, television advertising would help generate demand and create prosperity. To capture customers, advertisements needed to be interspersed in programmes with the widest appeal. By 1961 the average Briton spent thirteen hours a week watching television, which was now the most popular leisure activity. Most of the programmes they saw made no effort to tax the intellect or stimulate the imagination. This state of affairs seemed to fulfil the prophecies of those opposed to commercial television: the profit motive had done more harm than good. It was striking that there was now a body of middle-class opinion that was increasingly suspicious and sometimes contemptuous of the commercial world and its values.

The success of the Consumers' Association founded in 1957 and its magazine *Which?* was evidence of this new scepticism. The journal was compiled for 'the person who wants to know *what* he is buying' and wants to secure that eternal middle-class objective, value for money. *Which?* offered impartial, technical assessments of all kinds of products from lavatory paper ('not a gay subject, nor one much discussed in polite society') to electric kettles, cake mixes and sunglasses.[11] Within two years, *Which?* had seventy thousand subscribers. Not all gave their occupations, but among the first were 203 doctors, 125 officers from all three services, 32 clergymen and 10 professors. One early subscriber welcomed a publication run on 'ethical lines', another complained that the odds were now 'stacked against the consumer' and a third was disturbed by 'aggressive advertising'.[12]

Commercial ethics and marketing techniques were arousing the distrust of members of the middle class in the professions and public service. They were detached from the world of money-making and their misgivings about its morality and influence grew in scale and scope. Among the consequences were environmental movements dedicated to protecting townscapes and landscapes from commercial development and protecting wild life from the depredations of agri-business. The herbivores were striking back.

Meanwhile, Britons were getting richer. The consumer boom of the 1950s extended beyond the middle to the working classes whose lives were transformed in ways that would have been unimaginable twenty years before. In 1956 a journalist visited Wigan which, described by Orwell in the 1930s, had come to symbolise the human suffering of the recession. The 'town had changed from barefoot malnutrition to nylon and television, from hollow idleness to flush contentment'. In the local dance hall there were girls in off-the-shoulder dresses and smart Teddy Boys, one in a pale violet corduroy coat. 'The working classes have come a long way,' commented one drinker in a club. 'There's not far to go now.'[13] Life at the end of the road was revealed by another journalist in the new town of Harlow in Essex. He described working-class immigrants from the East End living in homes with three-piece suites, television sets, budgerigars and mass-produced china ornaments. They read the *Radio Times*, the *News of the World* and fashion magazines advertising objects of desire. The visitor concluded that the suburban, middle-class world was engrossing a large chunk of the old, urban working class.[14]

As in the past, the better-off working classes wanted the trappings of a middle-class life, and the more observant members of the Labour Party wondered whether new material comforts would soon change their political outlook. The traditional middle-class party, the Conservatives, hoped that it would and that the newly affluent would swell their ranks. A substantial number of people 'have never had it so good', the Prime Minister Harold Macmillan told voters in 1959. As he later explained, the Tories sympathised with 'the pride that comes with ownership . . . the wider horizons that open to families that get a car and for the first time see something of their country – even wider horizons that open to millions who can afford to take holidays abroad'.[15]

New cars, mortgaged houses and foreign holidays were among the components of the complementary consumer and credit revolutions which proved unstoppable. There were 2.26 million cars on the roads in 1950 and 11.5 million in 1970. By 1989 a good 85 per cent of households owned washing machines and 70 per cent coloured television sets. Superficially, history was repeating itself: cameras and bicycles had become gradually affordable by all but the poorest in the nineteenth century and likewise motor cars and radios between the wars. What was remarkable about the latest consumer revolution was the speed with which middle-class luxuries became affordable. In 1971 some 610,000 households possessed colour television sets, in 1995 the figure was twenty million.

Former status symbols appeared to lose their social lustre almost overnight. In 1962 Alec Issigonis, the designer of the immensely popular Mini, prophesied that within the next decade cars would cease to have any social cachet whatsoever, thanks to technical developments and a uniform design.[16] It seemed a logical conclusion, but it ignored something deep within the British psyche. This was that mixture of vanity and snobbery which had been exploited by advertisers in the past and would be again with even greater ingenuity. 'Executive' became the adjective attached to any product or service designed to boost the consumer's self-esteem by setting him apart from the common herd. In 1966 advertisements for the Ford Executive showed the vehicle with a party just about to attend an opera. A girls' private school with pupils in striped blazers was the backdrop for a 1968 advertisement for the Triumph Herald. The more expensive estate version appeared parked near the touchline of a rugby pitch on which two public school fifteens were playing.

'Every Englishman's a country gentleman at heart' ran the caption of a 1965 Austin Reed advertisement for such tweed jackets and cavalry twills. The two pretend squires in the photo were posed alongside a Hereford bull and against the background of a manor house. 'Stepping up in the world?' asked an advertisement for off-the-peg Hepworth suits (from twenty-two pounds) in 1968. The young proto-executive wearing the three-piece version certainly was, for he has a pretty girl, stands beside a sports car and is carrying golf clubs. In 1979 Crombie greatcoats were puffed as fit for 'officers and gentlemen', and perhaps the wearers imagined themselves setting out from a château to inspect the trenches.

Cars and clothes were well-established tokens of their owners' status. Yet advertisers and those who advised on such matters in the press steered away from blatant appeals to class pretensions and increasingly resorted to the neutral words 'lifestyle' or 'style'. Lifestyle could never be divorced from class and only the naive believed otherwise. Jeremy Bullmore, creative director of the J. Walter Thompson advertising agency, rescued Oxo from its post-war associations with making cheap meat palatable by giving it an unmistakable middle-class image. An enduring sequence of television commericals showed how the stock cube overcame the domestic crises faced by 'Katie', who was 'middle class with a nice home and a good cook'. In the late 1950s she spoke with a cut-glass accent which gradually vanished over the next thirty years.

The milieu of the upper-middle-class dinner party (increasingly imitated by those on the way up during the 1960s) was used to promote its perfect conclusion, the box of 'After Eight' mints. Test showings of the advertisements in Yorkshire were a success, which astonished Bullmore, for it was 'the area least likely to be swayed by that kind of gracious living'.[17] The sophisticated, often imported delicacies served on these occasions soon became everyday provender. In 1978 puffs for Brie and Camembert asked: 'Why should you wait for a dinner party to enjoy them?' They were ideal for luncheon, snacks and picnics.

Never before had the middle classes been so obsessed with food and never before were so many different cuisines available in restaurants and recipe books. 'Foreign' food which once had aroused disdain, especially among the lower-middle classes, became fashionable. Recipe suggestions for cauliflower in 1962 included cauliflower à la Niçoise alongside the conventional cauliflower cheese.[18] In the mid-1970s an eighth of British restaurants specialised in foreign dishes, mostly Chinese, Indian and Italian, and at least a half of these offered takeway meals.[19] By 1976 Chinese takeaways had overtaken fish-and-chip shops as the most popular source of fast food and, in turn, were being challenged by outlets selling kebabs.[20] The middle classes were keen to master the finer points of epicureanism and they learned them under the guidance of such experts as Elizabeth

David and Robert Carrier. Newspapers and journals ran regular columns in which bon vivants advised the untutored where best to eat out. In 1968 London gourmets were warned that the city's first Japanese restaurant made no concessions to the Western palate, which was a recommendation for metropolitan sophisticates.[21] Décor and ambience sometimes mattered as much as, and often more than, the virtuosity of chefs: the food at the Rupert was described as indifferent, but the surroundings were impressive with Victorian paintings, and 'dashing blades' and 'tally ho' types among the diners gave the place a raffish, upper-class atmosphere.[22] Much of what was spent in such establishments was paid for by corporate expense accounts.

In some quarters a gravitas attached to dining out. It manifested itself in the comments of subscribers to the *The Good Food Guide*, which had first appeared in 1951. Many, perhaps the majority, came from that section of the middle class who were unable to charge their bills to the company, that is to say professionals and those employed in public service. In the 1978 edition, one correspondent sniffily remarked that an otherwise agreeable rural restaurant was filled with 'businessmen' at lunchtime. Another regretted that his meal was interrupted by 'spontaneous singing in Welsh' and the presence of a party of BBC employees, 'some of whom were unruly'. There were also grizzles about piped music.[23] Complaints of this kind suggest that some middle-class 'foodies' had not shaken off the Puritanism of their mental forebears.

The entrances to many restaurants were now adorned with brightly coloured signs which announced that the proprietors took credit cards. Over the previous twenty years, the middle classes had discovered a new philosophy summed up by the advertisements for Access cards, which offered to 'take the waiting out of wanting'. American Express provided prestige as well as credit to their cardowners, who were guaranteed effusive welcomes at various exclusive hotels around the world. Within five years of their first appearance in 1966, Barclaycards were promising 'to make the good life better'.

Other forms of loans were easily obtainable and, by 1973, the total of personal debt was £37,200 million and rising. Bank advances accounted for £5,000 million, consumer credit (including hire purchase) £1,900 million, mortgages £19,000 million and other loans £10,500 million.[24] Thrift was not abolished, rather encouraged by the state, which gave the middle classes tax allowances for mortgage payments, pension contributions and life insurances. All these swelled the total of private assets which stood at £252,000 million in 1973, of which £96,000 million represented housing.

Inflation distorted these figures. From 1949 to 1969 it had stayed at a healthly 3 per cent, and between 1970 and 1983 it averaged 11, briefly leaping to 20 in 1975. The Retail Price Index jumped from 53 points in 1962 to 157 in 1976. Middle-class salaries outran inflation: the average weekly earnings for male white-collar workers rose from twenty-five pounds a week in 1970 to sixty-two in 1976. The figures for women were thirteen and thirty-eight pounds. The middle classes also enjoyed greater employment security, as they had done in the 1930s. The numbers of jobless in banking, finance and insurance fell slightly from 148,000 in 1971 to 145,000 in 1979. Overall unemployment figures rose from 620,000 to 1.2 million during the same period, largely as a result of the accelerated decay of manufacturing industry.

Not only did the middle classes weather the economic tempests of the 1970s, but they were growing in numbers. The remoulding of Britain's social demography had been under way before the war. Between 1931 and 1939, the numbers employed in the professions, commerce and central and local government rose from 7 to 11 per cent.[25] The expansion of middle-class occupations continued at a greater pace after the war. In 1978 the workforce totalled twenty-two million, of whom over a third were women. Just over six million were employed in professional and business services (3.6 million), social services including health (1.9 million), education (one million), insurance, banking and business services (one million) and the civil service (482,000).[26] During the previous decade the most striking expansion had been in financial, profession and scientific services, which had grown by nearly a million jobs. The numbers engaged in manufacturing industry dropped from eight million in 1968 to 7.1 million in 1976 and would continue to decline for the rest of the century. More and more men and women would spend their working lives at a desk or facing a computer screen, and fewer and fewer at a work bench or on an assembly line.

Never since the Industrial Revolution had there been such radical changes in employment patterns. Four factors had been catalysts: the growth of financial services, the recent penetration of the workplace by sophisticated technology, the demand for scientific research and the enlargement of national and local bureaucracies. New laws and the extension of state regulation into just about every area of human activity required legions of administrators. In 1935 around 23,000 officials had been required to deal with unemployment payments; in 1978 a total of 429,000 bureaucrats were needed to maintain the administrative machinery of the educational system. In terms of employment, the middle classes were beneficiaries of legislation designed to better the lives and opportunities of the working.

As in the earlier Industrial Revolution, new jobs were vulnerable to technology. Like their blue-collar counterparts on the shop floor, white-collar workers were being supplanted by machines. In 1979 Barclays Bank reported that a hundred cash-dispensing machines did the work of eighty staff.[27] The cashier and bank clerk could no longer look forward to a job for life, as their predecessors had in what the middle classes had traditionally seen as a secure occupation. It was the same elsewhere in the new world of business.

Its technical and management innovations were largely imported from America. This was a further reminder that Britain was now a country in international eclipse. Roughly between 1945 and 1970, Britain ceased to be a global power. The Empire, alternately a source of pride and moral responsibility, was dismantled with remarkably little trauma or bloodshed. The Suez debacle of 1956 proved beyond question that Britain was America's junior partner, and it has remained so ever since. Philip Larkin was among the few with qualms. In 1969 he wrote:

> Next year we are to bring the soldiers home
> For lack of money, and it is all right.

On the whole, the middle classes got on with the business of life
and enjoying themselves in new ways, without undue concern for
the shedding of imperial responsibility and the glory that sometimes
went with it. The disappearing Empire became the subject of
colourful, nostalgic pieces in the new Sunday newspaper supplements and the cinema. *Lawrence of Arabia* (1962), *Zulu* (1963) and
Khartoum (1966) entranced cinemagoers and, later, television audiences. In 1972 the BBC produced a lavish documentary on the
history of the Empire and, for those with a taste for its bravado,
there was *The Regiment*, a weekly drama series set in the previous
century.

In his earlier poem 'Annus Mirabilis', Larkin ruefully contemplated
another profound change in national life, the genesis and infancy of
what would be called the 'permissive' society.

> Sexual intercourse began
> In nineteen sixty-three
> (Which was rather late for me) –
> Between the end of the *Chatterley* ban
> And the Beatles' first LP.

Laissez-faire morality overtook Britain with amazing speed in less
than ten years. The process was so quick and the protests so few
that one wonders whether middle-class faith in the old moral order
had quietly decayed and all that remained was a façade. Perhaps it
was, but the middle-class belief that moral regulation was the cement
of an orderly society determined that in public at least conventions
were respected. In the immediate post-war years the nation's moral
watchdogs were still alert and had not lost their bark. In 1952 the
Church of England declared that artificial insemination was tantamount to adultery and should be treated as a crime.[28] A committee
of Blackpool shopkeepers guided by the mayor's chaplain vetted the
saucy postcards sold to holidaymakers, and similar bodies performed
this duty in Cleethorpes and Hastings.[29]

Those who found all this maddening or unnecessary had to be

circumspect. In 1958, when the Wolfenden committee recommended that homosexual acts between consenting males should be decriminalised, the liberal Conservative R. A. Butler was sympathetic but cautious. He reminded the Commons that there existed 'A very large section of the population who strongly repudiate homosexual conduct and whose moral sense would be offended by an alteration in the law'.[30] He was proved right by a fellow Tory who told the House that homosexuality had brought down the Roman Empire and Nazi Germany, which provoked laughter.[31]

This outburst might have been taken seriously fifty years before, but a new mood was gaining ground. It was detected in 1954 by the ultra-conservative Lord Chief Justice Goddard, who advised a jury to think as modern people, not in a 'priggish, high-minded, super correct mid-Victorian manner'.[32] 'Flog 'em' Fisher, the sometime headmaster of Repton and Archbishop of Canterbury, feared that some of the middle classes were neglecting their old responsibility for the moral tone of the nation. In 1959 he castigated the 'intelligentsia' for patronising a concert of 'ribald' seventeenth- and eighteenth-century songs held in the Festival Hall. If the middle classes tolerated such depravity, it was no wonder that the young were following their 'natural' instincts in such a wanton manner.[33] This was the era of Teddy Boys and Rock'n'Roll.

In Fisher's mind, the failure of at least one section of the middle class to set an example was a kind of trahison des clercs, and he was correct, save that his 'traitors' did not share his moral loyalties. They were members of the upper-middle class who subscribed to such bodies as the Progressive League and its offshoots, which included the Marriage Law Society, the Abortion Law Reform Society and the Society for Sex Education. Their ranks were filled with left-inclined men and women whose thinking was rooted in late-Victorian and Edwardian secular liberalism. Ironically all concurred with the Archbishop in their conviction that morality was just about sex. In 1959 they secured a triumph, a revision of the law which permitted literary or artistic merit to be invoked in defence of legal obscenity.

This revised law was tested the following year with the prosecution of Penguin Books for the publication of *Lady Chatterley's Lover*.

The crown's case was advanced half-heartedly: counsel added up the number of times that words like 'fuck' were used as if the old law still obtained and its language alone could condemn a book as obscence. The jury of nine men and three women read the novel and then listened to a pantheon of writers testify to its literary merits. John Robinson, the Bishop of Woolwich, declared that D. H. Lawrence's treatment of intercourse was in 'a real sense' the portrayal of sex as an 'act of Holy Communion'. This was how Christians ought to regard it and why they never made jokes about sex. A London parson announced that he would be glad for his children to read the book. The defence offered no witnesses to challenge the consensus on Lawrence the artist and lost the case.[34] Two hundred thousand copies of *Lady Chatterley's Lover* were released for publication and were quickly bought, not all by middle-class literary cognoscenti.

During the next eight years, homosexuality and abortion became legal and, when the Lord Chamberlain retired to purely ceremonial duties, theatre censorship had all but vanished. In 1961 science delivered the contraceptive pill, the National Health Service agreed to prescribe it and defenders of the new moral dispensation welcomed the arrival of a more tolerant society which at last had liberated itself from artificial shame. The state gave up playing the moral policeman, old rules and observances were discarded, but, as early-twenty-first-century Britain would painfully discover, demolition was never followed by reconstruction.

The donkey work of lobbying for the legislation which had ushered in the permissive society had been undertaken by a comparatively small but energetic body of the educated middle classes in the sincere belief that they were advancing personal freedom. People could be trusted to judge wisely without the intervention of magistrates and clerics. There was also a strong conviction that the past enforcement of moral orthodoxies had added greatly to the sum of human misery. In 1967, I encountered a rural solicitor who had been born seventy or so years before and recalled praying in church to make the Prince of Wales 'a good man'. Afterwards, he learned that Edward VII had been a decent fellow and was delighted to witness the moral revolution now in progress.

Younger generations of the middle class snatched at the chance to have a good time. A 1965 survey of a well-heeled Cheshire suburb revealed that sexual adventures had joined squash, golf and cocktail parties as a common weekend recreation.[35] If the increasingly explicit press and the proliferating magazines dedicated to sexual confessions were truthful, then wife swapping was replacing bridge in suburbia. Maybe it was not and the real sexual revolution was not about greater dissipation, but about a new candour in which individuals felt free to reveal their experiences and their secret desires without guilt.

Whether as a consequence of conviction or indifference, the mass of the middle classes were content with the permissive society which, in its elevation of sensuality, complemented the hedonistic new consumerism. Stage, cinema and film nudity came in quick succession, followed by page-three girls in the tabloids and novels crammed with descriptions of every kind of sexual activity. And there was *Playboy* and its rivals with their philosophy that sex was pure pleasure and nothing else, which of course it was for many of the liberated young, as Larkin enviously noticed in his 'High Windows' of 1967:

> When I see a couple of kids
> And guess he's fucking her and she's
> Taking pills or wearing a diaphragm,
> I know this is paradise.

For those among the middle classes who revered the former moral order, this pair's heaven was the way to hell. The *Chatterley* verdict had enraged many among the middle class, but organised resistance to permissive legislation was fitful and offered no more than breakwaters hurriedly constructed to stem what was becoming a tidal wave. In 1964 a Shropshire schoolmistress, Mrs Mary Whitehouse, launched her Clean Up TV Campaign which evolved into the National Viewers' and Listeners' Association. Its prime target was Sir Hugh Carleton Greene (Director-General of the BBC from 1960 to 1969), an upper-middle-class liberal whose daring and provocative innovations ruffled those for whom Reith was a saint. Out went

Children's Hour (in 1964) and in came disrespectful young satirists (one, Bernard Levin, called the Prime Minister, Sir Alec Douglas Home, a 'cretin') and plays by Dennis Potter. The National Viewers' and Listeners' Association recruited thirty thousand members within a year, and, Mrs Whitehouse boasted, a further three million silent sympathisers across the country. A new concept had appeared in public life: the silent majority, whose opinions were overridden by the vocal minority, and whose numbers were conveniently beyond calculation. For Mrs Whitehouse, her mute supporters were Christians who were dismayed by the devaluation of 'sinfulness', something brought home to her by a female pupil who told her that sex before marriage was all right so long as the couple were engaged.[36]

The National Viewers' and Listeners' Association developed into a Christian alliance of Protestant Evangelicals and Catholics who shared a fear that permissiveness endangered family life. There was something distinctly Victorian about the subsequent campaigns. Mrs Whitehouse allied with an elderly Catholic aristocrat, the Earl of Longford, to investigate pornography at first hand (much to the delight of the popular press) and published a damning report afterwards. In 1971 opponents of the new licentiousness held the Festival of Light in Trafalgar Square which was attended by at least twenty-five thousand, two-thirds of whom were under twenty-five. Yet the movement never gained the impetus of the great Victorian moral crusades and petered out into a number of protests against individual plays, films and television programmes.

A delayed and passionate backlash, expressed in MPs' constituency mail, helped persuade a Conservative government to draw a line and, towards the end of 1973, the Home Secretary Robert Carr introduced the Indecent Displays bill. Its objective was to halt the rapid spread of pornography. Sex magazines in newsagents and Underground advertisements for such films as *Danish Dentist on the Job* were a symptom of a wider 'collapse of the social order', warned William Deedes, Conservative member for Ashford and a future editor of the *Daily Telegraph*. Curiously, the bill intended to outlaw 'indecent sounds' and there were some delightful exchanges on the orgasmic sighs which accompanied Serge Gainsbourg and Jane Birkin's current hit, 'Je t'aime . . . moi non plus'.[37] Some wits wondered whether farting would become illegal, but the bill died with Edward Heath's government early the next year.

Christian moral absolutism had passed out of fashion and was not greatly mourned among the middle classes, Catholics apart. Protestant churchmen disagreed about the precise nature of the 'Christian way of life' which Mrs Whitehouse wished to be promoted in the media. Many Anglican and Presbyterian clerics, who had always counted themselves among the educated middle classes, were glad to shed the role of upholding moral dogmas which they and many in the pews considered misconceived and oppressive.

Some intellectuals who had fought the early battles for tolerance became disillusioned when they discovered that the literary results were often banality and sensationalism for its own sake. The playwright Ronald Duncan, who had had a work banned under the old laws, was dismayed by a Stratford production of *Troilus and Cressida* in which an invented homosexual relationship was intruded into the text. And there was the sheer vacuousness of many new plays like *A Day at the Nudist Camp* in which the cast removed their clothing down to fig leaves and a girl stripped completely.[38] This was known as a stage 'happening' and like so many others devised at the time had a significance for author and players which was not always appreciated by the audience.

The genesis of sexual liberation had coincided with a restless period of cultural experiment and change. Those who lived through the 1960s and 1970s were constantly reminded that they inhabited a Utopia in which everyone was now free to do their 'own thing' without inhibition or guilt. Mass-marketed pop music and ever-changing fashions in clothes diverted a generation of young sybarites. Youth and novelty became synonymous.

'Swinging' London was the microcosm and lodestar of the new age. It had glamour and excitement and was adorned by what, by 1965, was being identified as a 'New Aristocracy', or 'new class'. Its members were pop stars, models, photographers, designers, interior decorators, artists, hair stylists, film makers and style gurus. Most were under thirty and many, like the actor Terence Stamp, were working-class, although there was a scattering of public schoolboys like Lord Snowdon. They mingled in a mini-society in which a working-class background was chic. In 1966 'Jennifer', the social diarist of the *Tatler*, remarked that the appearance of the Beatles at a gathering would create a far greater stir than that of Lord Derby, and she was right.[39] Graver minds wondered whether this explosion of working-class talents confirmed the thesis that the class system was indeed a constraint on natural ability and, therefore, had to be demolished.

The new, creative elite was shoving aside the upper-middle classes and aristocracy. Their displacement was accompanied by savage ridicule. Their vices and platitudes were derided by former public schoolboys in *Private Eye*, which first appeared in 1961, and in the BBC's late-night satire show *That Was the Week That Was*, which ran for eighteen weeks during the winter of 1962 to 1963. Lampooning the old upper crust was made easy thanks to the Profumo scandal, which exposed its hypocrisy and the Edwardian isolation of Macmillan. The mischievous spirit of Gillray and Cruikshank was abroad again; rank no longer commanded deference.

Class was a target. Middle-class certitudes and habits had been excoriated in John Osborne's *Look Back in Anger*, which had been first performed in 1956. Class barriers handicapped the able and condemned the country to be ruled by the morally and intel-lectually bankrupt. Pop music knew no class divisions and classless-ness became the vogue among fans, who then proceeded to contrive their own tribal groupings. Mods, rockers, hippies, skinheads and, by the late 1970s, punks emerged, each defined by what they wore and listened to. All would have been insulted to be labelled middle-class, which many were. The self-hatred of the suburban young was translated into pop lyrics which jeered at suburbia and the fusty, empty lives of their inhabitants.[40] Yet the spirit of the times had infected the suburbs. In the late 1970s a model, who commuted from Seaford in Sussex to Chelsea where she worked at Vivienne Westwood's shop Sex, often stepped on to the train in stockings, suspenders and 'a rubber top'. 'Some of the commuters used to go absolutely wild, and they loved it.'[41]

While the young were forming their distinct, often transient and sometimes mutually hostile clans, a new and far more historically significant division appeared in society: race. From the mid-1950s there was an upsurge in immigration from the Indian sub-continent, the Far East and the former West Indian colonies. The new arrivals undertook low-paid work and were concentrated in the down-at-heel inner suburbs of London and the industrial Midlands and North, where they tended to stay thanks to economic pressures and communal loyalties. Would they remain there, or follow the path taken earlier in the century by Jewish immigrants from Eastern Europe? They had first settled in the poorest areas and then, as they prospered, shifted outwards to the middle-class suburbs of North London, Manchester and Leeds. In 1968 a stockbroker and former mayor of Bromley predicted that this pattern would repeat itself. 'In ten years middle-class Negroes will be waiting to move into suburban neighbourhoods.'[42]

The exodus from ghetto to middle-class suburb did occur, but it was a slow trickle. At a time when the number of white-collar jobs was growing, the majority of immigrants remained in manual occupations. In 1970 the proportion of Indians and West Africans in professional, managerial and clerical employment in the West Midlands was just under a fifth, less than half that of whites.[43] Social divisions opened up within the immigrant population: by the early 1980s the proportion of African Asians (many professional men and entrepreneurs expelled from Uganda in 1970) who were employers, managers and in the professions was 22 per cent, that of whites 19 per cent. By contrast, the figures for Pakistanis and West Indians were 10 and 5 per cent.

Fluency in English was a problem for large numbers of first-generation immigrants, but there was also race discrimination. It existed among all classes, although in 1974 the chairman of the Race Relations Board noticed that the odds against coloured applicants getting jobs in manufacturing were higher than for white-collar posts.[44] Absorption created social stress: there was mutual animosity and attacks on immigrants. In 1968 Enoch Powell, a Tory from a lower-middle-class Midlands background, predicted a civil war in characteristically florid language, but it did not occur. Anti-immigration parties like the National Front made little headway, most of it in inner-city, working-class districts.

Tensions emerged within the immigrant community: the manners and mores of permissive Britain were bewildering and shocking for people from Third World rural communities. Was assimilation desirable, or achievable, and if it was, what former values and habits had to be forfeited? For Muslims and West Indians brought up under strict moral codes these were difficult questions, and their resolution was made harder by the spasmodic hostility of many of their hosts. Class inevitably intruded into the tangle of loyalties: as many of the second and third generation of immigrants moved upwards into the middle classes, attachments to faith, family and the communities they had left were often strained. Of course similar conflicts of culture and allegiance had troubled and continued to trouble new arrivals in the white middle class.

On the whole British society absorbed the stresses of mass immigration remarkably well. It added to the complexity of society by creating racial divisions at a time when social ones were taking a battering. Yet predictions of the disappearance of the class system were premature: the hoped-for meritocracy that had emerged by 1979 did not demolish old barriers or sweep away social pretensions. Arrivistes continued to proclaim their elevation by flaunting the trappings of their new status. In 1966 a thirty-two-year-old managing director of a publishing company of lower-middle-class origins confessed to a paranoia about 'posh people' who looked down on him. He overcame it: 'I've got my Rolls, so bugger them. Life's great.'[45] He was an archetypal recruit to the thriving middle classes of the time.

3

The Decent Crowd: Tensions, 1918–1979

Social tensions persisted throughout the twentieth century. They existed between classes and within classes and varied in form and intensity. If hotheads and pessimists were to be believed, conflicts of interest between the middle and working classes nearly exploded into civil conflict on two occasions. On the eve of the General Strike in 1926, the *Scotsman* predicted that the Trade Union Congress (TUC) was taking 'the first steps towards Revolution'.[1] Early in 1974, when union militancy was at its most ferocious, an advertisement issued by the Aims of Industry lobby declared that 'The political wreckers want to smash our economy in order to destroy our free society.'[2] Both claims seemed credible at the time and gave the middle classes a bad turn.

Between 1918 and 1926 they were extremely jittery about the threat of revolution. Their rulers were equally disturbed and were taking no chances. In July 1920 on the eve of a miner's strike and at the onset of the General Strike in May 1926, the government appealed for volunteers to serve as auxiliary policemen and to maintain transport services. Working-class solidarity would be matched by middle-class patriotism. A fictional outcome was outlined in *The Middle Road* (1922) by the former war-correspondent Sir Philip Gibbs in which the government invites ex-officers to enlist in a defence corps. Its members were ready for a fight, as one explained:

> Us . . . meaning the Decent Crowd, anybody with a stake in the country, including the unfortunate Middle Classes. All of us. Well, we accept the challenge. We're ready to knock hell out of them . . . This clash has got to come. We must get the whole working classes back to their kennels. Back to cheap labour. Back to discipline. Otherwise we're done for.[3]

The interests of the nation and the middle class were the same, and the former would be saved by the determination of the latter. As readers of the thrillers of John Buchan and 'Sapper' knew, the workers were sound at heart, but were easily misled and manipulated by Bolshevik agitators, most of whom were foreigners, often Jews. 'I don't want anything to do with a man who listens to a lot of dirty foreigners and goes against his country,' Vi Gibbons tells her future husband Sam in Noël Coward's play *This Happy Breed* (1943). Sam is a Communist, and Vi's family are suburban lower-middle class. It is the time of the General Strike and her father has volunteered to drive a bus.

Vi's opinions echoed those of the Conservative press, which worked itself into a frenzy whenever a large strike was imminent. During January and February 1919, when there were disturbances among soldiers awaiting demobilisation and a miniature general strike in Glasgow, the *Morning Post* scared its upper-middle-class readers with rumours that the local police had been infiltrated by Bolsheviks. Red agitators from Russia, Sinn Fein terrorists and 'Councillor Shinwell, Polish Jew and Chairman of the Strike Committee' were about to achieve in Glasgow what Lenin had in Petrograd two years before.[4] In October 1920, the *Daily Graphic* likened the miners' strike to 'a Declaration of War against the Community' and accused the strikers of waging 'civil war' against women and children. Pictures of forced labour ('slavery') in Russian granaries reminded the paper's lower-middle-class readership of what the Reds had in store for them. As for the average working man, he was a simple soul. A cartoon showed him standing beside a newspaper placard announcing 'Racing Off' and observing: 'Then what's the good of striking?' None at all, thought the *Daily Graphic*, which ran a story of a Welsh miner and his three sons who were earning thirty pounds a week between them.[5]

Early in 1924 the working man secured his own government for the first time, a Labour–Liberal coalition. The middle classes were full of trepidation, despite Ramsay MacDonald's pledges of moderation. Four days before the October 1924 general election, residual anxieties broke surface when the *Daily Mail* published the Zinoviev letter. Probably a forgery, it suggested that the Soviet government regarded MacDonald as a Kerensky figure and that, if it won the election, Labour would unwittingly prepare the ground for a Communist revolution. It might have been the plot of a Buchan novel and again the middle classes shuddered, although it is unlikely that the Zinoviev canard tipped the electoral balance in favour of Stanley Baldwin and the Conservatives.

What is significant is that this kind of scaremongering was accepted by millions of otherwise level-headed men and women. They were ripe for conversion in so far as the middle classes imagined that they were on the defensive. Since 1914 they had seen their incomes shrink and those of the working class rise and feared that the pattern would continue after the war. There was a common perception that the middle classes had suffered most from wartime inflation and high tax levels. The incomes of professional men had been reduced by a quarter and the value of the residue was halved by price rises. By contrast, the workers were thriving because their unions had extorted excessive wage increases from a government which was willing to pay up rather than risk any disruption of wartime production. Union demands continued after the armistice and the middle classes expected further deprivation.[6] This was a crude view, but one which made sense to anyone who was finding it hard to make ends meet.

The middle classes had been frightened by Lenin's Bolshevik coup in Russia in 1917 and its (failed) imitations in Germany and Hungary in 1919 and 1920. Communist excesses were exposed in newspapers which also hinted that similar events might occur in Britain, where strike committees and mutinous soldiers defiantly called themselves 'soviets'. Labour leaders laced their speeches with the rhetoric of the barricades. 'Every union, without exception, would be thrown into the battle at once,' declared the railwaymen's leader a few days before the General Strike. In Glasgow, John Wheatley, a former Labour minister, told a May Day rally that the 'capitalist classes' were playing their last 'trump card' by deploying troops in readiness for the stoppage. For the previous eight years the working classes had been in retreat, the local MP Jimmy Maxton reminded his listeners; now they would regain ground.[7] One observer compared the atmosphere in London to that of August 1914, with young middle-class men keen for action of some kind. They had much to lose, for, if successful, the strike would be a signal victory for socialism.[8] Members of the Middle Class Union, the Citizens Union, the British Fascisti and the recently formed Organisation for the Maintenance of Supplies (OMS) rolled up their sleeves and prepared to do their duty. Many feared the worst; in February 1926 the York branch of the OMS appealed for volunteers with the warning that a general strike would lead to a government 'chosen by a Revolutionary element largely composed of aliens'.[9]

In all, the OMS fielded a hundred thousand volunteers during the strike and were augmented by a further quarter of a million reserve and special constables who were paid five shillings a day. Afterwards, strikers accused some of these of being belligerent and free with their truncheons and there were rumours that a few special constables had gone on patrol illicitly armed with revolvers.[10] Volunteers from polo clubs turned up on horseback, wearing pith helmets and carrying their mallets, looking as if they were about to pitch into rioters in India.

The overall picture of the General Strike as a rather jolly affair in which strikers played soccer with off-duty soldiers is a retrospective distortion. There was violence, and had the strike not ended within nine days, there would have been more. In London there were clashes between police and strikers attempting to impede trams, buses and food convoys. Edinburgh experienced two days of rioting in which cars were wrecked and the police attacked. A destroyer was ordered to berth in Leith harbour. There was rioting and looting of pubs and shops in Glasgow, where three special constables were badly injured. In Aberdeen the local BBC station warned women and children to keep off the streets after disturbances in which trams and cars had been stopped and smashed.[11] Yet nowhere did the police lose control, and the deployment of troops, armoured cars and, in London, tanks was an earnest that the government intended to preserve order and maintain food and fuel supplies at any cost.

Soon after the TUC called off the strike, the Home Secretary Joynson-Hicks announced a victory. Addressing the Primrose League in characteristically ebullient mood, he declared that 'once and for all the bogey of the General Strike' had been laid to rest.[12] It and the phantom of revolution had been exaggerated: the government had stockpiled fuel and food, the armed forces and the police were loyal and the potential insurgents lacked the necessary arms for a coup. None the less, these obvious factors did not prevent Joynson-Hicks from crowing and the middle classes from comforting themselves with the belief that their security was now restored. Not so the working classes. Their solidarity had not broken the resolve of the government, nor that of its middle-class supporters. Union membership, which had stood at 6.5 million in 1920, had fallen to 4.4 million by the time of the strike and would continue to decline over the next ten years as unemployment spiralled.

The social tensions of the immediate post-war years were a result of severe economic dislocation. Wartime systems were hurriedly dismantled, transport and coal mining were returned to private ownership and a degree of laissez-faire reappeared as the government attempted to distance itself from direct engagement in industrial relations. Hardly had the old order been partially restored than the country entered the slump of 1921; exports dropped and unemployment rose. Employers argued that the competitiveness needed to regain old markets required cuts in wages and extensions in hours worked. Governments endeavoured to reduce public expenditure to help repay wartime debts and were unwilling to subsidise stricken industries. Under the terms of the 1920 Employment Act, the state had to fund unemployment pay, a new and, as it turned out, heavy drain on the Exchequer. Between 1921 and 1931 the weekly dole for a single man was cut from a pound to fifteen shillings and three-pence, but this cheeseparing was not enough, and the government was driven to borrow £115 million to meet the bill.

The working classes were under siege. During the war, wages had just kept ahead of the cost of living, but after 1920 the margin narrowed. It was worst of all for the jobless as the dole was squeezed and governments strapped for cash resorted to the rigidly applied means test to hold down welfare payments. After 1934 the regulations were relaxed, but five years later a *Picture Post* analysis of the budget of an unemployed man, his wife and six children revealed a weekly expenditure of fifty-two shillings, which was nearly five shillings more than his allowances. Unlooked-for expenses were met by paring down the fuel and food budgets.[13]

If, as some of the more alarmist politicians and headline writers assumed, the class war was being waged during the inter-war years, then the working classes were losers. The General Strike had failed, both as a demonstration of power and as a device to prevent wage cuts for the miners, and the Labour Party fell apart over how to handle the financial and unemployment crises of 1931. Working-class frustration and anger vented themselves on Conservatives and their middle-class supporters. After the 1920 Northampton by-election, the government candidate accused his Labour opponent of 'preaching class hatred and class war' and inciting the 'poorest classes' against the rich.[14]

Social animosity fed on perceived and obvious injustices. Cuts in wages, war disability pensions and unemployment allowances were being implemented at the same time as the government shelled out huge cash rewards to generals who had lost battles and been care-less with other men's lives. The Prime Minister Lloyd George sold peerages to anyone who could afford them, including the million-aire Sir William Vestey, who had dodged wartime taxes by shifting his meat-packaging business to the Argentine.[15] Generosity to the haves was matched by meanness to the have-nots: on the day before the General Strike began, the annual meeting of the middle-class National Union of Ratepayers condemned the 'extravagant administration of poor relief' by Labour councils which supplemented the dole.[16]

Rancour expressed itself in different ways. Irrespective of whether their drivers had taken the government's advice and given lifts to commuters, cars were a favourite target during the General Strike. At the ball given by the Middlesex Yeomanry in the late 1930s, guests were hooted as they arrived at a hotel.[17] During the Second World War, officers found that many working-class soldiers blamed the Tories for everything that had gone wrong in their lifetimes from appeasement to unemployment.[18] The military authorities knew that they could no longer take for granted the patriotism and tractability of the other ranks and had to heed their grousing, much of which was rooted in social animosity. For the working classes, the legacy of the inter-war years was one of reverses and sour memories.

They were not exorcised by the war, Labour's post-war settlement and the mid-century boom. Old resentments resurfaced during the early 1970s, when all classes were determined to keep their incomes ahead of inflation and secure as large a share as possible of what appeared to be a diminishing national cake. There was social friction, and comparisons were made with the inter-war years. 'Sometimes it seems that 1926 was only the day before yesterday,' a journalist remarked after visiting a Welsh mining village towards the end of the four-week miners' strike in February 1972. The entire community was behind the strikers and ready to 'fight to the finish'.[19]

In the Commons the rhetoric of the class war was aired again. 'Class legislation' was how the far-left MP Eric Heffer described the Edward Heath government's efforts to impose wage controls. Neil Kinnock, a Welsh miner's son, declared that it was 'a government of capitalists for capitalists' and reminded the Commons of how its spiritual predecessor had starved strikers into submission in his father's time.[20] There was a buzz of excitement among Marxists who then held considerable sway in academe.[21] And a few wondered whether capitalism's final denouement had at last arrived. Britain was 'not yet in a revolutionary situation', but 'something resembling it' was emerging, alleged the *New Statesman*.[22] The Home Secretary had just activated the Emergency Powers Act and promised that troops would be deployed to 'maintain vital services' just as they had been in 1926. One Labour MP dramatically warned him that servicemen might not be biddable since many were former trade unionists and had kinsfolk who still were.[23]

There was no mobilisation of the middle classes, although during the next few years a handful of retired generals attempted to form units of volunteers ready to take on the strikers in the 1926 style. Recruits were scarce; suburbia had no desire to confront the Rhondda. Rather, the middle classes were sympathetic towards the miners. After a public opinion poll revealed a two-to-one majority in their favour, a *Daily Telegraph* cartoon showed Heath setting a dog labelled 'Public Opinion' on the miners' leaders and getting bitten himself by the animal.[24] The rest of the Conservative press was sympathetic, with the *Daily Mail* reflecting the widely held middle-class view that miners 'were poorly paid for grinding and dangerous work' and deserved more.[25]

On a cynical level, paying the miners more would not hurt the better off. They were generously treated by Heath's regime of wage controls, for income tax had just been cut and middle-class salary rises outpaced inflation. Between 1970 and 1974, the average weekly wages of manual workers rose by 17 per cent, while those of non-manual workers increased by an average of 23 per cent.[26] Power cuts in 1972 aroused some middle-class anger. A Durham miner on holiday in Newquay was accosted by a woman who hit him with her brolly 'cos I'd switched her electric off'. He replied, 'You silly old twat, my electric were off too,' and was struck again.[27]

Heady talk about class warfare and imminent revolution was a display of wishful thinking by the far left. The proliferating strikes of the 1970s were not a prelude to the collapse of capitalism, but by-products of its metamorphosis. The need for radical change within the structure and culture of British business had been obvious since the 1950s, when an American management consultant had brutally condemned the inertia and wastefulness of industry. A large section of the workforce was 'grossly underemployed in jobs that have not been needed' and was generously rewarded for this inactivity. Reorganisation and regeneration could be achieved only with mass redundancies, periods of high unemployment and the abandonment of derelict industries.[28] In his first two years in power, Heath had made tentative steps towards the wholesale modernisation of industry, but had come unstuck when he imposed constraints on pay rises.

There had been a contradiction in Heath's policies. On the one hand he wanted the state to regulate relations between labour and capital and, on the other, he believed that if left alone capitalism could save itself. Competitiveness was the key to this salvation, but it involved the eradication of much that the trade unions held dear. There were struggles over the closed shop, restrictive practices and fixed tea breaks, all of which were considered obstacles to efficiency. Inevitably, given collective historic memory, there was a class element in the contest between management and labour. Middle-aged and older union leaders and shop stewards who were children of the 1930s were encountering a new adversary: middle class technocrats. They were specialist managers and consultants, accountants and personnel officers who were full of new ideas (many from America and Japan) and determined to implement them. Their task was facilitated by rising unemployment, which, as in the 1930s, the left regarded as an instrument to coerce obstructive workers. The early days of the Industrial Revolution appeared to be returning, with workers being compared to Luddites, or lemmings bent on self-destruction.

Assertions of managerial authority and new criteria of efficiency helped weaken the old political consensus, which in part had been a response to the strife of the inter-war years when MacDonald and Baldwin had done all in their power to promote conciliation between the classes. When he returned to power in 1974, Harold Wilson, complete with Baldwinesque pipe, likened himself to that quintessential middle-class figure, the avuncular family doctor who would heal the country's ills. It was a conceit adapted by Mrs Thatcher after her election victory in May 1979, when she promised that her aims were those of St Francis of Assisi: 'where there is discord, may we bring harmony'.

4

One of Themselves: Mrs Thatcher and Tony Blair, 1979–2005

Mrs Thatcher's revelation of herself as a conciliator was unintentionally ironic. She had won the Conservative leadership in 1975 against a background of social and ideological turmoil within the party. This struggle generated tensions which persisted until her resignation at the end of 1990. On the whole she and her adherents prevailed; they ruthlessly pruned what they considered deadwood from the past and encouraged new growth. This husbandry was not to the liking of all the middle classes, although both Mrs Thatcher's friends and her enemies depicted her as their champion.

Since 1918 the Conservative Party had fulfilled its traditional function as the protector of the middle classes from collectivism and socialism. The 1945 general election had been a shock, although party analysts were soon sure that middle-class defectors would return to the fold once they realised that 'class hatred' was integral to Labour's creed.[1] By 1949 party pollsters were confident that the middle classes were rallying to the Conservatives in response to rationing, high taxes and excessive state regulation. The self-employed, proprietors of small businesses, farmers and shopkeepers stuck with the party, although in working-class districts the latter kept their opinions to themselves for fear of losing customers.[2]

The guardians of the shopkeepers' interests were aristocratic or upper-middle class and the party's tone was patrician. 'There are those of us born to lead and others to follow,' a Conservative officer explained to an audience of servicemen in 1944, adding that his party was progressive.[3] Little had changed since the days of Lord Salisbury: the party of 'one nation' was dominated by an elite educated at public schools (old Etonians were prominent) and Oxford or Cambridge. As a token acknowledgment of the egalitarian temper of wartime and post-war Britain, the Conservatives began to recruit candidates from outside the old circle. After the 1950 election, Lord Winterton (a grandee who had once served alongside Lawrence of Arabia) was gratified to find a sprinkling of the lower-middle classes among the new Conservative members. 'One very satisfactory feature of these young men was that several of them came from humble homes, and had made their way upwards solely by character and brains.'[4]

Among this new breed of Tory members were Edward Heath and Enoch Powell, both ex-grammar school boys, and, in time, they were followed by Margaret Thatcher, the daughter of a Grantham grocer, and by John Major, a former bank clerk. Party mandarins hoped that they would assimilate, absorbing the collective mindset of the rest of what was still an exclusive club. Its members agreed that the Conservatives were the natural party of government because they were a 'one nation' party devoted to the interests of the entire country and pragmatists free from the constraints of dogma. None the less, the Tories needed middle-class votes to win elections. 'Who are the middle classes?' Macmillan once asked. 'What do they want? How can we give it to them?'[5]

Answers were provided in a handbill circulated by local Conservatives during the 1958 Weston-super-Mare by-election which included three statements from local middle-class voters. An elderly farmer who had supported the party for forty years claimed that it had always worked for everyone, irrespective of class. A twenty-four-year-old hairdresser said that the Conservatives were the party of the young who wanted to get on in the world and rejected the 'dull levelling-down' of socialism. A butcher welcomed the slicing of 'red tape' and the boost now being given to the 'enterprising'.[6]

The middle classes trusted the Conservatives to take care of their interests. If they neglected to, then the dissatisfied would look elsewhere. They did so at the Orpington by-election of 1962 when disgruntled suburban voters plumped for a Liberal candidate. Explanations were provided in a sheaf of letters to Conservative Central Office which accused the government of caving in to the unions, overtaxation and extravagant spending. 'Not enough done for the middle classes', declared one protester. An overdue revolution at the top was imperative. A Yorkshire headmaster argued that 'The day of the Etonian, the industrial magnate, the landed gentry and the financial mogul has gone.' To survive, the Conservatives needed 'the votes of the prosperous, property owning lower middle and working classes which you have created'.[7] An official post-mortem on the Orpington reverse concluded that middle-class deserters felt that they were not getting 'a fair share of the cake' and were unable 'to keep up with the Jones's' because of higher fares, rates and fuel prices.[8]

Unperturbed by the restlessness among the middle classes and indifferent to the distaste aroused by the Profumo scandal, the Conservative leadership clung to its faith in deference. In 1963 the 14th Earl of Home succeeded Macmillan. Labour, which since 1935 had been successively led by Attlee (Haileybury and Oxford) and Hugh Gaitskell (Winchester and Oxford), broke with tradition and elected Harold Wilson, a former grammar schoolboy with a carefully cultivated Yorkshire accent. In contrast to Home the aristocratic amateur, Wilson projected himself as a technocrat from a lower-middle-class background who had made his way through natural ability and was impatient for change. He won the general elections of 1964 and 1966 as a modern man leading a modern nation towards a future that would be determined by releasing the talents of all its people. In 1965 the Conservatives imagined that they could trump Wilson with Edward Heath, another grammar schoolboy who was puffed as a moderniser. With television and carefully contrived advertising now playing a central part in political life, images mattered with an electorate which was now looking for reflections of themselves in their leaders. Heath sailing his yacht belonged to the present; a tweedy aristocrat totting up his bag of dead grouse on a Highland moorside did not.

While both Wilson and Heath proclaimed themselves politicians receptive to new ideas, each was constrained by the prevailing ethos of the post-1945 consensus. It blended well with old-style paternalism and 'one nation'Toryism because it promoted social harmony. Furthermore, consensus thinking had become the orthodoxy of that upper-middle-class intellectual aristocracy whose members dominated the cabinets of both parties and the higher civil service.[9] Their mental pedigree stretched back to the eighteenth-century Enlightenment, through the post-Arnoldian public schools and the Victorian universities. Their intelligence justified their influence and they believed themselves humane guardians of the rest of mankind, as had their ancestors. Their Olympian tolerance in matters relating to morals and crime often set a distance between them and those sections of the middle class which still cherished Puritan virtues.

In 1975 Conservative MPs discarded Heath, who departed into a curmudgeonly domestic exile, and replaced him with Margaret Thatcher. Her succession was significant in that she spoke proudly with the authentic voice of that section of the middle classes whose loyalty the party had for so long been taking for granted and whose opinions were commonly overlooked, or dismissed as ill-informed prejudice. Yet they were the pith and essence of the Conservative Party, as their fictional mouthpiece Leslie Titmuss announces to a selection committee:

> I went to a village school . . . Then I got a scholarship to Hartscombe Grammar. Weekends I used to get out on my bike and help people with their gardens. I grew up to understand the value of money because it took my father [an accounts clerk] five years to save up for our first second-hand Ford Prefect. Every night he finishes his tea and says to my mother, 'Very tasty, dear. That was very tasty' . . . You know what my parents are? They're true Conservatives! And I can tell you this. They're tired of being represented by people from the City or

folks from up at the Manor. They want one of themselves! You can forget the county families and the city gents and the river-side commuters. They'll vote for you anyway. What you need to win is my people. The people who know the value of money because they've never had it. The people who say the same thing every night because it makes them feel safe. The people who've worked hard and don't want to see scroungers rewarded or laziness paying off. Put it this way, ladies and gentlemen. You need the voters I can bring you! They are the backbone of the country. They aren't Conservative because of privilege or money, but because of their simple faith in the way we've always managed things in England.[10]

The date is the late 1960s. Within a few years and thanks to Heath's reorganisation of the local party machinery, the lower-middle classes were getting their hands on its levers. The cabals of rural landowners, retired officers and grandes dames who had held sway over Conservative Associations for over a century were gradually super-seded. Henceforward, selection committees were dominated by local businessmen, shopkeepers and solicitors who were more susceptible to candidates with similar backgrounds who echoed their views, espe-cially on law enforcement.[11] As the Labour MP Dennis Skinner drily noted, the estate agents had taken over from the estate owners.

After a by-election defeat by the Liberals in 1986, the Ryedale Conservatives rejected a public-school- and Oxford-educated barrister in favour of an ex-policeman who had been to a grammar school.[12] Such preferences changed the social composition of the Tory benches, but slowly. After the 1987 general election 68 per cent of Tory MPs had been to public schools, a proportion which fell to 62 per cent after the 1992 general election. None the less, the older generation of patrician Tories believed themselves embat-tled and spoke disdainfully of a 'peasants' revolt'.

The peasants were idealists armed with an ideology and, super-ficially, seemed somewhat out of place in a party which had always prized empiricism. Conservatives set a higher value on power and, by 1979, had ingested the radical ideas of a dynamic faction attached to Mrs Thatcher. Their solution to the country's intractable economic problems was an amalgam of libertarian principles, free-market economics and strict regulation of the money supply. Although these doctrines owed much to modern American economists, Mrs Thatcher repeatedly and unashamedly declared that they were a distillation of the middle-class virtues of the Victorian age which she had learned from her grandmother and seen applied by her father in his business and private life.

The famous Saatchi poster of the 1979 general election which declared that 'Labour isn't working' was an obituary notice for the post-war consensus. Past nostrums had failed and were tossed aside. 'What if the trades union leaders won't talk to Mrs Thatcher if she was Prime Minister?' voters asked Norman Tebbit during the 1979 campaign. 'So what – who cares?' was his answer.[13] Six months after her victory, Mrs Thatcher served notice that her task was to build 'a society of independent people' who owned their own houses, funded their own pensions, enjoyed a good standard of living and were free to enrich themselves. She warned that there was no place in this new world for those who believed in the mantra 'cast your burdens on the state and henceforth you will be absolved from all personal responsibility'.[14]

On the morning after the May 1979 election, dealers on the floor of the Stock Exchange cheered as the news came through of Tory victories, and some sang 'Land of Hope and Glory'.[15] During the day £1,000 million was added to share prices. There were further celebrations, for the Conservatives won three more general elections in 1983, 1987 and (narrowly) 1992 and champagne flowed in City wine bars. The drinkers were members of a growing section of the middle classes which was thriving thanks to Mrs Thatcher.

Not all the middle classes raised their glasses to Mrs Thatcher. She widened a rift within their ranks, admittedly along pre-existing fault lines. On one side were middle-class men and women engaged in business and finance and, on the other, their counterparts who worked in the public sector, particularly education and the welfare agencies. In 1987 between 56 and 60 per cent of middle-class private sector employees voted Conservative compared with between 36 and 40 per cent in the public.[16]

The divide was primarily cultural. The progressive and conscience-burdened herbivores had long been at odds with the carnivores, but now there was a significant difference: the former now felt excluded from a public arena in which their views were either ignored or dismissed as sentimentalist. Famously, when pressed during an interview on Christian responsibility, Norman Tebbit observed that it was the money in the good Samaritan's purse which enabled him to assist the stricken traveller. Only by allowing individuals to become rich could the state afford to help the poor and the sick. Many ardent Thatcherites pilloried public welfare systems as expensive, overmanned and inclined to perpetuate dependency and indulge the grumbling ('whingeing' was the common expression used by the right) of those who believed themselves alienated from society. In 1978 a television documentary aired the views of a prominent psychologist who claimed that an upsurge in violence among the young saw the genesis of the 'militant schoolkid', who, and this went without saying, needed sympathy and understanding. All this was interpreted by Kingsley Amis as 'a fucking tool of a trendy lefty psychologist talked about hooligans urged on by other fucking lefties'.[17] The country was going soft and too much energy and resources were being devoted to appeasing the disruptive, feckless and parasitic. Visceral Thatcherism disheartened and alarmed many public servants who found themselves isolated and undervalued by an administration which regarded 'social needs' as matters of secondary national importance.

Worse still, the public services were being compelled to conform to the ethos of the competitive market. They became 'providers' and their clients 'customers', and, particularly in health and education, employees had to submit to the regimen of 'performance indicators'. 'Targets' were set and the state borrowed from the world of football the concept of league tables. Those of schools, universities and hospitals were published. The ideals of public service were supplanted by the demands of the corporate world: college bursars became 'finance directors', 'action plans' and 'mission plans' had to be conjured up and everywhere the corridors of power were patrolled by cost-conscious accountants.[18] If, as the Thatcherites argued, the public services submitted to the disciplines of the market, they would provide value for money.

The perceived triumph of Mammon and its priorities ran counter to the growing middle-class concern for the environment which I shall discuss in the next chapter. Behind the Green movement of the 1970s and 1980s was a deeply rooted and frequently expressed fear that the commercial world considered the natural as a resource to be exploited regardless of long-term consequences. A high proportion of those engaged in environmental campaigns were middle-class men and women employed outside industry and commerce.[19]

Mrs Thatcher adored and did all in her power to help those who created wealth and multiplied choice, which she saw as the essence of freedom. She was a host to misgivings about the old upper-middle-class elites in the professions and the educational establishment who she thought wielded too much influence, lacked backbone and looked on the state as a milch cow. She considered local government as corrupt, profligate and a refuge for Marxists, which was why her government abolished the big metropolitan authorities and imposed controls over the expenditure of the rest.

With good reason, Mrs Thatcher suspected that all middle-class establishments haboured those who still hankered after the cosiness of consensus politics and were at heart hostile to the free market. Moreover, they subscribed to that old snobbery which looked askance at 'trade'. Her feelings broke surface in 1985 after a claque of Oxford dons had gracelessly refused her a customary honorary degree and inadvertently lost the university much private funding.[20] 'Cloister and common room . . . cannot stomach wealth creators,' she later remarked, adding that they were prejudiced against anyone who 'didn't have an Oxford accent' or the 'right connections'.[21] This sounded very much like the resentment of the hard-working, lower-middle class against those who had always treated it with condescension and pooh-poohed its conservatism, patriotism and faith in 'commonsense'. Yet Mrs Thatcher and her ideas were warmly applauded by a galaxy of intellectuals, including Sir Isaiah Berlin,

Kingsley Amis and Philip Larkin, and a coterie of articulate pundits who wrote on her behalf in the *Daily Telegraph, The Times* (from 1980), the *Spectator* and the *Economist.*

By dismissing much of 'one nation' Conservatism, Mrs Thatcher widened a gulf within the middle classes. Those employed in the public services found themselves beleaguered, dragooned into acceptance of the alien concepts of the market and forced to accept frozen budgets and salaries. The disaffected looked for new champions. There was the new Social Democratic Party of the centre left which offered a rehash of the old consensus politics and soon bonded with the Liberals to form the Liberal Democrats. In the 1992 general election, this alliance attracted the support of just under a quarter of the professional middle classes and just under a fifth of the managerial.[22]

None the less, a large swathe of the middle class welcomed Thatcherite policies as the lubricant of personal prosperity. Income tax fell (from 80 to 60 per cent on higher incomes and from 33 to 26 on lower), disposable incomes increased and, by 1984, there were 13.1 million owners of Visa cards and 11.4 million of Access cards. A new super-rich middle class was rapidly emerging from the City, where privatisation, deregulation (the 'Big Bang' of 1986) and the share boom were the mainspring of new fortunes. Mrs Thatcher was also propelling more and more people into the lower echelons of the middle class. Between 1980 and 1987 a million council houses were purchased by their tenants and the proportion of home owners soared from 52 to 66 per cent. Denationalisation swelled the number of private shareholders from three to eight million. Popular capitalism had arrived, or so its champions boasted. In fact, the proportion of individuals holding stock had fallen from 59 per cent in 1963 to 20 per cent in 1984. The slack was taken up by institutions, which owned 60 per cent of all shares.[23]

Many of the new stockholders in privatised utilities were working and lower-middle class, groups deliberately targeted by the 1986 'Tell Sid' advertising campaign for British Gas stock. This section of society had helped Mrs Thatcher to power in 1979 and kept her there, offsetting middle-class defections. Conservative analysts became engrossed in dissecting the preoccupations and aspirations of men and women who were poised on the lower edge of the middle class or had just entered it; they were classified as 'Essex Man', 'Mondeo Man' (after the popular family saloon) and 'Worcester Woman'. All lived in a vast psephological hinterland known as 'Middle England'. It became synonymous with the middle class, and the fate of governments hung on its concerns and ambitions. On the eve of the 1987 general election these were outlined by the *Sun*, a tabloid with a huge working-class readership. It was told what it owed to Mrs Thatcher:

> YOU wanted more money in your pay packet to spend as you choose.
> YOU wanted the firm control of the union bullies and the right to choose when and where you can go to work.

Now, you enjoyed 'the freedom to chose the best education, the best health care and the best home for your family'. The temper of the electorate was caught by Jean Rook in the *Daily Express* when she suggested that each voter would choose 'the party most likely to aid me personally to grab all I can'.

The ascendancy of Mrs Thatcher's free market in Britain coincided with the implosion of the alternative system, state socialism, in Russia and its Eastern European dependencies; capitalism was now the future and it worked. Collectivism was in retreat, much to the relief of the middle classes who had been give a nasty shock by the upsurge in union militancy during the late 1970s. Conservative legislation curbed the power of the trade unions: the closed shop was outlawed, compulsory secret ballots were held before strikes and unions were liable to fines if their members engaged in unofficial walk-outs. The reverses suffered by the miners in 1984–5 and the print workers in their disputes with Rupert Murdoch's News International (owner of the *Sun*) in 1986–7 demonstrated the new impotence of the unions. The middle classes were at last safe from the bogey of organised labour which had troubled them for a hundred years.

A revolution in the Conservative Party triggered one in the Labour Party. During the 1980s Labour had stumbled through the wilderness, peddling unpopular policies such as unilateral disarmament and nationalisation. It was obsessed with the past (the mind of its leader Michael Foot seemed frozen in the 1930s) and prone to internal squabbles. After 1987, the alternatives were permanent eclipse or modernisation. As the *New Statesman* commented, Labour had to stop listening to itself and instead heed an electorate for whom working-class solidarity and socialist orthodoxy were anachronisms.[24] A succession of reformers, Neil Kinnock, John Smith and Tony Blair (who in 1997 became the first ex-public school prime minister since Lord Home), set about discovering ways in which Labour could woo Middle England without abandoning its old conscience. Out went the trade union block vote and Clause Four (the 1918 pledge to nationalise major industries) and in came an acceptance of Tory trade union legislation, privatisation and a commitment to a free-market, competitive economy.

While Labour was reinventing itself, the Tories staggered from crisis to crisis. At the end of 1990 a baronial coup masterminded by Michael Heseltine and Geoffrey Howe (an alliance of the Mad Hatter and the Dormouse) overthrew Mrs Thatcher. Her successor John Major, a figure with lower-middle-class credentials and a simple honesty, won a majority of twenty-one at the 1992 general election and afterwards presided over one of the most ham-fisted administrations since Lord North's in the 1770s. Its blunders and lack of touch soon alienated a substantial section of the former Thatcherite constituency: in 1992 around 72 per cent of *Daily Telegraph* and 65 per cent of *Daily Mail* readers had voted Tory. These totals fell by 15 and 25 per cent in the 1997 general election.[25]

Tory defectors had ample grounds for disenchantment. The party had dramatically forfeited its ancient claim to be trusted with the management of the economy in September 1992 after the Exchange Rate Mechanism fiasco. The middle classes were again vulnerable and the Conservatives added to their woes. Value Added Tax was levied on fuel and an erratic property market sometimes left householders paying mortgages on properties worth far less than their original price. In 1991 the number of mortgage repossessions reached 74,000 and bankruptcies soared, reaching a peak of 47,000 in 1992.[26] The day after the feast was chill and disheartening for many who had dined well. They looked for a new saviour: in 1993 Labour's lead in the opinion polls soared to 33 per cent.

The Conservatives no longer offered the middle classes security and were now riven by internal wrangling, particularly over future relations with the European Union. Several prominent Conservatives were tarnished by scandals, mostly sexual, but two, involving Jonathan Aitken and Jeffrey Archer, were criminal. The sexual trespasses might have been overlooked had not John Major sermonised about moral regeneration, which he called 'Back to Basics'. It was a futile exercise given that most of the middle classes were content with the sexual revolution and were disinclined to reverse the new permissiveness. The new morality did not unduly disturb the Tories' old ally the Church of England, whose energies were now focused on inner-city poverty and a row over the ordination of women.

The Tories were soiled; New Labour appeared pristine. Like Mrs Thatcher, Tony Blair had a genius for courting the middle-class vote, which he rightly believed was essential to secure and hold power. New Labour assumed the role of the Conservatives: it was the enthusiastic partner of capitalism, pledged fiscal restraint, refused to reverse Thatcherite union laws and promised to address matters that were now disturbing the middle classes. These were the future funding and efficiency of public services, particularly health and education, on which they relied. In short, New Labour could be trusted to govern as the Tories had, but, as Blair repeatedly emphasised, with greater compassion. In his own words, New Labour would 'allow more people to become middle class' and prosper in an equitable society.[27] Voters gave the party two landslide victories in 1997 and 2002, although its manifestos would have dismayed Keir Hardie and Attlee. In September 2004 an opinion poll revealed that 72 per cent of the country imagined that New Labour was 'a middle-class party'.[28]

Blair has severely shaken old social/political allegiances. Middle-class loyalty to Conservatism has not been restored: between 1993 and 2004 the party's share of the popular vote has hovered around a third. Perhaps, like the Liberals at the close of the nineteenth century, the Tories have given the middle classes what they wanted and now have little else to offer them. The Liberal Democrats were now poaching Tory votes in the party's old heartlands in Southern and Western England, where in the 2004 European election there was a swing to the anti-European United Kingdom Independence Party, particularly among the middle classes. Many were over sixty and frightened by the growing influx of asylum seekers and the approach of a pan-European state.

New Labour has retained considerable middle-class support. Cynics wonder whether this is because Blair's leadership is an insurance against the return of socialism. Perhaps so, but middle-class loyalty is becoming increasingly strained as New Labour tentatively resuscitates old socialist policies of income redistribution and social engineering. High stamp duty and inheritance tax, together with the appointment in 2004 of an Orwellian-sounding 'regulator' whose task it is to compel universities to admit a fixed quota of working-class students (irrespective of their qualifications) are bound to perturb middle-class voters. Many have joined in the popular protests against the shifty political legerdemain which Blair used to involve Britain in the American invasion and subjugation of Iraq in 2003.

A university regulator with old Labour credentials who sees it as his duty to 'tackle class' and legislation to abolish hunting are a reminder that the concept of class war is still part of New Labour's genetic structure, whatever Blair may say to the contrary.[29] Old battlecries were heard again in the autumn of 2004 during the debate about hunting. Some Labour members regarded its abolition as a tit-for-tat for Mrs Thatcher's defeat of the miners in 1985. Speaking on the BBC, sometime social worker, collector of comics and MP for Ealing East George Pound spat out a declaration of war against 'braying Hooray Henries'. 'We're going after their 4x4s, ban pashminis – anyone with a contrasting silk lining on [*sic*] their suit, anyone who's called Ralph, we'll go after them.'[30] The accessories of wealth may be different, but the sentiments are those which Shakespeare placed in the mouths of Jack Cade's rebels.

Perhaps the class war is eternal. If it is, and Blair fails to bridle those of his followers who periodically deride 'toffs' and accuse their opponents of 'snobbery' whenever questions of moral or educational standards are raised, then the middle classes will look for a new defender. Accommodating middle-class demands will require extraordinary political gymnastics because of their sheer diversity. An attempt must be made, since winning over Middle England is essential to acquire and retain power.

Old political loyalties based upon class are dissolving and the result has been a series of often perverse contradictions. The middle classes want better public services, but are unwilling to submit to higher taxes. They approve of capitalism, but are fearful of the harm it can do to the environment and become indignant whenever individual capitalists reward themselves too generously. They cherish individual freedom and are suspicious of the power of the state, save when it is applied to criminals or deployed to frustrate developments that will threaten the ambience of their neighbourhoods.

The roots of these hopes and anxieties are not new; street crime and hooliganism arouse as much middle-class anxiety as they did a hundred or, for that matter, four hundred years ago. Yet the middle-class political animal of the early twenty-first century is a very different creature from his great-grandfather. He exists in a world in which the state has assumed more or less complete responsibility for much of his life, often, as in the cases of health and education, to his advantage. Security is not total, nor is it absolutely guaranteed, as many holders of private pensions have found to their cost. There are losers among the middle class, but, unlike their counterparts in the past who suffered at the hands of economic forces beyond their control or were victims of their own miscalculation, they seek compensation from the government. Heavy losses by largely upper-middle-class investors in Lloyd's on risks that were not altogether unforeseen led to pleas for government relief in the early 1990s. The individual had become less and less willing to accept responsibility for his own fate, even in the traditionally mutable world of underwriting. An Edwardian businessman would have been amazed, but he would also have been astonished to learn that it was the party of the working classes which now cultivated the middle, promising them what they had always wanted: freedom, safety and prosperity.

Don't Let Them Sch . . . on Britain: Good Causes

Like their Victorian predecessors, the twentieth-century middle classes contained a core of high-minded men and women who believed they represented the collective intelligence and conscience of the nation. United by the same sense of sometimes oppressive rectitude, the do-gooders proceeded along familiar lines: they identified abuses and then did all in their power to put them right through public meetings, petitions, letters to the press and political lobbying. It was a formula which, among other things, had outlawed slavery, provided sewers and halted the slaughter of Great Crested Grebes whose feathers were prized by Edwardian milliners.

Middle-class visions of a perfect world changed, as did their ideas of what was intolerable in the existing one. The likelihood of a second world war, more devastating than the first, drew thousands to pacifism during the 1930s. Similar alarms prompted the foundation of the Campaign for Nuclear Disarmament in 1958. Anti-war movements contained a strong Christian element, which was conspicuously absent from the conservation and environmental campaigns of the second half of the century. Architectural lobbies regularly identified the churches as villains whenever they neglected derelict places of worship. Among environmentalists there was a tendency to indulge in various 'New Age' cults which proliferated in the 1960s and whose ideology and practices were outside the Christian tradition. Middle-class Christian discontent with the sexual permissiveness and secular morality that also gained ground in the 1960s was channelled into various groups which concentrated on abortion, the spread of pornography and the nature of sexual education in schools. None enjoyed the same middle-class support as the environmental movement and none was anything like as successful.

Campaign tactics changed during this period. Experience taught that authority and the rest of society did not always respond to reasonable persuasion and so passive protest was gradually supplemented by active, which had the added virtue of attracting wide press and television coverage. Like the Chartists, the middle classes took to tramping the streets and holding mass rallies. Eighty thousand crowded into Trafalgar Square in 1980 in protest against Britain's nuclear arsenal, and in September 2002 the Countryside Alliance claimed that 400,000 of its members had marched through London. Zealots went further and picketed military bases, blockaded ports to stop the export of live animals, chained themselves to developers' bulldozers and uprooted genetically modified crops.

A few were arrested and sometimes sent to prison. Their immolation reflected extremes of exasperation, for the middle classes still retained their aversion to law breaking, whatever the cause or provocation. Most members of the overwhelmingly middle-class Campaign for Nuclear Disarmament preferred lobbying and marches to scrimmages at the gates of submarine bases.[1] Some of the women peace protesters camped outside the Greenham Common base in 1984 were discountenanced by the presence of extrovert lesbians and flamboyant punk rockers who simultaneously lowered the tone and invited press ridicule.[2] Complying with the law and an ingrained sense of seemliness acted as brakes on passion. There were no such inhibitions against borrowing weapons from the enemy; like the official and commercial interests they confronted, late-twentieth-century protesters hired professional political lobbyists and public relations agencies.

From mid-century onwards, the nuclear-disarmament and Green

movements captured the imaginations of many, particularly younger members of the middle classes. Both causes contained a strong element of cosmic Utopianism. Whereas Victorian reformers had hoped to civilise the post-industrial world, an influential section of modern environmentalists convinced themselves that it had become irredeemable. Those former handmaidens of progress, science and technology, assumed demonic qualities and, combined with capitalism, appeared to be driving the world towards self-destruction. The old middle-class optimism showed signs of faltering. A few pessimists succumbed to a mild form of paranoia and escaped the contaminated present for a pure and largely invented past. They took refuge in communes and smallholdings where they enjoyed a simplicity of life which they believed had been the common experience before the industrial age. They were not just modern Marie Antoinettes playing at milkmaids; some endeavoured to make their communities self-supporting. Some produced organic foodstuffs which, despite their comparatively high cost, found favour with the middle classes after a flurry of scares about fertilisers, insecticides and chemical additives in the closing years of the century. Again, capitalism was blamed.

Adherents of what was called the 'alternative' way of life were also haunted by apocalyptic nightmares induced by fears that an already disordered natural world was on the verge of collapse. An environmental journal of 1974 contained a plea from a young man fearful of the imminent 'end catastrophe' for a partner to 'share the remaining years of industrial civilisation'.[3] His pessimism was an extreme case of a loss of faith in the future. According to the various branches of the Green movement which gained impetus and converts after 1970, everyone was now living deracinated, unhealthy and spiritually arid lives in a competitive consumer society. Its insatiable demand for cheap energy was causing global warming, which, after the end of the Cold War in 1989, became the prime source of mass anxiety across the Western world.

Of course, there were many among the middle classes who still clung to their forebears' hope that all human problems could be solved by a mixture of inventiveness and reason. By mid-century these idealists' horizons had widened to encompass the entire globe.

As the British state shed its imperial responsibilities, the middle class formed charities to deliver material and moral assistance to what was being called the Third World. Like the poor of industrial Britain, the poor of Africa and Asia would not be allowed to drift into greater poverty and helplessness. There was long-term aid designed to foster economic growth and emergency appeals after natural disasters, chiefly famines. Donations were easy to secure, thanks to the television coverage of stricken regions which prompted the reaction: 'This is unspeakable, what can we do about it?' This was how the Victorians had behaved when they became aware of the horrors of say prostitution or cholera. The appeals of many overseas aid charities such as Oxfam had much in common with the Victorian tradition of self-help. Advertisements pointed to the fact that contributions were spent on schemes which enabled the recipients to become self-reliant and donors were sometimes invited to 'adopt' a specific child or its destitute grandparent.

Individual commitment was encouraged. The young were invited to penetrate the tropical equivalents of the slums and deliver enlightenment and practical help. The ex-sixth-former spending his gap year in a primary school in Botswana is the equivalent of the Victorian undergraduate who spent his vacation in a mission in Bermondsey. In each instance the benefits were mutual: the volunteers learned a sense of duty, saw at first hand what they and their kind had to do and gained self-knowledge. The recipients were helped and given a sense that the rich of the world had not completely abandoned them to their fate.

The expansion of international philanthropy coincided with the extension of official funding and control in domestic health and education, areas which had once been the prime concern of middle-class charities. These did not wither with the increase in state and local government engagement, but remained to work alongside statutory authorities. Moreover, the middle class retained its old belief in the duties which attached to status and individuals continued to serve on the increasing numbers of committees which supervised health and education authorities and, after 1945, town and countryside planning and patronage of the arts.

Wartime emergencies saw an extension in the local power of the middle class. From 1916 until 1918 the local administration of conscription was in the hands of committees of magistrates and local worthies who could decide whether a blacksmith was more valuable at his forge than at the front, or whether a pacifist's creed was sincere. In both world wars, the same respectable citizens sat on agricultural committees and presided over rallies to raise funds for servicemen's comforts. Between 1939 and 1945 the socially active middle classes allocated evacuee children to their hosts, managed events to raise cash for Spitfires and, through the Women's Voluntary Service, provided tea, hot food and kindliness to all who needed them everywhere.

Official recognition for such unpaid services had come in 1917 with the creation of the Order of the British Empire. It was organised on a hierarchical basis, like the older chivalric orders of the Bath and the Thistle, and recipients got a medal, a ribbon and the right to add CBE, OBE or MBE to their name. The 1928 New Year's Honours list included a CBE for the secretary of the Friends of the Poor Society, and MBEs for the chairman of the Nursing Council and members of local War Pensions Committees. In 1965 recipients of OBEs included Aberdeen's medical officer of health and the treasurer of the Scottish Amateur Athletic Association.

Like the aristocracy, the middle classes were enchanted by decorations and still are. Whenever the New Year or Queen's birthday lists are announced, the provincial press publishes the names and sometimes pictures of local recipients, many of whom say they are proud to accept their medals on behalf of their particular organisation. At the close of the century in the interests of what was called social 'inclusiveness', the Order of the British Empire was widened to embrace such humble servants of the community as lollipop ladies. Headteachers of state schools were occasionally made knights and dames, placing them on a level of worthiness equal to senior officers, diplomats, civil servants, academics and veteran actors and actresses. Attempts to transform the honours system into a national pantheon of virtue embracing all classes were hampered by the persistence of awards for political time-serving and to rich men who toady to the party in power.

★

Towering over all middle-class preoccupations during the nineteenth century had been the urban environment. By the middle of the twentieth, this concern shifted to the countryside and focused on preservation rather than renovation. The same was true in towns, where there was an awakening to the aesthetic harm being done by commercial development which was destroying so many comely and often distinguished old buildings. Societies sprang up to protect Georgian and Victorian architecture and townscapes on the grounds of their attractiveness (and the ugliness of much which replaced them) and their historic value. By 1973, one thousand local and national organisations had been set up to espouse public amenities ranging from the provision and protection of playing fields to the reintroduction of ospreys into Scotland. Successive governments responded sympathetically to these lobbyists: legislation created conservation areas – there were eight thousand in 1990 – in which development was supervised by local authorities under aesthetic guidelines.

The modern middle-class philosophy of conservation was rooted in the older romantic notion that the countryside represented certain timeless and wholly desirable qualities. Fields, woodlands, hedgerows, cottages and medieval churches stood for harmony and continuity. The middle classes had never found these qualities in towns and cities. From Tudor times, spirits disturbed by the pace and ruckus of urban money-making were refreshed through contact with Arcadia. Those who could afford to bought rural properties and those who could not visited the countryside for moments of refreshment.

After 1918 its therapeutic tranquillity became endangered to the point of extinction thanks to the middle-class love affair with the motor car. As predicted by early enthusiasts, mass motoring became a reality during the inter-war years and the new middle-class car owners flocked into the countryside. Mr Toad's open road was now everyone's highway, and motor manufacturers lured customers with rural images. A new model of 1931 was depicted being driven up a country lane away from a village in a valley, a theme repeated in a Fiat advertisement of 1968 which showed the vehicle being driven through the Yorkshire dales over the slogan 'You are free'.

The middle classes embraced this freedom. Car sales soared during the inter-war years, and after 1945 the better-off sections of the working class followed the middle classes on to the roads. There were 2.5 million private cars on the road in 1950 and more than four times that number in 1970. Most were comparatively cheap. In the 1930s a new two-seater Austin Eight cost as little as £125 and its equivalent thirty years later £400. Second-hand cars were half these prices.

Mass motoring created a Frankenstein's monster which threatened its creators. Its potential for mischief was clear during the 1920s when cars and their owners stripped rural Britain of the peace and seclusion which were its charms. New arterial roads brought ribbon development, strings of unsightly houses, petrol stations, giant hoardings and garish road houses for motorists, motor cyclists and charabanc parties. Slough, as reviled by John Betjeman, symbolised all the horrors of the new landscape of the automobile. The Council for the Preservation of Rural England, founded in 1926, attempted to stop the rot. One of its early postcards showed St George lancing a dragon labelled 'Cigarettes, petrol, tea, soap and pills' (all advertised on roadside hoardings) against the background of a garage.[4] Middle-class sensibilities were also jarred by the proliferation of working-class trippers, for whom the countryside was the town without pavements. They brought wind-up gramophones on which they played jazz, danced and left litter behind. Campaigns against noise and litter were soon under way.

Defending and rescuing the countryside became a focus for middle-class energies and remained so for the rest of the century. Just after the war, the conservationists placed their faith in the framework of national and local planning agencies, but inevitably these became embroiled in finding a balance between economic needs and aesthetic values. Moreover, as conservationists discovered to their fury, central government reserved the power to override even the most passionate and cogent local objections. By the mid-1960s a yet unfinished war of attrition was under way and the middle classes trooped into the opposing camps.

After one victory (the blocking of a 1970 scheme to knock down a section of the Elizabethan fortifications of Berwick to widen a road) the conservationists announced themselves as 'the authentic voice of the people'. The voice spoke in middle-class tones, for the prime objectors had been the local historical society and the Chamber of Trade.[5] An analysis of the readers of the new environmental magazine the *Ecologist* in 1971 revealed that 59 per cent were professional middle class (with a large proportion of teachers and scientists) and a third were students and school pupils. Well over a half read *The Times, Daily Telegraph* and *Guardian* and 2 per cent the *Financial Times*.[6] The absence of subscribers from commercial backgrounds is instructive, but not surprising. In an earlier issue of the *Ecologist* a writer had declared: 'Industry exists to exploit the environment and make profits.'[7] It was an assertion that would become widely accepted within the Green movement and by its middle-class sympathisers who made their living outside the world of business. In September 2004 a survey undertaken in Scotland showed that local authorities and conservation and community groups favoured a right of appeal against planning decisions made at the top, usually on economic grounds. Against such appeals were a legion of business interests, including British Petroleum, the National Farmers Union, the fish-farming industry, airport authorities and the Scottish Chamber of Commerce.[8]

The future of the environment split the middle classes. Superficially, romantics, nature lovers and aesthetes were ranged against the philistine money grubbers, although there were many landowners and farmers who encouraged wild life on their properties and companies which funded schemes for urban regeneration. Some firms tried to convince the middle classes that they were sympathetic to the environment. In the late 1930s Shell sponsored excellent county guidebooks (edited by John Betjeman and John Piper) and wildlife charts for schools. 'We're rather keen on the countryside,' declared an advertisement for High Speed Gas in 1970. Above was a Victorian painting of a rural scene with a milkmaid to remind everyone that gas pipelines 'don't spoil the view'.[9]

Roads and airports did. They generated noise and pollution and passionate middle-class resistance. The transport lobbies saw them as vital to economic survival. 'What we want are fifty-ton juggernauts,' proclaimed Joe Bamford in 1972. He was chairman of a farm machinery and earth-moving company who believed that the alternative to 'bigger and better and faster' lorries was the loss of business to European competitors.[10] Conservationists countered by demonstrating that these monsters wrecked towns and villages and destabilised ancient buildings; in 1977 it was feared that they would bring down the walls of York.[11] There had been no such middle-class objections to railway expansion, which had caused widespread demolition of property in towns and cities in the previous century.

An influential and vocal section of the middle class no longer shared their ancestors' faith in progress and wished to constrain it. Economic advantage was not a goal to be pursued at all costs. Those on the right disagreed: the shackling of enterprise would inevitably lead to job shortages (a powerful argument as unemployment rose in the 1970s) and stagnation. On the left, the Labour politician and public school class warrior Anthony Crosland claimed in 1971 that conservationists were a rich, upper-middle-class coterie bent on frustrating national growth to the detriment of the working class.[12] The subsequent history of middle-class environmental agitation has been one of tussles with commercial interests and government agencies whose duty it is to create jobs and expedite road and air transport for the masses.

The middle classes were facing a dilemma: should they allow progress to continue, despite frightening predictions of the consequences? Or should they demand a halt, even if this arrested living standards? Individual action provided some alternatives to these extremes. In 1970 the recently formed Friends of the Earth dumped throwaway bottles at the headquarters of Cadbury Schweppes with the slogan 'Don't let them Sch . . . on Britain'. Within twenty years the recycling of glass and much else had become fashionable and was officially encouraged at local and national level. The Green movement waged propaganda battles against the corporate world (for example, the proposed Rio Tinto Zinc plans for copper mining in Snowdonia in 1972) and physically obstructed roadworks and new developments.

'Middle-class, middle-aged hooligans from middle-England' was how *The Times* branded protesters at Fulbeck in Lincolnshire who were endeavouring to disrupt Nirex's efforts to bury nuclear waste near their homes in the autumn of 1986. The militants included a gentleman farmer, a squash-court manufacturer and the local parson and postmistress. All political parties were represented, including the vice-chairman of the local Tories. Nirex intended drilling at other sites and again found its way blocked by middle-class activists, forgivably given the Chernobyl catastrophe a few months before. There were mass vigils and human blockades, and some demonstrators chained themselves to equipment. At Elstow in Bedfordshire the middle classes mobilised under the chairmanship of a retired chief inspector of police. They held meetings, advertised in the press and mustered a band of distinguished scientists to counter Nirex's public relations offensive.[13]

The company secured legal injunctions against named demonstrators and these were enforced by the police, who arrested some. One declared: 'I haven't broken the law. I'm damned if I will vote Conservative again.' The rector of Fulbeck was astonished at the courtroom manoeuvres which quashed 'peaceful protest'.[14] Mrs Thatcher, a local girl, distanced herself from this middle-class revolt against capitalism, which *The Times* pompously declared placed 'local interests above national policy'. This was to profit from the disposal of nuclear garbage. Later, Tony Blair emphatically endorsed experiments in genetically modified crops as of vital national importance.

Middle-class custodians of town and countryside were unmoved. They asked what was the nation? Was it just a commercial concern, or an abstraction which embraced past, present and future? In 1996 thousands defended its past in the form of archaeological sites, two battlefields, and its present in the form of the habitat of badgers and rare snails and some breathtaking scenery, all of which were being destroyed by the Newbury bypass. There was much middle-class sympathy for the tactics of 'eco warriors' who perched in trees and burrowed underground. A headmaster who lived near by echoed many others when he asked: 'Who owns this country, anyway?' One of the policemen guarding the site observed: 'I feel guilty that our generation has allowed it to happen.'[15] The environment had become a moral issue: its protectors were defending a deep-rooted and essentially romantic vision of Britain, a nation whose soul was somehow embedded in the countryside. There was a spiritual dimension to the environmental movement which appealed to the middle classes in the same way as Evangelicalism had two hundred years before. Saving the earth was a chance to do good by protecting the rest of society from its follies and vices.

Middle-class rebellions against threats to the environment were often vilified as self-interested, in so far as the protesters' backyards were threatened, although hostility to genetically modified crops is now widespread. There were also assaults on the presumption of rectitude by groups which dictated what was good science and what was not, or what was unsightly and what was not. Caravan sites which crept along the coastline after the war were a source of pleasure to caravan owners (there were four and a half million in 1960) who could not understand why they should be curtailed on aesthetic grounds. Rows over such matters were an extension of those over the BBC and commercial television: could one relatively small segment of society claim a monopoly of taste and wisdom and impose both on everyone else? Matters were complicated by the fact that those who said they knew best prevented others from getting jobs, homes and the means of recreation. Was it right to balance an estuary where thousands of birds congregated in the winter with the demand for an airport from which thousands of working-class families could set off for cheap holidays on the Spanish coast in the summer?

Kicking up a fuss about the future of the countryside and what was grown there and how was fraught with problems. It had been relatively simple to denounce child labour or open sewers on moral and pragmatic grounds, but to tell the caravan owner that he was offending aesthetic canons was infinitely harder. So too was persuading farmers that intensive husbandry shattered fragile ecosystems when housewives were clamouring for cheap food. Such criticism assumed that the countryside had somehow reached a stage beyond which there could be no further evolution and denied the fact that its appearance had been radically changed in the past.

Preservationists of all kinds claimed a superior aesthetic judgment which grated on the ears of those who were expected to fall in line

with it. 'All posh and la–di–da' was how a villager described objectors to overspill housing and a new factory at Lavenham in Suffolk
in 1962. Its enchanting medieval and Tudor vernacular housing
attracted the middle classes, many of them retired. 'Everyone in the
village is about ninety and need shooting,' grumbled one village lad,
enraged by complaints about the jukebox in a local pub.[16] This did
not accord with the Chestertonian ambience the upper–middle class
expected from a country pub. Since the projected factory offered
thirty–five jobs at a time when agriculture was shedding men in
favour of machines, the row over Lavenham's future generated class
friction.

Another common source of tension was the understandable desire
of the middle classes to defend their surroundings. In 1972 the fifty–
five households of Dullatur near Dumbarton united to overturn
plans to end what one resident called their 'bucolic isolation' by the
construction of a 'mediocre housing estate'. The protesters were
'largely professional' and included university lecturers, bank officials
and a car salesman. Such objections often mystified or enraged developers and local authorities. When, in 1981, middle–class occupiers
of a terrace of well–maintained Victorian cottages in Langley Park
(Durham) resisted a scheme for their demolition, a local Labour
councillor observed: 'Between you and me, they've knocked their
houses together for wife–swapping!' Why the owners might prefer
to live in former working men's houses and restore them, rather
than in a modern development, was beyond his comprehension.[17]
Likewise, working–class locals in Cotswold villages are puzzled as to
why middle–class incomers pay high prices for decayed cottages with
few or limited facilities. None the less, they pocket the money and
use it to buy modern houses whose bland uniformity upsets the
sensitivities of middle–class aesthetes.

Riders of hobby–horses often collided. At the beginning of the
twenty–first century aesthetes locked horns with the Greens over
windfarms, which the former consider eyesores and the latter a
defence against global warning. Birdwatchers were at odds with
hedgehog lovers over a purge of these creatures from the Hebrides,
where they were eating the eggs of scarce waders. Internal snob-

bery among the middle classes also intruded. 'Help Stop These Global Warming Outsize Vehicles' was one of the slogans in the campaign to purge Hampstead of 4x4 cars in 2000. 'These cars damage the unique, liberal, sensitive intelligent face of Hampstead,' alleged one protester, well aware that their owners were City whizzkids whose mores (and wealth) distressed the left-inclining middle class.[18]

Active concern with the environment coincided with an upsurge in the numbers of people seeking recreation in the countryside. By the close of the century there were over five million anglers, bird-watchers and ramblers, all of whom were generously served with magazines and television programmes which often spotlighted the dangers of pollution and threats to wildlife habitats. Since the 1970s anecdotal evidence of the disappearance of birds, butterflies and wild flowers has been confirmed by scientific surveys. Middle-class news-papers now regularly publish lists of endangered species which are often described as the victims of intensive farming. Such farming has been blamed for the large-scale uprooting of hedgerows: in 1970 the Council for the Preservation of Rural England and the British Trust for Ornithology alleged that between 10,000 and 14,000 miles of hedgerow were being destroyed each year. The Ministry of Agriculture calculated that the total was only a thousand, a figure which, unsurprisingly, was agreed by the National Union of Farmers.[19]

A predominantly middle-class group, farmers were squeezed between demands for abundant food and pressure from ecologists to preserve the landscape and wildlife. The market wanted eggs from chickens reared in broiler houses which environmentalists condemned as cruel. Moreover, agriculture existed in an economic limbo thanks to subsidies, paid first by the state and then by the European Union. This system continued even after the Thatcherite free-market revo-lution, although many farmers have realised the potential of the middle-class market for organic and 'free-range' foodstuffs which simultaneously satisfied the purchaser's conscience and dispelled anxi-eties about 'unhealthy' eating. What was 'natural' was wholesome, whereas what had been produced with various forms of 'scientific' intervention was, at best, suspect.

Seen from the perspective of those who made their living there, the countryside was being forced to submit to standards imposed by an unsympathetic urban majority who wanted it to resemble a cross between the riverside of *Wind in the Willows* and the dreamworld 'shire' of Tolkien's *The Hobbit*. During the 1990s the spirit of urban meddling was embodied by the fictional Mrs Snell, a middle-class busybody from the suburbs in *The Archers* who devoted herself to preserving Ambridge and its surroundings with the help of planning regulations. Once, she symbolically waged war against a makeshift and ugly barn erected by the Grundys who were forever ingeniously if not successfully trying to earn a living from the land. In 1997 there was a rural rebellion against Mrs Snell and all that she represented in the form of the Countryside Alliance. It was essentially a middle-class movement: just under half its members came from the upper-middle and professional classes and three-fifths voted Conservative.[20] There were as many readers of *Country Living* (a magazine aimed at middle-class incomers seeking an appropriately rustic décor for their weekend cottages) as readers of *Farming Weekly*, if not more.

The Countryside Alliance's concerns over affordable rural housing, post offices, shops and transport facilities were overshadowed by the issue of field sports, particularly fox hunting. Mass demonstrations in London in 1998 and 2002 were focused on opposition to the ban on hunting with dogs which was finally passed towards the end of 2004. The debate was bad-tempered and riddled with the language and images of class war; with some justice the Alliance has argued that its enemies were driven by a loathing of the pursuers rather than any affection for the pursued. Parliamentary defeat prompted militants to pledge themselves to a campaign of civil disturbance. Just before the debate on hunting, a small knot of Countryside Alliance supporters disrupted the Commons proceedings while outside demonstrators were roughly used by policemen. Old taboos against belligerent protest were crumbling under the pressure of new, middle-class passions.

Like environmentalists, pacifists convinced themselves that they were prophets of global salvation. They were overwhelmingly middle-class: a breakdown of the Campaign for Nuclear Disarmament's

(CND) membership in 1968 showed that 83 per cent had non-manual jobs.[21] Ten years later the proportion had risen to 90 per cent, and three-quarters of all members had degrees or professional qualifications. In the 1980s, when CND's membership was rising (it totalled 85,000 in 1985), its followers were predominantly English with a third living in the South-East. Nearly all were employed in the public services and two-thirds voted Labour.[22] In brief, CND was home to the left-inclining schoolteacher or social worker who was deeply interested in politics and, in all likelihood, offered active support to Greenpeace or Friends of the Earth.

No social analyses exist of the tiny number of First World War Conscientious Objectors or the 136,000 signatories to the Peace Pledge in the mid-1930s. Both groups contained a strong Christian element with Quakers and nonconformists to the forefront together with socialist intellectuals who believed that men like themselves could solve the world's problems through reasoned argument. All agreed that war was utterly immoral and that the prospect of a second total war was so ghastly that it had to be prevented at all costs. Press support was minimal. The 1935 peace ballot, although supported in London by 'mayors, architects, doctors and *generally the best people in each borough* [my italics]' was given thin coverage in *The Times, Daily Telegraph* and *Morning Post,* and was ignored by the *Daily Mail.*[23] Events in Europe overtook and ultimately dissolved the inter-war pacifist movement. Nazi and Fascist aggression and the outbreak of the civil war in Spain in 1936 forced left-wing pacificists to reconsider their faith in Gandhian non-violence and its chances of success against ruthless forces bent on creating a universe in which might was right and the individual counted for nothing. Hitler and Mussolini did for British pacifism, which fell apart by 1939 with some of its followers drifting rightwards and offering apologies for German expansionism.

Founded in 1958, CND attracted veterans of the pre-war pacifist movement. In its goals and methods, it was the last of the Victorian moral crusades. It resembled the Anti-Corn Law League in its faith in public debates and lectures and pamphleteering and the anti-slavery movement in its assertion that once Britain gave a moral lead, the rest of the world would fall admiringly into line. By repudiating its nuclear arsenal, Britain would recover its traditional moral authority and a step would have been taken to pull the world back from self-destruction. There was, as with the environmental movements which were attracting middle-class support, a strong element of anti-Americanism within CND, especially among its Marxist adherents. Eighty thousand CND supporters gathered in London in 1984 to protest against the visit of President Reagan, and about the same number assembled at Molesworth two years later when the first American missiles were installed there.

CND made headlines but never converted the mass of the middle class. Like the rest of the country it equated nuclear disarmanent with taking a dangerous risk in an already precarious world. Press support was again sparse and when, in the 1980s, Labour flirted with unilateralist policies, they merely added to its electoral handicaps. Post-Cold War detente has made the movement largely irrelevant to political life, although its membership has been reactivated by the Anglo-American invasion of Iraq and has taken to the streets for mass demonstrations.

What is interesting about CND is that, like environmentalism, it was a symptom of middle-class apprehension about a world that seemed to be running out of control. The way ahead now led into a universe filled with ogres: global capitalism, consumer spending, disintegrating climate systems, a characterless and arid countryside, scientifically contaminated foods and the possibility that tampering with the environment might trigger new plagues, even an apocalypse. Consider the optimism contained in the first episode of 'Dan Dare: Pilot of the Future' which appeared in the new comic *Eagle* in 1952. It foresaw a unified world in which 'individual liberty and equality' were secured by a global federal government defended by an 'incorruptible' United Nations police force. Human ingenuity and science were concentrated on the elimination of 'poverty and squalor'.[24] This Utopia never came about. For the next fifty years *Eagle* readers were successively bombarded with dire warnings of man-made dangers; old friends like science and technology became new enemies; and reason, once a reliable ally, ceased to be trustworthy. In these circumstances, it was hard for those among the middle classes who gave thought to such matters not to feel uneasy about the future. Some attempted to halt or deflect the path of progress. Larger numbers retreated towards that romantic rusticity which was expressed in the 1970s by Laura Ashley fabrics and dresses (reminiscent of Kate Greenaway) and the uncomplicated world of James Herriot's stories of a veterinary practice in pre-war Yorkshire, which provided the scenarios for a much loved television series. Then and after, the middle classes endeavoured to relive the wholesomeness of that rural past (and incidentally promote their own health) by eating food which was organically grown and humanely reared. It was more expensive than 'industrial' comestibles, but a clear conscience was worth the price.

6

Freeing Us from Ourselves: Old Creeds and New Morals

Middle-class Christianity waned in the twentieth century. Its memorials are derelict churches, some boarded up against vandals, some turned into museums or community centres, others converted into business premises or homes, and a few to mosques. Many of these unwanted buildings were an embarrassment to their owners, who were glad to be rid of them and peeved when middle-class aesthetes clamoured for their preservation. As early as 1919 Arthur Winnington Ingram, the Bishop of London, established an Anglican tradition of philistinism by proposing to demolish some Wren and Hawksmoor churches in his diocese. A few years later he astonished the House of Lords by declaring that he wanted to build a bonfire of contraceptives and dance around it. Episcopal eccentricity thrived while congregations dwindled.

Statistics charted a decline in regular worshippers which had been detectable since the last century. The figures for England are set out in Table 6.

Table 6: Regular worshippers in British churches, 1911 and 1951

	Anglican	Methodist	Congregationalist	Roman Catholic
1911	2.3 million	786,300	288,000	1.7 million
1951	1.85 million	681,200	207,200	2.8 million

In Wales the falls were less pronounced, and, like the Catholics, the Church of Scotland gained ground. Its numbers doubled within forty years, peaking at 1.32 million in 1953.[1] On the whole, the slide was downwards and irreversible. According to the *U.K. Christian Handbook* of 1983, the national totals of those affiliated to the main denominations were: Anglicans 1.82 million, nonconformists and Church of Scotland 2.6 million and Catholics 1.8 million. There were a further million non-Christians, of whom 600,000 were Muslim. At the beginning of the twenty-first century, just under 8 per cent of the population were practising members of a church, compared with thirteen in 1931.[2] Yet the 2001 census revealed that 72 per cent of the population considered themselves Christians.

Given that so many congregations were predominantly middle-class, the arithmetic of church attendance suggests that its members were no longer inclined to submit to the discipline of communal worship. It plainly failed to capture the imagination; in 1938 a total of 67 per cent of the population were baptised, 26 confirmed and only 9 became regular communicants.[3] These figures did not indicate a decay of spirituality, merely that millions did not believe that it could be awakened or sustained by conventional observances. An awareness of God and inner equipoise were sought in other, novel ways as the century progressed. The quest was symbolised by the fate of the United Reform Church at Dent in the Yorkshire dales in the 1990s. Its congregation dwindled and its premises were taken over by a popular local meditation group, whose members included at least one former worshipper. As one explained:

We are not affiliated to any religion and there is no belief system imposed on anybody here. I was brought up a Christian,

but it held no real meaning for me. I would class myself as a
universalist, believing that all religions offer the same end. At
its simplest, meditation is giving the body and mind a very
deep level of rest, freeing us to be ourselves.[4]

This woman's revelation was typical and only possible after the 1960s,
when meditation, yoga and other forms of essentially personal spirituality began to fill the vacuum created by the decay of orthodox
Christianity.

Explanations for empty churches were the same as they had been
during the Victorian period: alternative diversions and disillusion. In
1926 a Presbyterian minister in Sunderland told his congregation
that the 'better ways of our fathers' were being discarded. The distractions of 'the world and all its interests' kept some away from services, and, more worryingly, there were others who gained nothing
from 'conventional church going', which they considered 'a disappointment and futility'.[5] Another clergyman thought the decline of
faith was more apparent than real, blaming flight from God on the
traditional 'shyness' and 'diffidence' of the English in spiritual matters.[6]

Dismay at the demise of old habits and faith was tinged with
anxiety about what would happen to the nation's moral framework.
Its joints were secured by Christian codes, so too were its laws. 'Without
religion there can be no morality and without morality there can be
no law,' declared Lord Denning, the nation's most distinguished jurist,
who was born at the close of the nineteenth century and lived through
most of the twentieth. It was an assertion which the Victorian middle
class would have endorsed, but for how long would it remain valid
in a nation in which an increasing proportion of the traditionally
church-going classes stayed at home on Sundays and were content
with various forms of vague deism?

They were not godless, nor indifferent. In 1963, the Catholic
journal the *Tablet* complained that in a country in the process of
'de-Christianisation' and where Sunday worship had been 'abandoned', there were plenty of individuals confidently expressing their
opinions about religion.[7] What disturbed the *Tablet* writer and
Catholics in general was a retreat from congregational worship and

prayer and the complementary erosion of moral absolutes based on scripture.

Rome would not compromise its ancient dogmas, but true to their intellectual traditions the Protestant churches were prepared to reconsider theirs. This was so of the Church of England, which remained deeply conscious of its unique role as a national church and a source of moral authority. To fulfil both it had to provide guidance on the problems which confronted individuals in the modern world. At the same time, it had to acknowledge that pronouncements from the pulpit no longer commanded attention and acquiescence. Like other Protestant clergy, the Anglican bishops faced two alternatives: to hold the pass come what may, or to adapt doctrines to entice the sceptical or indifferent into the pews. Both options were risky, for the former might encourage further defections and the latter could easily dilute traditional codes to the point where they ceased to be distinctively Christian. Redrawing moral boundaries was bound to upset those who expected to be told unambiguously what was right and what was wrong.

The upper reaches of the Anglican hierarchy plumped for tentative doctrinal revision. During the inter-war years and under the aegis of the future Archbishop of Canterbury William Temple, reports from successive Anglican Conferences on Politics, Economics and Citizenship endeavoured to formulate a theology which would show that the Church of England was in step with the times and a national body with answers to national problems. Some of the proposals were radical, which pleased many younger clergy and dismayed the old guard. Sex education in schools was favoured and, in a report of 1924, class divisions deplored. Their roots were regrettable and were a hindrance to 'proper relations' between different groups.[8] This was an astonishing turnabout by a church which had hitherto stressed that the social hierarchy was divinely ordained and vital for the order and prosperity of the nation. Then and for the rest of the century, conservatives among the clergy and laity detected what appeared to be a concerted lurch leftwards by leading churchmen.

Revised doctrines were accompanied by liturgical novelties. In

1934, Oxford undergraduates, bored by old-style services, flocked to churches which deviated from traditional forms and offered 'new ways' chosen to appeal to a younger generation.[9] Ahead lay the New English Bible, the colloquial Good News Bible and a new prayer book, all of which appeared between 1963 and 1966. Each was distinguished by banality of language, and none arrested the slide in church attendance. Swinging parsons attempted to entice the young into the pews with guitars, tokens that God was not fuddy-duddy. Their antics provoked ridicule: a *Private Eye* cartoon showed a trendy young clergyman announcing from the pulpit that God was not an old, white-bearded man in the sky, while above his head such a figure asks: 'What do you know about it?'

Yet from the new wave of Anglican worship there emerged the charismatic movement. Its forms of service looked back to the cavortings of the wilder seventeenth-century sects. Uninhibited by formal liturgy, the charismatics clapped their hands, danced and spoke in tongues, all expressions of the joyfulness of being Christian. Charismatic Christianity was vibrant, classless and proved to be very popular, particularly in urban areas.

Charismatic Anglicans were part of a church plunging deeper into turmoil. Its explorations of new theologies led to recurrent crises. The architects of a fresh or what they called 'relevant' approach to God and morality were from a clerical establishment with a common upper-middle-class, public school and Oxford and Cambridge background. They had learned the virtue of doing good and adding to human happiness and used what power they possessed to that end. In this respect (and for that matter in their upbringing and education) they were closer to those agnostic and atheist intellectuals who wanted to replace the old absolute morality with one which was humane and allowed individuals to make their own decisions. As the old moral order was dismantled in the 1960s, many senior Anglicans vied with each other to vaunt their radical open-mindedness. John Robinson (Marlborough and Cambridge), the Bishop of Southwark and defender of *Lady Chatterley's Lover*, later declared that *Playboy* performed 'a liberating function' in that it released 'all kinds of inhibitions about sex'. In 1967 he was outflanked in moral audacity by a future bishop, Hugh Montefiore (Rugby and Oxford), who told fellow churchmen that if Christ was homosexual then it would have been 'further evidence of God's self-identification with those who were unacceptable to the upholders of "the Establishment" and social convention'.[10]

Where did all these shifts leave the middle classes? Dismay at the crumbling of moral certainties was greatest among the lower-middle class.[11] They saw themselves as a sheet anchor, a self-image prized by Frank Gibbon in Noël Coward's *This Happy Breed* (1943), when he claims 'it's up to ordinary people to keep things steady'. The foundation of their steadfastness was a faith in tradition: 'we know what we belong to, where we come from, where we're going'. From the 1920s onwards, that path was far from clear and Gibbon's betters could no longer be depended upon to lead travellers because they were at odds over how to interpret the map. For the rest of the century, a section of the lower-middle classes was disheartened and sometimes infuriated by what appeared as tergiversation by the traditional custodians of the nation's morals. They abandoned absolutes and replaced them with a confusing variety of choices, many of which seemed to cock a snook at the codes that had gone before.

Like so many other respectable suburban families, the Gibbons were not quarantined from the ethos of their times. Frank's son tells his father that 'I don't hold with a God who just singles out a few to be nice to, and lets all the others rot.' His daughter Queenie leaves home to explore the world of glamour she has seen on the cinema screen and ends up living with a married man and having his child. Frank takes all this in his stride and affirms his faith in that mainstay of society, marriage.

Christian marriage was the touchstone for the moral health of society. On this all denominations were united, in principle at least. There were, however, disagreements over the permanence of the marriage oaths, the circumstances in which legal separation was permissible and what was the proper Christian attitude towards divorced men and women. In 1947 a total of 377 Anglicans in Chelmsford diocese were asked whether innocent parties in adultery cases should be allowed to take communion. They agreed, by a majority of one.[12] Evidence presented by various Christian groups to the 1951 Royal Commission on Divorce indicated a growing distress at its prevalence. The Methodist church conceded that it was not always possible for marriages to flourish, but the half-a-million-strong Anglican Mothers Union denounced divorce and mothers going out to work as threats to the family, which was the 'natural unit of society'. Within twenty-five years, its members agreed to admit divorced women. 'Flog 'em' Fisher, the Archbishop of Canterbury, blamed 'weak laws and unsound public opinion' for the devaluation of marriage. The Catholic Union concurred and predicted that the weakening of marriage would 'inflict grievous harm on the whole nation'.[13] These bleak prognoses were confirmed by a rise in the annual divorce rate from 2,700 in 1920 to 60,000 in 1947, a figure which was blamed on wartime infidelity.

Fisher's scapegoats were a greater tolerance and its reflection in the law. In 1924 the former was reflected in a purely pragmatic review of the current divorce laws by a female barrister in *Woman*, a somewhat raffish magazine for modern upper-middle-class women. In the following year a piece appeared which illuminated the attitudes of *Woman*'s younger readers towards marriage. 'Old repressions have gone forever, and the discontents that were formally hidden away as something disgraceful and inadmissible are now aired with a frankness' which bordered on the dangerous. The article concluded with speculation about whether Britain might follow certain American states and sanction divorce solely on the ground of incompatibility.[14] This was academic, since many lawyers happily colluded with couples whose chief reason for separation was mutual consent. It was a procedure approved by Marriage Guidance Councils, which had first appeared in 1938 and within nine years had a hundred branches.[15] From 1948, the new Legal Aid scheme gave access to divorce to the working classes: within three years, 87 per cent of all separations were between working-class couples, the rest between middle-class ones.[16]

In retrospect, the relaxation of the divorce laws was the most obvious instance of the retreat of moral standards based upon scriptural injunctions in the face of those which were secular and enforced by the state. To some extent these new moral codes reflected contemporary Protestant thought. Save in a handful of extreme sects, a compassionate, forgiving God was replacing the stern, unbending judge so often invoked by Victorian clergymen.

This was a blow for those Christians whose picture of the moral universe was rendered in black and white. The transformation of mainstream Christianity was slow and much of its impetus had come from a small body of liberal Protestant churchmen, who convinced themselves that it was better to temporise in favour of compassionate tolerance than resist in the name of dogmas which were ignored or rejected by the educated middle classes and to which the working class was largely indifferent. In broad historical terms, the second half of the twentieth century was engaged in a form of moral recividism, reverting back to the eighteenth. The intervening period of Evangelical zeal and the enforcement of Biblical moral codes had been an aberration. It had had substantial middle-class support, but this had all but dissolved by the 1960s. Thereafter, middle-class opinion did not on the whole fall in behind the successors of the Victorian purity movement.

Middle-class Catholics stood apart and were ready to follow their clergy and go against the flow. In 1953 an article in the *Tablet* castigated current attitudes to the 'unsavoury topic of homosexuality', which was discussed solely in relation to 'pagan principles and the ethics of rationalism'. The law was now blind to the Biblical divine injunctions against 'unnatural' crimes which demanded that the culprits repent their sinfulness and turn to God.[17] Likewise, marriage was moving from the divine sphere to the human. Commenting on a clause in the 1967 Matrimonial Causes bill which consigned divorce proceedings to lesser courts, the *Tablet* asked: 'Are marriages and families to be treated as accident cases . . . ?'[18]

From the reformation to the mid-nineteenth century, Catholicism had survived in the teeth of hostility from the state and public opinion. For most of this period the law excluded Catholics from civil society. Their admission was not accompanied by toleration. Victorian Protestants still feared the Pope (an alien autocrat) and regarded Catholics at home and abroad as perverse and degenerate. Ruskin's father (a sherry merchant) and his wife shunned the Catholic cantons in Switzerland on the ground that the accommodation was bound to be dirty.[19] Violent, predominantly working-class anti–Catholicism persisted in England's industrial centres until the early twentieth century, later in Scotland, and was always blended with racial antipathy towards Irish immigrants. To survive in a malevolent world, the Irish looked to their church as a source of solidarity and identity, and so working-class Catholicism flourished.

Before the Irish arrived, Catholicism had been largely confined to a handful of aristocratic and gentry families whose pedigrees and loyalty to their faith would later entrance Evelyn Waugh, an upper-middle-class convert. In time, many working-class Irish Catholic families moved upwards in society and a Catholic middle class had emerged which, like its Protestant counterpart, became actively engaged in national life. Until the 1960s participation in public affairs presented few difficulties for Catholics, but afterwards they found themselves living in a nominally Christian society in a state of moral flux. Rome stood aloof from the new ethical order and for the rest of the century affirmed old orthodoxies. Birth control was condemned and forbidden, as was sex outside marriage, and masturbation and homosexuality were classified as 'manifestations of moral disorder'.

The Catholic middle class was in a quandary. The ability to limit the size of one's family had become vital for the rest of the middle class, simply because it made it possible for them to husband their resources and maintain comfortable living standards. Catholic intellectuals were dismayed. Paul Johnson likened papal intervention on birth control to the 'disastrous episode' of the church's quarrel with Galileo when 'moral principles' had been applied to purely 'mechanical' matters. Auberon Waugh was also disturbed.[20] Catholic MPs sidestepped the issue by abstaining from the Commons vote on the 1967 Family Planning Act.[21] Neutrality became harder once the authorities were perceived as intruding into relations between parents and children. During the 1970s sexual education courses were introduced into schools which, unavoidably, included moral as well as clinical elements. Catholics had always considered education as vital for the preservation of their faith; in 2002 just under a third of the thirty-six public schools with denominational links were Catholic. Parents unable to afford fees or who lived in areas where there were no Catholic schools were alarmed about their children becoming exposed to a pragmatic sexual morality which overrode the tenets of their faith.[22] The same problem later troubled middle-class Muslim parents, who saw the solution in the form of Islamic schools with their own moral curriculum.

Pressure groups appeared both to express Catholic objections to the new moral climate and to reverse the laws which were shaping it. Most persistent was the Society for the Protection of the Unborn Child, founded in 1967 in opposition to the abortion laws. It belonged to the middle-class civic tradition of reasoned protest through public meetings, pamphlets, lobbying and fielding candidates at general elections. The society held mass rallies in London in 1974 and 1975, the last of which faced barracking by anarchists, homosexuals and lesbians. The latter two were beneficiaries of new legislation and were bitterly resentful of accusations that their sexuality was unnatural and intrinsically sinful. Anti-permissive lobbies regarded gays and lesbians as part of a sinister 'sexual left' whose long-term ambition was the destruction of the family.[23]

Significantly, no alliance developed between middle-class Christian pressure groups and the political right, as occurred in the United States during the 1990s. The Victorian axis between nonconformity and Liberalism was long dead and the Tory/Anglican rapport was in terminal decay by the 1970s. Even if they had wished to, the mainstream Protestant churches would have found it hard to resist the new morality. In 1970 a poll in Cheshire found that 60 per cent were in favour of contraceptive advice for everyone and only 25 per cent wanted it confined to married couples. A national poll two years later revealed that nearly two-thirds were happy for free birth control advice to be available to all men and women and a slightly smaller proportion welcomed sex education programmes.[24]

Anglican bishops stuck to the classic liberal case that individuals should be trusted to make up their own minds rather than submit to edicts from the pulpit. But could this principle be extended to the young? The bishops certainly thought so, as the spiralling numbers of teenage pregnancies suggested. By the late 1970s, anxieties about the promiscuity of youth were complemented by the fear that the agencies of the state were usurping the traditional role of parents as moral mentors to their offspring. One salient example of this encroachment was the 1979 decision by the Department of Health and Social Security to permit doctors to prescribe contraceptives to girls of sixteen and under without parental knowledge, if it was clinically imperative. Only by such means could the rise in teenage pregnancies be halted.[25]

Mrs Victoria Gillick resisted this trespass on the rights of parents. Funded by Legal Aid, she initiated an action against her local health authority after it had refused to assure her that its staff would never give contraceptive advice to her daughter. Mrs Gillick (born 1948) was a devout, middle-class Catholic housewife and the eventual mother of ten children. She admired Josephine Butler, who had campaigned against the Contagious Diseases Act in the 1870s.[26] Then, the law had been an accessory to wrongdoing, and Mrs Gillick believed that it was so again; handing out contraceptives to underage girls or advising them to seek abortions was an endorsement of crime and, by her canon, of sinfulness. Her action trundled upwards through the courts with some success until the House of Lords dismissed it in the summer of 1986.

The case raised moral issues dear to the middle classes. There was the primacy of individual conscience, as represented by Mrs Gillick. Against this was another strand of middle-class thinking which accepted that society had to pursue the greater good, even if that involved connivance with mischief. If, as Mrs Gillick believed, artificial birth control and abortion were sinful, was this not balanced by a greater social benefit, the reduction of unwanted pregnancies and the numbers of often very young single mothers who were ill provided to bring up their offspring? The state had now assumed many of the responsibilities once collectively shouldered by the middle classes. It was the heir of the old paternalism and had inherited its dilemmas. How far could agencies of the government go to protect individuals from their own waywardness or lack of foresight?

Many of the recipients of contraceptive advice were from the poorest sections of society. A general practitioner in a rural area told me that he prescribed the pill to a fifteen-year-old girl because he knew her to be incapable of judgment in sexual matters and suspected that there was incest in her family. 'We have to rely on doctors to act responsibly,' argued Mr Justice Woolf during an early hearing of the Gillick case, a presumption which lay at the heart of the middle-class concept of a profession.[27] Interestingly, the judgment of the clergyman in moral matters had been superseded by the physician's.

Professional organisations defended their members' integrity. The British Medical Association and the Royal College of Nursing opposed Mrs Gillick on the ground that she was intruding her private convictions into purely clinical concerns. As for her beliefs, they were antiquated. The Children's Legal Centre spoke for modern, middle-class enlightenment. 'The Victorian concept of absolute parental authority and control has been replaced by a new concept of partnership between parents and children.'[28] Other groups arrayed against Mrs Gillick included the London 'Mothers United against Mrs Gillick', professional women who believed that she was trying to reverse the process of female emancipation.[29] Inevitably, given her Catholicism, Mrs Gillick attracted the venom of feminist organisations and anyone else who considered papal injunctions on sexuality to be authoritarian and obscurantist.

Mrs Gillick's challenge to pragmatic, secular morality failed. Soon after the final verdict, she suffered a stroke of bad luck when a low Sunday tabloid published a photograph of one of her daughters sunbathing topless on a Mediterranean beach, a common enough pleasure for young girls. Nevertheless, her campaign had served as a warning shot, and the Conservative government noted it. The 1988 Local Authority Act included a loosely worded ban on lessons which 'unintentionally' or otherwise promoted homosexuality in schools. There have been no prosecutions under 'Clause 28', although it may have discountenanced teachers attempting to explain the king's passions in Marlowe's *Edward II*. Homosexual and lesbian lobbies were incensed by what they saw as a calculated slur and campaigned to have the clause revoked. The Scottish Parliament was sympathetic, but found itself under pressure from Catholic clergy and organisations which detest homosexuality.

By contrast, the Protestant churches have shown no collective will to resist either sexual permissivness or the state's accession to moral overlordship in such matters. Rather, they chose to re-evaluate Biblical doctrines which defined the nature of sin, gender and homosexuality. One unlooked-for consequence was that the Church of England, having admitted women priests in 1994, found itself under pressure to ordain and promote openly homosexual men. By 2003, a schism was opening, with the Evangelical wing of the church trenchantly opposed to a concession that would fly in the face of Old Testament and Pauline strictures.

By now middle-class attitudes to Christianity were ambivalent and sometimes contrary. Convictions may have weakened, but the force of social convention remained strong. Large numbers of the middle class still have their children baptised, hold their weddings in church and expect a clergyman to preside over their funerals. Those who rarely if ever attend a normal service flock to their church for Christmas services, specially when carols are sung, and at Easter. Millions listen to the annual Christmas Eve service broadcast from King's College, Cambridge, a comparatively modern but highly popular part of the season's celebrations.

Sunday has ceased to be the Sabbath. It has become part of the weekend, two days reserved for family relaxation and entertainment. The Fourth Commandment revered by the Victorians has been forgotten; a 1994 poll of eighteen- to thirty-five-year-olds revealed that only 3 per cent had even heard of it. This was inevitable since the laws which had enforced Sabbath observance had been successively repealed or amended over the previous sixty years by governments which no longer feared Christian lobbies. The 1932 Sunday Entertainments Act devolved the decision as to what was and what was not permitted to local authorities, and forty years later the law allowed all cinemas and theatres to open on a Sunday. During the next twenty years, prohibitions against Sunday trading and professional sports fixtures were removed. Save for people living close to football stadiums and Free Kirk congregations in the Western Isles, there were few objectors, although a strong feeling persists that Sunday should keep its character, even if this is as a day of recreation rather than of rest and worship.[30]

In most cities and towns, Sunday shoppers will find stores devoted to New Age literature and a range of products from Tarot cards to magical crystals. A substantial number of customers are middle-class and under fifty, and the wares on offer reflect the nature of the New Age movement which caught the imagination of the young in the late 1960s. By 1975, a fifth of the population claimed to be in some sort of pursuit of self-knowledge and realisation.[31] Journeys of self-discovery took many forms, many of which involved departing from familiar Judaeo-Christian traditions and investigating those of Eastern faiths. There was a common acceptance of God as a cosmic spirit who was latent within everyone and of individual perfectibility. New Age thinking tended to reject Enlightenment rationality and its confidence in science and its methodology. Instead, New Agers believed in the intuitive and spiritually elevating. Conventional medicine was dismissed in favour of treatments based upon notions of the quintessential wholeness of the patient's personality.

New Age reactions to modern medicine were an extension of that wider middle-class disillusion with progress and science which pervaded the contemporary environmental movement. Whatever their clinical value, the paraphernalia of holistic treatment, homeopathy and herbal nostrums were a rejection of modern scientific enquiry and methods. Implicit in their use was an admission of a supernatural world which lay beyond rational scientific or intellectual analysis. As one New Age votary explained: 'You cannot, unless highly gifted, explain to one outside a way of life how it *feels*.'[32] Intellectual rigour took second place to sensory perception.

The diversity of New Age obsessions and experiences was vividly illustrated when its middle-class followers advertised for soulmates. In 1978 a male research interviewer in his mid-twenties declared an interest in 'sociology, astrology, economics, transcendental meditation, whole foods' and motor bikes. A 'daring and compassionate' ex-public schoolboy listed Tolstoy, animals, music, Zola, plants and Konrad Lorenz as his interests. Prehistoric monuments, ancient cultures, comparative religion, art and writing fascinated a thirty-eight-year-old vegetarian woman.[33] Others found self- and cosmic revelation through psychedelic music and hallucinogenic drugs, or a combination of the two.

Underlying these eclectic passions were some common assumptions. The quest for interior awareness and peace could be undertaken only if the body was healthy, which was achieved through vegetarianism, consuming natural foodstuffs, exercise and purging one's system of the alleged 'poisons' found in commercial products. There was also an urge to trawl through past systems of belief to recover truths lost to the modern age. Its future rehabilitation would require humans to restore an imagined lost harmony with the natural world. This involved an emancipation of animals from what was considered unnatural and wicked exploitation; the animal rights movement was a by-product of New Age theories.

It is too early to assess the long-term consequences of the New Age movement for the middle classes. By emphasising the primacy of the senses, it had repudiated the educated middle class's faith in the application of reason as the answer to all human problems. New Agers also spurned materialism and in some cases exiled themselves from consumer society through rural self-sufficiency. An attempt to do so by a middle-class couple living in the suburbs was the subject of the television comedy series *The Good Life* which was immensely popular during the 1970s and 1980s.

In its infancy, New Ageism had been fiercely anti-capitalist, but it soon found itself in the market place. Corporations hired gurus and therapists who purveyed an updated form of Pelmanism to inspire executives and managers to release their hidden potential and work in concert as part of a team. In 1990 the University of Lancaster's Centre for the Study of Management Learning held a training course entitled 'Joining Forces: Working with Spirituality in Organisations'. A hundred and fifty attended and discovered among other things the wonders of 'Connecting with your Genes' and 'The I Ching: understanding and using its wisdom and magic'.[34] One is reminded of those pious Victorian factory owners who held services for their operatives.

What makes this exercise fascinating is its close resemblance to congregational worship. Although much of New Age thinking revolves around the self, New Age events are gregarious and often require participation in communal rituals. To this extent, they are similar to conventional religious formulae which fulfil those basic human needs: companionship and bonds of shared beliefs and objectives. Meditation and yoga sessions have this in common with, say, evensong or masonic rites, and groups pursuing common sensory experiences are not unlike those seventeenth-century Christian sectaries whose dancing and nudity so outraged the orthodox.

Since the 1990s it has been predicted that the 'holistic milieu' of the New Age may supplant conventional Christian worship by the mid-twenty-first century. Middle-class spirituality is alive and healthy, but less and less focused on the preparation for an afterlife. Instead, devotees of the New Age are predominantly concerned with the achievement of personal perfection in this world. This process takes for granted the uniqueness of each individual, which may help explain the speed with which the New Age movement has gained converts. It has flourished in a world under increasing, inescapable and often formidable pressure from the agencies of free-market capitalism which seek to advance mass consumption and taste. Consumers are treated as submissive, vain and gullible – recipients of what the educated middle classes commonly dismiss as trash, all of it modern and largely orginating (like so much popular entertainment) in America.

This being so, it is possible to interpret the New Ageism and the closely related environmental movement as a middle-class counter-offensive. In essence, it is a refusal by individuals to be cajoled by the conjuror's patter of the advertising and public relations industries and a rejection of their message that happiness is something which can be purchased. A middle-class revolution may be under way, but it still has far to go. At the beginning of the twenty-first century shopping is commonly recognised as a 'therapy' which can engender a sense of inner well-being in the same way as witnessing the sunrise from within a stone circle on Midsummer's Day.

7

Usefulness and Success: Education

Tom Barber left Eton in 1921 after making a name for himself as a star rugby player and entered the coal business. He was killed in a car crash in 1929. He was remembered as 'a man of fine physique and great vigour: he had many friends, for he was simple, loyal and kindly . . . his direct personality seemed to promise a life full of unselfish usefulness and success'.[1]

Here was ample proof that Arnoldian ideals were as strong as ever. The model public schoolboy was a figure who commanded respect and admiration throughout the middle classes and beyond. John Osborne's father, a down-at-heel commercial artist born in 1900, believed that the public schools 'had perfected a tried and tested way of turning out the very best type of man, who had learned to rough it, take it, not complain, take his medicine, be truthful and not put on airs when all around were not as good as you'.[2] The public schools were a mirror of what was best in the national character. 'Foreign countries were jealous of the wonderful feeling existing among all English public schoolboys,' the Duke of Connaught declared at Cheltenham's speech day in 1925. This spirit was a compound of 'doing what was right, what was honourable, and what was plucky and generous'.[3] In 1938 pupils at Canford heard Lord Cranborne praise the prefectorial system as perfect training for the exercise of judgment and authority. It complemented the team spirit, which was a much needed antidote to the 'herd spirit' now so prevalent.[4] If the public schools stayed true to their traditions, the nation and Empire would pass into the safe hands of new generations of upper-middle-class young men with honour and integrity.

They were admirably fitted to take command of the nation's industry. In the late 1920s ICI's ideal potential manager was an Oxford or Cambridge First or Second who had gained a blue in either rugger, soccer or cricket and had been president of his college junior common room. Such a man 'is not afraid of "losing his dignity" because he would bring his own dignity to whatever work he finds himself put to do, and is one of whom men inquire when he first appears in any gathering "who is that man?"'. The Cambridge University Appointments Board's version of this paragon portrayed him as a 'natural leader' whose sheer force of character would quash 'discontent' among the 'clerical staff who may see themselves super-seded'.[5]

His superiority and soundness were proclaimed by his distinctive bearing and presence. It was reproduced in countless contemporary advertisements where it symbolised the quintessence of sexually attractive manliness. The 'natural leader' is tall, athletic in frame, firm-jawed, with well-trimmed hair and often a clipped moustache, and his clothes are well cut and never flashy. His speech and accent convey natural authority and he smokes a straight-stemmed pipe which completes the impression of self-confidence and determination. Lesser men envy and admire him and women (of the right sort) adore him; many would have recognised him from the line drawings which illus-trated romantic fiction. John Buchan and Dornford Yates chose his type for their heroes. He appeared on the cinema screen in the form of Robert Donat or the young Michael Redgrave.

After 1945 this stereotype of the public school and varsity man went into what turned out to be a permanent eclipse. He represented a system and assumptions about natural authority and hierarchy which had been discredited along with much else from the inter-war years. His time had passed and within a generation his stiff upper lip would be derided. Discordant voices were in the ascendant and the public schools and Oxford and Cambridge were blamed for perpetuating social fragmentation and imposing the values of a narrow section of the middle classes on the rest of society. They were citadels of outmoded ideas and, above all, privilege.

So too were the grammar schools, which were eventually all but overwhelmed by an ideological assault along the same lines, despite having been opened to all children of ability by the 1944 Education Act. Two years after it had been passed, Dr Eric James, high master of Manchester Grammar School, defended schools like his own as invaluable to the country because they exposed the best minds to rigorous training. Academic fine tuning of the few ran against the grain in the age of the 'common man', claimed a training college principal, who wanted to preserve the 'togetherness' of the state primary schools. Older pupils needed to absorb 'social awareness, social knowledge and social service' rather than exercise their intellects.[6] Little was mentioned about leadership, although the armed forces still preferred public school and grammar school boys as national service officers.[7]

Possibly nothing has generated so much tetchy wrangling as the debate over whether state education should serve to create a meritocratic or an egalitarian society. On the one hand, there was the traditional middle-class view of free education as a device to open minds and propel the talented poor upwards to take their natural place in a society which flourished because ability was rewarded. On the other was the novel, essentially political concept of education as a battering ram which would knock down social barriers and clear the way for the complete equality which the left believed was the just reward for wartime sacrifice. This was the case advanced by middle-class Labour politicians such as Shirley Williams (Minister of Education from 1967 to 1969) and the trade unions. Once the policy of supplanting grammar with comprehensive schools was under way, the Conservatives acquiesced. By 1996 around 86 per cent of all secondary school pupils attended comprehensives. Champions of selection were accused of preserving social segregation since more middle- than working-class children passed the Eleven Plus.

Disagreements over the ultimate purpose of education coincided with a revival of older contentions about the nature of what should be taught. Should education exist and enjoy public funding for its own sake, or should it be deliberately tailored to fit utilitarian, economic needs? The spirit of Newman pervaded Oxford well into the century, but was criticised by the descendants of Gradgrind who wanted value for money. In 1934 an Oxford undergraduate noticed that few tutors knew anything of the world of business and so did not guide their pupils towards it. Vocational training was unthinkable since Oxford existed to produce graduates distinguished by their 'superior capacity for acquiring and using knowledge, not ready-made technical equipment.' This was appreciated by business, which saw Oxford and Cambridge as reservoirs of men of character rather than of specific expertise.[8] Attitudes changed radically in the wake of post-war anxieties about the efficiency of British industry. In 1951 the National Coal Board persuaded Leeds University to run courses in management training for graduates.[9]

Similar, essentially practical courses multiplied during the next fifty years. As universities came under financial pressure in the 1980s and 1990s, they were compelled to provide more to satisfy commercial sponsors and students who saw vocational degrees as visas for future jobs. 'Market-orientated' and 'demand-led' courses disregarded Newman's vision of a university and it had no place in the government's scheme of things. The left was host to reservations about institutions which smacked of privilege, and both right and left were dismissive of arcane subjects. 'I do not mind there being some mediaevalists around for ornamental purposes, but there is no reason for the state to pay them,' proclaimed the Education Secretary Charles Clarke in 2003. An alumnus of a minor public school and Cambridge, where he read Mathematics and Economics, his mindset was that of Gradgrind marinated in old-fashioned philistinism. Yet Clarke spoke for many within the Labour and Conservative parties who believed that education was a preparation for the serious business of work and nothing else.

Employers were less dogmatic. Many still treat degrees as assays of intellectual stamina and a capacity to reason from evidence – the qualities cultivated by the study of subjects such as Classics and History, which were preferred by a least one major global bank recruiting in Oxford in 2003.[10] At a lower level, modern employers periodically express their frustration at the dismal levels of literacy and numeracy among school leavers. This proven deterioration in standards of literacy and numeracy has been a source of middle-class anxiety and sometimes anger for at least fifty years. In 1951 Professor Colin Brogan cited copies of *Beano* and *Rainbow* lying around in NAAFI canteens as evidence of declining working-class literacy. The national service squaddies were the victims of novel educational theories which abjured compulsion and left children to discover reading when the mood took them.[11]

The progressive wing of the middle class approved; a survey of local authority primary schools in London in 1969 described one in Hampstead as 'unstructured', uncompetitive and, therefore, suitable to the neighbourhood.[12] What pleased Hampstead frightened much of the rest of the middle class, who feared that their children would only flourish under pressure from teachers, which of course augmented that applied at home.

For the mass of the middle classes, education was still all about getting on in the world. Parental ambition was as strong in the twentieth century as it had been in the nineteenth, if not stronger. The achievements of their children provide the middle classes with pride and a constant source of self-congratulation. Towards the end of the century it became the fashion each Christmas for middle-class families to send out circular letters which chronicle their members' activities during the previous year. These jaunty Pooteresque narratives gave prominence to degrees obtained, exams passed, musical grades accomplished, parts played in school plays, charity races run, triumphs on the playing field, mountains ascended and faraway places visited by sons and daughters.

Family aspirations have set parents against teachers who had swallowed theories which allowed children to develop at their own pace and find their own level, often with the minimum of supervision and correction. When middle-class parents talk about a 'good' school, they mean one in which their children learn in a happy but orderly environment, surrounded by modern equipment and with a competitive atmosphere in which the brightest are encouraged to surge ahead. To an extent, the grammar schools possessed these virtues and satisfied middle-class parents. Passing the Eleven Plus guaranteed that an able and hard-working boy or girl would secure the School Certificate and, later, passes at Ordinary and Advanced Level which were essential for further education or white-collar employment.

Discipline was strict in all state schools and, in many, pupils were coaxed into using the 'King's English'. In 1938 a prominent speech therapist urged all teachers to use 'correct' English in the classroom and stamp out dialect ('None of your Wiltshire here') and cinema-derived Americanisms such as 'Okay'. A thick accent could not offset a sheaf of certificates at a job interview, the expert concluded, and he was right.[13] In 1944 another writer on this subject deplored the lack of school-leaving tests in spoken English, but suggested that 'grammar school English' was unsuitable for the new secondary modern schools.[14] How one spoke was still a measure of education and background, which was why lower-middle-class parents sent young children to private elocution classes, often run by former actors or actresses. An article of 1946 advising parents on this sort of tuition mentioned that some were uneasy about their children learning to speak 'above their station'.[15] Given the exaggerated, cut-glass accents common on the stage at this time, this anxiety was understandable.

Audibility and clear vowels no doubt helped at the interviews which successful Eleven Plus candidates were given at their future schools. On the whole, the exam favoured the middle classes: they could pay for extra tuition and encourage their children with rewards, often new bicycles. They could also afford the uniforms, satchels, dictionaries, geometry sets and games kits which the grammar school boy and girl required. Equipped for their new existence, pupils found themselves in a world modelled on that of the public school. Instruction was formal and involved rote learning, and classes were streamed according to ability. The aim was to produce what, in 1947, the Parliamentary Secretary to the Minister of Education called 'experts with the characteristics of amateurs' (that is, not smart alecks) who had been exposed to that 'sunshine for the spirit', the arts.[16] The grammar school regime and hierarchy imitated the public schools. There were houses, prefects (sometimes with tasselled caps), colours, cross-country runs and team games. New boys endured initiations with varying degrees of humiliation, kind and unkind nicknames were given, weak teachers were ragged, miscreants suffered formal and informal corporal punishment and there was bullying.

Geography as well as intelligence dictated who passed the Eleven Plus. Grammar schools were randomly scattered about the country, and in areas where they were plentiful more candidates passed the exam. A survey of 1963 revealed that grammar schools were heavily concentrated in London, Middlesex and Wales, where the Eleven Plus pass rate was between 26 and 40 per cent. It was 32 per cent in Wallasey and only 13 in Burton-on-Trent.[17] The uneven spread of grammar schools made it impossible for them to have fulfilled R. A. Butler's dream that they would eventually eliminate Disraeli's 'two nations'; and, as their critics constantly claimed, the odds in the Eleven Plus were balanced in favour of the child of ambitious middle-class parents.[18] The numbers attending grammar schools rose from 492,100 in 1947 to 599,000 in 1958, and those at secondary moderns from 758,000 to 1.4 million, figures which in part reflect the immediate post-war baby boom.[19]

Even though it was unevenly applied, the principle of equal opportunity did break the near monopoly of public schoolmen in the professions, the higher civil service, senior management and the higher ranks of the armed services. In 1989 some 40 per cent of the country's business leaders had been educated at grammar schools and 24 per cent privately.[20] For many, a grammar school education was a chance to make modest moves up the social ladder. A social analyst, writing in 1968, described the progress of one working-class boy who had moved upwards after passing the Eleven Plus. After leaving school at fifteen with the requisite certificates, he joined an office equipment company and became a travelling salesman. Married at twenty-seven, he and his wife had a suburban home with typical lower-middle-class adornments. There was 'a pink plastic pelican on the front lawn' and, indoors, 'tasteless modern bric à brac'. He had recently joined the local branch of the Conservative Party and his children were in private nursery schools, which suggests ambitions for their future.[21]

The aside on décor was a salutary reminder that the snobbery of taste was still entrenched when other forms were being voiced in whispers or denounced. Selective schools preserved-social barriers, or so their champions claimed. The left-inclining middle classes agreed in theory, but had reservations about non-selective, comprehensive schools, at least when it came to the schooling of their own children. Inevitably, they would find themselves in classrooms alongside pupils with unambitious parents, or even, in some inner urban areas, who were hostile to the notion of education. There was unease too about unstreamed classes, which became the vogue in the 1970s and were blamed for shackling the brightest pupil to the pace of the dullest. Furthermore, and the middle classes were sometimes ashamed to admit this, many preferred their offspring to mix with their own kind.

In theory, these problems were alleviated by the 1980 Education Act, which allowed parental choice of local authority schools wherever it was possible, which in practice meant in the more densely populated urban areas. This law created moral quandaries for middle-class parents who now had to analyse the social geography of the catchment areas for schools and their individual philosophies. In 1985 the journalist Mary Kenny reflected wider misgivings when she complained of local authority schools 'where they have a gay rights counsellor for under-sevens and a multi-ethnic approach to faith and where the teachers must equate Fiji Animism with a Mozart Mass'.[22] Well-meaning but often crass attempts to engender racial and religious inclusiveness were being made by Labour councils and became known as 'political correctness'.

The new angst about education was echoed by Posy Simmons in one of her brilliant cartoons of metropolitan middle-class mores. In one, a mother who has just withdrawn her daughter from a local comprehensive and sent her to a private school in the country haltingly justifies her action to her leftish friend Wendy.

. . . Knew you'd be shocked . . . knew'd you think us traitors . . . but do try to understand . . . we were very worried about her at Fletcher. That school is so enormous, honestly, Wendy, she seemed overwhelmed . . . never quite fitted in . . . And those boys there . . . some of them charming . . . but Tara's bright . . . really she's the sort to flourish – away from that sort of thing . . . And I was desperately worried about her English . . . Not her accent! . . . although they did all have rather ghastly voices . . . no, I mean her native language. You do agree that's important, don't you, Wendy? And . . . you know me, I'm all for cultural mix . . . but at Fletcher . . . there did seem to be rather more, you know, ethnic children than one might . . . er . . .[23]

Put bluntly, there were too many working-class and coloured children, features of state schools which disturbed middle-class parents, although, like this mother, they were ashamed to say so directly. Even more disconcerting was the gradual disappearance of old forms of coercive discipline within state schools, particularly corporal punishment, and the failure to replace it with a system that deterred the rebellious and bloody-minded. From the 1980s onwards, the press regularly reported instances of schools tottering on the verge of anarchy with the intimidation of pupils and staff, assaults, drug dealing, vandalism and the disruption of lessons. The culprits were largely from the 'underclass', a recent name for the old phenomenon, that most impoverished and alienated section of the working class which lived on or within the margins of criminality. Its members often came from families in which unemployment was hereditary. A handful of pupils from this background could wreck lessons and hinder the progress of the majority. This problem has remained intractable. It has recently been proposed that unruly pupils should be transferred to flourishing comprehensives where, it was conjectured, the example of the co-operative would somehow implant a love of learning and trigger ambition. Many middle-class parents were unconvinced.

The social composition of a comprehensive in large part dictated its tone. In 1990 boys at the successful Brixton comprehensive school, which had once been the grammar school attended by John Major, frankly described themselves as middle class. One added that his parents were 'enlightened middle class', which indicates a political commitment to state schooling.[24] All admitted that in various ways they were unlike public schoolboys of their own age, and some felt inklings of inferiority.

By this date, parents choosing schools were helped by guidebooks whose judgments were later augmented by league tables that assessed the performance of state and private schools on the basis of results in public examinations. Good schools could be identified, and parents could either take steps to buy a house within the catchment area of one which appealed to them, or else attempt to secure a place through legerdemain. The 1989 *Good Schools Guide* recommended intensive lobbying of the head teacher, governors and the local authority and even suborning a sympathetic doctor to insist that a child's health would be impaired if it was not admitted to an over-subscribed school.[25]

Estate agents puffed properties within the catchment zones of first-rate schools and house prices rose accordingly. Anglican and Catholic primary schools were popular for their discipline and academic aspirations, and so prospective middle-class parents attached themselves to local churches to improve their children's chance of admission. A guide to long-distance commuting published by the *Sunday Telegraph* in conjunction with the railway companies in 2004 gave prominence to local schools in those areas where the Home Counties merged with the shires. Hertfordshire was 'stuffed with good schools', there were 'high-flying comprehensives' in Cambridgeshire and that magnet for the middle classes the Cotswolds had plenty of excellent grammar schools and comprehensives. The City executive could steel himself to buy an expensive season ticket and travel on wildly erratic train services in the knowledge that his children were at reliable schools. Or else he could strain the family budget and invest in a public school education.

Public schools were automatically listed in the *Sunday Telegraph* guides. They were profiting enormously from the endless period of flux through which state education was so painfully passing and from the exasperation of middle-class parents. Competition from the grammar schools had become acute immediately after the 1944 Education Act; between 1947 and 1965 the proportion of pupils at private schools had dropped sharply.[26] This economic threat receded in the next fifteen years and the market expanded as more and more middle-class parents abandoned comprehensives. By 2005, roughly 6 per cent of the nation's 9.9 million schoolchildren were being privately educated. They attended schools which dominated the summit of the new league tables: in 1996 a fifth of the top thousand schools graded on A Level results were fee-paying.[27]

Paying for schooling was a good investment and, next to house purchase, the largest ever undertaken by most middle-class families. The cost of private education soared. In 1947 charges for boarding schools ranged between £120 and £174 (Harrow), with day schools charging a third to a half of these figures. During the 1950s fees averaged about £400 (the cost of a family saloon) and they doubled over the next twenty years. They doubled again during the next decade so that in 1990 boarding schools were charging between £1,700 and £3,500 a year, and day schools between £700 and £2,500. The ascent continued, and by 2004 boarding schools were charging up to £20,000 and day schools £8,000. In 2005 a new company, Global Education Management Systems, promised lower fees for its schools. According to its founder, the cheapest day school (£5,000 a year) was 'for parents who want their children to go to good universities' and were uninterested in such extras as golf and squash courts.[28] University entrance was now the focus of middle-class ambitions.

Achieving them was expensive, although school-fee increases had been roughly commensurate with salary rises. Nearly all private schools were happy to go in for camel trading, especially if siblings were involved, and there were other sources of relief. From before the war, parents could finance school through insurance schemes: thirty-four pounds a year paid during the first twelve years of a child's life could finance five years of private schooling at a hundred a year.[29] After the Labour government withdrew state funds from direct grant grammar schools in 1979, the Conservatives redressed the balance by offering assistance for places at fee-paying boarding and day schools two years later. In 1996 this scheme was costing £115 million a year and over two-thirds of the recipients were from middle-class families.[30] Other alternatives were help from grandparents and, of course, scrimping and forgoing such luxuries as overseas holidays. Perhaps the commonest source of the extra cash was the wife's income. One of the side effects of the entry into the labour market of a growing number of graduate and vocationally trained women in the 1970s and 1980s was to make it possible for more middle-class families to afford fees that could not have been paid from a husband's salary alone.

With parents stretching their budgets to pay their bills, public schools had to justify themselves as never before in order to survive in a highly competitive market. Before, many had ambled along contentedly and complacently. At middle-ranking Oakham (£145 a year) in the mid-1940s, little appeared to have changed for fifty years. It took in day boys, mostly farmers' sons who were known as 'oiks' to the boarders (the term usually defined all non-public schoolboys), and the regime was Spartan, even by the standards of post-war austerity. The food was mediocre, the accommodation chilly and squalid, prefects governed, fags skivvied, and there was casual violence, bullying and 'homosexual intrigues'. Games mania was endemic, but the headmaster was more imaginative than most and fostered such hobbies as stamp collecting, archaeology, making model aircraft and puppetry. As in other similar schools, most boys left at sixteen with their certificates. National service followed at eighteen and meant commissions for Oakham old boys – 'you felt you were letting the side down' if you were not made an officer.[31]

This casual ambience was doomed. However much older staff and past generations of old boys disliked the concept, the public schools had to mirror changes in society, as Thomas Arnold had appreciated. If the public schools were to retain their middle-class patrons, they had to reflect the fiercely competitive spirit which was emerging. An Eton boy looking back over the 1960s concluded that the times had changed radically and that college leavers would 'have to struggle for a living' like everyone else. Perhaps ingenuously, he believed that 'breezy self-confidence' and relations in the boardroom were no longer the foundation of a successful city career.[32] Examination results were now what counted and procuring employment required a methodical approach. Like every other school, Eton set up the apparatus of a careers service.

It would have been impossible for public schools to have quarantined themselves from the pervasive youth culture which gained ground in the 1960s. It challenged just about everything the public schools had traditionally cherished by encouraging individual self-expression, hedonism and a cheeky disregard for authority. Mr Chips's counterparts faced classrooms full of long-haired, unkempt and insouciant adolescents whose heroes were the Rolling Stones and not the titans of the first XV. Skirmishes between cultures occurred, but on the whole the public schools coped well. A generation of younger and more flexible headmasters (born in the 1930s and 1940s) and staff reacted sympathetically to demands for reform, and there was a gradual liberalisation.[33]

A saner attitude to games crept in, prefects relinquished some of their powers (often gladly) and everyone relaxed, in so far as that was possible in schools where minds were now so concentrated on exams. Dances were held ('home' and 'away' matches with equivalent local girls' schools), even pop concerts, and bars were installed for sixth formers. Monasticism was abandoned by many boys' schools, which admitted girls, an innovation made partly in recognition of social change and partly to stimulate cash flow. Thomas Arnold would have approved: the public schools were continuing to accommodate themselves to the needs and ethos of the upper-middle class. Its members were now less concerned with placing sons in nurseries for Christian gentlemen and, instead, wanted to increase the odds on their sons (and daughters) securing the university place which was now the springboard for advancement in most prestigious and well-paid careers.

Every modern school magazine contains a list of university places secured by alumni alongside a catalogue of examination passes. Each summer, local newspapers print photographs of recent graduates from the area. Education is now all about an individual obtaining the means to earn his or her living. None the less, there are still many parents who congratualte schools for what they have accomplished for their child's character and self-confidence. Such metamorphoses are tremendously important but are sadly overshadowed by quantifiable results, much to the distress of teachers. The well-rounded 'whole man' once so prized by the middle classes (and the public and grammar schools) has been displaced.

A narrowly utilitarian spirit permeates all levels of education. When university teachers digress or raise some recondite but stimulating point, they are grumpily interrupted by students who ask whether the discussion will prove of value in their final exams. Intellectual adventurousness is treated as a luxury, which is understandable since nearly every student or his family is directly paying for his course. In 1997 graduates left university with an average debt of £5,800; in 2004 it stood at £11,800.[34]

These figures are one result of three coincidental revolutions in the world of higher education. It has expanded dramatically since 1960. In 1957–8 there were 27,700 university students. Thirty years later 243,000 were attending full-time higher education courses and 887,000 in 1996–7. The imperative for this growth has been economic. It was vital to create a highly qualified workforce for the various service industries that were superseding manufacturing. This requirement became even more urgent towards the close of the century as companies transferred unskilled jobs to overseas factories and agencies. There was less and less work for those with minimal qualifications or none at all. At the same time, all the professions were preferring graduates. According to a 2005 careers guide accountants, estate agents, film and television staff, and human resources and personnel departments expect new recruits to have degrees.[35]

Professionalisation has proliferated in business, public administration and the rapidly expanding leisure and entertainment industries. This trend is mirrored in university prospectuses which are crammed with courses designed to prepare the student for a specific job. Full-time study is replacing apprenticeships or training as you work. Sometime office boys who ascend to the boardroom or executive suite are becoming a rare species. The University of Stafford (one of the universities created by the 1992 policy to upgrade and merge former polytechnics and teacher training colleges) is typical. Degree courses offered for the academic year 2005–6 include Psychology and Sport, Environment Education and Outdoor Leadership, Exercise and Health, Midwifery and Technology for Robotics, Film Production, Sport and Cyberspace. Traditional subjects are recommended for their marketable value: the philosophy graduate will have learned 'analytical and communication' skills.

Competition in the graduate hiring fair is stiff, and so, in the hope of making themselves more attractive to employers, many graduates undertake additional degrees or diploma courses. It worked for one psychology graduate from Glasgow who invested £6,500 in taking a year's master's degree in public relations. 'It was a bit of a Mickey Mouse course, but I will always put it on my CV because it is recognised in the industry and it opened doors for me.'[36]

Opening doors has become very expensive. The post-1945 settlement had aimed to raise the number of graduates through generous allowances from public funds: university tuition fees were paid by local authorities which also provided means-tested grants, favourable to the middle classes. A student whose father had an annual salary of between £750 and £850 was given £90 to maintain himself at a time when his annual costs were calculated at just over £100.[37] The middle classes took advantage of the system and more and more of their children went to universities, colleges and polytechnics. The proportion of middle-class students increased from 36 per cent in the 1950s to 56 in the 1970s.

This middle-class preponderance remains despite the piecemeal reduction of state assistance to students' parents.[38] Mrs Thatcher's student loans and Mr Blair's insistence that they contribute substantially to tuition fees have not deterred the middle classes from encouraging their offspring to go to university. They are being true to their history. From the fifteenth century onwards they had always been willing to channel a large proportion of their resources into their children's education. Never has such expenditure been so vital. Universities now provide what the middle classes have always desired for their offspring: qualifications that propel them into well-paid careers which will sustain their position in the world. The degree is now the counterpart of an apprenticeship to a flourishing merchant or surgeon. It is also a passport to rewards, as the doggerel attached to a 1981 car advert suggested:

> Wanda hada Honda,
> Priscilla hada Porsche,
> Stephanie Lee's got a PH.D
> and drives a Colt of course.[39]

All this has created problems for modern governments chasing the vision of an inclusive society and simultaneously anxious to avoid the perpetuation of an unqualified, unemployable and therefore restless section of society. Every effort is being made to entice working-class youth into higher education and what the Victorians would have called 'usefulness'. Hurdles have been proposed to exclude middle-class entrants from universities on the grounds that they have been well taught in the best schools. Alongside threats of positive discrimination have been attempts to convince the working class to think like the middle classes and regard education at all levels as the guarantee that their children will secure well-paid and relatively secure livelihoods. Politicians lament the prevalence of a 'poverty of aspiration' among staff and pupils in comprehensives in the poorest districts – or, in other words, the absence of that middle-class confidence, initiative and drive which ensures that their children will get the best of whatever is available.

8

Bella Vista: The Suburban Universe

The suburbs are the habitat of preference for a large swathe of the middle classes, who have found that they contain all the elements needed for a contented life. They offer tranquillity, security and, above all, the assurance of living among others of similar tastes and outlook. Privacy can be balanced with neighbourliness, an equipoise represented by the cul de sac. One such cul de sac is the setting for the popular television soap opera of modern suburban life, *Brookside*, which was scrapped in 2003. It was the lineal descendant of the post-war radio serials of middle-class family life in the suburbs, *Mrs Dale's Diary* and *The Huggets*, which, in the mid-1950s, was transformed into the television serial, *The Groves*. All were mirrors of everyday life, sometimes punctuated by unlikely incidents, and a reminder that suburban life was not always as insular and boring as critics alleged.

Suburban architecture was dull. Houses and bungalows were more or less uniform, but this was more than compensated for by the pride of ownership and sense of status they aroused in their owners. They possessed modern homes which were easy to keep clean with airy rooms, gas and electricity, bathrooms and inside lavatories. These features made the suburban house especially attractive to families engaged in the transit from the working to the lower-middle class;

whatever else the semi might have been, it was infinitely more comfortable than the back-street terrace house. 'Healthy drudge-less living' promised an advertisement of 1935 for houses in what was still rural Kent. A smiling housewife looks out from a window on to trees. Her home was full of novel, labour-saving gadgetry, so she was fresh and glamorous when she welcomed her husband on his return from the City. A meal would be ready and perhaps a reviving gin and tonic or whisky. Suburban living offered a livelier sex life.[1]

Closeness to nature was one of the vital ingredients of suburban happiness. But it was nature that had been tamed for human convenience and kept under strict control. Privet hedges were clipped, grass verges trimmed and the trees which lined suburban roads were regularly pollarded. Gardening became a consuming passion of suburban man, transforming him at weekends into a countryman manqué. He mowed his lawns, laid out his rockery, dug ponds, spread compost, pruned, and coaxed growth from flowers and shrubs. He might even turn his plot into something with pretensions of grandeur with mass-produced sundials, birdbaths and statues which suggested the formal garden of a country house.

More commonly and particularly among the lower-middle class, there were flights of whimsy represented by the garishly coloured plaster (later plastic) gnomes which were imported from Germany during the inter-war years. These creations littered lawns and rockeries, some carrying fishing rods and others seated on toadstools, investing the suburban garden with fairytale magic. Real nature in the form of herons who ate the fish in ponds enraged the suburban gardener, as did the legions of pests who consumed his plants and whose elimination was one of his major tasks.

Outsiders envied him and wanted to become part of his world. Towards the end of the Second World War, a survey of young, unmarried servicewomen revealed a common dream of marriage, two or three children, their own home and 'a bit of garden'.[2] Eighty-five per cent of the population selected a suburban house as their ideal home, according to a poll taken in 1968.[3] At the beginning of the twenty-first century, another survey nominated Chorleywood as the setting for a perfect life. It is a quintessential suburb, leafier than most, set on the fringes of the Chilterns and forty minutes from London by tube. This was no surprise; for the past five hundred years the middling sort and their successors had been searching for such Edens. The appearance of suburbia may have changed, but the idea of it as a domestic retreat from city and office remains.

The modern suburb has appalled aesthetes and intellectuals, who have poured a stream of scorn on it and its inhabitants. For one architectural critic 'the jerry-built, pseudo-half-timbered, pseudo-Tudor house' symbolised 'modern ugliness' and was bleak evidence of the failure of 'architectural vision' between the wars.[4] What was galling was that so many of these buildings were designed by builders determined to give people what they wanted, rather than professional architects who had other ideas. Bogus bow windows and mock Elizabethan gables were façades for mediocrity, complacency and the abrasion of the human spirit. The suburbs were 'incubators of apathy and delirium', declared Cyril Connolly.[5] It was left to John Betjeman to plead for the serendipity he discovered in middle- and upper-middle-class Metroland.

Intellectual disdain for suburbia was reflected in fiction. The suburb was a gulag from which the bolder imprisoned souls sometimes broke free. George Orwell's hero, insurance salesman George Bowling, wants to escape from a nagging wife ('Butter is going up, and the gas bill is enormous, and the kids' boots are wearing out and there's another instalment due on the radio') and rows of uniform houses. Distinctiveness is provided by names which, ironically, have become as clichéd as their appearance: 'The Laurels', 'The Myrtles', 'Mon Repos' and 'Belle Vue'.[6]

Such names bestowed a status on those who had chosen them. In Winifred Holtby's *South Riding* (1936), Mr Mitchell, an insurance clerk compelled by unemployment to live in a seaside shack, names it 'Bella Vista' and so 'preserved his sense of still belonging to the middle classes'. Social prestige was attached to 'estates' (sometimes named after their former aristocratic owners who had sold the land to developers) and to the various 'drives', 'avenues' and 'parks' which criss-crossed the suburbs. This was the language of the rural country house and its grounds and it appealed to middle-class snobbery. A

Punch cartoon of 1935 showed a fireman climbing into a suburban bedroom and being reproved by its occupant: 'No, this is not Westbrook Terrace; this is Westbrook *Park* Terrace.'

Reginald Perrin, an executive at 'Sunshine Foods' and hero of David Nobbs's novel *The Death of Reginald Perrin* (1975), walks along 'Coleridge Close', 'Tennyson Avenue' and 'Wordsworth Drive' each morning to catch the Waterloo train. As the names imply, this is a superior suburb and Perrin inhabits a 'neo-Georgian' detached house with a garden planted with rhododendrons and lupins. He decamps and becomes another refugee from suburbia, fakes his suicide and reinvents himself before returning to the world he has spurned. Perrin is a classic comic figure, the discontented suburbanite with dreams of a new, exciting and possibly dangerous existence. Such dreams haunted Tony Hancock of 23 Railway Cuttings, Cheam, whose frus-trated intellectual pretensions were the source of much of the humour of the radio comedy series *Hancock's Half Hour*, which ran during the 1950s and early 1960s. He finally bounded to freedom in the film *The Rebel* (1960) and became an artist in a bohemian quarter of Paris, the antithesis of suburbia. Another fugitive, this time from a stifling, lower-middle-class suburban family in Yorkshire, is Billy Fisher, the hero of Keith Waterhouse's *Billy Liar* (1959), who finds refuge in a secret fantasy world.

Fisher's daydreams were an antidote to the sheer monotony of everyday suburban life. 'I hate living here,' declares Queenie, the wayward daughter, in Noël Coward's *This Happy Breed* (1943), 'in a house like all others, coming home from work on the Tube, washing up, helping mother darn father's socks.' Her quest for excitement ends in misery, for Coward's intention had been to vindicate suburban life and its virtues of dependability and performing one's duties without complaint. Adventure could be found in the suburbs for those with the knack of knowing where to look. It was found in abundance by Richmal Crompton's William and his appropriately named 'Outlaws'. These boys are mischiev-ous suburban guerrillas who, without malice, disrupt and confuse a staid middle-class world of tennis and bridge parties. It exists somewhere on the outer borders of suburbia (there are barns in which the Outlaws can devise their schemes) and is brilliantly depicted by Miss Crompton.

William began to torment his neighbourhood in 1919, the year which saw the start of the speculative housing boom in Southern England and the Midlands. Architectural styles were devised by builders with an instinct for what their customers wanted. There was a taste for a bucolic 'Merrie England' genre which Osbert Lancaster labelled 'Stockbroker Tudor' and harsher critics 'Jerrybethan'. Its prominent features were gables, latticed windows and half timbering. The 'Olde Worlde' theme was elaborated inside with brick fireplaces, mock-Jacobean furniture and, for those who could afford them, four-poster beds complete with testers and drapes, oak settles and refectory tables.

Modern functionalism crept in, slowly, and by the late 1930s a new generation of suburban houses appeared with plain façades, large metal-framed windows and sometimes flat roofs. Inside, the furnishings were Art Deco derivative: brick fireplaces were replaced by ones with shiny tiles with angular patterns. The Art Deco motif of the sunray was very popular, appearing on gates and in the mass-produced, stained-glass panels on front doors. Other favourite designs included galleons for the romantically inclined and owls and peacocks. Whatever the subject, these adornments provided a touch of individuality.

Suburban houses swallowed up the countryside on the outskirts of the larger cities, particularly London, and continued to do so until the Ribbon Development Act of 1935, by which time it was too late. Between 1919 and 1939 some 2.5 million new homes were constructed, most of them semis and bungalows. Their owners were predominantly middle class and they were paid for by mortgages. The outstanding balance on home mortgages rose from £84 million in 1924 to £360 million in 1931.[7] Levels of borrowing fell briefly after the 1930 slump, but soon regained their upward momentum in response to the demand for lower-middle-class housebuyers with incomes of between two and three hundred pounds.[8]

Prudent building societies (not all were) expected a 10 per cent deposit. Mortgage rates hovered around 4 per cent. The buyer of a three-bedroomed house costing £780 on the 'Winchester Park Estate' near Bromley paid just under a pound a week for the next twenty years. Cheaper houses meant smaller payments: the owner of a £690 house in Perivale paid seventeen shillings and eleven pence a week and the owner of a £470 house near West Wickham just over eleven shillings. This property was worth £6,700 in 1967, which was a good return, even allowing for wartime inflation.[9] The war interrupted the housing boom, but it quickly recovered its old momentum. One hundred and thirty thousand privately built houses were completed in 1958, and during the 1970s and 1980s the annual totals swung between 145,000 and 207,000. Mortgage interest rates crept up slowly from around 5 per cent in the 1950s to over 7 per cent in the 1970s and stabilising at between 5 and 6 per cent at the end of the century. Tax relief on mortgages offset the occasional violent fluctuations at times of national economic crisis.

The mortgage was a dependable and fruitful investment. The total amount borrowed rose steadily from £374 million in 1958 to £1.3 billion in 1997. This transfer of capital into housing, accelerated by the sale of council housing to sitting tenants after 1980, was the engine for a social revolution. By 1991 the total of owner-occupiers reached 14.3 million and that of council tenants had fallen to 4.6 million, a number which has continued to fall. If, as some claim, home ownership was a defining feature of middle-class identity, then two-thirds of the nation have become middle class. A suburb of one kind or another has become the home of a majority of the population, a fact which is dramatically clear to anyone looking through the window of an aeroplane approaching any of Britain's larger conurbations.

The purchase of a house on a mortgage simultaneously provided a family with a place to live and a nest egg for the future. In 1977 Sunley Homes was urging hesitant first-time buyers to take the plunge because 'houses are one of the few investments to keep ahead of inflation'.[10] On the whole this was true; in 1996 an average mortgage was costing the borrower just under twenty-nine pounds for every hundred he earned.[11] Market fluctuations intruded an element of risk into house buying; at this time there were a million house-owners whose property had fallen below the value of their original mortgage. Yet the future was bright, and by 2002 house prices were rising by an average of 7 per cent a year.[12]

Never before had the middle classes been so obsessed with the value of property. National and regional oscillations in house prices made headlines, and the traumas of house purchase became the staples of dinner-party conversations. Television companies produced programmes which traced the fortunes of buyers and sellers, and presenters frenziedly transformed interiors and gardens in attempts to entice potential buyers. Once a sitting room had merely been decorated and furnished for the owner's comfort; now external tastes were imposed to make it desirable for a buyer. These programmes will provide a rich source for students of middle-class discernment and dreams.

As modern buyers and sellers endeavouring to step on to or ascend the ladder of the property market understand too well, bricks and mortar can be a source of anxiety, even grief, as well as security. The roots of the trouble were always the same: overstretched budgets, unemployment and the consequent incapacity to repay credit. Mortgage foreclosures rose during periods of recession; in 1991 there were 74,000 and six years later, when the economy was reviving, there were 23,000.

Behind the statistics were human tragedies. In 1935 a judge attached to a suburban county court told a journalist that credit was demoralising the middle class, especially the 'small middle class' who took on debts they could never afford. He was astonished by the courage of men and women living on a 'narrow margin of security' without 'peace of mind'. Their misfortunes were aired in his court. There was an unemployed commercial traveller with a £1,400 mortgage and a maidservant who helped his invalid wife. He was in arrears in payments for his car, which, he argued, was vital for his work.[13] A contemporary *Punch* cartoon depicted a suburban garden with a typical middle-class man in a dressing gown and smoking a pipe who announces to his wife: 'Another sunny weekend! Let's let the encyclopedia bill slide and pay the instalment on the car.'[14]

Late-twentieth-century employment laws, statutory redundancy payments and state-funded unemployment allowances have reduced the financial trauma of losing a job. There has been a considerable relaxation of the bankruptcy laws and the penalties imposed on defaulters. Attitudes towards involvency have changed and to some extent it has ceased to be a source of disgrace and a mark of personal inadequacies. During and immediately after the First World War, middle-class clients entered pawnbrokers 'furtively' because, as one observed, pledging valuables carried a 'stigma of shame'.[15] Similar feelings inhibited the middle classes when it came to seeking assistance from the welfare agencies. In 1949, it was noted that it was hard for middle-class claimants to 'overcome their natural reluctance to detail their misfortunes to any official, however sympathetic'.[16] This shyness had disappeared by the early 1990s when victims of the Lloyd's insurance débâcle demanded some form of state relief to rescue them from bankruptcy.

Sixty years before, the middle class had still viewed insolvency through Victorian eyes. It represented a personal failure and a few took desperate measures to escape its consequences. At the beginning of 1931 a bank cashier and his wife committed suicide because of 'financial difficulties'.[17] Above the report of their deaths was an account of the trial of a commercial traveller, Alfred Rouse of Friern Barnet, who had bludgeoned a vagrant, placed him in his car and then set it alight. Rouse was strapped for cash; he earned twenty pounds a month, of which just over a third went in payments for his car. He had hoped that the corpse in the car would be assumed be his own and so he would be released from the obligations which were overwhelming him. His stratagem failed and he was hanged.

It was significant that a murderer from the middle-class suburbs killed to avoid the repercussions of heavy debts. Suburbia was inextricably linked with traditional middle-class notions of visible personal worth. Old snobberies took on new forms and a fresh lease of life in suburbia, inevitably since so many status-conscious middle-class families were in such close proximity. A cartoon of 1934 captured their temper. An elegantly dressed lady approaches a couple walking along a suburban road and the wife declares: 'Look, Stephen – here comes that odious Mrs Enderby, wearing her new suit at me.'[18]

This lady's pique would have aroused sympathy in Prestbury thirty-three years later. It was the 'poshest village' in Cheshire and was determined to stay that way, for its inhabitants rejected street lighting on the odd assumption that darkness 'keeps undesirable elements away'. Houses cost between £8,000 and £20,000 and included newly built 'Willowmead' bungalows. Some residents found it hard making ends meet and, according to one, there were a few with 'plenty of curtains at the bay window and bugger-all at the back'. It was worth it, for 'They'd rather be poor in Prestbury than rich in Pendleton.'[19]

Prestbury was unquestionably 'exclusive', an adjective extensively used in estate agents' puffs since the 1920s. It described the Keston Park Estate near Bromley, a complex of detached houses set in large gardens. Building began in 1924 and the developers imposed rules to safeguard the tone of the area: washing was 'to be kept out of sight' and wireless aerials banned. Defending these regulations in 1968, a local estate agent insisted that 'There are people who want to live in nice surroundings, you know, and frankly I think they're damn well entitled to.'[20] His sentiments echoed those of the residents of a private estate in the North Oxford suburb of Cutteslowe who, in 1934, erected a seven-foot wall crowned with iron spikes between themselves and an adjacent council estate. Its inhabitants were blamed for wandering dogs, noisy children and chalked graffiti. There was a row with the local council, but the wall stayed for the next twenty-five years. Checkpoints manned by officious ex-NCOs and equipped with barriers of the type which were found at frontier crossing points defended the Moor Park estate in North London during the 1970s and may still do. The excuse was that the residents of this plush corner of Metroland did not want through traffic passing their large detached houses.

Others might have interpreted these checkpoints as a blatant example of suburban aloofness. Lesser people had to be kept out and those whose work demanded their admittance were reminded of

The Wedding Morning by John Bacon, 1892. Final touches are put to the bride's dress in a lower-middle-class parlour; neighbours look on. Attention to the social niceties were important for families of this kind, moving upwards in the world and acutely conscious of respectability. *(Bridgeman Art Library)*

The original caption for this photograph of a middle-class family dinner was 'For what we are about to receive make us truly thankful – Cold mutton again!' This thrifty housewife has made the weekend joint spin out, as most did.
(Getty Images)

Lazing on a summer's afternoon: an upper-middle-class family pos after a game of tennis ir the 1890s. *(Getty Images)*

Victorian high noon: a late-Victorian upper-middle-class papa sits alongside his mother in widow's black, with his daughters at his feet and his wife standing to the right. His pose is stiff but he shows something of that confidence which distinguished men of his standing. *(Getty Images)*

Cycling mania: three middle-class cyclists bent on adventure in 1900. *(Getty Images)*

The General Strike, 1926

Doing their bit: middle-class volunteers peeling potatoes to feed strikebreakers.

Business as usual: a volunteer clippie takes fares from London office workers.

Safety first: one of Mr Baldwin's armoured cars protects a convoy of buses driven by volunteer drivers.

Off to the Continent: old patterns of middle-class holidays returned in the twenties. These burdened travellers have the comfort of knowing that they have a good stock of British cigarettes. *(University of St Andrews Library)*

The freedom of the road: this driver contemplates Stonehenge in 1938 in solitude. Such felicity was fast disappearing as more and more middle-class families were buying cars and heading for the countryside. *(University of St Andrews Library)*

'Who are the middle classes? What do they want? How can we give it to them?' Harold Macmillan considers the question which hold the key to the success of the Tories. *(Rex Features)*

Two of Macmillan's middle classes, perhaps considering their wants in 1959. *(The Advertising Archives)*

Consumer contentment: a middle-class family look forward to the open road.

Value for money in the market place: Margaret Thatcher on the campaign trail, determined to give the middle class both. *(Empics)*

he middle-class island in the sun: Tony and Cherie Blair take a break from their holiday or an official ceremony in Barbados, one of the many exotic destinations favoured by the middle classes. *(Empics)*

Parenthood defended: Victoria Gillick with her children. *(Empics)*

They shall not pass: an outnumbered protester stands in the way of the
Newbury bypass in 1997. *(Empics)*

their place in the scheme of things. Even the smaller semis had side gates conspicuously labelled 'Tradesmen's Entrance' through which errand boys passed. The sign's implication was recognised by one milkman: 'I suppose it's just that they've got a new house – they just think they're a cut above everybody else.'[21] There was nothing new in this: the middle classes had always believed that the rewards of their endeavours commanded respect, even deference.

Snobbery is part of a wider suburban stereotype. In its most exaggerated form it provided the basis of a 1990s television comedy series *Keeping Up Appearances*, in which Hyacinthe Bucket (pronounced 'Bouquet') strives to act as a grande dame, usually with ludicrous results. She was a slave to what has become another suburban stereotype: the imperative of 'Keeping up with the Joneses'. It was a new name for an old middle-class phenomenon, and it is worth remembering that participants in the race for status wished only to keep abreast of their neighbours rather than overtake them.[22]

Suburban man and woman inherited that vein of competitiveness which had long distinguished the middle class. Possessions were the outward sign of success: the latest model car, garden ornaments and the increasing range of household gadgets which became available and affordable (thanks to hire purchase) as the century advanced were the unmistakable tokens of prosperity. The radio sets and vacuum cleaners of the 1930s were augmented by refrigerators, washing machines, formica surfaces, televisions, fitted kitchens and central heating (and with it constant hot water), all of which came on the market in the late 1940s and 1950s. At the end of 1945 the housewife coping with rationing and shortages could read about home freezers and automatic dishwashers, luxuries then available in America.[23] Her daughter would possess both and regard them as necessities.

They *were* necessities, given the gradual disappearance of full-time female domestic servants. The numbers of such servants had fallen between 1914 and 1918 when many had flocked into the factories for better pay and greater freedom. After the war old patterns of employment were restored; the total of women in service rose from 1.1 million in 1921 to 1.4 million in 1931, a third of the female workforce.[24] This total fell to 790,000 in 1951, and in 1971, according to the census of that year, there were 46,000 'domestic housekeepers' and 169,000 maids and valets, many employed by hotels. Part-time charwomen and foreign au pair girls and nannies had replaced in part the old maidservant and, of course, are now invaluable in families in which husband and wife work full time.

Middle-class households no longer needed servants because new houses were easier to clean and more and more labour-saving devices were available. Servants' wages rose, so that by 1925 retaining a maid or housekeeper could consume as much as 45 per cent of a family's budget.[25] Current servant jokes reflected a changing and, for the middle-class housewife, distressing reversal of the old order. In one a lady has just purchased an off-the-peg gown and is exasperated by the hooks which keep coming undone. She asks the cook for help and is told: 'Yes 'm, they do, that's why I wouldn't have it myself when I tried it on at the shop.'[26] Such humour was against the grain for one parlourmaid who was so upset by servant jokes that she left her position.[27]

Full-time servants were replaced by part-timers. They added colour and amusement to *Mrs Dale's Diary* during the 1950s. Mrs Dale was the wife of a prosperous doctor, lived in a large suburban house and employed a lugubrious gardener called Monument, who sometimes gave horticultural tips to listeners, and a charwoman, Daisy Morgan. Speaking in stage cockney, she was a reservoir of down-to-earth wisdom and might easily have stepped from a *Punch* cartoon of a generation before. It was said that the Queen Mother listened regularly to the programme to discover how the middle classes lived and what they were thinking. What she heard was the humdrum trivia of everyday life, which was part of the appeal of the series to an audience which wanted to hear reflections of themselves and their world. This was why the 1944 film of Noël Coward's *This Happy Breed* was so popular with lower-middle-class cinemagoers.[28]

In their different ways the Dales and Coward's Gibbons revealed the conservative strain which ran through the suburbs. It was of course there for everyone to see: the architecture of suburbia is with few exceptions profoundly conservative. Everywhere there is a self-conscious desire to shun conspicuous novelty and a yearning for older styles, particularly those associated with the rural gentry and aristocracy. Consider two advertisements of 1984 for newly completed properties. A photograph of one from 'Three Beeches Wood' estate near Kingswood, Surrey shows a big detached house with Tudor gables and half-timbering which could have been built sixty years before. 'New period homes' at Lynden Gate, Putney were facsimile Regency villas each with an imposing porticoed doorway. Buyers simultaneously found themselves back in 'a gentle and civilised society' and looked forward to the rewards from 'an investment that will appreciate more surely than less distinctive contemporaries'.[29]

A 1988 advertisement for wrought-iron gates enticed the purchaser with the pledge that they would 'transform your garden into an elegant haven of tranquillity to match the grandest portals of the traditional English country garden'.[30] On opening the scrollwork gate, the suburban householder transformed himself into a country gentleman. In 1998 the developers Laing appealed to the daydreams of the suburban squire with a photograph of the centrally heated basement of one of their new 'luxury' homes which had been converted into a Victorian male den complete with billiard table and a suit of armour.[31]

Meanwhile, the suburb was reinventing itself as an authentic part of the romantic rural world. In 1998 'Traditional English Homes' were selling properties at 'The Village' complex at Bishop's Stortford. The 'traditional new community of St Michael's Mead . . . carefully recreates the vernacular of Hertfordshire's prettiest villages'. All that was missing was Miss Marple.[32] The appeal of the pre-industrial, rustic world which had so captivated the late-Victorian middle classes was as powerful as ever. Now, it could be reproduced exactly and not merely hinted at by gable ends and bow windows attached to semis.

'Period' homes were complemented by 'period' fittings. Reproduction Tudor and Georgian furniture has remained popular and every item is invariably advertised as having been made by craftsmen in a 'traditional' manner. 'Imagine the effect on your home', ran a 1977 puff for reproduction eighteenth-century Chinese wallpaper and fabrics, and, it went without saying, visitors would be impressed.[33] Claims for the 'Ambassador' silver-plated, mock-Georgian coffee and tea set were more direct: 'displayed proudly in the home', it was guaranteed to provide 'pleasure and pride'.[34] Similar emotions had been aroused by the originals when they had been used by a housewife to serve tea to her guests two hundred years before. Past and present were blended in the 1998 'Regency Style' fittings for a 'home office' which was advertised with a photograph of a computer sitting on an antique partner's desk.[35]

A few among the middle classes inherited the real thing and those who had not, but possessed the resources, could buy it. The rest made do with replicas, which were often sold as future 'heirlooms', a label commonly attached to modern sets of medallions or porcelain miniatures offered by mail-order firms. And then there were the trinkets, comestibles and toiletries sold in gift shops (many attached to National Trust properties) whose attractiveness lay in their apparent antiquity ('made according to an old recipe') and rusticity. Genuine or reproduction prints of game birds, dogs and sporting scenes enjoy an immense popularity because they are suggestive of the gun room. In the 1980s an antiques dealer told me that the striking portrait of a young Regency militia officer would, in all likelihood, be purchased by someone who would hang it in their home in the hope that the subject might be thought an ancestor.

Today's 'heritage' industry in all its manifestations is a response to middle-class demand. There is still something within the psyche of a wide segment of the middle-class which finds reassurance in being surrounded by objects from the past, whether original or not. Intellectuals and aesthetes have dismissed these traits as perverse, not least because they reflect that persistent philistinism which wilfully disregards or rejects much modern art.[36]

The middle-class home is a museum of the owner's taste, imagination, income and status, a truth which advertising copywriters continue to exploit. The 'smart people at no 61' had chosen a Kingston bath, ran a puff of 1965. Stick-in-the-muds who still saw a bathroom as utilitarian were warned that more and more people now 'realise just how important bathrooms are today and how much they're noticed'.[37] It was not merely keeping pace with the Joneses by imitating them. Many manufactures of furnishings and fittings stressed that their mass-produced items allowed some leeway for individual idiosyncrasies. 'With our furniture you can reflect your own tastes, use your imagination and make your house a home,' claimed Hülsta in 1987.[38]

Dissecting middle-class taste was essential for those whose living depended on satisfying it. In 1965 the designer Shirley Conran detected five broad types of interior then in fashion.[39] There were escapist 'Cottage modern' with pine furniture and 'unframed oil paintings' and the durable 'Decorator's modern' whose contents embraced anything from any period, so long as it was comfortable. 'Stark Scandinavian', which with its derivatives also survives, had subdued lighting and overawed the visitor. 'Everything is so plain and simple you know its wickedly expensive.' Fourth was 'Ginger Rogers Modern', which reflected the glitter and brassiness of 1930s Hollywood.

Last was 'Snob Junk Modern', garnered from junk shops and cluttered with cast-iron pub tables, roll-top desks and objets trouvés. It was destined for a long life, although by the end of the century Victoriana had become increasingly expensive and, therefore, was supplemented by twentieth-century bric-à-brac which once decorated suburban houses. Most of it and, for that matter its Victorian equivalent, was mass-produced and had only its age or quaintness to recommend it. The perpetual atavism of middle-class taste means that the Art Deco fireplace, an object of pride in the 1930s, blocked up in the 1960s, is now uncovered to become an admired 'period feature'.

The sitting-room fireplace was the focus of suburban family life between the wars. When advertisers wished to evoke the ethos of the middle class, they depicted the family gathered around the fire. The slippered husband sits in an easy chair (part of a three-piece suite), smoking his pipe and reading a newspaper. His wife is sewing or knitting and their two children are on the floor, the son puzzling over the intricacies of Meccano (he may soon ask his father for help) and the daughter either reading or playing with her dolls' house. All are listening to the wireless.

New and cheap technology changed this scene. During the 1950s the television replaced the wireless and within twenty years central heating had made every room in the house warm. Children withdrew to their bedrooms where they watched their own televisions, listened to pop music and later played computer games. Family breakfasts, lunches and dinners have ceased to be communal rituals: food may be consumed in front of the television, or by individuals at times of their own choosing, thanks to the microwave and pre-cooked supermarket meals. Each member of a family could now enjoy a degree of independence within the home.

The earlier image of the middle-class family gathered in one room inside a house barricaded by hedges and often isolated from its neighbours has conveyed the impression that suburbia was an atomised and insular community. Privacy was prized and everyone kept their distance. This was nonsense, although sociologists believed it and have argued that it stifled a spirit of community. The opposite was true: the inhabitants of the suburbs were doers and joiners, mixing enthusiastically to pursue common interests or just find friendship.

The pebble dash on the inter-war semis was hardly set before their occupants began forming gardening, cricket, bridge, bowls, tennis and amateur theatrical and operatic societies. Sometimes the latter had romantic names like Pinner's 'Vagabonds' who, in common with hundreds of others, performed Gilbert and Sullivan in church and school halls. Photographers, stamp collectors and amateur artists assembled to exhibit the results of their endeavours and discuss the esoteric aspects of their pastimes. During the winter, clubs and societies held annual dances and dinners. There were ninety-two clubs and societies active on the Coney Hall Estate near Wickham in Kent in the 1960s and dog-training classes. They had 150 pupils, including a large proportion of golden retrievers called Sandy, which must have been confusing at times.[40] Fashions in middle-class leisure were changing, and cooking and keep-fit classes were beginning to proliferate, to be followed by yoga and meditation.

Suburban domestic entertainment followed earlier patterns. Morning and afternoon tea parties were held in which wives gossiped and gained credit for the tidiness of their houses, their possessions and the politeness of their children. A 1947 guide to these occasions reminded mothers that 'children are no longer expected to be seen and not heard' and it was improper to talk about children as if they were absent. None the less, a degree of infant decorum was expected and children had to be warned against squirming and snatching the last piece of cake.[41] Not long afterwards, the Conservative Party contemplated using these tea parties held by young housewives as devices for spreading its message and gaining recruits.[42] This prototype of the later Tupperware party was not adopted.

The displacement of servants by labour-saving gadgets and the appearance of private caterers who would provide meals for such occasions extended the life of the dinner party. By the 1960s what had previously been a habit confined to the upper reaches of the middle classes was being adopted at lower levels. The dinner party was a taxing trial of a wife's capacity to organise and cook, but there was plenty of advice in women's magazines on procedures, props, menus and how to prepare them. All in all, the dinner party was an exercise in sophisticated ostentation which embraced laying out 'coffee table' books, arranging flowers, sculpting napkins and translating Elizabeth David's recipes into dishes which aroused admiration and envy in equal parts.

Continental cuisine penetrated the suburbs along with wine and the often ephemeral novelties associated with the acquisition of 'style'. Suburban houses underwent periodic redecoration, renovation and extensions to accommodate the needs and aspirations of new, younger occupants. Many undertook the work themselves. Do It Yourself (DIY) became increasingly popular from the mid-1960s onwards, not least because it was believed (not always correctly) that amateur improvements and additions raised the value of a property. Roughly two-thirds of middle-class males spent some time each week on some kind of DIY activity in 1993, slightly less than on gardening.[43]

★

The future of suburbia seems assured. It offers the middle classes an attractive environment, and the suburban house has proved a sound investment. The suburbs were the product of social and economic forces over the past two hundred years. Now, new forces are coming into play and creating a new middle-class habitat; the compact apartment suitable for single men or women (often divorced or separated and sometimes with one or two children), or childless couples. These groups are increasing in numbers. Between 1971 and 1991 the total of divorced men rose from 201,000 to 1.3 million and women from 321,000 to 1.6 million.

Housing developers have responded to this demographic change. Massive Victorian and Edwardian warehouses and institutions such as lunatic asylums and sanatoriums have been gutted and transformed into units of self-contained flats. In 1998 two- or three-bedroom apartments were being offered for £250,000 and upwards in 'Virginia Park' near Virginia Water in Surrey. The surrounding were rural, there were nearby golf courses, shops and restaurants and the complex included 'superb leisure facilities'. Buyers were promised 'a great lifestyle'. 'Life Swap' beckoned purchasers of apartments in 'Britannia Walk', a former converted warehouse near Islington. A strip cartoon showed two potential middle-class buyers, Marc (frustrated by commuting) and Hannah (seeking 'ample space' because she works from home), who meet at a sales promotion. They leave, having been persuaded to buy an apartment which instant mutual attraction means they will share. It is a happy ending. Hannah has a new home and 'a good looking guy' and the pair share a drink: 'They are looking forward to using the gym and movie suite [part of the complex] and inviting friends over to enjoy the local nightlife and their future together.'[44]

In essence, the priorities and dreams of this early-twenty-first-century couple are not unlike those of their counterparts who settled to their new life in Acacia Avenue eighty years before, save of course that the latter were already married.

9

Vulnerable, Dependent, Emotional Human Beings: Wives and Families

'The family life of our race . . . is strong, simple and pure,' asserted George V.[1] His tone and sentiments were Victorian: while he reigned and after, the family was still the bedrock of society and its moral healthiness was a measure of that of the entire nation. For this reason the family was under constant scrutiny by politicians, journalists and social analysts who regularly pronounced on its condition. Was it, some argued, a living organism capable of evolution and, if so, would it be weakened or strengthened by change? Moral conservatives believed that mutation would prove harmful and favoured the retention of older models of family life. Their structure and codes were Victorian and middle-class and did not wear well in the twentieth century.

After 1918 many sensed that all was not well with the family. Anglicans were appalled by the post-war climb in the divorce rate and wondered whether 'the idea of the family' was collapsing.[2] A Congregational minister from Lancashire deplored the 'frivolous spirit' of modern marriage and cited as evidence the indecorous 'giggling and cackling' he now endured at wedding breakfasts.[3] The war had created a large number of what we call 'single-parent' families brought up by widows who were said to over-indulge their offspring, particularly boys.[4]

The family remained the lowest level of the national hierarchy of discipline. Moral standards were learned in the home and, if parental examples and (usually paternal) coercion were lacking, an upsurge in youthful waywardness would follow. After the Second World War, an increase in juvenile delinquency was blamed on the enforced absence of fathers, often for several years on end. Some of the guilt extended to working mothers, whose inattention to their daughters had produced a generation of headstrong and flighty girls. The problem worsened and the breakdown of the family was identified as its root. At the beginning of the twenty-first century, the New Labour government passed laws to compel parents to take responsibility for their children, and those who had no idea of what was involved were ordered to attend classes in parenthood. It was one of many measures undertaken to curb that old bogey, the disorderly underclass.

Strictness did not always pay dividends or provide a pattern for future parents. A middle-class housewife born in 1936 recalled that her mother had struck her for swearing and her father had torn episodes of the salacious bodice-ripper *Forever Amber* from the newspaper. Approaching forty in 1975, she was prepared to allow her fifteen-year-old daughter to make up her own mind.[5] This was a long way from the middle-class Victorian notion of parenthood which assumed that innocence was natural in children, but accepted their vulnerability to corruption. It was an idea which persisted, despite the private doubts of many parents. 'I don't know whether I am a modest woman or a prude?' asked a mother in 1951, after she had removed paintings of nudes from a magazine to spare her family's blushes.[6]

Answers to such questions were found in the abundant literature on bringing up children and the advice columns of women's magazines. Agony aunts continued to fulfil their function as moral arbiters for middle-class women, now giving judgment on intimate, often clinical matters which would not have been aired previously. Advice had to take on board wider shifts in moral attitudes. In 1934 a mother who wished to know how to react to her daughter's request for a latchkey and the loan of lipstick was told that there had been a general 'emancipation' of women since the war and the old moral rules had been nullified. Now, the mother would be wisest to trust to the 'good sense' of her daughter, acknowledge her independence and exert a discreet influence. If needed, motherly cautions were those of a friend rather than a stern custodian of an absolute morality set in stone. Not all advice was so open-minded, and during the Second World War agony aunts pleaded with parents to take the severest line with daughters seeking the company of servicemen, particularly Americans.

The notion of the parent as a friendly confidant rather than a distant upholder and sometimes enforcer of fixed laws steadily gained ground among the middle classes after 1918. The new parenthood was advocated by *Parents*, an enlightened monthly journal which appeared during the 1930s and 1940s. It suggested that children were no longer restricted to their own domain of the nursery, where they had been supervised by servants and ate their own specially prepared pabulum. Instead, and this was facilitated by the radio and cars, parents were encouraged to offer their children companionship and common diversions. The commuter home from his office was called upon to read bedtime stories and, as his sons grew older, share with them the delights of Meccano, stamp collecting and masculine expeditions. In 1946 and in response perhaps to the unavoidable lapse of fatherhood during the war, fathers were told to interest their sons in 'man's things', which included football, aircraft modelling and car engines. As a boy approached adolescence, his father became 'A chap with whom one might share one's reaction to everyday topics and with whom conversation may take a deeper plunge than hitherto'.[7] The Olympian paterfamilias had become a sympathetic but wiser elder brother.

It was the mother's duty to introduce her daughter to the female world and prepare her for motherhood. Girls learned pastry making, knitting and sewing as they had done a hundred years before.[8] There were other lessons, for every 'good home' set the standard of children's future 'moral behaviour'. 'Direct simple explanations' were the best and only answer to sexual enquiries, which were natural and never to be discouraged. Adolescent relationships were inevitable and were treated calmly. In 1958 *Good Housekeeping* advised parents whose sons were about to enter university that homosexuals were not all maladjusted, although some were 'deliberately vicious', and that 'going too far' could lead to dangers. Girls were warned of the perils of losing their self-control during passionate petting.[9]

Parents accepted without question defined phases in their offspring's development: childhood, girlhood and boyhood. Each had its own characteristics which were catered for in comics and magazines for the young. During the inter-war years, the front cover of *Chums* showed three lads in cricket and soccer kit and one in motoring coat and goggles holding a motor bike. Between them were a large book (a stamp album?), a wireless set and models of a galleon and a railway engine. Here was the whole range of masculine activities for a twelve- to sixteen-year-old. Inside the magazine were yarns of boarding-school life, sport and high adventure. For girls, there were high jinks in boarding schools provided by Angela Brazil and her imitators. Younger children of both sexes shared intensely secret universes of adventures, mostly rural, created by Arthur Ransome and Enid Blyton.

Swallows and Amazons and the Famous Five were middle-class children. Keeping alive the ethos of their world and its virtues was one of the goals of Marcus Morris, a clergyman who founded the *Eagle* comic in 1951. Its publication was also a wholesome antidote to an invasion of garish and violent American comics which pessimists feared were corrupting a generation. Morris promised his readers 'good news, interest and entertainments' which embraced adventure serials and deliberately uplifting picture biographies of great men, including Baden-Powell and Alfred the Great.

The *Eagle*'s letters pages give a glimpse into the twilight of boyhood as it would have been enjoyed by William Brown and before him by readers of the *Boys' Own Paper*. In 1954 a group of eleven- and twelve-year-olds reported that during the summer holidays they had formed a club, established its headquarters in a hayloft, compiled a hand-written newspaper, played soldiers and, maybe to fund their pleasures, undertaken odd jobs such as window cleaning. Role models were regularly presented to these lads. They were the life stories of 'mugs', the cant word currently used by spivs for those who helped others. One selfless hero was an eleven-year-old 'cripple' who had managed to secure a grammar school place at the same time as caring for his invalid mother and six younger siblings.[10] Readers of *Girl*, *Eagle*'s counterpart, received an equally wholesome diet which reinforced the message of earlier girls' comics and magazines by concentrating on the achievements of women in the past. *Girl*'s cartoon biographies included Queen Margaret of Scotland and Mary Slessor.

The spirit of individual inventiveness, energetic outdoor activity and improving enquiry filled the pages of *Young Elizabethan*, a monthly magazine aimed at a middle-class teenage audience during the 1950s. There were articles on current events, short stories and serials by distinguished authors such as Geoffrey Trease, and the subversive comments of Nigel Molesworth of St Custard's prep school. Readers' correspondence reflected wholesome preoccupations: advice on future careers, questions about holidays spent working in children's villages in Switzerland and pet maintenance. A reader asked where a bush baby could be purchased and was told that one could be bought from the Army and Navy Stores for fifteen pounds and ten shillings (a shock for parents) and could be sustained on meal worms, sponge cake and fruit.[11] There were profiles of role models, including Antarctic explorers; and, for the venturesome, a Raleigh bicycle promised the buyer that 'Adventure lies ahead.' It might be keeping a 'flower diary' or brass rubbing, both recommended by the magazine.

In 1958 the tocsin for this world of individually inspired, middle-class enthusiasms was sounded by a poem written by a fourteen-year-old girl whose heroes were Elvis Presley and Tommy Steele. 'It's rocking 'n' rolling that keeps them alive,' she wrote of her contemporaries, who wore 'sloppy jumpers and luminous socks' and 'scorned their frocks'.[12] Within a decade, the Victorian concept of a progression from childhood through to adulthood had been superseded. 'Young adults' were drawn into the expanding world of 'style' and consumption. 'Fashion for the schoolroom' had arrived, announced an advertisement of 1961 which offered uniforms that combined 'practical virtues with fashion flair'.[13] 'Lock up your sons,' warned a puff for Judy clothes which produced fashions for 'fives-to-teens' in 1966.[14] The next year, a fashion guru told parents that 'pre-teens' would no longer be 'fobbed off' with their sisters' hand-me-downs and were demanding 'mini skirts and chic'.[15] For the first time since the late eighteenth century, children were dressed like their parents.

Levels of pocket money were rising and many parents were happy to acquiesce in their children's demands to keep pace with new fashions and fads. One advertising executive felt ashamed of his 'humiliating' exercise of paternal power in forbidding his fourteen-year-old daughter to attend a Beatles concert in 1969. He compensated by buying her a complete set of the group's LPs.[16] Such appeasement was common and in some quarters was considered to mark the beginning of the collapse of the family. Others saw it as welcome evidence of the final demise of the authoritarian and male-dominated family.

The stream of new fashions for the young and their absorption into a distinctive youth culture of pop music and hedonism was part of an acceleration of social change that was already having significant repercussions for the middle classes. Placed in perspective (which they rarely were at the time) the 1960s were the culmination of a series of revisions and re-evaluations of social attitudes and habits that had been under way since the start of the century. What was remarkable was not the pace of the latest changes, but the fact they had taken so long to gather momentum.

Two opposing historical forces had been at work. The first was essentially conservative and treated the Victorian social and family order as a model for the present, not to be tampered with. Freezing the past was fraught with difficulty, given the tendency of one age to regard itself as superior in enlightenment to its predecessors. The pious and industrious Victorian middle classes had looked with disdain on the irresponsible and immoral world of the eighteenth century. The point was made by Thackeray in his *The Four Georges* (1855). Lytton Strachey applied a similar irreverent and sceptical hindsight, and his *Eminent Victorians* (1918) found an audience receptive to the mockery of what their grandparents had stood for. Likewise, the satirists (mostly university and public school educated) of the 1960s ridiculed what had been revered by the previous generation.

Making fun of their elders and their ways appealed to the younger,

educated elements within the middle classes, and was either tolerated as a feature of the impatience of youth or else dismissed as
'cleverness' without responsibility. The lower-middle class was less
sanguine. It adhered more tenaciously to traditional ethical values
because they were part and parcel of the respectability which defined
its standing, and it was indignant whenever they were challenged
or ridiculed. Nevertheless, after 1918 there was a sense that the
twentieth century would no longer be beholden to the past. The
new mood was reflected within the upper reaches of the middle
class by the antics of various 'fast' sets bent solely on pleasure.

Partially emancipated, educated middle-class women were beneficiaries of the new ethos. 'The old repressions have gone away for
ever,' announced a columnist in *Woman* in 1925, and her sex now
enjoyed the freedom to express their innermost feelings without
shame. In the same issue, another writer identified new fashions in
underclothing as banners of liberation. 'Bygone' discomforts had
been banished and 'her grandmother would hold up her Victorian
hands in horror' at today's black knickers. 'Prejudice' had been routed
and the 'frivolous road' taken by lingerie led to greater freedom.[17]
Fun was in the ascendant and Victorian grandmamas were successively appalled by flappers, the Charleston and girls puffing cigarettes and sipping cocktails.

Among them may have been the independent 'new' woman
profiled in 1931. She was young, unmarried, earned five hundred
pounds a year, and rented a flat in London equipped with an electric cooker, refrigerator, toaster and tea-maker. She could not afford
a cleaner, which was understandable since her hobbies were
motoring, flying, winter sports and stamp collecting.[18] She had plenty
of spare time, as did her married counterpart who was lucky enough
to live in a modern 'electric' home with a washing machine, a
Hoover, an electric bedwarmer, heated towel rails, cooker, alarm
clock and tea-maker, and electric fires with bogus glowing coals and
logs.[19] Physical emancipation was not always accompanied by intellectual. In 1924 the middle-class mother was advised to encourage
her adolescent daughter to play outdoor games 'rather than sitting
around reading'.[20]

New female freedoms existed in a limbo. Victorian ideals of marriage still carried considerable weight: husbands assumed primacy and wives were judged by their achievements as mothers and home-makers. As late as 1965, a *Times* article on female education remarked that many middle-class fathers still judged their daughters according to 'standards of womanhood' set by their mothers, and so dispatched them to 'lightweight schools' which fostered such models. Yet things were about to change, and the author predicted that equal competition between boys and girls was imminent.[21]

Such an idea would have been wormwood for many between the wars. Marriage remained a woman's proper destiny and, when necessary, authority stepped in to enforce it. Women civil servants, teachers and doctors were dismissed the moment they married on the ground that running a household and doing a job were incompatible. Women may have taken men's jobs during the war and were applauded for doing so, but this had been an aberration created by an emergency, not a precedent for the future. There was also the visceral feeling that employed married women were depriving men of jobs. Males were still the natural breadwinners. In 1923 the Labour local authority in Rhondda sacked twenty-three married teachers for these reasons.[22] Even if they had kept their jobs, the law did not allow them or other women equal pay.

Married male teachers whose salaries had been pared after the 1931 economic crisis found themselves discussing contraception with their wives as one way to keep down costs.[23] Birth control had gained ground with all classes; between 1920 and 1924 around 58 per cent of married women or their husbands were employing some form of birth control and the average family size had fallen to 2.4. For middle-class newlyweds, unplanned children could upset budgets finely balanced to cover hire purchase and mortgage instalments. The alternative was an extended engagement during which the couple saved money and strove to maintain chastity. In 1920, the wife of a junior RAF officer wrote to Marie Stopes saying that she needed to work so that the couple could afford to live in a manner appropriate to their status. Dr Stopes directed her towards Harrods, which sold pessaries.[24] The *Economist* objected on eugenic grounds.

If the middle class produced fewer children, the nation's future would be jeopardised.[25]

It was an idea that probably did not cross the minds of newly married women who made their way to Harrods or responded to coy advertisements offering 'Protective Necessities' by mail order. Their decision to postpone a family would have probably been made in consultation with their husbands. If these women read the opinions on marriage in their magazines, they would have been aware that it was now a shared enterprise whose success would rest on mutual respect and companionship. It was a concept which had its roots in the last century, but it spread slowly and unevenly. Young men interviewed in the early 1950s tended to see marriage as a 'co-operative' venture undertaken by equal partners, some observing that this had not been the view of their parents.[26]

Brides were always conscious that their husbands had high expectations of their domestic competence. 'Are you trying to poison me?' asked a furious young husband in an advertisement of 1951 after tasting his wife's custard. She then discovered Cremeola and harmony was restored. In another advertisement, a fiancé spills coffee on some new pillowcases and his future bride washes them with Surf on the advice of the wife of the grocer. On presenting him with the clean linen, she receives a kiss on the hand from her future husband who is impressed by her housewifely flair.[27] This marriage would surely flourish, or so the copywriters hoped. They had had a hundred years of learning how to exploit the middle-class housewife's wish to please her husband.

Many wives found domestic chores as tedious as they were onerous. In 1938 the *Lancet* exposed perturbing levels of neuroses among suburban housewives, who were bored and frustrated by routines and loneliness. Their symptoms were often an exaggerated concern for the welfare of children, an obsession with order and cleanliness in the house and clinically inexplicable pains. The same ennui and frustration was endured in the 1960s, when there were new sources of stress. Wives waited at suburban stations for the invariably overdue commuter train and worried about a dinner about to be ruined – 'charred roast, wizened chicken or obliterated soufflé'.

One experience from 1966 reflected others. 'Louise', a twenty-nine-year-old former journalist married to an advertising executive and with one child, confessed to being overwhelmed to the point of despair by the sheer monotony of her daily life. She sought respite through reading, listening to Classical music and conjuring up erotic fantasies. Hours were consumed planning meals for her husband's return and, when he did appear, he often fell asleep exhausted in front of the television. Their sex life was in abeyance and when his train was late Louise downed cocktails.[28] Others like Louise pestered their doctors for anti-depressants and tranquillisers.[29]

As an educated woman, she felt demeaned by housework. Its status was being devalued as growing numbers of women of her background, married or not, were beginning to pursue careers beyond the home. Many were competing with men in areas they had once thought their own.

Successful women saw themselves as liberated, the ultimate heiresses of the movement for female emancipation which had started in the middle years of the previous century. Its intellectual roots had been in the minds of the educated liberal middle classes and it had followed a course dictated by their ideals. In essence women's emancipation was a pursuit of natural justice and those who gained from it were expected to fulfil that essentially middle-class concept of reciprocity. They used their talents for the greater good of society. This was why in the 1920s girls at the fee-paying Sutton High School were encouraged to seek spiritual rather than material rewards and be prepared to place duty before self. Those who followed careers entered teaching, medicine and the civil service.[30]

Mary Butt summed up her education at St Leonard's School in St Andrews at the beginning of the century as being presented with 'a pair of sensible walking shoes wrapped up in a brown paper parcel'.[31] Worthy and practical, this footwear suited many middle-class girls. It would have appealed to Winifred Holtby. A Yorkshire farmer's daughter who attended local private schools, she served in the Women's Auxiliary Army Corps before going up to Somerville in 1919, and followed a career of public usefulness. She campaigned (sometimes speaking at Hyde Park Corner) in support of the League of Nations, pacifism and the rights of blacks in South Africa and was involved in voluntary educational and welfare work.

Thanks to the 1919 and 1928 Representation of the People Acts, women in theory were fully integrated into political life; in the 1929 general election female voters outnumbered male by a million. They were the majority in South Kensington, where they secured the seat for a Tory who had been a co-respondent in a recent divorce case, which raised some eyebrows.[32] Yet, for the most part, women hovered on the fringes of political life, working outside Parliament and through their own lobby groups. These were often powerful: the Anglican and morally conservative Mothers Union had half a million members by 1939 and the National Federation of Townswomen's Guilds three hundred thousand. Their principal interests were causes connected to the family and public welfare. Women MPs were rare: they comprised just 4 per cent of the Commons between 1945 and 1983.

Scarce on front and back benches, women were nevertheless gradually colonising regions traditionally occupied by men. The deadweight of custom and its mouthpiece prejudice were still evident in 1958, according to an article on women seeking careers in engineering. Anecdotal wisdom alleged that women could never understand mathematics or machines, and so teachers and parents advised girls to steer clear of engineering. Yet major companies, including English Electric and Vickers Armstrong, welcomed women either as apprentices or as graduates.[33]

In the long term, economic forces prevailed with the assistance of the state. The Equal Opportunities and Employment Protection Acts of 1970 and 1975 and their successors made work more attractive for women, not least through the provision of maternity leave. Careers need no longer be terminated by having children, and the demand for educated women was growing with the expansion of service industries and the public sector. Again, the state was already playing its part through an education system which had recognised merit rather than gender as the yardstick for college or university entrance. In 1965 some 15,000 women were admitted to university compared with 38,000 men and, in all, roughly one-eighth of women born between 1954 and 1968 gained degrees.[34] In terms of subject choice, language, arts and social science courses were the most popular. Women were competing with men on equal terms and, strikingly, began to outpace them in terms of examination results. In 1981–2 around 10 per cent of girls left school with three or more A Levels and 11 per cent of boys. By 1992–3, the order had been reversed, with girls leading boys by 23 to 21 per cent.[35]

Sprinters' shoes had replaced walkers'. Confident, qualified and ambitious women were joining the workforce in increasing numbers and they were no longer content to settle for inferior opportunities. They even found their way into such closely guarded male enclaves as the City and the superior echelons of the press. In 1971 a total of 44 per cent of women were in full or part-time employment; in 1994, the figure was 53 per cent. The number of households in which both husband and wife worked rose from 8.3 million in 1978 to 12.8 million in 2002.

An employment revolution was bound to be a catalyst for a social one. The old pattern of middle-class marriage in which the husband was expected to be the only breadwinner dissolved in less than forty years. A working wife was no longer a token that a man could not support his family, rather it was the means to maintain and enhance social status. Talents and experience acquired before marriage were not allowed to rust. 'I wanted to occupy my mind,' confessed a businessman's wife in 1975 after she had established her own catering firm. Her husband was a weekly commuter and, revealingly, she felt obliged to arrange her work to fit in with family obligations.[36] A 1991 survey of working, middle-class wives revealed that 40 per cent needed the additional money to meet bills or fund luxuries, 22 per cent enjoyed their jobs, 17 per cent wished to continue their careers and 10 per cent spent their earnings on themselves. Just over a half employed paid child carers.[37]

Middle-class reactions to the new pattern of female employment varied immensely. Old stereotypes endured in the minds of those who had been brought up to accept them, but not always. In the mid-1980s a commercial traveller born at the turn of century insisted that a woman's place was always in the home, but an engineer of the same generation was happy to fly in an aeroplane piloted by a woman. A City banker born in the 1950s believed women to be unfitted to the world of finance because they crumpled under extreme stress. A middle-aged bank manager thought women were best teaching small children, and a science lecturer believed that their minds were somehow untuned to technology, although he could not explain why.[38]

Economic parity within marriage inevitably raised the issue of the demarcation of domestic responsibilities and labour. There were and are myriad individual responses to this dilemma, but, by and large, the economic revolution did not prompt a domestic one. The stove and the sink were still the 'natural' lot of many working wives, some married to husbands who prided themselves on their open-mindedness. In 1991, about 36 per cent of husbands with working wives admitted to helping with shopping, 29 per cent with cleaning, 23 per cent with cooking and just 19 per cent with washing clothes.[39] Given that children tend to follow models set by their own parents, this balance of labour may change within the middle classes within the next two or three generations.

For modern feminists, the unequal sharing of chores was proof of a wider disparity of the sexes whose roots lay in still vibrant traditions of male dominance. Fresh opportunities for women and their greater engagement in the economic life of the nation were a deceptive façade behind which historic assumptions of male superiority lurked, as ingrained as ever. It pervaded what, in 1970, Germaine Greer, an Australian academic and feminist polemicist, called the 'patriarchal family structure' and, indeed, the entire framework of the society which it underpinned.[40] Time out of mind, women had been compelled to suppress their individuality and conform to standards imposed for masculine convenience. The experience of many educated, middle-class women confirmed many feminist arguments, if not their extension into a wilder anti-male polemic.

What particularly irked the feminist advance guard and drove them to ignite bras and wear boiler suits was the dictatorship of fashion. It is easy to see why. 'That's what I call a lovely figure,' declares one of a pair of suave males eyeing a girl in 1949. 'Where there's admiration . . . there's a JB foundation.'[41] In 1966 another corset manufacturer promised a forlorn middle-aged woman 'we'll make you look 26 . . . around the waist'.[42] Some years before, a couturier had repeated what his kind had known for hundreds of years: 'women's clothes are no good until they have sex'.[43] Dress designers and copywriters consciously treated women as 'sex objects' and in doing so were upholding a basic tenet of masculine orthodoxy.

Feminists fervently hoped that women would dissolve old stereotypes and their justifications through discovering their own sexuality. In the words of Germaine Greer, 'one of the chief mechanisms in the suppression of female humanity is the obliteration of female sexuality'. To an extent and like many feminists of the time, she was tilting at windmills: the female capacity for sexual pleasure had been discussed by writers such as Marie Stopes since the 1920s, albeit somewhat circumspectly. At the same time, women were becoming less modest about their bodies and were prepared to show more and more of them on beaches or in swimming pools, often wearing revealing beachware based upon Hollywood models.[44] Yet, while a healthy body was a source of pride, unchastity remained one of shame and there were plenty of middle-class women who remained ignorant of the mechanics of sex, let alone the possibility that it might be enjoyable.

The pleasures of sex and its pitfalls (for the young) were increasingly exercising legal and medical minds by 1960. During the previous decade, there had been evidence of a swift relaxation of old constraints. By a twist of what the feminists would have ridiculed as peculiarly masculine logic, teenage boys declared that they considered it perfectly all right for engaged couples to sleep together, but wanted their own wives to be virgins.[45] By 1959, pregnancies among girls under sixteen (mostly working class) had risen by nearly a third, a statistic which was blamed on inadequate sex education.[46] Those responsible for instruction no longer had any faith in delivering fierce moral warnings and demanding self-control. In 1961 a lady magistrate told a conference of youth leaders that the young needed to know how far to go. 'I tell young people that if they laugh and joke when they are petting it is all right. It is when they become earnest that it is time to break it up.'[47] Quite so, but it must have been hard to think of a quip in the heat of passion.

Sexual misunderstandings within marriage were pushing up the divorce rate. They were dissected and discussed at a conference held by the British Academy of Forensic Sciences in 1963, which concluded that there were still plenty of women who had never understood the mechanics of sex, or knew what was 'normal'. Margaret Puxon, the distinguished family lawyer, told listeners that non-consummation was commoner than imagined and that there were husbands who abstained from sex for fear of shattering their wives' 'femininity'.[48] Individual doctors confirmed these facts from their own experience. The bien-pensant middle classes demanded the classic remedies: further analysis of the problem by professional experts and additional education – and, given the enlightened temper of the times, a willingness to show sympathetic understanding more freely than blind censure.

The appearance of oral contraceptives added immensely to the complexities of the problem. In 1963 the privately run Brook Advisory Centres prescribed them to unmarried girls, and six years later the Family Planning Association did likewise. Both took patients referred to them by National Health Service clinics. The pill was seen as an agent of female emancipation: in future the individual woman alone decided if and when she would have children, and to choose when, how often and with whom she had sexual relations without fear of the consequences. Opponents of contraception, echoing historic fears that female sexuality was a Pandora's Box, were mortified. Feminists announced that the opportunity was at hand for women at last to explore and exploit their sexuality.

Middle-class parents faced new quandaries. These were aired in the advice columns of women's magazines, mostly along the lines of how far parents could allow their children to go. A garage manager's wife was happy for her fifteen-year-old daughter to go on the pill, although a too easy-going attitude to her elder brother had led to the police catching him with cannabis. Another mother kept her daughter under close surveillance, for fear that meeting boys would inevitably lead to pregnancy, venereal infection and abortion. A photographer insisted that his sixteen-year-old son knuckled under and, among other things, had a haircut. His wife disagreed, not wishing to 'suppress' the boy's personality. Patriarchy was preserved by the son: 'Recently, I became a Christian, so I tend to obey my parents more often.'[49] There were no hard-and-fast answers, plenty of tantrums and some heartache.

Advice and suggestions on sexual techniques became freely available once the censorship laws had been relaxed. *Forum* offered both and an early edition inspired a letter from a cleaning lady who had found it in her boss's office, much to her amusement, for he seemed a stuffy sort. It cost seven shillings and sixpence, it was clearly for the middle classes and its contents would never be taken seriously by working women, who were 'too busy worrying about getting a meal on the table for our husbands'.[50] She missed the edition in which James Hemming, the chairman of the British Humanist Council, and a psychiatrist advised readers that the variety of marriage patterns was diverse and recommended group sex.[51]

It was all too much for the wife of an engineer who successfully sued for divorce in 1975 on the grounds of being asked to play strip poker and dance naked at parties.[52] Others had no objections to such goings-on: one middle-class wife concluded dinner parties in Cheshire with a strip-tease show. Her performances did not deter hostesses from asking her again.[53]

The middle-class man was adrift in an unfamiliar world filled with new pleasures and new terrors. In 1978 one woman journalist imagined that men had suddenly been exposed as 'vulnerable, dependent, emotional human beings' judged (not always favourably) on their sexual performance.[54] Some women believed that they too had been devalued. A divorced teacher in her thirties complained that 'Nowadays, you go out with a man and simply it's assumed that you are an emancipated woman who will fall into bed.' Romance had disappeared.[55] It had staged a recovery by 1988 when a survey of 21,000 predominantly middle-class single women revealed that only 6 per cent went to bed with a man on their first date. Just under a half waited weeks or months.[56] Fears that the pill would open the floodgates of reckless promiscuity had been premature: in 1990 it was found that only a fifth of girls were taking the pill when they first had sex.[57] Of course, by that date five years of sometimes manic official propaganda about AIDS had created anxieties about casual sex.

What is most fascinating about the survey of single women was that 52 per cent of them believed that marriage was important, 38 per cent regarded cohabitation as the same thing and only 8 per cent considered wedlock to be redundant. Statistics gathered in 1993–4 confirmed this picture: only 5 per cent of women were living with a partner, while 56 per cent were married. 'Living in sin' had obviously lost its stigma, which was inevitable given the decline in the authority of the churches. Their more pessimistic followers had repeatedly predicted the impending collapse of marriage and with it the rest of the social order. Yet marriage survived the prolonged shock of the gradual easing of the divorce laws and the more recent revision of attitudes towards sexuality, and it is accommodating the upswing in the numbers of working wives.

What enabled middle-class marriage to survive the twentieth century was its flexibility. This explanation would have shocked those moral absolutists who spent much of the period insisting that it had reached perfection and that change could only be harmful. It was a view which steadily lost ground because it went against the grain among the educated and liberal-minded middle classes. At the risk of piling generalisation on generalisation, the evolution of marriage and the gradual emancipation of women can be explained as consequences of a peculiarly middle-class enlightenment. Since the eighteenth century, its components had been a questioning spirit, a tendency to measure all human institutions by their usefulness, a faith in reason as the key to solving any problem and a belief in individual freedom. Apply these criteria to the notion of female subordination and the nature of marriage and both were bound to change, particularly as religious dogma was in retreat.

Yet, in spite of the transformation of marriage, there is still general agreement that a loving and stable partnership offers the best way of bringing up children, even if it is unconsecrated or without formal legal sanction. The cycle of change continues to run: the twenty-first century will continue to see more and more single-parent families and married and unmarried women will remain integral to the economic life of the nation. Not everyone in the middle class is happy with these developments, nor with the ideas which have made them possible. In varying degrees, Catholics and Muslims adhere to doctrines about marriage and the rights of women which are akin to those of the nineteenth or, for that matter, the seventeenth century.

10

Have a Capstan and Make Friends: Pleasures and Anxieties

During the 1950s smoking was an acceptable social pleasure for just about everyone. Offering a cigarette was a gesture of friendship and an invitation to familiarity, hence the slogan. 'Have a Capstan and Make Friends'. Smoking was the norm at nearly every social occasion. An advertisement for State Express showed a packet being shared by a party in a box at the opera. Such behaviour is now unthinkable: smokers have become pariahs, their indulgence is vilified as a danger to their own and others' health and it is in the process of being prohibited from public places. Middle-class smokers are a diminishing species. Thanks to chilling warnings about the connections between smoking and lung cancer, repeatedly and vehemently made by the medical profession, smoking has lost both its innocence and its popularity.

The middle classes treat their pleasures seriously, their health more so. The twentieth century has given them more time for leisure, an ever-expanding range of diversions and more money to spend on them. The most popular pastimes are sedentary and three, watching television and listening to the radio and to recorded music, depend on modern technology. Television is the universal consumer of spare time for all classes, according to a survey of 1993. Next in popularity came visiting and entertaining friends and family and then listening to radio and music on tapes and discs, a common diversion of just over 80 per cent of the middle classes. Roughly the same proportion were avid readers of books, a habit which separated the middle from other classes; less than half the skilled and unskilled working classes read books frequently.[1]

Recreational time has increased, although fitfully. In the 1970s executives and managers were working a forty-two- to forty-four-hour week, just as they had done for the previous fifty years. Over the same period, holiday allowances had extended from two or three weeks to four, but not universally. Middle-class leisure time shrank during the 1980s and 1990s, particularly at the managerial and executive levels, as companies became intoxicated by the Japanese 'corporate warrior' ethos which demanded longer hours at desk and computer. The pseudo-samurai also took more and more work home, and there were widespread complaints that the time left for relaxation and recuperation was being squeezed.[2] Doctors, particularly general practitioners, wilted under similar burdens and in 2004 a quarter were allegedly suffering from symptoms of stress.[3] It was tough at the top, which explains why those who earned most rewarded themselves most generously when it came to leisure.

Providing leisure in all its forms has become a growth industry which, by 1995, was employing 10 per cent of the workforce and accounted for a quarter of all consumer expenditure. Over ten billion pounds was spent on sport alone, with admission charges, gambling and sportswear each contributing roughly two billion.[4] The slice of the average middle-class budget reserved for relaxation grew. Between 1925 and 1949 it hovered at around a tenth and then rose rapidly to a quarter in the next fifty years.[5] The proportion was even higher for those with large incomes, rising to an astonishing 58 per cent for those earning more than £300 a week in 1985.[6]

The middle classes became swamped by choice as to how they used their spare time, but there was always plenty of advice at hand. The literature of leisure has kept pace with the inflation of entertainment and is now enormous. There were eight hundred different magazines on sale at Victoria station in 1996, nearly all concerned with leisure. Seventy titles concerned music and hi-fi gadgetry, forty home computing and twelve the Internet.[7] From the early 1970s, middle-class newspapers began to provide sections on travel, regular features on such popular pastimes as gardening and birdwatching, introductions to others and lists of entertainments and places to visit.

These reflected the proliferation and variety of commercial diversions, particularly for families. Choices for the 1983 May Bank Holiday included the National Leisure Festival at Knebworth Park, where there were displays of aerobatics and morris dancing (presumably not simultaneous), barbecues, barn dances and discos. At Beaulieu antique steam engines and fairground organs reverberated and armoured knights jousted at Sudeley Castle. There was mock combat in the grounds of Ripley Hall, where over two thousand members of the Sealed Knot staged a battle between Roundheads and Cavaliers. Near by was a reconstructed seventeenth-century village street with stalls.[8] Merrie England, or a sanitised version of it, was very popular and the owners of country houses and estates were glad to market it to offset death duties and maintenance expenses.

Revealingly, the top tourist attraction for 1995 was Alton Towers (owned by the Tussaud Group), which offered rollercoaster rides and 'Old MacDonald's Farm' as well as gardens. At Warwick Castle, also run by the Tussaud Group, there was the interior filled with the usual aristocratic accumulations of furniture, paintings and tapestries. Outside, men and women in fifteenth-century costume enacted a form of tableau vivant showing Warwick the Kingmaker and his followers preparing for another round in the Wars of the Roses.[9]

There was an element of educational improvement in these fun days out for the family. Residual Victorian Puritanism still permeates middle-class attitudes towards leisure. Pure hedonism has made considerable headway, most obviously since the 1960s. In 1977 picnickers were invited to surrender to the 'unashamed pleasure' of the French al fresco meal and spend hours 'feasting, drinking and chatting' in the shade of a tree. Abandonment was not total; the contented picnickers were enjoined to clear up the detritus of eating before leaving.[10]

Superior pleasure derived from activities which offered mental and physical benefits. Gardeners justified their endeavours on aesthetic grounds and with crops of home-grown fruit and vegetables, and stamp collectors claimed that they were enlarging their knowledge of the world and its peoples. It was sometimes difficult to draw a line between what was and what was not beneficial. The fashion for sunbathing which caught on during the inter-war years was defended as healthy and denounced as a decadent fad which would stimulate promiscuity. A press photograph of men and women 'sun worshippers' on a beach in 1936 had the comment that their shorts and one-piece costumes 'would have aroused a storm of protest' a few years before.[11] Passions had also run high on nudism (a largely middle-class pursuit), but it too was accepted as a healthy if eccentric pastime. But not for long; by the turn of the century there was a steady stream of medical caveats pointing to the connection between over-exposure to the sun and skin cancer.

The dangers of mountaineering, rock climbing and modern 'Thrill Sports' such as hang-gliding were also justifiable. Undergoing self-inflicted ordeals was a form of therapy in which participants discovered their mental as well as physical limits. Overcoming fear and developing self-confidence paid dividends, but the intitial investment was costly. In 1978 novice hang-gliders needed between £400 and £800 for their machines, which could be hired for six or seven pounds a day, as well as money for training courses.[12]

Leisure has remained inseparable from status. Every pastime has its accoutrements and gadgets which advertised not only commitment but the wherewithal to support it. This was proclaimed by manufacturers' labels prominently displayed on everything from trainers to birdwatchers' binoculars. At the close of the century, seekers of adventure and pleasure could equip themselves with, among other things, a map plotter (£199), a mountain bike repair kit (£44.95p), a digital compass (£219), a waterproof watch suitable for surfing (£99.99p) and an 'owl scope' for observing nocturnal wild life (£149.95p).[13]

The accessories of middle-class leisure may have multiplied, but its basic ingredients have stayed constant. They were listed in 1970 as the arts, fashion, food, motoring, sport and 'the home' in *Accent on*

Good Living, a journal devoted to advising 'busy people' on the best choices for 'living and leisure'. To what was essentially a Victorian recipe for pleasure could be added association and conviviality. Gregariousness remains at the heart of leisure. The fisherman may stand alone in the trout stream and treasure his solitary communion with nature, but afterwards he will share his experiences with others of his kind, or anyone else who will listen. Holidaymakers still send postcards to friends and family and, when they return home, may sometimes entertain the recipients with slides and video films.

Like their predecessors, the modern middle class love each other's company. A *Punch* cartoon of 1950 said it all when it showed a scene at a private viewing in an art gallery at which all the guests had gathered together in the centre of the room and were chattering, drinking and smoking. No one was even glancing at the paintings on the walls. Mark Cocker's recent intimate account of the world of birdwatchers is revealingly subtitled 'Tales of a Tribe'. Its members existed within a self-contained universe in which they met and talked about their passion, often using an argot incomprehensible to outsiders. Readers will recognise or be members of other tribes, each with its own camaraderie, language and, invariably, competitiveness. Opera aficionados vie with each other, recount the finer points of past performances and argue about which was definitive. Golfers congregate in club houses to drink, relive golden moments, share advice and speculate about the might-have-beens of past rounds.

Dressing up and observing rituals remain integral to convivial middle-class leisure. Knowing the rules was vital and those who infringed them, unwittingly or not, risked disapproval or even ostracism. The embarrassment of the ignorant was at the heart of the cruel social humour of the cartoonists H. M. Bateman and 'Fougasse', who mocked middle-class customs between the wars. Once, Fougasse exposed the humiliation of an amateur cricketer who appeared at a match in his club colours rather than in the obligatory medley of striped blazers, caps and ties from school and university teams nonchalantly worn by his team mates.[14] This innocent did not know the form, like H. M. Bateman's famous figure who lit his cigar before the loyal toast at a City banquet.

The rules have withered somewhat. Jackets, waistcoats and ties are now discarded and braces exposed at dinner dances and balls, mostly by the young. Nevertheless, neuroses about the niceties of protocol still disturb the middle classes. As Fougasse and Bateman understood, conduct and dress appropriate to the occasion are an assay of status and upbringing. For this reason, middle-class newspapers and journals retain columnists who answer readers' questions about etiquette.

Wedding protocol and matching dress to event cause considerable angst, but other arcane dilemmas are posed. In the mid-1990s a *Spectator* reader wondered whether glancing through previous entries in a house visitors' book was a 'social faux pas'. The new sexual frankness created fresh problems. One enquirer, aware that those twin high priests of social propriety Radio Four and the *Daily Telegraph* commonly used the word 'willy', wanted to know what was now the polite term for its female counterpart.[15] Old quandaries remained; in 1999 *The Times*'s etiquette guru was asked to legislate on the proper disposal of a soiled table napkin.[16] Punctilio matters to the modern middle classes who submit to the primacy of a correct way of doing things. A minority of bold spirits dissent and deviate, either because they consider themselves bohemians free from the constraints of convention, or because they are so self-confident that they can overlook them. The rest of the middle class prefers the safety of conformity.

Alcohol remains the lubricant of middle-class sociability, perhaps more so than at any time. Drink consumption among all classes has risen since the 1950s, and during the same period there was a sudden and rapid upsurge in the consumption of wine. Imports rose from 27.9 million gallons in 1964 to 66.4 million in 1977. By 2001 this total had trebled to 9,534,000 hectolitres and is continuing to rise. Between the mid-1960s and the mid-1980s, the average yearly individual intake of alcohol nearly doubled to just over nine litres.[17] Middle-class buyers led the way in the new mass market for wine, but they trod warily, acutely aware of the snobberies of the wine world. Guidance was on hand from expert newspaper and magazine columnists who took care to respond to their readers' spending power. Wines sold in the new chain stores such as Augustus Barnett and supermarkets were commonly reviewed. 'Party size' bottles and 'boxes' of 'plonk' were graded by one expert as 'acceptable' or 'good' and another assessed a Tesco Bardolino as 'perfect for summer slurping'.[18] This was for everyday consumption with meals or social drinking, particularly by women who were now offering a glass of wine to visiting friends as an alternative to tea.[19] Wine supplemented and to some extent replaced cocktails and spirits as an aperitif and became the norm at receptions. In the mid-1980s it was estimated that twenty thousand bottles of wine were consumed annually at the three hundred private gallery viewings held in London. Here and on other occasions, waiters were encouraged to be generous to swell their employers' takings.[20]

Wine has its distinctive snobbery and so connoisseurs proffered their arcane knowledge, palates and experience to purchasers who wanted prestige. Just as their eighteenth-century predecessors had vaunted their claret and port, modern hosts drew attention to their selection of table wines and invited their guests' opinions. Current middle-class preoccupations with the purity of what they ate soon extended to wine. As with food, the market responded and by 1995 'organic' wine was on the shelves.[21] There were other perils to drinking wine, and, for that matter, all kinds of alcohol.

In 1981 what the director of the National Council for Alcoholism called the new 'recreational freedom' was behind a spreading epidemic of drunkenness.[22] The scale of the problem and the alarm it caused have escalated steadily. By 1996, a senior police officer alleged that alcohol was somehow involved in two-thirds of crimes.[23] An old nightmare was returning to unsettle the middle classes: drunken youths brawling in the streets, menacing passers-by and smashing public and private property. The experience of a Friday evening in the dormitory town of Bishop's Stortford during the summer of 2000 was repeated across the country. Yobs swigged lager in doorways, threw bottles, broke glass and shouted, 'Get your tits out!' and other obscenities. Girls as well as boys were involved, including two solicitors' secretaries.[24] It was a scene that had occurred over the past five centuries, but was nonetheless still frightening.

The return of Hogarth's England struck other observers favourably. There was speculation about whether the national character was reverting to a 'national type' which had existed before the nineteenth century when the British had been famed for their uninhibited exuberance. Evidence of this was the flourishing 'club' life of the cities and the cheerful, sometimes raucous gatherings in restaurants. The middle classes were recovering their capacity to enjoy themselves, or so it seemed.[25] Continental café society was being reproduced in Britain.

Meanwhile, the old middle-class Puritanism was resurrected, but in mutated form. Once concerned with redeeming souls, it was now concentrated on rescuing bodies from the dire consequences of saturated fats and junk food. Middle-class valetudinarianism has had a long and occasionally comic history. Its persistence is proved by the sheer number of advertisements for patent medicines, universal panaceas and tonics which appeared in the eighteenth- and nineteenth-century press. Health fears spawned an extraordinary gullibility which led the middle classes to swallow the outrageous claims of advertisers as readily as they did their worthless nostrums. These were gradually proscribed by law. Restoratives for unspecific conditions survived. Lucozade restored energy and Horlicks overcame 'night starvation' and, according to the strip cartoons which accompanied its puffs, rescued many flagging careers. In 1954 a new but happily curable form of debility briefly appeared: 'Exhaustipation'.[26]

The National Health Service did not shake the middle class's belief that the individual was responsible for his or her well-being. This was confirmed by a survey of 1984 in which middle-class respondents expressed a wish to get fitter through giving up smoking, taking regular exercise, eating better-quality food, dieting and drinking less.[27] Resolve was strengthened by the alarms about chemical additives in everyday foods which were being disseminated by the Green movement, and within the next decade there would be successive scares over salmonella in eggs, BSE in beef and excessive cholesterol in all sorts of products, particularly the mass-produced, cheap and convenient comestibles. Sugar became a villain: in 1983 it was blamed for encouraging criminality in those who ate too much, and, as ever, there were statistics and chemical data to back up this supposition.[28]

The middle classes were by turns scared and bewildered. On one hand, they had a historic respect for conclusions based upon empirical science, which led them to accept the links between smoking and cancer. On the other hand, encouraged by the Green movement and the anti-rational elements of New Ageism, there was a growing suspicion of science, which was reflected in the widespread dismissal of the scientific assurances about the safety of genetically modified crops. There was agreement that ultimately the individual was master of his or her metabolism and that, through knowledge and self-discipline, it was possible to contrive 'a healthy life style'. It was a compound of exercise, dieting and moderate drinking. In came a vast literature of guides to dieting (packed with scientific information about such crucial matters as calories), an abundance of often exotic greenstuffs (nearly all restaurants offered some form of salad as a side dish) and scientifically planned regimes of exercise. Some were undertaken daily in gymnasiums under the supervision of personal 'coaches' by those who could afford both. Lawmakers in Brussels obliged by insisting that every kind of packaged food had a label which provided buyers with a chemical breakdown of what they were about to eat.

There is a parallel between the modern middle class's fixation with physical fitness and its Victorian predecessor's concern for spiritual salvation. Both were taken to extremes, generated a vast literature and were translated into campaigns to instruct and convert an ignorant or indifferent working class. Today's nutritionist exhorting the poor to eat fruit summons up Gustave Doré's famous image of a clergyman reading passages from the Bible to the derelicts in a Victorian doss house. Having discovered the benefits of a healthy life, the middle class felt duty bound to share their good fortune. Governments concurred.

This mission was most fervently pursued early in 2005 in a television series in which 'celebrity chef' Jamie Oliver devised nourishing meals for working-class schoolchildren in London. Initially there was resistance because the eaters preferred their familiar industrial pabulum ('Turkey Twizzlers') to what was good for them. The press correctly detected the hand of middle-class paternalism.[29] It was also present in the official war against obesity among the young, which seemed to approach a pandemic thanks to the reckless consumption of processed sugars and fats and inert hours spent in front of screens of one kind or another.

The 'two nations' had returned, now divided by waistlines and the contents of supermarket trolleys. Margaret Driscoll, a journalist visiting her supermarket in Hackney in 2004, observed one trolley filled with coriander, fruit and parma ham destined for a middle-class table and another packed with Coco Pops, white long-life bread, 'Chicken Tonight' and bottles of Tango which would be consumed in a council flat.[30] The evidence of the check-out was confirmed by statistics: on average the middle classes were leaner and fitter and lived longer than the working class.[31]

There had always been 'two nations' when it came to holidays. Victorian patterns of social segregation at resorts persisted and, during the last quarter of the century, were extended overseas as more and more of the working class took foreign holidays. Foremen and the middle classes of West Yorkshire stayed at Morecambe while the working classes went to Blackpool. Scarborough had its own zones, with the upper-middle class occupying the north of the resort, the rest of the middle class the North Bay and the working class the area around the fishing port.[32] The local authorities did all in their power to preserve the social ambience; in 1921 Westgate banned Punch and Judy shows to preserve its respectable image.[33] Travel writers continued to tell their readers who as well as what to expect on holiday. In 1936 an 'invasion of trippers' threatened that sedate backwater, the Isle of Wight.[34]

Abroad, the middle classes prized peace, seclusion and authenticity, while the working class preferred beaches, sunshine, cheap drink and the sort of fun (and food) they enjoyed at home. On the whole the middle classes were appalled and shifted elsewhere. 'The flavour of Miami and Benidorm is infiltrating' the more popular Caribbean islands, complained one travel writer in 1987. None the less, Nevis remained 'untouched', with cheery and deferential natives.[35] As air travel became cheaper, the discriminating holidaymaker penetrated hitherto remote regions. 'Nothing I had seen or smelt had been familiar,' reported one correspondent after a tour of eastern Turkey in 1988, which recommended the region to anyone sick of 'English' bars and chip shops. 'Twentieth-century dross' had not yet reached the region, but, if past experience was anything to go by, it soon would.[36] It permeated the Aegean Islands in 1999, where another correspondent had dreamed of discovering true 'Greekness'. Instead, he was stunned by the 'epitome of tourist hell' at Mykonos. There were more motorbike rental outlets than grocery stores, and bars and restaurants outnumbered churches.[37]

After 1918 the old patterns of middle-class foreign holidays were restored, with cruises (twenty-five pounds for seven days on the Nile and eighty guineas for six weeks in the Caribbean) and far cheaper weekly and fortnightly package trips to France, the Alps and Italy. Adventurous and exotic tastes were also catered for: in 1932 the Soviet Intourist agency offered 'The Golden Road to Turkestan' and a cruise on an icebreaker through Arctic waters.[38] For the more conventional, Continental hotels offered tennis courts, croquet lawns and proximity to gold courses. Air travel made short breaks possible: in 1937 the fight from Croydon to Deauville took less than an hour and cost five pounds return. The Second World War and post-war restrictions on travel allowances interrupted the expansion of air travel and foreign holidays in general.

By the mid-1950s and thanks to lower air fares and larger, if less comfortable, aircraft the middle classes were again venturing abroad. The working class followed closely behind, with the same dream of continual sunshine, beaches and cheap hotels. In 1954 a visitor to a Spanish seaside resort could pay as little as a shilling a day for board and pay the same amount for a bottle of local wine.[39] By contrast, the average daily charge at a British seaside boarding house was between thirty and forty shillings and there was no guarantee of sunshine. A revolution in holidaymaking soon gathered momentum: in 1963 Hotelplan was offering fifteen days in a Costa Brava hotel and air fares for just under thirty-five pounds.[40] In the next thirty years and thanks to the jumbo jet, the exodus to the sun continued and extended to such faraway places as Thailand and Goa.

Some among the middle classes were so enchanted by what they found that they stayed. Retirement homes and those hybrid properties 'time shares' were purchased in and around popular holiday areas. The result was small expatriate communities which enjoyed a foreign climate, but adopted a 'cantonment' mentality by surrounding themselves with trappings of Britishness such as bars selling Guinness, golf clubs and imported comfort foods. An English couple who bought a village store in the Dordogne found that the middle-class expatriate community beat a path to their door to purchase Shredded Wheat and Walker's Crisps.[41] The buyers must have been the direct descendants of those Victorian tourists who demanded their cups of tea and were uneasy about local delicacies. As with holidays abroad, the middle-class emigrants strove to keep ahead of the masses. The price of exclusiveness was high; those seeking an 'idyllic, unhurried and inexpensive' life in Crete in 2005 were warned that they would need to be fluent in Greek.[42]

The middle classes remain addicted to the educational holiday which blended recreation with instruction. During the 1970s craft schools in suitably rural surroundings offered amateurs expert instruction in weaving, pottery and wrought-iron working.[43] Amateur artists were invited to learn from professionals, again in appropriate surroundings; in 1989 painting holidays were advertised in France, Spain, Italy and Turkey. They were expensive: eleven days in Assisi cost just under eight hundred pounds and a fortnight in China nearly two thousand.[44] There were also tours for music buffs which provided first-class accommodation and a programme of concerts and/or operas in Central and Eastern Europe and Italy. Often combined with organised visits to museums, galleries and historic buildings, these holidays were a modern equivalent of the Grand Tour. The visitor returned refreshed in spirit as well as body.

To judge by the numbers advertised, birdwatching holidays dominate the market for improving holidays. This is unsurprising given the spectacular growth of this pastime. In 1939 the Royal Society for the Protection of Birds had fewer than 5,000 members, a total which rose to 29,000 in 1965. Thereafter growth spiralled to 100,000 in 1973 and a million in 1998.[45] Almost nine-tenths of the new members joined as a consequence of apprehension about the dwindling numbers of familiar birds, victims of intensive scientific agriculture. The environmental damage and economic dislocation caused by mass tourism has disturbed the greenish middle classes. Their fears have been alleviated by specialist companies like Kudu Travel and Richard Randall Tours which stress their sensitivity to the environment and contribute to local projects.

Mass tourism has always disfigured seascapes and landscapes. The golden era of seaside holidays roughly between the 1920s and the late 1950s left behind a rash of caravan parks and coastal bungalows. The traditional British seaside holiday with its familiar accoutrements of spades and buckets, beach huts, piers, pierrots and candy floss has passed into terminal decay. It had never really appealed to the middle class, which has always been uncomfortable among noisy crowds. When the middle classes stayed at home they chose the isolation and simple charms of small, picturesque fishing villages in Cornwall, Norfolk and Suffolk and their Scottish equivalents. Many have been colonised by the middle classes and their needs are satisfied by delicatessens, gourmet pubs and restaurants, art galleries and antique shops. Some of the premises advertised their former economic function with names like 'The Old Bakehouse' or 'The Smithie'. Many of the larger resorts such as Bournemouth and Torquay contain settlements of the retired middle class and have endeavoured to survive through the promotion of language schools and conference centres.

Childhood holidays are one of the staples of media nostalgia. It has become an essential ingredient in television schedules, whether for the seaside (*Fawlty Towers* and *Hi-De-Hi!*), or for more gracious and perhaps more innocent periods (*The Jewel in the Crown*, *Brideshead Revisited* and dramatisations of Jane Austen and Trollope). Television has become the dominant source of entertainment for every class, as had been predicted in the 1950s. Its arrival was also accompanied by bleak prophecies that reading would pass into terminal decline, and there was a brief fall in borrowing from libraries which had picked up by 1963 with a striking increase in non-fiction loans.[46]

By this date, over fourteen million people were watching television each Sunday evening.

The cinema lost to television. Ticket sales had risen to a peak of over a thousand million in 1956 and then slumped steadily for the next thirty years. Like television, the cinema had to survive by enticing a mass audience and, for this reason alone, fell foul of upper-middle-class cultural snobbery. Films were not art, asserted C. A. Lejeune, the *Observer*'s film critic, in 1947; they were 'vulgar and illiterate rubbish' which provided 'good entertainment'. This succeeded only when it provided romance and escapism. 'I can see no merit in bringing misery into our recreation.'[47]

Realism with attendant misery and sometimes outrage crept into the cinema, the theatre and television during the 1950s and 1960s and the middle class accepted them, just as it had the new realism of the Edwardian theatre. Working-class ('kitchen sink') scenarios and the candour of young 'angry' playwrights transformed middle-class theatregoers into social anthropologists and stirred their consciences. In 1964 Dennis Potter's television play *Vote, Vote, Vote for Nigel Barton* was widely applauded for its brusque honesty.[48] The play ended with the hero thrusting two fingers in the face of the Conservative candidate Captain Archibald Lake after he had made a platitudinous speech at a dinner dance. There was also a sequence in which Barton is told by a working-class housewife: 'Well, we're Labour, we're all for keeping the blacks out.'

Older middle-class sensibilities lingered on and even in the permissive 1970s theatre impresarios were nervous about going too far. They rejected (understandably perhaps) *The Beard*, a surrealist play which revolved around cunnilingus between Jean Harlow and Billy the Kid, but accepted the nudity of *Oh! Calcutta!* Observing the trend, one actor remarked: 'I am an actor. I don't want to be known for the size of my prick.'[49] Avant-garde playwrights could ignore commercial inhibitions thanks to BBC2, which televised plays by John Arden, Joe Orton and Dennis Potter.

Institutional patronage of the arts had expanded since 1945. Its most powerful godfather was the Arts Council, founded in 1945 to perpetuate wartime support for the arts. By 1970 this predominantly middle-class body had an annual budget of over nine million pounds and subsidiary committees responsible for music, the theatre and literature.[50] Its vast patronage was augmented by that of public and private institutions in which middle-class influence was strong. County councils, universities and schools were among the principal buyers of the modern paintings sold by the new Lincoln Gallery during 1961.[51] Ceramic sculptures commissioned during 1989 were for display in school playgrounds, churches, a library, a railway station, a crematorium, a hospital and an accountancy firm's office.[52] It was art for everyone, but choosing it was delegated to committees in which the middle class was well represented. By the end of the century, a new breed of expert was emerging to help them make up their minds; in 1997 the City University was offering an MA in 'Arts Criticism and Management'.

The private market for decorative art has survived. It was about eight million strong according to an academic and was wholly middle class, made up of professionals and men and women who had had 'higher education'. They were 'enlightened' towards the arts and happy to spend between forty and four hundred pounds per item.[53] Publicly funded bodies could afford to be more open-handed. In 1997 Hackney Council offered ten thousand pounds each to 'craftspeople' to design hats for the borough's annual May Bank Holiday celebrations.[54]

In theory, spending the ratepayers' cash in this way was an extension of the Victorian middle-class principle that the arts civilised society. Previous confidence as to what kind of art best achieved this purpose had wilted under the heat of political considerations. Were subsidies to be dispensed on opera, ballet and concerts which attracted well-heeled audiences? More importantly, these forms of entertainment and much else which received assistance were being traduced as elitist, which became a pejorative term in the late twentieth century. Defenders of publicly funded culture lamely responded with utilitarian arguments designed to placate politicians and voters rather than assert the inspirational value of the arts to the individual human spirit. Henceforward, arts programmes were deliberately favoured on the ground that they somehow promoted social inclusion. None the less, special exhibitions of medieval, Renaissance and later artworks produced for aristocratic patrons attract vast audiences whenever they are held.

Judgments about relative worth and quality lay at the root of elitism and were shunned. 'No leisure activity is intrinsically superior to any other' was the breathtaking conclusion of a conference held by the Arts Council and the Library Association. By the 1990s it had become, as Richard Hoggart has suggested, snobbish to assert that *Paradise Lost* was superior to the lyrics of the Beatles.[55] The prevailing atmosphere was hostile towards critical aesthetic connoisseurship. 'The bestowal of [public] money for the arts', observed the poet Roy Fuller, 'inevitably attracts the idle, the dotty, the minimally talented, the self promoted.'[56] True enough, but private purses have made a fortune for the authors of that recent farrago of fantasy and cod history, *The Da Vinci Code*.

There are still some among the educated middle classes who are willing to risk accusations of mandarin superiority when it comes to artistic judgments. Revealingly, they are condemned for social rather than aesthetic reasons. 'Irritable knee-jerk snobbery' was how *The Times* responded to Antonia Byatt's suggestion that Jeffrey Archer's novels were not worth preserving.[57] Perhaps so, but his oeuvre is evidence of the tastes of a huge number of readers, many of them middle-class. That class has always read trite, banal and sensationalist fiction.

Today, the middle class reads more books and newspapers than ever. Eighty thousand books were published in 1994, a tenth of them novels, and, between 1945 and 1994, the readership of the quality daily newspapers more than doubled to 2.6 million. By contrast, and in pursuit of policies aimed at inclusiveness, local authority libraries are buying fewer books. Older ones are sometimes censured if they appear to deny inclusiveness or reflect values now out of favour in leftish circles. 'Old-fashioned books' which portrayed women as the 'weaker sex' have been removed from some shelves, and School Library Services have been encouraged to include material with 'positive images of disabled people'. Whether this excludes *Treasure Island* is not known.

The cult of inclusiveness has made no impact on the old cultural hierarchy of high, middle and low brow. A glance along the shelves of any bookstore proves this, as do bestseller lists and the weekly ratings of television programmes. Book buyers are overwhelmingly middle class and their tastes remain eclectic and diverse. Victorian patterns of reading have been perpetuated, but with some significant changes. Religious books command little attention, but manuals of self-help have multiplied, particularly during the last quarter of the twentieth century. There has been a steady flow of texts promising to revitalise the reader's life through diet and courses of mental and physical exercise. Sometimes, they promise the path to ultimate self-understanding. Older traditions of self-help have been kept alive through the equally numerous handbooks on individual business success, each offering magic formulae, many with New Age ingredients. These are hilariously analysed in Francis Wheen's *How Mumbo Jumbo Conquered the World* (2004). If the sheer amount of such self-improving literature is anything to go by, the middle classes are still seeking a balance between personal achievement (and with it the admiration of others) and internal spiritual harmony.

There have been changes in the nature of middle-class fiction. Three new genres have come into prominence: science fiction, fantasy and espionage thrillers. Each reflected the neuroses of their times: futuristic novels pointed the dangers and advantages of scientific progress, while fantasy works, most famously those of Tolkien, conducted readers into universes filled with sorcery and wonderful creatures and in which good and evil were in perpetual conflict. Spy thrillers penetrated the murky but frightening world of power politics and conspiracies, which were thwarted by superheroes such as John Buchan's Richard Hannay and Ian Fleming's James Bond. Invented conspiracy theories based upon actual mysteries such as the murder of the Russian royal family and multiple appearances of what may be alien spaceships have recently gained a considerable following. Much of this is bunkum, but it is further evidence of a wider willingness to suspend rational disbelief and accept the untested.

Both world wars generated an ever-expanding literature embracing memoirs, narrative histories, analyses of strategy and tactics and, most mesmeric of all, studies of Adolf Hitler and his Third Reich. Since the 1960s there has been a continual cross-fertilisation between war literature and television documentaries and film dramas with wartime themes. The same has applied in other subjects, particularly natural history, and fiction. Old and new novels have been translated into films and television serials with varying degrees of authenticity and success. The urge to entice a large audience has sometimes led to dilution and distortion: one scriptwriter admitted in 2004 that *Pride and Prejudice* was about 'girls in nighties talking about love' and that the 'macho' in Mr Darcy needed development. Some of his middle-class listeners gasped at what seemed to affirm the highbrow belief that the media was bent on 'dumbing down' the classics.

The novel has continued to hold up a mirror to middle-class life and morals and readers have yet to tire of recitations of the common-place whose latest manifestations have been the 'Aga saga' and 'chick lit', both aimed at female, middle-class readers interested in their own kind. Historical fiction thrives, especially when it contains the romance and high adventure so brilliantly blended by Georgette Heyer, C. S. Forester, Patrick O'Brian and George Macdonald Fraser. All have had some of their works made into highly popular films and television series. It remains a matter of contention whether these authors produce 'serious' literature and, if not, what are its vital ingredients. Such matters engage the minds of middle-class book circles, whose members read a book and then assemble to dissect and discuss it, often over glasses of wine. Such gatherings are comparatively new phenomena, but with an ancient pedigree. The convivial exchange of knowledge and ideas among the like-minded in search of self-improvement has remained one of the most perfect recipes for middle-class pleasure.

11

I'm Proud of Being Middle-Class: Identities, Past and Future

'Mrs Weber' and 'Alex' are cartoon characters who occupy opposite and mutually hostile poles of the modern middle class. They reveal much about its present state of evolution and its mental heritage. Mrs Weber, her family and friends were created in the late 1970s by Posy Simmonds for a strip cartoon which appeared in the *Guardian*. Its readers looked into a mirror which reflected their passions, idiosyncrasies and moral quandaries. Mrs Weber is a feminist, ex-nurse and aspiring children's writer married to a bearded sociology lecturer at a London polytechnic. Their progressive mindset was formed in the 1960s when they were 'flower children' and they inhabit a terrace house in a district of London in the process of gentrification, a word they would not like because it implies a graded society. They take great pains not to appear stand-offish towards old residents.

In their eyes the Webers embody modern enlightenment. Their daughter Belinda sees them as living anachronisms from the 1960s. 'My parents really are peasants! They look so scruffy and unkempt . . . they never buy things that last.' Belinda is 'sick of lentils, old denim, Batik prints' and her parents' obsession with sex, and regrets that they and their kind have transformed the neighbourhood into 'an urban village'. It was the setting for a street party for which Mrs

Weber had prepared quiches ('the vegetarian ones are at the front') and at which 'Marks and Sparks' plonk' is served. Genuine locals sip gin and tonics and smile indulgently at 'the peasants'. George Weber's former colleague Kevin Penwallet has retired to live among real peasants at Tresoddit on the Cornish coast, where he is a shopkeeper-cum-missionary selling 'morally wholesome foods'. The locals want none of them and continue to consume such 'bio-cultural poisons' as frozen chips and instant whips.

Other heretics reject the Webers' well-meaning creed. When they rebuke Belinda's punkish boyfriend Jasper for his 'sexist' remarks, he snarls at them:

> . . . you woolly liberals! Look at you! All your soft, frayed, patched, ethnic, woolly comfortable, old clothes sum up your attitude to life! Whenever controversy comes your way, you swaddle it in woolly deference and smother it with a cushion of irreproachable tolerance! Your bile never bubbles! Your gorge never boils! . . . you sit on the bloody fence! You're tepid!

Mrs Weber sadly wonders whether 'woolly liberals' are destined to become 'moth eaten'.[1]

Alex would have applauded Jasper's tirade. He was created by Charles Peattie and Russell Taylor and first appeared in the *Independent* in 1987. Alex is a predatory carnivore employed by a City corporate finance company and is moving upwards in the world thanks to his instinctive ruthlessness and duplicity. Alex worships money and the prestige it buys. He is proud of his wad of credit cards, complains to a restaurant waiter that his bill is 'too small' and, when offered the latest hi-fi, tells the salesman that he is seeking 'something more ostentatious'.

Alex's landscape is peopled by winners like himself and losers like his fellow bankers, whom he plies with dud shares, and beggars and Tube buskers. When one of them sings 'Money can't buy you love', Alex passes him a note which reads, 'How would you know, pauper?' He takes a coin from the cap of a beggar as a 'consultation fee' after telling him to buy a mouth organ. Once, Alex rings up the Samaritans to tell them that he earns forty thousand pounds a year and owns a BMW, adding by way of explanation, 'I just thought you might like to hear some good news for a change.' His holiday on a remote and untouched Greek island is made perfect by locals touching their forelocks as he drives past. Alex is a natural philistine; invited to the opera by his rivals at Metrobank, he and they treat the perform-ance as an endurance test. He judges paintings solely by how much they cost.[2]

Of course, Alex is an exaggeration, but like the best caricatures he reflects reality. He sincerely believes that his intelligence and endeavour deserve rich rewards and that life is a Darwinian struggle in which the ablest succeed. Those who do not, and depend upon the charity of others, are parasites. There were and are many within the middle classes who share his opinions. Alex would have further justified his salary on the ground that he was taking risks, not only with other people's money but with his own future. In later episodes he is made redundant (as were many like him) and forced to find a new post. George Weber was paid far less (in the late 1970s lecturers earned between five and eight thousand pounds a year) and, as a public employee, enjoyed security of employment and a generous pension. Security of employment disappeared in the next two decades.

Alex and the Webers are witty reminders of two significant and enduring divisions within the middle class. Real Webers were plen-tiful and distinctive. A sociologist's impression of the herbivorous middle class compiled in 1970 characterised them as well educated, prosperous, open-minded, radical, prone to identify themselves with outsiders, hostile to organised religion, outwardly dismissive of social rituals and uncomfortable about competition. Their indulgences enriched body and soul and included: 'muesli, Renault Fours, au pairs, brass rubbings, along with sauna baths, *Which?*, discussion groups, nut salads . . . a croft in the Shetlands, painless childbirth, wholemeal bread, encounter therapy, finger painting, dabbling in the occult, nudity . . .'[3]

Like the Webers, these creatures lived within the penumbra of bohemianism and, in all likelihood, earned their living as servants of the state, although they would have preferred the word 'community'.

They participated in public affairs, felt a responsibility for society's waifs and casualties, which was perhaps tinged with guilt, and made a fuss whenever they uncovered injustice or found their environment imperilled. Their influence exceeded their numbers and they flattered themselves that they were the conscience of the nation, which was why, in May 2005, a substantial number abandoned New Labour for the Liberal Democrats because of the Iraq war.

The bien-pensant middle class has had other grounds for political disenchantment. The institutions which they cherish and work for have been penetrated by the ethos of competitive business with its opaque jargon of performance, targets and 'solutions'. Solace and compassion have no columns in the balance sheet. Moreover, and this concerns the entire middle class, the state is failing to live up to expectation in the free provision of welfare and education. Bureaucratic structures buckle, costs escalate and there is a feeling that the scale and complexities of the problems render them uncontrollable.

Alex is exempt from anxieties about the facilities provided by the state: he pays for them from his own pocket. He too had a distinctive pedigree which stretched back to the hard-nosed manufacturers and entrepreneurs of the Industrial Revolution and beyond to the buccaneering merchants and financiers of the seventeenth and eighteenth centuries. Their drive, acumen, ambition and ruthlessness were inherited by the young 'masters of the universe' who made fortunes in the City during the 1980s. Audacity and nerve paid dividends: in 1992 one London speculator claimed that he had made half a million pounds on the day of the ERM fiasco.[4] Such coups were exceptional, but the everyday rewards were enough to tempt the keenest minds. In 1971 a total of 114 Oxford and Cambridge graduates went into the City; in 1994 a further 446 followed in Alex's path. The numbers entering teaching and the public sector plummeted.[5]

The young men and women who became accountants, commercial and corporate lawyers, and merchant bankers coalesced into a new, extremely rich superclass which was metropolitan and meritocratic. Its upwardly mobile members were called 'Yuppies' and they attracted a mixture of envy and admiration from the poor. 'Jammy bastards' and 'nice work if you can get it' were two reactions of 1988 to the Yuppy phenomenon.[6]

Older Yuppies who scooped up directorships, share options and self-awarded perks during the privatisations of the 1980s and 1990s provoked jealousy laced with rage. Cedric Brown, the chairman of British Gas, was nicknamed 'Cedric the Pig' by the press for his apparent greed (in 1994 he was earning £475,000 a year) and others of his kind were labelled 'fat cats'. Brown's director of retailing, Norman Blacker, got by on £250,000 and, perhaps tactlessly, told show-room workers that they were overpaid.[7] Defenders of strato-spheric salaries argued that they offered true value to their compan-ies, a claim which was undermined by the fact that some highly paid executives presided over declining firms. There was a moral revulsion against rewarding incompetence and failure. A cynical but common reaction was expressed by the comedian Alexis Sayle, who observed that top men rewarded themselves prodigally for the same reason as a dog licked its balls, simply because it knows it can. More politely, Simon Jenkins, the former editor of *The Times*, described their behaviour as an 'insult to those who worked hard for fixed pay'.[8] The middle-class orthodoxy that rewards should be commen-surate with intelligence and effort still holds strong.

Alex, the Webers, their actual counterparts and those executives who overvalue their ability are all part of a middle class which, since 1914, has found that the forces of history were on its side. Their favours were not always apparent. There were moments when the middle classes felt the pinch and, whenever economic crises co-incided with working-class militancy, periods of acute nervousness about the future. Making long-term provision for their own and their children's futures has been a constant feature of the middle-class psychology, yet they succumbed easily to short-term panics. Present anxieties about Muslim terrorism and immigration are proof of this.

Taxation has been a perpetual bugbear to the middle class. After the First World War, alarmists had predicted that it would strangle the middle class, and similar jeremiads were heard over the next ninety years, invariably in the Tory press. In 1985 the *Daily Mail* denounced Labour plans to 'help the poor by hammering the rich' as a 'sting' which would cripple the entire middle class.[9] It was a familiar allegation and was guaranteed to throw the middle classes on the defensive and into the arms of the Conservatives, which explains why in the last three general elections New Labour has vigorously contested claims that it intended to increase taxation.

Behind the intermittent political rows over how much tax was paid by the middle classes was a wider and more significant question about the nature of society. In the years immediately before 1914 the Liberals had introduced legislation based upon the principle that the state should oversee the redistribution of income from the rich to the poor in the interests of a fairer society. Since then a vast amount of political energy has been concentrated on evolving a system which achieved this to the satisfaction of all. It was not a matter of squaring a circle, since the middle classes and their press and Parliamentary tribunes accepted (sometimes with sighs) the concept of what became known as social justice. It is important to remember this, for it illustrates a willingness to compromise that helps reveal why the middle classes were able to survive comparatively unharmed in a democracy in which, until the end of the twentieth century, they were a minority. Acceptance of state-regulated social justice was facilitated because traditionally the middle classes had never been prepared to leave the poor to sink or swim. Furthermore, during the second half of the century, the middle classes relied upon health and educational services provided by the state.

Transferring money from the better off to the poorest was at the heart of the egalitarian society of which socialists dreamed. Thanks to a national emergency, it was achieved during and immediately after the war when the government decreed how people spent their money and what they could eat. It was an experience which the middle class disliked. The suspension of economic inequality was seen on the left as a step towards the end of class divisions. In 'Dawn for Jessica', a serial run in *Woman's Own* in 1943, a rich woman is horrified when her son announces his intention to marry a working-class WAAF girl. A friend tells her that her objections are outdated: 'The old barriers of class and well, money are just disappearing. It's character, courage and sympathy and other qualities that count.'[10] That was the message of the 1943 film *Millions Like Us*, in which an upper-middle-class girl (Anne Crawford) falls in love with her foreman (Eric Porter), a working-class Yorkshireman. The story ends on a cautious note: when the couple discuss marriage, the foreman suggests waiting until the war is over, for only then will it be clear whether class divisions have permanently disappeared.

Those class divisions, and those implied assessments of individual worth which sustained them, had been firmly in place before the war. In 1916 Major Darwin, the son of the scientist, had told fellow eugenicists that judged by their intelligence the 'well-to-do-classes' were innately superior to those at the bottom of the 'economic scale'.[11] In 1939 a middle-class housewife (the daughter of a brick-layer) found that there was 'too much snobbery' in Marlow where she lived, yet she accepted the small town's distinctive hierarchy. At its summit were those earning between eight and twelve pounds a week who were the 'nicest' of all because they were intelligent, but not too well educated. Then came those on between five and eight pounds a week, struggling to acquire a car and the status it bestowed, and beneath them were the 'crude, dirty and irresponsible' working class.[12] Those who would have been shocked by her judgment blamed the public schools for perpetuating a rigid hierarchy. According to *Picture Post* in 1939 they provided 'a class education and a class outlook' and were still doing so in 1966 when the Labour writer Ted Willis accused them of being 'citadels' of class.[13]

Deference had withered, but slowly. One who had been conditioned to expected it groused in 1919 about the decline in the use of 'Sir' and 'Madam' even by servants.[14] Frank Richards, the creator of Billy Bunter, concluded a diatribe against the disasters of the inter-war years ('the General Strike, the outbreak of sex chatter . . . make-up') with the assertion that 'It is an actual fact that, in this country at least, noblemen generally are better fellows than commoners.'[15] Some women appeared to agree. Shortly before the 1945 general election the *Economist* thought that female shopkeepers and servants believed that 'only the rich and glamorous are fit to govern' and would, presumably, vote Tory.[16]

The antics of the 'rich and glamorous' have continued to arouse the curiosity of the middle and lower reaches of the middle classes, if the popularity of gossip columns is anything to go by. In August 1931 readers of the *Daily Sketch* discovered that Prince Rispoli, 'the handsomest man in Hollywood', was taking a holiday on the Adriatic. At home, Lord and Lady Carlisle were hosting a shoot at Naworth Castle.[17] All that is new about the current celebrity cult is the social origins of its subjects. The foibles of royalty were depicted with almost comic obsequiousness. In 1954 *Illustrated* described Princess Alexandra as 'a beautiful young woman' who was learning from her mother 'the art of being graceful in company'. Another piece revealed that 'Prince Charles, already six, understands how a Briton treats his dog. "I think Sugar is thirsty. Someone had better show her where to get a drink."'[18]

Respect for their subjects (and by implication for the social order of which they occupied the summit) gradually disappeared from the gossip columns after the 1960s, and within twenty years royalty was exposed to the sort of prying and ridicule it had not suffered since the Regency. Gossip became synonymous with scandal, as it had been in the eighteenth-century press. Towards the end of the 1980s, a new elite suddenly appeared. They were 'celebrities' who were and are predominantly young, whose fame is almostly entirely the consequence of fortunes made in the worlds of sport (particularly football), fashion, pop music and showbiz, or, in the instances of Jeffrey Archer and Mrs and Mrs Neil Hamilton, public notoriety.

All celebrities depend upon a public relations apparatus which strives to keep their names in the public consciousness. *Hello!* magazine, its imitators and gossip columnists chronicle their lives, provide the prurient with tales of their sexual adventures and allow the envious and curious to inspect their homes and learn about their domestic trivia. Some celebrities have volunteered for public humiliation in television programmes in which they are placed in undignified predicaments. What in 1991 the *Economist* called the 'celebristocracy' had supplanted the aristocracy as a source of public interest.[19] One fascinating aspect of this phenomenon is that reports of celebrity scandals are now regularly carried by serious newspapers with an upper-middle-class readership.

The changing intellectual character of the middle-class press was a source of contention in a libel suit brought in 1990 by Andrew Neil (Paisley Grammar School and Glasgow University), the editor of the *Sunday Times*, against Sir Peregrine Worsthorne (Stowe and Peterhouse), editor of the *Sunday Telegraph*. Worsthorne was appalled by Neil's 'celebrity' lifestyle, which included a relationship with Pamella Bordes, an alleged courtesan. The world of the playboy was utterly inappropriate for the editor of a serious newspaper, who, Worsthorne insisted, needed to be a cultured figure, intimate with such establishment luminaries as the Archbishop of Canterbury and the heads of Oxford and Cambridge colleges. Night clubs were out, save for Annabel's because 'it was frequented by the aristocracy', whom Worsthorne admired. He lost the case, which had been a skirmish between the old upper-middle class and its new, meritocratic wing which refused to be intimidated by starchy conventions.[20] Neil versus Worsthorne was a signal reminder that the more arcane nuances of class still mattered.

A year after this lawsuit, an opinion poll revealed that Britons believed by a majority of five to one that a classless society would never be created.[21] During the 1970s a similar investigation yielded a similar result: half the population thought class divisions were 'desirable' and over three-quarters considered them 'inevitable'.[22] The British were contented living with class, in spite of dire warnings during and after the war that it retarded progress. Surveying Britain's wobbling economy in 1978, the German Chancellor Helmut Schmidt declared: 'As long as you maintain that damned class-ridden society of yours, you will never get anywhere.'[23] Yet within two decades the British economy was flourishing and the German drifting as a consequence of over-generous welfare programmes, or so its critics alleged.

The economic resurgence of the 1980s had, however, chipped away at the social hierarchy, according to an analysis made in 1994.

New business organisational structures borrowed from Germany and Japan had encouraged 'democracy' and 'equality' which had led to a 'blurring of socio-economic class divisions'. If this was so, then in time corporate loyalties would supersede social and tribal ones.[24] This accorded with Mrs Thatcher's social vision. In 1985 she had told an audience of Eton boys that 'My hope is that people would become less concerned with status and more concerned with performance.'[25]

This has not happened, nor will it according to the most recent study of the subject.[26] The pursuit of status was one of the features which defined the middle class, observed one working man in 1970. 'They look down on people who work with their hands and spend all their time worrying about holidays in Spain, getting an "1100" and so on.' The latter still holds true, although the car will now be a '4x4' and the holiday destination will probably be Thailand or New Zealand.

But do the middle classes still 'look down' on others? On a public level, the middle classes pay lip-service to the abstract notion of equality, but on another, they are still inclined to make private judgments which assume differences of moral worth and intelligence. It was a subject which both fascinated and tormented the playwright Dennis Potter. He was a miner's son and grammar schoolboy who went to Oxford in 1956 where he found himself surrounded by upper-middle-class public schoolboys. Once, he introduced his working-class fiancée to them and wrote afterwards: 'She must have felt like I once felt as a private in an officer's mess . . . she was ill-at-ease with them and they were ill-at-ease with her.' Potter was acutely uncomfortable about his relations with his scout; he did not want to patronise him, but was anxious that his servant should not discover his working-class background. Other grammar schoolboys swam with the current and Potter condemned them as 'creeps, adopting as many mannerisms of Oxford as they could and distancing themselves from their past'. 'Like most people from the working classes', Potter hoped to escape and yet somehow retain his old 'identity'.[27]

He made a name for himself by laying bare social prejudices

which were felt but left unspoken for the sake of politeness and which, among other things, drove him to spit on parked Rolls-Royces. Potter unburdened himself on television and wrote a book (*The Glittering Coffin*) about his experiences. His outspokenness may have touched some raw nerves and caught the spirit of the times, for, as a female undergraduate from a similar background observed: 'Being working class at the end of the Fifties . . . was the thing . . . we flaunted it to great effect.'[28] In 1960 *Queen* magazine made as much of the background of the young novelists Keith Waterhouse ('his father sold greengroceries from a horse-drawn cart') and Alan Sillitoe ('left school to work in a bicycle factory') as the content of their books.[29]

They were members of a generation of working-class writers whose novels were welcomed for their forthrightness and, above all, 'grittiness', a form of directness found among the Northern working class which made them refreshing and appealing. There was nothing to be ashamed of in a working-class background. It became glamorous, which may be why, in 1976, Nicholas Cutter, the owner of a small business, declared: 'I'm proud of being middle-class, not one of those people . . . who insinuate that they had a working-class background.' He lived near Wilmslow in Cheshire and proudly affirmed that 'if there wasn't a middle-class, we'd be Britain, full stop. There'd be very little of the "Great" left, wouldn't there?'[30] Cutter also had a nostalgia for the Victorian heyday of the middle class when Britain barked orders to the rest of the world and sent out gunboats to enforce them. His views were not uncommon: many members of the middle class still consider themselves to be the backbone of the nation.

There was comfort too in the knowledge that entry into the middle class was the goal of the ambitious working class. Yet, as Ferdinand Mount has remarked, this ascent involves clambering up the foothills of the lower-middle class. Its associations with suburbia have been unfortunate, which is why, in Mount's words: 'People are quite happy to describe themselves as having been born into the lower-middle class — but only if they have climbed out of it.'[31] As he explains, this is because for over a century the upper reaches of the middle classes have identified the suburbs as nurseries of narrow-minded philistines. Even in the upper strata of the middle class, there were fine distinctions of status and prestige. In 1985, Colonel Gordon Palmer of Huntley and Palmers told an audience of Etonians: 'People are quite prepared to say they are a stockbroker [*sic*] at Lloyd's but not to say that they run an engineering works.'[32]

However much it is deplored, snobbery will not fade away. It remains deeply embedded in the national sense of humour. The ignorance, ineptitude and inarticulacy of the lower orders drew laughs from Elizabethan theatregoers, filled eighteenth-century books of jests and were the stock-in-trade of *Punch*. The middle classes have laughed at rustic chawbacons, dim-witted servants and, most recently, Essex girls, 'chavs' and, in Scotland, 'Neds'. All are young and working-class and their habits, tastes and appearance are ridiculed without inhibition. It remains perfectly acceptable to jeer at the idiosyncrasies of class or to express contempt for an individual or group on grounds of class. Yet the law forbids such licence when it comes to race and, if legislation proposed in 2005 is passed, religion.

Mockery blended with condescension entertained television audiences during the summer of 2003. The contents of one programme (*You Are What You Eat*), ostensibly about working-class feeding habits, struck the journalist Ron Liddle as grotesque. It consisted of 'ripping the piss out of the staggering thick, feckless and fat British *untermensch*'. Viewers had the opportunity to 'laugh at the chavs *and* to watch them being repeatedly smacked about the head for their manifest irresponsibilities by clever middle-class people'. These were represented by a bossy female nutritionist who castigated overweight, working-class Yvonne for the follies of her sugary diet. Her degradation was complete when her stool was inspected and condemned for lack of substance. A crash diet soon produced what Liddle called 'a firm and bulky middle-class turd'.[33]

The 'underclass' is not funny, quite the opposite. Like its predecessors, it occupies the bottom of the social pile and its violence seems to threaten the security of the middle classes. Newspapers inflate their anxieties and politicians promise protection. In 1995 the shadow Home Secretary Jack Straw announced that he would purge the streets of 'aggressive begging, of winos, addicts and squeegee merchants' so that the 'law-abiding citizen' could walk abroad undisturbed. Similar declarations could have been made in 1895 or 1595.

Jokes about chavs and spasmodic media jitters about the criminal underclass indicate that early-twenty-first-century Britain is still a layered society. It is, but far less so than it was ninety, even fifty years ago. Many of the superficial distinctions between the classes have vanished or become blurred. In 1931 an advertisement for the deodorant Odo-Ro-No promised to eliminate the 'social stigma' of unwashed flesh and, twenty years later, the working classes had one bath a week.[34] Nowadays and thanks to modern hot-water systems, just about everyone has a daily bath or shower, although unease about 'personal freshness' persists. Likewise, the washing machine and modern fabrics mean that the cleanliness of clothes no longer indicates social status.

What you wear does indicate status, however, simply because dress continues to fulfil its ancient function of proclaiming wealth and status. George Orwell's insurance salesman George Bowling – in his worn grey suit, fifty-shilling overcoat and bowler hat – knew that he could never be mistaken for a 'gentleman'. 'Well-educated', 'intelligent' and 'well-motivated' were the reactions of personnel staff to a young man in a pinstripe suit and bowler hat in a survey of job applications made in 1968. Another candidate in denim jeans was automatically considered to be an applicant for a labouring or maintenance job.[35]

The social language of dress remains complex. Spending power is obviously important, as the *Economist* pointed out in 1992 with its hierarchy of shirts: 'drip dry', 'cotton rich' and 'all cotton'.[36] Other considerations come into play, particularly the pressures to conform to peer groups and keep up with fashion, which are obsessions for the young and anyone wishing to assert their status. These groups find reassurance in the 'designer' label, which is the modern counterpart of the silk hat, kid gloves and silver-mounted cane with which D. H. Lawrence's brother impressed his former neighbours. The gold chain and hunter conspicuously displayed in the waistcoat pocket have been replaced by the 'state-of-the-art' mobile phone. Both attract envy and thieves.

Different classes and subspecies within classes have adopted different uniforms to say who they are (or think they are) and secure acceptance by their own kind on formal and informal occasions. For the same reasons, the young have their own uniforms which declare attachment to styles of pop music. Neutral or 'classless' items such as jeans, T-shirts and baseball caps revealingly derive from America, but, like the rest of modern dress, can be graded according to cut and therefore price.

Dress has always disguised or embellished nature. Now it is possible to counterfeit it through plastic and cosmetic surgery. Such surgery erases the stigmata of ageing, guaranteeing some kind of perpetual youth, and remoulds curves and bumps to conform to an individual's ideal of beauty. In 2004 some 65,000 such operations were performed in Britain, nine-tenths of them on women. This sort of treatment is expensive and most popular among the lower-middle and richer working classes. Their paradigms of perfection are film actresses or models.[37] Nothing better illuminates contemporary obsessions with celebrities than this form of imitation.

Fluency and vocabulary still distinguish different classes, accents less so than in the past. As a ranker in the RAF in the 1930s, T. E. Lawrence was sometimes egged on by his working-class comrades to use his 'toffology' against their superiors. Language was a weapon deployed by 'them' against 'us' and it was heartening to have the tables turned. One who knew Lawrence remembered that he spoke with the 'accent of the ascendancy', that is to say the received pronunciation of the BBC which derived from late-Victorian and Edwardian public schools and Oxford and Cambridge. Its tone was authoritative and was used by BBC newsreaders and cinema newsreel commentators.

This accent gradually disppeared from the airwaves after 1960. Its demise was inevitable, for while it had been cultivated in many grammar schools, it was not adopted in the comprehensives which succeeded them. In 1963 boys at an LCC (London County Council) boarding school in Suffolk were noted as speaking in 'a neutral

David Frost accent' which made them 'genuinely classless'. Some still feared that their native working-class culture was being 'ironed out', and this was a period when it was becoming fashionable.[38]

Paradoxically at a time when the external trappings of status were so passionately sought after and acquired, the audible ones lapsed. The middle-class accent, now only heard when films produced between and immediately after the war are shown on television, has become a handicap. It conveyed a sense of superiority, which contradicted the egalitarian spirit of the times. The middle-class young in search of 'coolness' and, in the 1980s, 'street credibility' mimicked working-class accents and speech patterns. The outcome was the spread of 'Estuary' English, a singsong South London twang. Inarticulateness is emphasised through a superfluity of redundant 'likes' in every sentence.

By 2004 drama schools found themselves overwhelmed by pupils whose slovenly and indistinct speech rendered them incapable of playing classical roles. Rescue courses had to be assembled to teach the old received pronunciation. It was extremely hard to find a newcomer to play the role of Tom Brown for a television version of his schooldays.[39] In the end a public schoolboy was uncovered who could speak the lines in an approved manner, which was ironic since the Tom Brown of the 1830s may well have spoken with the burr of his native Devon. Those seeking public favour used 'neutral' accents to avoid sounding 'posh' which, it was believed, now alienated those who had once been reassured by an educated accent. Clement Attlee's passage through public school and Cambridge was stamped on his speech; modern Labour politicians who have made the same journey now go to great lengths to hide it. To do otherwise is to risk charges of condescension. During the May 2005 general election, Michael Brown, a former Tory MP, noted approvingly that a public-school- and Oxford-educated candidate for his party gave no hint of his background as he canvassed in casual clothes. In public life it is now a handicap to sound even remotely like Bertie Wooster; a BBC producer excluded one distinguished figure from a book programme on the ground that listeners might take against her 'posh' accent.[40]

★

In terms of the history of the middle classes, the distinctive upper-middle-class accent has had a brief life. Its rise and fall coincided with sporadic agitation against 'privilege'. It was a word commonly employed by thinkers and writers of the left whenever they wished to expose or eradicate what they regarded as the inherent unfairnesses within society. Privilege symbolised inequality and in particular the concentration of resources within the pockets of the middle classes. They had more money and so secured the best of everything, particularly education. It was a generalisation that could have been justified during the inter-war years, but even then it denied the fact that the patterns of wealth distribution were changing. The proliferation of the suburbs and cheap cars on the road were clear evidence of this.

Then and afterwards statistics which showed that relatively small groups owned a disproportionate amount of the nation's wealth were paraded to prove that 'privilege' survived. The residue available for the rest was increasing and filtered down through the middle and working classes. Merlyn Rees, a Labour MP and future minister, sensed the change and its impact on his working-class constituents during the late 1950s. 'The possession of a cheque book and of a building society pass book do tend to make people conscious of their status.' Women, he noted, were acutely aware of the 'new social milieu and how to respond to it'.[41] This was confirmed by a sociologist who observed a tendency among women to upgrade their social position when questioned for surveys.[42]

The need for such misrepresentation diminished during the next fifty years; the middle classes were growing in number for reasons I have explained earlier. Now, they are a sprawling mass making up perhaps as much as two-thirds of society. A version of classlessness has been achieved simply through more and more people becoming middle-class. This transformation of society has not lessened assaults on privilege. New Labour may have embraced free-market capitalism, but it has not entirely discarded its party's ancestral egalitarianism. On the one hand, its policies encourage competition, private investment, consumer credit, house ownership and customer choice, all dear to a large section of the middle classes. On the other, the party's leadership is outraged if middle-class individuals choose to employ their resources to secure better versions of what the modern state provides, education and health.

At the heart of this debate is the assumption that everyone shares or ought to share middle-class aspirations. This ambition has been repeatedly endorsed and encouraged by Mrs Thatcher and Tony Blair, but it creates political problems. Those already in the middle classes want their children to get on and provide them with whatever 'advantages' (for example, books, the exercise of discipline and encouragement) will assist their progress. They do this out of choice and, in the process, sometimes have to practise self-denial. This is always worth remembering whenever the left raises the issue of 'privilege' or 'advantage'.

New Labour has decided to overcome this problem by compelling universities to restrict the entry of students from public schools, irrespective of scholastic attainment. Proposals which deny the middle-class belief that talent should rise freely were expressed in the argot (for example, 'targets' and 'penalties') of the competitive market, also dear to the middle classes. In return for obeying the state, universities were free to respond to market forces by raising tuition fees. Independent public institutions of the kind which the Victorian middle class did so much to foster have become agents of the state. Sensitive to middle-class disquiet, at the May 2005 general election the Liberal Democrats promised a return to state provision of tuition fees, which may have helped it garner middle-class votes.

The middle classes now hold the political balance and will have to decide whether they can survive and prosper in a nation in which a centralised state exercises more power than ever in peacetime and plans to engross more under the guise of the 'war' against fundamentalist Muslim terrorism. Nearly all our political and personal liberties have been secured through middle-class agitation, and sections of that class, particularly lawyers, have been in the forefront of resistance to the far-reaching and, some would argue, authoritarian constitutional and legal measures recently proposed by New Labour. The historic middle-class conscience has been deeply offended by the invasion and subjugation of Iraq; there was a swing away from New Labour by the professional and educated middle class during the May 2005 election. Afterwards, pundits wondered whether Tony Blair had lost his instinctive flair for sensing middle-class feeling. On the other hand, disenchantment with New Labour has not persuaded the middle classes to rekindle their love affair with the Tories, although the party made headway in its traditional heartland in South-Eastern England.

Entering the middle class remains a goal for talented outsiders. The actor Michael Gambon, a former apprentice toolmaker, defended himself against charges that he was over-zealous about how much he was paid by asserting that such matters no longer concerned him. 'I've joined the middle classes now. I've accepted a knighthood. I'm a member of the Garrick Club for God's sake.'[43] This was an accomplishment always worth celebrating, but what does it mean today?

There is no easy answer, nor has there ever been. The middle class remains a sprawling, complex organism in a state of continuing evolution. It is split along political, cultural, economic, religious and generational lines. Passage into the middle class has been and remains a goal of immigrants. There are Jewish, Italian, Sikh, Hindu, African, Afro-Caribbean and Muslim middle classes, the last two smaller, but growing. They are among many, often transient sub-species such as the Sloane Rangers or Young Fogeys whose tastes and behaviour caught the attention of style gurus. These 1980s phenomena are reminders that clannishness, conformity and imitation have been constant features of middle-class life.

So too has diversity of conviction. Aesthetes clash with environmentalists over wind farms and secularists battle with Christians and Muslims over the primacy of the state as the arbiter of morality. Some within the middle class are open-minded towards the new, others shrink from it. The Alexes are happy to give full rein to market forces, the Webers want to bridle them. Taste arouses bile. On a new housing estate on Teesside in 2004, one owner of a semi embellished it with cheery but garish Christmas illuminations. His neighbours were apoplectic: one wrote anonymously that everyone who lived in a semi was 'common' and another declared: 'Your house looks like a cross between a bingo hall and a brothel.'[44]

The myriad divergences within the middle class have been and are deceptive. Those divergences and the class's capacity for mutation have provided that flexibility which has made it possible for it to maintain its ascendancy in society. The middle classes' power is still vast and obvious; they are the organisers and servants of society who get things done. They provide specialised knowledge, operate the machinery of the state and direct every form of commercial enterprise.

No single philosophy has ever guided the middle class which, on the whole, gravitates towards pragmatism and compromise. Nevertheless, there have been and are articles of faith which, while never universally accepted, provide an insight into the mainsprings behind middle-class thought and action.

First is a belief that together the middle classes represent the enterprise and genius of the nation; they are the people who recognise what needs to be done and set about achieving it. Throughout its history, the middle class has believed in the rights of the individual to think and do as he wished (within the bounds of reason and law) and in government by consent. The middle classes insist that the state should protect them and their property and wish everyone to be free to ascend as far as their talents allow, and for this reason they have an enormous faith in education. They want their children to get on and will do all in their power to assist them.

The middle classes resist any real or imaginary infractions of their own rights or impediments to personal ambition. They relish the pleasures of consumption, the deserved reward of hard work, but a substantial portion feel that their material indulgences have been and are paid for by the suffering of others. Conscience tempers selfishness. Above all, the middle classes have a resilient confidence in themselves, and with good reason. For over five hundred years they have provided order, direction and momentum to the life of the nation.

Abbreviations in Notes and Sources

BL: British Library
BLO: Bodleian Library Oxford
BPP: British Parliamentary Papers
CBS: Centre for Buckinghamshire Studies
CCO: Conservative Central Office
CSP: Calendar of State Papers
GHRO: Guildhall Record Office
GL: Guildhall Library
HCJ: *House of Commons Journals*
HMC: Historic Manuscripts Commission
HP: History of Parliament
ILN: *Illustrated London News*
LA: Lambeth Archives
NA: National Archives
NAS: National Archives of Scotland
NLS: National Library of Scotland
SR: Statutes of the Realm
TES: *Times Educational Supplement*
TLS: *Times Literary Supplement*
VCH: Victoria County History
WI: Wellcome Institute

Notes

Part One: Roots and Antecedents: 1350–1720

Chapter 1: Strings upon a Harp: Order and Change
1. Brown, *Popular Piety*, 16–17.
2. NA, STAC, 3/5, 62.
3. *Lancashire and Cheshire Wills*, 39, 185,
4. *Harrison's Description of England in Shakespeare's Youth*, 137.
5. *Reports from the Lost Notebooks of Sir James Dyer*, 1, 129.
6. HMC, *12th Report*, Appendix, 9, 443–4.
7. Owst, 558.
8. Owst, 551.
9. Liedl, 590–1.
10. Ashby, 4, 10, 20, 89, 95.
11. Cooper, *Land*, 44.
12. CSP, *Domestic, 1641–43*, 66.

Chapter 2: Duty and Order: The Hierarchy of Discipline
1. *Manners and Meals*, 240; *Yorkshire Diaries and Autobiographies*, 67; *Gent*, 12.
2. Owst, 362.
3. *England in the Reign of Henry VIII*, 2, 110.
4. HMC, *Welsh Language*, 1, iii.

5. Dyer, English Medieval Village, 427.

6. McRee, 111–12.

7. Friedburg, 374.

8. Sharp, 188.

9. Sharp, 28; *Calendar of Assize Records . . . Kent*, 355.

10. *SR*, 4, ii, 893.

11. *Rogues and Vagabonds*, 41.

12. *HCJ*, 13, 1.

13. Hindle, 137, 141.

14. *Calendar of Memoranda Rolls*, 138.

15. Griffiths, 163.

16. Wall, 75.

17. Tittler, 138, 152–3.

18. *Poverty*, 9–10; Clark, 'Ramoth Gilead', 257; Friedberg, 354–6.

19. *Somerset Wills*, 3, 214.

20. VCH, *Cambridge*, 9, 15, 22, 180, 191.

Chapter 3: Common Consent: Hierarchy and Power

1. Baskerville, 49.

2. HP, *Commons 1660–1690*, 1, 203.

3. HP, *Commons 1660–1690*, 1, 70.

4. HP, *Commons 1660–1690*, 1, 3.

5. *HCJ*, 10, 399.

6. Fear, 422.

7. James, *Society*, 196.

8. Sharp, 130–1.

9. Clarendon, 2, ii, 339.

10. Hill, *World*, 64.

11. Hill, *World*, 119.

12. Woodhouse, 123–124.

13. Woodhouse, 120–1.

14. Hill, *World*, 329.

15. *Surrey Quarter Sessions*, 307.

16. Greaves, 161.

17. *Surrey Quarter Sessions*, 271, 274–5.

18. *Bedfordshire Schoolchild*, 15.

19. *Bedford Moravian Church*, 38.

20. CSP, *America and West Indies, 1717–18*, 102.

21. CSP, *America and West Indies, 1717–18*, 184.
22. *Earl Marshal's Papers*, 30.
23. *Joe Miller's Jests* (1739), 47, 52–3.

Chapter 4: *Those of Eminent Blood: The Gentry*
 1. Cooper, *Land*, 59.
 2. Legh, 22–3.
 3. Barnes, 24.
 4. CSP, *America and West Indies, 1700*, 193.
 5. Cliffe, 18–19.
 6. Harrison, *Description*, 128–9.
 7. *Select Collection of Old English Plays*, 6, 537.
 8. *Rogues and Vagabonds*, 102–3.
 9. *Earl Marshal's Papers*, 35.
10. *Reports of Heraldic Cases*,
11. Lambard, 10, 66.
12. Stone, *Crisis*, 51.
13. *Two East Anglian Diaries*, 208.
14. *Select Collection of Old English Plays*, 9, 23–5.
15. *Manners and Meals*, 71.
16. Holles, 42.
17. Cooper, *Land*, 33.
18. Cooper, *Land*, 33–4.
19. Cliffe, 5, 13, 16.
20. BL, Ragford Ballads, 2, 170.
21. *Inventories of Bedfordshire Houses*, 3.
22. *Visitation of Northampton*, 92–3.
23. Quitt, 641–2.
24. Thomas, Numeracy, 111.
25. J. Wilson, 24.
26. Caryll, 2, 485.
27. *Select Cases on Defamation*, 47.
28. Sharpe, 21.
29. Wood, Poore Men, 75.

Chapter 5: *Golden Hooks: The Professions*
 1. Burrell, 161.
 2. *Universal Jester*, 164.

3. Brown, *Physick*, 10.

4. *Select Collection of Old English Plays*, 6, 283.

5. *Calendar of Memoranda Rolls*, 127.

6. Baker, 25.

7. *Reports from the Lost Notebooks of Sir James Dyer*, 2, 293–4.

8. Stell, 8, 20.

9. Razi, 77, 78n, 123, 147.

10. *Paston Letters*, 1, xlii–xliii, xlv; 2, 549, 551.

11. Ives, 7.

12. Brooks, Common Lawyers, 53.

13. BL, Lansdowne 2335, 1–8.

14. Broadway, *passim*.

15. Girouard, *Smithson*, 5–6.

16. Strong, *English Icon*, 177.

17. Colvin, 658.

18. Colvin, 543.

19. Webb, *Burlington Magazine*, 100, 115.

20. Vertue, 3, 258–9.

21. Vertue, 5, 248–9.

22. Barnes, 59–60.

23. *Yorkshire Biographies*, 198.

24. *Swaledale Wills*, 281.

25. *Somerset Wills*, 3, 146.

Chapter 6: A Heavy Purse: Buying and Selling

1. Dekker, 3, 235–6.

2. Muldrew, 19.

3. Burke, Popular Culture, 39.

4. Cooper, 97.

5. Owst, 358.

6. HP, *Commons 1509–1558*, 3, 124–6, 127–8; VCH, *Oxfordshire*, 6, 295.

7. *Josselin*, 33.

8. GL, Ms 12,017, 5.

9. Ellis, Bold Adventurer, 119.

10. *Two East Anglian Diaries*, 204–8, 245.

11. Hanham, 4–5.

12. Field, Migration, 33–6.

13. *Bedford Moravian Church*, 215–33 (obituary of Ann Okely).

14. GL, Ms 12,017, *passim*.

15. Ellis, Bold Adventurer, *passim*; Hughes, *North Country, passim*.

Chapter 7: Dexterous Men: Credit and Money Men

1. John, London Assurance, 127n.

2. Muldrew, 200.

3. *Swaledale Wills*, 114–15; *Ipswich Inventories*, 42–3.

4. Muldrew, 101.

5. Muldrew, 97.

6. Simpson, *passim*.

7. Defoe, *Tradesman*, 1, 57.

8. *Josselin*, 517, 535.

9. *Yorkshire Diaries and Autobiographies*, 36, 50, 55.

10. *Athenian Mercury*, 7 November 1693.

11. Pepys, 2, 61–2; 4, 199–200; 5, 174, 359; 7, 425–6; 8, 487.

12. Muldrew, 117.

13. Gough, 85, 131, 185.

14. Dekker, 3, 25.

15. Muldrew, 130.

16. H. R. French, 61–2.

17. Swift, *Examiner*, 5–7.

18. *London Journal*, 13–16 July 1720.

19. Swift, *Examiner*, 6.

20. HMC, *Portland*, 4, 545.

21. Swift, *Examiner*, 134.

22. Defoe, *Tradesman*, 1, 24.

23. Anderson, Provincial, 21.

Chapter 8: Diverse Be Their Wits: The Value and Uses of Learning

1. Clark, 'Ramoth Gilead', 266; Houston, 241; Pearlman and Shirley, 51.

2. Spufford, 413.

3. Ingram, Reformation, 53.

4. Haigh, 151.

5. *Gentleman's Magazine*, May 1737.

6. *Bedfordshire Schoolchild*, 34–5.

7. *Yorkshire Diaries*, 188.

8. Greene, 19.

9. *Testamenta Eboracensia*, 5, 167–8; Quitt, 640.

10. Spufford, 416–17.

11. *Universal Jester*, 147; *Joe Miller's Jests* (1739), 40; *Joe Miller's Complete Jest Book* (1832), 132; Thomas, *TLS*, 21 January 1977.

12. Orme, 145.

13. Orme, 83, 107.

14. *Early Yorks. Schools*, 2, 224.

15. *Early Yorks. Schools*, 2, 385.

16. *Records of King Edward's School*, 81, 85.

17. *Early Yorks. Schools*, 2, 427; *Bedfordshire Schoolchild*, 25.

18. Leach, 152.

19. *Parson and Parish*, 9, 59, 116.

20. *Bedfordshire Schoolchild*, 13, 16.

21. Barron, 139.

22. *Oxford Apprentices*, 59–64.

23. *White-hall Evening Post*, 7 March 1719.

24. BL, Ragford Ballads, 2, 10.

25. *Post-Man*, 25–27 March 1701.

26. *City Mercury*, 13 March 1693.

27. *The Old Whig, Or The Consistent Protestant*, 12 January 1738.

Chapter 9: Godly Matrons: Wives and Daughters

1. *Reports of the Heraldic Cases*, 12–17.

2. *Lincoln Wills*, 389; *Bailiff's Minute Book*, 20.

3. Newman, 126–7.

4. H. R. French, 401–2.

5. *Manners and Meals*, 39–40.

6. Rowlands, 2, 32.

7. See p. 210.

8. Razi, 58–9, 65–6; 69.

9. *Rogues and Vagabonds*, 41.

10. M. Ingram, Reformation of Manners, 60.

11. Palliser, 82.

12. M. Ingram, Reformation of Manners, 45.

13. Griffiths, 152–3.

14. Pepys, 1, 311.

15. *Joe Miller's Jests* (1739), 36.

16. *Two East Anglian Diaries*, 48, 69, 117.

17. NA, STAC 8/57, 17.
18. Capp, Double Standard, 117–18.
19. Rogers, 69.
20. BL, Ragford Ballads, 3, 45, 47.
21. *Athenian Mercury*, 4 November 1693.
22. Atkinson and Stoneman, 197–8.
23. Cliffe, 11–12.
24. *Athenian Mercury*, 29 January 1695.
25. *Daily Courant*, 22 January 1719; *Country Journal or Craftsman*, 7 February 1738.
26. *Athenian Mercury*, 11 October 1693.
27. *Cely Letters*, 151–2.
28. Macfarlane, 265, 276.
29. Macfarlane, 306–7.
30. Aubrey, 212.
31. Brodsky, 122, 139.
32. Macfarlane, 162.
33. Brodsky, 126–7.
34. Macfarlane, 257–8.
35. *Athenian Mercury*, 15 and 25 July 1693.

Part Two: The Middle Class Emerges: 1720–1832

Chapter 1: The Gigantic Power of Man: A New Age

1. Southey, *Sir Thomas More*, 2, 242.
2. *Scotsman*, 22 September 1830.
3. Rubenstein, British Millionaires, 206–7.
4. Williams, *Our Iron Roads*, 33.
5. Williams, *Our Iron Roads*, 27.
6. *The Railway Companion*, 15.
7. Southey, *Sir Thomas More*, 1, 170.
8. *United Trades Cooperative Journal*, 1, xviii, xix (June–July 1830).
9. Thomas, *Man and the Natural World*, 66.
10. Marshall, 93, 132.
11. *Magazine of Natural History*, 1, February 1828, 4, 6.
12. Pellew, 3, 243.
13. NA, HO 40/27, 28.

Chapter 2: Benefits to the Country: Revolutions

1. BPP, *Reports by Inspectors of Factories . . . 1835–1841*, Report of January 1839, 98.
2. CBS, QS/JC/6, 115–22.
3. *Farming Magazine*, 1 (July 1800), 328–34.
4. Wasson, 91.
5. *Scotsman*, 1 March 1817.
6. *Felix Farley's Bristol Journal*, 25 July 1789; *Bath Chronicle*, 23 July 1789.
7. *World*, 5 September 1793.
8. Bamford, 1, 43–4.
9. *Public Advertiser*, 7 December 1793.
10. *Political Register*, 2 November 1816.
11. NA, HO 40/29, 397.
12. NA, HO 44/2, 171.
13. *True Briton*, 14–15 June 1797.
14. Rohstedt, 107, 109.
15. Poole, 73–4, 79; *Morning Post*, 3 January 1794.
16. *Morning Post*, 3 August 1795.
17. Rohstedt, 5, 14.
18. Godber, 157.
19. NAS, AD 14/1/2.
20. NA, HO 40/12, 67.
21. *Black Dwarf*, 30 June 1819.
22. Pellew, 3, 254.
23. Grime, 99, 103.
24. *The Times*, 14 September 1830.
25. *The Times*, 18 March 1831.
26. Hansard, 3rd Series, 12, 7–8.
27. Beckett, 76–8.
28. CBS, D 85/12/12.
29. NA, HO 40/29, 476.
30. NA, HO 40/29, 483.
31. NA, HO 40/30, 4–5, 17–18.
32. NA, HO 40/29, 190.
33. Hansard, 3rd Series, 12, 421–2.
34. Hansard, 3rd Series, 12, 254, 277.
35. O'Gorman, 177.

Chapter 3: Usefulness: Identities and Aspirations

1. *A Poll of the Electors . . . Borough of Aylesbury, 1818; ibid., 1835.*
2. *General Evening Post*, 16 September 1775.
3. NA, HO 42/28, 108.
4. *Recollections of Nineteenth-Century Buckinghamshire*, 22.
5. *Gentleman's Magazine*. 101, March 1831.
6. H. R. French, 64.
7. *Present State*, 167.
8. Boswell, 1, 109.
9. I am indebted to Professor Nick Roe for this verse.
10. Davidoff and Hall, 330–1.
11. *World*, No. 18, 3 May 1753.
12. *Rambler*, 1, No. 116 (27 April 1751); No. 123 (21 May 1751).
13. *General Evening Post*, 9 March 1776.
14. Corfield, 43.
15. *Statistical Account*, 2, 28, 31.
16. Warren, 67.
17. Harden, 111.
18. Parkes, 377.
19. *General Evening Post*, 18 January, 1 February, 16 November 1776.
20. *London Chronicle*, 18–21 April 1767.
21. *Statistical Account*, 2, 47, 57.
22. *Swinney's Birmingham Chronicle*, 23 January 1817.
23. NA, Mepo 4/29, 5, 189.
24. Cobbett, *Advice*, 15, 17, 69.
25. *Weekly Miscellany*, 20 May 1737; GHRO, London and Southwark Coroner's Inquests, Box 32, 13.
26. *Lady's Magazine*, October 1777.
27. *Mechanic's Magazine*, 1, 11 October 1823.
28. Southey, *Sir Thomas More*, 1, 165.
29. Brown, *English Letter-Writer*, 45–6, 89.
30. Goldsmith, 3, 355–6.
31. *Rambler*, 1, No. 9 (17 April 1750); No. 21 (29 May 1750).
32. *Monthly Gazette of Health*, 1 January 1816.
33. *Mechanic's Magazine*, 1, 30 August 1823.
34. Wade, 178–9.

Chapter 4: Genteel Chimney Pieces: Patterns of Consumption

1. Trusler, 89.
2. *Lady's Magazine*, May 1798.
3. Harrison, *Drink*, 38.
4. Woodforde, 2, 105.
5. *Blackwood's Magazine*, 1, iv, July 1817.
6. *Georgian Public Buildings*, 75.
7. *Felix Farley's Bristol Journal*, 6 and 13 January 1787.
8. *Aberdeen Journal*, 9 January 1817.
9. *World*, 5 September 1793.
10. *Aberdeen Journal*, 4 February 1793.
11. *Statistical Account*, 10, 150, 499.
12. *Aberdeen Journal*, 7 June 1773.
13. *Statistical Account*, 2, 55.
14. Harden, 105–6.
15. Woodforde, 1, 197, 198, 201, 217, 218, 324–325; 2, 19.
16. Cobbett, *Rural Rides*, 229.
17. *Statistical Account*, 2, 22 ff.
18. Berg, 53–4.
19. Morris, 293.
20. Brewer, 506.
21. Pigot Papers.
22. *Scotsman*, 3 January 1827.
23. *Quarterly Musical Magazine and Review*, 3, 67–8.

Chapter 5: Improvement in Friendship and Knowledge: Association and Reading

1. *Magazine of Natural History*, 1, May 1828.
2. *Transactions of the London Institute for the Encouragement of Arts, Manufactures and Commerce*, 15, 61, 273.
3. *Farmer's Magazine*, 17, 12 February 1816.
4. *Minute Books of the Spalding Gentleman's Society*, ix–xi.
5. Fawcett, 16–17.
6. *Gentleman's Magazine*, 94, February 1824.
7. Uglow, 309.
8. Becker, 69.
9. Clark, *Alehouse*, 235.
10. Goldsmith, 3, 12–13.

11. Farrington, 1, 151–2.

12. Jacob, 58–9, 65.

13. *Gentleman's Magazine*, 2nd Series, 69, February 1799.

14. *Gentleman's Magazine*, 2nd Series, 69, April 1799.

15. Pigot Papers, dated 1 April 1771.

16. *Gentleman's Magazine*, 2nd Series, 6, October 1836.

17. *Morning Post*, 12 March 1796.

18. *London Chronicle*, April 1767; *The Times*, 6 January 1825.

19. *The Stranger in Liverpool*, 88–92.

20. Brewer, 181–2.

21. *Chester Chronicle*, 29 May 1775.

22. *Morning Post*, 6 January 1796.

23. *Quarterly Review*, 8, xiii.

24. Cobbett, *Advice*, 294–5.

25. Plant, 58.

26. *Memoir of John Bowdler*, 320.

27. T. Bowdler ed., *Gibbon's History*, 1, ix–x.

28. More, *Coelebs*, 2, 33.

29. Houghton, 125–6; 131.

Chapter 6: *Worthy Labours: Christianity, Coercion and Charity*

1. Giles, 6.

2. *Memoir of John Bowdler*, 295.

3. GL, Ms 5762, I, nn.

4. GHRO, London and Southwark Coroner's Inquests, Box 32, 40.

5. *Present State*, 147–8.

6. Gray, *Admission*, 19.

7. *Lady's Magazine*, January 1805.

8. Ambler, 322.

9. Smith, Occupational, *passim*.

10. Wadsworth, 107.

11. Holyoake, 1, 33.

12. Thomas, *Sermon*, 6, 7, 14.

13. Pellew, 3, 196–7.

14. Roberts, Victorian Morals? *passim*.

15. Smith, *Works*, 131.

16. Leneman, 50.

17. *True Briton*, 11 February 1797.

18. Phillips, Good Men, 133–5.

19. NAS, JC 26/137.

20. GHRO, London and Southwark Coroner's Inquests, Box 2, 175.

21. *Morning Post*, 3 August 1795.

22. NA, HO 44/1, 9.

23. CBS, QS/JC/3, 171–2.

24. Eden, 1, 491–3.

25. *Morning Post*, 24 July 1795.

26. *To the Freeholders and Inhabitants of Nantwich* (BL Cat. No. 8285 g 21).

27. Williams, Midland, 270.

28. Anderson, *Christian Philanthropy*, 10, 15.

29. *Farmer's Magazine*, 17, 12 February 1816.

30. Parkes, 101, 106, 108–9.

31. Wilberforce, 455.

32. More, *Strictures*, 1, 16–18; 2, 53.

Chapter 7: Domestic Happiness: Marriage, Children and Morality

1. *Annual Register 1836* (Chronicle), 136.

2. Leneman, 50.

3. Trusler, 64.

4. 'Mira', 9, 21–2, 227.

5. Parkes, 206.

6. *Lady's Magazine*, 4, January 1773.

7. *Lady's Magazine*, 4, February 1773.

8. Burn, 32–3.

9. *The Oracle, or British Advertiser*, 2 July 1798.

10. Young, 1, 104–6.

11. Ashford, 12.

12. Ashford, *passim*.

13. Brown, *English Letter-Writer*, 28–30.

14. GL, Ms 5762, 12, 11 July 1830.

15. Kelly ed., 93–4.

16. Solomon, 222–3.

17. *The Literary Courier of Grub Street*, 2 February 1738.

18. *Felix Farley's Bristol Journal*, 27 June, 1 August 1789.

19. GL, Ms 15,819.

20. Galbraith, *passim*.

21. *Scotsman*, 4 April 1827.

22. Holyoake, 1, 9–11.

23. Brown, James Williams, 21.

24. Leneman, 41–2.

25. Eden, 1, 626–7.

26. Booth, 351, 372.

27. *Devizes Division*, 112–13.

28. *The Educator*, 81.

29. *The Educator*, 48.

30. McLaren, *passim*.

31. *Bulldog*, No. 3, 9 September 1826.

32. Himmelfarb, 73–6.

33. Solomon, 188–9, 197, 211.

34. *Bulldog*, No. 3, 9 September 1826.

35. *True Briton*, 16 April 1797.

36. McLaren, 11; Booth, 441.

37. Place, 58, 75–6, 78.

38. Hansard, 3rd Series, 146, 1355.

39. Hansard, 3rd Series, 56, 1339–41, 1343.

Chapter 8: A Post Hoffice Directory . . . Man: Snobberies
  1. *Gentleman's Magazine*, 2nd Series, 5, June 1836.

  2. *Gentleman's Magazine*, 2nd Series, 5, April 1836.

  3. *Lancet*, 12 April 1828.

  4. Boswell, 2, 151

  5. Phillips, 136.

  6. Phillips, 136.

  7. Phillips, 136.

  8. *Scotsman*, 21 June 1817.

  9. Holyoake, 1, 21.

10. *Northern Star*, 13 January 1838.

11. NA, Mepo 4/29, 157.

Part Three: The Triumph of the Middle Classes, 1832–1914

Chapter 1: Work: Middle-Class Values
  1. Himmelfarb, 3–4.

  2. Shipway, 51.

  3. *Building News*, 1 January 1892.

4. Williams, *Our Iron Roads*, 211.

5. Houghton, 4–5.

6. Cockman, 56.

7. GL, Ms 19,019, 12 June 1844; 23 August 1848.

8. *Country Life*, 3 August 1901.

9. Church, 8.

10. *The Times*, 20 August 1912.

11. Barker, Urban Transport, 158.

12. Davidoff and Hall, 305–6.

13. Houghton, 243–4, 253.

14. *Manchester Guardian*, 4 October 1866.

15. Burn, 315.

16. *Trial of William Palmer*, 17.

17. Buchanan, 183.

18. Burn, 171.

19. *Saturday Review*, 10 November 1860.

20. *Banbury Gaol Records*, 153–63.

21. Bunker, 91.

22. Galbraith, *passim*.

23. Porter, 'Bureau', *passim*.

24. Falkus, 135.

25. Blewett, 400.

Chapter 2: Exclusiveness: Social Arithmetic

1. LA, Norwood Conservative Association, IV/166/1/13.

2. Turton, 62, 69–70.

3. *Victorian City*, 1, 371.

4. BPP, *Reports . . . Industrial Factories*, 497.

5. Sanger, 30.

6. *Victorian City*, 1, 368.

7. *Builder*, 6 October 1894.

8. *Victorian City*, 1, 67.

9. Bunker, 72.

10. Gourvish, Rise, 20.

11. *Saturday Review*, 3 January 1885.

12. Booth, 335, 336, 354.

13. Miles, 52.

14. Griffen, 63, 65.

15. *Statistical Abstract . . . 1891 to 1905*, 39.
16. Hollams, 149–50.
17. *Devizes Division, passim*; detailed individual tax returns from this period are rare.
18. Saville, 377; *TES*, 4 October 1910; 5 September 1911.
19. *The Times*, 12 May 1866.
20. *Medical Times*, 10 October 1864.
21. Booth, 441; MacKenzie and Mathew, 159–65.
22. Griffen, 44.
23. *Army Medical Department Report for the Year 1899*, 38–9.
24. MacKenzie and Mathew, 167–70, 209–10, 247.
25. Morrison, *passim*; Colmore, *passim*; Layard, *passim*.

Chapter 3: A Good Time Coming: Class Politics, 1832–1885

1. Trollope, *Dr Thorne*, chapter XXVII.
2. *Edinburgh Review*, 98, No. 200 (October 1853), 573, 578, 583, 597.
3. Grime, 14–15.
4. *Guardian*, 13 January 1886.
5. *Annual Register 1835*, Chronicle, 6–7, 86–8.
6. Beckett, 80; *The Times*, 9 August 1886.
7. *National Observer*, 2 July 1892.
8. Hansard, 3rd Series, 97, 331.
9. Hansard, 3rd Series, 98, 293.
10. NA, HO 44/38, 1070.
11. *Northern Star*, 3 and 17 September 1842.
12. *Northern Star*, 1 July 1848.
13. Searle, Edwardian Liberal Party, 23.
14. Grime, 172.
15. *Northern Star*, 4 July 1846.
16. Harrison, *Memoirs*, 1, 287.
17. Holyoake, 1, 20–1.
18. Burn, 94.
19. NAS, SC 40/51/25, 131–5.
20. Lee, 5.
21. Cannadine, 88.
22. *Punch*, 20, 240, 247.
23. Trinder, 142.

24. Hansard, 3rd Series, 168, 1321.

25. Burn, 39.

26. *Guardian*, 20 January 1886.

27. *School Board Chronicle*, 15 December 1877; 17 December 1881.

28. Chamberlain, 1, 15.

29. *The Times*, 4 August 1886.

30. *Saturday Review*, 19 April 1873.

31. *Victorian Cities*, 2, 783.

32. Hansard, 3rd Series, 294, 1824–6.

Chapter 4: Private Property Is Public Robbery: New Politics and Old Tensions, 1886–1914

1. Harrison, *Memoirs*, 1, 18.

2. *Victorian City*, 2, 575.

3. *Victorian City*, 2, 576–7.

4. Blewett, 301–2.

5. *Black and White*, 11 August 1900.

6. Blewett, 302.

7. Richards, *Candidates*, 46.

8. LA, Norwood Conservative Association IV/166/1/13.

9. Howe, Liberal Party Organisation, 117.

10. *Edinburgh Courant*, 11 February 1880.

11. Peddar, 275–6.

12. LA, Norwood Conservative Association IV/166/1/4.

13. Lawrence, *passim*.

14. *Black and White*, 6 October 1900.

15. Lawrence, 644.

16. *Cardiganshire County History*, 3, 2–3.

17. King, Popular Violence, *passim*.

18. *Daily Graphic*, 3 and 4 July 1898.

19. I owe this point to the late Professor Gwyn Williams.

20. *National Observer*, 30 July 1895.

21. *Builder*, 3 November 1894.

22. Blewett, 14.

23. *National Observer*, 2 July 1892.

24. *Saturday Review*, 29 January 1910.

25. Blewett, 89.

26. Searle, Edwardian Liberal Party, 31.

27. *Spectator*, 2 February 1901.
28. Blewett, 16.
29. Masterman, 77 ff.
30. *TES*, 3 January 1911.
31. Blewett, 405–6.
32. *Spectator*, 3 December 1910.
33. *East of Fife Record*, 15 December 1910.
34. *Spectator*, 10 December 1910.
35. *Blackwood's Magazine*, December 1910, 188.
36. Blewett, 414.
37. Bowyer, 110.
38. Pennybacker, 53–5.
39. *TES*, 6 September 1910.
40. Snowden, 1, 44.
41. Meyer, *passim*.

Chapter 5: Dangerous Classes: Correction and Compassion

1. NAS, SC 40/51/7, 65–6.
2. Harrison, *Peaceable Kingdom*, 87.
3. NA, Mepo 4/6, 135d–36.
4. *The Times*, 31 July 1872.
5. Lee, 3–4.
6. Sanger, 77–8.
7. Hansard, 3rd Series, 56, 659–60.
8. NAS, SC 15/51, *passim*.
9. *Daily Graphic*, 29 November 1897.
10. Wells, 61–3.
11. Bosanquet, 4.
12. NAS, SC 36/56/86, 251, 258.
13. Dunning and Sheard, 43.
14. Mason, *Association Football*, 43.
15. Mason, *Association Football*, 163.
16. *Building News*, 20 April 1894.
17. Schwarz, 104.
18. *School Board Guardian*, 2 May 1879.
19. Harrison, *Peaceable Kingdom*, 250.
20. NAS, GD 409/28/11, Report for Year 1900, Edinburgh, 19; ibid., Glasgow, 28.

21. *ILN*, 15, 20, 29 April, 20 May, 3 June 1871; *Saturday Review*, 27 May 1871.
22. *Fifeshire Journal*, 28 September 1854.
23. Hansard, 4th Series, 17, 1256, 1400.
24. *Daily Graphic*, 6 July 1897.
25. NAS, AD 15/02/62.
26. *Guardian*, 5 October 1898.
27. Gorsky, 178, 203.
28. Harrison, *Peaceable Kingdom*, 249.
29. Harrison, *Peaceable Kingdom*, 250.
30. *Guardian*, 25 November 1903.
31. Wilson, *Victorians*, 264–6.
32. *Banbury Gaol Records*, 162.
33. Harrison, *Peaceable Kingdom*, 411.
34. Harrison, *Peaceable Kingdom*, 411, 419.
35. Bosanquet, 61–2.
36. *Black and White*, 23 May 1891.
37. *Cambridge Review*, 11 March 1880.
38. Bartley, 147–9.
39. NAS, GD 409/28/11, Report for the Year 1900, Edinburgh, 23.
40. *Guardian*, 8 July 1903.
41. Harrison, *Peaceable Kingdom*, 223; Jones, *Victorian Boyhood*, 40.
42. *Daily Graphic*, 21 July, 6, 19, 20 and 25 August, 6 September 1898.
43. *Eugenicist*, 1 (1909–10), 39–41, 206.
44. *Life and Work*, 11, 4 (April 1904) (Women's Branch Reports).
45. Gorsky, 223.
46. *Life and Work*, October 1913 (Women's Guild Supplement).

Chapter 6: Put Your Playthings Away: Faith and Morals

1. Houghton, 136.
2. Taylor, *Autobiography*, 149.
3. Memoir of William Smith, 184.
4. Bradley, *Abide with Me*, 124.
5. *Journal of the Royal Statistical Society*, 74, 130.
6. Hansard, 3rd Series, 135, 25–6.
7. *Bishop Wilberforce's Visitation*, 36.
8. McGarvie, 299–300.
9. Brown and Brown, 94–5.

10. Sneyd-Kinnersley, 13.

11. *Edinburgh Review*, 98, No. 200 (October 1853), 289–90.

12. *Spectator*, 27 February 1869.

13. Maxwell, *Evening Memories*, 57.

14. *Alma Mater: Aberdeen University Magazine*, 12 November 1884.

15. Bowyer, 78.

16. *Bishop Wilberforce's Visitation*, 114.

17. Sturrock, 127.

18. *Church Union Journal*, 3 November 1911.

19. *Guardian*, 1 July 1903.

20. Sayers, 85.

21. Hansard, 3rd Series, 146, 333–4, 1152.

22. Roberts, Morals, 613.

23. NA, Mepo 3/935.

24. Hyam, 69.

25. Maxwell, *Evening Memories*, 45.

26. NA, HO 45/6628.

27. NA, HO 45/6628.

28. *Daily Graphic*, 15, 16 October 1896.

29. *Guardian*, 15 December 1911.

30. NA, Mepo 2/1691.

31. *Lancet*, 31 March 1894.

32. Himmelfarb, 198.

Chapter 7: To Live Decently before His Fellows: The Triumph of the Public Schools

1. Barnett, *Audit*, 218.

2. *Cambridge Review*, October 1892.

3. *Guardian*, 21 January 1891.

4. *TES*, 4 October 1910.

5. *Guardian*, 12 October 1898.

6. *Country Life*, 1 December 1906.

7. *TES*, 3 October; 7 November 1911.

8. *TES*, 6 February 1912.

9. Barnett, *Audit*, 213–14.

10. Burn, 22.

11. Honey, 55.

12. *Saturday Review*, 8 December 1860.

13. *Everyday Life in Our Public Schools*, 187.
14. *Cambridge Review*, October 1889.
15. *Cambridge Review*, February 1880.
16. Dunning and Sheard, 134; Mason, 22–3.
17. Mason, 80, 86.
18. *Black and White*, 22 December 1894.
19. Gray, *Public School*, 12–13.
20. For example, during the notorious 1933 Test series against Australia, England was captained by D. R. Jardine and 'Larwood' was the body-line bowler.
21. Barnett, *Collapse of British Power, passim.*
22. *Repton School Register, 1620–1894*, 117–19.
23. *Sedbergh School Register, 1546 to 1895*, 303–8.
24. *Haileybury School Register, 1862–1900*, 323–31.
25. *Biographical History of Gonville and Caius College*, 291–8.
26. *Biographical History of Gonville and Caius College*, 480–7.
27. *Guardian*, 21 January 1891.
28. *Summoned by Bells*, 17.
29. I have seen manuscript school registers that record expulsions for sexual indiscretion: the information was not reproduced in published registers of alumni.
30. *Memoirs of John Addington Symonds*, 97, 100, 288.
31. Maugham.
32. Newsome, 45.
33. Burn, 266–7.
34. *School Board Chronicle*, 5 March, 23 April 1881.
35. *TES*, 9 April 1911.
36. Richards, *Happiest Days, passim.*

Chapter 8: The New Woman: Marriage and Its Alternatives

1. *Work and Leisure for the Enjoyment and Recreation of Working Women,* cover.
2. *Studio*, 3 (1905), 307–8.
3. Collett, 513.
4. Layton, 518–19.
5. Jordan, 385.
6. *Home Sweet Home*, 29 October 1898.
7. *Home Sweet Home*, 20 January 1900.

8. St John, 212.

9. *The Times*, 18, 21 November 1861; Guerriro Wilson, 466.

10. Hammerton, 278–9.

11. Burn, 250.

12. *The Times*, 1, 2, 3, 4 August 1876.

13. *The Times*, 1, 9 August 1889.

14. *Guardian*, 22 July 1903.

15. Houghton, 350–1.

16. Jalland, 259.

17. Illustrated in Wilson, *Victorians*.

18. Brittain, 39.

19. I am indebted to the late Mrs Charlotte Williams for this point.

20. *Royal Commission on University Education in Wales*, 98.

21. Dyhouse, *No Distinction*, 17.

22. *Lancet*, 4, 19 May, 8 June 1894.

23. *Lancet*, 2, 23 November 1895.

24. *Practitioner*, December 1895.

25. *Saturday Review*, 3 December 1870.

26. Pennybacker, 27, 255.

27. For example, Rosen.

28. Rosen, 237.

29. 9 & 10 Geo 5, Ch. 71.

30. *Cycle and Camera*, 11 September 1897.

31. *Wheelwoman*, 12 December 1896.

32. *Beauty and Health*, October 1903.

33. *Cycle and Camera*, 5 June 1897.

34. *Daily Graphic*, 11 October 1895.

35. *Daily Graphic*, 23 December 1895.

36. *Wheelwoman*, 2 January 1897.

37. *Beauty and Health*, April 1904.

38. Dyhouse, Mothers, 35.

39. Bland, 123–4.

40. WI, Stopes, PP/MCS, A 6.

41. WI, Stopes, PP/MCS, A 182.

42. McLaren, 11.

43. McLaren, 126.

44. *Report . . . Physical Deterioration*, 38–9.

45. Weeks, 45–6.

46. Weeks, 45.

47. McLaren, 11.
48. Weeks, 41.
49. Madox Ford, 11, 16.
50. Jordan, 385.

Chapter 9: Be Imaginative: Diversions, Mostly Outdoors

1. *Country Life*, 25 August 1905.
2. *Murray's Handbook of Greece*, 6, 13–16.
3. *A Handbook for the Traveller in Turkey*, 34.
4. *A Handbook for the Traveller in France*, xxxiv.
5. Hare, 3, 345.
6. *ILN*, 7 August 1890.
7. *Murray's Handbook of Greece*, 1–2.
8. *A Handbook for the Traveller in Turkey*, 11.
9. GL, Ms 19,019, 20 August 1855.
10. King, George Goodwin, 101.
11. *Pictures of the Year 1914*, 12.
12. *The Times*, 30 April 1931.
13. NLS, 14,366.
14. *Cycle and Camera*, 22 May 1897.
15. Suffling, 3.
16. VCH, *Sussex*, 6, i, 95.
17. *Saturday Review*, 1 September 1866.
18. *The Times*, 8, 11 July 1870; *Saturday Review*, 12 July 1870.
19. *The Times*, 3, 14, 16, 17, 19 September 1870.
20. *The Times*, 2 November 1892.
21. Burn, 30: Most casualties were people who wandered on to lines or fell from trains.
22. *Cardiganshire County History*, 307.
23. King, George Goodwin, 102–3.
24. *A Handbook for the Traveller in Kent and Sussex*, 196.
25. *Black and White*, 29 August, 12 September 1891.
26. Ritvo, 227.
27. *ILN*, 26 July 1890.
28. *Work and Leisure, passim*.
29. *Consumer Expenditure . . . 1900 to 1919*, 161.
30. Ibid.
31. Killingray, 67–9.

32. *Golf*, 5 June 1891.

33. *Motor*, 22 August 1905.

34. *Economist*, 13 April 1912.

35. *Spectator*, 11 June 1904.

36. *Motor Cycling and Motor*, 12 November 1902.

37. *Buffalo Review and Lodge Reporter*, 1 August 1881.

38. Lee, 6.

39. *Spectator*, 6 August 1892.

40. *ILN*, 13 August 1881.

41. *ILN*, 3 June 1893.

42. GL, Ms 19,019, 16, 18 November 1852.

43. GL, Ms 15,819.

Chapter 10: Philistines: Middle-Class Cultures

1. Girouard, *Sweetness and Light*, 175–6.

2. Trewin, 31.

3. *ILN*, 2 October 1886.

4. *Connoisseur*, March 1902.

5. King, George Goodwin and the Art Union, *passim*.

6. *Art Journal*, December 1852.

7. *Graphic*, 17 March 1894.

8. *Daily Graphic*, 4 October 1895.

9. *The Year's Art, 1901*, 294–303.

10. *Art Journal*, 17, 233.

11. *Magazine of Art*, 8 (1885), 346–7.

12. *Magazine of Art*, 9 (1886), 361–3.

13. *Studio*, 15 July 1914.

14. *The Studio Yearbook of Decorative Art, 1911*, 3, 4–5.

15. Helland, 151, 153.

16. *The Year's Art, 1911*, 260.

17. *Listener*, 8 August 1934.

18. I am indebted to the late A. V. Williams for this observation.

19. *Athenaeum*, 9 March 1901.

20. *Spectator*, 4 July 1914.

21. White, *Fortnightly*, 776.

22. Tennyson, *passim*.

23. *Athenaeum*, 11 January 1913.

24. *Scottish Art and Letters*, November 1911.

25. *Bohemian*, 1 July 1893.

26. McCarthy, 605, 608–9.

27. Trewin, 31

28. Madox Ford, 47–8.

29. *Spectator*, 26 February 1910.

30. *Punch*, 2 and 9 March 1910.

31. Low and Manvell, 2, 24, 26.

32. Terry, 10.

33. *Home Sweet Home*, 10 September 1898.

34. *Buffalo Review*, August and November 1882.

35. Hopgood, *passim*.

36. SRO, GD 412/1/2.

37. MacCormick Edwards, *passim*.

38. Cork, 154.

39. Cork, 23–30.

Chapter 11: Am I Making Progress?: Happiness, Identity and Prospects in 1914

1. *The Times*, 29 June 1914; *Scotsman*, 29 June 1914.

2. *Victorian City*, 1, 300.

3. *Everyman*, 18 October 1912.

4. Frank, 43, 72–3.

5. Offer, 97–8.

6. Minois, 319.

7. Ogle, 114.

8. Ogle, 108–9; Woods, 29–30.

9. Rapp, 219–22, 237.

10. *Small Beginnings*, 32–3, 39.

11. Brown, *Life*, 7.

12. Worthen, 1, 84.

13. *Report . . . on Physical Deterioration*, 183.

14. D'Aeth, *passim*.

15. Beveridge, 451–3.

16. Bowyer, 2–10.

17. *Victorian City*, 1, 63.

18. Humphries, 37.

19. *Guardian*, 7 July 1909.

20. Woolf, 145.

21. *Saturday Review*, 4 July 1914.

22. *Practitioner*, December 1900.

23. *Lancet*, 3 June 1910.

24. 'Notes on the English Character', in Forster, *Abinger Harvest*, 19–20.

25. Muggeridge, 21, 31.

26. *Decorators and Painters Magazine*, 15 May, 16 July 1903.

27. Hopgood, 525.

28. *Guardian*, 9 July 1909.

29. Miles, 7, 24, 39.

Part Four: Stress and Survival, 1914–2005

Chapter 1: People Seem to Lose their Way: Continuity and Change, 1914–1951

1. Russell, 131.

2. *Saturday Review*, 5 September 1914.

3. *Saturday Review*, 29 August 1914.

4. *TES*, 2 January 1919.

5. *Spectator*, 20 April 1918.

6. Petter, 143.

7. *Morning Post*, 23 April 1920.

8. *The Times*, 31 October 1919.

9. The best survey is G. J. De Groot, *Blighty: British Society in the Era of the Great War* (1996).

10. *Horizon*, 1940, 293.

11. *Saturday Review*, 9 November 1918.

12. *Saturday Review*, 25 January 1919.

13. *Morning Post*, 2 January 1919.

14. *Morning Post*, 26 June 1920.

15. *Political Quarterly*, 22, 161–2.

16. Riddell, 10–11.

17. Simmat, 4.

18. Gray, *Worst of Times*, 128,

19. Graves and Hodges, 15.

20. *TES*, 8 August 1931.

21. Russell, 128.

22. Crossman, *Backbench Diaries*, 209.

23. Crossman, *Diaries*, 109, 666; *Backbench Diaries*, 743.

24. Orwell, *Coming Up for Air*, 13.

25. NA, Mepo 3/946.

26. *Daily Sketch*, 4 September 1931.

27. NA, Mepo 3/2323.

28. *Picture Post*, 11 March 1939.

29. *Parents*, July 1934.

30. *Royal Commission on Marriage and Divorce*, 367.

31. Graves and Hodge, 241.

32. *Morning Post*, 28 February 1933.

33. *BBC Year Book 1932*, 19.

34. *Listener*, 3 November 1938.

35. *This England*, 29.

36. *Morning Post*, 2 March 1933.

37. *BBC Year Book 1947*, 58; *Radio Times*, 13 June 1947.

38. Carpenter, 35.

39. Priestley, 401.

40. *Ministry of Labour Report for the Year 1935*, 99.

41. Floud, 33.

42. *Picture Post*, 5 and 12 April 1941.

43. NAS, HH 55/43, PWD/1/1/2/108, 5.

44. NAS, HH 55/43, PWD/1/1/2/110, 11.

45. BLO, CCO 180/2/1, Public Opinion Survey No. 1 (January 1949), 6.

46. Adonis and Pollard, 23.

47. BLO, CCO 180/2/1, Public Opinion Survey 2 (February 1949), 5.

48. *New Statesman*, 23 September 1933.

49. NAS, HH 55/42, PWD/1/1/2/105, 8.

Chapter 2: Make the Good Life Better: Prosperity and Permissiveness, 1951–1979

1. NAS, HH 55 / 48, PWD/1/1/2/127, nn.

2. Frayn, 331.

3. *Illustrated*, 24 March 1951.

4. Weight, 244–5.

5. Hansard, 5th Series (House of Lords), 188, 236.

6. Hansard, 5th Series (House of Lords), 188, 250, 355–6.

7. *Punch*, 24 March 1954.

8. Hansard, 5th Series, 522, 51.

9. Weight, 251.

10. Weight, 316–17.

11. *Which*, July 1959.

12. *Which*, Winter 1957.

13. Young, *Encounter*, June 1956.

14. Young, *Encounter*, June 1956.

15. BLO, CCO 500/14/2, Macmillan's address to the Conservative Women's Association, April 1961.

16. *Sunday Times*, Supplement, 15 April 1961.

17. *Queen*, 3 January 1968.

18. *Sunday Times*, Supplement, 15 April 1961.

19. Offer, 86.

20. *Good Food Guide, 1977*, ix.

21. *Queen*, 3 January 1968.

22. *Queen*, 28 February 1968.

23. *Good Food Guide, 1978*, 218–19.

24. *Royal Commission on the Distribution of Income and Wealth*, 82.

25. *Economist*, 9 June 1945.

26. *Monthly Digest of Statistics*, No. 391 (July 1976).

27. *Economist*, 21 January 1979 (Barclay's Briefing Supplement).

28. *Royal Commission on Marriage and Divorce*, 139, 149.

29. *Illustrated*, 17 July 1954.

30. Hansard, 5th Series, 596, 370.

31. Hansard, 5th Series, 596, 437.

32. *The Times*, 28 October 1960 (quoted in the *Lady Chatterley* trial).

33. Weight, 313–14.

34. *The Times*, 28 and 29 October 1960; *Spectator*, 4 November 1960.

35. *New Society*, 8 April 1965.

36. Newburn, 17–18.

37. Hansard, 5th Series, 864, 319–20, 348, 404.

38. *Queen*, 23 October 1968.

39. *Observer*, Supplement, 23 October 1966.

40. Medhurst, 264; Simonelli, 131–2.

41. Medhurst, 283.

42. *Sunday Times*, Supplement, 11 February 1968.

43. Goulbourne, 82–4; Brown, *Brown Black and White*, 197.

44. *The Times*, 4 November 1977.

45. *Observer*, Supplement, 23 October 1966.

Chapter 3: The Decent Crowd: Tensions, 1918–1979

1. *Scotsman*, 3 May 1926.
2. *Spectator*, 16 February 1974.
3. Florey, 81.
4. *Morning Post*, 25 and 30 January, 3 February 1919.
5. *Daily Graphic*, 15, 16, 17, 18, 20 and 21 October 1920.
6. *Saturday Review*, 9 November 1918.
7. *Scotsman*, 3 May 1926.
8. *Spectator*, 8 May 1926.
9. Hills, 3.
10. Florey, 121.
11. *Scotsman*, 6, 7, 10 and 11 May 1926.
12. Florey, 121.
13. *Picture Post*, 21 January 1939.
14. *Morning Post*, 1 April 1920.
15. Florey, 84.
16. *The Times*, 4 May 1926.
17. I am indebted to the late Charlotte Williams for this point.
18. Calder and Sheridan, 215 ff.
19. *The Times*, 14 February 1972.
20. Hansard, 5th Series, 849, 572–3.
21. *New Society*, 24 February 1972.
22. Hansard, 5th Series, 849, 1344.
23. *New Statesman*, 18 February 1972.
24. *Daily Telegraph*, 15 February 1972.
25. *Daily Mail*, 11 February 1972.
26. *Monthly Digest of Statistics*, No. 391 (July 1976), 391.
27. Geary, 121.
28. *Economist*, 29 June 1972.

Chapter 4: One of Themselves: Mrs Thatcher and Tony Blair, 1979–2005

1. BLO, CCO 180/2/1, Public Opinion Survey No. 12 (December 1949), 2.
2. BLO, CCO 180/2/1, Public Opinion Survey No. 1 (January 1949), 6.
3. Calder and Sheridan, 223.
4. Roth, 63.
5. Kavanagh, 39.
6. BLO, CCO 500/18/16.

7. BLO, CCO 500/18/52, 3 ff.

8. BLO, CCO 500/18/52, 7.

9. Cf. Annan, *passim*.

10. Mortimer, 298–9.

11. I am indebted to James Goodsman for his memories of Conservative organisation during this period.

12. Butler and Kavanagh, *The British General Election of 1987*, 196.

13. Tebbit, 152.

14. *Now!*, 5–11 October 1979.

15. *Sunday Telegraph*, 6 May 1979.

16. Savage, 41, 49.

17. Amis, 846.

18. Hoggart, 37–8.

19. Private information.

20. Kavanagh, 291.

21. Hudson and Williams, 128.

22. Hudson and Williams, 198.

23. Hudson and Williams, 62, 65.

24. *New Statesman*, 19 June 1987.

25. Butler and Kavanagh, *The British General Election of 1997*, 161.

26. Hudson and Williams, 69.

27. Adonis and Pollard, 4.

28. *The Times*, 27 September 2004.

29. *The Times*, 21 September 2004.

30. *The Times*, 5 October 2004.

Chapter 5: Don't Let Them Sch . . . on Britain: Good Causes

1. Byrne, 135.

2. *New Society*, 6 September 1984.

3. *Ecologist*, March 1974.

4. Matlass, 27.

5. *Scotsman*, 7 November 1970.

6. *Ecologist*, March 1971.

7. *Ecologist*, December 1970.

8. *Sunday Herald*, 14 November 2004.

9. *New Statesman*, 20 March 1970.

10. *Scotsman*, 1 December 1972.

11. *Sunday Times*, 13 February 1977.

12. *Ecologist*, February 1973.
13. *The Times*, 14 August, 20 and 23 September 1986; *Sunday Times*, 24 August 1986.
14. *New Society*, 5 September 1986; *The Times*, 19 September 1986.
15. *New Statesman*, 19 January 1996; *TES*, 23 February 1996.
16. *Sunday Times*, Supplement, 19 March 1962.
17. *Scotsman*, 29 November 1972; *Private Eye*, 13 February 1981.
18. *New Statesman*, 4 September 2000.
19. *The Times*, 3 November 1970; *New Statesman*, 2 January 1971.
20. Weight, 799.
21. Veldman, 115, 127n.
22. Byrne, 54–5, 71–2, 95.
23. *Minutes of Evidence Taken before the Royal Commission on the Press*, 1st and 2nd Days, 31–2.
24. *Eagle*, 18 April 1952.

Chapter 6: Freeing Us from Ourselves: Old Creeds and New Morals

1. Wolffe, 71.
2. Wolffe, 71.
3. Davies, 337.
4. *The Times*, 2 November 2004.
5. *Christian World Pulpit*, 26 August 1926.
6. *Guardian*, 14 June 1927.
7. *Tablet*, 2 February 1963.
8. Norman, 30.
9. *Spectator*, 8 June 1934.
10. Norman, 443, 446.
11. Weeks, 261.
12. *Royal Commission on Marriage and Divorce*, 509.
13. *Royal Commission on Marriage and Divorce*, 80–1, 160, 428.
14. *Woman*, February 1925.
15. *Royal Commission on Marriage and Divorce*, 23, 546, 777.
16. *Royal Commission on Marriage and Divorce*, 873–8.
17. *Tablet*, 12 December 1953.
18. *Tablet*, 15 April 1967.
19. I am indebted to A. N. Wilson for this point.
20. *Nova*, July 1966.
21. Perman, 179.

22. *Tablet*, 21 August 1963.

23. *TES*, 12, 26 September 1986.

24. *Lancet*, 5 December 1970; 20 January 1973.

25. *British Medical Journal*, 26 October 1985.

26. *Sunday Times*, 2 June 1985.

27. *Practitioner*, December 1983.

28. *Lancet*, 30 November 1985.

29. *The Times*, 19 June 1985.

30. Field, Opinion Polls, 1–8.

31. Heelas, 141.

32. *Alive*, May 1978.

33. *Alive*, July, October 1978.

34. Heelas, 154–5.

Chapter 7: Usefulness and Success: Education

1. *Eton Chronicle*, 30 January 1930.

2. Osborne, 245.

3. *TES*, 4 July 1925.

4. *TES*, 9 July 1938.

5. Quail, 181.

6. *TES*, 3, 10 January, 2, 16 February 1946.

7. Royle, 101–2.

8. *Spectator*, 8 June 1934.

9. *TES*, 29 June 1951.

10. Private information.

11. *TES*, 5 June 1951.

12. *Queen*, 21 August 1969.

13. *TES*, 4 June 1938.

14. *TES*, 8 July 1944.

15. *Parents*, December 1946.

16. *TES*, 9 January 1947.

17. *Sunday Times*, Magazine, 10 November 1963.

18. Adonis and Pollard, 20.

19. Logan and Goldberg, 326.

20. Hudson and Williams, 104.

21. *Radio Times*, 4 February 1968.

22. *Tablet*, 17 August 1985.

23. Simmonds, *Very Posy*, n.p.

24. Adonis and Pollard, 34–5.

25. *Good Schools Guide 1989*, 8–9.

26. *Economist*, 10 October 1957; *TES*, 23 June 1972.

27. Adonis and Pollard, 23–4.

28. *The Times*, 29 January 2005.

29. *Parents*, March 1934.

30. Adonis and Pollard, 48–9.

31. Baker, 12–16.

32. *Eton Chronicle*, 2 February 1968.

33. *TES*, 23 June 1972.

34. *Independent*, 18 August 2004.

35. *Careers 2005*, n.p.

36. *Independent*, 20 January 2005.

37. *Daily Mail Scholarship Guide, 1947*, 131.

38. Adonis and Pollard, 23.

39. *Now!*, 9–16 January 1981.

Chapter 8: Bella Vista: The Suburban Universe

1. Oliver, Davies and Bentley, 85, 101.

2. BL, CCO 1/1/2, 115.

3. Edward, 243–4.

4. *The Studio Yearbook of Decorative Art, 1938*, iii.

5. Clapson, 151–2; Medhurst, 241.

6. Orwell, *Coming Up for Air*, 7.

7. *Economist*, 11 June 1932.

8. *Economist*, 23 November 1935.

9. *Sunday Times*, Magazine, 11 February 1968.

10. *Sunday Times*, 24 April 1977.

11. *Economist*, 9 March 1996.

12. *Economist*, 31 August 2002.

13. Gibbs, 92–5.

14. *Punch*, 12 June 1935.

15. Hirst, 285–6.

16. *Good Housekeeping*, May 1949.

17. *The Times*, 31 January 1931.

18. *Punch*, 28 March 1934.

19. *Observer*, Magazine, 9 April 1967.

20. *Sunday Times*, 11 February 1967.

21. *Long March of Everyman*, 234.
22. Oliver, Davies and Bentley, 191–2.
23. *ILN*, 29 December 1945.
24. Lewis, 212.
25. Connor, 475, 483.
26. *Punch*, 29 October 1919.
27. *Saturday Review*, 23 November 1923.
28. Medhurst, 245–6.
29. *Sunday Times*, 4 March 1984.
30. *Observer*, Magazine, 6 March 1988.
31. *Sunday Times*, 3 May 1998.
32. *Sunday Times*, 13 June 1999.
33. *Sunday Times*, 10 April 1977.
34. *Sunday Times*, 24 April 1977.
35. *Sunday Times*, 3 May 1998.
36. Richards, *Castles*, 57.
37. *Observer*, Magazine, 4 April 1965.
38. *Observer*, Magazine, 4 October 1987.
39. *Observer*, Magazine, 11 April 1965.
40. *Sunday Times*, Magazine, 11 February 1968.
41. *Parents*, April 1947.
42. BLO. CCO 170/1/1/4, 43.
43. *General Household Survey 1993*, 155.
44. *Independent*, 9 February 2005.

Chapter 9: Vulnerable, Dependent, Emotional Human Beings: Wives and Families
1. Weeks, 214.
2. *Guardian*, 8 May 1919.
3. *Daily Graphic*, 1 October 1920.
4. Hirst, 75–6.
5. *Woman's Own*, 15 February 1975.
6. *Illustrated*, 13 January 1951.
7. *Parents*, January 1935; October 1946; March 1947.
8. *Parents*, March 1947.
9. *Good Housekeeping*, March 1958.
10. *Eagle*, 13 April 1951.
11. *Young Elizabethan*, April 1958.
12. *Young Elizabethan*, September 1958.

13. *TES*, 7 July 1961.

14. *Nova*, September 1966.

15. *Observer*, Magazine, 5 February 1967.

16. *Woman's Own*, 15 February 1975.

17. *Woman*, February 1925.

18. *Sphere*, 29 August 1931.

19. *Woman*, February 1925.

20. *Woman*, December 1924,

21. *The Times*, 21 June 1965.

22. Lewis, 214–16; *TES*, 12 May 1923.

23. Hirst, 71.

24. WI, Stopes PP/MCS/A7.

25. *Economist*, 27 March 1920.

26. Logan and Goldberg, 337.

27. *Illustrated*, 24 July 1954.

28. *Nova*, September 1966.

29. Greer, 48.

30. Spencer, 81, 83, 84–6.

31. I am indebted to my wife Mary for this quotation.

32. *The Times*, 29 May 1929.

33. *Good Housekeeping*, January 1958.

34. Crompton, 57; *Social Focus on Women*, 25.

35. Crompton, 57.

36. *Woman's Own*, 4 January 1975.

37. Corti, Laurie and Dex, 63.

38. Walczak, 67–74.

39. Corti, Laurie and Dex, 64.

40. Greer, 35–6.

41. *Good Housekeeping*, February 1949.

42. *Nova*, May 1966.

43. *Illustrated*, 23 January 1954.

44. Horwood, *passim*.

45. Logan and Goldberg, 338.

46. *TES*, 7 July 1961.

47. *TES*, 14 July 1961.

48. *Lancet*, 10 August 1963.

49. *Woman's Own*, 4 January 1975.

50. *Forum*, 2, viii, 54–5.

51. *Forum*, 2, iv, 6–9.

52. *Scottish Daily News*, 8 May 1975.
53. Private information.
54. *Cosmopolitan*, February 1978.
55. *Cosmopolitan*, December 1978.
56. *Cosmopolitan*, October 1988.
57. *Social Focus on Women*, 11.

Chapter 10: Have a Capstan and Make Friends: Pleasures and Anxieties
 1. *General Household Survey 1993*, 144, 156.
 2. Gratton and Taylor, 40–3.
 3. *The Times*, 18 August 2004.
 4. Gratton and Taylor, 19.
 5. Caradog Jones, 463, 477; *Good Housekeeping*, January 1949.
 6. Hudson and Williams, 122–3; *Economist*, 12 September 1992.
 7. Seymour-Ure, 4.
 8. *The Times*, 28 May 1983.
 9. *The Times*, 15 May 1995.
10. *Sunday Times*, 2 July 1978.
11. *Sphere*, 12 September 1936.
12. *Sunday Times*, 9 July 1978.
13. *Sunday Times*, 23 May 1999.
14. *Punch*, 14 May 1934.
15. *Spectator*, 18 September 1993; 20 September 1994.
16. *New Statesman*, 12 July 1999.
17. *Economist*, 13 September 1986.
18. *Observer*, Supplement, 4 March 1984.
19. *Economist*, 13 September 1986.
20. *Art and Artists*, May 1986.
21. *The Times*, Magazine, 13 May 1995.
22. *Now!*, 16–23 April 1981.
23. *Economist*, 13 November 1996.
24. *New Statesman*, 10 July 2000.
25. *The Times*, Magazine, 5 August 2003.
26. *Illustrated*, 10 July 1954.
27. *Observer*, Magazine, 7 October 1984.
28. *The Times*, 1 August 1983.
29. For example, *Independent*, 10 March 2005.
30. *Sunday Times*, 21 November 2004.

31. *Sunday Times*, 21 November 2004.

32. Walton, 53.

33. Walton, 159.

34. *Sphere*, 12 September 1936.

35. *Country Life*, 24 September 1987.

36. *Observer*, Magazine, 24 October 1984.

37. *Sunday Times*, 23 May 1999.

38. *Sphere*, 25 June 1932.

39. *Illustrated London News*, 29 May 1954.

40. *Listener*, 26 December 1963.

41. *Sunday Telegraph*, 23 January 2005.

42. *Independent*, 2 February 2005.

43. *Crafts*, January/February 1975.

44. *Art and Artists*, February and April 1989.

45. *Birds*, July/August 1966; September/October 1973; Spring 1998.

46. *Listener*, 18 November 1954; 26 September 1963.

47. *Sight and Sound*, Autumn 1956.

48. Carpenter, 173–4.

49. *Theatre Quarterly*, January/March 1971.

50. Harris, 52–4, 84.

51. *Studio*, October 1962.

52. *Crafts*, July/August 1989; September/October 1989.

53. *Crafts*, July/August 1989.

54. *Crafts*, May/June 1997.

55. Hoggart, 55.

56. Hoggart, 57.

57. Hoggart, 339.

Chapter 11: *I'm Proud of Being Middle-Class: Identities, Past and Future*

1. Simmonds, *Mrs Weber's Diary, passim.*

2. Peattie and Taylor, *Alex* (1987), *passim.*

3. Punch, *passim.*

4. *New Statesman*, 6 November 1992.

5. Adonis and Pollard, 4.

6. *New Society*, 20 May 1988.

7. Adonis and Pollard, 93.

8. *Spectator*, 3 December 1994.

9. *Daily Mail*, 22 April 1985.

10. McAleer, 237.

11. *Eugenics Review*, 8, 302.

12. Calder and Sheridan, 160–1.

13. *Picture Post*, 11 March 1939; *Observer*, Supplement, 30 October 1966.

14. *Morning Post*, 29 January 1919.

15. *Horizon*, 1, iv (1940), 350.

16. *Economist*, 30 June 1945.

17. *Daily Sketch*, 24 August 1931.

18. *Illustrated*, 21 August and 8 September 1954.

19. *The Economist*, 12 September 1992.

20. *The Times*, 25, 26 and 31 January 1990.

21. Adonis and Pollard, 4.

22. Roberts, Cooke, Clark and Semenoff, 44–5.

23. *Daily Telegraph*, 4 December 1978.

24. Fenton-O'Creevy and Nicholson, i, 6.

25. *Eton Chronicle*, 15 February 1985.

26. Botton, *passim*.

27. Carpenter, 55–6, 73, 80–2.

28. Carpenter, 92–3.

29. *Queen*, 15 March 1960.

30. *Sunday Times*, Magazine, 25 January 1976.

31. Mount, 159.

32. *Eton Chronicle*, 25 October 1985.

33. *The Times*, Review, 3 July 2004.

34. *Daily Sketch*, 1 July 1931; Logan and Goldberg, 334.

35. *Sunday Times*, Magazine, 7 January 1968.

36. *Economist*, 12 September 1992.

37. *Sunday Herald*, 'Fresh', 9 January 2005.

38. *Sunday Times*, Magazine, 10 November 1963.

39. *Sunday Telegraph*, 8 August and 21 October 2004.

40. Private information.

41. Rees, *Political Quarterly*, 294.

42. Hall and Caradog Jones, 48–9.

43. *Sunday Telegraph*, 8 May 2005.

44. *Independent*, 16 December 2004.

Sources

Unpublished

Bodleian Library Oxford
Conservative Central Office Papers.

British Library, London
Additional, Egerton and Lansdowne Manuscripts.
Berney Collection of Early Newspapers.
Ragford Ballad Collection.

Centre for Buckinghamshire Studies, Aylesbury
Diary of John Pope Fordon [D/X 992/9].
Diary of Joseph Townsend [D 85/12/1].
Quarter Session Papers [QS/JC].
A Poll of the Electors of the Borough of Aylesbury 1818 (Aylesbury, 1818).
A Poll of the Freeholders of the County of Buckingham at the Election of Knights of the Shire . . . May 1831 (1832).
A Poll of the Electors of the Borough of Aylesbury . . . 1835 (Aylesbury, 1835).
Pigott's Guide to Buckinghamshire (1831).

Guildhall Library, London
Diary of Thomas Rogers [Ms 19,019].

Diary of William Rowsell [Ms 24,458].
Diary of Samuel Elliot [Ms 15,819].
Diary of Charles Churchill [Ms 5762].
Autobiography of Sir John Fryer [Ms 12,017].
Diary of Elizabeth Tirell [Ms 14,951].

Guildhall Record Office, Guildhall, London
London and Southwark Coroners' Inquests, 1787–1837.

Lambeth Archives, Knatchbull Road, Lambeth
Papers of the Norwood Conservative Association, 1876–1914.

National Archives, Kew, London
HO [Home Office] 40, 42, 44, 55; Mepo [Metropolitan Police] 3 and 4.
STAC [Star Chamber] 3 and 8.

National Archives of Scotland, Edinburgh
Anti-Militia Riots, affidavits [AD 14/1/1].
Police Surveillance Files, 1945–1951 [HO 55 series].
Scottish NSPCC Papers [GD 409/28/11].
Scottish Commercial Travellers Association Papers [GD 412/1/2].
Sheriff's Court Proceedings [SC series].

National Library of Scotland, Edinburgh
Ms. 8919 (Motorist's log book, 1904).
Ms. 19,366 (Traill Diary).

Wellcome Institute, London
Stopes Collection [PP/MCS].

Privately Owned
Pigot Papers.

Published

Except where otherwise stated, all books are published in London.
All annuals, year books, journals, magazines and newspapers are cited
by name and date in the Notes.

P. Addison, *Now the War Is Over* (1995 edn).

A. Adonis and S. Pollard, *A Class Act: The Myth of Britain's Classless Society* (1997).

J. E. Allen, Some Changes in the Distribution of National Income during the War, *Journal of the Statistical Society of London*, 83 (1920).

R. C. Allen, The Growth of Labour Production in Modern English Agriculture, *Explorations in Economic History*, 25 (1998).

R. W. Ambler, From Ranters to Chapel Builders: Primitive Methodists in the South Lincolnshire Fenland, *Studies in Church History*, 23 (1986).

The Letters of Kingsley Amis, ed. Z. Leader (2000).

D. Amos, The 'Good Old Days': The Victorian Working Class Diet in Nottingham, *Transactions of the Thoroton Society*, 106 (2002).

B. L. Anderson, Provincial Aspects of the Financial Revolution of the Eighteenth Century, *Business History*, 11 (1969).

J. S. M. Anderson, *Christian Philanthropy* (1835).

N. Annan, *Our Age: Portrait of a Generation* (1990).

Anon [A Tourist], *The Railway Companion* (1833).

Army Medical Department Report for the Year 1899 (1901).

M. Arnold, *Culture and Anarchy*, in *The Works of Mathew Arnold*, VI (1907).

George Ashby's Poems, ed. M. Bateson (Early English Text Society, 1899).

Mrs Ashford, *Life of a Licensed Victualler's Daughter* (1842).

C. B. Atkinson and W. P. Stoneman, 'These griping greefes and pinching pangs': Attitudes to Childbirth in Thomas Bentley's *The Monument of Matrones* (1582), *Sixteenth Century Journal*, 21 (1990).

J. Aubrey, *Brief Lives*, ed. R. Barber (1975 edn).

G. Aylmer, *The King's Servants: The Civil Service of Charles I, 1625–1642* (1974 edn).

The Bailiff's Minute Book of Dunwich, 1404–1430, ed. M. Bailey (Suffolk Record Society, 24, 1992).

J. H. Baker, The English Legal Profession 1450–1550, in W. Prest ed., *Lawyers in Early Modern Europe and America* (1981).

The Autobiography of Samuel Bamford, ed. W. H. Chaloner (2 vols, 1967).

Banbury Gaol Records, ed. P. Renold (Banbury Historical Society, 21, 1987).

T. C. Barker, Urban Transport, in M. J. Freeman and D. H. Aldcroft eds, *Transport in Victorian Britain* (Manchester, 1988).

Memoirs of the Life of Mr Ambrose Barnes (Surtees Society, 50, 1867)

C. Barnett, *The Audit of War* (1986).

C. Barnett, *The Collapse of British Power* (Gloucester, 1984 edn).

C. M. Barron, The Education and Training of Girls in Fifteenth-Century London, in D. E. S. Dunn ed., *Courts, Counties and the Capital in the Later Middle Ages* (Stroud, 1996).

J. Barry ed., *The Tudor and Stuart Town: A Reader in English Urban History* (1990).

P. Bartley, Moral Regeneration of Women: Women and the Civic Gospel in Birmingham, 1880–1914, *Midland History*, 25 (2000).

S. W. Baskerville, Elections and the Yeoman: The Changing Identity of the English County Voter. 1700 to 1850, *Parliamentary History*, 17 (1998).

W. H. Beadle, *Behind the Counter: A Practical Guide to Shop Assistants* (1925).

M. B. Becker, *The Emergence of Civil Society in the Eighteenth Century* (Bloomington, 1995).

J. V. Beckett, Aristocrats and the Electoral Control of the East Midlands, 1660–1914, *Midland History*, 17 (1993).

The Bedford Moravian Church in the Eighteenth Century, ed. E. Welch (Bedfordshire Historical Records Society, 68, 1980).

The Bedfordshire Schoolchild: Elementary Education before 1902, ed. D. Bushby (Bedfordshire Historical Records Society, 67, 1988).

C. Behagg, Custom, Class and Change: The Trade Societies of Birmingham, *Journal of Social History*, 4 (1979).

M. Bennett, Careerism in Late-Mediaeval England, in J. Rosenthal and C. Richmond eds, *People, Politics and Community in the Later Middle Ages* (Gloucester, 1987).

M. Berg, *The Age of Manufactures, 1700–1820* (1996 edn).

J. de Berners, *The Book Containing the Treatises of Hawking, Hunting, Coat-Armour, Fishing and the Blazing of Arms* (1810: facsimile of the 1496 printed edn).

J. Betjeman, *Summoned by Bells* (1960).

A. Beveridge, Life in the Asylum: Patients' Letters from Morningside, 1873–1908, *History of Psychiatry*, 9 (1998).

Biographical History of Gonville and Caius College, II (1713–1897), ed. J. Venn (1898).

Bishop Wilberforce's Visitation of the Oxford Archdeaconry in the Year 1854, ed. E. D. Baker (Oxfordshire Record Society, 1954).

Black's Picturesque Tourist of Scotland (Edinburgh, 1882).

L. Bland, Marriage Laid Bare: Middle-Class Women and Marital Sex, 1880–1914, in J. Lewis ed., *Labour and Love: Women's Experience of Home and Family, 1850–1946* (1986).

N. Blewett, *The Peers, the Parties and the People: The General Elections of 1910* (1972).

R. Blythe, *The Age of Illusion* (1963).

L. Bonfield, R. M. Smith and K. Wrightson eds, *The World We Have Gained: Essays Presented to Peter Laslett on his Seventieth Birthday* (Oxford, 1986).

C. Booker, *The Neophiliacs* (1970 edn).

C. Booth, Occupations of the People of the United Kingdom, 1831–1881, *Journal of the London Statistical Society*, 49 (1886).

A. Borsay, A Middle Class in the Making: The Negotiation of Power and Status at Bath's Georgian General Infirmary, c 1729–65, *Eighteenth Century History*, 24 (1999).

H. Bosanquet, *Social Work in London 1869 to 1912: A History of the Charity Organisation Society* (1914).

J. Boswell, *The Life of Samuel Johnson* (9th edn, 4 vols, 1822).

A. de Botton, *Status Anxiety* (2005 edn).

Memoir of the Late John Bowdler Esq., to which is added some account of the late Thomas Bowdler Esq., Editor of the Family Shakespeare (1825).

T. Bowdler ed., *Gibbon's History of the Decline and Fall of the Roman Empire for the Use of Families and Young Persons* (5 vols, 1826).

W. Bowyer, *Brought Out in Evidence: An Autobiographical Summing-up* (1940).

BPP, *Health and Medical Profession*, 1 (Shannon, 1968).

BPP, *Parliamentary Papers: Account of the Population of Great Britain in the Years 1801, 1811, 1821, 1831* (Shannon, 1968).

BPP, *Reports from Committees of Enquiry: Industrial Factories*, 30 (Shannon, 1968).

BPP, *Reports by Inspectors of Factories . . . 1835–1841* (Shannon, 1969).

I. Bradley, *Abide with Me: The World of Victorian Hymns* (1997).

J. Brash, The New Scottish Electors in 1832: An Occupational Analysis, *Parliamentary History*, 15 (1996).

N. Breton, *A Mad World My Masters*, ed. U. Kentish-Wright (2 vols, 1929).

J. Brewer, *The Pleasures of the Imagination: English Culture in the Eighteenth Century* (1997).

A. Briggs, The Language of Class in Early-Nineteenth Century England, in M. W. Finn and T. C. Smout eds, *Essays in Social History* (Oxford, 1974).

B. Brittain, *The Woman at Oxford* (1960).

A. A. Broadbridge, The Sources of Railway Capital, in M. C. Reed ed., *Railways and the Victorian Economy* (Newton Abbot, 1969).

J. Broadway, John Smyth of Nibley: A Jacobean Man of Business and His

Service to the Berkeley Family, *Midland History*, 24 (1999).

M. Brock, *The Great Reform Act* (1973).

V. Brodsky, Widows in Late Elizabethan England: Remarriage, Economic Opportunity and Family Orientations, in L. Bonfield, R. M. Smith and K. Wrightson eds, *The World We Have Gained: Essays Presented to Peter Laslett on his Seventieth Birthday* (Oxford, 1986).

C. W. Brooks, The Common Lawyers in England 1558–1642, in *Lawyers in Early Modern Europe and America*, ed. W. Prest (1981).

A. D. Brown, *Popular Piety in Late Mediaeval England* (Oxford, 1995).

C. Brown, *Black and White Britain: The Third PSI Survey* (1984).

C. Brown, James Williams, 1798–1888: Profile of a Victorian Sculptor, *Proceedings of the Suffolk Institute of Archaeology*, 36 (1985).

G. Brown, *The English Letter-Writer, or, The Whole Art of General Correspondence* (1785).

J. Brown, *Life on the Road: My Experiences as a Commercial Traveller* (1885).

P. S. and D. Brown, The Anti-Vaccination Movement in Weston-super-Mare, *Notes and Queries for Somerset and Dorset*, 35, part 365 (2002).

S. E. Brown, 'A Just and Public Commerce': Moral Economy and the Middle Class in Eighteenth-Century London, *Journal of British Studies*, 32 (1993).

T. Brown, *Physick Lies a Bleeding, or the Apothecary turned Doctor* (1697).

A. Bryson, The Rhetoric of Status, in L. Gent and N. Llewellyn eds, *Renaissance Bodies: The Human Figure in English Culture c 1540–1660* (1990).

C. A. Buchanan, John Bowen and the Bridgwater Scandal, *Somerset Archaeological and Historical Society Transactions*, 138 (1995).

The Bull Dog: A Weekly Expositor of Humbug (1826).

V. L. Bullough, Prostitution and Reform in Eighteenth-Century England, *Eighteenth Century Life*, 9 (1985).

S. Bunker, *Strawopolis: Luton Transformed, 1840–1876* (Bedfordshire Historical Record Society, 78, 1999).

P. Burke, Popular Culture in Seventeenth Century London, in B. Reay ed., *Popular Culture in Seventeenth Century England* (1985).

W. L. Burn, *The Age of Equipoise* (1968 edn).

T. Burnet, *An Account of a Journey to London [1729]*, (Miscellany of the Third Spalding Club, 2 (Aberdeen. 1940)).

F. Burney, *Evelina*, ed. E. A. Bloom (Oxford, 1968).

Extracts from the Diary of Timothy Burrell, ed. R. W. Blencow, *Sussex Archaeological Collections*, 3 (1850).

G. M. Burrows, *Observations on the Comparative Mortality of Paris and London* (1815).

D. Butler and D. Kavanagh, *The British General Election of 1987* (1987).

D. Butler and D. Kavanagh, *The British General Election of 1997* (1997).

P. Byrne, *The Campaign for Nuclear Disarmament* (1988).

P. J. Cain, Railways 1870–1914: The Maturity of the Private System, in M. J. Freeman and D. H. Aldcroft eds, *Transport in Victorian Britain* (Manchester, 1988).

A. Calder and D. Sheridan, *Speak for Yourself: A Mass Observation Anthology, 1937–1949* (1984).

Calendar of Assize Records, Essex Indictments, Elizabeth I, ed. J. S. Cockburn (1978).

Calendar of Assize Records, Kent Indictments, Elizabeth I, ed. J. S. Cockburn (1979).

Calendar of Assize Records, Surrey Indictments, Elizabeth I, ed. J. S. Cockburn (1980).

Calendar of Plea and Memoranda Rolls of the City of London, 1423–1437, ed. A. H. Thomas (Cambridge, 1943).

D. Cannadine, *Class in Britain* (1998).

G. Cannan, *Round the Corner* (New York, 1923 edn).

B. Capp, The Double Standard Revisited: Plebeian Women and Male Reputation in Early Modern England, *Past and Present*, 162 (1999).

B. Capp, Separate Domains? Women and Authority in Early Modern England, in P. Griffiths, A. Fox and S. Hindle eds, *The Experience of Authority in Early Modern England* (1996).

D. Caradog Jones, The Cost of Living of a Sample of Middle Class Families, *Journal of the London Statistical Society*, 91 (1928).

Cardiganshire County History, 3: Cardiganshire in Modern Times, ed. G. H. Jenkins and I. G. Jones (Cardiff, 1998).

H. Carpenter, *Dennis Potter: A Biography* (1998).

Report of the Cases of John Caryll, ed. J. H. Baker (2 vols, Selden Society, 1999–2000).

M. Ceadal, *Pacifism in Britain 1914–1945: The Decline of a Faith* (Oxford, 1980).

The Cely Letters, ed. A Hanham (Early English Text Society, 1975).

Mr Chamberlain's Speeches, ed. C. W. Boyd (2 vols, 1914).

G. Chaucer, *The Canterbury Tales*, trans. N. Coghill (Penguin, 1954 edn).

R. Church, Markets and Marketing in the British Motor Industry before 1914 with Some French Comparisons, *Journal of Transport History*, 3 (1982).

M. Clapson, The Suburban Aspiration of England since 1919, *Contemporary British History*, 14, i (2000).

Lord Clarendon, *History of the Great Rebellion* (6 vols, Oxford, 1712).

C. Clark, Further Data on the National Income, *Economic Journal*, 44 (1934).

P. Clark, *The English Alehouse: A Social History 1200–1830* (1983).

P. Clark, Popular Protest and Disturbance in Kent, 1558–1640, *Economic History Review*, 29 (1976).

P. Clark, 'The Ramoth-Gilead of the Good': Urban Change and Political Radicalism in Gloucester, 1540–1640, in J. Barry ed., *The Tudor and Stuart Town: A Reader in English Urban History* (1990).

E. Clarke, Social Welfare and Mutual Aid in the Mediaeval Countryside, *Journal of British Studies*, 33 (1994).

J. T. Cliffe, *The Yorkshire Gentry from the Reformation to the Civil War* (1969).

W. Cobbett, *Advice to Young Men and (Incidentally) to Young Women in the Middle and Higher Ranks of Life* (1872 edn).

W. Cobbett, *Rural Rides* (1967 edn).

M. Cocker, *Birders: Tales of a Tribe* (2001).

F. G. Cockman, *The Railway Age in Bedford* (Bedfordshire Historical Records Society, 53, 1974).

C. Collett, The Social Status of Women's Occupations, *Journal of the London Statistical Society*, 71 (1908).

G. Colmore. £800 a Year, *Cornhill Magazine*, New Series, 10 (1901).

H. Colvin, *A Biographical Dictionary of British Architects, 1600–1840* (1978).

L. R. Connor, On certain Aspects of the Distribution of Income . . . 1914 to 1924, *Journal of the London Statistical Society*, 81 (1928).

C. Cooper, *Land, Men and Beliefs*, ed. G. E. Aylmer and J. S. Morrill (1982).

J. F. Cooper, *Men and Beliefs* (1983).

P. J. Corfield, Class by Name and Number in Eighteenth-Century Britain, *History*, 72 (1987).

R. Cork, *Art Beyond the Gallery in Early 20th Century England* (1985).

L. Corti, H. Lawrie and S. Dex, *Highly Qualified Women* (1995).

W. Coster, *Kinship and Inheritance in Early Modern England: Three Yorkshire Parishes* (York, 1993).

D. D. Cottingham-Taylor, *A Guide to a Better Diet* (1933).

N. Coward, *Plays Four* (1979).

D. Cressy, *Birth, Marriage and Death: Ritual, Religion and the Life-Cycle in Tudor and Stuart England* (Oxford, 1999 edn).

D. Cressy, Kinship and Kin Interaction in Early Modern England, *Past and Present*, 112 (1986).

R. J. Croft, The Nature and Growth of Cross-Channel Traffic through Calais and Boulogne, *Journal of Transport History*, 6 (1973).

R. Crompton, Where Did All the Bright Girls Go? Women's Higher Education and Employment since 1975, in N. Abercrombie and A. Warde eds, *Social Changes in Contemporary Britain* (1992).

The Backbench Diaries of Richard Crossman, ed. J. Morgan (1981).

The Crossman Diaries, ed. A. Howard (1981 edn).

CSP, *Domestic, 1641–43* (1887).

CSP, *America and West Indies, 1700* (1908).

CSP, *America and West Indies, 1717–18* (1930).

H. Custance, *Riding Recollections and Turf Stories* (1894).

G. G. D'Aeth, Present Tendencies of Class Differentiation, *Sociological Review*, 3 (1910).

Daily Mail Scholarship Guide, 1947 (1947).

L. Darwin, Quality *not* Quantity, *Eugenics Review*, 8 (1916).

L. D. Davidoff and C. Hall, The Architecture of Public Life: English Middle-Class Society in a Provincial Town, 1780 to 1850, in D. Fraser and A. Sutcliffe eds, *The Pursuit of Urban History* (1983).

H. Davies, *Worship and Theology in England: The Ecumenical Century 1900–1965* (Princeton, 1965).

J. F. R. Day, Primers of Honour: Heraldry, Heraldry Books, and English Renaissance Literature, *Sixteenth Century Journal*, 21 (1990).

D. Defoe, *The Complete English Tradesman* (1841 edn, 2 vols).

D. Defoe, *Family Instructor* (1841 edn, 2 vols).

The Dramatic Works of Thomas Dekker, ed. F. Bowers (vols 1–3, Cambridge, 1953–58).

P. Dele-Thomas, The Landed Estates of Somersetshire since 1871, *Somerset Archaeology and History*, 138 (1995).

Devizes Division Income Tax Assessment, 1842–1860, ed. R. Colley (Wiltshire Record Society, 55, 2002).

G. C. Dickinson and C. J. Longley, The Coming of Cheap Transport: A Study of Tramway Fares and Municipal Systems in British Provincial Towns, 1900–1914, *Transport History*, 6 (1973).

T. Dickson, *Scottish Capitalism: Class, State and Nation from before the Union to the Present* (1980).

J. Dillon, *Theatre, Court and City, 1595–1610: Drama and Social Space in London* (Cambridge, 2000).

R. Dinn, 'Monuments Answerable to Men's Worth': Burial Patterns, Social Status and Gender in Late-Mediaeval Bury St Edmunds, *Journal of Ecclesiastical History*, 46 (1995).

B. Disraeli, *Coningsby* (1907 edn).

B. Disraeli, *Sybil* (1907 edn).

E. J. Dobson, *English Pronunciation 1500–1700* (2 vols, Oxford, 1968).

B. M. Doyle, Urban Liberalism and the 'Lost Generation': Politics and Middle Class Culture in Norwich, 1900–1935, *Historical Journal*, 38 (1995).

E. Dunning and R. Sheard, *Barbarians, Gentlemen and Players: A Sociological Development of Rugby Football* (1979).

C. Dyer, The English Mediaeval Village Community and Its Decline, *Journal of British Studies*, 33 (1994).

Reports from the Lost Notebooks of Sir James Dyer, ed. J. H. Baker (Selden Society, 2 vols, 1994).

M. Dyer, *Men of Property and Intelligence: The Scottish Electoral System Prior to 1884* (1996).

C. Dyhouse, Mothers and Daughters in the Middle Class Home, c. 1870–1914, in J. Lewis ed., *Labour and Love: Women's Experience of Home and Family, 1850–1940* (1986)

C. Dyhouse, *No Distinction of Sex? Women in British Universities 1870–1939* (1995).

H. J. Dyos, *Exploring the Urban Past*, ed. D. Cannadine and D. Reader (Cambridge, 1982).

The Earl Marshal's Papers at Arundel Castle, ed. F. W. Steer (Harleian Society, 1964).

Early Trade Directories of Wiltshire, ed. K. H. Rogers and J. H. Chandler (Wiltshire Record Society, 47, 1992).

Early Yorkshire Schools, 2, ed. A. F. Leech (Yorkshire Archaeological Society, 39, 1903).

East End, West End: The Face of Leeds during Urbanisation 1684–1842, ed. M. Beresford (Thoresby Society, 70–1, 1985–6).

F. Eden, *The State of the Poor, or A History of the Labouring Classes in England* (3 vols, 1797).

The Educator: Prize Essays on the Expediency and Means of Elevating the Profession of Educator in Society (1839).

A. M. Edwards, *The Design of Suburbia* (1981)

E. L. Eisenstein, *The Printing Press as an Agent of Change* (Cambridge, 1997 edn).

J. Ellis, A Bold Adventurer: The Business Fortunes of William Clesworth, c 1668–1726, *Northern History*, 27 (1981).

A. Elton, *Leeds Cyclists and Cycle Makers, 1880–1901* (Thoresby Society, 1995).

T. Elyot, *The Boke named The Governour*, ed. H. H. Cope (2 vols, 1880).

England in the Reign of King Henry the Eighth (Early English Text Society, 1878).

English Gilds, ed. L. Toulmain Smith (Early English Text Society, 1870).

Everyday Life in Our Public Schools, ed. C. Pascoe (1881).

M. Falkus, The Development of Municipal Trade in the Nineteenth Century, *Business History*, 19 (1977).

The Diary of Joseph Farrington, ed. K. Garlick and A. MacIntyre (8 vols, 1978).

T. Fawcett, Measuring the Provincial Enlightenment: The Case of Norwich, *Eighteenth Century Life*, 8 (1982).

M. R. Fear, The Election at Great Marlow in 1640, *Journal of Modern History*, 14 (1942).

M. Fenton O'Creevy and N. Nicholson, *Middle Managers: Their Contribution to Employee Involvement* (1994).

N. Ferguson, *The Cash Nexus: Money and Power in the Modern World 1700–2000* (2001).

C. D. Field, 'The Secularised Sabbath' Revisited: Opinion Polls as Sources for Sunday Observance, *Contemporary British History*, 13 (2001).

R. K. Field, Migration in the Later Middle Ages: The Case of the Hampton Lovett Villeins, *Midland History*, 8 (1983).

M. Finn, Men's Things: Masculine Possession in the Consumer Revolution, *Journal of Social History*, 25 (2000).

A. Fletcher, *A County Community in Peace and War: Sussex 1600–1660* (1975).

M. W. Flinn and T. C. Smout eds, *Essays in Social History* (Oxford, 1974).

R. A. Florey, *The General Strike of 1926* (1980).

R. Floud, The Dimensions of Inequality: Height and Weight Variation in Britain, 1700–2000, *Contemporary British History*, 16, ii (2002).

E. M. Forster, *Abinger Harvest* (1967 edn)

E. M. Forster, *Howards End* (1963 edn).

E. Foss, *A Biographical Dictionary of the Judges of England* (1870)

F. F. Foster, *The Politics of Stability: A Portrait of the Rulers of Elizabethan London* (1977).

J. Foster, Nineteenth Century Towns: A Class Division, in M. W. Flinn and T. C. Smout eds, *Essays in Social History* (Oxford, 1974).

R. H. Frank, *Luxury Fever* (New York, 1999).

D. Fraser and A. Sutcliffe, *The Pursuit of Urban History* (1983).

M. Frayn, Festival, in M. Sissons ed. *The Age of Austerity* (1963 edn).

M. J. Freeman and D. H. Aldcroft, *Transport in Victorian Britain* (Manchester, 1988).

H. R. French, 'Ingenious and Learned Gentlemen': Social Perceptions and Self-Fashioning among Parish Elites in Essex, 1680–1740, *Journal of Social History*, 25 (2000).

K. L. French, Maiden's Lights and Wives' Stones: Parish Guilds in Late-Mediaeval England, *Sixteenth Century Journal*, 29 (1998).

R. v. Friedburg, Reformation of Manners and the Composition of Offenders in an East Anglian Village: Earl's Colne, Essex, 1531–1642, *Journal of British Studies*, 29 (1990).

P. Frost, Yeomen and Metalsmiths: Livestock in the Dual Economy in South Staffordshire, 1560–1720, *Agricultural History Review*, 29 (1981).

T. R. Fyvel, The Stones of Harlow, *Encounter* (June 1956).

S. Galbraith, Dr Joshua Parsons (1814–1892) of Beckington, Somerset, General Practioner, *Somerset Archaeological and Natural History Proceedings*, 140 (1990).

J. Gay, *The Beggar's Opera* (1922 edn).

R. Geary, *Policing Industrial Disputes, 1893–1985* (1986 edn).

General Household Survey 1993 (1995).

The Life of Mr Thomas Gent, Printer of York (1832).

The Georgian Public Buildings of Leeds and the West Riding, ed. K. Brady (Thoresby Society, 62, 1987).

Georgian Tiverton: The Political Memoranda of Beavis Wood, 1768–1798, ed. J. Bourne (Devon and Cornwall Record Society, 29, 1986).

P. Gibbs, *England Speaks* (1935).

The Diary and Memoirs of John Allen Giles, ed. D. Bromwich (Somerset Record Society, 2000).

M. Girouard, *Robert Smithson and the Elizabethan Country House* (1983 edn).

M. Girouard, *Sweetness and Light: The Queen Anne Movement 1860–1900* (1977).

G. Gissing, *New Grub Street* (1927 edn).

J. Godber, *Some Documents Relating to Riots* (Miscellanea, Bedfordshire Historical Record Society, 49, 1970).

O. Goldsmith, Life of Robert Nash, in *Collected Works*, ed. A. Friedman, 3 (Oxford, 1966).

The Good Food Guide, 1977 (1978).

N. Goose, Household Size and Structure in Early Stuart Cambridge, in J. Barry ed., *The Tudor and Stuart Town: A Reader in English Urban History* (1990).

J. Gordon Kelter, The Lay Presence: Chancery and Privy Seal Personnel in the Bureaucracy of Henry VI, *Mediaeval Prosopography*, 10, i (1989).

M. Gorsky, *Patterns of Philanthropy: Charity and Society in Nineteenth-Century Bristol* (1999).

S. Gosson, *Pleasant Quippes for Upstart Newfangled Gentlemen* (1847 edn).

J. W. Gough, *The Rise of the Entrepreneur* (1969).

H. Goulbourne, *Race Relations in Britain since 1945* (1998).

T. R. Gourvish, Railways 1830–1870: The Formative Years, in M. J. Freeman and D. H. Aldcroft eds, *Transport in Victorian Britain* (Manchester, 1988).

T. R. Gourvish, The Rise of the Professions, in T. R. Gourvish and A. O'Day eds, *Later Victorian Britain* (1993 edn).

R. Grassby, The Personal Wealth of the Business Community in Seventeenth Century England, *Economic History Review*, 23 (1970).

C. Gratton and P. Taylor, *Economics of Sport and Recreation* (2001 edn).

R. Graves and A. Hodge, *The Long Weekend: A Social History of Britain 1918–1939* (1995 edn).

H. B. Gray, *The Public School and Empire* (1913).

J. Gray, *The Admission of Dissenters to the Universities* (Oxford, 1834).

N. Gray, *The Worst of Times* (1985).

R. L. Greaves, *Enemies Under His Feet: Radicals and Nonconformists in Britain, 1664–1677* (Stanford, Calif, 1990).

R. Greene, *A Groats-Worth of Witte, The Repentance of Robert Greene, 1592*, ed. G. B. Harrison (1923).

G. Greer, *The Madwoman's Underclothes: Essays and Occasional Writings 1965–85* (1986 edn).

R. Griffen, Further Notes on the Progress of the Working Class in the Last Half Century, *Journal of the Statistical Society of London*, 49 (1886).

P. Griffiths, Masterless Young People in Norwich, in P. Griffiths, A. Fox and S. Hindle eds, *The Experience of Authority in Early Modern Britain* (1996).

P. Griffiths, A. Fox and S. Hindle eds, *The Experience of Authority in Early Modern Britain* (1996).

R. Grime, *Memory Stretches: History of Oldham Parliamentary Elections, 1832–1852* (Oldham, 1887).

C. Grover and K. Soothill, 'A Murderous Underclass?' The Press Reporting of Sexually Motivated Murders, *Sociological Review*, 44 (1996).

R. Guerriro Wilson, Women's Work in Offices and the Preservation of Men's 'Breadwinning' Jobs in Early-Twentieth Century Glasgow, *Women's History Review*, 10 (2001).

P. Gurney, The Middle Class Embrace: Language, Representation and the Contest over Cooperative Farms in Britain, c. 1860–1914, *Victorian Studies*, 37 (1993–4).

C. Haigh, *English Reformations: Religion, Politics and Society under the Tudors* (Oxford, 1995 edn).

Haileybury School Register, 1862–1900 (1900).

Hall's Chronicles, Containing the History of England (1809).

J. Hall and D. Caradog Jones, Social Grading of Occupations, *British Journal of Sociology*, 1 (1950).

L. A. Hall, *Hidden Anxieties: Male Sexuality 1900–1950* (1991).

A. J. Hammerton, Victorian Marriage and the Law of Matrimonial Cruelty, *Victorian Studies*, 33 (1989).

A Handbook for the Traveller in France (John Murray, 1856 edn).

A Handbook for the Traveller in Kent and Sussex (1858).

A Handbook for the Traveller in Northern Italy (1874).

A Handbook for the Traveller in Turkey (n.d.).

A. Hanham, *The Celys and Their World* (Cambridge, 1985).

Jesse Harden's Journal, ed. W. Park (The Book of the Old Edinburgh Club, 30, 1959).

A. J. C. Hare, *The Story of My Life* (6 vols, 1896–1900).

J. S. Harris, *Government Patronage of the Arts in Britain* (Chicago, 1970).

Harrison's Description of England in Shakespeare's Youth, ed. E. J. Furnivall (New Shakespeare Society, 1, 1877).

B. Harrison, *Drink and the Victorians: The Temperance Question in Victorian England 1815–1872* (1971).

B. Harrison, *Peaceable Kingdom: Stability and Change in Modern Britain* (Oxford, 1982).

F. Harrison, *Autobiographical Memoirs* (2 vols, 1911).

E. Hawkes, 'She will . . . protect her rights bodily by law and reason: Women's Knowledge of Common Law and Equity Courts in late Mediaeval England, in N. J. Menage ed., *Mediaeval Women and the Law* (Woodbridge, Suffolk, 2000).

D. Hay and F. Snyder, *Policing and Prosecution in Britain 1750–1850* (Oxford, 1989).

P. Heelas, The Sacralization of Self and New Age Capitalism, in N. Abercrombie and A. Warde eds, *Social Change in Contemporary Britain* (1992).

J. Helland, Locality and Pleasure in Landscape: A Study of Three Nineteenth Century Scottish Watercolourists, *Rural History*, 8 (1997).

C. Hill, *The World Turned Upside Down: Radical Ideas during the English Revolution* (1972 edn).

R. I. Hills, *The General Strike in York* (York, 1980).

G. Himmelfarb, *The Demoralization of Society* (New York, 1996).

S. Hindle, The Political Culture of the Middling Sort in English Rural Communities, c 1550–1700, in T. Harris ed., *The Politics of the Excluded* (2001).

F. W. Hirst, *The Consequences of the War to Great Britain* (Oxford, 1934)

The Historical Collections of a London Citizen, ed. J. Gairdner (Camden Society, 1876).

HMC, *12th Report*, Appendix, Part 9 (1891).

HMC, *Portland*, 4 (1897).

HMC, *Report on Manuscripts in the Welsh Language* (1898).

D. Hoak ed., *Tudor Political Culture* (Cambridge, 1995).

J. Hoeppner-Moran, Literacy and Education in Northern England, 1350–1520, *Northern History*, 27 (1983).

R. Hoggart, *The Way We Live Now* (1995).

B. A. Holderness, *Pre-Industrial England: Economy and Society, 1500–1750* (1976).

B. A. Holderness, Credit in English Rural Society before the Nineteenth Century with Special Reference to the Period 1605–1720, *Agricultural History Review*, 24 (1976).

J. Hollams, *The Jottings of an Old Solicitor* (1906).

G. Holles ed., *Memorials of the Holles Family* (Camden Society, 3rd Series, 1937).

W. Holtby, *South Riding* (1949 edn).

G. J. Holyoake, *Sixty Years of an Agitator's Life* (2 vols, 1893).

J. R. de S. Honey, *Tom Brown's Universe: The Development of the English Public School* (1977).

C. P. Hopgood, The 'Knights of the Road': Commercial Travellers and the Culture of the Commercial Room in Late-Victorian and Edwardian England, *Victorian Studies*, 37 (1993–4).

J. Hoppit, *A Land of Liberty? England 1689–1727* (Oxford, 2000).

C. Horwood, Girls Who Arouse Dangerous Passions: Women and Bathing 1900–1939, *Women's History Review*, 9 (2000).

W. G. Hoskins, *Essays in Leicestershire History* (Liverpool, 1950).

W. E. Houghton, *The Victorian Frame of Mind 1830–1870* (1970 edn).

House of Commons Journals (55 vols, 1803).

R. A. Houston, Illiteracy in the Diocese of Durham, 1663–89 and 1750–62: The Evidence of Marriage Bonds, *Northern History*, 28 (1982).

D. Howarth, *Images of Rule: Art and Politics in the English Renaissance, 1485–1649* (1997).

J. R. Howe, Liberal Party Organisation in Gloucestershire before 1914, *Southern History*, 9 (1987).

P. P. Howe, The Circulating Libraries: Their Complaint and Code, *Nineteenth Century*, 74 (1913).

HP, *The House of Commons, 1386–1421*, ed. J. S. Roskell (3 vols, 1992).

HP, *The House of Commons, 1509–1558*, ed. S. T. Bindoff (3 vols, 1982).

HP, *The House of Commons, 1660–1690*, ed. B. Henning (3 vols, 1983).

R. Hudson and A. M. Williams, *Divided Britain* (1995 edn).

F. Hughes, *North Country Life in the Eighteenth Century, The North East 1700–1750* (Oxford, 1969).

S. Humphries, *Hooligans or Rebels? An Oral History of Working-Class Childhood and Youth, 1889–1939* (Oxford, 1981).

R. Hyam, *Empire and Sexuality* (Manchester, 1992 edn).

K. S. Inglis, Patterns of Religious Worship in 1851, *Journal of Ecclesiastical History*, 11 (1960).

M. Ingram, The Reform of Popular Culture, in B. Reay ed., *Popular Culture in Seventeenth-Century England* (1985).

M. Ingram, The Reformation of Manners in Early Modern England, in P. Griffiths, A. Fox and S. Hindle eds, *The Experience of Authority in Early Modern England* (1996).

Inventories of Bedfordshire Country Houses, 1714–1830, ed. J. Collett-White (Bedfordshire Historical Record Society, 74, 1995).

Inventories of the Worcestershire Landed Gentry, 1537–1786, ed. M. Wanklyn

(Worcestershire Historical Society, 1998).

Ipswich Probate Inventories, 1583–1631, ed. M. Reed (Suffolk Record Society, 22, 1981).

E. W. Ives, *The Common Lawyers of Pre-Reformation England; Thomas Kabell, A Case Study* (Cambridge, 1983).

M. C. Jacob, *Living in the Enlightenment: Freemasonry and Politics in Eighteenth Century Europe* (Oxford, 1991).

P. Jalland, *Women, Marriage and Politics, 1860–1914* (Oxford, 1986).

L. James, *Warrior Race: A History of the British at War* (2002).

M. James, *Society, Politics and Culture: Studies in Early Modern England* (Cambridge, 1986).

R. R. James, *The British Revolution: British Politics 1880–1939* (1978 edn).

H. H. Jewell, 'The Bringing Up of Children in Good Learning and Manners': A Survey of Secular Education in the North of England, c. 1350–1550, *Northern History*, 28 (1982).

Johan Johan the Husband (Malone Society, 1972).

A. H. John, The London Assurance Company and the Marine Insurance Market of the Eighteenth Century, *Economica*, 25 (1958).

S. Johnson, *The Rambler* (3 vols, 1806).

L. E. Jones, *A Victorian Boyhood* (1955).

S. Jones, The Cotton Industry and Joint Stock Banking in Manchester in 1825 to 1850, *Business History*, 20 (1978).

E. Jordan, 'The Great Principle of English Fair Play?' Male Champions of the English Women's Movement and the Admission of Men to the Pharmaceutical Society in 1879, *Women's History Review*, 7 (1998).

The Diary of Ralph Josselin, 1616–1683, ed. A. Macfarlane (1976).

The Justicing Notebook of William Hunt, 1744–1749, ed. E. Crittall (Wiltshire Record Society, 37, 1982).

D. Kavanagh, *Thatcherism and British Politics: The End of Consensus* (Oxford, 1987).

S. Kelly ed., *The Life of Mrs Sherwood* (1844).

A. J. Kidd, 'Local History' and the Culture of the Middle Classes in North-West England, c 1840–1900, *Transactions of the Historical Society of Lancashire and Cheshire*, 147 (1997).

A. J. Kidd and D. Nicholls, The Making of the Middle Class? (Stroud, 1998).

D. Killingray, Rights, 'Riot' and Ritual: The Knole Park Access Dispute, Sevenoaks, Kent, 1883–1885, *Rural History*, 5 (1994).

A. King, George Goodwin and the Art Union, London, *Victorian Studies*, 8 (1964–5).

J. E. King, 'We Could Eat the Police!': Popular Violence in the North Lancashire Cotton Strike of 1878, *Victorian Studies*, 28 (1985).

C. Kingsley, *Yeast* (1879 edn).

C. Kitson Clark, *The Making of Victorian England* (1977 edn).

W. Lambard, *Eirenarcha, or The Office of the Justice of the Peace* (1599 edn).

Lancashire and Cheshire Wills, 1572 to 1696, ed. J. P. Earwaker (Chetham Society, 1893).

Law and Order in Georgian Bedfordshire, ed. E. Stockdale (Bedfordshire Historical Records Society, 61, 1982).

J. Lawrence, Class and Gender in the Making of Urban Toryism, 1880–1914, *English Historical Review*, 108 (1993).

G. S. Layard, A Lower-Middle Class Budget, *Cornhill Magazine*, New Series, 10 (1901).

W. T. Layton, Changes in the Wages of Domestic Servants during the Past Fifty Years, *Journal of the London Statistical Society*, 71 (1908).

A. F. Leach, *English Schools at the Reformation, 1546–8* (1896).

R. Lee, Revolution and Restoration: Paternalism, Disgrace and Dignity in the Victorian Church, *Norfolk Archaeology*, 44 (2002).

Leeds Friends Minute Book 1692 to 1712, ed. J. and R. Mortimer, *Yorkshire Archaeological Society*, 139 (1977–8).

A. Leggatt, *Citizen Comedy in the Age of Shakespeare* (Toronto, 1973).

G. Legh, *The Accedens of Armory* (1562).

Leland's Itinerary of England and Wales, ed. L. Toulmin Smith (5 vols, 1964).

L. Leneman, 'A tyrant and tormentor': Violence against Wives in Eighteenth-Century and Early-Nineteenth-Century Scotland, *Continuity and Change*, 12 (1997).

Letters and Papers, Foreign and Domestic of the Reign of Henry VIII, 14, ii (1895).

J. Lewis, Women between the Wars, in F. Gloversmith ed., *Class, Culture and Social Change: A New View of the 1930s* (Brighton, 1980).

The Letters of Henry Liddell to William Cotesworth, ed. J. H. Ellis (Surtees Society, 2001).

J. Liedl, The Penitent Pilgrim: William Calverley and the Pilgrimage of Grace, *Sixteenth Century Journal*, 24 (1994).

Lincoln Wills, 1532–1534, ed. D. Hickman (Lincoln Record Society, 2001).

R. F. L. Logan and E. M. Goldberg, Rising Eighteen in a London Suburb: A Study of Some Aspects of the Life and Health of Young Men, *British Journal of Sociology,* 4 (1953).

The London Assize of Nuisance, 1301–1431, ed. H. M. Chew and W. Kellaway (London Record Society, 1973).

The Long March of Everyman 1750–1960, ed. T. Barker (1978 edn).

R. Low and R. Manvell, *The History of the British Film* (vols 1 and 2, 1997).

J. McAleer, *Popular Reading and Publishing in Britain* (Oxford, 1992).

T. B. Macaulay, *Critical and Historical Essays* (3 vols, 1843).

D. McCarthy, The Censorship of Plays, *New Quarterly,* 2 (1909).

M. C. McClendon, 'Against God's Word': Government, Religion and the Crisis of Authority in Early Reformation Norwich, *Sixteenth Century Journal,* 25 (1994).

N. McCord, Some Aspects of Change in the Nineteenth Century North East, *Northern History,* 31 (1995).

L. MacCormick Edwards, *Herkomer: A Victorian Artist* (Aldershot, 1999).

S. MacDonald, Further Progress with the Early Threshing Machines: A Rejoinder, *Agricultural History Review,* 26 (1978).

A. Macfarlane, *Marriage and Love in England: Modes of Reproduction* (Oxford, 1986).

M. McGarvie, A Religious Disturbance of 1874, *Somerset and Dorset Notes and Queries,* 333 (1994).

W. L. MacKenzie and E. Mathew, *Medical Inspection of Children* (Edinburgh, 1904).

R. McKibbin, *Classes and Cultures: England 1918–1951* (Oxford, 1998).

A. McLaren, *Birth Control in Nineteenth Century England* (1978).

E. N. McRee, Religious Gilds and Regulation of Behaviour in Late Mediaeval Towns, in J. Rosenthal and C. Richmond eds, *People, Politics and Community in the Later Middle Ages* (Gloucester, 1987).

F. Madox Ford, *A History of Our Own Times,* ed. S. Berinfield and S. J. Stang (1989).

Manners and Meals in Olden Times (Early English Text Society, 1868).

W. Marshall, *The Rural Economy of the West of England* (2 vols, 1796).

T. Mason, *Association Football and English Society, 1863–1915* (Brighton, 1980).

The Plays of Philip Massinger, ed. C. Gibson, II (Oxford, 1976).

C. F. G. Masterman, *The Condition of England* (1910).

D. Matlass, *Landscape and Englishness* (1998).

R. Maugham, *Escape from the Shadows* (1981 edn).

H. Maxwell, *English Memories* (1932).

A. Medhurst, Negotiating the Gnome Zone: Versions of Suburbia in British Popular Culture, in R. Silverstone ed., *Visions of Suburbia* (1997).

D. Mellor, Arts in the 1930s: Some Political and Cultural Structures, in F. Gloversmith ed., *Class, Culture and Social Change: A New View of the 1930s* (Brighton, 1980).

N. J. Menage, *Mediaeval Women and the Law* (Woodbridge, 2000).

W. R. Meyer, *Charles Henry Wilson: The Man Who Was Leeds* (Thoresby Society, Leeds, 1998).

T. Middleton, *Michaelmas Term*, ed. R. Levin (1967).

G. Miège, *The New State of England under our Present Monarch William III* (1699).

A. Miles, *Social Mobility in Nineteenth and Early-Twentieth Century England* (Basingstoke, 2001).

Joe Miller's Complete Jest Book (1832).

Joe Miller's Jests: or, the Wit's Vade Mecum (1739).

Ministry of Labour Report for the Year 1935 (1936).

G. Minois, *The History of Suicide* (Baltimore, 1999).

The Minute Book of the Spalding Gentlemen's Society, ed. D. Owen and S. W. Woodward (Lincolnshire Record Society, 73, 1981).

Minutes of the Board of Directors of the Reading, Guildford and Reigate Railway Company, ed. E. Course (Surrey Record Society, 33, 1987).

Minutes of Evidence Taken before the Royal Commission on the Press (1948).

'Mira', *The Wife* (1756).

W. N. Molesworth, *A History of England from the Year 1830 to 1874* (3 vols, 1875).

H. More, *Coelebs in Search of a Wife* (2 vols, 1809 edn).

H. More, *Strictures on the Modern System of Female Education* (2 vols, 1799).

K. O. Morgan, *The People's Peace: British History 1945–1989* (Oxford, 1990).

R. J. Morris, The Middle Class in British Towns and Cities of the Industrial Revolution, 1780–1870, in D. Fraser and A. Sutcliffe eds, *The Pursuit of Urban History* (1983).

A. Morrison, Family Budgets: I, A Workman's Budget, *Cornhill Magazine*, New Series, 10 (1901).

R. Mortimer, *Paradise Postponed* (1986 edn).

F. Mount, *Mind the Gap* (2004).

M. Muggeridge, *The Green Stick* (1973 edn).

C. Muldrew, *The Economy of Obligation: The Culture of Credit and Social Relations in Early Modern England* (1998).

Murray's Handbook of Greece (1876).

J. Murray MacDonald, The Economic Decay of Britain, *Contemporary Review*, 79 (1901).

A Myrour to Lewde Men and Wymmen. ed. V. Nelson (Heidelberg, 1981).

T. Newburn, *Permission and Regulation: Law and Morals in Postwar Britain* (1992).

E. S. Newman, Between Pit and Pedestal: Images of Eve and Mary in Mediaeval Cornish Church Drama, in E. E. Dubruck ed., *New Images of Mediaeval Women* (Lampeter, 1989).

D. Newsome, *Godliness and Good Learning: Four Studies on a Victorian Ideal* (1961).

E. R. Norman, *Church and Society in England 1770–1970* (Oxford, 1976).

A. Offer, Body Weight and Self-Control in the United States and Britain since the 1950s, *Society for the History of Medicine*, 14 (2001).

M. Ogborn, *Spaces of Modernity; London's Geographies, 1680–1780* (New York, 1998)

W. Ogle, Suicides in England and Wales in Relation to Age, Sex, Season and Occupation, *Journal of the Statistical Society of London*, 49 (1886).

F. O'Gorman, The Electorate before and after 1832, *Parliamentary History*, 12 (1993)

P. Oliver, I. Davies and I. Bentley, *Dunroamin: The Suburban Semi and its Enemies* (1994 edn).

S. Olson, Family Linkages in the Structure of the Local Elite in the Mediaeval and Early-Modern Village, *Midland History*, 13, ii (1992).

N. Orme, *Education and Society in Mediaeval and Renaissance England* (1984).

G. Orwell, Boys' Weeklies, *Horizon*, 1, iii (1940).

G. Orwell, *Coming Up for Air*, in *Complete Works*, 8, ed. P. Davison (20 vols, 1986–98),

J. Osborne, *Damn You, England: Collected Prose* (1994).

G. R. Owst, *Literature and the Pulpit in Mediaeval England* (Cambridge, 1933).

Oxford City Apprentices 1697–1800, ed. M. Graham (Oxford Historical Society, 31, 1987).

T. Paine, *The Rights of Man*, ed. A. Seldon (1963).

D. M. Palliser, Civic Mentality and the Environment in Tudor York, *Northern History*, 28 (1982).

The Trial of William Palmer, ed. G. H. Knott (1912).

S. Parker, *The Sociology of Leisure* (1976).

W. Parkes, *Domestic Duties or Instructions to Young Married Ladies* (1825).

Parson and Parish in Eighteenth Century Hampshire: Replies to the Bishop's Visitations, ed. W. R. Ward (Hampshire Record Series, 13, 1995).

Paston Letters and Papers of the Fifteenth Century, ed. N. Davies (2 vols, Oxford 1971 and 1976).

V. Pearl, Change and Stability in Seventeenth Century London, in J. Barry ed., *The Tudor and Stuart Town: A Reader in English Urban History* (1990).

J. Pearlman and D. Shirley, When Did New Women Acquire Literacy?, *William and Mary Quarterly*, 48 (1991).

G. Pearson, *Hooligan: a History of Respectable Fears* (1983).

J. Pearson ed., *Belief beyond Boundaries: Wicca, Celtic Spirituality and the New Age* (2002).

O. C. Peattie and R. Taylor, *Alex* (1987); *The Unabashed Alex* (1988).

D. C. Peddar, Intensive Electioneering, *Contemporary Review* (January 1910).

G. Pellew, *The Life and Correspondence of the Right Honourable Henry Addington, First Viscount Sidmouth* (3 vols, 1847)

H. Pelling, *The Social Geography of British Elections 1885–1910* (1967).

S. D. Pennybacker, *A Vision for London 1889–1914: Labour, Everyday Life and the LCC Experience* (1995).

D. Pepper, *The Roots of Modern Environmentalism* (1984).

The Diary of Samuel Pepys, ed. R. C. L. Lethan and W. K. Matthews (11 vols, 1974–94).

S. and R. Percy, *London or Interesting Memorials of its Rise, Progress and Present State* (3 vols, 1823).

D. Perman, *Change and the Churches: An Anatomy of Religion in Britain* (1977).

M. Petter, Temporary Gentlemen, *Historical Journal*, 37 (1994).

D. Phillips, Good Men to Associate, Bad Men to Conspire: Associations for the Prosecution of Felons in England, 1760–1860, in D. Hay and F. Snyder eds, *Policing and Prosecution in Britain 1750–1850* (Oxford, 1989).

K. C. Phillips, *Language and Class in Victorian England* (1984).

Pictures of the Year 1914 (1914).

The Autobiography of Francis Place (1771–1854), ed. M. Thale (Cambridge, 1972).

M. Plant, *The English Book Trade* (1939).

The Pleasant Conceited Comedy of George a Green, the Pinner of Wakefield (Malone Society, 1911).

S. Poole, Pitt's Terror Reconsidered: Jacobinism and the Law in Two South-Western Counties, 1791–1803, *Southern History*, 17 (1995).

B. Porter, 'Bureau and Barrack': Early Victorian Attitudes toward the Continent, *Victorian Studies*, 27 (1984).

R. Porter, *Enlightenment* (2000 edn).

R. Porter, 'The Secrets of Generation Display'd: Aristotle's Masterpiece in Eighteenth Century England, *Eighteenth Century Life*, 9 (1984–5).

Poverty in Early Stuart Salisbury, ed. P. Slack (Wiltshire Record Society, 31, 1975).

The Present State of Great Britain and Ireland (7th edn, 1731).

W. Prest, Legal Education of the Gentry, 1560–1640, *Past and Present*, 36 (1967).

W. Prest, The English Bar 1550–1700, in W. Prest ed., *Lawyers in Modern Europe and America* (1981).

J. B. Priestley, *English Journey* (1934).

Probate Inventories of Lincoln Citizens 1661–1714, ed. J. A. Jackson (Lincoln Records Society, 80, 1991).

Proceedings in Quarter Sessions, 1660–1696, ed. H. J. Johnson and N. J. Williams (Warwick County Records, 9, 1964).

M. Punch, Who Is the intellectual When He Is At Home? *New Society*, 12 November 1970.

J. M. Quail, From Personal Patronage to Public School Privilege, in A. J. Kidd and D. Nicholls eds, *The Making of the Middle Class* (Stroud, 1998).

H. H. Quitt, Immigrant Origins of the Virginia Gentry: A Study of Cultural Transmission and Innovation, *William and Mary Quarterly*, 45 (1988).

The Railway Companion describing a journey on the Liverpool line (1833).

D. Rapp, The Early Discovery of Freud by the British General Educated Public, *Social History of Medicine*, 3 (1990).

Z. Razi, *Life, Marriage and Death in a Mediaeval Parish Economy: Society and Demography in Halesowen 1270–1400* (Cambridge, 1980).

W. J. Reader, *Professional Men* (1966).

B. Reay, Popular Religion, in B. Reay ed., *Popular Culture in Seventeenth-Century England* (1985).

Recollections of Nineteenth-Century Buckinghamshire, ed. I. Toplis, G. Clarke,

I. Bennett and H. Henley (Buckinghamshire Record Society, 31, 1988).

Records of King Edward's School, Birmingham, 3, ed. W. F. Carter and E. A. B. Bernard (Dugdale Society, 1933).

Records of Old Aberdeen MCCXCVIII–MCMIII, ed. M. Munn (New Spalding Club, Aberdeen, 1909).

Religious Worship in Norfolk: The 1851 Census of Accommodation and Attendance at Worship, ed. J. Ede and N. Virgoe (Norfolk Record Society, 72, 1998).

Remains of the Early Popular Poetry of England, ed. W. C. Hazlitt (4 vols, 1864).

Report of the Inter-Departmental Committee on Physical Deterioration, 1 (1904).

Reports of the Heraldic Cases in the Court of Chivalry 1632–1732, ed. G. P. Squibb (Harleian Society, 107, 1956).

The Repton School Register 1620–1894 (1895).

H. C. Richards, *The Candidates and Agents Guide to Contested Elections* (1894).

J. Richards, *Happiest Days: The Public Schools in English Fiction* (Manchester, 1988).

J. M. Richards, *Castles on the Ground: The Anatomy of Suburbia* (1973 edn).

M. S. Riddell, *A First Year Nursing Manual* (1931).

H. Ritvo, Pride and Pedigree: The Evolution of the Victorian Dog Fancy, *Victorian Studies*, 29 (1986).

K. Roberts, F. G. Cooke, S. C. Clark and E. Semenoff, *The Fragmentary Class Structure* (1977).

M. J. D. Roberts, Morals, Art and the Law: The Passing of the Obscene Publications Act, *Victorian Studies*, 28 (1985).

M. J. D. Roberts, Victorian Morals? The Society for the Suppression of Vice and Its Critics, *Historical Studies* (Melbourne), 21 (1984).

D. Rogers, *Matrimonial Honour: or, The Mutual Crowne and Comfort of Godly Loyall and Chaste Marriage* (1642).

The Rogues and Vagabonds of Shakespeare's Youth, ed. E. Viles and F. J. Furnivall (New Shakespeare Society, 1880).

J. Rohstedt, *Riots and Community Politics in England and Wales, 1790–1810* (Cambridge, Mass., 1983).

The Roll of the Royal College of Physicians of London, ed. W. Munk (3 vols, 1878).

A. Rosen, *Rise Up Women! The Militant Campaign of the Women's Social and Political Union, 1903–1914* (1974).

J. Rosenthal and C. Richmond, *People, Politics and Community in the Later Middle Ages* (Gloucester, 1987).

G. Rosser, Going to the Fraternity Feast: Commensability and Social Relations in Late-Mediaeval Britain, *Journal of British Studies*, 33 (1994).

A. Roth, *Enoch Powell: Tory Tribune* (1970).

The Complete Works of Samuel Rowlands, 1598–1628 (3 vols, Hunterian Club, 1880).

Royal Commission on Marriage and Divorce (1956).

Royal Commission on the Taxation of Public Income (2nd Report, 1954).

Royal Commission on University Education in Wales: Appendix to the First Report (1917).

T. Royle, *The Best Days of Their Life* (1988 edn).

W. B. Rubenstein, Britain's Elites in the Inter-War Period, *Contemporary British History*, 12 (1998).

W. B. Rubenstein, British Millionaires, 1809–1949, *Bulletin of the Institute of Historical Research*, 48 (1974).

W. B. Rubenstein, Wealth, Elites and the Class Structure of Modern Britain, *Past and Present*, 74 (1977).

The Collected Papers of Bertrand Russell, 28, ed. A. G. Bone, (2003).

D. F. St John, Educate or Domesticate? Early Twentieth Century Pressures on Girls in Elementary Schools, *Women's History Review*, 3 (1994).

'Lord' George Sanger, *Seventy Years a Showman* (c. 1910).

M. Savage, Making Sense of Middle-Class Politics: A Secondary Analysis of the 1987 British General Election Survey, *Sociological Review*, 39, i (1991).

M. Savage, P. Watt and S. Arber, Social Class, Consumption Divisions and Housing Mobility, in R. Burrows and C. March eds, *Consumption and Class* (1992).

R. Saville, *The Bank of Scotland: A History 1695–1995* (Edinburgh, 1996).

The Letters of Dorothy L. Sayers, 1899–1936: The Making of a Detective Novelist, ed. D. Reynolds (New York, 1995).

M. Scammell. The Phenomenon of Political Marketing: The Thatcher Contribution, *Contemporary Record*, 8, i (1994).

B. Schwarz, Night Battles: Hooligan and Citizen, in M. Nava and A. O'Shea eds, *Modern Times: A Reflection on English Modernity* (1996).

G. R. Searle, The Edwardian Liberal Party and Business, *English Historical Review*, 98 (1983).

G. R. Searle, *Entrepreneurial Politics and Mid-Victorian Britain* (Oxford, 1993).

Sedbergh School Register, 1546 to 1895 (Leeds, 1895).

Select Cases on Defamation to 1600, ed. R. H. Helmholz (Selden Society, 1985).

A Select Collection of Old English Plays, ed. W. Carew Hazlitt (10 vols, 1874–6).

C. Seymour-Ure, *The British Press and Broadcasting since 1945* (1996).

B. Sharp, *In Contempt of All Authority: Rural Artisans and Riot in the West of England 1586–1660* (Berkeley, Calif., 1980).

J. A. Sharpe, Disruption in the Well-Ordered Household: Age, Authority and Possessed Young People, in P. Griffiths, A. Fox and S. Hindle eds, *The Experience of Authority in Early Modern England* (1996).

M. Shaw, *The Clear Stream: A Life of Winifred Holtby* (1999).

Mrs Sherwood, *The History of the Fairchild Family, or, The Child's Manual* (1818).

Mrs Sherwood, *The History of Milner; A little boy who was not brought up according to the Fashions of the Times* (1825).

M. Shipway, *The Adoption of the Public Libraries Act in Leeds, 1861–1868* (Thoresby Society, Leeds, 1998).

R. Silverstone ed., *Visions of Suburbia* (1997).

P. Simmat, *Personal Salesmanship* (1930).

D. Simonelli, Anarchy, Pop and Violence: The Punk Rock Subculture and the Rhetoric of Class, *Contemporary British History*, 16, ii (2002).

P. Simmonds, *Mrs Weber's Diary* (n.d.).

P. Simmonds. *Very Posy* (1987).

A. Simpson, Thomas Cullum 1587–1664, *Economic History Review*, 11 (1958).

R. Sinclair, C. Ryan and M. Walker, Continuity, Change and Consumption: British Economic Trends 1945–1995, *Contemporary British History*, 10 (1996).

Small Beginnings, or the Way to Get On (c. 1880).

J. Q. Smith, Occupational Groups among the Early Methodists of the Keighley Circuit, *Church History*, 57 (1988).

R. M. Smith, The Court and its Neighbourhood: Royal Policy and Urban Growth in the Early Stuart West End, *Journal of British Studies*, 30 (1991).

The Works of the Reverend Sydney Smith (1850 edn).

The Memoir of William Smith, ed. B. S. Trinder, *Transactions of the Shropshire Archaeological Society*, 58 (1965–8).

E. M. Sneyd-Kinnersley, *HMI: Some Passages in the Life of One of HM Inspectors of Schools* (1908).

P. Snowden, *An Autobiography* (2 vols, 1934).

Social Focus on Women (1995).

S. Solomon, *A Guide to Health . . . to which is added an address to Boys, Young Men, Parents, Tutors and the Guardians of the Young* (c. 1810).

Somerset Medieval Wills, ed. F. W. Weaver, Somerset Record Society, 1 (1901), 2 (1903), 3 (1904).

R. Southey, *Journal of a Tour of Scotland in 1819*, ed. C. H. Herford (1929).

R. Southey, *Sir Thomas More or, Colloquies on the Progress and Prospects of Society* (2 vols, 1829).

Speak for Yourself: A Mass Observation Anthology, 1937–1949, ed. A. Calder and N. Sheridan (1984).

S. Spencer, Advice and Ambitions in a Girl's Public Day School: The Case of Sutton High School 1884–1924, *Women's History Review*, 9 (2000).

M. Spufford, First Steps in Literacy: The Reading and Writing Experiences of the Humblest Seventeenth-Century Autobiographers, *Journal of Social History*, 4 (1979).

Statistical Abstract for the United Kingdom in Each of the Last Fifteen Years from 1891 to 1905 (1906).

The Statistical Account of Scotland, ed. D. J. Withrington and I. Grants.

Statutes of the Realm, vols 2–9 (1816–22).

P. Stell, *Medical Practice in Mediaeval York* (York, 1996).

L. Stone, *The Crisis of the Aristocracy* (1965).

The Stranger in Liverpool with Plates of the Principal Buildings (1820).

R. Strong, *The English Icon: Elizabethan and Jacobean Portraiture* (1969).

R. B. Sturrock, *Looking Back: A Series of Reminiscences, Sketches and Studies* (Paisley, 1910).

E. R. Suffling, *The Land of the Broads* (c. 1890).

Surrey Quarter Sessions Records 1661–1663 (Surrey Record Society, 36, 1935).

R. S. Surtees, *Handley Cross* (2 vols, 1899 edn).

Swaledale Wills and Inventories, 1522–1600, ed. E. K. Berry (Yorkshire Archaeological Society, 152, 1998).

J. Swift, *The Examiner*, ed. H. Davies (Oxford, 1946).

The Memoirs of John Addington Symonds, ed. P. Grosskurth (1984).

R. Symons, *A Commercial Traveller's Reminiscences* (1884).

J. Taylor, *Autobiography of a Lancashire Lawyer* (Bolton, 1883).

N. Tebbit, *Upwardly Mobile* (1988).

C. Tennyson, The Libraries and Censorship, *Contemporary Review*, 97 (1910).

R. C. Terry, *Victorian Popular Fiction, 1860–80* (1983).

Testamenta Eboracensia, 5, ed. R. Raine (Surtees Society, 79, 1884).

J. Thirsk, *The Rural Economy of England* (1984).

This England, ed. M. Bateman (1969).

K. Thomas, *Man and the Natural World: Changing Attitudes in England, 1500–1800* (1983).

K. V. Thomas, Numeracy in Modern England, *Transactions of the Royal Historical Society*, 37 (1987).

K. V. Thomas, The Place of Laughter in Tudor and Stuart England, *Times Literary Supplement*, 21 January 1977.

V. Thomas, *A Sermon Preached at St Mary's Oxford, June 4 1835* (Oxford, 1835).

E. P. Thompson, Time, Work, Discipline and Industrial Capitalism, *Past and Present*, 38 (1967).

F. M. L. Thompson, The Social Distribution of Landed Property in England in the Sixteenth Century, *Economic History Review*, 79 (1966).

P. Thompson, Snatching Defeat from the Jaws of Victory: The Last Post of the Old City Elite, in A. J. Kidd and D. Nicholls eds, *The Making of the Middle Class?* (Stroud, 1998).

E. Tilney, *A Briefe and Plesaunt Discourse of the duties in Mariage* (1568).

R. Tittler, Political Culture and the Built Environment of the English County Town, in D. Hoak ed., *Tudor Political Culture* (Cambridge, 1995).

To the Freeholders and Inhabitants of Nantwich (Nantwich, *c.* 1816).

Tradesmen in Early-Stuart Wiltshire, ed. N. J. Williams (Wiltshire Archaeological and Natural History Society Records, 15, 1960).

T. G. Trewin, *The Edwardian Theatre* (1976).

B. Trinder, *Victorian Banbury* (Banbury Historical Society, 1982).

A. Trollope, *Doctor Thorne* (Oxford, 1963 edn).

J. Trusler, *The Progress of Society* (1791).

Tudor Royal Proclamations, ed. P. L. Hughes and J. E. Larkin (3 vols, 1969).

B. J. Turton, Crewe New Town in 1851, *North Staffordshire Journal of Field Studies*, 16 (1976).

Two East Anglian Diaries 1641–1729, Isaac Archer and William Coe, ed. M. Storey (Suffolk Record Society, 16, 1994).

J. Uglow, *Hogarth: A Life and World* (1997).

UK Christian Handbook 1983 (1984)

UK Christian Handbook 2002/2003 (2004).

The Universal Jester: Or, A Complete Book of Jests (1718).

VCH, *County of Cambridge and the Isle of Ely*, 9 (1989).

VCH, *Oxfordshire*, 4 (1959).

VCH, *Sussex*, 6, i (1980).

M. Veldman, *Fantasy, the Bomb and the Greening of Britain; Romantic Protest, 1945–1980* (Cambridge, 1994).

G. Vertue, *Anecdotes of Painting in England* (6 vols, 1786).

The Victorian City, ed. H. J. Dyos and M. Wolff (2 vols, 1973).

The Visitation of the County of Northampton in the Year 1681, ed. H.T. Longdon (Harleian Society, 87, 1935).

W. Wade, *History of the Middle and Working Class with a Popular Exposition of the Economical and Political Principles which have influenced the past and present condition of the Industrious Orders* (1833).

A. P. Wadsworth, The First Manchester Sunday Schools, in M. W. Flinn and T. C. Smout eds, *Essays in Social History* (Oxford, 1974).

V. Walczak, *He and She: Men in the Eighties* (1988).

A. Wall, *Power and Protest in England 1525–1640* (2000).

C. Wall, H. C. Cameron and E. Ashworth Underwood, *A History of the Worshipful Society of Apothecaries of London*, 1 (1963).

S. Waller, Censors and Photography in the Third Republic of France, *History of Photography* 27 (2003).

R. Wallis, 'Goal Displacement' and 'Rentinisation of Cleansing' in the Nationwide Festival of Light, *Scottish Journal of Sociology*, 1 (1977).

J. K. Walton, *The British Seaside: Holidays and Resorts in the Twentieth Century* (2000).

E. Ward, *The Quack Vintners or, a Satyr against Bad Wine* (1712).

J. R. Ward, *The Finance of Canal Building in Eighteenth-Century England* (Oxford, 1974).

L. E. Warren, Turning Reality Around: Guides to Conversation in Eighteenth Century England, *Eighteenth Century Studies*, 8 (1983).

E. A. Wasson, The Third Earl Spencer and Agriculture, *Agricultural History Review*, 26 (1978).

K. Waterhouse, *Billy Liar* (1959 edn).

M. Webb, Henry Sheere, Henry Scheemakers and the Apprenticeship Lists, *Burlington Magazine*, 99 (1957).

M. Webb, Henry Sheere, Sculptor and Businessman, *Burlington Magazine*, 100 (1958).

J. Weeks, *Sex, Politics and Society* (1989 edn).

R. Weight, *Patriots: National Identity and Britain 1940–2000* (2002).

R. Wells, Popular Protest and Social Crime: The Evidence of Criminal Gangs in Rural Southern England, *Southern History*, 13 (1991).

H. A. White, Moral and Merry England, *Fortnightly Review*, 45 (1885).

W. Wilberforce, *A Practical View of Prevailing Religious Systems of Professed Christians in the Higher and Middle Classes contrasted with real Christianity* (1797).

D. E. Williams, Midland Hunger Riots in 1766, *Midland History*, 3 (1975).

F. S. Williams, *Our Iron Roads: Their History, Construction and Social Influence* (1852).

Wills and Inventories from the Registry of the Archdeaconry of Richmond, ed. J. Raine (Surtees Society, 26, 1852).

A. N. Wilson, *The Victorians* (2003).

J. Wilson, *The State of England Anno Dom 1600*, ed. F. J. Fisher (Camden Miscellany, 14, 1936).

K. Wilson, Citizenship, Empire and Modernity in the English Provinces, *Eighteenth Century Studies*, 29 (1995).

C. Withers and E. Matthews, The Geography of Apprenticeship Migration in Gloucestershire, 1680–1830, *Transactions of the Bristol and Gloucestershire Archaeological Society*, 110 (1992).

J. Wolffe, *God and Greater Britain: Religion and National Life in Britain and Ireland, 1843–1945* (1994).

J. Woodfield, *English Theatre in Transition 1884–1914* (1984).

The Diary of a Country Parson: The Reverend John Woodforde, ed. J. Beresford (5 vols, Oxford, 1924–1931).

A. S. P. Woodhouse, *Puritanism and Liberty* (1950).

R. Woods, Physician, Heal Thyself: The Health and Mortality of Victorian Doctors, *Social History of Medicine*, 9 (1996).

V. Woolf, *A Passionate Apprenticeship: The Early Journals, 1897–1909*, ed. M. A. Lacska (1990).

Work and Leisure for the Enjoyment and Recreation of Women Workers (1887).

The World (1753).

J. Worthen, *D. H. Lawrence: The Early Years 1885–1912* (Cambridge, 1991).

S. Wright, 'Holding Up Half the Sky': Women and their Occupations in Eighteenth-Century Ludlow, *Midland History*, 14 (1989).

K. Wrighton, The Politics of the Parish in Early Modern England, in P. Griffiths, A. Fox and S. Hindle eds, *The Experience of Authority in Early Modern England* (1996).

Yorkshire Diaries and Autobiographies (Surtees Society, 65, 1877).

W. Young, Return to Wigan Pier, *Encounter*, 6 (June 1956).

Index